CHARLIE=
    Hope you enjoy this book as
a Christmas present,
                Best wishes,
                Walter LeConte

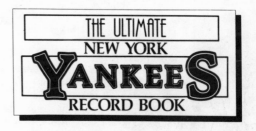

THE ULTIMATE
NEW YORK
YANKEES
RECORD BOOK

A publication of
Leisure Press.
597 Fifth Avenue: New York, N.Y. 10017

Copyright © 1984 Leisure Press
All rights reserved. Printed in the U.S.A.

Library of Congress Cataloging in Publication Data

LeConte, Walter.
The ultimate New York Yankees record book.

Bibliography: p.
1. New York Yankees (Baseball team)—History. 2. New York Yankees (Baseball team)—Records. 3. Baseball—United States—Records. I. Title. II. Title: New York Yankees record book. III. Title: Yankees record book.
GV875.N4L42 1984 796.357'64'097471 84-47520
ISBN 0-88011-231-X

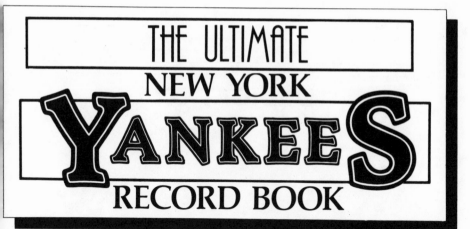

THE ULTIMATE NEW YORK YANKEES RECORD BOOK

WALTER LE CONTE

LEISURE PRESS

NEW YORK

DEDICATION

I wish to dedicate this book to some very special people in my life: First of all, to my beloved mother, Anna Mae Chatelain LeConte, to whom I owe everything and without whom I could not have realized my potential. Although she no longer lives in this world, I am most assured that her spirit lives on in the company of her Maker.

Secondly, to my best friend (who also just happens to be my wife), Jeanie W. LeConte, who daily gives me the support, love and understanding I so deeply cherish. Jeanie is truly the treasure of my life.

Thirdly, to Franklin Norwood, who may not realize the impact he has made in my life, for seeing me through one of my biggest crises. With Frank's support and guidance in my time of need, I was able to learn much about myself as well as learning about others. Although we are apart now, I will always be grateful and indebted to his aid in my time of personal need.

Finally, to my father, Walter L. LeConte Sr, whom I love very deeply; to Etna, Al and Lonnie, who saw me through much of my younger years; and to Camille, that wonderful and warm human being, may you rest in peace.

TABLE OF CONTENTS

INTRODUCTION

The New York Yankees. The very utterance of their name conjures images of greatness and phenomenal success. With this work, I have encapsulated every Yankee season and have included every score of all 12,545 Yankee games from 1903 through 1983, some 81 seasons.

Ever since I was a child growing up in the Ninth Ward of New Orleans, the Yankees were always my favorite sports team. It was in my late teenage years that I conceived the idea for this book. It was, however, just this year that I realized the publication of my first book would be possible.

Over ten years ago, May 1973 to be more exact, I began to research the daily games of the Yankees as a hobby. The first season researched (and appropriately so) was the daily log of the 1927 Yankees, commonly referred to in baseball annals as "Murderer's Row." As the season unfolded before me, I was thoroughly fascinated as I was able to "relive," so to speak, this truly remarkable club on a daily basis. Using various newspapers on microfilm, I was able to research any season I so desired. Generally, it took an average of about four research hours to complete each season's day by day scores.

A majority of the work in this book was completed while I was in pursuit of a college degree at Southeastern Louisiana University (S.L.U.) in Hammond. I am indebted to Linus Sims Memorial Library on the S.L.U. campus for the use of their resources. The remainder of the research was completed while in graduate school at Louisiana State University (L.S.U.) in Baton Rouge. The Troy Middleton Library at L.S.U. proved to be most helpful in my endeavor as well.

As the years went on, my completed day by day logs (which, in addition to the game score, included idle dates, tie games and postponed games) began to accumulate. What facilitated my research was the discovery of the official American League schedules in the early newspapers. One by one, the Yankee schedules for each season were copied onto a day by day sheet, which was standardized to include a vertical column for each month of the season with their accompanying dates affixed accordingly. Space was allowed to enter the site of the game, the Yankee score, the opponent's score, and special notations for extra-inning or less than nine inning games. Also, a notation was made when a doubleheader was scheduled for a specific date. Historical Yankee data was also noted as needed. Thus, a completed sheet would provide a month by month tabulation versus each Yankee opponent for both home and away games. Also, cumulative won-lost records for each month for all games was made available at a glance.

To ensure my accuracy with scores, resources such as *The Baseball Encyclopedia* (Macmillan), various baseball guides and record books, as well as statistics found in newspapers, were utilized. From these sources, the official record of Yankee runs as well as the runs of their opponents could be obtained. It was then just a matter of cross-checking the official records with my own scores obtained through my research. When discrepancies were found in my research, it was sometimes laborious to determine my error. In most cases, these errors were found and corrected. The reader should note that the run and opponent run totals included at the end of each day by day scoresheet (only data prior to 1920) were obtained using statistics obtained from the Baseball Hall of Fame Library in Cooperstown, New York. I have made every effort to ensure the accuracy of my research but this is indeed difficult when considering the vast number of discrepancies found by me (as well as by other researchers) in the early "official" records. Readers are encouraged and welcomed to write the author regarding any such discrepancies or errors on my part which they may discover . . .

Previous baseball books about the Yankees have usually focused on a day by day history, or on individual Yankee teams or players. No book about the Yanks (or any other team for that matter) has included *all* of the actual daily scores for each season. In addition to the scores, I have also included other Yankee statistics and records that I feel to be genuinely original. In this Special Record Section, the box scores, statistics and other data are of special interest to the author and are not intended to reflect the interest of Yankee fans in general. For example, lists of *all* 1–0 Yankee wins and losses, greatest shutout scores (wins and losses), greatest margins of victory and defeats, season opening games, plus other various records researched extensively by the author are included.

It is hoped that the reader shall gain greater understanding of Yankee history in reviewing each season's narratives as well as a greater appreciation of the incredible success of this fabulous team as reflected in the day by day scores.

In summation, the scope of this book is intended to be informative and attempts to embellish the success of America's most famous sports team—the New York Yankees. I can only hope that the reader finds this volume as fascinating as I have found researching it to be.

Walter L. LeConte

ACKNOWLEDGMENTS

I would like to take the opportunity to thank the following people who in some way helped to create this book:

Jeanie W. LeConte—Without her help I could not have completed this book. Jeanie unselfishly gave up much of her leisure time to assist with the typing of the scores, narratives and tables of seemingly repetitive statistics. Her unconditional support of this work is greatly appreciated. Thanks, Jeanie, and I love you dearly.

Dorothy Taylor—Without her expert typing, the final manuscript would have been delayed. Thanks to Dorothy (and her husband Raymond), my first book shall become a reality.

Fred Stein—Fred is a fellow Society for American Baseball Research (SABR, for short) member and was the actual catalyst for the publication of this book. It was he who encouraged my contact with Mark Gallagher. Through Fred's suggestion, I was able to assist Mark in his book, *Day by Day in New York Yankees History*. Thank you very much, Fred.

Mark Gallagher—Another SABR member, Mark provided me with reassurance and support that my ideas could actually be presented in published form. It was Mark who helped to put my foot in the door at Leisure Press, my publisher. Mark, thanks for your support and "good words." Many of the photos included in this volume are from Mark's own personal collection. Many thanks again to you, Mark.

Arthur Schott—His support and vast expertise as Louisiana's Official Baseball Historian was truly helpful in this enterprise. His warmth and hospitality given to me upon each visit to his "Cooperstown, Jr." is deeply appreciated. With every visit to the home of this fine man, my interest in baseball research is strengthened immensely. Art is also a very active SABR member in New Orleans.

Paul Szeflinski and Jim Curtis—These two research assistants at the Baseball Hall of Fame Library at Cooperstown, New York have been very thorough with the materials they have provided, contributing much to the accuracy of my statistical analysis of the early years of Yankee baseball.

Jay Gauthreaux—Thanks to Jay for sharing his wealth of personal Yankee photographs used throughout this book. Jay is another New Orleans SABR member.

Finally, Jim Peterson, Ph.D., and Gary L. Miller, Ph.D., both of Leisure Press, are to be thanked for the opportunity given to me to publish my first (of many, hopefully) book. All my thanks to Jim, Gary, and the people of Leisure Press.

HOW TO USE THIS BOOK

This book is divided into 2 major sections. The first focuses on 3 main areas: 1) a summary season narrative for each season, 2) the DAY BY DAY scoresheet citing every game score, and 3) a CLUB VS. CLUB chart that is to be used as a supplement to the DAY BY DAY scoresheet. The second section deals with selected special records of the Yankees. Standard abbreviations are used in the narrative section: ERA (Earned Run Average), RBI (Run Batted In), A.L. (American League), N.L. (National League), and so forth. The following club abbreviations are used throughout this volume:

HOME/away	CLUB	INCLUSIVE DATES	TOTAL YEARS
BAL–bal	BALTIMORE ORIOLES	1954–NOW	30
BOS–bos	BOSTON RED SOX	1903–NOW	81
CAL–cal	CALIFORNIA ANGELS	1965–NOW	19
CHI–chi	CHICAGO WHITE SOX	1903–NOW	81
CLE–cle	CLEVELAND INDIANS	1903–NOW	81
DET–det	DETROIT TIGERS	1903–NOW	81
KC–kc	KANSAS CITY ATHLETICS	1955–1967	13
KC–kc	KANSAS CITY ROYALS	1969–NOW	15
LA–la	LOS ANGELES ANGELS	1961–1964	4
MIL–mil	MILWAUKEE BREWERS	1970–NOW	14
MIN–min	MINNESOTA TWINS	1961–NOW	23
OAK–oak	OAKLAND ATHLETICS	1968–NOW	16
PHI–phi	PHILADELPHIA ATHLETICS	1903–1954	52
STL–stl	SAINT LOUIS BROWNS	1903–1953	51
SEA–sea	SEATTLE MARINERS	1977–NOW	7
SEA–sea	SEATTLE PILOTS	1969 Only	1
TEX–tex	TEXAS RANGERS	1972–NOW	12
TOR–tor	TORONTO BLUE JAYS	1977–NOW	7
WAS–was	WASHINGTON SENATORS	1903–1960	58
WAS–was	WASHINGTON SENATORS	1961–1971	11

INTERPRETING THE DAY BY DAY SCORESHEET

Below are instructions on how to understand and interpret the DAY BY DAY scoresheets. I have devised a hypothetical example illustrating every possible situation arising throughout a season's play. The example is divided into 3 columns which I have called A, B and C.

EXAMPLE FOR DAY BY DAY SCORESHEET

A	B	C
April, 1984		
29 DET	L	3–8
30 DET	W	12–6h
May, 1984		
1 DET		*
2 NG		
3 chi	L	3–6a
" chi	TG	3–3e

COLUMN A

In this column the month, year and the month's date are noted and should be obvious to the reader. A ditto mark beneath a date (see May 3 in example) signifies the second game of a doubleheader played on the same day. Also in column A is the Yankee opponent, with the specific club abbreviation given (i.e. BAL, CLE, etc., see previous abbreviations). Yankee home games are represented by ALL CAPITAL letters, for example, April 29, 30, and May 1, when Detroit (DET) played at New York; conversely, all small letters signify a Yankee game away from home (i.e. May 3 when the Yanks visited Chicago (chi) playing 2 games on that date). The symbol NG means that No Game was scheduled on that date.

COLUMN B

The three game outcomes—1) Wins, 2) Losses, or 3) Ties are the only items noted in this column. Wins, losses, and ties are *always* from a Yankee perspective; that is, the symbol represented reflects either a Yankee win (W), Yankee loss (L), or Yankee tie (TG). For example (see column B), the Yankees lost (L) to Detroit (DET) at New York on April 29 and won (W) the following day, April 30. On May 3, the Yanks lost at Chicago (chi) in the first game of a double-header and tied (TG) the second game.

COLUMN C

Column C represents the score of the game and whether the game is either postponed or consists of more or less than the usual nine innings. The exception to this is when there is a tie game, in which case the number of innings is always given. For example, the 2nd game of May 3 at Chicago, which being a tie game has a symbol representing the number of innings played—in this case, a 9 inning game. To determine the score, the first number is always the Yankee score. For example, the Yankees scored 3 runs on April 29 and 12 runs on April 30 (see example). The other number represents the run total of the Yankee opponent. For instance, (see example) Detroit scored 8 runs against N. Y. on April 29 and 6 on April 30.

To the immediate right of the score (see column C), there is an INNING SYMBOL to be found, but only if applicable. Using the inning symbol legend (see legend), locate the appropriate inning total for that game. For example, on April 30, the Yanks beat Detroit in 12 innings (h); likewise, the Yanks lost the 1st game of a double-header at Chicago in 5 innings (the letter a). All tie games throughout the DAY BY DAY section are given an inning symbol. In the example, the 2nd game of May 3 at Chicago was a 3–3, nine-inning (e) tie. Finally, an asterisk (*) signifies that the game scheduled for that day was postponed. In the example, the May 1st game with Detroit at New York was cancelled.

The won-lost record of the Yankees at the traditional ALL-STAR break (beginning in 1933) is cited on the appropriate date on the DAY BY DAY scoresheet.

CLUB VS. CLUB MONTHLY RECORDS

Immediately following each DAY BY DAY scoresheet is the chart of CLUB VS. CLUB monthly records for each season. The year of the season is shown in the heading of each season as indicated by the letter A in the example. As in the DAY BY DAY example, the club record is divided into columns for the purpose of explanation and clarity, and in addition is also subdivided into horizontal rows, F and G. Each of these will be represented by a letter in the following example:

EXAMPLE FOR CLUB VERSUS CLUB SHEET

A		APR	MAY	JUN	JUL	AUG	SEP	OCT	C HOME	D AWAY	E TOTAL
WAS	H	1–0	3– 2	2–0	xxx	xxx	1– 2	xxx	7– 4	xxx	
	A	xxx	2– 5	xxx	0– 2	2– 0	xxx	xxx	xxx	4– 7	11–11
F TOTAL:	H	7–1	16– 3	5– 0	15– 6	15– 3	4– 2	xxx	62–15	xxx	
	A	3–2	2– 5	15– 8	5– 8	8– 2	12– 7	xxx	xxx	45–32	107–47
GRAND TOTAL:		10–3	18– 8	20– 8	20–14	23– 5	16– 9	xxx	xxx	**TIE GAMES:**	1
G CUMUL TOTAL:		10–3	28–11	48–19	68–33	91–38	107–47	xxx	xxx	det-Sep	

H

COLUMN A

Column A in the CLUB VS. CLUB records shows the club abbreviation for the opposing teams , and the initials H and A stand for home and away games, respectively.

COLUMN B

Column B includes all of the months of the season in which games were played. Under each month are the totals of wins and losses at home and away against each opponent. The first number in each set is the number of Yankee wins, with the second number representing the Yankee losses in that month against that opponent. For example, in the month of June, New York won a total of 5 home games versus Washington (see row F), while losing none. Away games are interpreted in exactly the same manner. The marks *xxx* indicate that no games were played against that opponent in that month.

COLUMN C

Column C is the total of all Yankee wins and losses played in New York during the entire season against each opposing team. The example illustrates that New York won 7 home games while losing 4 versus the Washington club.

COLUMN D

Column D is read essentially the same way as column C, but it is the total Yankee win/loss record of away games. In the example, New York shows 4 wins and 7 losses against Washington while on the road.

COLUMN E

Column E is the season total of Yankee wins/losses against each team and combines home and away games. So, as in the example, if New York won 7 home games and 4 away games against Washington, the total of wins in Column E would be 11. Likewise, 4 losses at home and 7 losses in the away column (D) add up to a total in Column E of 11.

ROW F

Row F runs horizontally across columns B, C, D, and E and shows the monthly totals of home/away victories of the Yanks against all opponents. For example, in April, New York shows a month total of 7 wins and 1 loss of games played at home. Away games shows totals of 3 wins and 2 losses. Again, this row is the monthly total against all opponents. The intersection of Columns C, D, and E with row F show season totals of home/away victories and losses. For example, under Column C, the Yankees show 62 home victories and 15 home losses for the season against all opponents. Likewise, Column D shows 45 away victories and 32 on-the-road losses for the Bronx Bombers. Column E—Row F indicates season totals of win/loss records, or the summation of Columns C and D: 62 + 45 wins = 107; 15 + 32 losses = 47.

ROW G

Row G is divided into two sections, the grand total row, which indicates the monthly totals of wins/losses of both home and away games, and the cumulative total row, which gives a running total of wins and losses as the season progresses. For example, in the grand total row, the grand total for the month of May shows 18 victories and 8 losses for the New Yorkers against all opponents. Going to the cumulative total section, the example shows that by the end of July, the Yankees had won a total of 68 and had lost a total of 33 games, both at home and away.

PART H

The final part of our example is Part H. H is the record of tie games for the season. The total number of ties is shown as a number and the opponent tied is shown by the club abbreviation. In addition, the month in which the game is played is also shown immediately after the club abbreviation. So, in the example, New York tied Detroit (det) in September and we know the game was played in Detroit because the opponent is shown in small letters rather than in capitals, as it would be if played in Yankee Stadium, just as in the DAY BY DAY scoresheet. Most seasons have had no tie games; for those specific seasons the word "NONE" is found, signifying no tie games in that specific season. The reader should note that the statistical charts presented in the last section of this book are updated through the 1983 season unless noted otherwise. The period included in the tabulation of such statistics begins in 1903 and includes the 1983 season, a period of 81 years.

ABBREVIATIONS

HOME/away	CLUB
BAL–bal	BALTIMORE ORIOLES
BOS–bos	BOSTON RED SOX
CAL–cal	CALIFORNIA ANGELS
CHI–chi	CHICAGO WHITE SOX
CLE–cle	CLEVELAND INDIANS
DET–det	DETROIT TIGERS
KC–kc	KANSAS CITY ATHLETICS
KC–kc	KANSAS CITY ROYALS
LA–la	LOS ANGELES ANGELS
MIL–mil	MILWAUKEE BREWERS
MIN–min	MINNESOTA TWINS
OAK–oak	OAKLAND ATHLETICS
PHI–phi	PHILADELPHIA ATHLETICS
STL–stl	SAINT LOUIS BROWNS
SEA–sea	SEATTLE MARINERS
SEA–sea	SEATTLE PILOTS
TEX–tex	TEXAS RANGERS
TOR–tor	TORONTO BLUE JAYS
WAS–was	WASHINGTON SENATORS (OLD)
WAS–was	WASHINGTON SENATORS (NEW)

A.L.–American League
N.L.–National League

DAY BY DAY SCORESHEET/
CLUB VS.CLUB

NG	– No Game	A	– Away
*	– Game Postponed	"	– 2nd game of double-header
W	– Won	xxx	– No game this month
L	– Lost		(club vs. club only)
TG	– Tie Game	TOT	– Total
H	– Home	CUMUL	– Cumulative Total

INNING SYMBOLS:

INN	SYM
5	a
6	b
7	c
8	d
9	e
10	f
11	g
12	h
13	i
14	j
15	k
16	l or L
17	m
18	n
19	o
20	p
22	q

All other abbreviations are traditional in baseball, such as those found in box scores, etc.

Babe Ruth—"The Sultan of Swat" clouted 714 career home runs and 659 in his 15 years as a Yankee. He holds many records, including the Major League slugging mark of .847 in 1921. Babe smashed 60 homers in 1927 and was a charter member of the Hall of Fame in 1936. He remains an American folk hero even after all these years.

THE NEW YORK YANKEES SEASONS 1903 THROUGH 1983

Clark Griffin—"The Old Fox" was a pitcher in 5 Yankee seasons and was their first ever manager for the then New York Highlanders in 1903. He was elected to baseball's Hall of Fame in 1946.

1903

THE BIRTH OF THE YANKEES

This season marked the birth of what was to become America's most famous sports team in history—the New York Yankees. No other sports franchise in American history shall approach the Yankees' unprecedented success over the next several decades. However, in 1903, the New York Club was in its infancy. In January of this year a very significant change will occur in the structure of the American League.

After playing the two previous seasons in Baltimore, New York City would become the new home of the troubled Orioles club. The first New York owners, Frank Farrell and William "Big Bill" Devery, bought the faltering Baltimore club on January 9, 1903 for a sum of $18,000 and on March 12, 1903, the New York club was officially voted into the American League. It should be noted that this franchise shift would be the only one in either league until 1953 when the Boston Braves of the National League moved to Milwaukee. Ironically, it was Baltimore in the American League which was the recipient of the transferred St. Louis club in 1954 and represented the first change of A.L. teams since 1903. Thus, Baltimore, which 51 years hence lost their franchise to New York, was again a member of the Junior Circuit.

Under the direction of their first manager, Clark Griffith, "The Old Fox," the Highlanders* finished in 4th place, 17 games behind the frontrunning Boston Red Sox (or Pilgrims as they were known then).

---

*To be consistent throughout this work, the author has chosen to use the name "Yankees" rather than "Highlanders" even though the former nickname was not officially adopted until the start of the 1913 season. However, prior to 1913 "The Highlanders" was New York's official monicker, much to the chagrin of newspaper typesetters. The nickname "Highlanders" (which is usually credited to New York's first club president, Joseph W. Gordon) had no shortened version (as does Yanks). In addition to the Highlanders, the New York club was referred to in print as the Hilltoppers, the New York Americans, the Kilties and the Invaders, since they had "invaded" the territory of already established New York teams, namely Brooklyn and the New York Giants.

In this their first season, the Yanks would play a 140-game schedule, and conclude the year with a 72–62 record. They shall play only one other season (1919) with but 140 games regularly scheduled.

The New Yorkers began their inaugural A.L. campaign at Washington on April 22. "Wee Willie" Keeler scored the first Yankee run in regular season play in the first inning; New York took a 1–0 lead. However, Washington, behind Al Orth's pitching, emerged victorious, beating Jack Chesbro and New York, 3–1. The following day the New Yorkers had their first victory, beating Washington 7–2 with Harry Howell chalking up the win. On the final day of April, Hilltop Park, located on Manhattan's highest elevation at Washington Heights (hence, the nickname "Highlanders") was dedicated with more than 16,000 in attendance. The Yanks downed the Washington Senators 6–2 with Jack Chesbro picking up the victory, besting Jack Townsend. In this inaugural contest at New York, Ban Johnson, American League president, tossed out the first ball in opening game ceremonies. Johnson was the A.L. president until resigning in October 1927.

Hilltop Park was the Yankees' home turf until 1913 when they moved to the Polo Grounds to share occupancy with the rival New York Giants of the National League. At Hilltop Park (or American League Park as it was commonly called in New York), the Yankees drew 211,808 for 58 home dates for an average attendance of about 3,652 fans per home opening in 1903. By comparison, the Yankees of the 70's and 80's attracted that many spectators in but a four-game series in the thick of a pennant race.

During the course of the 1903 season, the Yanks fielded three future Hall of Famers. Their pitcher-manager, Clark Griffith, was New York's field marshal in each of their first five seasons and part of their sixth. He was inducted into the Hall of Fame at Cooperstown, New York, in 1945 as the fourth Yankee to be so honored since one George Herman "Babe" Ruth's election in 1936. The second Hall of Famer on the 1903 club was William Henry Keeler, commonly known in baseball circles as "Wee Willie" and famous for his adage "hit 'em where they ain't." Standing at 5'5'', "Wee Willie" was considered one of the most effective place hitters in the early era of baseball. Playing most of his 19-year career (and seven with the Yankees) as an outfielder, Keeler was elected into the Hall of Fame with Lou Gehrig in 1939. Only the Babe preceded these two Yankees into the hallowed halls of Cooperstown. The third and final Hall of Famer on this 1903 club was pitcher John "Jack" Chesbro, who was elected in 1946 (along with Frank Chance, New York's 1913 player-manager). "Happy Jack," as he was nicknamed by his teammates, won 21 games in 1903 and became New York's first 20-game winner. Chesbro had jumped to New York from Pittsburgh prior to the 1903 season. In six full seasons with the

Yanks, Chesbro won 20+ games 3 times and pitched 169 complete games in 228 starts, a 74.1% completion ratio.

Statistically, Keeler placed fifth in A.L. batting with a .318 mark and third in runs scored with 95. Third baseman Wid Conroy had 33 stolen bases to finish 5th in that department.

As a club, the Yanks hit but 18 home runs, with outfielder Herm Mc-Farland leading the team with 5 roundtrippers. The team could muster only a .249 batting mark, placing fifth among other A.L. opponents.

On the mound, Jack Chesbro was New York's only representative in any league pitching department. He tied for third in the league with 21 victories and was tied for second place with 33 complete games.

The club's ERA of 3.08 ranked seventh overall in the American League. Their fielding abilities were only average at best. New York turned its first triple play in history on May 5 against Philadelphia at Hilltop Park. This triple killing occurred in the final inning of New York's 11–3 win over the Athletics. First baseman John Ganzel and shortstop Herman Long participated in that first historic Yankee triple play.

This season had an oddity of sorts. This was the only year in Yankee history that they would play 2 games in non-American League cities. On May 17, they played at Columbus, Ohio and were defeated by Cleveland, 9–2. Later that year, on August 16, a game was played at Toledo, Ohio versus Detroit. The Tigers won 12–8. The Yanks played one other game in a "foreign" city when they traveled to Newark, New Jersey on July 17, 1904. This time they beat Detroit, 3–1 (in the late sixties, the Yankees would travel to Milwaukee to take on the Chicago White Sox for 2 contests).

An important date in Yankee history was May 7 of this season. On that day, the greatest rivalry in sports was initiated with the Yankees invading the home field of the Boston Red Sox. The Boston club defeated the Yanks 6–2.

This year represented a beginning for the New York based American League club. It would take several painful seasons before success becomes synonymous with the Yankee name. Their showing next season would be much improved thanks to Jack Chesbro's incredible season.

The 1903 DAY BY DAY scores follow:

DAY BY DAY, 1903 NEW YORK YANKEES

April, 1903

22	was	L	1- 3
23	was	W	7- 2
24	was	L	1- 7
25	was	W	11- 1
26	NG		
27	phi	L	0- 6
28	phi	L	3- 7
29	phi	W	5- 4
30	WAS	W	6- 2

May, 1903

1	WAS	W	8- 3
2	WAS	L	3- 4
3	NG		
4	PHI	W	4- 3
5	PHI	W	11- 3
6	PHI	L	1- 6
7	bos	L	2- 6
8	bos	W	6- 1
9	bos	L	5- 12
10	NG		
11	det	W	8- 2
12	det	L	4- 8
13	det	L	1- 7
14	det	L	6- 9
15	cle	L	3- 5
16	cle	W	3- 2
17	cle#	L	2- 9

#Col umbus,OH

18	cle	L	3- 7
19	NG		
20	chi	W	5- 2
21	chi	*	
22	chi	L	1- 2g
23	stl	W	3- 1
24	stl	W	4- 1
25	stl	L	1- 6
26	NG		
27	NG		
28	phi	W	5- 2
29	phi	W	3- 2c
30	phi	L	0- 1f
"	phi	L	3- 4
31	NG		

June, 1903

1	BOS	L	2- 8
2	BOS	L	0- 9
3	BOS	L	3-9
4	CLE	L	3- 6
5	CLE	W	8-7
6	CLE	L	4- 8
7	NG		
8	STL	*	
9	STL	W	3-1
10	STL	*	
11	DET	W	4-3
12	DET	*	
13	DET	W	3-2
14	NG		
15	CHI	*	
16	CHI	W	1-0
17	CHI	W	1- 0
18	NG		
19	det	L	0-7
20	det	*	
21	det	*	
22	cle	*	
23	cle	*	
24	cle	W	6-3
"	cle	L	0- 3
25	chi	TG	6- 6n
26	chi	L	2- 3
27	chi	L	4- 7
28	chi	W	12-2
"	chi	L	1-2g
29	stl	W	6- 3
30	stl	W	2-1

July, 1903

1	stl	W	7- 3
2	stl	W	3- 2
3	NG		
4	CHI	W	5- 3
"	CHI	W	5-3
5	NG		
6	CHI	W	4- 2
7	CHI	L	2-3f
8	STL	L	1-6
9	STL	W	5-4

July, 1903

10	STL	W	3- 1
11	STL	W	5 4g
12	NG		
13	DET	L	3- 4
14	DET	W	5- 4f
15	DET	L	4- 7
16	DET	L	2-10
17	CLE	L	4-11
18	CLE	*	
19	NG		
20	CLE	W	7- 3
"	CLE	L	0- 2
21	CLE	W	9- 3
22	BOS	*	
23	BOS	L	1- 6
"	BOS	W	4- 2
24	BOS	L	2- 8
25	BOS	L	5- 7
26	NG		
27	bos	L	0- 5
28	bos	L	0- 3
29	bos	W	15-14
30	bos	W	12- 1
31	PHI	W	3- 1

August, 1903

1	PHI	W	3- 2
2	NG		
3	PHI	L	2- 5
4	PHI	*	
5	was	W	2- 1
6	was	W	4- 0c
7	was	W	10- 4
8	WAS	W	7- 2
9	NG		
10	WAS	W	6- 1
11	WAS	W	16- 1
12	NG		
13	cle	L	2- 5
"	cle	L	2- 8
14	cle	L	0- 3
15	cle	L	5- 6
16	det#	L	8- 12

#Toledo, Ohio

August, 1903

17	det	L	3- 6
18	det	W	1- 0
"	det	W	8- 1
19	stl	*	
20	stl	W	6- 1
"	stl	L	2- 4
21	stl	L	3- 8
22	chi	W	9- 6g
23	chi	W	6- 5
"	chi	L	1- 3
24	chi	L	5- 9d
25	NG		
26	WAS	L	1- 2
27	WAS	W	6- 5
28	WAS	*	
29	phi	*	
30	NG		
31	phi	*	

September, 1903

1	phi	W	5- 1
"	phi	TG	1- 1e
2	was	W	11- 3d
3	was	W	3- 1
4	was	L	1- 8d
5	WAS	W	10- 3
"		*	
6	NG		
7	BOS	L	0- 4
"	BOS	W	5- 0
8	BOS	W	1- 0
9	PHI	W	4- 0
"	PHI	W	6- 3c
10	PHI	L	2- 5
11	PHI	L	4- 7
12	bos	L	1-10
13	NG		
14	bos	W	4- 2
15	bos	L	3-12
16	CHI	*	
17	CHI	*	
18	CHI	W	7- 1
"	CHI	W	6- 3
19	CLE	W	3- 1

September, 1903

20	NG		
21	CLE	L	4- 8
22	CLE	L	4- 5
23	STL	L	4- 7
"	STL	W	4- 1
24	STL	W	6- 2
"	STL	W	8- 6
25	STL	W	8- 2
26	DET	L	8-13
"	DET	W	5- 1b
27	NG		
28	DET	W	7- 6
29	DET	W	10- 4

END OF 1903

RUNS: 579

OPP RUNS: 572

CLUB VS. CLUB AND MONTHLY RECORDS OF THE NEW YORK YANKEES' 1903 SEASON FOR HOME AND AWAY GAMES

CLUB		APR	MAY	JUN	JUL	AUG	SEP	OCT	HOME	AWAY	TOTAL
BOST	H	xxx	xxx	0- 3	1- 3	xxx	2- 1	xxx	3- 7	xxx	7- 13
	A	xxx	1- 2	xxx	2- 2	xxx	1- 2	xxx	xxx	4- 6	
CHIC	H	xxx	xxx	2- 0	3- 1	xxx	2- 0	xxx	7- 1	xxx	11- 7
	A	xxx	1- 1	1- 3	xxx	2- 2	xxx	xxx	xxx	4- 6	
CLEV	H	xxx	xxx	1- 2	2- 2	xxx	1- 2	xxx	4- 6	xxx	6-14#
	A	xxx	1- 3#	1- 1	xxx	0- 4	xxx	xxx	xxx	2- 8	
DET	H	xxx	xxx	2- 0	1- 3	xxx	3- 1	xxx	6- 4	xxx	9-10%
	A	xxx	1- 3	0- 1	xxx	2- 2%	xxx	xxx	xxx	3- 6%	
PHIL	H	xxx	xxx	xxx	1- 0	1- 1	2- 2	xxx	6- 4	xxx	10- 8
	A	1- 2	2- 2	xxx	xxx	xxx	1- 0	xxx	xxx	4- 4	
STL	H	xxx	xxx	1- 0	3- 1	xxx	4- 1	xxx	8- 2	xxx	15- 5
	A	xxx	2- 1	2- 0	2- 0	1- 2	xxx	xxx	xxx	7- 3	
WAS	H	1-0	1- 1	xxx	xxx	4- 1	1- 0	xxx	7- 2	xxx	14- 5
	A	2-2	xxx	xxx	xxx	3- 0	2- 1	xxx	xxx	7- 3	
TOTAL:	H	1- 0	3- 2	6- 5	11-10	5- 2	15- 7	xxx	41-26	xxx	72-62
	A	3-4	8-12	4- 5	4- 2	8-10	4- 3	xxx	xxx	31-36	
GRAND TOT:		4-4	11-14	10-10	15-12	13-12	19-10	xxx	xxx	xxx	
CUMUL TOT:		4-4	15-18	25-28	40-40	53-52	72-62	xxx	xxx	xxx	

TIE GAMES: 2
chi-Jun; phi-Sep

#INCLUDES ONE LOSS AT COLUMBUS, OHIO, MAY 17
%INCLUDES ONE LOSS AT TOLEDO, OHIO, AUGUST 16

1904

"HAPPY JACK" CHESBRO WINS 41 GAMES AND ALMOST A PENNANT FOR NEW YORK

In their second season in New York, the Yankees finished in second place, just 1½ games behind the Boston Club. Having played most of the season neck and neck, Boston clinched the A.L. pennant on the last day of the campaign, in which Jack Chesbro unleashed a wild pitch allowing the eventual winning (and pennant-clinching) run to score.

However, it seems many baseball historians point to that wild pitch in disfavor, seeming to minimize "Happy Jack's" accomplishments during the season prior to that final game. Day in and day out, throughout the entire pennant race, Chesbro was a marvel of consistency, winning 41 of New York's 92 victories (or 44.6%). Chesbro set A.L. standards for games started with 51, and completed games with 48, a completion ratio of 94.1%. He pitched a staggering total of 454⅔ innings which ranks second in American League history (only Ed Walsh's total of 464 in 1908 with Chicago is greater). During the middle part of the season, Chesbro won 14 consecutive games and was involved in a pitching decision (that is, winning or losing the game) in all but one game (a 3–3 tie at Chicago) in which he pitched; a truly remarkable statistic. Chesbro's winning percentage of .774 (41–12) made him the first Yankee to lead the league in that category. In addition, he became the only pitcher in Major League history to pace both leagues in percent of games won, having led with Pittsburgh in the National League in 1902. Such a pitching performance today would surely win both a Cy Young Award as well as the Most Valuable Player Crown.

The pitching staff had two 20 game winners, the first time for New York. Chesbro paced the league with 41 wins, while Powell secured 23 victories.

Through 1983, the Yankees never had 3 twenty-game winners in the same year, which seems unusual when considering the large number of games they have won through the years. No other Yankee players other than Chesbro led the league in any major statistical department, but the team ERA of 2.57, fifth in the league in 1904, established a mark that continues to be a club record. In addition, the pitching staff completed 123 of its 155 games, a 79.4% completion ratio, another club record.

The 1904 season, although disappointing in its final outcome for the Yanks, embellished a phenomenal season by Chesbro, who almost single-handedly led New York to their first pennant in only their second year in existence. New Yorkers would never see their team higher in the standings in the latter games of the season (except for 1906) until 1920, their first pennant-clinching year.

The 1904 DAY BY DAY scores follow:

DAY BY DAY, 1904 NEW YORK YANKEES

April, 1904
14 BOS W 8- 2
15 BOS L 1- 4
16 BOS L 6-12
17 NG
18 PHI L 1- 5
19 PHI W 5- 4
20 PHI *
21 phi L 2- 3h
22 was W 2- 0
23 was W 4- 3
24 NG
25 was W 4- 1
26 was *
27 PHI *
28 phi *
29 phi *
30 phi L 2- 6
May, 1904
1 NG
2 WAS W 5- 0
3 WAS W 8- 2
4 WAS W 6- 3
5 WAS L 4- 9
6 bos L 2- 5
7 bos W 6- 3
8 NG
9 bos *
10 bos W 2- 1
11 CLE W 4- 3
12 CLE L 0- 7
13 CLE W 7- 6
14 CLE W 10- 1
15 NG
16 DET L 6-11
17 DET W 5- 1
18 DET L 1- 6
19 DET *
20 CHI W 3- 2h
21 CHI L2- 11
22 NG
23 CHI L 2- 6
24 STL W 3- 0

May, 1904
25 STL L 4- 7
26 STL W 6- 5g
27 PHI L 5- 7
28 PHI W 1- 0
29 NG
30 PHI W 7- 4
" PHI L 0- 1
31 NG
June, 1904
1 det W 5- 3
2 det W 5- 4
3 det L 4- 5f
4 det W 5- 1
5 NG
6 cle L 1- 5
7 cle *
8 cle W 4- 1
9 cle W 3- 2
10 chi L 5- 8
11 chi W 6- 3
12 chi W 2- 0
13 chi L 1- 2
14 NG
15 stl L 1- 6
16 stl W 10- 3
17 NG
18 stl *
19 stl W 4- 3
" stl L 0- 1
20 NG
21 was W 3- 0
22 was W 11- 6
23 was W 7- 4
24 was W 5- 3f
25 bos W 5- 3
26 NG
27 bos W 8- 4
28 bos L 2- 5
29 bos *
30 WAS *
July, 1904
1 WAS W 8- 3

July, 1904
2 WAS L 2- 3
" WAS W 11- 6
3 NG
4 phi W 9- 3
" phi W 5- 2
5 phi W 6- 3
6 phi W 7- 1
7 BOS L 1- 4
8 BOS L 3-12
9 BOS L 1- 2
10 NG
11 BOS W 10- 1
12 CLE L 1- 3
13 CLE L3- 16
14 CLE W 21- 3
15 CLE W 3- 2k
16 DET W 9- 8f
17 DET W##3- 1
18 DET L 4- 8
19 DET W 2- 1g
20 DET L4- 11
21 CHI L 3- 5
22 CHI L 5- 6
23 CHI L 4- 5
24 NG
25 CHI W 1- 0
26 STL *
27 NG
28 STL *
29 STL W 2- 0
30 STL W 9- 2
" STL W 3- 2f
31 NG
August, 1904
1 det L 6- 8
2 det W 2- 1f
3 det W 5- 2
4 det W 6- 1
5 cle W 5- 0
6 cle W 4- 3
7 NG
8 cle L 1- 9

August, 1904
9 cle L 3- 6
10 chi L 1- 5
11 chi L 0- 1
12 chi W 2- 1
13 chi TG 3- 3a
14 stl W 2- 1
15 stl W 3- 1
16 stl W 4- 1
17 stl L 1- 3
18 NG
19 CHI W 6- 1
20 CHI L 2- 4
21 NG
22 CHI W 4- 3
23 CHI W 1- 0
24 STL W 9- 1
25 STL W 2- 1g
26 STL W 3- 2g
27 STL L 2- 7
" STL L 3- 4
28 NG
29 CLE L 2- 4
30 CLE W 1- 0
31 CLE W 3- 1
September, 1904
1 DET W 4- 2
2 DET W 12- 6c
3 DET W 2- 1
4 NG
5 PHI W 2- 1
" PHI L 2- 7
6 PHI W 5- 2
" PHI W 2- 1
7 phi L 0- 3
8 phi W 3- 2
" phi W 5- 1
9 phi L 2- 3
" phi L 1- 5
10 WAS L 2- 3
" WAS W 6- 5
11 NG
12 WAS W 4- 2

September, 1904
13 NG
14 bos W 3- 1
" bos TG 1- 1a
15 bos L 2- 3
" bos TG 1- 1e
16 bos W 6- 4
" bos L 2- 4
17 WAS W 6- 5
18 NG
19 was W 4- 3
20 was W 3- 2g
" was W 5- 1b
21 was L 2- 4
22 NG
23 cle TG 1- 1e
24 cle *
25 NG
26 cle L 3- 4
" cle L 2- 6
27 det W 4- 1g
28 det L 0- 5
29 det W 5- 0
30 chi L 0- 4
October, 1904
1 chi W 7- 2
2 chi L 1- 7
" chi W 6- 3c
3 stl W 3- 0
4 stl W 6- 0
5 stl W 8- 1
6 NG
7 BOS W 3- 2
8 bos L2- 13
" bos L 0- 1c
9 NG
10 BOS L 2- 3
" BOS W 1- 0f

END OF 1904
RUNS: 598
OPP RUNS: 526

##At Newark, New Jersey

CLUB VS. CLUB AND MONTHLY RECORDS OF THE NEW YORK YANKEES' 1904 SEASON FOR HOME AND AWAY GAMES

CLUB:		APR	MAY	JUN	JUL	AUG	SEP	OCT	HOME	AWAY	TOTAL
BOST	H	1- 2	xxx	xxx	1- 3	xxx	xxx	2- 1	4- 6	xxx	10- 12
	A	xxx	2- 1	2- 1	xxx	xxx	2- 2	0- 2	xxx	6- 6	
CHIC	H	xxx	1- 2	xxx	1- 3	3- 1	xxx	xxx	5- 6	xxx	10-12
	A	xxx	xxx	2- 2	xxx	1- 2	0- 1	2- 1	xxx	5- 6	
CLEV	H	xxx	3- 1	xxx	2- 2	2- 1	xxx	xxx	7- 4	xxx	11- 9
	A	xxx	xxx	2- 1	xxx	2- 2	0- 2	xxx	xxx	4- 5	
DET	H	xxx	1- 2	xxx	3- 2	xxx	3- 0	xxx	7- 4##	xxx	15- 7##
	A	xxx	xxx	3- 1	xxx	3- 1	2- 1	xxx	xxx	8- 3	
PHIL	H	1- 1	2- 2	xxx	xxx	xxx	3- 1	xxx	6- 4	xxx	12- 9
	A	0- 2	xxx	xxx	4- 0	xxx	2- 3	xxx	xxx	6- 5	
STL	H	xxx	2- 1	xxx	3- 0	3- 2	xxx	xxx	8- 3	xxx	16- 6
	A	xxx	xxx	2- 2	xxx	3- 1	xxx	3- 0	xxx	8- 3	
WAS	H	xxx	3- 1	xxx	2- 1	xxx	3- 1	xxx	8- 3	xxx	18- 4
	A	3-0	xxx	4- 0	xxx	xxx	3- 1	xxx	xxx	10- 1	
TOTAL:	H	2-3	12- 9	xxx	12-11	8- 4	9- 2	2- 1	45-30	xxx	92- 59
	A	3-2	2- 1	15- 7	4- 0	9- 6	9-10	5- 3	xxx	47-29	
GRAND TOT:		5-5	14-10	15- 7	16-11	17-10	18-12	7- 4	xxx	xxx	TIE GAMES: 4
CUMUL TOT:		5-5	19-15	34-22	50-33	67- 43	85-55	92-59	xxx	xxx	chi-Aug; bos-Sep (2); cle-Sep

##INCLUDES ONE WIN AT NEWARK, NEW JERSEY, JULY 17

1905

A SIXTH PLACE FINISH

In 1905, the Yankees finished in 6th place, some 21½ games behind Connie Mack's Philadelphia Club. Attendance at Hilltop Park slumped drastically but would increase again in 1906.

Only Willie Keeler, the Yankees' steadiest batter over the first three seasons, led the league with his stat work. Hitting over .300 for the third straight campaign, Keeler got the most singles in the league (147). He also had the most one-base hits in 1904, with 164. The club as a whole stole 200 bases, tops in the Junior Circuit.

The pitching staff finished dead last in the eight club pennant race, with a combined ERA of 2.93. By today's standards, such a team ERA would probably lead almost any league in that department.

1905 was a most unproductive year in all aspects. The 1906 club, although finishing higher in the American League standings, did not win their first A.L. pennant.

The 1905 DAY BY DAY scores follow:

DAY BY DAY 1905 NEW YORK YANKEES

April, 1905
14 was W 4- 2
15 was W 4- 0d
16 NG
17 was W 13- 7
18 phi *
19 phi L 6- 7
20 phi L 1- 8
21 WAS *
22 WAS W 5- 3
23 NG
24 WAS L 3- 4
25 WAS W 6- 5
26 PHI W 4- 3
27 PHI W l- 0
28 PHI L 5- 7
29 PHI *
30 NG

May, 1905
1 BOS L 3- 4g
2 BOS L 4- 9
3 BOS W 3- 2
4 BOS L 4- 9
5 bos L 2- 4
6 bos L 2- 8
7 NG
8 bos W 9- 3
9 bos L 2- 5
10 NG
11 NG
12 chi W 7- 3
13 chi TG 0- 0g
14 chi L 3- 9
15 chi L 4-10
16 stl W 3- 2
17 stl L 2-10
18 stl L 1- 3
19 stl W 3- 0
20 det L 0- 6
21 NG
22 det W 3- 0
23 det L 4- 5
24 det L 6-12
25 cle L 1- 9
26 cle L 0- 1f
27 cle L 3- 6
28 NG
29 phi L 1- 2
30 phi L 5- 6
31 phi W 8- 3

June, 1905
1 BOS W 15- 5
2 BOS *
3 BOS L 3-10
4 NG
5 BOS W5- 2
6 CLE *
7 CLE *
8 CLE L 0- 4
9 CLE L 2- 4
10 STL W 9- 3
11 NG
12 STL *
13 STL *
14 STL W 7- 5
15 CHI L 1- 5
16 CHI W 3- 0
17 CHI L 3- 6
18 NG
19 CHI L 6- 9
20 DET L 3- 5f
21 DET *
22 DET *
23 DET W 7- 0
24 bos L 0- 3
25 NG
26 bos *
27 bos *
28 bos W 5- 2f
" bos W 3- 1
29 PHI W 13- 4
30 PHI L 4- 7

July,1905
1 PHI L 0- 1
" PHI L 2- 3g
2 NG
3 PHI W 3- 0
4 WAS W 8- 5
" WAS W 3- 2
5 WAS L 1- 8
6 was *
7 was W 3- 0
" was W 5- 1
8 was W 6- 4
" was TG 5- 5j
9 NG
10 det W 3- 0
11 det L 1- 3
12 det W 7- 0
13 det L 3- 6
14 cle L 2- 7
15 cle W 6- 5
16 NG
17 cle L 1- 4
18 cle W 2- 0
19 chi W 2- 1
20 chi L 4- 6
21 chi L 1- 2h
22 chi L 1- 2
23 stl W 5- 2
24 stl W 10- 5
25 stl W 10- 4
26 stl *
27 NG
28 NG
29 CLE W 7- 0
" CLE W 10- 9
30 NG
31 CLE *

August, 1905
1 CLE W 3- 2
2 CLE W 4- 3
3 STL W 5- 4g
4 STL W 7- 3
5 STL W 3- 1
" STL W 6- 5
6 NG
7 STL W 14- 4
8 CHI *
9 CHI *
10 CHI L 2- 8
11 CHI W 2- 1
12 DET W 2- 1
" DET L 1- 2f
13 NG
14 DET W 7- 1
15 DET L 4- 6
" DET *
16 DET *
17 cle W 2- 1
18 chi L 0- 6b
19 chi W 4- 2f
20 chi L 1- 2g
21 chi W 5- 3
22 stl *
23 stl L 0- 5
" stl W 1- 0h
24 stl L 1- 2
" stl W 3- 1
25 cle W 3- 1g
26 cle L 0- 1
27 NG
28 cle L 4- 5
29 det L 0- 2
30 det L 3- 5
31 det L 0- 5

September, 1905
1 NG
2 BOS W 1- 0
3 NG
4 BOS L 4- 9
" BOS W 8- 5c
5 was W 7- 4
6 was W 2- 0
7 was L 6-11
" was L 2-10
8 was L 5- 6
9 phi L 2- 6
" phi TG 7- 7e
10 NG
11 phi *
" phi *
12 phi L 3- 5
" phi W 7- 4
13 WAS W 6- 1
14 WAS W 7- 6
15 WAS L 2- 6
16 WAS W 5- 2
" WAS L 0- 3f
17 NG
18 PHI *
19 PHI W 5- 0
" PHI L 0- 3
20 PHI W 1- 0
21 CHI L 2- 3
" CHI L 2- 6d
22 CHI W 5- 2
23 CHI L 1- 3
" CHI L 1-10c
24 NG
25 STL W 13-10
26 STL L 3- 6
" STL L 2- 7d
27 STL L 2- 7
28 CLE W 9- 4
" CLE L 1- 3f
29 CLE L 0- 1
30 CLE W 7- 5
" CLE L 0- 1a

October, 1905
1 NG
2 DET L 2- 7
" DET L 1- 7
3 DET W 3- 0
" DET W 10- 1
4 NG
5 bos L5- 10
6 bos L 1- 3
7 bos L 6- 7f
" bos L 9-12h

END OF 1905
RUNS: 587
OPP RUNS: 622

CLUB VS. CLUB AND MONTHLY RECORDS OF THE NEW YORK YANKEES' 1905 SEASON FOR HOME AND AWAY GAMES

CLUB:		APR	MAY	JUN	JUL	AUG	SEP	OCT	HOME	AWAY	TOTAL
BOST	H	xxx	1– 3	2– 1	xxx	xxx	2– 1	xxx	5– 5	xxx	8–13
	A	xxx	1– 3	2– 1	xxx	xxx	xxx	0– 4	xxx	3– 8	
CHIC	H	xxx	xxx	1– 3	xxx	1– 1	1– 4	xxx	3– 8	xxx	7–15
	A	xxx	1– 2	xxx	1– 3	2– 2	xxx	xxx	xxx	4– 7	
CLEV	H	xxx	xxx	0– 2	2– 0	2– 0	2– 3	xxx	6– 5	xxx	10–12
	A	xxx	0– 3	xxx	2– 2	2– 2	xxx	xxx	xxx	4– 7	
DET	H	xxx	xxx	1– 1	xxx	2– 2	xxx	2– 2	5– 5	xxx	8–13
	A	xxx	1– 3	xxx	2– 2	0– 3	xxx	xxx	xxx	3– 8	
PHIL	H	2–1	xxx	1– 1	1– 2	xxx	2– 1	xxx	6– 5	xxx	8–11
	A	0– 2	1– 2	xxx	xxx	xxx	1– 2	xxx	xxx	2– 6	
STL	H	xxx	xxx	2– 0	xxx	5– 0	1– 3	xxx	8– 3	xxx	15– 7
	A	xxx	2– 2	xxx	3– 0	2– 2	xxx	x xx	xxx	7– 4	
WAS	H	2–1	xxx	xxx	2– 1	xxx	3– 2	xxx	7– 4	xxx	15– 7
	A	3–0	xxx	xxx	3– 0	xxx	2– 3	xxx	xxx	8– 3	
TOTAL:	H	4–2	1– 3	7– 8	5– 3	10– 3	11–14	2– 2	40–35	xxx	71–78
	A	3–2	6–15	2– 1	11– 7	6– 9	3– 5	0– 4	xxx	31–43	
GRAND TOT:		7–4	7–18	9– 9	16–10	16–12	14–19	2– 6	xxx	xxx	
CUMUL TOT:		7–4	14–22	23–31	39–41	55–53	69–72	71–78	xxx	xxx	

TIE GAMES: 3
chi–May; was–Jul; phi–Sep.

1906

CHALLENGING THE "HITLESS WONDERS"

As in 1904, the Yankees concluded the season in second place, three games behind the Chicago White Sox, the "Hitless Wonders." The Yankees' team batting average was 36 points higher than Chicago, .266 versus only .230 for Fielder Jones' White Sox.

Keeler again led the league in one-base hits with 166, thus becoming the only Yankee batter in history to win the one-base hit "crown" for three consecutive seasons. Bobby Richardson later matched this singles total, but in three non–consecutive seasons, 1961, 1962, and 1964.

The Yankees laid down 178 sacrifice hits, an all-time club record. Fielding–wise, New York turned the fewest double plays in their history, 69, or about one twin-killing every 2¼ games.

Al Orth anchored the pitching staff with a league-leading 27 wins, the only Yankee hurler to win a major pitching stat this season. Overall, the club knocked 77 triples, first in the American League. During a six day period, from August 30 through September 4, the New Yorkers won 5 consecutive doubleheaders, a Major League standard that stands even to this day. For the first time in their four year history, the Yankees won twenty games in a month, having a 20–11–2 mark for September. This feat happened in the midst of a fifteen game winning streak which concluded on September 10.

The Yankees could not overcome the steady pitching of Chicago's moundsmen. An even more disappointing season was in store for 1907.

The 1906 DAY BY DAY scores follow:

DAY BY DAY, 1906 NEW YORK YANKEES

April, 1906
14 BOS W 2- 1h
15 NG
16 BOS W 4- 3
17 bos W 4- 3
18 bos TG 3- 3g
19 bos L 0- 2
" bos L 1- 3
20 phi L 3-11
21 phi L 1- 3
22 NG
23 phi *
24 phi W 7- 4
25 was L 2- 7
26 was L 3- 5
27 was L 2- 5
28 was W 5- 1
29 NG
30 BOS L 4-13

May, 1906
1 BOS W 8- 0
2 PHI *
3 PHI W 6- 5f
4 PHI W 6- 2
5 PHI L 3- 9
6 NG
7 WAS W 7- 2
8 WAS L 3- 8
9 WAS *
10 WAS *
11 CLE L 3- 6
12 CLE L 0- 2g
13 NG
14 CLE *
15 CLE W 5- 4
16 STL W 5- 2
17 STL W 4- 2
18 STL W 14- 4
19 STL W 8- 3
20 NG
21 CHI L 6- 7
22 CHI W 8- 2
23 CHI W 4- 1
24 DET W 8- 6
25 DET W 15- 5
26 DET W 10- 2
27 NG
28 DET *
29 WAS W 5-2
30 WAS W 9-2
" WAS W 7-6
31 PHI W 7-3

June, 1906
1 PHI W 10-2
2 PHI W 14-4
" PHI L 1- 7
3 NG
4 stl W 1- 0c
5 stl L 5-9
6 stl L 0-5
7 stl W 6-4i
8 chi W 6-2
9 chi W 2- 1
10 chi L 0- 1
11 chi W 3-0
12 cle L 4- 5h
13 cle W 3-2
14 cle L 2-3
15 cle L 2-5
16 det W 6-2
17 NG
18 det L 2-9
19 det L 1-4
20 det L 1-3
21 NG
22 was L 1-2
23 was W 3-2
24 NG
25 was W 2-0
26 was *
27 BOS W 6-5
28 BOS W 7-4
29 BOS W 8-4
30 bos *

July, 1906
1 NG
2 phi L 4-5
" phi W 5-1e#
#FORFEITED TO
NEW YORK IN 9TH
3 phi *
4 phi L 1-3
" phi W 2-1
5 bos W 8-3
6 bos W 4-0
" bos W 8-0
7 STL L 6- 8
8 NG
9 STL W 2- 0a
10 STL *
11 STL W 4-2
" STL L 0-6
12 CHI W 4-3
13 CHI L 1- 3
14 CHI W 9-8
15 NG
16 CHI L 4- 7f
17 CLE *
18 CLE W 6-4
19 CLE L 0-5
" CLE L 2-3
20 CLE W 5-4
21 DET L 1-6
22 NG
23 DET W 4-2
24 DET W 1-0
25 DET W 5- 4f
" DET W 9-0
26 NG
27 cle *
28 cle W 6-4
29 NG
30 cle W 6-4
31 cle L 0-2

August, 1906
1 det L 1-2
2 det W 11-1
3 det L 2- 3f
4 det W 2- 1
5 stl L 1- 2
6 stl W 8- 6
7 stl *
8 stl L 1- 2f
9 stl *
10 chi L 1- 2
11 chi L 1- 8
12 chi L 0- 3
13 chi TG 0- 0e
14 NG
15 DET W 10- 2
16 DET L 1- 2g
17 DET L 0- 6
18 CHI L 0-10
19 NG
20 CHI L 1- 4
21 CHI *
22 CHI L 1- 6
" CHI L 6-11
23 CLE W 3- 1
24 CLE *
25 CLE W 2- 0
" CLE W 2- 0
26 NG
27 STL W 2- 1
28 STL L 1- 3
29 STL W 5- 4
30 WAS W 5- 0
" WAS W 9- 8f
31 WAS W 7- 5
" WAS W 20- 5b

September, 1906
1 WAS W 5- 4
" WAS W 5- 3
2 NG
3 PHI W 4- 3
" PHI TG 3- 3e#
#FORFEITED TO
NEW YORK IN 9TH
4 bos W 7- 0
" bos W 1- 0
5 bos W 6- 1
6 BOS W 6- 5
7 PHI W 3- 2
8 PHI W 11- 4
9 NG
10 BOS L 1- 4
11 BOS W 11- 3
12 BOS L 2- 4
13 was W 4- 2c
14 was L 1- 5
15 was L 1- 3
" was W 6- 1c
16 NG
17 stl W 4- 3
18 stl L 2- 7
19 stl W 3- 0
20 stl TG 5- 5d
21 chi W 6- 3
" chi W 4- 1b
22 c hi L 1- 7
23 chi W 1- 0
24 det L 4- 7
25 det L 5- 6
26 det L 0- 2
27 cle L 1-10
" cle TG 2- 2c
28 cle W 2- 0
" cle L 1- 2
29 cle W 4- 1
30 NG

October, 1906
1 NG
2 phi L 3- 4
3 phi W 7- 5
" phi L 0- 3b
4 phi *
5 bos W 6- 4
6 bos W 5- 4

END OF 1906
RUNS: 641
OPP RUNS: 543

CLUB VS. CLUB AND MONTHLY RECORDS OF THE NEW YORK YANKEES' 1906 SEASON FOR HOME AND AWAY GAMES

CLUB:		APR	MAY	JUN	JUL	AUG	SEP	OCT	HOME	AWAY	TOTAL
BOST	H	2-1	1- 0	3- 0	xxx	xxx	2- 2	xxx	8- 3	xxx	17- 5
	A	1-2	xxx	xxx	3- 0	xxx	3- 0	2- 0	xxx	9- 2	
CHIC	H	xxx	2- 1	xxx	2- 2	0- 4	xxx	xxx	4- 7	xxx	10-12
	A	xxx	xxx	3- 1	xxx	0- 3	3- 1	xxx	xxx	6- 5	
CLEV	H	xxx	1- 2	xxx	2- 2	3- 0	xxx	xxx	6- 4	xxx	11-10
	A	xxx	xxx	1- 3	2- 1	xxx	2- 2	xxx	xxx	5- 6	
DET	H	xxx	3- 0	xxx	4- 1	1- 2	xxx	xxx	8- 3	xxx	11-11
	A	xxx	xxx	1- 3	xxx	2- 2	0- 3	xxx	xxx	3- 8	
PHIL	H	xxx	3- 1	2- 1	xxx	xxx	4- 0	xxx	9- 2	xxx	13- 8
	A	1- 2	xxx	xxx	2- 2	xxx	xxx	1- 2	xxx	4- 6	
STL	H	xxx	4- 0	xxx	2- 2	2- 1	xxx	xxx	8- 3	xxx	13- 8
	A	xxx	xxx	2- 2	xxx	1- 2	2- 1	xxx	xxx	5- 5	
WAS	H	xxx	4- 1	xxx	xxx	4- 0	2- 0	xxx	10- 1	xxx	15- 7
	A	1- 3	xxx	2- 1	xxx	xxx	2- 2	xxx	xxx	5- 6	
TOTAL:	H	2-1	18- 5	5- 1	10- 7	10- 7	8- 2	xxx	53-23	xxx	90-61
	A	3-7	xxx	9-10	7- 3	3- 7	12- 9	3- 2	xxx	37-38	
GRAND TOT:		5-8	18- 5	14-11	17-10	13-14	20-11	3- 2	xxx	xxx	
CUMUL TOT:		5-8	23-13	37-24	54-34	67-48	87-59	90-61	xxx	xxx	

TIE GAMES: 4
bos-Apr; chi-Aug;
stl-Sep; cle- Sep;

1907

A DISAPPOINTING SEASON

After challenging for the pennant the preceding year, the Yankees finished a disappointing 5th with a 70–78 record. The Hughie Jennings-led Detroit Club finished 21 games ahead of the New Yorkers.

In a front office change, Frank Farrell replaced Joe Gordon as club president, remaining in that capacity until January of 1915. Farrell, in addition, remained co-owner of the club with William Devery.

Al Orth had one of his worst seasons as a pitcher, with a league-leading 21 losses. This was but a gauge of this season's futility. The club had the worst fielding marks of any A.L. Club with .947, also leading the way with 334 errors afield. Even Keeler, usually very reliable, failed to produce by not being able to "hit 'em where they ain't."

The year 1907 was a harbinger of things to follow for the next season as one of the Yankees' two worst seasons in their illustrious history awaited them.

The 1907 DAY BY DAY scores follow:

DAY BY DAY, 1907 NEW YORK YANKEES

April, 1907	May, 1907	July, 1907	August, 1907	September, 1907
11 was W 3–2	23 chi *	1 WAS W 16– 15	4 NG	8 NG
12 was *	24 ch i *	" WAS W 8– 4	5 CHI W 8– 4	9 was W 10– 0
13 was TG 4–4f	25 chi L 1– 3	2 PHI W 8– 7f	6 CHI L 2– 6	" was W 2– 0
14 NG	26 chi L 1– 8a	3 PHI L 1– 3	7 STL L 4– 8	10 was W 1– 0
15 was L 4– 9	27 NG	4 PHI L 1– 3	8 STL W 6– 5	" was W 5– 3
16 PHI L 6– 9	28 was W 2– 1	" PHI W 7– 3c	9 STL *	11 was W 4– 2
17 PHI W 5–4	29 was W 2– 0	5 cle L 1– 2	10 STL L 5– 7	12 WAS L0– 2
18 PHI W 8–4	30 was W 3– 1	6 cle L 0– 4	" STL TG 6– 6e	13 WAS L 2–10
19 BOS *	" was L2– 9c	7 NG	11 NG	14 WAS W 8– 2
20 BOS W 8–1	31 bos W 4– 1	8 cle W 5– 4	12 CLE L 3– 5	15 NG
21 NG	**June, 1907**	9 cle W 3– 1	13 CLE L 6–15	16 phi W 3– 2
22 PHI W 8– 7	1 bos L 0– 2	10 det L 4– 9	14 CLE W 2– 1	17 phi W 11– 3
23 PHI *	2 NG	11 det *	15 det W 2– 1	18 phi *
24 WAS L 1–5	3 bos *	12 det L 0– 1	16 det W 4– 2	19 PHI *
25 WAS W 11–2	4 CLE L 3– 4	" det W 8– 3	17 det W 5– 3f	20 DET L 0– 1
26 WAS W 4–0	5 CLE *	13 det L3– 7	18 det L 6–13	21 DET W 8– 2
27 WAS L 2–3f	6 CLE L0– 5	14 NG	19 stl L 0– 1	" DET L 2– 7c
28 NG	7 CLE L4– 6	15 chi L 0–15	20 stl W 6– 3	22 NG
29 bos L 1–2	8 DET L0– 6	16 chi L 2– 3i	21 stl W 4– 3	23 DET *
30 bos W 3– 1	9 NG	17 chi L 4– 5	22 NG	24 CLE W 4– 2c
May, 1907	10 DET W 9– 3	" chi W 5– 1	23 chi L 0– 4	25 CLE L1– 3
1 bos L 3–4	11 DET L 2–10	18 chi W 11– 2	24 chi L 2– 5	26 CLE L0– 6
2 bos W 5–2	12 DET L 4–16	" chi W 4– 0	25 chi L 2– 3	27 STL L6– 7
3 phi W 4–3f	13 CHI L 3– 4	19 stl L 2– 4	26 NG	28 STL L1– 3
4 phi W 8–0	14 CHI *	20 stl L 2– 6	27 BOS W 5– 1	" STL L 2– 5b
5 NG	15 CHI W 2– 0	21 stl W 7– 2f	28 BOS L3– 5	29 NG
6 phi *	16 NG	22 stl W 6– 4	" BOS W 1– 0	30 STL L2– 4
7 phi *	17 CHI W 4– 3g	23 NG	29 PHI W 5– 2	**October, 1907**
8 NG	18 STL W 6– 1	24 CLE W 7– 6	30 PHI L 3– 6	1 CHI W 3– 1
9 cle L 2–5	19 STL L 0– 9	25 CLE W 9– 4	31 PHI L 0– 3	2 CHI W 4– 3
10 cle L 1–5	20 STL L 6– 9	26 CLE L 5– 7	**September, 1907**	3 CHI W 8– 0
11 cle L 2–6	21 STL L 3– 7	" CLE L 3– 8	1 NG	4 BOS W 3– 1
12 NG	22 bos L 2–12	27 CLE L10– 11g	2 BOS L 1–12	5 BOS TG 3– 3f
13 cle W 7–1	23 bos *	28 NG	" BOS *	" BOS *
14 det L 3–4	24 bos W 9– 8	29 DET *	3 BOS L 2– 3	END OF 1907
15 det *	" bos W11– 3	30 DET L 1– 6	" BOS W10– 5c	RUNS: 605
16 det L 0–1	25 bos W 3– 2	31 DET W 2– 1	4 phi L 2– 4	OPP RUNS: 668
17 det W 5–3	26 bos L 2– 6	**August, 1907**	5 phi W 6– 3	
18 stl W 4–3	27 WAS W 15– 7	1 DET L 3– 4	" phi TG 2– 2e	
19 stl W 7–6	28 WAS L 5–16	2 CHI W 7– 5	6 phi L4– 6	
20 stl L 2–3	29 WAS *	3 CHI L 3– 6	" phi L2– 6	
21 stl L 0–3	30 NG	" CHI L 3– 5	7 phi L3– 8	
22 NG				

CLUB VS. CLUB AND MONTHLY RECORDS OF THE NEW YORK YANKEES' 1907 SEASON FOR HOME AND AWAY GAMES

CLUB:		APR	MAY	JUN	JUL	AUG	SEP	OCT	HOME	AWAY	TOTAL
BOST	H	2-0	xxx	xxx	xxx	2-1	1-2	1-0	6-3	xxx	xxx
	A	1-1	2-1	xxx	3-3	xxx	xxx	xxx	xxx	6-5	12-8
CHIC	H	xxx	xxx	xxx	2-1	2-3	xxx	3-0	7-4	xxx	xxx
	A	xxx	0-2	1-3	xxx	xxx	2-3	xxx	xxx	3-8	10-12
CLEV	H	xxx	xxx	1-3	1-2	1-3	xxx	xxx	3-8	xxx	xxx
	A	xxx	1-3	1-1	xxx	xxx	2-3	xxx	xxx	4-7	7-15
DET	H	xxx	xxx	1-2	xxx	1-2	1-3	xxx	3-7	xxx	xxx
	A	xxx	1-2	xxx	2-2	2-2	xxx	xxx	xxx	5-6	8-13
PHIL	H	2-1	xxx	1-2	xxx	xxx	2-2	xxx	5-5	xxx	xxx
	A	xxx	2-0	xxx	1-2	2-2	xxx	xxx	xxx	5-4	10-9
STL	H	xxx	xxx	0-3	1-3	1-3	xxx	xxx	2-9	xxx	xxx
	A	xxx	2-2	xxx	2-1	xxx	2-2	xxx	xxx	6-5	8-14
WAS	H	2-2	xxx	xxx	2-1	2-2	xxx	xxx	6-5	xxx	xxx
	A	1-1	3-1	xxx	2-0	xxx	3-0	xxx	xxx	9-2	15-7
TOTAL:	H	6-3	xxx	5-11	7-6	6-9	4-12	4-0	32-41	xxx	xxx
	A	2-2	11-11	3-3	8-10	6-7	8-4	xxx	xxx	38-37	70-78
GRAND TOT:		8-5	11-11	8-14	15-16	12-16	12-16	4-0	4-0	32-41	70-78
CUMUL TOT:		8-5	19-16	27-30	42-46	54-62	66-78	70-78	70-78		

TIE GAMES: 4
was-Apr; STL-Aug;
phi-Sep; BOS-Oct;

1908

AN "EXPLETIVE DELETED" SEASON

If 1907 was a disappointing season, then the 1908 campaign was beyond adjectival description. The Yankees set a still-standing club mark of 103 losses, coming in dead last behind Detroit some 39½ games out of the lead.

After guiding New York to a 24–32 (.429) record in their first 56 games, Clark Griffith, the Yank's only manager since their transfer from Baltimore in 1903, was replaced by Norman "The Tabasco Kid" Elberfeld. Elberfeld's tenure as player-manager can be considered pathetic, at best, as New York lost 71 of their final 98 games, a   horrendous .276 winning percentage.

Other records of futility were set this year also and discredit should be given where it is due. Cy Young hurled the first no-hitter ever against the Yanks on June 30, Boston winning 8–0. In a four day span in September, Walter Johnson, "The Big Train," shut out New York at home thrice, Washington winning 3–0 (6 New York hits) on September 4, 6–0 (4 New York hits) on September 5 and 4–0 (2 New York hits) in the first of two games September 7. Johnson pitched his fourth season shutout against the Yanks later in October. The "not yet" Bronx Bombers lost twenty games in two consecutive months for the *only* time in their history. In June, they lost 21 while winning but 7 and in July experienced the worst month in their history, losing 24 of 30 games played, an un-Yankee-like winning percent of .200.

With a bat in their hands, the Yankees set club records for futility which read   as follows: fewest runs scored (458), fewest runs batted in (372), fewest doubles (142), and fewest batters with bases on balls (288).

No batter or pitcher led in any major statistical area. On the other side of the coin, Joe Lake, Yankee righthander, suffered through a league-leading 22 defeats.

This was, indeed, a season most diehard Yankee fans would rather forget. The Yanks 1909 season was a substantial improvement, but it seemed that almost any season would be after the 1908 debacle.

The 1908 DAY BY DAY scores follow:

DAY BY DAY, 1908 NEW YORK YANKEES

April, 1908

14 PHI	W	1- 0h
15 PHI	*	
16 PHI	W	2- 1
17 PHI	L	2- 8
18 WAS	W	6- 5g
19 NG		
20 WAS	W	4- 3
21 WAS	W	16-13
22 phi	L	2- 3
23 phi	W	5- 3
24 phi	L	2- 3g
25 phi	L	5- 9
26 NG		
27 BOS	W	1- 0
28 BOS	W	7- 4
29 BOS	L	1- 5
30 BOS	*	

May, 1908

1 was	W	9- 4
2 was	L	3- 6
3 NG		
4 was	W	11- 5
5 was	*	
6 bos	L	0- 4
7 bos	*	
8 bos	W	3- 0
9 bos	W	2- 1
10 NG		
11 bos	W	3- 0
12 CLE	L	0- 2
13 CLE	W	7- 2
14 CLE	W	3- 1
15 CLE	*	
16 DET	W	7- 6
17 NG		
18 DET	L	6- 11
19 DET	W	6- 1
20 DET	*	
21 CHI	L	2- 9
22 CHI	*	
23 CHI	W	4- 0
24 NG		
25 CHI	L	3- 9
26 STL	L	3- 5f
27 STL	L	2- 7
28 STL	L	3- 4
29 PHI	W	6- 5
" PHI	L	0- 1
30 PHI	*	
" PHI	*	
31 NG		

June, 1908

1 BOS	W	2- 0
2 BOS	L	0- 7
" BOS	L	5- 6
3 BOS	L	1- 6
4 cle	L	1-10
5 cle	L	4- 6
6 cle	W	6- 2
7 NG		
8 cle	W	6- 1
9 det	W	5- 3
10 det	L	6- 7h
11 det	L	1- 3
12 det	L	2- 5
13 chi	L	1- 5
14 chi	L	4- 5
15 chi	L	1- 2
16 chi	L	2- 3
17 chi	W	5- 2
18 stl	L	6-12
19 stl	L	0- 4
20 stl	L	2- 4
21 stl	L	1- 5
22 NG		
23 phi	L	6- 9
24 phi	TG	6- 6e
25 phi	L	0- 3
" phi	W	2- 1
26 phi	L	2- 6
27 BOS	W	7- 6
28 NG		
29 BOS	L	1- 4g
30 BOS	L	0- 8

July, 1908

1 BOS	L	3- 4
2 was	L	3- 4
" was	L	3- 5
3 was	L	4- 7
4 was	W	5- 1
" was	L	2- 6
5 NG		
6 phi	L	3- 6
7 DET	L	3- 8
" DET	L	4- 11
8 DET	L	3- 6
9 DET	L	8-10
10 DET	L	2- 8
11 CLE	W	3- 2
" CLE	W	3- 2
12 NG		
13 CLE	L	0- 3
14 CLE	*	
15 CLE	L	1- 16
" CLE	L	2- 3
16 STL	W	10- 1
17 STL	W	5- 3
18 STL	L	1- 7
19 NG		
20 STL	L	3- 8
21 CHI	L	3- 6
" CHI	W	6- 3
22 CHI	*	
23 CHI	L	2- 6
" CHI	L	3- 6d
24 NG		
25 det	L	3- 5
26 det	L	2- 6
27 det	L	2- 4
28 NG		
29 NG		
30 cle	L	2- 3j
31 cle	L	3- 16

August, 1908

1 cle	L	3- 4f
2 NG		
3 cle	L	0- 2
4 stl	*	
5 stl	L	2- 5
" stl	L	1- 6
6 stl	L	1-3
7 stl	*	
8 chi	W	4-1
9 chi	L	3- 4
10 chi	L	1- 2
11 chi	L	1-6
12 NG		
13 NG		
14 CLE	L	2-4
15 CLE	L	4-5g
16 NG		
17 CLE	L	1-5
18 DET	L	3-7
19 DET	W	8-0
20 DET	W	4-3
21 STL	L	3-4
22 STL	*	
23 NG		
24 STL	L	2-4
" STL	W	6-4
25 STL	W	3-1
26 CHI	*	
27 CHI	*	
28 CHI	W	1-0
" CHI	L	1-2
29 CHI	L	0-1
" CHI	L	2-6
30 NG		
31 PHI	L	0-1
" PHI	L	1-2

September, 1908

1 PHI	W	4-3h
" PHI	L	0-4
2 PHI	L	2-5
3 PHI	W	2-1
4 WAS	L	0-3
5 WAS	L	0-6
6 NG		
7 WAS	L	0-4
" WAS	L	3-9
8 phi	L	5-6
9 phi	W	9-6
10 NG		
11 bos	W	4- 2
" bos	L	1- 5
12 bos	W	l- 0
13 NG		
14 bos	L	1- 2
15 bos	W	1- 0
16 NG		
17 det	L	4- 7
18 det	W	5- 1
19 det	W	6- 5
20 det	L	1- 2
21 cle	L	3- 5
22 cle	L	0- 7
23 cle	L	3- 9
24 chi	W	1- 0
25 NG		
26 chi	L	0- 12
27 stl	*	
28 stl	L	1-12
" stl	W	3- 2c
29 stl	L	0- 6
" stl	L	1- 2
30 NG		

October, 1908

1 WAS	W	2- 1
2 WAS	L	2-12
3 WAS	W	2- 1
" WAS	W	3- 2
4 NG		
5 bos	L	0- 4
6 bos	L	3- 11
7 was	L	0- 1g
" was	L	4- 9
8 was	L	5- 7

END OF 1908

RUNS: 458

OPP RUNS: 713

CLUB VS. CLUB AND MONTHLY RECORDS OF THE
NEW YORK YANKEES' 1908 SEASON FOR HOME AND AWAY GAMES

CLUB:		APR	MAY	JUN	JUL	AUG	SEP	OCT	HOME	AWAY	TOTAL
BOST	H	2-1	xxx	2-5	0-1	xxx	xxx	xxx	4-7	xxx	10-12
	A	xxx	3-1	xxx	xxx	xxx	3-2	0-2	xxx	6-5	
CHIC	H	xxx	1-2	xxx	1-3	1-3	xxx	xxx	3-8	xxx	6-16
	A	xxx	xxx	1-4	xxx	1-3	1-1	xxx	xxx	3-8	
CLEV	H	xxx	2-1	xxx	2-3	0-3	xxx	xxx	4-7	xxx	6-16
	A	xxx	xxx	2-2	0-2	0-2	0-3	xxx	xxx	2-9	
DET	H	xxx	2-1	xxx	0-5	2-1	xxx	xxx	4-7	xxx	7-15
	A	xxx	xxx	1-3	0-3	xxx	2-2	xxx	xxx	3-8	
PHIL	H	2-1	1-1	xxx	xxx	0-2	2-2	xxx	5-6	xxx	8-14
	A	1-3	xxx	1-3	0-1	xxx	1-1	xxx	xxx	3-8	
STL	H	xxx	0-3	xxx	2-2	2-2	xxx	xxx	4-7	xxx	5-17
	A	xxx	xxx	0-4	xxx	0-3	1-3	xxx	xxx	1-10	
WAS	H	3-0	xxx	xxx	xxx	xxx	0-4	3-1	6-5	xxx	9-13
	A	xxx	2-1	xxx	1-4	xxx	xxx	0-3	xxx	3-8	
TOTAL:	H	7-2	6-8	2-5	5-14	5-11	2-6	3-1	30-47	xxx	
	A	1-3	5-2	5-16	1-10	1-8	8-12	0-5	xxx	21-56	51-103
GRAND TOT:		8-5	11-10	7-21	6-24	6-19	10-18	3-6	xxx	xxx	
CUMUL TOT:		8-5	19-15	26-36	32-60	38-79	48-97	51-103	xxx	xxx	

TIE GAMES: 1
phi.-Jun.

1909

WHAT AN IMPROVEMENT!

After that woeful 1908 season, the Yankees won 23 more games in 1909 (74) and lost 26 fewer (77) to finish in a more respectable 5th place finish behind the Detroiters.

The Yankees were led by a new manager, George Stallings, their third field general, as he replaced Kid Elberfeld. This season, the Yanks played before 501,000 fans at Hilltop Park. This attendance mark was the highest until 1919 when New York (the American League version) drew 619,164 at the Polo Grounds.

As in the two preceding seasons, the Yanks finished last in team fielding. Through the 1983 season, the Yanks finished last in fielding just twice more, in 1912 and again in 1967.

Again, as in preceding seasons, the New Yorkers placed no batters or pitchers at the top in any of the major categories.

The 1909 edition of the Yankees showed marked improvement over the preceding year. This positive development would continue but for a couple more years.

The 1909 DAY BY DAY scores follow:

DAY BY DAY, 1909 NEW YORK YANKEES

April, 1909

12	was	L	1- 4
13	was	W	5- 0
14	was	*	
15	was	W	4- 1
16	phi	W	1- 0
17	phi	L	4- 6
18	NG		
19	phi	W	4- 2
20	phi	*	
21	WAS	*	
22	WAS	W	8- 1
23	WAS	*	
24	WAS	W	17- 0
25	NG		
26	bos	L	0- 1
27	bos	W	4- 3
28	bos		L2- 12
29	bos		L4- 10
30	PHI	*	

May, 1909

1	PHI	*	
2	NG		
3	PHI	W	9- 6
4	PHI	W	11- 3
5	BOS	W	2- 0
6	BOS	L	3- 4
7	BOS	W	4- 3h
8	BOS	L	4- 6
9	NG		
10	det	*	
11	det	L	5-16
12	det	L	4-11
13	det	W	6- 4
14	cle	*	
15	cle	W	4- 3
16	NG		
17	cle	W	6- 5h
18	cle	W	4- 2b
19	stl	W	5- 1
20	stl	L	1- 2
21	stl	L	1- 2
22	stl	W	2- 1
23	chi	L	3- 7
24	chi	L	1- 2
25	chi	*	
26	chi	*	
27	chi	TG	2- 2f
28	NG		
29	was	W	4- 2
30	NG		
31	was	*	
"	was	L	1- 8

June, 1909

1	was	W	4- 0
"	was	L	0- 2
2	STL	W	3- 1
3	STL	W	7- 5
4	STL	*	
5	STL	*	
6	NG		
7	DET	W	5- 1
8	DET	L	4- 5g
9	DET	*	
10	DET	L	1- 2
11	CHI	L	0- 1
12	CHI	L	3- 5
13	NG		
14	CHI	W	7- 5
15	CHI	L	3- 7
16	CLE	L	3- 4
17	CLE	L	2- 3
18	CLE	L	4-10
19	WAS	L	4- 7
"	WAS	W	6- 3
20	NG		
21	WAS	L	4- 6
"	WAS	W	3- 2
22	bos	L	6- 9
23	bos	L	5-14
24	phi	L	3- 5
25	phi	W	12- 2
26	phi	L	0- 3
"	phi	L	1- 4
27	NG		
28	phi	W	2- 1
29	WAS	L	1- 3
"	WAS	W	11- 3
30	WAS	W	4- 2

July, 1909

1	WAS	W	2- 1f
2	WAS	W	3- 0
3	PHI	L	2- 5
"	PHI	L	0- 7
4	NG		
5	PHI	L	2- 7
"	PHI	L	3- 4
6	PHI	L	2- 3
7	BOS	L	6- 9
8	NG		
9	stl	W	5- 2
10	stl	*	
11	stl	L	2- 8
"	stl	L	0- 1
12	stl	W	5- 0
I3	chi	W	5- 1
"	chi	L	2- 6
14	chi	W	4- 3
"	chi	L	2- 8
15	chi	L	0- 9
16	chi	L	1- 3
17	det	L	2- 9
18	det	L	3- 4i
19	det	W	5- 3
20	det	W	6- 1
21	det	L	0- 2
22	cle	W	1- 0
"	cle	*	
23	cle	*	
"	cle	*	
24	cle	L	0- 2
"	cle	W	3- 2
25	NG		
26	cle	L	1- 2
27	BOS	W	6- 0
28	BOS	L	2- 8
29	DET	W	11- 2
30	DET	W	6- 0
31	DET	W	7- 2
"	DET	L	4- 7

August, 1909

1	NG		
2	STL	*	
3	STL	W	5- 4
"	STL	L	3- 7
4	STL	*	
5	STL	W	5- 0
"	STL	L	0- 4
6	CLE	W	8- 0
7	CLE	W	5- 2
8	NG		
9	CLE	W	3- 0
10	CLE	L	I- 4
11	CHI	W	2- 1
12	CHI	L	0- 2
13	CHI	L	3- 4
I4	CHI	L	3- 7
15	NG		
16	BOS	*	
17	BOS	*	
18	BOS	L	0- 3
"	BOS	L	3- 6
19	BOS	W	7- 6
"	BOS	W	2- 1f
20	NG		
21	chi	L	4- 5i
22	chi	W	6- 5
23	chi	L	1- 5
24	stl	L	0- 3
25	stl	L	0- 1f
26	stl	W	5- 1
27	det		L6- 17
28	det	L	1- 2
29	det	L	3- 7
30	NG		
31	cle	W	4- 1
"	cle	L	1- 2

September, 1909

1	cle	*	
2	cle	W	6- 1
"	cle	L	1- 2
3	NG		
4	bos	W	8- 6
5	NG		
6	bos	L	9-10
"	bos	W	9- 6
7	phi	W	8- 6
8	phi	L	6- 8
9	phi	L	3-11
10	was	*	
"	was	*	
11	was	W	3- 0
"	was	W	2- 1
12	NG		
13	PHI	L	2-10
14	PHI	L	4- 5
"	PHI	L	2- 3d
15	PHI	W	3- 2
16	CLE	W	2- 1
17	CLE	W	10- 0
18	CLE	W	5- 3
19	NG		
20	CLE	W	9- 4
21	CHI	W	5- 0
22	CHI	*	
23	CHI	W	4- 2
"	CHI	W	7- 1
24	DET	*	
25	DET	L	1- 2
"	DET		L4- 10c
26	NG		
27	DET	*	
"	DET	W	4- 1
28	DET	L	0- 5
29	STL	W	5- 2
"	STL	W	11- 0
30	STL	TG	4- 4e

October, 1909

1	STL	W	6- 0
"	STL	W	11- 4b
2	bos	W	6- 5
"	bos	L	1- 6
3	NG		
4	NG		

END OF 1909

RUNS: 589

OPP RUNS: 587

CLUB VS. CLUB AND MONTHLY RECORDS OF THE NEW YORK YANKEES' 1909 SEASON FOR HOME AND AWAY GAMES

CLUB:		APR	MAY	JUN	JUL	AUG	SEP	OCT	HOME	AWAY	TOTAL
BOST	H	xxx	2- 2	xxx	1- 2	2- 2	xxx	xxx	5- 6	xxx	
	A	1-3	xxx	0- 2	xxx	xxx	2- 1	1- 1	xxx	4- 7	9-13
CHIC	H	xxx	xxx	1- 3	xxx	1- 3	3- 0	xxx	5- 6	xxx	
	A	xxx	0- 2	xxx	2- 4	1- 2	xxx	xxx	xxx	3- 8	8-14
CLEV	H	xxx	xxx	0- 3	xxx	3- 1	4- 0	xxx	7- 4	xxx	
	A	xxx	3- 0	xxx	2- 2	1-1	1- 1	xxx	xxx	7- 4	14- 8
DET	H	xxx	xxx	1- 2	3- 1	xxx	1- 3	xxx	5- 6	xxx	
	A	xxx	1- 2	xxx	2- 3	0- 3	xxx	xxx	xxx	3- 8	8-14
PHIL	H	xxx	2- 0	xxx	0- 5	xxx	1- 3	xxx	3- 8	xxx	
	A	2- 1	xxx	2- 3	xxx	xxx	1- 2	xxx	xxx	5- 6	8-14
STL	H	xxx	xxx	2- 0	2- 0	2- 2	2- 0	2- 0	8- 2	xxx	
	A	xxx	2- 2	xxx	2- 2	1- 2	xxx	xxx	xxx	5- 6	13- 8
WAS	H	2-0	xxx	4- 3	2- 0	xxx	xxx	xxx	8- 3	xxx	
	A	2-1	1- 1	1- 1	xxx	xxx	2- 0	xxx	xxx	6- 3	14- 6
TOTAL	H	2-0	4- 2	8-11	6- 8	8- 8	11- 6	2- 0	41-35	xxx	
	A	5-5	7- 7	3- 6	8-11	3- 8	6- 4	1- 1	xxx	33-42	74-77
GRAND TOT:		7-5	11- 9	11-17	14-19	11-16	17-10	3- 1	xxx	xxx	
CUMUL TOT:		7-5	18-14	29-31	43-50	54-66	71-76	74-77	xxx	xxx	

TIE GAMES: 2 chi-May; STL-Sep.

1910

IMPROVEMENT CONTINUES

Under the guidance of George Stallings and later Hal Chase, the Yankees concluded the season in second place for the third time. Connie Mack's Philadelphia Athletics ran away with the pennant, finishing 14½ games ahead of runner-up New York. Manager Stallings resigned late in the season after an ongoing dispute with Hal Chase throughout most of the campaign. "Prince Hal" finally assumed the role of manager the final eleven games of the season.

The Yankees continued to demonstrate a poor showing regarding placement of their players in top statistical categories, again having no pitchers or batters finishing first. However, as a club, the Yanks paced the Junior Circuit in stolen bases with 288 to establish a team record (which still stands through 1983) and which in all probability will never be surpassed. Leading the way with thefts was Bert Daniels with 41, Hal Chase with 40, and Harry Wolter with 39. Eleven Yankees stole 10 or more bases. Defensively, the Yanks advanced from last place to a fourth place tie with a .956 fielding mark.

On August 30, Thomas Hughes pitched the first Yankee no-hitter for nine full innings, New York losing the game to Cleveland in 11 innings, 0–5.

In 1910, the Yankees continued to show progress,but the next year saw New York again slipping. A reversal of the advances made by New York was more and more evident in the next few seasons.

The 1910 DAY BY DAY scores follow:

DAY BY DAY, 1910 NEW YORK YANKEES

April, 1910

14	BOS	TG	4- 4j
15	BOS	L	2- 3
16	BOS	W	4- 2
17	NG		
18	phi		*
19	phi		*
20	phi	L	0- 6
21	phi	W	1- 0
22	was	W	3- 1
23	was	TG	0- 0b
24	NG		
25	was	W	5- 2
26	was	L	7- 9
27	PHI		*
28	PHI	W	7- 3
29	PHI		*
30	PHI	L	2- 4g

May, 1910

1	NG		
2	WAS	W	3- 2f
3	WAS	L	3- 8
4	WAS	W	4- 2
5	bos		*
6	bos	W	11- 0
7	bos	W	4- 1f
8	NG		
9	bos	L	0- 10
10	DET	L	3- 5f
11	DET	W	2- 0
12	DET	W	5- 3
13	DET	L	3- 5
14	STL	W	14- 0
15	NG		
16	STL	W	5- 3
17	STL	W	8- 7g
18	STL	W	6- 3
19	CLE	W	4- 3f
20	CLE	W	3- 2
21	CLE	W	5- 4k
22	NG		
23	CLE		*
24	CHI	TG	5- 5h
25	CHI	W	5- 0
26	CHI	W	4-3
27	CHI	L	1-2
28	WAS	L	3-4
29	NG		
30	WAS	W	3-1
"	WAS	W	3-0
31	WAS	W	5- 1

June, 1910

1	NG		
2	chi		*
3	chi	L	1- 3
4	chi	W	3-2
5	chi	W	2-0
6	stl	W	2- 1
7	stl	W	4-0
8	stl	TG	4- 4c
9	stl		*
10	det	L	3-4f
11	det	W	4- 3
12	det	L	3-8
13	det	L	1-5
14	NG		
15	cle	W	3-0
16	cle	L	3-5
17	cle	L	6-7
18	cle	W	5-2
19	NG		
20	NG		
21	PHI	L	4- 7
"	PHI	L	1- 7
22	PHI	L	0-8
"	PHI	L	2-9
23	PHI	W	12- 5
24	PHI	W	2-1
25	was	W	7-4
26	NG		
27	was	W	4- 3f
"	was	L	1-2
28	was	W	9-7
29	was	W	2-1
30	NG		

July, 1910

1	phi	L	0- 2
"	phi	L	3- 4
2	phi	L	3- 8
"	phi	L	1- 8
3	NG		
4	phi	W	7- 3
"	phi	L	1- 8
5	BOS	W	3- 2
6	BOS	W	3- 2
"	BOS	L	3- 5
7	BOS	L	4- 13
8	CHI	W	13- 4
9	CHI	L	2- 5
"	CHI	W	3- 2g
10	NG		
11	CHI	W	8- 4
12	CHI	W	4- 3
13	CLE	L	2- 9
14	CLE	W	4- 1
15	CLE	W	8- 7
16	CLE	W	5- 3
"	CLE	L	4- 9
17	NG		
18	STL	L	3- 4
19	STL	W	5- 1
20	STL	W	2- 1f
21	STL	W	19- 2
22	DET	W	11- 8
23	DET	L	2- 6
24	NG		
25	DET	L	4- 8
26	DET	L	0- 1
27	bos	L	4- 5
"	bos	W	6- 3g
28	bos	W	5- 4
29	bos	W	3- 1
30	bos	L	4- 5f
31	NG		

August, 1910

1	cle	W	4- 2
2	cle	W	5- 2
3	cle	L	2- 4
4	cle	L	5- 6
5	det	L	6- 9
6	det	L	0- 5
7	det	L	1- 4
8	det	L	1- 2
9	stl	L	0- 1
"	stl	W	8- 0
10	stl	L	6-10
"	stl	L	0- 3
11	stl	W	3- 1f
12	stl	L	4- 5
13	chi	W	1- 0
14	chi	L	1- 4
"	chi	W	5- 1
15	chi	L	2- 3
16	chi	W	7- 1
17	NG		
18	STL		*
19	STL	W	6- 0
20	STL	W	5- 3
"	STL	W	2- 1
21	NG		
22	DET	L	5- 8
23	DET	W	3- 2
24	DET	W	6- 0
25	CHI	W	8- 4
26	CHI		*
27	CHI	W	4- 3
"	CHI	TG	6- 6d
28	NG		
29	CLE		*
30	CLE	W	4- 1
"	CLE	L	0- 5g
31	CLE	W	2- 1

September, 1910

1	BOS		*
2	BOS	W	6- 5
3	BOS		*
4	NG		
5	PHI	W	5- 2
"	PHI	L	1- 2
6	PHI	W	3- 2
7	was	L	1-2
8	was	W	8- 2
9	was	W	3-1
10	bos	W	6- 3
"	bos	L	3- 5
11	NG		
12	bos	L	0-4
"	bos	L	5-6
13	bos	W	7- 5
14	NG		
15	stl	W	9-3
16	NG		
17	stl	W	5- 1
18	stl	L	3-6
19	chi	L	0- 1
20	chi	L	0-3
21	chi	L	4-6
22	cle	W	2- 1
23	cle	L	2-7
24			*
25	NG		
26	det	W	3- 1g
27	det	W	10-2
28	det	W	6-5
29	NG		
30	WAS	L	3-6

October, 1910

1	WAS	W	7-2
2	NG		
3	WAS	L	0-4
4	WAS	W	8-5
5	phi	W	7- 4
6	phi	W	3-1
7	phi		*
8	BOS	W	4-1
"	BOS	W	6-5

END OF 1910

RUNS: 626

OPP RUNS 557

CLUB VS. CLUB AND MONTHLY RECORDS OF THE
NEW YORK YANKEES' 1910 SEASON FOR HOME AND AWAY GAMES

CLUB:		APR	MAY	JUN	JUL	AUG	SEP	OCT	HOME	AWAY	TOTAL
BOST	H	1-1	xxx	xxx	2- 2	xxx	1- 0	2- 0	6- 3	xxx	
	A	xxx	2- 1	xxx	3- 2	xxx	2- 3	xxx	xxx	7- 6	13- 9
CHIC	H	xxx	2- 1	xxx	4- 1	2- 0	xxx	xxx	8- 2	xxx	
	A	xxx	xxx	2- 1	xxx	3- 2	0- 3	xxx	xxx	5- 6	13- 8
CLEV	H	xxx	3- 0	xxx	3- 2	2- 1	xxx	xxx	8- 3	xxx	
	A	xxx	xxx	2- 2	xxx	2- 2	1- 1	xxx	xxx	5- 5	13- 8
DET	H	xxx	2- 2	xxx	1- 3	2- 1	xxx	xxx	5- 6	xxx	
	A	xxx	xxx	1- 3	xxx	0- 4	3- 0	xxx	xxx	4- 7	9-13
PHIL	H	1-1	xxx	2- 4	xxx	xxx	2- 1	xxx	5- 6	xxx	
	A	1-1	xxx	xxx	1- 5	xxx	xxx	2- 0	xxx	4- 6	9-12
STL	H	xxx	4- 0	xxx	3- 1	3- 0	xxx	xxx	10- 1	xxx	
	A	xxx	xxx	2- 0	xxx	2- 4	2- 1	xxx	xxx	6- 5	16- 6
WAS	H	xxx	5- 2	xxx	xxx	9- 2	0- 1	2- 1	7- 4	xxx	
	A	2- 1	xxx	4- 1	xxx	xxx	2- 1	xxx	xxx	8- 3	15- 7
TOTAL:	H	2-2	16- 5	2- 4	13- 9	9- 2	3- 2	4- 1	49-25	xxx	88-63
	A	3-2	2- 1	11- 7	4- 7	7-12	10- 9	2- 0	xxx	39-38	
GRAND TOT:		5-4	18- 6	13-11	17-16	16-14	13-11	6- 1	xxx	xxx	88-63
CUMUL TOT:		5-4	23- 10	36-21	53-37	69-51	82-62	88-63	xxx	xxx	

TIE GAMES: 5
BOS-Apr; CHI-May
CHI-Aug; stl-June
was-Apr.

1911

PROGRESS IN THE WRONG DIRECTION

In his first (and only) full season as player-manager, Hal Chase guided New York to a 76–76 ledger for the season. The Yanks settled into sixth place, 25½ games behind pennant-winning Philadelphia.

The Yanks continued to have difficulty defensively, again placing near the bottom (6th) in fielding. Continuing to keep the base paths busy, New York swiped 270 bases, six less than league-leading Detroit. Birdie Cree led the club with 48 pilfers, followed by Bert Daniels with 40, and manager Hal Chase with 38 swipes. As in 1910, eleven Yanks stole ten or more bases. In fact, they stole fifteen bases in one game at New York versus St. Louis, beating the Brownies 18–12. Included in that stolen base total, which is a post-1900 Major League record, was six steals in the second inning alone, two short of the A.L. record of 8, set by Washington versus Cleveland in 1915. The Yanks led the league in triples for the second time (1906 was the first time with 77) with 96 three-baggers.

In 1911, the Yankees continued their slide downward. 1912 will follow as probably the overall worst season in New York Yankee history.

The 1911 DAY BY DAY scores follow:

DAY BY DAY, 1911 NEW YORK YANKEES

April, 1911	May, 1911	June, 1911	August, 1911	September, 1911
12 phi W 2- 1	23 chi W 4- 3h	29 bos W 3- 1	" CHI W 8- 2	8 was W 2- 1
13 phi W 3- 1	24 chi W 5- 3	" bos L 2- 3	2 CLE L 8-10	9 was W 5- 1i
14 phi *	25 chi L 2- 3f	30 bos L 6- 7	3 CLE L10-11	10 NG
15 phi W 7- 4f	26 NG	**July, 1911**	4 CLE L 3-10	11 PHI L5- 12
16 NG	27 phi L 1- 8	1 bos W 8- 2	5 CLE W 8- 7	12 PHI L1- 10
17 was W 6- 3f	" phi W 8- 3	2 NG	6 NG	13 PHI L 0- 2
18 was L 0- 2	28 NG	3 PHI L 7- 8h	7 DET L 6- 7	14 NG
19 was *	29 phi L 1- 4	" PHI L 1- 5	8 DET W 6- 4	15 DET *
20 WAS *	30 phi L 0- 3	4 PHI L 4- 7	" DET W 2- 1	16 DET L 3- 5
21 WAS L 0- 1	" phi L 5- 8	" PHI L9- 11g	9 DET L 3- 8	" DET W 4- 3
22 WAS *	31 was L 2- 3b	5 PHI W 9- 8	10 DET W 12- 5	17 NG
23 NG	**June, 1911**	6 NG	11 was L 1- 3	18 DET L 4- 9
24 WAS W 5- 3	1 STL W 11- 8	7 chi L 3- 5	" was L 2- 3g	19 CLE TG 3- 3e
25 bos L 3- 5	2 STL W 6- 3	8 chi L 2- 5	12 was W 4- 0	20 CLE L 9-12
26 bos L8- 11	3 STL W 3- 2	" chi L 0- 7	13 NG	" CLE W 5- 4c
27 bos W 4- 3	4 NG	9 chi W 5- 2	14 was L 0- 3	21 CLE L 1- 8
28 bos W 2- 1	5 STL *	10 chi W 5- 2g	15 was W 6- 1d	22 CLE W 4- 3f
29 PHI L 6-10	6 CHI *	11 stl W 8- 3	16 NG	23 CHI L 2- 3
30 NG	7 CHI *	12 stl W 12- 2	17 cle W 6- 2	24 NG
May, 1911	8 CHI L 2- 7	13 stl L 1- 6	18 cle L 4- 5	25 CHI W 7- 3
1 PHI *	9 CHI W 9- 2	14 stl L 3- 4	19 cle L 2- 3	26 CHI L 4- 5
2 PHI W 2- 1	10 CLE W 2- 1	15 cle L 4-12	20 det W 5- 3	27 STL *
3 PHI L 4-13	11 NG	16 cle L 2- 6	21 det L 4- 5g	28 STL W 18-12
4 BOS L 0- 2	12 CLE W 4- 1	17 cle L 1- 2	22 det W 9- 4	29 STL *
5 BOS L 5-14	13 CLE W 5- 1	18 cle L 6- 9	23 NG	30 STL L 4- 5
6 BOS W 6- 3	14 DET W 5- 3	19 NG	24 chi L 3- 5	" STL W 7- 2
7 NG	15 DET W 5- 0	20 det W 8- 6	25 chi L 5- 6	**October, 1911**
8 BOS L 0- 4c	16 DET *	21 det W 6- 4	26 chi W 3- 2	1 NG
9 det L0- 10	17 DET W 3- 2	22 det W 8- 7j	27 stl W 4- 2	2 BOS *
10 det W 6- 2	18 NG	23 det W 7- 4	28 stl W 4- 2	3 BOS L 1- 4
11 det W 6- 0	19 BOS L 3- 6	24 NG	29 stl W 7- 4	" BOS L 0- 7
12 det L 5- 6	20 BOS W 9- 8	25 STL W 3- 2	30 NG	4 BOS L 4- 6d
13 cle L 6-12	21 BOS L 3-11	26 STL L 6- 7	31 NG	5 phi L 0- 1
14 cle L 3-14	22 BOS W 7- 0a	" STL W 5- 1	**September, 1911**	6 phi L 4- 5
15 cle W 6- 3	23 WAS W 3- 2	27 STL W 5- 4	1 WAS W 6- 0	7 phi *
16 cle L 1- 2	24 WAS W 11- 6	28 CHI L 5- 7j	2 WAS L 1-11	END OF 1911
17 NG	" WAS W 9- 2	29 CHI L2- 10	3 NG	RUNS: 683
18 stl W 3- 1	25 NG	" CHI L 7- 8f	4 bos W 6- 3	OPP RUNS: 723
19 stl W 10- 6	26 WAS W 3- 1	30 NG	" bos W 5- 1	
20 stl W 6- 2	27 WAS L 2- 5	31 CHI L0- 13	5 bos W 4- 3	
21 stl L 4- 5f	" WAS L 3- 6	**August, 1911**	6 WAS L 2- 6	
22 chi *	28 bos *	1 CHI W 4- 3	7 was W 5- 2	

CLUB VS. CLUB AND MONTHLY RECORDS OF THE
NEW YORK YANKEES' 1911 SEASON FOR HOME AND AWAY GAMES

CLUB:		APR	MAY	JUN	JUL	AUG	SEP	OCT	HOME	AWAY	TOTAL
BOST	H	xxx	1- 3	2- 2	xxx	xxx	xxx	0- 3	3- 8	xxx	
	A	2-2	xxx	1- 2	1- 0	xxx	3- 0	xxx	xxx	7- 4	10-12
CHIC	H	xxx	xxx	1- 1	0- 4	2- 0	1- 2	xxx	4- 7	xxx	
	A	xxx	2- 1	xxx	2- 3	1- 2	xxx	xxx	xxx	5- 6	9-13
CLEV	H	xxx	xxx	3- 0	xxx	1- 3	2- 2	xxx	6- 5	xxx	
	A	xxx	1- 3	xxx	0- 4	1- 2	xxx	xxx	xxx	2- 9	8-14
DET	H	xxx	xxx	3- 0	xxx	3- 2	1- 2	xxx	7- 4	xxx	
	A	xxx	2- 2	xxx	4- 0	2- 1	xxx	xxx	xxx	8- 3	15- 7
PHIL	H	0-1	1- 1	xxx	1- 4	xxx	0- 3	xxx	2- 9	xxx	
	A	3-0	1- 4	xxx	xxx	xxx	xxx	0- 2	xxx	4- 6	6-15
STL	H	xxx	xxx	3- 0	3- 1	xxx	2- 1	xxx	8- 2	xxx	
	A	xxx	3- 1	xxx	2- 2	3- 0	xxx	xxx	xxx	8- 3	16- 5
WAS	H	1-1	xxx	4- 2	xxx	xxx	1- 2	xxx	6- 5	xxx	
	A	1-1	0- 1	xxx	xxx	2- 3	3- 0	xxx	xxx	6- 5	12-10
TOTAL:	H	1-2	2- 4	16- 5	4- 9	6- 5	7-12	0- 3	36-40	xxx	
	A	6-3	9-12	1- 2	9- 9	9- 8	6- 0	0- 2	xxx	40-36	76-76
GRAND TOT:		7-5	11-16	17- 7	13-18	15-13	13-12	0- 5	xxx	xxx	
CUMUL TOT:		7-5	18-21	35-28	48-46	63-59	76-71	76- 76	xxx	xxx	

TIE GAMES: 1
CLE-Sep.

1912

SLIPPING INTO THE ABYSS AGAIN

After a .500 season in 1911, the Yankees ended the season at 50–102, a record very similar to their one in 1908. The winning percentage of .329 beat the .331 of 1908 as the worst in their history. As in 1908 also, New York finished in the cellar 55 games, a club record, behind first place Boston. Harry Wolverton guided New York through this entire atrocious season. This was the last year that New York lost 100 + games and they will not finish in last place again until 1966, when they wound up at the bottom of nine other teams.

Defensive, offensive, and pitching performances were pathetic. Their .940 fielding average was again last in the A.L.; not until 1967 will New York finish last defensively again. Their lack of defensive prowess did not end there. The poorly-fielding club committed 382 errors,with Hal Chase leading first basemen with 27 miscues and Ed Sweeney's 34 muffs leading all A.L. catchers.

There were no individual offensive records of note and the pitching staff mustered but 50 victories, a club record for fewest wins in a season. All thirteen New York moundsmen totaled but 3 complete game shutouts of opponents, another all-time club low.

Ironically, it was one pitcher, Ray Caldwell, who recorded all three of the team's shutouts. To add insult to injury, Russell Ford led the A.L. in losses with 21.

This was New York's final season playing at Hilltop Park. In ten seasons at Hilltop, New York drew 3,451,542. Next season they moved into the Polo Grounds to share occupancy with their rivals, the New York Giants.

The 1912 DAY BY DAY scores follow:

DAY BY DAY, 1912 NEW YORK YANKEES

April, 1912			May, 1912			June, 1912			July, 1912			September, 1912		
11 BOS	L 3- 5		21 CHI	W 9- 8		27 phi	L 0- 4		29 stl	L 1- 2		2 BOS	L 1- 2	
12 BOS	L 2- 5		22 CHI	L 5-11		28 bos	L 4- 5		30 stl	L 1- 5		" BOS	L 0- 1	
13 BOS	L 4- 8		23 CHI	L 4-10		" bos	L 4- 6		31 chi	W 12- 3		3 BOS	*	
14 NG			24 WAS	W 11- 6		29 bos	L 6-13		**August, 1912**			4 PHI	W 6- 1	
15 WAS	L 0- 1		25 WAS	W 6- 3		" bos	L 0- 6c		1 chi	L 1-2		5 PHI	L 9-19	
16 WAS	L 3-10		" WAS	W 9- 5		30 NG			2 chi	L 3-5		" PHI	L 2- 5b	
17 WAS	*		26 NG			**July, 1912**			3 chi	W 2- 1		6 PHI	L 2- 4	
18 bos	*		27 WAS	W 10- 5		1 bos	L 1- 4		4 det	L 1- 4		7 PHI	L 8-10g	
19 bos	*		28 WAS	L 3- 8		2 bos	W 9- 7		5 det	L 2- 4		" PHI	*	
" bos	*		29 PHI	L 4- 7b		3 was	L 2- 3		6 det	L 2- 6		8 NG		
20 bos	L 6- 7g		30 PHI	L 1- 7		" was	L 2-10		7 det	L 0- 7		9 NG		
21 NG			" PHI	*		4 was	L 1-12		8 cle	L 5- 8		10 stl	W 8- 3	
22 PHI	*		31 NG			" was	L 5-12		9 cle	L 1-3		11 stl	W 5- 4	
23 PHI	W 3- 0		**June, 1912**			5 was	L 5-6 L		10 cle	L 1- 5		12 stl	L 0- 3	
24 PHI	L 0- 7		1 det	L 3- 9		6 WAS	L 7- 8		11 cle	L 3- 8		13 chi	L 0- 2	
25 PHI	L 4- 5i		2 det	W 6- 3		7 NG			12 NG			14 chi	L 1- 4	
26 was	W 10- 2d		3 det	L 1- 4		8 NG			13 DET W	3-2		15 chi	L 2- 4	
27 was	L 0- 5		4 det	L1- 14		9 DET	L 2- 6		14 DET	L 3-6		16 NG		
28 NG			5 cle	L 0- 7		10 DET	L3- 11		" DET W	3-1		17 det	*	
29 was	L 0- 2		6 cle	L 3- 8		11 DET	*		15 DET W	5-4		18 det	L 4- 7	
30 was	*		7 cle	W 7- 0		12 STL	W 4- 1		16 DET	9-8		" det	L 2- 4	
May, 1912			8 cle	L 0- 1		13 STL	W 5- 4		17 STL	W 16-9		19 det	L 5- 6	
1 phi	W 3- 2		9 chi	L 1--2		" STL	L 1- 6		" STL	W 7-0c		20 cle	L 8- 9	
2 phi	W 11- 5		10 chi	W 5- 1		14 NG			18 NG			21 cle	L 4- 5f	
3 phi	L15-18		11 chi	W 6- 3		15 STL	W 5- 3		19 STL	*		22 cle	*	
4 phi	L 5-10		12 chi	L2- 11		16 STL	L 1- 5		20 STL	L 3-4		23 NG		
5 NG			13 stl	*		" STL	L 1- 3		" STL	W 2-1		24 bos	W 5- 2	
6 BOS	*		14 stl	W 7- 5f		17 CLE	L 1- 5		21 CHI	W 6-1		" bos	L 1- 3	
7 STL	*		15 stl	L 1- 2		18 CLE	*		22 CHI	L 4-9		25 bos	L 0- 6	
8 STL	*		16 stl	*		19 CLE	W 4- 3f		23 CHI	L 2-4		26 bos	L12-15d	
9 STL	*		17 NG			20 CLE	W 4- 3		24 CHI	W 7- 6		27 NG		
10 STL	W 3- 2		18 NG			" CLE	W 4- 0		25 NG			28 phi	L 4- 5f	
11 DET	L 5- 9		19 BOS	L 2- 5		21 NG			26 CLE	TG 8- 8e		" phi	L 2- 4	
12 NG			20 BOS	L 8-15		22 CHI	W 13- 3		27 CLE	W 8- 4		29 NG		
13 DET	W 15- 4		21 BOS	L 3-11		23 CHI	L 4- 6		" CLE	W 6- 4		30 phi	L10-11g	
14 DET	L 1- 5		22 BOS	L 2-13		24 CHI	W 4- 3		28 CLE	L 3-6		**October, 1912**		
15 DET	L 4- 8		" BOS	L 3-10		25 CHI	L 4- 6f		" CLE	W 4-2		1 phi	L 3- 4	
16 CLE	*		23 NG			26 NG			29 was	L 1-2		2 NG		
17 CLE	W 8- 3		24 phi	L 1- 3		27 stl	W 7- 5		30 was	L 2-7		3 WAS	L 3- 4	
18 CLE	L7- 10f		25 phi	*		" stl	L 1- 6		31 was	W 1-0		4 WAS	L 2- 4	
19 NG			26 phi	W 6- 5		28 stl	W 9- 4		**September, 1912**			5 WAS	W 8- 6	
20 CLE	L 3- 6		" phi	L 1-11		" stl	W 6- 3		1 NG			6 NG		

END OF 1912

RUNS: 630

OPP RUNS: 842

CLUB VS. CLUB AND MONTHLY RECORDS OF THE
NEW YORK YANKEES' 1912 SEASON FOR HOME AND AWAY GAMES

CLUB:		APR	MAY	JUN	JUL	AUG	SEP	OCT	HOME	AWAY	TOTAL
BOST	H	0- 3	xxx	0- 5	xxx	xxx	0- 2	xxx	0-10	xxx	2- 19
	A	0- 1	xxx	0- 4	1- 1	xxx	1- 3	xxx	xxx	2- 9	
CHIC	H	xxx	1- 2	xxx	2- 2	2- 2	xxx	xxx	5- 6	xxx	9- 13
	A	xxx	xxx	2- 2	1- 0	1- 2	0- 3	xxx	xxx	4- 7	
CLEV	H	xxx	1- 2	xxx	3- 1	3- 1	xxx	xxx	7- 4	xxx	8- 13
	A	xxx	xxx	1- 3	xxx	0- 4	0- 2	xxx	xxx	1- 9	
DET	H	xxx	1- 3	xxx	0- 2	4- 1	xxx	xxx	5- 6	xxx	6- 16
	A	xxx	xxx	1- 3	xxx	0- 4	0- 3	xxx	xxx	1-10	
PHIL	H	1- 2	0- 2	xxx	xxx	xxx	' 1- 4	xxx	2- 8	xxx	5- 17
	A	xxx	2- 2	1- 3	xxx	xxx	0- 3	0- 1	xxx	3- 9	
STL	H	xxx	1- 0	xxx	3- 3	3- 1	xxx	xxx	7- 4	xxx	13- 9
	A	xxx	xxx	1- 1	3- 3	xxx	2- 1	xxx	xxx	6- 5	
WAS	H	0- 2	4- 1	xxx	0- 1	xxx	xxx	1- 2	5- 6	xxx	7- 15
	A	1- 2	xxx	xxx	0- 5	1- 2	xxx	xxx	xxx	2- 9	
TOTAL:	H	1- 7	8-10	0- 5	8- 9	12- 5	1- 6	1- 2	31- 44	xxx	50-102
	A	1- 3	2- 2	6-16	5- 9	2-12	3-15	0- 1	xxx	19-58	
GRAND TOT:		2-10	10-12	6-21	13-18	14-17	4-21	1- 3	xxx	xxx	
CUMUL TOT:		2-10	12-22	18-43	31-61	45-78	49-99	50-102	xxx	xxx	

TIE GAMES: 1
CLE-AUG.

1913

NEXT STOP, THE POLO GROUNDS AND A NEW NICKNAME

Assuming his first year as Yankee skipper, Frank Chance, the sixth New York manager, led his team to a seventh place finish, one game from the cellar. The Yanks' attendance in their first season at the Polo Grounds was not appreciably better than previous seasons at Hilltop Park. New York, the American League version, would draw 357,551. The Yanks remained at the Polo Grounds through 1922 until moving into their new home, Yankee Stadium. In April 1913, the official nickname of Yankees was adopted with the name of Highlanders being dropped forever.

In 1913, the "not yet" Bronx Bombers hit only nine home runs the entire season; Harry Wolter and Ed Sweeney shared the club lead with but two homers each! So, New York finished last in the league in home runs (9), triples, (45), doubles (154), batting average (.237), and slugging percentage (.293). New York scored one more run than the St. Louis club which tallied 528 runs, fewest in the league. New York batsmen, however, garnered the most walks in the A.L. with 534.

No pitchers finished among the statistical leaders. New York set another club record by recording 13 consecutive losses in a row (with one tie game in between) from May 15 through June 6. The Yanks finally won a game June 7, beating Chicago.

New York's first season at the Polo Grounds was fairly uneventful. The 1914 club will make a slight improvement in their record and will see the appointment of their first official team captain.

The 1913 DAY BY DAY scores follow:

DAY BY DAY, 1913 NEW YORK YANKEES

April, 1913			May, 1913			June, 1913			August, 1913			September, 1913		
10 was	L	1–2	21 stl	L	0– 5	27 bos	L	3–10	1 CHI		*	" was	L	0– 1
11 was		*	22 stl	L	0– 7	" bos	L	4– 6	2 CHI	L	1– 4	6 was	L	1– 9
12 was		*	23 NG			28 bos	L	6– 9	3 NG			7 NG		
13 NG			24 BOS	TG	3– 3f	" bos	W	7– 6	4 DET	W	6– 4	8 was	W	4– 0
14 bos	L	1–2	25 NG			29 NG			5 DET	L5–	10	9 STL	W	6– 5
15 bos	W	3–2	26 BOS	L	1– 3	30 PHI	L	0– 6	6 DET	L	1– 2	10 STL	L	7–10
16 bos		*	27 BOS		*	**July, 1913**			7 DET	W	5– 1	11 STL	W	4– 0
17 WAS	L	3–9	28 BOS		*	1 PHI	L	1– 2	8 STL	L	4– 6	12 STL	W	10– 3
18 WAS	L	5–7	29 phi	L	5– 6	2 PHI	L	5– 8	9 STL	W	6– 5	13 DET	W	4– 3
19 WAS	L	0–3	30 phi	L	2– 3	3 PHI	L	4– 8	10 NG			14 NG		
20 NG			" phi	L	4– 7	4 WAS	L	0– 5	11 STL	W	6– 2	15 DET	L	5– 7
21 WAS	L	4–8	31 phi	L	2–12	" WAS	W	5– 2	12 STL	L	2– 7	16 DET	L	3– 4
22 phi	L	4–7	**June, 1913**			5 WAS		*	13 NG			17 CHI	L	3– 9
23 phi	W	4– 0	1 NG			6 NG			14 chi	W	2– 0	" CHI	W	3– 2
24 phi	L	1–4	2 BOS	L	3– 4	7 WAS	W	5– 2	15 chi	L	2– 3	18 CHI	W	6– 3
25 phi	L	0–4	" BOS	L	6– 8	" WAS	L	1– 8	16 chi	L	0– 2	19 CHI		*
26 BOS	L	5–8	3 CLE	L	2– 8	8 NG			17 chi	W	3– 2h	20 CLE	W	7– 3
27 NG			4 CLE	L	5– 9	9 chi	L	0– 2	18 stl	W	4– 2	21 NG		
28		*	5 CLE	L	3– 5f	10 chi	W	2– 1	19 stl		*	22 CLE	L	4– 5
29		*	6 CLE	L	1– 2	11 chi	W	11– 1	20 stl	L	1– 2	23 CLE	W	3– 1
30 BOS	L	1–8	7 CHI	W	3– 2	12 stl	L	1– 2	" stl	L	0– 7	24 NG		
May, 1913			8 NG			13 stl	W	3– 2	21 det		*	25 WAS	L	2– 5
1 PHI	L	2– 4	9 CHI	W	4– 1	14 stl	L	1–11	22 det	L	4– 7	26 WAS	L	0– 3
2 PHI	L	5– 6	10 CHI	L	1– 5	15 stl	L	0– 3	" det	W	12– 7	27 WAS	L	3– 8
3 PHI	L	6– 8	11 CHI	L	0– 1	16 cle	L	0– 5	23 det	L	1– 8	28 NG		
4 NG			12 DET	W	2– 1	" cle	W	4– 2	" det	W	4– 2	29 BOS	W	3– 1
5 PHI	L	1–8	13 DET	W	4– 2	17 cle	W	7– 1	24 cle	L	0– 4	" BOS	W	5– 1d
6 NG			14 DET	L	5– 6f	18 cle	W	5– 2	25 cle	L	2– 6	30 BOS	L	2– 3
7 det	W	6– 0	15 NG			19 cle	L	1– 2	26 cle	L	0– 3	" BOS	L	0– 3d
8 det	L	1– 3	16 DET	L	3– 5	20 det	W	10– 5	27 NG			**October, 1913**		
9 det	W	9– 0	17 STL	L	4– 7	21 det	L	1– 6	28 PHI	L	3– 9	1 BOS		*
10 det	W	10– 9f	18 STL	W	5– 1	22 det	L	0– 2	29 PHI		*	2 phi		*
11 cle	L	2– 7	19 STL	W	10– 4	23 det		*	30 PHI	W	5– 0	3 phi		L10–13
12 cle	W	4– 3	20 was	W	9– 3	24 NG			" PHI	W	6– 4d	" phi	W	2– 1b
13 cle	W	8–5	" was	W	9– 3	25 CLE	L	2– 3i	31 NG			4 phi	W	10– 8
14 cle	TG	2–2k	21 was	L	1– 4	26 CLE	W	4– 3	**September, 1913**					
15 chi	L	2–3	" was	L	0– 6	27 NG			1 bos	L	0– 6	END OF 1913		
16 chi	L	0– 7	22 NG			28 CLE		*	" bos	L	3– 4g	RUNS:		529
17 chi	L	3– 6	23 was		*	29 CLE	L	2– 6	2 bos	L	2– 4	OPP RUNS:		668
18 chi	L	3–5	24 was	L	0– 3d	" CLE	L	3– 6	3 bos	W	11– 4			
19 stl	W	8–6	25 bos	W	5– 2	30 CHI	W	3– 0	4 was	W	3– 2			
20 stl	W	6– 3	26 bos		*	31 CHI	W	3– 1	5 was	L	2– 3			

CLUB VS. CLUB AND MONTHLY RECORDS OF THE NEW YORK YANKEES' 1913 SEASON FOR HOME AND AWAY GAMES

CLUB:		APR	MAY	JUN	JUL	AUG	SEP	OCT	HOME	AWAY	TOTAL
BOST	H	0- 2	0- 1	0- 2	xxx	xxx	2- 2	xxx	2- 7	xxx	
	A	1- 1	xxx	2- 3	xxx	xxx	1- 3	xxx	xxx	4- 7	6-14
CHIC	H	xxx	xxx	2- 2	2- 0	0- 1	2- 1	xxx	6- 4	xxx	
	A	xxx	0- 4	xxx	2- 1	2- 2	xxx	xxx	xxx	4- 7	10- 11
CLEV	H	xxx	xxx	0- 4	1- 3	xxx	2- 1	xxx	3- 8	xxx	
	A	xxx	2- 1	xxx	3- 2	0- 3	xxx	xxx	xxx	5- 6	8-14
DET	H	xxx	xxx	2- 2	xxx	2- 2	1- 2	xxx	5- 6	xxx	
	A	xxx	3- 1	xxx	1- 2	2- 2	xxx	xxx	xxx	6- 5	11-11
PHIL	H	xxx	0- 4	0- 1	0- 3	2- 1	xxx	xxx	2- 9	xxx	
	A	1- 3	0- 4	xxx	xxx	xxx	xxx	2- 1	xxx	3- 8	5-17
STL	H	xxx	xxx	2- 1	xxx	2- 2	3- 1	xxx	7- 4	xxx	
	A	xxx	2- 2	xxx	1- 3	1- 2	xxx	xxx	xxx	4- 7	11-11
WAS	H	0- 4	xxx	xxx	2- 2	xxx	0- 3	xxx	2- 9	xxx	
	A	0- 1	xxx	2- 3	xxx	xxx	2- 3	xxx	xxx	4- 7	6-16
TOTAL:	H	0- 6	0- 5	6-12	5- 8	6- 6	10-10	xxx	27- 47	xxx	
	A	2- 5	7-12	4- 6	7- 8	5- 9	3- 6	2- 1	xxx	30-47	57-94
GRAND TOT:		2-11	7-17	10-18	12-16	11-15	13-16	2- 1	xx x	xxx	**TIE GAMES: 2**
CUMUL TOT:		2-11	9-28	19-46	31-62	42-77	55-93	57-94	xxx	xxx	BOS–MAY; cle–MAY

1914

PLAYING A LITTLE BIT BETTER

The Yankees placed sixth in a tie with Chicago at 70–84 (.455), thirty games in back of frontrunning Philadelphia. The managerial duties were split between Frank Chance and Roger Peckinpaugh, the latter coming in as manager for the season's last seventeen games. Peckinpaugh also began serving as New York's first official team captain. He remained in that position through the 1921 season.

Displaying one of the poorest demonstrations of hitting in their history, the team as a whole managed only a paltry .229 club average, dead last in the league. Having their lowest slugging percentage in their history (.287), the Yankees mustered but 1,433 total bases, one of their worst totals ever.

Fritz Maisel set a Yankee club record with a league-leading 74 stolen bases. As a team, the Yankees pilfered 251 bases, most in the American League.

The pitching staff paced the league in complete games (97) and with the fewest walks allowed (390). However, opponent pitchers had an easy time with the Yanks tossing a club record 27 shutouts against New York. In the month of May alone, opponents whitewashed the Yanks eight times, which surely must be close to some sort of record for futility. New York also lost nine 1–0 games, an American League record that still stands.

This was a disappointing year for New York. The start of the next season will mark the advent of one of the Yankee trademarks, the famous pinstriped uniform.

The 1914 DAY BY DAY scores follow:

DAY BY DAY, 1914 NEW YORK YANKEES

April, 1914			May, 1914			June, 1914			July, 1914			September, 1914		
14 PHI	W	8- 2	25 CHI	L	0-1	29 was	L	0-1	30 cle	W	3- 2f	4 WAS	L	0- 1
15 PHI	W	*	26 CHI	L	1-2	30 was	L	1- 2g	" cle	W	8- 6	5 WAS	L	1- 4i
16 PHI		*	27 CHI		*	**July, 1914**			31 cle	W	7- 2	6 NG		
17 PHI	W	4- 0	28 CHI	W	6-1	1 was	L	4- 7	**August, 1914**			7 BOS	L	1- 5
18 WAS	L	1- 4	29 PHI	L	2- 6	2 was	W	6- 1	1 cle	L	0- 7	" BOS	W	7- 1c
19 NG			" PHI	L	0- 3	3 phi	L	0-2	" cle	W	9- 2	8 BOS	L	5- 6
20 WAS		*	30 PHI	L	0- 8	" phi	L	0-1	2 det	L	3- 4	9 was	L	0- 1
21 WAS	W	3- 2f	" PHI	W	10-5	4 phi	W	7-5	3 det	L	1- 4	10 was	W	6- 4
22 WAS	L	1- 2	31 NG			" phi	L	2-6	4 det	L	3- 9	11 was	L	2- 4
23 phi	W	5- 3	**June, 1914**			5 NG			5 det	W	14- 4	12 PHI	W	2- 1
24 phi	L	6- 7g	1 PHI	L	8-9h	6 phi	L	0- 2	6 NG			13 NG		
25 phi		*	" PHI	W	4-2	7 CLE		*	7 stl	W	4- 3	14 PHI	L	1- 2
26 NG			2 WAS	L	8-9	8 CLE	W	7- 1	8 stl	W	2- 1i	15 PHI	L	1- 3
27 phi	L	4- 5	3 WAS	L	0-2	9 CLE	W	7- 4	9 stl	L	0- 2	16 NG		
28 BOS		*	" WAS	L	3-5	" CLE	TG	3- 3f	10 stl	L	1- 4	17 chi	W	7- 2
29 BOS	W	1- 0	4 WAS		*	10 CLE	L	2- 7	11 NG			18 chi	L	5- 7
30 BOS		*	5 NG			" CLE	W	1- 0b	12 NG			19 chi	W	4- 1
May, 1914			6 chi	TG	1- 1d	11 CHI	W	9-4	13 bos	W	1- 0	20 stl	L	2- 3f
1 BOS	W	6- 0	7 chi	L	0-4	12 NG			14 bos	W	7- 6	21 stl	W	4- 3
2 was	L	1- 14	8 chi	L	0-1	13 CHI	L	0-2	15 bos	L	0- 1	22 stl		*
3 NG			9 chi	L	4-7	" CHI	W	3-1	16 NG			23 stl	W	9- 2
4 was	W	8- 2	10 stl	W	5-3	14 CHI		*	17 WAS	L	0- 1	24 det		*
5 was	L	0- 6	11 stl	L	1-3	15 CHI	L	2-3	" WAS	W	4- 3	25 det	W	5- 4
6 was	W	4- 0c	12 stl	L	3-9	" CHI	W	2- 1d	18 CLE	L	3- 4	26 det	L	3- 6
7 bos	L	0- 2	13 stl	L	4- 5	16 STL	W	6-4	19 CLE	W	7- 5	" det	W	4- 3
8 bos	L	0- 3	14 det	L	1- 3	17 STL		*	20 CLE	L	8-11	27 cle	L	3- 5
9 bos	W	3- 2	15 det	L	1- 4	18 STL	W	5-2	21 CLE		*	" cle	W	5- 2
10 NG			16 det	L	0- 3	19 NG			22 CHI	W	5- 2	28 cle	L	2- 5
11 bos	W	6- 2	17 det	W	4- 3	20 STL	L	1-3	23 NG			29 NG		
12 DET	L	0- 4	18 cle		*	" STL	L	2- 6	24 CHI	L	1- 2	30 bos		*
13 DET		*	19 cle		*	21 DET	W	7- 5	25 CHI	W	9- 0	**October, 1914**		
14 DET	L	1- 3	20 cle	W	7- 1	22 DET	W	3-1	26 STL	W	2- 1h	1 bos	W	5- 3
15 DET	L	2- 4	21 cle	L	3-7	" DET	W	8-5	27 STL	L	4- 5h	" bos	L	2- 4
16 STL	W	2- 1	22 cle		*	23 DET	TG	1-1e	28 STL	W	9- 5	2 bos	L	5-11
17 NG			23 NG			24 NG			29 DET	W	6- 5	3 bos	W	3- 2
18 STL	L	2- 4	24 BOS	L	0-3	25 chi	L	0- 1i	30 NG			4 NG		
19 STL	L	0- 3	" BOS	W	3-2	26 chi	W	1- 0	31 DET	L	6- 9i	5 phi	L	0- 2
20 STL	W	3- 1	25 BOS	W	3- 2	" chi	L	3-7	" DET	W	3- 2c	6 phi	W	2- 1
21 CLE	W	5- 2	" BOS	L	3-4	27 chi	W	5-0	**September, 1914**			7 phi	L	0- 10
22 CLE	L	2- 3	26 BOS	L	1-2f	28 chi	L	2-6	1 DET	L	2- 3	END OF 1914		
23 CLE	W	10- 9	27 BOS	L	3-5	29 cle	W	6-2	2 DET	L	5- 6	RUNS:		536
24 NG			28 NG			" cle	W	10-6	3 WAS	W	10- 4	OPP RUNS:		550

CLUB VS. CLUB AND MONTHLY RECORDS OF THE NEW YORK YANKEES' 1914 SEASON FOR HOME AND AWAY GAMES

CLUB:	APR	MAY	JUN	JUL	AUG	SEP	OCT	HOME	AWAY	TOTAL
BOST H	1- 0	1- 0	2- 4	xxx	xxx	1- 2	xxx	5- 6	xxx	11–11
BOST A	xxx	2- 2	xxx	xxx	2- 1	xxx	2- 2	xxx	6- 5	
CHIC H	xxx	1- 2	xxx	3- 2	2- 1	xxx	xxx	6- 5	xxx	10–12
CHIC A	xxx	xxx	0- 3	2- 3	xxx	2- 1	xxx	xxx	4- 7	
CLEV H	xxx	2- 1	xxx	3- 1	1- 2	xxx	xxx	6- 4	xxx	14– 8
CLEV A	xxx	xxx	1- 1	5- 0	1- 1	1- 2	xxx	xxx	8- 4	
DET H	xxx	0- 3	xxx	3- 0	2- 1	0- 2	xxx	5- 6	xxx	9–13
DET A	xxx	xxx	1- 3	xxx	1- 3	2- 1	xxx	xxx	4- 7	
PHIL H	2- 0	1- 3	1- 1	xxx	xxx	1- 2	xxx	5- 6	xxx	8–14
PHIL A	1- 2	xxx	xxx	1- 4	xxx	xxx	1- 2	xxx	3- 8	
STL H	xxx	2- 2	xxx	2- 2	2- 1	xxx	xxx	6- 5	xxx	11–11
STL A	xxx	xxx	1- 3	xxx	2- 2	2- 1	xxx	xxx	5- 6	
WAS H	1- 2	xxx	0- 3	xxx	1- 1	1- 2	xxx	3- 8	xxx	7–15
WAS A	xxx	2- 2	0- 2	1- 1	xxx	1- 2	xxx	xxx	4- 7	
TOTAL: H	4- 2	7-11	3- 8	11- 5	8- 6	3- 8	xxx	36-40	xxx	70–84
TOTAL: A	1- 2	4- 4	3-12	9- 8	6- 7	8- 7	3- 4	xxx	34-44	
GRAND TOT:	5-4	11-15	6-20	20-13	14-13	11-15	3- 4	x xx	xxx	
CUMUL TOT:	5-4	16-19	22-39	42-52	56-65	67-80	70-84	xxx		

TIE GAMES: 3 chi–June; CLE–July; DET–July

1915

THE ARRIVAL OF RUPPERT, HUSTON AND PINSTRIPES

In January of 1915, Tillinghast L'Hommedieu Huston and Jacob Ruppert purchased the Yankee franchise. An amount of some $460,000 was paid to the first New York owners, Frank Ferrell and William Devery. Ruppert assumed the role of club president until his death in 1939. Harry Sparrow was appointed as first general manager, a position he held until his passing in 1920.

"Wild Bill" Donovan took over as the eighth Yankee manager, remaining three full seasons with his club finishing no better than fourth place. Taking the field in pinstriped uniforms for the first time, the Yanks placed fifth, 32½ games behind the Red Sox.

At the gate, New York experienced the worst season while at the Polo Grounds, drawing but 256,035 paying customers. In 66 playing dates at home, that averaged out to a crowd of 3,879 per opening. To illustrate this point, at home on September 21 versus St. Louis, New York drew but 321 fans for a doubleheader. A breakdown of that attendance is as follows: 267 in the lower stands, 11 in the upper stands and just 43 in the bleachers! This was undoubtedly one of the smallest (if not *the* smallest) crowds in the history of the Polo Grounds.

For the first time in their history, New York paced the league in fielding percentage with a mark of .966. In addition, the New Yorkers committed the league's fewest errors with 217.

Offensively, the emergence of the Bronx Bombers was evident as New York led the league in homers with 31 roundtrippers. The Yankees went on to lead the league in homers in 33 other seasons through 1983. They dominated 34 of 47 league home run titles from 1915 through 1961, leading the league a remarkable 72% of the time during that span.

In 1915, New York began to display power that will eventually be their trademark over the next several decades. The evolution of the Bronx Bombers was taking place.

The 1915 DAY BY DAY scores follow:

DAY BY DAY, 1915 NEW YORK YANKEES

April, 1915

14 was	L	0-7
15 was	W	3-1
16 was	L	2-3
17 phi	W	9-1
18 NG		
19 phi	W	11-6
20 phi	L	2-6
21 phi	W	8-0
22 WAS	L	1-5
23 WAS	*	
24 WAS	W	4-0
25 NG		
26 WAS	W	9-2
27 bos	W	2-0
28 bos	*	
29 bos	W	6-4
30 bos	*	

May, 1915

1 PHI	W	11-3
2 NG		
3 PHI	W	8-4
4 PHI	*	
5 PHI	L	l-2
6 BOS	W	4-3i
7 BOS	L	3-5
8 BOS	W	10-3
9 NG		
10 BOS	L	1-3
11 cle	L	1-3
12 cle	W	4-2
13 cle	W	6-1
14 NG		
15 cle	W	4-2
16 det	W	6-2
17 det	*	
18 det	*	
19 det	L	1-3
20 stl	W	4-2
21 stl	L	4-5
22 stl	L	2-6
23 stl	L	3-4
24 chi	L	4-5
25 chi	*	
26 chi	L	6-7
27 chi	L	2-8
28 NG		
29 was	*	
30 NG		
31 was	W	11-4
" was	W	4-1

June, 1915

1 BOS	L	3-4i
2 BOS	L	1-7
3 BOS	*	
4 DET	L	0-3
5 DET	L	2-11
6 det	L	4-6
7 DET	L	2-3
8 DET	W	4-1
9 CHI	L	0-13
10 CHI	L	4-5
11 CHI	W	10-9
12 STL	W	9-5
13 NG		
14 STL	W	12-7
" STL	W	5-4
15 STL	W	9-4
16 NG		
17 CLE	W	7-3
18 CLE	*	
19 CLE	W	5-4
" CLE	L	4-5
20 NG		
21 phi	L	6-7f
" phi	L	7-12
22 phi	*	
23 phi	W	3-2f
" phi	W	15-7
24 phi	W	7-6f
25 bos	L	5-9
26 bos	W	5-1
" bos	L	2-4
27 NG		
28 bos	W	3-2
" bos	L	3-6
29 bos	L	3-4f
30 WAS	W	4-1

July, 1915

1 WAS	L	3-5
2 WAS	W	1-0
3 WAS	L	7-8g
" WAS	W	4-1
4 NG		
5 PHI	L	2-4
" PHI	L	1-2
6 PHI	L	6-7
7 PHI	W	13-5
" PHI	L	5-6
8 NG		
9 cle	L	3-4
10 cle	W	4-0
11 cle	W	5-2h
12 cle	W	7-4
13 det	L	2-3
" det	W	10-8
14 det		L3-12
15 det	*	
16 NG		
17 stl	L	3-4
18 stl	*	
19 stl	W	10-3
" stl	W	4-1
20 stl	L	2-3
21 NG		
22 chi	L	1-3
" chi	L	1-4
23 chi	L	2-3
24 chi	*	
25 chi	*	
26 NG		
27 DET	L	3-7
28 DET	W	6-4
29 DET	L	6-7
30 CHI	L	4-6
31 CHI	W	2-1

August, 1915

1 NG		
2 CHI	W	3-2
3 CHI	*	
4 STL	*	
5 STL	W	3-1
" STL	W	2-0
6 STL	*	
7 STL	L	1-6
" STL	TG	4-4f
8 NG		
9 CLE	TG	1-1b
10 CLE	W	2-0
" CLE	L	2-3
11 CLE	W	2-1
12 CLE	L	4-6
13 PHI	W	3-2h
14 PHI	W	9-5
15 NG		
16 PHI	L	0-2
17 NG		
18 stl	*	
19 stl	*	
20 stl	*	
21 chi	L	0-1g
" chi	W	3-2
22 chi	L	2-5
" chi	L	0-5
23 chi	L	3-4g
24 cle	L	0-6
25 cle	W	3-2
26 cle	W	6-5
27 det	L	1-8
" det	L	3-11
28 det	W	1-0
" det	L	2-6
29 det	L	4-7
30 NG		
31 was	L	1-4
" was	L	2-3g

September, 1915

1 was	L	1-2g
2 was	W	1-0
3 was	L	0-2
4 was	L	3-4
5 NG		
6 bos	W	4-0
" bos	W	5-2
7 bos	W	8-3
8 WAS	L	0-1
9 WAS	L	3-5
" WAS	L	1-4
10 STL	L	1-3
11 DET	L	3-4
12 NG		
13 DET	L	0-2
14 DET	L	2-3
15 DET	L	2-4
16 CHI	W	3-2
17 CHI	W	3-2
18 CHI	L	3-7
" CHI	L	1-4
19 NG		
20 CHI	W	3-2
21 STL	W	3-0
" STL	L	3-5
22 STL	L	2-4
" STL	L	1-3
23 STL	W	7-0
" STL	W	5-1
24 CLE	L	1-4
25 CLE	L	5-6
" CLE	W	6-1
26 NG		
27 CLE	L	2-9
28 NG		
29 NG		
30 NG		

October, 1915

1 phi	*	
2 phi	*	
3 NG		
4 BOS	W	5-1
" BOS	W	3-2
5 BOS	*	
6 BOS	L	0-2
" BOS	L	2-4
7 BOS	W	4-3

END OF 1915

RUNS: 584

OPP RUNS: 588

CLUB VS. CLUB AND MONTHLY RECORDS OF THE NEW YORK YANKEES' 1915 SEASON FOR HOME AND AWAY GAMES

CLUB:		APR	MAY	JUN	JUL	AUG	SEP	OCT	HOME	AWAY	TOTAL
BOST	H	xxx	2- 2	0- 2	xxx	xxx	xxx	3- 2	5- 6	xxx	12-10
	A	2-0	xxx	2- 4	xxx	xxx	3- 0	xxx	xxx	7- 4	
CHIC	H	xxx	xxx	1- 2	1- 1	1- 0	3- 2	xxx	6- 5	xxx	7- 15
	A	xxx	0- 3	xxx	0- 3	1- 4	xxx	xxx	xxx	1-10	
CLEV	H	xxx	xxx	2- 1	xxx	2- 2	1- 3	xxx	5- 6	xxx	13- 9
	A	xxx	3- 1	xxx	3- 1	2- 1	xxx	xxx	xxx	8- 3	
DET	H	xxx	xxx	1- 3	1- 2	xxx	0- 4	xxx	2- 9	xxx	5-17
	A	xxx	1- 1	0- 1	1- 2	1- 4	xxx	xxx	xxx	3- 8	
PHIL	H	xxx	2- 1	xxx	1- 4	2- 1	xxx	xxx	5- 6	xxx	11- 9
	A	3-1	xxx	3- 2	xxx	xxx	xxx	xxx	xxx	6- 3	
STL	H	xxx	xxx	4- 0	xxx	2- 1	3- 4	xxx	9- 5	xxx	12-10
	A	xxx	1- 3	xxx	2- 2	xxx	xxx	xxx	xxx	3- 5	
WAS	H	2-1	xxx	1- 0	2- 2	xxx	0- 3	xxx	5- 6	xxx	9-13
	A	1-2	2- 0	xxx	xxx	0- 2	1- 3	xxx	xxx	4- 7	
TOTAL:	H	2-1	4- 3	9- 8	5- 9	7- 4	7-16	3- 2	37- 43	xxx	69-83
	A	6-3	7- 8	5- 7	6- 8	4-11	4- 3	xxx	xxx	32-40	
GRAND TOT:	H	8- 4	11-11	14-15	11-17	11-15	11-19	3- 2	xxx	xxx	69-83
CUMUL. TOT:	A	8- 4	19-15	33-30	44-47	55-62	66-81	69-83	xxx	xxx	

TIE GAMES: 2 CLE-Aug; STL-Aug.

1916

NEW YORK'S FIRST HOME RUN KING

New York improved its record over 1915, winning 80 games while losing 74 to finish in fourth place, eleven games behind the champion Boston Club. New York's hitting prowess was exemplified for the first time with the acquisition of Frank Baker. Team hitting power was gradually replacing team speed as was evidenced in numerous league home run crowns by New York over the next several years.

Prior to the start of the 1916 campaign, Frank "Home Run" Baker was purchased from the Athletics of Philadelphia. Baker, who had led the league in homers in the past four seasons, lost his home run title to Wally Pipp. Pipp was thus the Yankees' first league home run season leader with 12 roundtrippers to his credit. Baker finished second in the league with ten four-baggers. At Boston, George Foster became the second pitcher to toss a no-hitter against the Yankees on June 21, the Red Sox winning 2–0.

The Yanks, for the second straight season, banged out the most homers in the Junior Circuit hitting 35. Together, Pipp and Baker formed a nucleus around which other players gathered to form future championship clubs.

The 1916 DAY BY DAY scores follow:

DAY BY DAY, 1916 NEW YORK YANKEES

April, 1916

12 WAS	L	2- 3g	
13 WAS		*	
14 WAS		*	
15 WAS	W	3- 1	
16 NG			
17 PHI		*	
18 PHI	W	4- 2	
19 PHI	W	2-1	
20 was		L4- 12	
21 was	W	5- 3c	
22 was	W	3- 2g	
23 NG			
24 WAS	L	2- 8	
25 BOS	L	3- 4f	
26 BOS	W	9- 0	
27 BOS		*	
28 BOS	L	2- 3g	
29 phi	W	4- 2f	
30 NG			

May, 1916

1 phi	L	2- 4	
2 phi	W	9- 4	
3 phi	L	2- 3	
4 bos	L	0- 3	
5 bos	W	8- 4i	
6 bos	W	5- 4	
7 NG			
8 bos	W	4- 0	
9 CHI	L	4- 5	
10 CHI	L	2- 5	
11 CHI	W	2- 1	
12 CHI	W	2- 0	
13 CLE	L	2- 4	
14 NG			
15 CLE	L	4- 6	
16 CLE		*	
17 CLE		*	
18 DET		*	
19 DET	TG	2- 2L	
20 DET	W	2- 1	
21 NG			
22 STL	L	5- 9	
23 STL		*	
24 STL	W	10- 1	
25 STL	W	7- 5	
26 BOS	W	2- 1	
" BOS	W	6- 5f	
27 BOS	W	4- 2	
28 NG			
29 BOS	L	0- 3	
30 PHI	W	7- 2	
" PHI	L	0- 1	
31 PHI	W	8- 7	
" PHI	W	9- 5	

June, 1916

1 PHI	L	0- 5	
2 NG			
3 chi	W	5- 0	
4 chi		L4- 12	
5 chi	W	3- 2	
6 stl		*	
7 stl	L	5- 6h	
8 stl		*	
9 stl	L	2- 3i	
10 det		*	
11 det	L	1- 4	
12 det	L	6- 8	
13 det	W	4- 2	
14 det	L	2- 6	
15 cle	L	2- 3f	
16 cle		*	
17 cle	W	5- 3	
18 cle	W	19- 3	
19 cle	W	7- 6	
20 bos	W	4- 1	
21 bos	L	0- 2	
22 bos	L	0- 1	
23 WAS	W	6- 5	
" WAS	W	5- 1	
24 WAS	W	2- 1	
" WAS	W	4- 3	
25 NG			
26 WAS	L	8- 9g	
27 WAS	W	3- 2	
28 phi	W	9- 7	
29 phi	W	5- 0	
30 phi	W	7- 0	

July, 1916

1 phi	W	5- 4	
2 NG			
3 was	W	1- 0g	
4 was	W	1- 0	
" was	L	4- 6	
5 was	W	9- 1	
6 CHI	W	4- 3	
7 CHI	W	4- 3h	
8 CHI	L	1- 2	
9 NG			
10 CLE	L	2- 3	
11 CLE	W	8- 2	
" CLE	L	2- 4	
12 CLE	L	0- 1	
" CLE	L	3- 6	
13 CLE	W	6- 3d	
14 DET	L	2- 6h	
" DET	W	4- 3h	
15 DET	L	7- 9	
16 NG			
17 DET	W	2- 0	
" DET	W	3- 2	
18 DET	L	0- 4	
19 STL	W	5- 0	
" STL	W	5- 4	
20 STL	L	2- 4	
21 STL		*	
22 STL		*	
" STL	W	1- 0	
23 NG			
24 NG			
25 chi	L	8-13	
26 chi	L	0- 2	
27 chi	W	8- 6	
28 chi	W	5- 3	
29 stl	L	2- 3	
" stl	L	1- 3	
30 stl	L	1- 2	
" stl	L	0- 2	
31 stl	L	2- 4	

August, 1916

1 stl	L	2-3j	
2 NG			
3 det	L	1-2	
4 det	L	2-5	
5 det	L	2-3j	
6 det	W	4-2	
7 cle	W	3-2	
8 cle	L	4- 9	
9 cle	L	3- 5	
10 cle	L	2- 3	
11 NG			
12 PHI	L	3-9	
" PHI	L	0-2	
13 NG			
14 PHI	W	4-3	
15 PHI	W	6-2	
16 CLE	W	5- 3	
17 CLE	W	5- 4	
18 CLE	W	4-3i	
19 CHI	L	1-3	
20 NG			
21 CHI	W	6-2	
22 CHI	W	7-6	
23 CHI	W	5-4	
24 STL	L	4- 5	
" STL	W	4- 2	
25 STL	L	2-5	
26 STL	W	10-6	
27 cle	L	1-5	
28 DET		*	
29 DET	L	1-9	
" DET	L	1-4	
30 DET	W	5-2	
31 DET	L	3-7	

September, 1916

1 BOS	W	7-3	
2 BOS	L	3-5	
3 NG			
4 BOS	L	1- 7	
" BOS	W	4-3	
5 was	L	0-2	
6 was		*	
7 was	L	1-5	
" was	W	3-2	
8 phi	L	2-8	
9 phi	W	4-1	
" phi	W	4-0	
10 NG			
11 NG			
12 NG			
13 det	L	1-4	
14 det	W	4-2	
15 det	L	2-4	
16 cle	W	4-3	
17 cle	L	7-9	
18 NG			
19 stl	W	4- 3k	
20 stl	L	3- 7	
21 stl	W	5-4	
22 chi	L	3-6	
23 chi	W	7-2	
24 chi	L	1-2	
25 chi	L	1-5	
26 NG			
27 bos	L	2- 3f	
28 bos	W	4- 2f	
29 bos	L	0-3	
30 bos	L	0-1f	

October, 1916

1 NG			
2 WAS	W	5-1	
3 WAS	TG	9-9g	
4 WAS	W	4-3	
" WAS	W	5-1	

END OF 1916

RUNS: 577

OPP RUNS: 561

CLUB VS. CLUB AND MONTHLY RECORDS OF THE NEW YORK YANKEES' 1916 SEASON FOR HOME AND AWAY GAMES

CLUB		APR	MAY	JUN	JUL	AUG	SEP	OCT	HOME	AWAY	TOTAL
BOST	H	1-2	3-1	xxx	xxx	xxx	2-2	xxx	6-5	xxx	11-11
	A	xxx	3-1	1-2	xxx	xxx	1-3	xxx	xxx	5-6	
CHIC	H	xxx	2-2	xxx	2-1	3-1	xxx	xxx	7-4	xxx	12-10
	A	xxx	xxx	2-1	2-2	xxx	1-3	xxx	xxx	5-6	
CLEV	H	xxx	0-2	xxx	2-4	3-0	xxx	xxx	5-6	xxx	10-12
	A	xxx	xxx	3-1	xxx	1-4	1-1	xxx	xxx	5-6	
DET	H	xxx	1-0	xxx	3-3	1-3	xxx	xxx	5-6	xxx	8-14
	A	xxx	xxx	1-3	xxx	1-3	1-2	xxx	xxx	3-8	
PHIL	H	2-0	3-1	0-1	xxx	2-2	xxx	xxx	7-4	xxx	15-7
	A	1-0	1-2	3-0	1-0	xxx	2-1	xxx	xxx	8-3	
STL	H	xxx	2-1	xxx	3-1	2-2	xxx	xxx	7-4	xxx	9-13
	A	xxx	xxx	0-2	0-5	0-1	2-1	xxx	xxx	2-9	
WAS	H	1-1	xxx	5-1	xxx	xxx	xxx	3-0	9-2	xxx	15-7
	A	2-2	xxx	xxx	3-1	xxx	1-2	xxx	xxx	6-5	
TOTAL:	H	4-3	11-7	5-2	10-9	11-8	2-2	3-0	46-31	xxx	80-74
	A	3-2	4-3	10-9	6-8	2-8	9-13	xxx	xxx	34-43	
GRAND TOT:		7-5	15-10	15-11	16-17	13-16	11-15	3-0	xxx	xxx	
CUMUL TOT:		7-5	22-15	37-26	53-43	66-59	77-74	80-74	xxx	xxx	

TIE GAMES: 2 DET-May; WAS-Oct.

1917

PIPP FLEXES HIS MUSCLES AGAIN

In this, their 15th season, the Yankees ended the season in sixth place after showing an improvement the previous year. With a worksheet of 71–82 (.464), New York closed 28½ games behind the Chicago White Sox. Bill Donovan served his last season as Yankee skipper.

For the third consecutive season, the Yankees won the league home run title, this time deparking 27 four-baggers. Wally Pipp again paced the American League with 9 roundtrippers, one of the lowest totals to win the home run crown. Despite New York's periodic flash of power, the club came in last in team batting with a .239 average. At Boston on April 24, George Mogridge became the first Yankee lefthander to hurl a no-hitter, beating the Red Sox 2–1. It will take some 66 years (1983) until Dave Righetti duplicates Mogridge's feat as a southpaw.

As in many previous seasons, 1917 was, for the most part, uneventful and quite a disappointing campaign. The Yankee dynasty was soon to be emerging under the skillful management of Miller Huggins, who will arrive on the scene in 1918.

The 1917 DAY BY DAY scores follow:

DAY BY DAY, 1917 NEW YORK YANKEES

April, 1917

```
11 BOS   L 3-10
12 BOS   L 1- 6
13 BOS        *
14 BOS   W 7- 2
15 NG
16 WAS        *
17 WAS   W 2- 1
18 WAS   W 7- 5
19 WAS   W 3- 2f
20 bos        *
21 bos   L 4- 6
22 NG
23 bos   W 9- 6
24 bos   W 2- 1
25 PHI   L 2- 4
26 PHI        *
27 PHI        *
28 PHI   L 0- 1
29 NG
30 was   W 4- 3f
```

May, 1917

```
 1 was   L 2- 3
 2 was   W 2- 0
 3 was   L 1- 3
 4 phi        *
 5 phi        *
 6 NG
 7 phi   W 9- 4
 8 phi   W 4- 2
 9 NG
10 chi   W 1- 0
11 chi   W 6- 1
12 chi   L 1- 2
13 chi   L 0- 1
14 stl   W 6- 2
15 stl   W 7- 4
16 stl   W 5- 2g
17 stl   W 7- 3
18 det   W 7- 3
19 det   TG 9- 9g
20 det   L 0- 1
21 det        *
22 det        *
23 cle        *
24 cle   L 0-2
25 cle   L 5-6
26 cle   W 4-3
27 cle   L 3-7
28 phi        *
29 phi   L 0-4
30 phi   L 3-4
 " phi   W 2- 0k
 " phi   W 6- 0
31 DET   L 0-2
```

June, 1917

```
 1 DET        *
 2 DET   W 8-4
 3 det   L 4-5
 4 det   W 6-5
 5 det   W 5-1
 " det   L 4-6
 6 CLE   L 1-6
 7 CLE        *
 8 CLE   W 7-4
 9 CLE   L 0-2
10 NG
11 CHI        *
12 CHI   W 4-3h
13 CHI   W 7-6f
14 CHI        *
15 STL   W 5-1
16 STL   W 8-4
17 STL   L 1-2
18 STL   L 0-1
19 NG
20 BOS   W 3-2
 " BOS   L 1- 3
21 BOS   W 5- 4
22 BOS   L 1-2
23 PHI   W 10- 4
 " PHI   W 2- 1
24 NG
25 PHI   W 1-0
 " PHI   W 7-5
26 PHI   W 7- 6
27 PHI   L 1- 3
28 bos   L 2- 3
 " bos   L 0- 5
29 bos   L 1- 2f
30 bos   L 2- 9
```

July, 1917

```
 1 NG
 2 bos   TG 4- 4g
 3 WAS        *
 4 WAS   L 4- 6
 " WAS   L 4- 5
 5 WAS   L 1- 2
 " WAS   W 5- 4i
 6 NG
 7 stl   L 0- 1
 8 stl   L 2- 8
 9 stl   W 2- 1
10 stl   W 7- 5m
11 chi        *
12 chi   L 1- 2f
 " chi   L 3- 5
13 chi   W 6- 5g
14 chi   L 1- 4
15 cle   W 4- 0
 " cle   W 8- 2
16 cle   L 2- 3
17 cle   L 1- 2
18 cle   W 12- 7f
19 det   L 0- 2
20 det   W 3- 1
21 det   L 3- 4f
 " det   L 2-11
22 det   W 7- 5i
23 NG
24 NG
25 CHI   L 1- 4
 " CHI   L 1- 5
26 CHI   W 6- 5j
27 CHI   L 5- 9
28 CHI   W 5- 4
 " CHI   W 4- 3
29 NG
30 STL   W 3- 2
31 STL   W 4-1
```

August, 1917

```
 1 STL        *
 2 STL   L 0- 3
 " STL   W 3- 1
 3 DET   L 3- 10
 4 DET   L 0- 3
 5 NG
 6 DET   W 5- 3
 7 DET   W 7- 1
 8 CLE   W 8- 2
 " CLE   L 1- 2
 9 CLE   L 2-5f
10 CLE   L 7- 8j
11 CLE   L 1- 4
12 NG
13 was   L 5- 9
14 was   L 0- 1
 " was   L 1- 10
15 NG
16 NG
17 stl   W 4- 1
18 stl   L 1- 7
19 stl   L 1- 4
20 det   L 2- 3
21 det   W 3- 1f
22 det   L 0- 2
23 cle   L 2- 4
24 NG
25 cle   W 3- 0
26 chi   L 3- 8
27 chi   L 0- 3
28 chi   L 3- 4
29 NG
30 WAS        *
31 WAS   L 1- 4
 " WAS   L 3- 6g
```

September, 1917

```
 1 WAS        *
 2 NG
 3 bos   W 1- 0
 " bos   W 4- 1
 4 bos   L 2- 4
 " bos   W 7- 3
 5 was   L 0- 3
 6 was        *
 7 was   L 0-6
 " was   W 4-1
 8 was   W 2-0
 " was   L 0-3
 9 NG
10 phi   W 10-1
 " phi   W 5-1
11 phi   W 1-0
 " phi   W 4- 1
12 phi   L 1- 7
13 BOS   W 13- 7
14 BOS   L 5- 6
15 BOS   L 3- 8
16 NG
17 BOS   L 1-6
18 CLE   L 4-5
19 CLE   L 0-2
20 CLE   L 2-6
21 STL   W 9-6
22 STL   L 2-4
 " STL   L 0-3
23 NG
24 NG
25 DET   L 2-4
26 DET   L 1-5
27 NG
28 CHI        *
29 CHI   W 12-8
 " CHI   L 1-3
30 NG
```

October, 1917

```
 1 CHI   W 4-2
 2 PHI   W 3-2
 3 PHI   L 1- 3
 " PHI   W 3- 2
END OF 1917
RUNS:        524
OPP RUNS:    558
```

CLUB VS. CLUB AND MONTHLY RECORDS OF THE NEW YORK YANKEES' 1917 SEASON FOR HOME AND AWAY GAMES

CLUB:		APR	MAY	JUN	JUL	AUG	SEP	OCT	HOME	AWAY	TOTAL
BOST	H	1-2	xxx	2-2	xxx	xxx	1-3	xxx	4-7	xxx	
	A	2-1	xxx	0-4	xxx	xxx	3-1	xxx	xxx	5-6	9-13
CHIC	H	xxx	xxx	2-0	3-3	x	1-1	1-0	7-4	x	
	A	x	2-2	x	1-3	0-3	x	x	x	3-8	10-12
CLEV	H	x	x	1-2	xxx	1-4	0-3	xxx	2-9	xxx	
	A	xxx	1-3	xxx	3-2	1-1	xxx	xxx	xxx	5-6	7-15
DET	H	xxx	0-1	3-1	xxx	2-2	0-2	xxx	5-6	xxx	
	A	xxx	1-1	0-1	2-3	1-2	xxx	xxx	xxx	4-7	9-13
PHIL	H	0-2	xxx	5-1	xxx	xxx	xxx	2-1	7-4	xxx	
	A	xxx	4-2	xxx	xxx	xxx	4-1	xxx	xxx	8-3	15-7
STL	H	xxx	xxx	2-2	2-0	1-1	1-2	xxx	6-5	xxx	
	A	xxx	4-0	xxx	2-2	1-2	xxx	xxx	xxx	7-4	13-9
WAS	H	3-0	xxx	xxx	1-3	0-2	xxx	xxx	4-5	xxx	
	A	1-0	1-2	xxx	xxx	0-3	2-3	xxx	xxx	4-8	8-13
TOTAL:	H	4-4	0-1	15-8	6-6	4-9	3-11	3-1	35-40	xxx	
	A	3-1	13-10	0-5	8-10	3-11	9-5	xxx	xxx	36-42	71-82
GRAND TOT:		7-5	13-11	15-13	14-16	7-20	12-16	3-1	xxx	xxx	
CUMUL TOT:		7-5	20-16	35-29	49-45	56-65	68-81	71-82	xxx	xxx	

TIE GAMES: 2
det-May; bos-Jul.

1918

MILLER HUGGINS ASSUMES YANKEE MANAGERIAL DUTIES

Miller Huggins, one of the Yankees' most successful field generals, took over the club, becoming their ninth manager. In this war-shortened season, New York ended up in fourth place behind manager Ed Barrow's Boston Club, who went on to win the World Series. Under American League President Ban Johnson's orders, the 1918 season was ended on September 2. In 126 games, New York won 60, lost 63 and three contests ended in a tie.

This year, no individual Yankee players set the league afire in any major statistical category. However, as a club, New York concluded 1918 in second place in fielding percentage with a .970 mark, .001 points behind league-leading Boston. In addition, four Yanks ranked as the best in double plays: Pratt led all A.L. second basemen with 82 twin killings, Peckinpaugh bests all shortstops with 75, Gilhooley paces all outfielders with eight and Hannah tops all catchers with 16 double plays. New York also recorded a league-high 137 double plays, one more than Philadelphia.

Miller Huggins' presence as manager was evident this season, with New York playing almost .500 ball. Team progress will continue to be apparent over the next few seasons, 1919 being no exception.

The 1918 DAY BY DAY scores follow:

DAY BY DAY, 1918 NEW YORK YANKEES

April, 1918
15 was   W   6- 3
16 was   L   6-7
17 was   W   8-7h
18 was   '*
19 bos   L   1-2
" bos   L   5-9
20 bos   L   3-4
21 NG
22 bos   W 11- 4
23 bos   L   0-1
24 WAS W   5-4
25 WAS L   5-7
26 WAS L   4-9
27 WAS W   2-1
28 NG
29 PHI   *
30 PHI W   2- 0

May, 1918
1 PHI   *
2 PHI   L   5-7
3 BOS W   3-2g
4 BOS W   5-4
5 NG
6 BOS W 10-3
7 phi   W   9-1
8 phi   L   2-5
9 phi   W   7-3
10 DET L   3-5
11 DET W   6- 5
12 NG
13 DET W   3-2
14 DET   *
15 STL L   4-5h
16 STL W   1-0
17 STL W   4-2
18 STL L   5-6
19 NG
20 CHI L   2- 6
21 CHI   *
22 CHI W   1- 0j
23 CHI   *
24 CLE L   2- 3o

May, 1918
25 CLE W   2-1
26 cle   W   9- 3
27 CLE W   7- 1
28 CLE L   2-3
29 PHI W   7-2
" PHI W 12-2
30 PHI W   2-1
31 NG

June, 1918
1 chi   W   6- 3
2 chi   L   2- 6
3 chi   L   2-9
4 chi   L   4-5
5 stl   W   5-2
6 stl   W   5-2f
7 stl   W   1-0
8 stl   W   4-3
9 stl   L   4-5h
10 NG
11 cle   L   3- 4h
12 cle   L   5- 7
13 cle   W   3- 2f
14 det W 11-6
15 det L   0-4
16 det W   5-2
17 det TG 5- 5d
18 NG
19 WAS W   9-0
20 WAS L   1-4
21 WAS L   2- 3i
22 WAS W   5- 3
23 NG
24 BOS W   3-2
25 BOS L   3-7
26 BOS W   3-1
27 BOS W   7-5
28 phi   W 10-2
29 phi   L   1-2
30 NG

July, 1918
1 phi   W   9- 2
2 phi   L   0- 5

July, 1918
3 was   L   3- 4
4 was   W   7- 0
" was   L   3- 4
5 was   L   1- 2
6 CHI   W   3- 1
" CHI   L   2- 3
7 NG
8 CHI   W   6- 5
9 CHI   W   6- 4
" CHI   L   3- 4f
10 CHI L   4- 5
11 CLE L   0- 1
12 CLE W   6- 1
13 CLE W   4- 3
14 cle   L   1- 7
15 CLE L   3- 5
16 DET L   1-12
" DET L   1- 4
17 DET   *
18 DET L   1- 4
" DET W   3- 2f
19 STL   *
20 STL L   2- 5
" STL W   5- 3
21 NG
22 STL TG 4- 4k
23 STL W   4- 1
24 NG
25 cle   *
26 cle   L   3- 8
27 cle   L   6- 7f
28 cle   TG 2- 2f
29 det L   2- 3
30 det L   0- 3
31 det W   5- 3
" det L   2- 6

August, 1918
1 det   W   7- 0
2 stl   L   2- 3
3 stl   L   5- 8
4 stl   L   6- 7
" stl   L   3- 5

August, 1918
5 NG
6 chi   L   4- 5k
7 chi   L   4- 8
" chi   L   0- 4
8 NG
9 NG
10 bos W   5- 1f
" bos W   4- 1
11 NG
12 bos W   2- 1
13 NG
14 CLE L   2- 7
15 CLE W   3- 2
16 CLE L4- 12
17 CHI L   4- 7
" CHI W   7- 2
18 NG
19 CHI L   1- 4
20 NG
21 DET W   5- 2
22 DET W   5- 3
23 NG
24 DET L   4- 5
" DET W   2- 0
25 NG
26 STL L   0- 2
27 STL W   4- 2
" STL W   7- 6h
28 STL L   2- 4
29 was   W   6- 4
30 was   L   1- 6
31 was   L   3- 6

September, 1918
1 was   L   3- 5
2 BOS   L   2- 3
" BOS W   4- 3##

END OF 1918
RUNS: 493
OPP RUNS: 475

##SEASON SHORTENED
DUE TO WORLD WAR I

CLUB VS. CLUB AND MONTHLY RECORDS OF THE NEW YORK YANKEES' 1918 SEASON FOR HOME AND AWAY GAMES

CLUB:		APR	MAY	JUN	JUL	AUG	SEP	OCT	HOME	AWAY	TOTAL
BOST	H	xxx	3– 0	3– 1	xxx	xxx	1– 1	xxx	7– 2	xxx	
	A	1–4	xxx	xxx	xxx	3– 0	xxx	xxx	xxx	4– 4	11– 6
CHIC	H	xxx	1– 1	xxx	3– 3	1– 2	xxx	xxx	5– 6	xxx	
	A	xxx	xxx	1– 3	xxx	0– 3	xxx	xxx	xxx	1– 6	6–12
CLEV	H	xxx	2– 2	xxx	2– 2	1– 2	xxx	xxx	5– 6	xxx	
	A	xxx	1– 0	1– 2	0– 3	xxx	xxx	xxx	xxx	2– 5	7–11
DET	H	xxx	2– 1	xxx	1– 3	3– 1	xxx	xxx	6– 5	xxx	
	A	xxx	xxx	2– 1	1– 3	1– 0	xxx	xxx	xxx	4– 4	10– 9
PHIL	H	1–0	3– 1	xxx	xxx	xxx	xxx	xxx	4– 1	xxx	
	A	xxx	2– 1	1– 1	1– 1	xxx	xxx	xxx	xxx	4– 3	8– 4
STL	H	xxx	2– 2	xxx	2– 1	2– 2	xxx	xxx	6– 5	xxx	
	A	xxx	xxx	4– 1	xxx	0– 4	xxx	xxx	xxx	4– 5	10–10
WAS	H	2–2	xxx	2– 2	xxx	xxx	xxx	xxx	4– 4	xxx	
	A	2–1	xxx	xxx	1– 3	1– 2	0– 1	xxx	xxx	4– 7	8–11
TOTAL:	H	3–2	13– 7	5– 3	8– 9	7– 7	1– 1	xxx	37–29	xxx	
	A	3–5	3– 1	9– 8	3–10	5– 9	0– 1	xxx	xxx	23– 34	60–63
GRAND TOT:		6–7	16– 8	14–11	11–19	12–16	1– 2	xxx	xxx	xxx	
CUMUL TOT:		6–7	22–15	36–26	47–45	59–61	60–63	xxx	xxx	xxx	

TIE GAMES 3
STL-Jul; det-Jun; cle-Jul.

1919

MOVING UP TO THIRD PLACE

Playing a 140-game schedule for only their second time (1903 was the other), Huggins piloted New York into third place, 7½ games off pennant-winning Chicago's pace. In twelve seasons as manager, Huggins eventually won six pennants and three World Series. New York's attendance at the Polo Grounds continued to rise, attracting some 337,117 more fans than in 1918. This increase was a 120% gain over the preceding year.

With a pitching staff shored by veterans Jack Quinn and Bob Shawkey, New York hurlers allowed the fewest runs by opponents, with a league-leading total of 514. This was the first of many seasons that the New York pitching staff would permit the fewest runs in the league. On the other side of the pitching ledger, Ray Caldwell pitched the third no-hitter against New York, Cleveland winning 3–0 on September 10 at the Polo Grounds.

New York lost twenty-one games in the month of July (they won 13). This marked the last time (through 1983) that twenty or more losses were suffered in any month. Prior to 1919, this "feat" of 20+ losses in a month was attained on six previous occasions.

This season proved to be the last "dead ball" year for New York for some time. Supporting this notion was the additon of one new Yankee to the fold in 1920, one George Herman Ruth.

The 1919 DAY BY DAY scores follow:

DAY BY DAY, 1919 NEW YORK YANKEES

April, 1919

23 BOS	L	0–10
24 BOS		*
25 BOS		*
26 BOS		*
27 NG		
28 PHI	W	3– 2h
29 PHI	L	1– 7
30 PHI	W	5– 3

May, 1919

1 bos	W	7– 3
2 bos	W	3– 1
3 bos	L	2– 3
4 NG		
5 bos	W	5– 1
6 phi	L	2– 3f
7 phi		*
8 phi	W	2– 0
9 WAS		*
10 WAS		*
11 WAS	TG	0– 0h
12 WAS	TG	4– 4k
13 NG		
14 det	W	1– 0
15 det	W	4– 3
16 det		*
17 cle	W	8– 3
18 cle	L	3– 4
19 cle	W	7– 0
20 cle		*
21 chi		*
22 chi	L	0– 1
23 chi	L	0– 5
24 chi	W	2– 1
25 stl	L	5– 6
26 stl	L	1– 2f
27 stl	L	3– 5
28 NG		
29 was	W	5– 4f
30 was	W	4– 2f
" was	W	6– 2
31 was	W	6– 5f

June, 1919

–1 was	L	2– 5
2 phi	W	7– 0
" phi	W	10– 5
3 phi	W	10– 9
4 phi	W	10– 7
5 CHI	L	1– 5
6 CHI		*
7 CHI	W	6– 4
8 CHI	W	4– 0
9 NG		
10 DET	W	2– 1
11 DET	W	7– 0
12 DET	W	6– 1
13 DET	L	5– 6
14 STL	W	7– 2
15 STL	L	0– 1
16 STL	W	4– 3f
17 STL	W	5– 2
18 CLE	L	3–13
19 CLE	L	3– 4
20 NG		
21 CLE	W	2– 1
22 BOS	W	6– 2
23 PHI	W	11– 4
24 PHI	W	9– 0
25 PHI	W	4– 3
26 PHI		*
27 BOS		*
28 BOS	L	0– 2
" BOS	W	4– 1
29 BOS	L	3– 5
30 BOS	W	7– 4
" BOS	W	4– 2

July, 1919

1 was	W	1– 0
2 was	L	4– 6
3 was	L	0– 1
4 WAS	W	8– 2
" WAS	W	6– 5
5 WAS	W	6– 4
" WAS	L	5– 11

July, 1919

6 WAS	L	1– 3
7 WAS	W	3– 2
8 NG		
9 cle	L	0– 2
10 cle	W	1– 0
" cle	L	3– 7
11 cle	L	1– 5
12 det	L	5– 8
13 det	L	4– 5
14 det	L	0– 3
" det		*
15 det	L	2–13
" det	W	3– 0b
16 stl	L	0– 5
17 stl	L	6– 7m
18 stl	W	4– 3
19 stl	W	9– 8
20 chi	L	1– 2f
21 chi	L	4– 5f
" chi	L	6– 7
22 chi	W	6– 1
23 NG		
24 bos	L	3– 4
25 bos	L	6– 8
26 bos	W	8– 5
27 NG		
28 bos	L	1– 5
29 CHI	W	10– 1
30 CHI	W	6– 5f
" CHI	L	3– 5f
31 CHI	L	2– 7

August, 1919

1 DET	W	5– 4
2 DET	L	8– 14f
3 DET	W	10– 2
4 NG		
5 STL		*
6 STL		*
7 STL	L	3– 6
" STL	W	8– 2d
8 STL	W	6– 1

August, 1919

9 CLE	L	4– 6
10 CLE	W	11– 4
11 CLE	L	9–15
12 CLE	L	1– 2
13 NG		
14 det	W	5– 4k
15 det	L	0– 7
16 det	L	2– 3
17 cle	W	6– 2
18 cle	L	1– 2
19 cle	L	1– 5
20 stl		*
21 stl	W	3– 2
" stl	L	1– 2j
22 stl	W	5– 2
23 chi	L	2–10
24 chi	L	1– 4
25 chi	W	6– 5
26 NG		
27 WAS		*
28 WAS	W	5– 4j
" WAS	W	5– 3
29 WAS	W	4– 1
" WAS	W	5– 1
30 PHI	W	5– 2
31 PHI	W	6– 0

September, 1919

1 phi		*
" phi	W	5– 2
2 bos		*
3 bos		*
4 NG		
5 NG		
6 was	L	1– 4
7 was	W	3– 2
8 BOS	L	1– 3
" BOS	L	0– 3
9 CLE		*
10 CLE	L	2– 3
" CLE	L	0– 3
11 CLE	W	2– 1

September, 1919

12 STL		*
13 STL	W	4– 1
" STL	W	9– 6
14 STL	W	8– 1
15 NG		
16 CHI		*
17 CHI	L	0– 2
" CHI	L	2–11
18 CHI	W	6– 4
19 DET	W	7– 0
20 DET	W	6– 3
21 DET	W	4– 3
22 NG		
23 BOS		*
24 BOS	L	0– 4
" BOS	W	2– 1i
25 PHI	W	4– 0
26 PHI	W	8– 2
27 phi	W	4– 1
" phi	W	9– 2
28 NG		
29 phi	W	4– 2

END OF 1919

RUNS:	578
OPP RUNS:	506

CLUB VS. CLUB AND MONTHLY RECORDS OF THE NEW YORK YANKEES' 1919 SEASON FOR HOME AND AWAY GAMES

CLUB:	APR	MAY	JUN	JUL	AUG	SEP	OCT	HOME	AWAY	TOTAL
BOST H	0-1	xxx	4- 2	xxx	xxx	1- 3	xxx	5- 6	xxx	
BOST A	xxx	3- 1	xxx	1- 3	xxx	xxx	xxx	xxx	4- 4	9-10
CHIC H	xxx	xxx	2- 1	2- 2	xxx	1- 2	xxx	5- 5	xxx	
CHIC A	xxx	1- 2	xxx	1- 3	1- 2	xxx	xxx	xxx	3- 7	8-12
CLEV H	xxx	xxx	1- 2	xxx	1- 3	1- 2	xxx	3- 7	xxx	
CLEV A	xxx	2- 1	xxx	1- 3	1- 2	xxx	xxx	xxx	4- 6	7-13
DET H	xxx	xxx	3- 1	xxx	2- 1	3- 0	xxx	8- 2	xxx	
DET A	xxx	2- 0	xxx	1- 4	1- 2	xxx	xxx	xxx	4- 6	12- 8
PHIL H	2- 1	xxx	3- 0	xxx	2- 0	2- 0	xxx	9- 1	xxx	
PHIL A	xxx	1- 1	4- 0	xxx	xxx	4- 0	xxx	xxx	9- 1	18- 2
STL H	xxx	xxx	3- 1	xxx	2- 1	3- 0	xxx	8- 2	xxx	
STL A	xxx	0- 3	xxx	2- 2	2- 1	xxx	xxx	xxx	4- 6	12- 8
WAS H	xxx	xxx	xxx	4- 2	4- 0	xxx	xxx	8- 2	xxx	
WAS A	xxx	4- 0	0- 1	1- 2	xxx	1- 1	xxx	xxx	6- 4	14- 6
TOTAL: H	2-2	xxx	16- 7	6- 4	11- 5	11- 7	xxx	46-25	xxx	
TOTAL: A	xxx	13- 8	4- 1	7-17	5- 7	5- 1	xxx	xxx	34-34	80-59
GRAND TOT:	2-2	13- 8	20- 8	13-21	16-12	16- 8	xxx	xxx	xxx	
CUMUL TOT:	2-2	15-10	35-18	48-39	64- 51	80-59	xxx	xxx	xxx	

TIE GAMES: 2
WAS-Apr (2).

1920

THE BABE ARRIVES ON THE SCENE

The 20's began with a new addition to the Yankees' lineup, one Mr. George Herman Ruth, affectionately called the Babe. With the Babe in their fold, the Yankees finished in third place, 3 games behind A.L. champion Cleveland. Up to this season, the New Yorkers had never won so many games (95) since emerging victorious in 92 contests way back in 1904. Their 95–59 ledger (.617) was their best ever to this point in Yankee history.

Babe Ruth, who is probably without question the greatest namesake in baseball history, was acquired from the Boston Red Sox (as were many other Yankee mainstays through the years) late in 1919. Ruth's acquisition by Ruppert and Huston was easily the single greatest deal in New York Yankee history. After the scandalous Black Sox fiasco of 1919, the Babe was to become a savior of sorts of the game of baseball. Babe's home run prowess, which prior to this year was unparalleled in baseball annals, refocused the attention of a nation to the more positive aspects of our National Pastime, thus maximizing the chances of its future success and survival. In this, Ruth's first season in New York, he batted a very respectable .376, fourth best in the league. He led both leagues in RBI with 137, walks with 148, runs with 158 and an incredible slugging percentage of .847! The latter slugging mark looks like a typesetter's error but it is not. His .847 figure remains the all-time slugging mark and in all probability will never be surpassed. That translates into 388 total bases in 458 times at bat; simply astonishing! Ruth also connected for a previously unheard of 54 homers, eclipsing his own A.L. mark of 29 set the previous year. His influence allowed New York to become the first club in Major League history to hit over 100 + (115) home runs in a season.

1920 marked the first occasion that the Yankees hit 100 + homers; they will accomplish this feat some 58 more times through 1983, representing a 63 year span. As far as slugging average goes, the Bombers will go on to win 27 more of those titles between 1920 and 1962.

In terms of Yankee pitching, Carl Mays (26–11), Bob Shawkey (20–13), and Jack Quinn (18–10), anchor New York's A.L. top ERA staff with 3.31. The club paced the league with 16 shutouts of their opponents, Mays leading the league individually with 6 whitewash jobs, becoming the first Yankee hurler to do so. Bob Shawkey was the first Yankee to win an A.L. ERA title, posting a fine 2.45 mark.

On a tragic note, Cleveland's Ray Chapman was struck by a Carl Mays pitch on August 16, Chapman passing away the next day. He never regained consciousness before his death. In all of recorded baseball history, this was the only known playing fatality.

In a game on July 6 at Washington, the Yankees scored fourteen runs in the fifth inning to post a 17–0 victory. That run total in an inning was the American League mark until tied by two other clubs. However, all of these totals were surpassed by Boston's 17-run seventh inning versus Detroit on June 18, 1953.

Another club milestone was passed in 1920. Playing at the Polo Grounds, the Yanks drew a then Major League record attendance of 1,289,422 for one season. They outdrew their co-tenants,the Giants,for the first time in their history. This increased attendance must surely be correlated to the Babe's arrival in New York.

After six seasons as Yankee General Manager, Harry Sparrow died and Ed Barrow assumed the role of second New York GM, remaining in that capacity until 1945.

This season can be best described in two words—Babe Ruth. His domination of the game of baseball was indeed felt during the course of the season. New York Yankee fans needed to wait only one more season for the club's first of many pennants. The seeds for future pennant-winning Yankee teams were now taking root in the Bronx.

The 1920 DAY BY DAY scores follow:

DAY BY DAY, 1920 NEW YORK YANKEES

April, 1920	May, 1920	July, 1920	August, 1920	September, 1920
14 phi L 1-3	25 DET W 4- 3	1 phi W 9- 5	6 det W 11- 7	15 NG
15 phi W 4-1	26 DET W 4- 1	2 phi W 7- 4	7 det W 7- 3	16 chi L 3- 8
16 phi *	27 bos W 6- 1	3 phi W 5- 0	8 det L 0- 1	17 chi L 4- 6
17 phi *	28 bos W 4- 3	" phi W 4- 2	9 cle W 6- 3	18 chi L 9-15
18 NG	29 bos W 4- 3	4 was L 2- 5	10 cle *	19 stl L 1- 6
19 bos L 0-6	" bos W 8- 3	5 was L 3- 4	11 cle W 7- 4f	20 stl W 4- 3g
" bos L 3- 8	30 NG	" was L 3- 9	12 cle W 5- 1	21 stl W 8- 3
20 bos L 2- 3	31 WAS W 7- 6	6 was W 17- 0	13 cle W 4- 3	22 NG
21 bos *	" WAS W 10- 7	7 NG	14 was W 3- 2	23 NG
22 PHI W 8-6	**June, 1920**	8 DET L 3- 4	15 was L 4- 6	24 WAS L 1- 3
23 PHI *	1 WAS W 14- 7	9 DET W 9- 3	16 CLE L 3- 4	" WAS W 2- 1
24 PHI W 3-2f	2 WAS W 8- 1	10 DET W 7- 6f	17 NG	25 WAS L 2- 5
25 PHI L 1-2	" WAS L 6- 7	11 DET W 6- 5	18 CLE W 4- 3	26 WAS W 9- 5
26 WAS W 3-2	3 PHI W 5- 4	12 NG	19 CLE L 2- 3	27 phi W 3-0
27 WAS *	4 PHI W 12- 5	13 STL L 4- 6	20 NG	28 phi *
28 WAS *	5 PHI *	" STL W 7- 2	21 DET L 3-10	29 phi W 7- 3
29 WAS L 1-2	6 PHI W 12- 6	14 STL L 3- 7	22 DET L 9-11	" phi W 9- 4g
30 BOS L 2-4	7 PHI W 3- 1	15 STL W 13-10g	23 DET W 10- 0	
May, 1920	" PHI L 5- 6	16 STL L 2- 5	24 DET L 3- 5	END OF 1920
1 BOS W 6- 0	8 det W 13- 6	17 CHI W 20- 5	25 NG	RUNS: 837
2 BOS W 7- 1	9 det W 11- 3	18 CHI W 8- 4	26 CHI L 4-16	OPP RUNS: 629
3 BOS L 1-3	10 det W 7- 5d	19 CHI W 8- 2	27 CHI W 6- 5h	
4 BOS W 6-1	11 det W 5- 0	" CHI L 5- 8	28 CHI W 3- 0	
5 was W 7-1	12 cle L 4- 5	20 CHI L 5- 7	29 STL W 4- 3	
6 was L 1-4	13 cle W 14- 0	" CHI W 6- 3	30 NG	
7 was L 5-6	14 cle L 1- 7	21 CLE W 4- 3	31 STL L 2- 3	
8 was L 0-3	15 cle L2- 10	22 CLE W 11- 3c	**September, 1920**	
9 was W 5-3	16 chi W 7- 4	23 CLE W 6- 3	1 STL W 2- 0	
10 NG	17 chi W 7- 2	24 CLE L 2- 4g	2 bos L 2- 6	
11 CHI W 6-5	18 chi W 3- 2	25 BOS W 8- 2	3 bos W 5- 3	
12 CHI W 14-8	19 chi L 5- 6f	26 BOS L 0- 9	4 bos W 5- 3	
13 CHI *	20 stl W 4- 3	27 NG	" bos L 5- 6	
14 CHI *	21 stl *	28 stl L 0- 1	5 NG	
15 CLE W 2- 0	22 stl L 3- 9	29 stl L 3- 4	6 PHI W 4- 1	
16 CLE L 2- 8	23 stl W 6- 3	" stl W 6- 4	" PHI W 5- 0	
17 NG	24 NG	30 stl W 19- 3	7 PHI W 2- 0	
18 CLE W 11- 0	25 BOS L 3- 6	31 stl L 8-13	8 NG	
19 CLE L 0-5	26 BOS W 14- 0	**August, 1920**	9 cle L 4-10	
20 STL W 8-3	27 BOS W 7- 5	1 chi L 0- 3	10 cle W 6- 1	
21 STL *	28 NG	2 chi W 7- 0	11 cle W 6- 2	
22 STL L 1-2	29 BOS W 6- 5	3 chi L 1- 3	12 det W 13- 6	
23 STL W 3-2	30 phi W 6- 5	4 chi L3- 10	13 det W 4- 2	
24 DET L 1-3	" phi W 10- 6	5 det L 1- 7	14 det W 13- 3	

CLUB VS. CLUB AND MONTHLY RECORDS OF THE NEW YORK YANKEES' 1920 SEASON FOR HOME AND AWAY GAMES

CLUB		APR	MAY	JUN	JUL	AUG	SEP	OCT	HOME	AWAY	TOTAL
BOST	H	0-1	3- 1	3- 1	1- 1	xxx	xxx	xxx	7- 4	xxx	13- 9
	A	0-3	4- 0	xxx	xxx	xxx	2- 2	xxx	xxx	6- 5	
CHIC	H	xxx	2- 0	xxx	4- 2	2- 1	xxx	xxx	8- 3	xxx	12-10
	A	xxx	xxx	3- 1	xxx	1- 3	0- 3	xxx	xxx	4- 7	
CLEV	H	xxx	2- 2	xxx	3- 1	1- 2	xxx	xxx	6- 5	xxx	13- 9
	A	xxx	xxx	1- 3	xxx	4- 0	2- 1	xxx	xxx	7- 4	
DET	H	xxx	2- 1	xxx	3- 1	1- 3	xxx	xxx	6- 5	xxx	15- 7
	A	xxx	xxx	4- 0	xxx	2- 2	3- 0	xxx	xxx	9- 2	
PHIL	H	2-1	xxx	4- 1	xxx	xxx	3- 0	xxx	9- 2	xxx	19- 3
	A	1-1	xxx	2- 0	4- 0	xxx	3- 0	xxx	xxx	10- 1	
STL	H	xxx	2- 1	xxx	2- 3	1- 1	1- 0	xxx	6- 5	xxx	12-10
	A	xxx	xxx	2- 1	2- 3	xxx	2- 1	xxx	xxx	6- 5	
WAS	H	1-1	2- 0	2- 1	xxx	xxx	2- 2	xxx	7- 4	xxx	11-11
	A	xxx	2- 3	xxx	1- 3	1- 1	xxx	xxx	xxx	4- 7	
TOTAL:	H	3-3	13- 5	9- 3	13- 8	5- 7	6- 2	xxx	49-28	xxx	95-59
	A	1-4	6- 3	12- 5	7- 6	8- 6	12- 7	xxx	xxx	46-31	
GRAND TOT:		4-7	19- 8	21- 8	20-14	13-13	18- 9	xxx	xxx	xxx	TIE GAMES: NONE
CUMUL TOT:		4-7	23-15	44-23	64-37	77-50	95-59	xxx	xxx	xxx	

1921

THE FIRST OF MANY YANKEE PENNANTS

The year 1921 brought New York their first pennant in their nineteenth season. Huggins guided his troops to a then Yankee record of 98 wins, heading the second place Cleveland club by 4½ games. Baseball had its first commissioner, Kenesaw Mountain Landis, who served in that capacity until his death in November of 1944.

As with the previous season, Babe Ruth dominated league statistics. "The Sultan of Swat" led the A.L. in the following categories: home runs (59),eclipsing his Major League record he set just the previous year; runs scored (177),an American League record today still unthreatened; bases on balls (144); runs batted in (171) and an incredible slugging percentage of .846, just .001 below his 1920 all-time Major League total. In addition, Babe set another league (and Major League) standard accounting for 457 total bases on 85 singles, 44 doubles, 16 triples and 59 home runs, the latter three totals combining for 119 long hits, another Major League record. Quite a season!

As a team, New York paced the league with 948 runs, 134 homers, 861 runs batted in, and a .464 slugging percentage. In pitching statistics, Carl Mays won a league high 27 victories, with 9 defeats, a .750 A.L.-topping winning percentage. Composite pitching figures had the Yankees winning their second consecutive team ERA mark, with 3.79. Also, Yankee hurlers had the most A.L. complete games and strikeouts, 92 and 481, respectively.

Although eventually losing out to the Giants in the first "Subway" World Series, this Yankees season was their most successful to date. However, they would have to wait until 1923 to clinch their first of 22 (through 1983) unprecedented World Series championships.

The 1921 DAY BY DAY scores follow:

DAY BY DAY, 1921 NEW YORK YANKEES

April, 1921	May, 1921	June, 1921	August, 1921	September, 1921
13 PHI W 11- 1	24 stl L 4- 8	30 BOS *	7 CHI W 2- 0a	11 BOS L 1- 3
14 PHI L 3- 4	25 stl L 6- 7	**July, 1921**	8 CHI W 7- 0	" BOS W 5- 1
15 PHI *	26 NG	1 BOS *	" CHI L 4- 5	12 NG
16 PHI W 3- 1	27 was W 11- 4	2 BOS W 5- 3	9 CHI L 4- 5	13 CHI L 2- 6
17 BOS W 4- 0	28 PHI W 5- 1	" BOS W 5- 1	10 CHI W 14- 8	14 CHI W 11- 8
18 BOS *	" PHI W 6- 2	3 NG	11 phi W 7- 3	15 STL W 10- 6
19 BOS *	29 PHI W 9- 4	4 PHI W 6- 4	12 phi L 6- 8	" STL W 13- 5
20 BOS W 8- 4	30 was W 2- 1	" PHI W 14- 4	13 phi W 7- 2	16 STL L3- 10
21 phi W 6- 1	" was L 0- 1	5 PHI W 7- 5	" phi W 13- 7	17 NG
22 phi L 4-11	31 was L 5-12	6 NG	14 NG	18 DET W 4- 2
23 phi *	**June, 1921**	7 NG	15 NG	19 DET L6- 10
24 was L 1- 3	1 was L 7- 8	8 chi L 1- 4	16 NG	20 DET W 4- 2
25 WAS L 3- 5	2 STL W 7- 2	9 chi L 9-10L	17 chi W 11- 3c	21 DET *
26 WAS L 4- 5	3 STL L 8- 9	10 chi L 1- 4	18 chi L 6- 7	22 DET W 12- 5
27 WAS L 3- 5	4 STL W 9- 4	11 chi W 4- 0	19 chi L 9-13	23 CLE W 4- 2
28 WAS W 9- 5	5 STL W 5- 4	12 stl W 6- 4	20 stl W 5- 2	24 CLE L 0- 9
29 bos *	6 STL L 1- 5	13 stl W 11- 1	21 stl L 4- 5	25 CLE W 21- 7
30 bos *	7 CLE W 9- 2	14 stl *	" stl L 0-10	26 CLE W 8- 7
May, 1921	8 CLE W 4- 3	15 stl W 7- 3	22 stl W 10- 2	27 STL L 0- 2
1 NG	9 CLE L 4-14	16 det W 5- 4	23 cle W 6- 1	28 NG
2 bos L 1- 2	10 CLE L 6- 8g	17 det W 8- 5	24 cle W 3- 2f	29 phi W 5- 0
3 bos W 2- 0	11 DET W 7- 6	18 det W 10- 1	25 cle L 1-15	30 phi
4 was *	12 DET W 12- 8	19 det W 6- 5	26 det W 10- 2	**October, 1921**
5 was *	13 DET W 13- 8	20 cle W 7- 1	27 det W 7- 5	1 PHI W 5- 3
6 was W 9- 2	14 DET W 9- 6	21 cle L 8-17	28 det L 3- 7	" PHI W 7- 6g
7 was W 6- 5	15 CHI L 2- 7	22 NG	29 NG	2 BOS W 7- 6
8 PHI L 4- 5j	16 CHI W 7- 3	23 cle L 0- 3	30 WAS W 10- 3	
9 NG	17 CHI *	24 cle W 7- 3	31 WAS W 17- 9	**END OF 1921**
10 det W 2- 1	18 CHI L 3- 4	25 NG	**September, 1921**	RUNS: 948
11 det L 1- 2	19 CHI L 4- 6	26 STL *	1 WAS W 6- 3	OPP RUNS: 708
12 det W 11-10	20 bos W 7-6f	27 STL L 5- 7	" WAS W 8- 1	
13 det W 6- 4	21 bos L 3- 8	28 STL W 6- 0	2 WAS W 9- 3	
14 cle W 6- 4	" bos L 1- 6	29 STL *	3 WAS W 9- 3	
15 cle W 8- 2	22 bos W 8- 2	30 CLE L1- 16	4 was *	
16 cle W 6- 3	" bos L 1- 5	31 CLE W 12- 2	5 bos W 8- 0	
17 cle L 2- 4	23 bos W 6- 1	**August, 1921**	" bos L 2- 8	
18 chi L 2-12	24 WAS W 9- 3	1 CLE W 5- 2	6 bos L 1- 2	
19 chi W 11- 4	25 WAS L 4- 6	2 CLE *	7 BOS W 6- 2	
20 chi L 5- 6	26 WAS W 9- 1	3 DET *	" BOS W 7- 2	
21 chi W 7- 4	27 NG	4 DET L 3- 8	8 phi L 5- 6	
22 stl W 6- 5f	28 WAS *	5 DET W 7- 3	9 phi W 14- 5	
23 stl W 6- 4	29 BOS W 8- 5	6 DET L 8- 9	10 phi W 19- 3	
	" BOS W 5- 3f			

CLUB VS. CLUB AND MONTHLY RECORDS OF THE
NEW YORK YANKEES' 1921 SEASON FOR HOME AND AWAY GAMES

CLUB:		APR	MAY	JUN	JUL	AUG	SEP	OCT	HOME	AWAY	TOTAL
BOST	H	2-0	xxx	2-0	2-0	xxx	3-1	1-0	10-1	xxx	15-7
	A	xxx	1-1	3-3	xxx	xxx	1-2	xxx	xxx	5-6	
CHIC	H	xxx	xxx	1-3	xxx	3-2	1-1	xxx	5-6	xxx	9-13
	A	xxx	2-2	xxx	1-3	1-2	xxx	xxx	xxx	4-7	
CLEV	H	xxx	xxx	2-2	1-1	1-0	3-1	xxx	7-4	xxx	14-8
	A	xxx	3-1	xxx	2-2	2-1	xxx	xxx	xxx	7-4	
DET	H	xxx	xxx	4-0	xxx	1-2	3-1	xxx	8-3	xxx	17-5
	A	xxx	3-1	xxx	4-0	2-1	xxx	xxx	xxx	9-2	
PHIL	H	2-1	3-1	xxx	3-0	xxx	xxx	2-0	10-2	xxx	17-5
	A	1-1	xxx	xxx	xxx	3-1	3-1	xxx	xxx	7-3	
STL	H	xxx	xxx	3-2	1-1	xxx	2-2	xxx	6-5	xxx	13-9
	A	xxx	2-2	xxx	3-0	2-2	xxx	xxx	xxx	7-4	
WAS	H	1-3	xxx	2-1	xxx	xxx	4-0	xxx	7-4	xxx	13-8
	A	0-1	4-2	0-1	xxx	2-0	xxx	xxx	xxx	6-4	
TOTAL:	H	5-4	3-1	14-8	7-2	5-4	16-6	3-0	53-25	xxx	
	A	1-2	15-9	3-4	10-5	12-7	4-3	xxx	xxx	45-30	
GRAND TOT:		6-6	18-10	17-12	17-7	17-11	20-9	3-0	xxx	xxx	98-55
CUMUL TOT:		6-6	24-16	41-28	58-35	75-46	95-55	98-55	xxx	xxx	

TIE GAMES: NONE

1922

SECOND STRAIGHT PENNANT

The year 1922 again found New York in first place, concluding the season but one game in front of the St. Louis Browns. The Yankees clinched their second pennant on September 30, winning at Boston 3–1 on the second to last day of the season. This was one of the most exciting pennant chases in American League history. After serving in May for 6 games as Yankee captain, Babe Ruth was replaced by Everett Scott, New York shortstop, who would retain that important title until 1925.

Individually, Babe again topped the league slugging list, tapering off (!) to .672. Whitey Witt and Ruth finished 1–2 in bases on balls with 89 and 84 respectively. Pitching-wise, "Bullet Joe" Bush was victorious 26 times (suffering 8 defeats)for .788 and the Junior Circuit lead. The New York pitching staff as a whole allowed but 618 runs by their opponents and pitched 98 rout jobs, both A.L. marks for 1922.

Another fine season came to pass. Again, the Yanks lost out to the Giants in the World Series; next season would be a different story.

The 1922 DAY BY DAY scores follow:

DAY BY DAY, 1922 NEW YORK YANKEES

April, 1922

Date	Opp	Result
12	was	L 5- 6
13	was	W 5- 2
14	was	*
15	was	W 5- 3
16	NG	
17	bos	*
18	bos	W 10- 8
19	bos	L 3- 5
"	bos	W 6- 1
20	WAS	W 10- 3
21	WAS	W 1- 0
22	WAS	W 4- 2
23	WAS	W 3- 0
24	PHI	W 6- 4q
25	PHI	W 6- 0
26	PHI	L 2- 4
27	NG	
28	BOS	W 10- 3
29	BOS	L 2- 5j
30	BOS	L 1- 2

May, 1922

Date	Opp	Result
1	BOS	L 2- 5
2	BOS	W 12- 6
3	phi	L 2- 4
4	phi	*
5	phi	W 5- 4
6	phi	W 2- 0
7	was	W 8- 1
8	CHI	W 7- 5
9	CHI	W 8- 7f
10	CHI	L 1- 2g
11	CHI	W 4- 1
12	DET	W 10- 8
13	DET	L 5- 8i
14	DET	L 2- 8
15	DET	L 1- 6
16	CLE	W 3- 0
17	CLE	W 6- 4
18	CLE	*
19	CLE	W 12- 4
20	STL	L 2- 8
21	STL	W 6- 5f
22	STL	W 4- 3i
23	STL	L 3-11
24	WAS	L 3- 5
25	WAS	W 6- 4
26	was	L 1- 3
27	was	W 3- 1
28	was	L 3- 4f
29	PHI	W 7- 4
30	PHI	W 3- 2
"	PHI	L 3- 4
31	NG	

June, 1922

Date	Opp	Result
1	BOS	W 5- 4
2	BOS	*
3	BOS	L 2- 6c
"	BOS	*
4	PHI	W 8- 3
5	NG	
6	chi	W 3- 1
7	chi	W 9- 7
8	chi	W 7- 2
9	chi	L 6-10
10	stl	W 14- 5
11	stl	W 8- 4
12	stl	L 1- 7
13	stl	L4- 13
14	det	L 2- 6
15	det	L 1- 2
16	det	L 4- 9
17	det	L 8- 9
18	cle	L 2- 9
19	cle	L 2- 4
20	cle	W 6- 5
21	cle	W 7- 3
22	bos	L 2- 6
23	bos	L 4- 5
24	bos	L 7-12
"	bos	L 2- 5
25	NG	
26	bos	W 6- 4
27	NG	
28	was	L 0- 1
29	was	W 6- 4f
30	NG	

July, 1922

Date	Opp	Result
1	phi	W 4- 1
"	phi	W 7- 4
2	PHI	W 9- 3
3	phi	W 12- 1
4	phi	L 1- 3
"	phi	W 6- 1
5	phi	*
6	CLE	W 10- 3
"	CLE	W 11- 3
7	CLE	W 1- 0
8	CLE	L 1- 3
9	CLE	L 7- 9i
10	NG	
11	STL	W 2- 1
12	STL	L 4- 7
13	STL	*
14	STL	W 4- 0
15	CHI	L 2- 3h
16	CHI	L 0- 4
17	CHI	L 7- 8g
18	CHI	W 14- 4
19	DET	L 1- 5
20	DET	W 5- 1
21	DET	W 7- 5
22	DET	L 0- 2
23	BOS	W 11- 7
24	NG	
25	stl	L 0- 8
26	stl	W 11- 6
27	stl	W 6- 5g
28	stl	W 7- 3
29	chi	W 6- 2
30	chi	L 5- 6
31	chi	L 2- 3

August, 1922

Date	Opp	Result
1	chi	*
2	cle	W 5- 1
3	cle	W 10- 9f
4	cle	W 7- 5
5	cle	W 7- 1
6	det	W 11- 6
7	det	W 4- 3
8	det	L 1- 2
9	det	W 8- 3
10	NG	
11	PHI	W 3- 2
12	PHI	*
13	was	L 2- 3
14	NG	
15	DET	W 2- 1f
16	DET	L 3- 7
17	DET	W 7- 1
18	CHI	W 8- 7f
19	CHI	W 12- 5
20	CHI	W 7- 5
21	NG	
22	CLE	L 2- 6
23	CLE	L 1- 4
24	CLE	W 7- 3
25	STL	L 1- 3
"	STL	W 6- 5
26	STL	W 9- 2
27	STL	*
28	STL	W 2- 1g
29	WAS	W 3- 1
30	WAS	W 5- 4
31	WAS	W 3- 1

September, 1922

Date	Opp	Result
1	NG	
2	phi	W 11- 6
"	phi	L 0- 6
3	NG	
4	BOS	*
"	BOS	*
5	BOS	L 3- 4
"	BOS	L 5- 6
6	BOS	W 9- 2
7	NG	
8	WAS	W 8- 1
9	WAS	W 3- 2f
10	PHI	W 10- 3
"	PHI	W 2-1
11	phi	W 9-4
12	NG	
13	chi	L 3-7
"	chi	W 6- 3
14	chi	W 4-1
15	chi	L 1- 2
16	stl	W 2-1
17	stl	L 1-5
18	stl	W 3-2
19	det	W 4- 3
20	det	W 6-5
21	det	W 9-8
22	cle	W 9-3
23	cle	W 7-6
24	cle	L 0-3
25	NG	
26	NG	
27	NG	
28	bos	L 1-3
29	bos	L 0-1
30	bos	W 3- 1

October, 1922

Date	Opp	Result
1	was	L 1-6

END OF 1922

RUNS: 758
OPP RUNS: 618

CLUB VS. CLUB AND MONTHLY RECORDS OF THE NEW YORK YANKEES' 1922 SEASON FOR HOME AND AWAY GAMES

CLUB:		APR	MAY	JUN	JUL	AUG	SEP	OCT	HOME	AWAY	TOTAL
BOST	H	1- 2	1- 1	1- 1	1- 0	xxx	1- 2	xxx	5- 6	xxx	9- 13
	A	2- 1	xxx	1- 4	xxx	xxx	1- 2	xxx	xxx	4- 7	
CHIC	H	xxx	3- 1	xxx	1- 3	3- 0	xxx	xxx	7- 4	xxx	13- 9
	A	xxx	xxx	3- 1	1- 2	xxx	2- 2	xxx	xxx	6- 5	
CLEV	H	x	3- 0	x	3- 2	1- 2	x	x	7- 4	x	15- 7
	A	x	x	2- 2	x	4- 0	2- 1	xxx	xxx	8- 3	
DET	H	xxx	1- 3	xxx	2- 2	2- 1	xxx	xxx	5- 6	xxx	11- 11
	A	xxx	xxx	0- 4	xxx	3- 1	3- 0	xxx	xxx	6- 5	
PHIL	H	2- 1	2- 1	1- 0	1- 0	1- 0	2- 0	xxx	9- 2	xxx	17- 5
	A	xxx	2- 1	xxx	4- 1	xxx	2- 1	xxx	xxx	8- 3	
STL	H	xxx	2- 2	xxx	2- 1	3- 1	xxx	xxx	7- 4	xxx	14- 8
	A	xxx	xxx	2- 2	3- 1	xxx	2- 1	xxx	xxx	7- 4	
WAS	H	4- 0	1- 1	xxx	xxx	3- 0	2- 0	xxx	10- 1	xxx	15- 7
	A	2- 1	2- 2	1- 1	xxx	0- 1	xxx	0- 1	xxx	5- 6	
TOTAL:	H	7- 3	13- 9	2- 1	10- 8	13- 4	5- 2	xxx	50-27	xxx	94-60
	A	4- 2	4- 3	9- 14	8- 4	7- 2	12- 7	0- 1	xxx	44-33	
GRAND TOT:		11- 5	17- 12	11-15	18- 12	20- 6	17- 9	0- 1	xxx	xxx	
CUMUL TOT:		11- 5	28- 17	39-32	57-44	77-50	94-59	94-60	xxx	xxx	

TIE GAMES: NONE

1923

FINALLY BEATING THE GIANTS AND THE STADIUM IS DEDICATED

The Yankees concluded the 1923 season as the World Champions, defeating their rivals, the New York Giants, in the World Series. Their first World Championship was not to be denied this year as was the case the two previous years. The most famous sports arena, Yankee Stadium, was dedicated April 18 before an enormous crowd, with the Yanks beating Boston 4–1. Fittingly, it was the Babe who would lead New York to this first victory in "The House That Ruth Built" with a homer. For the third consecutive season, the Yankees won the A.L. pennant, finishing 16 games ahead of second place Detroit. Fielding their fewest players ever over an entire season (25—also in 1927), the Yankees had their most productive season to date, winning 98 while losing 54 (.645).

In May, 1923, Til Huston sold his half-ownership of the Yankees to Jacob Ruppert, who thereby became the sole New York owner. In addition, Ruppert served in the capacity of club president until 1939. For the third time, a Yankee pitcher tossed a no-hitter. Sam Jones pitched hitless ball against Philadelphia at New York on September 4, winning 2–0.

The pitching staff led the league with 102 complete games and 506 strikeouts. The staff as a whole led the A.L. with a 3.66 ERA. Pennock led A.L. pitchers with a .760 winning percentage and a 19–6 record.

Babe Ruth reached base safely 379 times during the season, a Major League record, on 205 hits, 170 walks (another Major League mark) and 4 hit by pitch. Ruth led also in runs (151), homers (41), RBI (131), total bases (399), and slugging percentage (.764). As a result of his consistency throughout the season, Ruth won the League Award. As a team, the Yanks finished first in the league with 105 homers and a .422 slugging percentage.

Afield, the Yankees finished tops in the league, the first time since 1915. With a percentage of .977, the Yanks committed a league low 144 errors. For the next two seasons, New York was first in the A.L. in fielding percentage as well as the fewest errors.

1924 began a brief hiatus as far as pennant winning goes. They are to win the A.L. flag again in 1926, for their first of 3 straight. In 1924 and 1925, the Yanks will finish behind Bucky Harris' Washington Club.

The 1923 DAY BY DAY scores follow:

DAY BY DAY, 1923 NEW YORK YANKEES

April, 1923

18	BOS	W	4-	1
19	BOS	W	8-	2
20	BOS	W	4-	3
21	BOS	W	7-	6
22	WAS	L	3-	4
23	WAS	L	1-	2
24	WAS	W	4-	0
25	WAS	W	7-	1
26	bos	L	4-	5
27	bos	W	4-	2
28	bos	L	3-	5
29	NG			
30	was	W	17-	4

May, 1923

1	was	W	8-	7
2	was	L	0-	3
3	was	W	3-	2
4	PHI	L	6-	8f
5	PHI	W	7-	2
6	PHI	L	1-	5
7	NG			
8	cle	W	3-	2c
9	cle		*	
10	cle	W	13-	4
11	cle		*	
12	det	W	3-	2
13	det	L	1-	4
14	det	W	16-	11h
15	det	W	9-	5
16	stl	W	4-	1
17	stl	W	9-	2
18	stl	W	9-	4
19	stl	W	6-	5f
20	chi	W	3-	2
21	chi	W	5-	0
22	chi	W	3-	1k
23	NG			
24	phi	L	0-	1
25	phi	L	2-	4
26	phi	W	10-	8g
27	was	W	8-	1
28	NG			
29	was	W	4-	2
30	was	W	6-	4
"	was	W	9-	5
31	BOS	W	8-	1

June, 1923

1	BOS	L	0-	5
2	BOS	L	3-	7
3	BOS		*	
4	was	L	2-	5
5	CHI	W	7-	6f
6	CHI	L	1-	4
7	CHI		*	
8	CHI	L	3-	7
9	CLE	L	3-	13
10	CLE	W	8-	7
11	CLE	L	3-	4
12	CLE	L	4-	8
13	STL	W	5-	0
14	STL	L	1-	3
15	STL	W	10-	0
16	STL	W	9-	4
17	DET	W	9-	0
18	DET	L	3-	11
19	DET	W	6-	5
20	DET	L	7-	9
21	NG			
22	bos	W	4-	2
23	bos	W	4-	0
24	NG			
25	bos	W	14-	6
26	bos	L	1-	3
27	NG			
28	PHI	W	4-	2
29	PHI	W	10-	9
30	PHI	W	6-	1

July, 1923

1	phi	W	4-	0
2	WAS	W	13-	1
3	WAS	W	2-	1k
4	WAS	W	12-	6
"	WAS	W	12-	2
5	NG			
6	stl	W	5-	2
7	stl	L	3-	13
8	stl	W	6-	4
9	stl	W	9-	3
10	chi	W	3-	2
11	chi	W	3-	1
12	chi	W	10-	6
13	chi	L	3-	4f
14	cle	L	2-	4
"	cle	W	10-	7
15	cle	W	4-	2
16	cle	L	0-	6
"	cle	W	11-	7
17	cle	L	0-	13
18	det	W	4-	1
19	det	L	2-	9
20	NG			
21	det	W	3-	2
22	det	W	7-	4
23	NG			
24	phi	W	9-	2
25	phi	W	5-	4
26	phi	W	4-	3
27	phi	W	7-	3
28	CHI		*	
"	CHI	L	1-	3
29	CHI	L	2-	3
"	CHI	W	8-	2
30	CHI	W	5-	3
31	CHI		*	

August, 1923

1	CLE	L	3-	5
2	CLE	W	4-	2
3	CLE		*	
4	CLE	L	7-	15
5	STL	W	9-	8i
6	STL	W	5-	3
7	STL		L10-	12
8	STL	L	3-	4
9	DET	L	3-	11
10	DET		*	
11	DET	W	10-	4
"	DET	W	9-	8f
12	DET	L	2-	5
13	NG			
14	NG			
15	stl	L	3-	5
16	stl	W	3-	1
17	stl	W	5-	4
18	chi	W	6-	5
19	chi	L	3-	4
20	chi	W	16-	5
21	chi		*	
22	det	L	3-	6
23	det	L	1-	2
24	det	W	7-	1
25	cle	L	2-	5
26	cle	L	3-	4
27	cle	W	10-	3
28	NG			
29	NG			
30	WAS	W	4-	3
31	WAS	W	4-	2

September, 1923

1	WAS	W	6-	1
2	was	L	2-	7
3	PHI	W	2-	1i
"	PHI	W	7-	4
4	PHI	W	2-	0
5	PHI	W	6-	3
6	NG			
7	NG			
8	was	L	0-	4
9	BOS	W	6-	2
"	BOS	W	4-	0
10	BOS	W	8-	1
11	BOS	L	0-	3
12	CHI	W	2-	1
"	CHI	W	5-	3
13	CHI	W	9-	5
14	CHI	L	4-	7
15	CHI	W	10-	4
16	CLE	W	4-	2
"	CLE	W	3-	2
17	CLE	L	2-	6
18	CLE	L	3-	8
19	NG			
20	STL	W	4-	3
21	NG			
22	STL		*	
23	STL		*	
24	DET	W	12-	4
25	DET	L	4-	5
26	DET	L	3-	8f
27	bos	W	8-	3
28	bos	W	24-	4
29	bos	L	4-	5
"	bos	L	2-	3L
30	NG			

October, 1923

1	NG			
2	NG			
3	NG			
4	PHI	L	6-	7
5	PHI	W	8-	4
6	PHI	W	3-	1
7	PHI	L	7-	9

END OF 1923

RUNS: 823

OPP RUNS: 622

CLUB VS. CLUB AND MONTHLY RECORDS OF THE NEW YORK YANKEES' 1923 SEASON FOR HOME AND AWAY GAMES

CLUB:		APR	MAY	JUN	JUL	AUG	SEP	OCT	HOME	AWAY	TOTAL
BOST	H	4-0	1-0	0-2	xxx	xxx	3-1	xxx	8-3	xxx	14-8
	A	1-2	xxx	3-1	xxx	xxx	2-2	xxx	xxx	6-5	
CHIC	H	xxx	xxx	1-2	2-2	xxx	4-1	xxx	7-5	xxx	15-7
	A	xxx	3-0	xxx	3-1	2-1	xxx	xxx	xxx	8-2	
CLEV	H	xxx	xxx	1-3	xxx	1-2	2-2	xxx	4-7	xxx	10-12
	A	xxx	2-0	xxx	3-3	1-2	xxx	xxx	xxx	6-5	
DET	H	xxx	xxx	2-2	xxx	2-2	1-2	xxx	5-6	xxx	12-10
	A	xxx	3-1	xxx	3-1	1-2	xxx	xxx	xxx	7-4	
PHIL	H	xxx	1-2	3-0	1-0	xxx	xxx	2-2	7-4	xxx	16-6
	A	xxx	1-2	xxx	4-0	xxx	4-0	xxx	xxx	9-2	
STL	H	xxx	xxx	3-1	xxx	2-2	1-0	xxx	6-3	xxx	15-5
	A	xxx	4-0	xxx	3-1	2-1	xxx	xxx	xxx	9-2	
WAS	H	2-2	xxx	xxx	4-0	2-0	1-0	xxx	9-2	xxx	16-6
	A	1-0	6-1	0-1	xxx	xxx	0-2	xxx	xxx	7-4	
TOTAL:	H	6-2	2-2	10-10	7-2	7-6	12-6	2-2	46-30	xxx	98-54
	A	2-2	19-4	3-2	16-6	6-6	6-4	xxx	xxx	52-24	
GRAND TOT:		8-4	21-6	13-12	23-8	13-12	18-10	2-2	xxx	xxx	
CUMUL TOT:		8-4	29-10	42-22	65-30	78-42	96-52	98-54	xxx	xxx	

TIE GAMES: NONE

1924

RUTH LEADS THE LEAGUE IN BATTING

After a disappointing season, the Yanks fell to second place behind Washington, two games back. They finished the season with an 89–63 worksheet (.586). Babe Ruth became the first Yankee to lead the league in batting with a .378 mark, getting 200 hits in 529 at bats (in the National League, Rogers Hornsby batted an astonishing .424 in 143 games for St. Louis to pace the Senior Circuit). In addition to the batting title, Ruth scored the most A.L. runs (143), hit the most homers (41), gathered the most total bases (391), and won his seventh consecutive slugging title, five of those with New York. Babe also walked the most frequently (142) and struck out a league leading 81 times. Wally Pipp hit the most three-baggers in the A.L. (19) to become the first Yankee to lead the league in that department.

As a club, New York won its eighth home run title in a decade as well as its fourth slugging title in five seasons. Defensively, the Yanks finished atop the A.L. with a .974, committing the least miscues, 156. The pitching staff whiffed 487 opponent batters and blanked the competition 13 times, both league highs. Regarding strikeouts, the New York batters fanned only 420 times, an all-time Yankee record.

The 1924 year proved more of an eventful season for the Babe than for the Yankees as a whole. Next season, an eating binge by Ruth will prove devastating to the Yankee pennant chances.

The 1924 DAY BY DAY scores follow:

DAY BY DAY, 1924 NEW YORK YANKEES

April, 1924			May, 1924			June, 1924			July, 1924			September, 1924		
15 bos	W	2- 1	26 DET	W	8- 2	30 phi	W	10- 4	31 stl	L	1- 2	4 PHI	L	3- 8
16 bos	L	6- 9	27 was		*	" phi		L3- 10	" stl	L	4- 5	5 NG		
17 bos	L	1- 9	28 was	W	7- 4	**July, 1924**			**August, 1924**			6 PHI	W	10- 7
18 bos		*	" was	L	1- 6	1 phi	W	7- 0	1 stl	W	3- 2	7 PHI	L	1- 2
19 was	L	2- 7	29 was		*	2 phi	L	8- 9	2 stl	L	8-12	8 bos	W	2- 0
20 was		L3- 12	30 PHI	W	6- 0	" phi	W	10- 1	3 det	L	2- 5	9 bos	W	5- 4
21 was	W	4- 2	" PHI	L	4- 5	3 phi	L	5-10	4 det	W	9- 8g	10 bos		*
22 was	W	6- 3	31 PHI	W	5- 0	4 was	W	4- 2	5 det	W	9- 2	11 bos	W	4- 3
23 BOS	W	13- 4	" PHI	L	3- 5	" was	W	2- 0	6 det	L	2- 5a	" bos	W	8- 3
24 BOS	W	6- 3	**June, 1924**			5 was	W	2- 0	7 cle	W	7- 5	12 NG		
25 BOS	W	5- 2f	1 NG			" was	L	2- 7	8 cle	L	8-10	13 chi	W	16- 1
26 BOS	W	4- 3g	2 NG			6 was	W	7- 4	9 cle	W	5- 1	14 chi	L	2- 5
27 PHI	W	11- 2	3 chi	W	6- 3	7 NG			10 cle	L	1- 7	15 chi	W	2- 0
28 phi	W	11- 6	4 chi	L	3- 4	8 CHI		L2- 10	11 NG			16 stl		*
29 phi		*	5 chi		*	" CHI	W	8- 5	12 STL		*	17 stl	W	7- 3
30 phi		*	6 chi	W	5- 3	9 CHI	L	6- 8	13 STL	W	1- 0	" stl	W	8- 7
May, 1924			7 stl	L	3- 6	10 CHI	W	6- 1	" STL	W	2- 1	18 stl	W	2- 1f
1 WAS	L	2- 3	8 stl	L	0- 5	" CHI	W	18- 5	14 STL	L	5- 8	19 det	L	5- 6
2 WAS	L	4- 6	9 stl	L	3- 5	11 CHI	W	12- 9	15 NG			20 det	L	5- 6
3 WAS	W	5- 4	10 stl	W	5- 0	12 STL	W	4- 2	16 CHI	W	3- 2	21 det	L	3- 6
4 NG			11 det	L	2- 7	13 STL	W	6- 2	17 CHI	W	2- 1	22 cle	W	10- 4
5 PHI	W	10- 5	12 det	W	10- 4	14 STL	W	7- 3	18 CHI	W	2- 0	23 cle	W	8- 2
6 PHI	W	3- 2	13 det	W	10- 6##	" STL	L	4- 9	19 NG			24 cle	W	2- 0
7 PHI	W	7- 4	14 det	W	6- 2	15 STL	W	5- 4	20 NG			25 NG		
8 PHI		*	15 cle	L	3-10	16 CLE	L	3- 4	21 DET		*	26 phi	W	7- 1
9 WAS		*	16 cle	L	1- 2	17 NG			22 DET	L	6- 8h	27 phi	L	3- 4
10 CHI	W	2- 1f	17 cle	W	7- 5	18 CLE	L	2- 9	23 DET	W	8- 1	28 NG		
11 CHI		*	18 cle	L	5- 6	" CLE	W	7- 2	24 DET	L	2- 7	29 phi		*
12 CHI		*	19 NG			19 CLE	W	10- 5	25 CLE	W	8- 3	30 phi		*
13 CHI	L	5- 7	20 BOS		*	20 CLE	W	4- 1	26 CLE		*	END OF 1924		
14 STL	L	1-11	21 BOS	W	5- 3	" CLE	W	10- 4	27 CLE	L	0- 1	RUNS:		798
15 STL	L	1- 2	" BOS	TG	3- 3a	21 DET	L	7- 9	" CLE	W	5- 4	OPP RUNS:		667
16 STL		*	22 BOS	L	2- 6	22 DET	L	1- 3	28 WAS		L6- 11			
17 STL	W	7- 2	23 WAS	L	3- 5	23 DET	W	4- 3g	29 WAS	L	1- 5			
18 CLE	W	8- 0	" WAS	L	2- 4	24 DET	L	4- 5d	30 WAS	W	2- 1			
19 NG			24 WAS	L	3- 4f	25 NG			31 WAS	L	2- 4f			
20 CLE		*	25 WAS	L	2- 3c	26 chi	W	5- 4j	**September, 1924**					
21 CLE		*	26 bos	L	5- 8	27 chi	L	6- 7	1 BOS	W	3- 0			
22 CLE	W	6- 3	27 bos	W	12- 7	28 chi	W	8- 3	" BOS	W	12- 2			
23 DET	W	7- 6	" bos	W	10- 5	" chi	W	12-10	2 BOS	L	6-14			
24 DET	L	3- 7	28 bos	W	4- 3h	29 chi	W	9- 4	" BOS	W	5- 2			
25 DET	L	5- 6	29 NG			30 stl		*	3 BOS	W	11- 6			

##FORFEITED TO
NEW YORK

CLUB VS. CLUB AND MONTHLY RECORDS OF THE NEW YORK YANKEES' 1924 SEASON FOR HOME AND AWAY GAMES

CLUB:		APR	MAY	JUN	JUL	AUG	SEP	OCT	HOME	AWAY	TOTAL
BOST	H	4-0	xxx	1-1	xxx	xxx	4-1	xxx	9-2	xxx	17-5
	A	1-2	xxx	3-1	xxx	xxx	4-0	xxx	xxx	8-3	
CHIC	H	xxx	1-1	xxx	4-2	3-0	xxx	xxx	8-3	xxx	16-6
	A	xxx	xxx	2-1	4-1	xxx	2-1	xxx	xxx	8-3	
CLEV	H	xxx	2-0	xxx	4-2	2-1	xxx	xxx	8-3	xxx	14-8
	A	xxx	xxx	1-3	xxx	2-2	3-0	xxx	xxx	6-5	
DET	H	xxx	2-2	xxx	1-3	1-2	xxx	xxx	4-7	xxx	9-13
	A	xxx	xxx	3-1	xxx	2-2	0-3	xxx	xxx	5-6	
PHIL	H	1-0	5-2	xxx	xxx	xxx	1-2	xxx	7-4	xxx	12-8
	A	1-0	xxx	1-1	2-2	xxx	1-1	xxx	xxx	5-4	
STL	H	xxx	1-2	xxx	4-1	2-1	xxx	xxx	7-4	xxx	12-10
	A	xxx	xxx	1-3	0-2	1-1	3-0	xxx	xxx	5-6	
WAS	H	xxx	1-2	0-4	xxx	1-3	xxx	xxx	2-9	xxx	9-13
	A	2-2	1-1	xxx	4-1	xxx	xxx	xxx	xxx	7-4	
TOTAL:	H	5-0	12-9	1-5	13-8	9-7	5-3	xxx	45-32	xxx	
	A	4-4	1-1	11-10	10-6	5-5	13-5	xxx	xxx	44-31	89-63
GRAND TOT:		9-4	13-10	12-15	23-14	14-12	18-8	xxx	xxx	xxx	TIE GAMES: 1
CUMUL TOT:		9-4	22-14	34-29	57-43	71-55	89-63	89-63	xxx	xxx	BOS-June

Lou Gehrig takes a mighty swing for photographers. The great Gehrig connected for 439 homers in his career and formed an unbelievable hitting tandem with Babe Ruth in their many seasons together.

1925

ONE HEADACHE AND HOT DOG TOO MANY

In 1925, the Yankees plummeted to seventh place thanks largely to Ruth's indulgence prior to the start of the season. Suffering from a stomach illness due mostly to excessive amounts of food consumption, Babe had the worst season in pinstripes spanning his entire 15 years with New York. Ruth played but 98 games, hitting a non-Ruthian total of 25 homers.

One June 1, Pee Wee Wanninger was pinch-hit for by Lou Gehrig. The following day, Wally Pipp, Yankee first baseman, suffered a headache and was removed from the game, Gehrig filling his vacated position. The rest is history. Any baseball fan worth his salt already knows these facts as well as Lou's feat of 2,130 consecutive games played. "The Iron Horse" eventually ended this incredible endurance record on May 1, 1939, some 14 years later. It seems that Lou's streak is probably the safest to never be broken of all individual records through the years.

The Yankees finished 1924 at 69–85 (.448)—their worst record since '18—hit 110 homers, leading the league yet another time. Bob Meusel, Yankee outfielder, banged out 33 roundtrippers to pace the A.L. This was Meusel's only homer title. "Long Bob" also won the RBI crown with 138.

Because of Ruth's absence for much of the season, the Yankees' offensive power was severely hindered. However, defensively, New York won, finishing first in the league for a third consecutive time, the only time they will ever accomplish this. Making the fewest A.L. miscues (160), they matched the previous year's fielding figure of .974. Pitching-wise, Jones lost the most games (21) in the A.L.

On June 17, the Tigers defeated New York, 19–1, for the worst home loss in Yank history, a record later suffered at the hands of Toronto in 1977, the Blue Jays winning 19–3.

This was truly a disastrous season, to put it mildly. The emergence of Gehrig was a key factor in the later development of "Murderer's Row." The 1925 DAY BY DAY scores follow:

DAY BY DAY, 1925 NEW YORK YANKEES

April, 1925
14 WAS W 5- 1
15 WAS L 2- 5b
16 WAS L 5- 7
17 WAS L 1- 6
18 BOS W 6- 3
19 BOS *
20 BOS *
21 BOS W 5- 1
22 was L 1-10
23 was L 1- 2
24 NG
25 was l7- 8
26 was W 3- 2
27 phi L 0- 8
28 phi *
29 phi *
30 bos *

May, 1925
1 bos L 5- 7f
2 bos L 4- 5
3 PHI L 0- 1
4 PHI L 7- 8
5 PHI W 8- 4
6 PHI L 2- 6f
7 NG
8 stl W 12- 0
9 stl TG 1- 1c
10 stl W 13- 1
11 stl L10-19
12 chi L 4- 5f
13 chi L 0- 4
14 chi L 0- 1
15 chi W 6- 5
16 det W 12- 3d
17 det L 2- 3
18 det W 9- 7
19 det L 5-11
20 cle L 9-10
21 cle W 6- 3
22 NG
23 cle W 7- 6
24 cle *
25 NG
26 BOS L 2- 3
" BOS W 6- 1
27 BOS W 4- 3
28 BOS L 1- 3
" BOS W 7- 2
29 phi L 4- 6
" ph i *
30 phi L 7- 9
" phi L 5- 6j
31 BOS L 6- 9h

June, 1925
1 WAS L 3- 5
2 WAS W 8- 5
3 WAS W 6- 4h
4 W AS L 3- 8
5 STL W 10- 7
6 STL W 11- 9
7 STL L 2- 5
8 STL W 6- 5f
9 NG
10 CLE W 6- 5f
11 CLE L 1- 4
12 CLE L2- 5
13 CLE W 7- 4
14 DET W 8- 3
15 NG
16 DET L 3- 5
17 DET L 1-19
18 DET L 3- 6
19 CHI W 4- 3g
20 CHI W 12- 2
21 CHI L 2- 9
22 CHI L 1- 6
23 was L 1- 8
24 was W 5- 3
25 was L0- 1
26 NG
27 bos W 10- 5
" bos W 5- 1
28 NG
29 bos L 5-10
30 bos W 3- 0

July, 1925
1 bos W 11- 8
2 PHI L 3- 6
3 PHI W 1- 0
4 PHI W 1- 0k
" PHI L 5- 8
5 was L 2- 7
6 NG
7 stl L 2-12
" stl L 5- 6
8 stl W 6- 4
9 s tl *
10 stl L 8- 9
" stl L3- 13
11 chi W 5- 3d
12 chi L 0- 3
13 chi L 4- 8
14 chi L 0- 3
15 cle L 4- 5h
" cle W 9- 4
16 cle L 9-17
17 cle W 5- 1
18 det L 3- 7
19 det L12-18
20 det L 5- 9
21 det W 5- 4g
22 NG
23 WAS W 11- 7
24 NG
25 W AS *
26 WAS L 4- 7
" WAS L 3- 4g
27 NG
28 STL W 6- 2
29 STL W 8- 7h
30 STL W 9- 2
31 STL *

August, 1925
1 CLE W 8- 3
2 CLE L 2- 3
3 CLE W 3- 2
4 CLE W 4- 1
5 DET *
6 DET W 10- 4
7 DET L 1- 3
8 DET L 3- 9
" DET L 2- 3
9 CHI L 3- 4h
10 NG
11 CHI L 2-15
12 CHI W 2- 0
13 CHI *
14 was L 0- 2
15 was L 1- 6
16 was W 3- 2
17 NG
18 det W 5- 2
19 det L 3- 4
20 det *
21 cle L 1- 2
22 cle L 4- 5
23 cle L 6- 7
24 cle L 1- 5
25 chi W 7- 4
26 chi L 0- 1
27 chi L 5- 6
28 stl L 0- 1
29 stl W 4- 1
30 stl L 6- 7
31 NG

September, 1925
1 BOS W 2- 1
2 BOS W 4- 2
3 NG
4 NG
5 PHI W 3- 0
6 PHI W 4- 3
7 bos L 1- 5
" bos *
8 bos W 5- 4
" bos W 7- 4
9 bos L 4- 5
10 phi W 7- 3
" phi L 4- 5h
11 phi L 2- 3
12 phi W 7- 2
" phi L6- 10
13 BOS L 1- 2
14 phi W 3- 1
15 CLE *
16 CLE W 8- 0
" CLE W 4- 3f
17 CLE W 5- 0
18 STL W 4- 2
19 STL L 6- 9
" STL L 3- 4
20 STL L 0- 5
21 NG
22 CHI W 11- 6
" CHI L 2- 4
23 CHI W 7- 6
24 CHI W 6- 5f
25 NG
26 DET W 3- 1
27 DET L 5-10
" DET TG 1- 1a
28 DET L 2- 6
" DET W 7- 6
29 NG
30 NG

October, 1925
1 NG
2 phi L0- 10
3 PHI W 9- 8
END OF 1925
RUNS: 706
OPP RUNS: 774

CLUB VS. CLUB AND MONTHLY RECORDS OF THE NEW YORK YANKEES' 1925 SEASON FOR HOME AND AWAY GAMES

CLUB:		APR	MAY	JUN	JUL	AUG	SEP	OCT	HOME	AWAY	TOTAL
BOST	H	2-0	3- 3	xxx	xxx	xxx	2- 1	xxx	7- 4	xxx	
	A	xxx	0- 2	3- 1	1- 0	xxx	2- 2	xxx	xxx	6- 5	13- 9
CHIC	H	xxx	xxx	2- 2	xxx	1- 2	3- 1	xxx	6- 5	xxx	
	A	xxx	1- 3	xxx	1- 3	1- 2	xxx	xxx	xxx	3- 8	9-13
CLEV	H	xxx	xxx	2- 2	xxx	3- 1	3- 0	xxx	8- 3	xxx	
	A	xxx	2- 1	xxx	2- 2	0- 4	xxx	xxx	xxx	4- 7	12-10
DET	H	xxx	xxx	1- 3	xxx	1- 3	2- 2	xxx	4- 8	xxx	
	A	xxx	2- 2	xxx	1- 3	1- 1	xxx	xxx	xxx	4- 6	8-14
PHIL	H	xxx	1- 3	xxx	2- 2	xxx	2- 0	1- 0	6- 5	xxx	
	A	0- 1	0- 3	xxx	xxx	xxx	3- 3	0- 1	xxx	3- 8	9-13
STL	H	xxx	xxx	3- 1	3- 0	xxx	1- 3	xxx	7- 4	xxx	
	A	xxx	2- 1	xxx	1- 4	1- 2	xxx	x xx	xxx	4- 7	11-11
WAS	H	1-3	xxx	2- 2	1- 2	xxx	xxx	xxx	4- 7	xxx	
	A	1-3	xxx	1- 2	0- 1	1- 2	xxx	xxx	xxx	3- 8	7-15
TOTAL:	H	3-3	4- 6	10-10	6- 4	5- 6	13- 7	1- 0	42-36	xxx	
	A	1-4	7-12	4- 3	6-13	4-11	5- 5	0- 1	xxx	27-49	69-85
GRAND TOT:		4-7	11-18	14-13	12-17	9-17	18-12	1- 1	xxx	xxx	69-85
CUMUL TOT:		4-7	15-25	29-38	41-55	50-72	68-84	69-85	xxx	xxx	69-85

TIE GAMES: 2
stl-May; DET-Sept.

1926

THE GREAT COMEBACK

After a dismal finish in 1925, the Yankees rebounded, soundly winning their fourth pennant. Winning 91 games and losing but 63 (.591), New York concluded the season 3 games ahead of second place Cleveland. With the Babe back on track, the Yankees were a tough unit. Although winning the A.L. flag, they could not beat the Cardinals in the World Series.

A healthy Ruth again led the league in runs scored (139), RBI (145), homers (47), total bases (365) and his traditional slugging crown with a mark of .737. Lou Gehrig, in his first full season with the Yanks, paced the league with 20 triples, the most during his incredible 17 years as a Yankee.

As a team, the Yankees' display of offensive abilities was evidenced by leading the A.L. in each of the following categories: runs (847), homers (121), RBI (794), walks (642) and slugging percentage (.437). Defensively, after having the best fielding club in the A.L. the last three seasons, the Yankees plunged to seventh, making 50 more errors than the previous year.

The year 1926 marked the arrival of Michael Joseph "Pete" Sheehy on the Yankee scene. Pete remains as equipment manager even as of this writing.

The magnificent comeback in 1926 was but an omen for things to come. The next season will unveil what most experts (and myself) believe to be the greatest team in baseball history, the 1927 New York Yankees.

The 1926 DAY BY DAY scores follow:

DAY BY DAY, 1926 NEW YORK YANKEES

April, 1926

Date	Opp	Result
13	bos	W 12–11
14	bos	L 7– 8
15	bos	*
16	bos	W 3– 2
17	was	W 8– 6
18	was	L 2– 3g
19	was	*
20	was	W 18– 5
21	BOS	W 8– 5
22	BOS	L 8– 9f
23	BOS	W 5– 1
24	BOS	W 9– 1
25	PHI	W 7– 2
26	PHI	*
27	PHI	W 8– 2
28	PHI	W 3– 0
29	WAS	W 8– 5
30	WAS	W 7– 2

May, 1926

Date	Opp	Result
1	WAS	W 4– 1
2	NG	
3	phi	L 3– 8
4	phi	L 5–10
5	phi	L 3– 5
6	WAS	L 3– 5
7	DET	W 7– 6g
8	DET	L 5– 7
9	DET	L10–14
10	DET	W 13– 9
11	CLE	*
12	CLE	W 6– 5f
13	CLE	W 13– 9
14	CLE	W 2– 1
15	CHI	W 10– 1
16	CHI	*
17	CHI	W 5– 3
18	CHI	W 5– 3
19	STL	W 6– 2
20	STL	W 5– 4
21	STL	W 7– 2
22	STL	W 7– 6
23	BOS	W 8– 3
24	bos	W 4– 2
25	bos	W 5– 3
26	bos	W 9– 8
27	NG	
28	PHI	L 1– 2
29	PHI	L 5– 6
30	PHI	W 9– 3
31	WAS	*

June, 1926

Date	Opp	Result
1	WAS	*
2	WAS	W 9– 5
"	WAS	W 5– 4
3	BOS	W 8– 5
4	NG	
5	cle	L 3–15
6	cle	W 6– 5c
7	cle	L 2– 5
8	det	W 11– 9g
9	det	W 4– 3
10	det	W 8– 1
11	det	W 9– 3
12	stl	L 5– 6
13	stl	W 6– 5
14	stl	L 3– 7
15	stl	W 6– 1
16	NG	
17	chi	L 2– 6
18	chi	W 10– 2
19	chi	W 6– 5
20	chi	L 3– 4
21	NG	
22	was	L 7– 8
"	was	W 9– 1
23	NG	
24	bos	L 5– 6g
25	bos	W 12– 2
"	bos	W 11– 4
26	bos	*
27	BOS	W 7– 1
28	phi	L 1– 7
29	phi	W 7– 5
30	phi	L 4– 5

July, 1926

Date	Opp	Result
1	WAS	W 3– 2
"	was	L 5–12
2	was	L 5– 6
3	was	W 5– 4
4	was	TG 4– 4b
5	phi	L 1– 2
"	phi	L 3– 6
6	NG	
7	NG	
8	CLE	L 1– 6
9	CLE	W 8– 2
10	CLE	W 4– 3h
11	CLE	L 3– 8
12	CLE	L 2– 6
13	DET	L 4– 5
14	DET	W 7– 6h
15	DET	L 1– 7
16	DET	W 4– 3
17	STL	W 3– 2
18	STL	L 0– 4
19	STL	W 11– 2
20	STL	L 6– 7
21	CHI	L 3– 4
"	CHI	W 5– 4
22	CHI	W 13–10
23	CHI	W 11– 3
24	CHI	W 7– 4
25	CHI	W 2– 1
26	NG	
27	stl	W 6– 5
28	stl	W 3– 2
29	stl	W 10– 7
30	stl	W 10– 8g
31	chi	W 2– 1

August, 1926

Date	Opp	Result
1	chi	W 8– 4
2	chi	L 1– 2
3	chi	W 7– 6
4	cle	L 2– 4
5	cle	W 8– 2
6	cle	W 8– 7
7	det	L 4– 6
8	det	L 3– 8
9	det	W 9– 8
10	det	L 3– 5c
11	was	L 4– 5
"	was	L 4– 5g
12	was	L 2– 5
13	was	W 7– 5
14	WAS	W 4– 2
"	WAS	L 5–10
15	BOS	W 4– 2
"	BOS	L 3– 5
16	NG	
17	CHI	L 3– 5a
18	CHI	*
19	NG	
20	STL	W 10– 4
21	STL	W 3– 1
22	STL	*
23	CLE	W 3– 2
24	CLE	*
25	CLE	L 0– 6
26	NG	
27	DET	W 4– 1
28	DET	L 4– 8
29	DET	W 6– 1
30	WAS	L 6–12
31	PHI	L 5– 8

September, 1926

Date	Opp	Result
1	PHI	W 6– 4
2	phi	*
3	phi	L 2– 7
"	phi	W 7– 4
4	phi	W 3– 0
5	NG	
6	PHI	L 2– 5
"	PHI	W 2– 1
7	BOS	W 4– 2
8	BOS	L 2– 5
9	BOS	W 10– 0
10	NG	
11	det	W 10– 8
12	det	*
13	det	L 3– 4
"	det	L 1– 4
14	NG	
15	cle	W 6– 4
"	cle	*
16	cle	L 1– 2
"	cle	L 0– 5
17	cle	L 1– 5
18	cle	L 1– 3
19	cle	W 8– 3
20	chi	L 3– 7
"	chi	L 3– 4
21	chi	W 14– 0
22	chi	L 1– 2
23	NG	
24	s tl	*
25	stl	W 10– 2
"	stl	W 10– 4
26	stl	L 1– 6
"	stl	L 2– 6
27	NG	

END OF 1926

RUNS: 847

OPP RUNS: 713

CLUB VS. CLUB AND MONTHLY RECORDS OF THE NEW YORK YANKEES' 1926 SEASON FOR HOME AND AWAY GAMES

CLUB		APR	MAY	JUN	JUL	AUG	SEP	OCT	HOME	AWAY	TOTAL
BOST	H	3–1	1– 0	2– 0	xxx	1– 1	2– 1	xxx	9– 3	xxx	17– 5
	A	2–1	4– 0	2– 1	xxx	xxx	xxx	xxx	xxx	8– 2	
CHIC	H	xxx	3– 0	xxx	5– 1	0– 1	xxx	xxx	8– 2	xxx	14– 8
	A	xxx	xxx	2– 2	1– 0	2– 1	1– 3	xxx	xxx	6– 6	
CLEV	H	xxx	3– 0	xxx	2– 3	1– 1	xxx	xxx	6– 4	xxx	11–11
	A	xxx	xxx	1– 2	xxx	2– 1	2– 4	xxx	xxx	5– 7	
DET	H	xxx	2– 2	xxx	2– 2	2– 1	xxx	xxx	6– 5	xxx	12–10
	A	xxx	xxx	4– 0	xxx	1– 3	1– 2	xxx	xxx	6– 5	
PHIL	H	3– 0	1– 3	xxx	xxx	0– 1	2– 1	xxx	6– 5	xxx	9–13
	A	xxx	0– 3	1– 2	0– 2	xxx	2– 1	xxx	xxx	3– 8	
STL	H	xxx	4– 0	xxx	2– 2	2– 0	xxx	xxx	8– 2	xxx	16– 6
	A	xxx	xxx	2– 2	4– 0	xxx	2– 2	xxx	xxx	8– 4	
WAS	H	2– 0	1– 1	2– 0	1– 1	1– 2	xxx	xxx	7– 4	xxx	12–10
	A	2– 1	xxx	1– 1	1– 1	1– 3	xxx	xxx	xxx	5– 6	
TOTAL	H	8–1	15– 6	4– 0	12– 9	7– 7	4– 2	xxx	50– 25	xxx	91–63
	A	4–2	4– 3	13–10	6– 3	6– 8	8–12	xxx	xxx	41–38	
GRAND TOT:		12–3	19– 9	17–10	18–12	13–15	12–14	xxx	xxx	xxx	
CUMUL TOT:		12–3	31–12	48–22	66–34	79–49	91–63	xxx	xxx	xxx	

TIE GAMES: 1 was–July

1927

THE ARCHETYPAL SUPERTEAM

The 1927 New York Yankees are generally considered the greatest team in baseball history. This amazing conglomerate of athletes commonly referred to as "Murderer's Row," led by Ruth and Gehrig, bested all American League opposition by winning the pennant in a landslide 19 games ahead of Connie Mack's Philadelphia Athletics. Guiding his club to the most American League victories (110) in a season in history up to that point (Cleveland eventually wins 111 in 1954), manager Miller Huggins won his fifth A.L. pennant since arriving on the Yankee scene in 1918. Only the 1936 Yankees won an A.L. pennant by more games (19½) than did the '27 Yanks (excluding A.L. divisional play beginning in 1969). The Yanks winning percentage of .714 (a number which most sports fans connect with Ruth's career homer total) is the second best in A.L. history, being surpassed only by the 1954 Cleveland Indians with a .721 winning mark.

This season is usually best remembered as the Babe's sixty homer year. Babe was to best his previous record of 59 roundtrippers, set in 1921, his second season as a Yankee. Ruth's homer feat was usually regarded as one of baseball's most cherished records and when surpassed in 1961 by Roger Maris, Commissioner Ford Frick felt it appropriate to place an asterisk beside Maris' total of 61 since he had required a 162-game schedule to achieve his record while Ruth had attained his 60 homers in a 154 game season.

In addition to his 60 homers, the Babe, together with teammate Lou Gehrig, form an unbelievable hitting tandem. Ruth and Gehrig finished 1–2 respectively in the A.L. with: slugging percentage (.772, .765), bases on balls (138, 109), and runs scored (158, 149). Centerfielder Earle Combs finished third in the A.L. in runs scored behind Ruth and Gehrig with 137 tallies. Between them, Ruth, Gehrig, and Combs accounted for 444 of the Yanks' 975 league-leading run total, or about 46% of New York's scoring for the season. Not to be outdone, Gehrig outshadowed the Babe with a league-high 447 total bases (Ruth was second with 417 and Combs next with 331) and Lou outdistanced Ruth with 175 RBI to Ruth's 164, finishing 1–2 in the league. Gehrig, who won this year's League Award, also placed third with a .373 batting mark and became the first Yankee ever to lead the league in doubles with 52, a still-standing club record for a season. The great Lou was not finished with his hitting exploits, finishing second to Combs' A.L. high in triples (23) with 18 three-baggers. Combs' total of 23 triples is also a club record as is his league-leading singles total for 1927, 166, tying Keeler's mark of 1906. Gehrig, with his 218 hits, is second to Combs with 231, yet another club mark.

In addition to the hitting prowess of Ruth, Gehrig, and Combs, Bob Meusel and Tony Lazzeri each totaled more than 100 RBI with 103 and 102 RBI, respectively. In addition, Lazzeri places third in A.L. homers with 18, a paltry total in comparison to Ruth's 60 and Gehrig's 47. Meusel, in stealing 24 bases, finished second to St. Louis' George Sisler's total of 27 pilfers, with Lazzeri adding 22 to tie for third place in A.L. steals with two other players.

The Yanks paced the A.L. in team batting (.309), team slugging (.489, a club and Major League record), runs scored (975), triples (103), homers (158), hits (1,644), RBI (908), and bases on balls (635). Also, their 110 victories, .714 winning percentage and but 44 losses are all Yankee season marks.

What made this team so remarkable was that its hitting was only partially responsible for its success. Their pitching was something else, too! Four of the top hurlers in A.L. winning percentage wore pinstripes, led by Waite Hoyt's .759 (22 wins, 7 losses), followed in order by Urban Shocker's .750 (18–6), Wilcy Moore's .731 (19–7) and Herb Pennock's .704 (19–8). Between them, these four pitchers won 78 of New York's 110 games, some 71% of the Yankee victories in 1927. Hoyt's total of 22 wins tied with Ted Lyons of Chicago as A.L. leader, with Yankees Moore and Pennock tied for third with 19 victories apiece (Tommy Thomas of Chicago also had 19 wins). To complete his sweep of the pitching "Triple Crown" (that is, leading in winning percentage, ERA and wins), Hoyt placed first in individual ERA with a 2.63 mark, followed by Shocker's 2.84 in the runner-up slot, being tied with Lyons of Chicago. Waite Hoyt also finished third overall in the A.L. with 23 complete games, with teammate Herb Pennock coming in fifth with 18 route jobs along with Cleveland's Willis "Ace" Hudlin.

As a team, the pitching corps finished with the lowest ERA, 3.20, and demonstrated the best control, walking a league low 409 A.L. batters. The Yankee moundsmen also yielded the league's fewest runs with 599.

Defensively, the Yanks finished in a third place tie with Washington in fielding percentage, both with a .969 mark.

In 1927, Yankee domination and intimidation of their opponents did not end with the conclusion of the regular season. There was also the World Series to consider. Pitted against manager Donie Bush and his Pirates, the Hugmen (as the Yankees were called under Miller Huggin's guidance) entered the Series as heavy favorites to cop the Fall Classic in easy fashion. It has been written many times that Pittsburgh actually lost the World Series before the first game was ever played. It seems that Pittsburgh players witnessed the Yankees taking batting practice. The Pirate players were so awed and intimidated by the Yankee display of raw power that they accepted inevitable defeat in the World Series then and there. The Bronx Bombers did in fact live up to the Pirate's expectations, vanquishing Pittsburgh in four straight games! Yankees hurlers permitted but 10 Pirate runs in the four games. This was the Yanks' first of three non-consecutive Fall Classic appearances in which they defeated their opponents in four straight games, a World Series record. The next two occasions they would manage this feat was next season, and then in the 1932 World Series against the Cubbies of Chicago.

Hitting the century mark in victories (for the first of fourteen times through 1983), the 1927 season was one of remarkable personal performances as well as a year of excellent all-around team play. The consistency of hitting for power as well as for average was complemented with superb pitching throughout the season. Although there is dispute about other teams being better than the 1927 Yankees, this edition of the New Yorkers receives my vote as the greatest team in all of baseball history.

The 1927 DAY BY DAY scores follow:

DAY BY DAY, 1927 NEW YORK YANKEES

April, 1927

12	PHI	W	8- 3
13	PHI	W	10-4
14	PHI	TG	9-9f
15	PHI	W	6-3
16	BOS	W	5-2
17	BOS	W	14-2
18	BOS	W	3-0
19	BOS	L	3-6
20	phi	L	5-8
21	phi	W	13-6
22	phi	*	
23	phi	L	3- 4
24	was	W	6-2
25	WAS	L	4- 5
26	WAS	*	
27	WAS	*	
28	bos	*	
29	bos	W	9-0
30	bos	L	2-3

May, 1927

1	PHI	W	7-3
2	was	W	9-6
3	was	W	6-4
4	was	L	4-7
5	was	L	1-6
6	NG		
7	chi	W	8-0
8	chi	W	9- 0
9	chi	L	1- 2f
10	stl	W	8-7
11	stl	W	4- 2
12	stl	W	4- 3
13	stl	W	3-1
14	det	*	
15	det	*	
16	det	W	6- 2
17	det	W	9- 2
18	cle	*	
19	cle	W	4-3
20	cle	L	1- 2
21	cle	L	4- 5h
22	cle	W	7- 2

May, 1927

23	was	L	2- 3
24	PHI	*	
25	PHI	*	
26	NG		
27	WAS	L	2- 7
"	WAS	W	5- 0
28	WAS	W	8- 2
"	WAS	L	2- 3
29	BOS	W	15- 7
30	phi	L	8- 9
"	phi	W	6- 5g
31	phi	W	10- 3
"	phi	W	18- 5

June, 1927

1	phi	W	2- 1
2	DET	W	2- 0
3	DET	L	1- 3
4	DET	*	
5	DET	W	5- 3
6	NG		
7	CHI	W	4- 1
8	CHI	W	12-11g
9	CHI	W	8- 3
10	CHI	L	2- 4
11	CLE	W	6- 4
12	CLE	L	7- 8
13	CLE	W	14- 6
14	CLE	*	
15	NG		
16	STL	W	8- 1
17	STL	W	3- 2
18	STL	W	8- 4
19	STL	*	
20	bos	*	
21	bos	W	7- 3
"	bos	W	7- 1
22	bos	W	7- 4
"	bos	W	3- 2
23	bos	W	11- 4
24	NG		
25	PHI	L	6- 7
"	PHI	L	2- 4

June, 1927

26	PHI	L	2- 4
"	PHI	W	7- 3
27	PHI	W	6- 2
28	PHI	W	9- 8
29	BOS	W	8- 2
30	BOS	W	13- 6

July, 1927

1	BOS	W	7- 4
2	BOS	W	3- 2
3	was	L	5- 6
4	WAS	W	12- 1
"	WAS	W	21- 1
5	WAS	W	7- 6
6	NG		
7	NG		
8	det	L	8-11
"	det	W	10- 8
9	det	W	19- 7
"	det	L	4-14
10	det	L	3- 6
11	det	W	8- 5
12	cle	W	7- 0
13	cle	W	5- 3
14	cle	L	1- 4
15	cle	W	10- 9
16	stl	W	5- 2
17	stl	W	5- 4
18	stl	W	10- 6
19	stl	W	6- 1
20	NG		
21	chi	W	4- 1
22	chi	L	5- 7
23	chi	W	5- 2
24	chi	W	3- 2
25	NG		
26	STL	W	15- 1
"	STL	W	12- 3
27	STL	W	4- 1
28	STL	W	9- 4
29	CLE	L	4- 6
30	CLE	W	7- 3
"	CLE	W	5- 0
31	CLE	*	

August, 1927

1	CLE	L	1- 2b
2	NG		
3	DET	L	5- 6
"	DET	W	8- 6
4	DET	L	2- 6
5	DET	W	5- 2
6	CHI	L	3- 6
7	CHI	W	4- 3
8	CHI	*	
9	phi	L	1- 8
10	was	W	4- 3
11	was	L	2- 3g
12	NG		
13	was	W	6- 3
14	was	W	6- 2
15	NG		
16	chi	W	8- 1
17	chi	W	3- 2g
18	chi	W	5- 4h
19	chi	L	2- 3
20	cle	L	8-14
21	cle	L	4- 7
22	cle	L	4- 9
23	NG		
24	det	W	9- 5
25	det	W	8- 2
26	det	W	8- 6
27	stl	W	14- 4
28	stl	W	10- 6
29	stl	W	8- 3
30	NG		
31	BOS	W	10- 3

September, 1927

1	BOS	*	
2	phi	W	12- 2
3	phi	L	0- 1
4	NG		
5	bos		L11-12n
"	bos	W	5- 0a
6	bos	W	14- 2
"	bos	L	2- 5
7	bos	W	12-10

September, 1927

8	STL	W	2- 1
9	STL	W	9- 3
10	STL	W	1-0
11	STL	L	2-6
12	NG		
13	CLE	W	5-3
"	CLE	W	5-3
14	CLE	W	4-1
15	CLE	L	2-3
16	CHI	W	7-2
17	CHI	W	3-2
"	CHI	W	8- 1
18	CHI	W	2-1
"	CHI	W	5- 1
19	NG		
20	NG		
21	DET	L	1-6
22	DET	W	8-7
23	NG		
24	DET	W	6-0
25	DET	L	1-6
26	NG		
27	PHI	W	7-4
28	NG		
29	WAS	W	15-4
30	WAS	W	4-2

October, 1927

1	WAS	W	4-3

END OF 1927

RUNS: 975

OPP RUNS: 599

CLUB VS. CLUB AND MONTHLY RECORDS OF THE NEW YORK YANKEES' 1927 SEASON FOR HOME AND AWAY GAMES

CLUB		APR	MAY	JUN	JUL	AUG	SEP	OCT	HOME	AWAY	TOTAL
BOST	H	3–1	1–0	2–0	2–0	1–0	xxx	xxx	9–1	xxx	
	A	1–1	xxx	5–0	xxx	xxx	3–2	xxx	xxx	9–3	18–4
CHIC	H	xxx	xxx	3–1	xxx	1–1	5–0	xxx	9–2	xxx	
	A	xxx	2–1	xxx	3–1	3–1	xxx	xxx	xxx	8–3	17–5
CLEV	H	xxx	xxx	2–1	2–1	0–1	3–1	xxx	7–4	xxx	
	A	xxx	2–2	xxx	3–1	0–3	xxx	xxx	xxx	5–6	12–10
DET	H	xxx	xxx	2–1	xxx	2–2	2–2	xxx	6–5	xxx	
	A	xxx	2–0	xxx	3–3	3–0	xxx	xxx	xxx	8–3	14–8
PHIL	H	3–0	1–0	3–3	xxx	xxx	1–0	xxx	8–3	xxx	
	A	1–2	3–1	1–0	xxx	0–1	1–1	xxx	xxx	6–5	14–8
STL	H	xxx	xxx	3–0	4–0	xxx	3–1	xxx	10–1	xxx	
	A	xxx	4–0	xxx	4–0	3–0	xxx	xxx	xxx	11–0	21–1
WAS	H	0–1	2–2	xxx	3–0	xxx	2–0	1–0	8–3	xxx	
	A	1–0	2–3	xxx	0–1	3–1	xxx	xxx	xxx	6–5	14–8
TOTAL:	H	6–2	4–2	15–6	11–1	4–4	16–4	1–0	57–19	xxx	
	A	3–3	15–7	6–0	13–6	12–6	4–3	xxx	53–25	110–44	
GRAND TOT:		9–5	19–9	21–6	24–7	16–10	20–7	1–0			
CUMUL TOT:		9–5	28–14	49–20	73–27	89–37	109–44	110–44			

TIE GAMES: 1
PHI-Apr

1928

WHAT AN ENCORE!

After that unbelievable 1927 season, 1928 proved just as eventful. The Yankees clinched their third consecutive pennant and second straight Fall Classic. Just as in the previous World Series, the Yanks again defeated their opponents, this time the St. Louis Cardinals, in four straight games. Finishing with a 101–53 (.656) ledger, the Yanks defeated a determined Philadelphia Club by a scant 2½ games. 1928 had Ernest Barnard replacing Ban Johnson as the second American League president. Johnson had served in that capacity since the inception of the league in 1901.

Babe Ruth again dominated the A.L. statistics, finishing first in five major areas. He banged out 54 homers, exactly twice more than teammate Lou Gehrig, who was second in the A.L. Ruth also rated tops with 163 runs scored, 142 RBI (tied with Lou Gehrig), 380 total bases, and a slugging average of .709. Gehrig became the only Yankee in history to lead the league in doubles two consecutive seasons, this year tying Manush (St. Louis) with 47 two-baggers. Not to be outdone, Earle Combs hit 21 triples to lead the A.L. Bob Meusel hit for the cycle (homer, triple, double, and single in same game) for an American League record third time in 1928, having accomplished this previously in 1921 and 1922.

As far as pitching, Herb Pennock, "The Knight of Kennett Square," hurled a league-leading five shutouts. The pitching staff placed second with a team ERA of 3.74.

As usual, the Yankees led in total homers for the sixth straight season, this time leading with 133 roundtrippers. In team batting, the Yanks finished first for the second straight year with a .296 mark. In addition, they scored the most often (894), walked the most (562) and drove across the most runs (817). The latter two categories were dominated by the New Yorkers for the third consecutive year. Slugging percentage, their forte, was also claimed with a .450 average.

On the negative side of the ledger, the Cleveland Indians scored more runs in a game against the Yanks than any other club in history on July 29. The Indians pounded out a 24–6 rout at Cleveland against 5 Yankee hurlers, Pipgras being the starter and eventual losing pitcher. Getting 27 hits off Yankee moundsmen, Cleveland became *the only* club to score 20 or more runs against the Yanks in their history; the Yankees will return the favor against their opponents some nineteen times, an American League record.

This season was again an enormously successful campaign for the Yankees. 1929 will prove to be quite a different story.

The 1928 DAY BY DAY scores follow:

DAY BY DAY, 1928 NEW YORK YANKEES

April, 1928	May, 1928	June, 1928	July, 1928	August, 1928
11 phi W 8– 3	21 BOS L 4– 8	" BOS L 1– 7	25 det L 2– 3	28 NG
12 phi *	" BOS W 3– 2	24 BOS W 4– 0	" det L7– 10	29 NG
13 phi W 8– 7	22 BOS W 14– 4	25 NG	26 det W 12– 1h	30 was L 1– 3
14 phi *	23 BOS W 2– 1	26 NG	" det L10–13	31 NG
15 NG	24 phi W 9– 7	27 phi W7– 4	27 det *	**September, 1928**
16 bos W 7– 2	" phi L 2– 5	28 phi W 10– 4	28 cle W 6– 2	1 was W 8– 3
17 bos *	25 phi W 4– 2	29 phi L 4– 6	" cle L 4– 9	2 was L 0– 2
18 bos W 10– 7	" phi W 9– 2	30 bos W 11– 4	29 cle L 6–24	3 BOS W 8– 7
19 bos L 6– 7	26 phi W 7– 4	" bos W 7– 6	30 cle L 2– 4	" BOS L 3– 4
" bos W 7– 2b	27 NG	**July, 1928**	31 cle W 12– 9	4 NG
20 PHI L 1– 2	28 phi W 11– 4	1 PHI W 12– 6	**August, 1928**	5 WAS L 1– 3
21 PHI L 0–10	29 WAS W 3– 2	" PHI W 8– 4	1 stl W 12– 1	" WAS W 8– 3
22 PHI *	" WAS W 12– 3	2 was L 3– 4	2 stl L 3– 4k	6 WAS *
23 WAS W 4– 0	30 WAS L 0– 5	3 was W 7– 6	3 stl L 0– 8	7 WA S L 0–11
24 WAS W 12– 4	" WAS *	4 was L 2– 5	4 chi W 8– 6f	" WAS L 1– 6
25 WAS *	31 WAS W 4– 0	" was W 5– 4	5 chi L 4– 5	8 WAS W 6– 3
26 BOS W 9– 4	**June, 1928**	5 NG	6 chi L 4– 5k	9 PHI W 5– 0
27 BOS *	1 NG	6 STL *	7 chi W 6– 3	" PHI W 7– 3
28 BOS *	2 det W 5– 2	7 STL W 6– 5	8 NG	10 NG
29 was W 7– 5	3 det W 7– 2	" STL W 1– 0	9 bos W 7– 1	11 PHI W 5– 3
30 was W 8– 4	4 det *	8 STL L4– 10	10 bos W 5– 2	12 PHI L 3– 4
May, 1928	5 det *	" STL L 3– 5	11 bos W 5– 2	13 NG
1 was W 8– 5	6 cle W 8– 3	9 STL W 4– 0	12 BOS W 8– 0	14 NG
2 was L 5– 9	7 cle W 8– 2	" STL L6– 12	13 NG	15 stl L 5– 6
3 NG	8 cle *	10 DET *	14 CHI L 2– 5	16 stl W 7– 5
4 CHI W 10– 4	9 cle W 7– 3	11 DET L 2– 4	15 CHI L 4– 8	17 stl W 12– 2
5 CHI W 7– 0	10 chi L 6– 8	" DET W 6– 5	16 CHI W 11– 1	18 stl W 14–11
6 CHI W 4– 2	11 chi L 1– 6	12 DET L 2– 4	17 CLE *	19 NG
7 CHI W 8– 5	12 chi W 15– 7	13 DET *	18 CLE W 8– 5	20 chi L 3– 4h
8 CLE L 0– 3	13 chi W 8– 6	14 CLE *	19 CLE L 2– 3f	21 chi W 5– 2
9 CLE *	14 stl W 4– 3	15 CLE W 3– 0	" CLE W 10– 2	22 chi L 2– 5
10 CLE W 4– 2	15 stl L 4– 5	" CLE W 6– 4	20 NG	23 cle W 5– 0
11 CLE W 7– 6f	16 stl L 5– 7	16 CLE W 7– 3	21 STL W 3– 1	24 cle L 3– 4
12 DET W 8– 7	17 stl W 6– 2	" CLE W 6– 2	22 STL *	25 cle W 10– 1
13 DET W 7– 2	18 NG	17 CLE W 4– 2	23 STL *	26 NG
14 DET W 7– 5	19 PHI *	18 CHI W 9– 8	24 STL L 2– 5	27 det W 4– 3
15 DET W 12– 8	20 PHI L 5–10	19 CHI W 6– 4	" STL L 1– 3	" det W 8– 5c
16 NG	" PHI W 9– 3	20 NG	25 DET L 3– 9	28 det W 11– 6
17 STL W 4– 3	21 PHI W 4– 0	21 CHI W 2– 0	" DET W 7– 0c	29 det L10–19
18 STL *	" PHI *	22 CHI L 4– 6	26 DET *	30 det W 7– 6
19 STL *	22 PHI *	23 bos L 3– 8	27 DET W 4– 3	**END OF 1928**
20 STL W 9– 3	23 BOS L 4– 8	24 bos W 5– 3	" DET W 5– 2	RUNS: 894
				OPP RUNS: 685

CLUB VS. CLUB AND MONTHLY RECORDS OF THE NEW YORK YANKEES' 1928 SEASON FOR HOME AND AWAY GAMES

CLUB:		APR	MAY	JUN	JUL	AUG	SEP	OCT	HOME	AWAY	TOTAL
BOST	H	1- 0	3- 1	1- 2	xxx	1- 0	1- 1	xxx	7- 4	xxx	16- 6
	A	3- 1	xxx	2- 0	1- 1	3- 0	xxx	xxx	xxx	9- 2	
CHIC	H	xxx	4- 0	xxx	3- 1	1- 2	xxx	xxx	8- 3	xxx	13- 9
	A	xxx	xxx	2- 2	xxx	2- 2	1- 2	xxx	xxx	5- 6	
CLEV	H	xxx	2- 1	xxx	5- 0	2- 1	xxx	xxx	9- 2	xxx	16- 6
	A	xxx	xxx	3- 0	2- 3	xxx	2- 1	xxx	xxx	7- 4	
DET	H	xxx	4- 0	xxx	1- 2	3- 1	xxx	xxx	8- 3	xxx	15- 7
	A	xxx	xxx	2- 0	1- 3	xxx	4- 1	xxx	xxx	7- 4	
PHIL	H	0- 2	xxx	2- 1	2- 0	xxx	3- 1	xxx	7- 4	xxx	16- 6
	A	2- 0	5- 1	2- 1	xxx	xxx	xxx	xxx	xxx	9- 2	
STL	H	xxx	2- 0	xxx	3- 3	1- 2	xxx	xxx	6- 5	xxx	12-10
	A	xxx	xxx	2- 2	xxx	1- 2	3- 1	x xx	xxx	6- 5	
WAS	H	2- 0	3- 1	xxx	xxx	xxx	2- 3	xxx	7- 4	xxx	13- 9
	A	2- 0	1- 1	xxx	2- 2	0- 1	1- 1	xxx	xxx	6- 5	
TOTAL:	H	3- 2	18- 3	3- 3	14- 6	8- 6	6- 5	xxx	52-25	xxx	101-53
	A	7- 1	6- 2	13- 5	6- 9	6- 5	11- 6	xxx	xxx	49-28	
GRAND TOT:		10- 3	24- 5	16- 8	20-15	14-11	17-11	xxx	xxx	xxx	
CUMUL TOT:		10- 3	34- 8	50-16	70-31	84-42	101-53	xxx	xxx	xxx	

TIE GAMES: NONE

1929

THE DEATH OF MILLER HUGGINS

After twelve seasons at the Yankee helm, Miller Huggins passed away at the age of 50 in the latter stages of the season. Art Fletcher assumed the managerial reins the season's final eleven games. As a tribute to this great man, Miller Huggins, all American League games were postponed on September 27, the date of Huggins' funeral.

The pennant race was really no contest with Connie Mack's A's finishing an incredible 18 games ahead of second place New York. In spite of this finish, the Yanks continued to dominate the home run race for the 7th straight season, banging out 142 this time. Mr. Ruth again led in home runs with 46 and with a slugging percentage of .697. Combs led the league in one base hits with 151 for the second time in three seasons.

For the first time in baseball history, the Yankees played throughout the season with numerals on their uniforms.

This season was indeed a sad one for the Yanks both on and off the field. Frustration and disappointment will beset the Yankee franchise over the next few seasons.

The 1929 DAY BY DAY scores follow:

DAY BY DAY, 1929 NEW YORK YANKEES

April, 1929	May, 1929	June, 1929	August, 1929	September, 1929
16 BOS *	24 bos L 0- 5	28 phi *	3 CLE *	7 DET L 4- 5
17 BOS *	25 bos L 8-10	29 phi W 7- 5	4 CLE W 12- 0	" DET W 11- 7
18 BOS W 7- 3	" bos W 8- 3	30 bos W 6- 4	" CLE L 6-14	8 DET W 9- 3
19 PHI W 2- 1	26 bos W 15- 4	**July, 1929**	5 NG	9 DET *
20 PHI *	27 NG	1 BOS W 3- 2	6 WAS L 9-13	10 DET L 4- 8
21 PHI L 4- 7a	28 was W 12- 7	2 BOS W 4- 3f	" WAS W 8- 0	" DET W 10- 9
22 PHI *	29 was L 3- 8	3 BOS W 6- 5	7 phi L 2- 4	11 STL L 0- 5
23 bos L 2- 4	30 was L 5- 8	4 WAS W 8- 4	" phi W 13- 1	12 STL W 5- 2
24 bos W 9- 3	" was L 3- 4	" WAS W 14- 4	8 phi W 6- 4	13 STL *
25 bos *	31 NG	5 NG	9 NG	14 STL L 3-12
26 phi L 2- 5	**June, 1929**	6 stl W 3- 1	10 cle W 4- 2	" STL W 4- 2
27 phi W 9- 7	1 CHI W 8- 1	7 stl L 2- 7	11 cle L 5- 6	15 CLE W 1- 0
28 was W 7- 2	2 CHI W 6- 1	8 stl W 10- 3	12 cle L 7-11	" CLE L 0-10
29 phi L 1-10	3 CHI W 1- 0	9 stl W 8- 7	13 cle L 2- 3	16 CLE L 2- 4
30 WAS W 10- 9f	4 CHI W 4- 2	10 chi L 3- 6	14 det L13-17	17 CLE *
May, 1929	5 CLE W 6- 5g	11 chi *	15 det L 0- 3	18 CLE W 9- 7
1 WAS *	6 CLE L 7- 9	12 chi W 12- 2	16 det W 12- 2	" CLE W 12- 2
2 WAS *	7 CLE L 3- 7	13 chi W 4- 2	17 det W 7- 2	19 CHI L 0- 7
3 NG	8 CLE *	" chi W 6- 5j	18 chi L 2- 3	20 CHI *
4 chi W 11- 9	9 STL W 17- 2	14 det L 3- 7	19 chi W 3- 2	21 CHI W 8- 5
5 chi W 8- 3	10 STL W 3- 2	15 det W 7- 6	20 chi W 5- 4	22 CHI L 4- 7
6 chi W 7- 6f	11 STL W 11- 5	16 det W 11- 7	21 chi L 3- 4	" CHI W 3- 1
7 s tl W 6- 5	12 STL L 4- 9	17 det L 8- 9f	22 stl L 0-10	23 NG
8 stl W 8- 1	13 DET W 8- 5	18 cle *	23 stl L 0- 5	24 bos W 5- 3
9 stl W 7- 3	14 DET W 15- 4	19 cle W 7- 2	24 stl L 0- 4	25 bos W 11-10g
10 det W 10- 5	15 DET L 2- 9	" cle L 3-11	25 stl L 2- 3	26 was W 10- 3
11 det L 7-13	16 DET W 11- 7	20 cle L 4- 8	26 NG	27 was *
12 det L 7- 9	17 NG	" cle W 11- 6	27 PHI W 2- 0	28 was L 4- 6
13 cle L 3- 4	18 BOS W 9- 0	21 cle L 4- 6	28 PHI L 7- 9	" was L 3- 6
14 cle *	" BOS L 4- 7	22 NG	29 WAS W 5- 4	29 was W 3- 0
15 cle L 1- 7	19 BOS W 13- 2	23 DET W 7- 5	" WAS L 4- 8	30 NG
16 NG	20 NG	24 DET W 7- 5	30 WAS *	**October, 1929**
17 BOS L 3- 5h	21 PHI L1- 11	25 DET *	31 WAS W 4- 0	1 NG
18 BOS W 5- 2	" PHI W 8- 3	26 STL W 9- 0	" WAS W 13- 3	2 NG
" BOS W 5- 0	22 PHI L 3- 7	27 STL W 5- 3	**September, 1929**	3 NG
19 BOS W 3- 0a	" PHI W 4- 3j	28 STL W 7- 6h	1 bos W 6- 4	4 NG
" BOS *	23 PHI L 4- 7	29 NG	2 phi L 3-10	5 PHI L 4- 8
20 NG	24 NG	30 CHI W 7- 3	" phi L 5- 6	6 PHI L 2- 5
21 WAS *	25 was *	31 CHI W 16- 2	3 phi L 2-10	END OF 1929
22 WAS L 2-10	26 was W 7- 0	**August, 1929**	4 NG	RUNS: 899
" WAS L2- 3	" was L 3- 4	1 CHI L 2- 3	5 NG	OPP RUNS: 775
23 bos W 7- 6	27 phi L 3- 6	2 CLE L 8- 9	6 NG	

CLUB VS. CLUB AND MONTHLY RECORDS OF THE NEW YORK YANKEES' 1929 SEASON FOR HOME AND AWAY GAMES

CLUB:		APR	MAY	JUN	JUL	AUG	SEP	OCT	HOME	AWAY	TOTAL
BOST	H	1-0	3-1	2-1	3-0	xxx	xxx	xxx	9- 2	xxx	17- 5
	A	1-1	3-2	1-0	xxx	xxx	3-0	xxx	xxx	8- 3	
CHIC	H	xxx	xxx	4-0	2-0	0-1	2-2	xxx	8-3	xxx	16- 6
	A	xxx	3-0	xxx	3-1	2-2	xxx	xxx	xxx	8- 3	
CLEV	H	xxx	xxx	1-2	xxx	1-2	3-2	xxx	5-6	xxx	8-14
	A	xxx	0-2	xxx	2-3	1-3	xxx	xxx	xxx	3- 8	
DET	H	xxx	xxx	3-1	2-0	xxx	3-2	xxx	8-3	xxx	13- 9
	A	xxx	1-2	xxx	2-2	2-2	xxx	xxx	xxx	5- 6	
PHIL	H	1-1	xxx	2-3	xxx	1-1	xxx	0-2	4-7	xxx	8-14
	A	1-2	xxx	1-1	xxx	2-1	0-3	xxx	xxx	4- 7	
STL	H	xxx	xxx	3-1	3-0	xxx	2-2	xxx	8-3	xxx	14- 8
	A	xxx	3-0	xxx	3-1	0-4	xxx	xxx	xxx	6- 5	
WAS	H	1-0	0-2	xxx	2-0	4-2	xxx	xxx	7-4	xxx	12-10
	A	1-0	1-3	1-1	xxx	xxx	2-2	xxx	xxx	5- 6	
TOTAL:	H	3-1	3-3	15-8	12-0	6-6	10-8	0-2	49-28	xxx	88-66
	A	3-3	11-9	3-2	10-7	7-12	5-5	xxx	xxx	39-38	
GRAND TOT:		6-4	14-12	18-10	22-7	13-18	15-13	0-2	xxx	xxx	
CUMUL TOT:		6-4	20-16	38-26	60-33	73-51	88-64	88-66	xxx	xxx	

TIE GAMES: NONE

1930

SCORING RUNS IS NOT ENOUGH

The opening of the 30's proved disheartening for New York, again finishing behind Philadelphia but this time in third place, 16 games off the lead. As their eleventh manager, Bob Shawkey, former Yankee pitcher, guided his club to an 86–68 record (.558). This was his only year as Yankee manager, never assuming the role again of field general.

This edition of the Yankees was without a doubt one of the best third-place teams in history. Scoring an impressive 1,062 times in 154 games (almost 7 runs a contest), the Yankees established some club standards. Nine Yankee hitters batted .300 or more; their .309 team batting average is the best in New York history, .002 points ahead of the '27 club. Yankee pitchers allowed opponents the most runs, 898, another club record. Offensively, the Bombers pounded out 1,683 hits and 110 triples, both team marks and best in the A.L. in 1930. In addition to leading in batting, this club was tops in the league in RBI (986), slugging percentage (.488) and walks (with 644). Individually, the Babe led the league in slugging percentage and homers with .732 and 49, respectively. Gehrig won two important categories, heading the RBI list with 174 and total bases with 419. The duo of Babe and Lou represented an incredible combination of awesome power and consistency in most of their years as teammates. For the third time in the past 4 seasons, Combs paced the Junior Circuit in triples with 22. He thus became the only Yankee in history to lead the A.L. in triples on three separate occasions.

In the pitching department, Pipgras tied for the league lead with 3 shutouts. This shutout total represents the least whitewashes to lead the league in A.L. history. In no other A.L. season have so few shutouts represented the highest league total for individual pitchers. The Yankees club mark of the highest staff ERA (4.88, 741 earned runs) was set in 1930.

As a whole, the Yankee defense and pitching staff did not embellish their hopes for a pennant. This season was dominated by the hitter. Winning would require more than scoring runs in large numbers. In 1931, the Yanks will again play second fiddle to Connie Mack's Philadelphia A's.

The 1930 DAY BY DAY scores follow:

DAY BY DAY, 1930 NEW YORK YANKEES

April 1930
15 phi	L	2– 6
16 phi		*
17 phi		*
18 bos		*
19 bos	L	3– 4k
" bos	L	2– 7
20 was	L	3– 6
21 NG		
22 PHI	L	6– 7
23 PHI		*
24 PHI		*
25 BOS	W	3– 2f
26 BOS	W	8– 3
27 BOS	L	7– 8
28 was	L	5– 6
29 was	L	8–11
30 was	W	9– 0

May, 1930
1 NG		
2 CHI	L	1–10
3 CHI	W	5– 3
4 CHI	W	7– 4
5 CHI	W	4– 1
6 CLE	L	6– 7
7 CLE	W	8– 7
8 CLE		*
9 DET	L	4– 5
10 DET	W	14– 5
11 DET	W	7– 6
12 DET	W	7– 0
13 STL	W	4– 1
14 STL		*
15 STL		*
16 bos	L	4– 5
17 bos	W	3– 2
18 bos	W	11– 0
19 bos		*
20 bos	W	7– 4f
21 phi	L	7–15
" phi	L	1– 4
22 phi	W	10– 1
" phi	W	20–13

May, 1930
23 NG		
24 PHI	W	10– 6
" PHI	W	11– 1
25 PHI	L	3– 10
26 WAS	L	7–10
27 WAS	L	2– 7
28 WAS		*
29 WAS	W	4– 2
30 BOS	W	6– 5
" BOS	W	7– 3
31 BOS	W	5– 2

June, 1930
1 BOS	L	4– 7
2 NG		
3 chi	W	13– 7
4 chi	L	7– 8f
5 chi		*
6 chi		*
7 stl	W	12– 5
8 stl	L	4– 5
9 stl	W	8– 5
10 stl	W	5– 3
11 det	L	7–13
12 det	W	14– 2
13 det	W	10– 9
14 cle	W	11– 7
15 cle	W	17–10
16 cle		*
17 cle	W	17– 2
18 NG		
19 DET	W	5– 4
20 DET	L	6–11
21 DET	W	3– 0
22 STL	W	5– 4
" STL	L	2– 5
23 STL	W	15– 0
" STL	L	6–10
24 STL		*
25 STL	W	5– 4
" STL	W	16– 4
26 CLE	W	13–11
27 CLE	L	7–11

June, 1930
28 CLE	W	13– 1
" CLE	W	14– 2
29 CLE	W	7– 6
30 CHI	W	15– 4

July, 1930
1 CHI		*
2 CHI	W	5– 1
" CHI	L	4– 15
3 phi	L	4– 5
4 was	L	0– 8
" was	L	3– 7
5 was	L	2– 3
6 was	L	2– 3f
7 NG		
8 PHI	L	0– 4
" PHI	W	9– 4
9 PHI	W	12– 6
10 PHI	L	1– 9
11 NG		
12 chi	L	6–11
" chi	W	11– 7
13 chi	W	7– 5
14 chi	L	9– 10
" chi	W	7– 2
15 chi	W	9– 5
16 stl	W	2– 1
17 stl	W	16– 7
18 stl	L	6–14
19 stl	W	13– 7
20 cle	L	8– 9
21 cle	W	7– 3
22 cle	L	5– 6
" cle	L	8– 10
23 cle	L	6–10
24 det	W	5– 2
25 det	W	14– 7
26 det	L	8–12
27 det	L	3– 7
28 phi	L	5– 6h
29 phi	W	12– 3
30 bos	W	8– 2f
" bos	W	10– 1

July, 1930
31 bos	W	14–13

August, 1930
1 bos	W	4– 1
2 WAS	L	3– 9
" WAS	L	5– 9
3 PHI	W	9– 3
4 WAS		*
5 WAS	L	4– 6
" WAS	W	7– 1
6 BOS	W	4– 2
7 BOS	W	5– 1
8 STL	W	5– 3
9 STL	W	9– 8
10 STL	W	14–11
11 STL	L	5– 10
12 DET	W	6– 5
13 DET	W	10– 8
14 DET	L	1– 5
15 DET		*
16 CHI		*
17 CHI	W	8– 7f
" CHI	L	1– 6a
18 CHI	W	11– 4
19 CHI	W	3– 0
20 NG		
21 CLE	L	5– 6h
22 CLE	L	4– 5
23 CLE		*
24 CLE	W	5– 3g
" CLE	L	2– 4
25 NG		
26 NG		
27 NG		
28 was	L	3– 6
29 NG		
30 was	L	6–12
31 was	L	1– 5

September, 1930
1 PHI	L	2– 3
" PHI	W	2– 0
2 NG		
3 WAS	W	10– 7

September, 1930
4 WAS	L	2– 3
5 WAS	L	5–14
6 WAS	W	3– 2
7 BOS	L	3– 5
" BOS	W	5– 2
8 NG		
9 cle	W	8– 6
10 cle	W	7– 2
11 cle	L	5– 9
12 det	L	4– 5
13 det	L	10–11
" det	L	4– 9b
14 det	W	10– 3
15 det	W	5– 3
16 stl	W	19–10
17 stl	L	8– 9
18 stl	W	7– 6f
19 chi	W	18– 9
20 chi	L	7– 10
21 chi	L	7– 15
22 NG		
23 NG		
24 NG		
25 phi	L	3–13b
26 phi	L	6– 7
27 phi	W	10– 8
28 bos	W	9– 3
END OF 1930		
RUNS:		1062
OPP RUNS:		898

CLUB VS. CLUB AND MONTHLY RECORDS OF THE
NEW YORK YANKEES' 1930 SEASON FOR HOME AND AWAY GAMES

CLUB:		APR	MAY	JUN	JUL	AUG	SEP	OCT	HOME	AWAY	TOTAL
BOST	H	2–1	3– 0	0– 1	xxx	2– 0	1– 1	xxx	8– 3	xxx	16– 6
	A	0–2	3– 1	xxx	3– 0	1– 0	1– 0	xxx	xxx	8– 3	
CHIC	H	xxx	3– 1	1– 0	1– 1	3– 1	xxx	x xx	8– 3	xxx	14– 8
	A	xxx	xxx	1– 1	4– 2	xxx	1– 2	xxx	xxx	6– 5	
CLEV	H	xxx	1– 1	4– 1	xxx	1– 3	xxx	xxx	6– 5	xxx	12–10
	A	xxx	xxx	3– 0	1– 4	xxx	2– 1	xxx	xxx	6– 5	
DET	H	xxx	3– 1	2– 1	xxx	2– 1	xxx	xxx	7– 3	xxx	13– 9
	A	xxx	xxx	2– 1	2– 2	xxx	2– 3	x xx	xxx	6– 6	
PHIL	H	0–1	2– 1	xxx	2– 2	1– 0	1– 1	xxx	6– 5	xxx	10–12
	A	0–1	2– 2	xxx	1– 2	xxx	1– 2	xxx	xxx	4– 7	
STL	H	xxx	1– 0	4– 2	xxx	3– 1	xxx	xxx	8– 3	xxx	16– 6
	A	xxx	xxx	3– 1	3– 1	xxx	2– 1	xxx	xxx	8– 3	
WAS	H	xxx	1– 2	xxx	xxx	1– 3	2– 2	xxx	4– 7	xxx	5–17
	A	1–3	xxx	xxx	0– 4	0– 3	xxx	xxx	xxx	1–10	
TOTAL:	H	2–2	14– 6	11– 5	3– 3	13– 9	4– 4	xxx	47–29	xxx	86–68
	A	1–6	5– 3	9– 3	14–15	1– 3	9– 9	xxx	xxx	39–39	
GRAND TOT:		3–8	19– 9	20– 8	17– 18	14–12	13–13	xxx	xxx	xxx	
CUMUL TOT:		3–8	22–17	42– 25	59–43	73–55	86–68	xxx	xxx	xxx	

TIE GAMES: NONE

1931

ENTER JOSEPH V. McCARTHY

In 1931, Joseph V. McCarthy began his 16 year reign as New York field manager, the longest such tenure in Yankee history. The Yanks, although winning 94 games of 155 (.614), concluded the season some 13½ games behind Philadelphia. In spite of their second place finish, New York had an incredible season from a statistical standpoint. This 1931 Yankee team went down as one of the greatest runners-up in baseball history.

In 1930 and 1931, the Yanks scored an amazing 2,129 runs in 309 games for an average of 6.9 tallies per outing! In 1931 alone, six New York players scored 100 + runs, an A.L. record. Those half dozen players, led by Lou Gehrig's A.L. high 163, accounted for 754 of the A.L. record 1,067 runs, for 71% of New York's entire club total.

The Yankees set a Major League record by leading the A.L. in club homers for the 9th straight season dating back to 1923 (they will later eclipse this record with 12 consecutive home run crowns from 1936 thru 1947). This season they banged out 155 four-baggers and led the league in team batting and slugging (.297, .457) as well as with 138 stolen bases, displaying an unusual combination of awesome power and great team speed. Ben Chapman led the A.L. in steals with 61. The Yanks also hit 1,157 singles, a team record, and drove home 990 runs, high in the A.L. for 1931, as was their 1,667 basehit total.

Individual league standouts were, you guessed it, Gehrig and Ruth. Lou led in runs (163), hits (211), total bases (410) and an American League record 184 RBI. Ruth was the best home run hitter for the 6th straight season, a Major League record. Gehrig shared the homer title with the Babe, both deparking 46 circuit jobs. In addition, Babe won his 13th and final slugging championship,having won 13 of fourteen such crowns. Only St. Louis' Kenneth Williams' .613 (a paltry total by Ruthian standards!)

slugging mark in 1925 prevented Ruth's total domination of this stat from 1918 through 1931, some fourteen years! No player in baseball history can surpass the Babe's reign as the ultimate slugging champion for an entire career.

As a unit, New York pitchers struck out a league high 686 enemy batters, finishing second in overall team ERA with 4.20. In the field, the Yanks finished in third place and for the first and only time in Major League history suffered no passed balls the entire season.

William Harridge replaced the deceased Ernest Barnard as the third A.L. president since 1901.

The 1931 edition of the Bronx Bombers became one of the greatest baseball teams of all time. In 1932, New York will reign again in the American League after a four year hiatus.

The 1931 DAY BY DAY scores follow:

Joseph Vincent McCarthy—"Marse Joe" managed the Yanks in 16 different seasons, winning 8 A.L. pennants and 7 World Series. One of the greatest field managers in baseball history, Joe was elected to the Hall of Fame in 1957.

DAY BY DAY, 1931 NEW YORK YANKEES

April, 1931
14 BOS W 6- 3
15 BOS W 8- 7
16 BOS W 2- 1
17 NG
18 BOS L 4- 5k
19 PHI L 2- 3
20 PHI W 5- 4
21 PHI W 12- 1
22 bos W 7- 5
23 *
24 bos W 7- 4
25 bos L 4- 5f
26 was L 7- 9
27 was L 8- 9h
28 was TG 7- 7j
29 was L 5- 9
30 phi W 7- 2

May, 1931
1 phi L 0- 4
2 phi *
3 BOS W 8- 3
4 WAS L 3- 7
5 WAS W 18- 8
6 WAS W 10- 7
7 NG
8 chi *
9 chi W 13- 9
10 chi *
11 chi *
12 stl *
13 stl W 3- 2
14 stl W 14- 2
15 det L 0- 2
16 det L 1- 3b
17 det W 8- 5
18 det W 20- 8
19 cle W 8- 6
20 cle *
21 cle W 7- 6
22 NG
23 WAS W 7- 6

May, 1931
24 PHI L 3- 7
25 phi L 2- 4
" phi L4- 16
26 phi W 6- 2
27 phi L 5- 6
28 phi L 4- 5
29 NG
30 was L 2- 3
" was W 9- 8
31 was W 4- 2c

June, 1931
1 was *
2 STL W 9- 2
3 STL L 6- 8
4 STL L 6- 8
5 STL W 8- 7
6 CLE L 5- 7
7 CLE W 5- 1
8 CLE L 1- 4
9 CLE *
10 CHI *
11 CHI *
12 CHI W 11- 2
14 CHI W 11- 6
14 DET L 2- 4f
15 DET L 5- 8
16 DET *
17 bos *
" bos *
18 NG
19 stl W 16- 5
20 stl W 9- 1
21 stl L 7- 9
" stl L 2- 8
22 stl L10-14
23 chi W 8- 6
" chi W 9- 4
24 chi W 10- 3
25 chi W 10- 9
" chi W 9- 2
26 cle *

June, 1931
27 cle L5- 12
" cle L 1- 2
28 cle W 9- 5
29 cle L 6-15
" cle L 2- 4
30 det L 7- 8g

July, 1931
1 det W 4- 2
2 det W 13- 1
3 NG
4 WAS W 6- 1
" WAS W 7- 4
5 BOS L 3- 6g
6 BOS *
7 BOS *
8 BOS W 13- 3
" BOS W 9- 4
9 PHI W 9- 4
10 PHI L 6- 8j
11 PHI W 3- 1
12 was W 10- 4
13 NG
14 CLE W 19- 2
" CLE L 1- 5
15 CLE W 5- 4
16 CLE L 8- 9
17 CLE L 1- 2d
18 STL *
19 STL W 10- 9
" STL W 8- 2
20 STL W 8- 5
21 STL *
22 DET L 2- 3
" DET W 9- 5
23 DET W 7- 6i
24 DET W 6- 5
25 DET W 10- 7g
26 CHI L 4- 5
" CHI W 22- 5
27 CHI L 7- 8f
" CHI W 12- 3

July, 1931
28 CHI L12-14
29 CHI W 10-4
30 NG
31 bos W 4- 1

August, 1931
1 bos L 2- 9
2 bos W 4- 1
" bos L 0- 1
3 bos W 9- 8
4 NG
5 bos L 1- 5
" bos W 4- 1
6 PHI W 5- 3
7 NG
8 PHI W 3- 2
9 PHI L 3- 5
10 NG
11 cle *
12 cle W 18- 1
" cle L 7-17
13 cle *
14 cle L7- 13
" cle L 1- 9
15 det W 7- 5L
16 det W 9- 6
17 det L 2- 8
18 det L 4- 5g
19 stl L 3- 7
20 stl W 7- 3
21 stl W 11- 7
22 stl W 8- 6g
23 chi W 10- 4
" chi W 9- 1
24 chi W 8- 5
25 chi W 8- 0
26 chi L 5- 8
27 NG
28 phi L 4- 5
29 phi L 4- 7
30 bos W 14- 4
31 WAS L 5- 6

September, 1931
1 BOS W 11- 3
" BOS W 5- 1
2 BOS W 7- 6
3 NG
4 was L 4- 5f
5 was W 7- 0
" was W 7- 3
6 was L 1- 4
7 phi W 15- 3
" phi W 9- 4
8 NG
9 NG
10 CHI *
11 CHI L 1- 3
12 CHI L 5- 8i
" CHI TG13-13f
13 DET W 2- 1
" DET W 4- 3
14 DET W 2- 1
15 DET W 9- 2
16 NG
17 STL W 17- 0
" STL W 6- 1
18 STL W 14- 4
19 STL W 3- 0
20 CLE W 7- 1
" CLE W 10- 4c
21 CLE L 1- 5
22 NG
23 WAS L 2- 3
24 WAS *
25 WAS W 8- 3
26 WAS W 7- 2
" WAS W 8- 3
27 PHI W 13- 1
END OF 1931
RUNS: 1067
OPP RUNS: 760

CLUB VS. CLUB AND MONTHLY RECORDS OF THE NEW YORK YANKEES' 1931 SEASON FOR HOME AND AWAY GAMES

CLUB:		APR	MAY	JUN	JUL	AUG	SEP	OCT	HOME	AWAY	TOTAL
BOST	H	3- 1	1- 0	xxx	2- 1	xxx	3- 0	xxx	9- 2	xxx	16- 6
	A	2- 1	xxx	xxx	1- 0	4- 3	xxx	xxx	xxx	7- 4	
CHIC	H	xxx	xxx	2- 0	3- 3	xxx	0- 2	xxx	5- 5	xxx	15- 6
	A	xxx	1- 0	5- 0	xxx	4- 1	xxx	xxx	xxx	10- 1	
CLEV	H	xxx	xxx	1- 2	2- 3	xxx	2- 1	xxx	5- 6	xxx	9-13
	A	xxx	2- 0	1- 4	xxx	1- 3	xxx	xxx	xxx	4- 7	
DET	H	xxx	xxx	0- 2	4- 1	xxx	4- 0	xxx	8- 3	xxx	14- 8
	A	xxx	2- 2	0- 1	2- 0	2- 2	xxx	xxx	xxx	6- 5	
PHIL	H	2- 1	0- 1	xxx	2- 1	2- 1	1- 0	xxx	7- 4	xxx	11-11
	A	1- 0	1- 5	xxx	xxx	0- 2	2- 0	xxx	xxx	4- 7	
STL	H	xxx	xxx	2- 2	3- 0	xxx	4- 0	xxx	9- 2	xxx	16- 6
	A	xxx	2- 0	2- 3	xxx	3- 1	xxx	xxx	xxx	7- 4	
WAS	H	xxx	3- 1	xxx	2- 0	0- 1	3- 1	xxx	8- 3	xxx	13- 9
	A	0- 3	2- 1	xxx	1- 0	xxx	2- 2	xxx	xxx	5- 6	
TOTAL:	H	5- 2	4- 2	5- 6	18- 9	2- 2	17- 4	xxx	51-25	xxx	94-59
	A	3- 4	10- 8	8- 8	4- 0	14-12	4- 2	xxx	xxx	43-34	
GRAND TOT:		8- 6	14-10	13-14	22- 9	16-14	21- 6	xxx	xxx	xxx	
CUMUL TOT:		8- 6	22-16	35-30	57-39	73-53	94-59	xxx	xxx	xxx	

TIE GAMES: 2 CHI-SEP; was-APR;

1932

PENNANT NO. 7

Under the expert directorship of Manager Joe McCarthy, New York won their seventh pennant in 12 seasons. Winning 107 of 154 games (.695), the Yankees made shambles of the pennant race, besting runner-up Philadelphia by thirteen games. More importantly, the Yanks captured their fourth World Series, beating the Chicago Cubs four games to none. Beating their opponents four straight on 3 different occasions (also in 1927 and 1928) set a World Series record for most consecutive games won with 12.

As a club, New York scored more than 1,000 runs for the third time (1,002). They will score 1,065 in 1936, their fourth 1,000 + run season, a Major League record. They set a club record 766 walks by batters to pace the A.L., led by Ruth's league-topping 130 bases on balls. The Yanks drove in 955 runs, the league high, with Ruth and Gehrig accounting for 288 RBI between them. After nine straight home run crowns, the Yanks finished second overall to Philadelphia who banged out 173 roundtrippers, thirteen more than the Yanks. No Yankees won any significant batting crowns. Chapman led the A.L. in steals with 38.

On the mound, the staff topped all other A.L. clubs with a 3.98 composite ERA. Johnny Allen placed atop A.L. hurlers in winning percentage with a .810 figure on 17 wins and but 4 defeats. Gomez and Ruffing finished second and third, respectively, in that category.

Red Ruffing became the first Yankee to lead the league in strikeouts with 190 whiffs. The New York staff also placed first in total strikeouts (780), shutouts (11) and complete games (95), tied with Philadelphia in the latter category.

1932 saw the Yankees win their fourth World Series in 7 attempts. The consistency of the pitching staff in conjunction with clutch-hitting solidified the Yankees' pennant-winning season. Although the next season will be fairly productive, the pennant will not be theirs again until 1936.

The 1932 DAY BY DAY scores follow:

DAY BY DAY, 1932 NEW YORK YANKEES

April, 1932

12	phi	W 12– 6	
13	phi	*	
14	phi	*	
15	phi	L 8– 9	
16	bos	W 14– 4	
17	bos	*	
18	NG		
19	bos	L 5– 6	
"	bos	W 6– 3	
20	PHI	W 8– 3	
21	PHI	L 6– 8	
22	NG		
23	PHI	W 16– 5	
24	BOS	W 9– 2	
25	WAS	*	
26	WAS	W 6– 5	
27	WAS	*	
28	BOS	W 5– 1	
29	BOS	W 8– 7	
30	BOS	W 6– 3	

May, 1932

1	was	L 2– 4	
2	was	L3– 10	
3	was	L 4– 5	
4	NG		
5	NG		
6	DET	W 1– 0	
7	DET	W 4– 1	
8	DET	*	
9	STL	*	
10	STL	W 10– 3	
11	STL	W 3– 0	
12	CHI	*	
13	CHI	*	
14	CHI	W 6– 0	
15	CLE	W 5– 0	
16	CLE	W 8– 0	
17	CLE	W 3– 2	
18	CLE	W 3– 2f	
19	WAS	L 6– 8f	
"	WAS	L 7–12	
20	WAS	W 6– 3	

May, 1932

21	WAS	W 14– 2	
"	WAS	W 8– 0	
22	PHI	L 2– 4	
23	PHI	W 6– 5	
24	PHI	W 3– 1	
25	NG		
26	was	W 5– 0	
27	was	*	
28	was	L 1– 5	
"	was	L 5–13	
29	was	W 11– 8	
30	BOS	W 7– 5	
"	BOS	W 13– 3	
31	NG		

June, 1932

1	phi	L 7– 8L	
"	phi	L 6– 7	
2	phi	W 5– 1	
3	phi	W 20–13	
4	phi	L7– 10	
"	phi	W 7– 4	
5	BOS	W 12– 1	
6	NG		
7	det	W 9– 2	
8	det	W 5– 4	
9	det	L 4– 5	
10	det	W 8– 7g	
11	cle	L 3– 6	
12	cle	W 13– 5	
13	cle	W 8– 7	
14	cle	W 7– 6	
15	chi	L 1– 2	
16	chi	W 6– 1	
17	NG		
18	chi	W 4– 2	
19	chi	W 1– 0	
20	stl	W 3– 1	
21	stl	W 11– 8	
22	stl	L10–17	
23	stl	L10–14	
24	NG		
25	PHI	W 7– 4	

June, 1932

26	PHI	W 6– 2	
27	NG		
28	WAS	W 5– 2	
29	WAS	W 6– 5	
30	bos	W 15– 4	

July, 1932

1	BOS	L 6–11	
2	BOS	W 8– 5	
"	BOS	L 5– 6	
3	BOS	W 13– 2	
4	was	L 3– 5	
"	was	L 6–12	
5	NG		
6	DET	*	
7	DET	L 5– 8f	
8	DET	W 3– 2	
9	DET	W 7– 6	
"	DET	W 14– 9	
10	STL	L 7– 8f	
"	STL	L 9–10	
11	STL	W 15– 4	
12	STL	W 4– 2	
13	STL	W 5– 3	
14	CLE	L 3–11	
15	CLE	W 8– 5	
16	CLE	L 1– 8	
17	CHI	W 4– 3h	
"	CHI	W 3– 2	
18	CHI	W 6– 4	
19	CHI	W 6– 3	
20	CHI	W 7– 2	
21	BOS	L 2– 3	
22	BOS	*	
23	BOS	W 4– 3k	
"	BOS	W 5– 4	
24	PHI	W 9– 3	
25	phi	L 7– 8	
26	cle	*	
27	cle	L 1– 2	
"	cle	L10–12	
28	cle	W 10– 1	
29	cle	L 3– 4	

July, 1932

30	det	W 5– 4	
31	det	W 12– 8	

August, 1932

1	det	VOID 6– 3##	
2	det	*	
3	chi	L 2– 3f	
4	chi	W 15– 3	
5	NG		
6	chi	L 5–10	
"	chi	W 4– 1	
7	stl	W 11– 5	
"	stl	W 9– 4	
8	NG		
9	stl	W 5– 3	
10	stl	W 7– 6	
11	NG		
12	NG		
13	was	W 1– 0	
14	was	W 5– 4	
15	NG		
16	DET	W 13– 8	
"	DET	W 7– 3	
17	DET	W 8– 3	
18	DET	*	
19	DET	L 3– 4	
"	DET	W 6– 5	
20	STL	W 5– 0	
21	STL	W 3– 1	
22	STL	L 1– 5	
23	STL	W 8– 7	
24	CLE	W 9– 3	
25	CLE	W 4– 3	
26	CLE	W 4– 2	
27	CLE	W 5– 4	
28	CHI	L 2– 5	
"	CHI	W 11– 5	
29	CHI	W 10– 3	
"	CHI	W 4– 3	
30	CHI	W 6– 5	
31	NG		

##GAME VOIDED BUT
SCORE COUNTS

September, 1932

1	WAS	L 2– 6	
2	WAS	L 1– 7	
3	WAS	W 6– 5	
4	BOS	W 8– 2	
5	PHI	W 8– 6	
"	PHI	W 6– 3	
6	NG		
7	NG		
8	det	W 6– 4j	
"	det	TG 7– 7c	
9	det	L13–14j	
"	det	L 1– 4a	
10	det	W 11–10	
"	det	W 4– 1f	
11	cle	L 4– 5	
12	cle	W 8– 3h	
13	cle	W 9– 3	
14	chi	W 3– 2	
15	chi	L 5– 8	
16	chi	W 4– 1	
17	stl	W 6– 4	
18	stl	W 7– 2	
"	stl	L 1– 2f	
19	NG		
20	NG		
21	phi	L 4– 8	
22	phi	W 8– 7f	
23	bos	W 3– 0	
24	bos	W 8– 2	
25	bos	L 3– 8	
26	PHI	W 6– 2	
27	NG		
28	WAS	W 5– 2	
29	WAS	W 6– 5	
30	bos	W 15– 4	

END OF 1932
RUNS: 1002
OPP RUNS: 724

CLUB VS. CLUB AND MONTHLY RECORDS OF THE NEW YORK YANKEES' 1932 SEASON FOR HOME AND AWAY GAMES

CLUB:		APR	MAY	JUN	JUL	AUG	SEP	OCT	HOME	AWAY	TOTAL
BOST	H	4-0	2-0	1-0	2-1	xxx	1-0	xxx	10-1	xxx	17-5
	A	2-1	xxx	1-0	2-2	xxx	2-1	xxx	xxx	7-4	
CHIC	H	xxx	1-0	xxx	5-0	4-1	xxx	xxx	10-1	xxx	17-5
	A	xxx	xxx	3-1	xxx	2-2	2-1	xxx	xxx	7-4	
CLEV	H	xxx	4-0	xxx	1-2	4-0	xxx	xxx	9-2	xxx	15-7
	A	xxx	xxx	3-1	1-3	xxx	2-1	xxx	xxx	6-5	
DET	H	xxx	2-0	xxx	3-1	4-1	xxx	xxx	9-2	xxx	17-5
	A	xxx	xxx	3-1	2-0	xxx	3-2	xxx	xxx	8-3	
PHIL	H	2-1	2-1	2-0	1-0	xxx	2-0	xxx	9-2	xxx	14-8
	A	1-1	xxx	3-3	0-1	xxx	1-1	xxx	xxx	5-6	
STL	H	xxx	2-0	xxx	3-2	3-1	xxx	xxx	8-3	xxx	16-6
	A	xxx	xxx	2-2	xxx	4-0	2-1	xxx	xxx	8-3	
WAS	H	1-0	3-2	2-0	xxx	xxx	1-2	xxx	7-4	xxx	11-11
	A	xxx	2-5	xxx	0-2	2-0	xxx	xxx	xxx	4-7	
TOTAL:	H	7-1	16-3	5-0	15-6	15-3	4-2	xxx	62-15	xxx	107-47
	A	3-2	2-5	15-8	5-8	8-2	12-7	xxx	xxx	45-32	
GRAND TOT:		10-3	18-8	20-8	20-14	23-5	16-9	xxx	xxx	xxx	
CUMUL TOT:		10-3	28-11	48-19	68-33	91-38	107-47	xxx	xxx	xxx	

TIE GAMES: 1 det-Sep

1933

THE END OF THE CONSECUTIVE-SCORING STREAK

In their 31st season, the New Yorkers wound up in second place (91–59, .607) behind Joe Cronin's Washington club. The Yanks finished seven games out of first place.

Babe Ruth, in the twilight of his remarkable career, led the A.L. in bases on balls for the eleventh and final time, a Major League record that still stands. He totaled 114 passes this season. Ben Chapman, with a scant 27 stolen bases, became the only Yankee in history to lead the A.L. in steals for three consecutive seasons, having won previously with 61 in 1931 and 38 in 1932.

Scoring a league pacing 927 runs, the Yankees' string of 308 consecutive games without being shutout was finally broken on August 3, Philadelphia and Lefty Grove winning 7–0. The streak, which is an all-time Major League mark, began on August 3, 1931, with Wilcy Moore blanking New York at Boston 1–0 (2nd game) the day before. Their 144 homers led the league for the 16th time and their 849 total RBI ranked first overall. Gehrig finished first with 138 runs scored. In addition, on August 17 at St. Louis, Lou broke the then record of consecutive games played held by former Yankee Everett Scott with his 1,308th straight game in which he played. Gehrig will continue to amass 822 more straight games before his incredible streak ends with 2,130.

For the second straight season, a Yankee pitcher won the strikeout crown, this year the honors going to Lefty Gomez with 163. As a unit, the pitching staff again topped the league in strikeouts with 711 whiffs of enemy batters.

After a World Series victory the previous year, 1933 was quite a setback to their pennant strivings. For two more seasons, no new A.L. pennants will fly in Yankee Stadium.

The 1933 DAY BY DAY scores follow:

DAY BY DAY, 1933 NEW YORK YANKEES

April, 1933	May, 1933	June, 1933	July, 1933	September, 1933
12 BOS　　*	20 STL　L 2– 4	22 stl　　L 4– 5	" bos　　L 4– 9	1 BOS　L 2– 4h
13 BOS W 4– 3	21 STL　L 4– 8	23 stl　W 10– 6	27 was　　L 2– 3f	2 BOS W 2– 1
14 BOS W 6– 2	22 CLE　W 3– 0	" stl　　L 4– 5	28 was　　　*	3 PHI　　*
15 PHI　W 7– 3	23 CLE　W 8– 6	24 stl　W 8– 4	29 was　　L 5–11	4 phi　　*
16 PHI　W 5– 4	24 CLE　　*	25 det　　L 5– 6h	30 was　W 7– 2	" phi　　*
17 NG	25 CHI　　*	" det　W 3– 0b	31 was　W 13– 9	5 phi　　L 1– 6
18 PHI　W 2– 1	26 CHI　L 6– 8	26 det　　　*	**August, 1933**	" phi　W 9– 6
19 PHI　　*	27 CHI　W 15–11	27 det　W 9– 8	1 NG	6 STL　W 3– 2
20 NG	28 CHI　W 2– 1	28 det　W 10– 7	2 PHI　L 3–16	7 STL　W 12– 8
21 bos　W 7– 5	" CHI　W 9– 7	29 cle　W 9– 3	3 PHI　L 0– 7	8 STL　W 5– 3
22 bos　W 2– 1	29 NG	30 cle　　L12–13	4 NG	9 STL　TG 6– 6e
23 was　L 4– 5	30 was　W 3– 2f	**July, 1933**	5 PHI　　L 3– 8	10 DET　W 2– 1
24 was　　L10–11	" was　　　*	1 cle　W 4– 2	6 BOS W 5– 4	" DET　W 9– 1
25 was　W 16– 0	31 was　L 7–12	2 cle　W 7– 3	7 WAS W 6– 5	11 DET　　L 1– 5
26 phi　　*	" was　W 9– 7	3 NG	" WAS W 5– 4	12 DET　W 5– 3
27 phi　W 5– 2	**June, 1933**	4 WAS　L 5– 6f	8 WAS　L 1– 5	13 NG
28 WAS　L 3– 4f	1 NG	" WAS　L 2– 3	9 WAS　L 1– 4	14 CLE　　*
29 WAS　L 3– 6	2 PHI　W 5– 4	5 ALL-STAR BREAK	10 phi　　*	15 CLE　　*
30 BOS W 1 1– 2	3 PHI　W 17–11	6 WON-45, LOST-28	11 phi　　*	16 CLE　　*
" BOS W 8– 3	4 PHI　W 3– 2	7 DET　L 4– 9	12 phi　　L 9–11f	" CLE　　*
May, 1933	" PHI　W 6– 0	8 DET　L 2– 5	" phi　W 8– 6	17 CLE　W 3– 2
1 NG	5 NG	9 DET　W 11– 7	13 was　　L 3– 4	" CLE　W 6– 1
2 det　　L 2– 3	6 BOS W 4– 0	" DET　W 7– 6	14 NG	18 CHI　W 6– 1
3 det　　*	" BOS W 8– 4	10 DET　W 10– 6	15 stl　W 8– 5	" CHI　　L 3– 4
4 det　W 5– 2	7 NG	11 STL　W 5– 4	16 stl　　L 3–13	19 CHI　W 10– 1
5 cle　　*	8 phi　　L10–14	12 STL　W 4– 2	17 stl　　L 6– 7f	" CHI　W 10– 3
6 cle　　L 6– 7	9 phi　W 7– 6	13 STL　W 12– 0	18 stl　W 8– 3	20 CHI　W 5– 3
7 cle　　L 6– 7	10 phi　　L 5– 9	14 STL　W 11– 6	19 chi　　L 7– 8h	21 NG
" cle　W 8– 4	" phi　　L 7– 8	15 CHI　W 11– 2	20 chi　W 14– 3	22 NG
8 chi　W 7– 3	11 bos　W 8– 7	16 CHI　　*	" chi　W 11– 3	23 bos　W 16–12
9 chi　　*	" bos　　L 9–11b	17 NG	21 chi　TG 3– 3n	24 bos　　L 8–10
10 chi　　L2– 10	12 NG	18 CHI　W 9– 4	22 cle　W 4– 3	25 NG
11 chi　　*	13 bos　L 5– 6	19 CHI　　L 4– 8	23 cle　　L 1– 2	26 NG
12 stl　　*	14 bos　L 5–13	20 CLE　　L 1– 3	24 cle　W 10– 1	27 phi　W 7– 0
13 stl　　*	15 bos　L 5– 8	21 CLE　W 10– 2	25 cle　　L 4– 6	" phi　　L 1–10c
14 stl　　L 1– 5	16 NG	22 CLE　　L 1– 2	26 det　W 9– 5	28 WAS W 11– 9
" stl　W 9– 5	17 chi　W 8– 3	23 CLE　W 8– 1	27 det　　L 3– 4	29 WAS　L 5– 8
15 NG	18 chi　W 6– 4	" CLE　W 8– 1	" det　W 12– 2	30 WAS　L 2– 7
16 DET　　*	" chi　　L 4– 5f	24 bos　　*	28 det　　L 1– 6	**October, 1933**
17 DET W 4– 1	19 chi　　L 3– 4	25 bos　　*	29 det　W 11– 9	1 BOS W 6– 5
18 DET W 5– 1	20 chi　W 15– 8	" bos　　*	30 NG	END OF 1933
19 STL　W 6– 5	21 stl　W 5– 3i	26 bos　W 2– 0	31 BOS　　L 2–15	RUNS:　　　927
				OPP RUNS:　768

CLUB VS. CLUB AND MONTHLY RECORDS OF THE
NEW YORK YANKEES' 1933 SEASON FOR HOME AND AWAY GAMES

CLUB:		APR	MAY	JUN	JUL	AUG	SEP	OCT	HOME	AWAY	TOTAL
BOST	H	4- 0	xxx	2- 0	xxx	1- 1	1- 1	1- 0	9- 2	xxx	14- 8
	A	2-0	xxx	1- 4	1- 1	xxx	1- 1	xxx	xxx	5- 6	
CHIC	H	xxx	3- 1	xxx	2- 1	xxx	4- 1	xxx	9- 3	xxx	15- 7
	A	xxx	1- 1	3- 2	xxx	2- 1	xxx	xxx	xxx	6- 4	
CLEV	H	xxx	2- 0	xxx	3- 2	xxx	2- 0	xxx	7- 2	xxx	13- 7
	A	xxx	1- 2	1- 1	2- 0	2- 2	xxx	xxx	xxx	6- 5	
DET	H	xxx	2- 0	xxx	3- 2	xxx	3- 1	xxx	8- 3	xxx	15- 7
	A	xxx	1- 1	3- 1	xxx	3- 2	xxx	xxx	xxx	7- 4	
PHIL	H	3-0	xxx	4- 0	xxx	0- 3	xxx	xxx	7- 3	xxx	12- 9
	A	1-0	xxx	1- 3	xxx	1- 1	2- 2	xxx	xxx	5- 6	
STL	H	xxx	1- 2	xxx	4- 0	xxx	3- 0	xxx	8- 2	xxx	14- 7
	A	xxx	1- 1	3- 2	xxx	2- 2	xxx	xxx	xxx	6- 5	
WAS	H	0-2	xxx	xxx	0- 2	2- 2	1- 2	xxx	3- 8	xxx	8-14
	A	1-2	2- 1	xxx	2- 2	0- 1	xxx	xxx	xxx	5- 6	
TOTAL:	H	7-2	8- 3	6- 0	12- 7	3- 6	14- 5	1- 0	51-23	xxx	91-59
	A	4-2	6- 6	12-13	5- 3	10- 9	3- 3	xxx	xxx	40-36	
GRAND TOT:		11-4	14- 9	18-13	17-10	13-15	17- 8	1- 0	xxx	xxx	
CUMUL TOT:		11-4	25-13	43-26	60-36	73-51	90-59	91- 59	xxx	40-36	

TIE GAMES: 2
STL-Sep; chi-Aug

1934

LOU WINS THE FIRST YANKEE TRIPLE CROWN AND THE BABE DEPARTS THE SCENE

The year 1934 marked the end of a Yankee era with the departure of George Herman "Babe" Ruth after 15 fabulous seasons in pinstripes. The Yankees can do no better than second best for the second straight season. New York won 94, lost 60 for a .610 winning percentage, some 7 games off Detroit's pace.

Lou Gehrig won one of baseball's most coveted awards, the Triple Crown. Hitting the most homers (49) and RBI (165), Lou became the second Yankee in history to lead the A.L. in batting with a .363 mark (Babe Ruth was the first New York A.L. Bat King with .378 in 1924). In addition, Lou placed highest in slugging percentage (.706) on 409 total bases. Chapman led the A.L. in triples with 13.

The pitching staff, anchored by Lefty Gomez's sensational season, tossed the most shutouts (13), complete games (83) and gathered the most strikeouts with 656, all A.L. high marks for 1934. Their 3.76 ERA and league low 669 opponent runs further illustrated their consistency, both American League leads. Defensively, the New Yorkers chalked up the fewest errors in the league with 157, or about one miscue per game.

Lefty Gomez had one of the best overall seasons by a pitcher in New York history. Gomez finished first in each of the following league departments: winning percentage (.839) with a 26–5 won-lost worksheet, strikeouts (158), complete games (25), innings pitched (281$2/3$), shutouts (6, tied with Cleveland's Mel Harder) and ERA, a fine 2.33. Gomez surely would have walked away with the Cy Young Award had it been in existence back then.

This season's departure of the Great Babe paved the way for Lou Gehrig to assume the club's overall player leadership to an even greater degree. The Babe closed out his illustrious career after his 1935 season with the Boston Braves of the National League. Ruth's effect upon the game of baseball can never be measured but it sure can be very much appreciated and treasured throughout history. His records, which speak for themselves, and love for the great game of baseball remain a legacy to all who cherish our national pastime.

The 1934 DAY BY DAY scores follow:

Lou Gehrig—"The Iron Horse" played in an incredible 2,130 consecutive games spanning some 15 seasons! Lou had an A.L. record 184 RBI in 1931. He played his entire 17 years in pinstripes and was elected to the Hall of Fame in 1939.

DAY BY DAY, 1934 NEW YORK YANKEES

April, 1934

17 phi	L 5- 6
18 phi	W 11- 5
19 phi	W 10- 4
20 bos	*
21 bos	L 6- 9
22 bos	W 8- 1
23 NG	
24 PHI	W 1- 0
25 PHI	W 3- 2
26 PHI	L 2- 3
27 BOS	*
28 BOS	L 2- 4
29 BOS	W 3- 2
30 was	W 7- 4

May, 1934

1 was	W 10- 5
2 was	L 2- 6
3 DET	*
4 DET	W 3- 0
5 DET	W 10- 6
6 STL	W 6- 5
7 STL	W 14- 1
8 STL	W 8- 3
9 STL	L 8- 9
10 CHI	W 13- 3
11 CHI	W 7- 6j
12 CHI	W 4- 3f
13 CLE	W 8- 0
14 CLE	*
15 CLE	*
16 NG	
17 det	L 4- 5
18 det	L 8- 10
19 det	W 8- 3
20 cle	L 5- 8
21 cle	L 5- 9
22 cle	L 1- 5
23 chi	L 2-14
24 chi	W 2- 1
25 chi	L 5- 7
26 stl	W 4- 1
27 stl	L 7-16
28 stl	W 13- 9
29 NG	
30 WAS	L 0- 1
" WAS	W 5- 4g
31 WAS	L 3- 9

June, 1934

1 phi	L 5-10
2 phi	W 9- 8f
3 phi	W 5- 3
4 NG	
5 bos	L 3- 8
6 bos	W 15- 3
" bos	L 4- 7
7 bos	*
8 PHI	W 11- 4
9 PHI	L 2- 4
10 PHI	W 7- 3
11 NG	
12 STL	*
13 STL	W 6- 2
14 STL	W 7- 0
15 STL	W 6- 3
16 DET	W 8- 4
17 DET	W 3- 2
" DET	L 2- 5
18 DET	L 5- 6
19 DET	*
20 CLE	W 3- 2
" CLE	W 3- 0
21 CLE	L 5- 9
22 CLE	L 1- 4
23 CLE	W 6- 3
24 CHI	W 5- 0
25 CHI	W 13- 2
26 CHI	W 6- 2
27 CHI	W 8- 7g
28 was	W 4- 0
29 NG	
30 was	*

July, 1934

1 was	W 5- 2
2 BOS	W 5- 0
3 BOS	L9- 10g
4 bos	L 5- 8
" bos	W 10- 4
5 WAS	W 8- 3
6 WAS	L 8- 9
7 WAS	W 7- 4
8 WAS	W 6- 3
9 ALL-STAR BREAK	
10 WON-47,LOST-27	
11 cle	W 9- 4
12 det	L 2- 4
13 det	W 4- 2
14 det	L 11-12
15 det	L 3- 8
16 cle	W 7- 4
17 cle	L 5-13
18 cle	L 14-15
19 chi	W 4- 3
20 chi	L 6- 7i
21 chi	W 6- 2
22 chi	W 8- 2
" chi	W 15- 2
23 stl	W 5- 2
24 stl	L 2- 4
25 stl	W 5- 4
26 stl	W 3- 1
27 NG	
28 phi	L 3- 4
" phi	W 2- 1
29 phi	L 3- 6
30 NG	
31 BOS	W 11- 2
" BOS	W 2- 1

August, 1934

1 BOS	L 4- 7
2 BOS	W 12- 4
3 PHI	W 5- 1
4 PHI	W 5- 1
5 PHI	W 3- 1
6 NG	
7 was	W 4- 3
" was	L 3- 6
8 was	L 2- 9
9 was	*
10 bos	W 10- 3
11 bos	L 2- 3i
12 bos	L 4- 6
" bos	W 7- 1
13 NG	
14 DET	L 5- 9
" DET	L 3- 7
15 DET	W 8- 2
16 DET	*
17 DET	W 5- 0
" DET	L 0- 2
18 STL	W 2- 1h
19 STL	W 9- 3
" STL	W 2- 1
20 NG	
21 STL	L 6- 8
22 CLE	W 9- 0
" CLE	L 4-10
23 CLE	W 9- 2
24 CLE	*
25 CLE	L 3- 5
" CLE	W 9- 3
26 CHI	W 9- 5
" CHI	W 2- 0
27 CHI	W 3- 2
28 NG	
29 CHI	L 1- 3
30 WAS	W 8- 2
31 WAS	W 3- 1

September, 1934

1 WAS	L 1- 5
2 WAS	L 3- 9
3 PHI	W 11- 7
" PHI	L 3-10
4 NG	
5 NG	
6 chi	W 5- 3
7 chi	L 5- 6
8 chi	W 7- 1
9 stl	W 6- 5j
" stl	W 2- 1b
10 stl	*
11 stl	W 7- 4
" stl	L 3- 7
12 NG	
13 cle	W 3- 1
14 cle	L5- 12
15 cle	W 2- 1
16 cle	L 2- 5
17 det	L 0- 3
18 det	L 0- 2
19 det	W 5- 2
20 det	W 11- 7
21 NG	
22 BOS	*
23 BOS	W 1- 0
" BOS	W 5- 4f
24 BOS	L 0- 5
25 phi	W 5- 0
26 phi	W 4- 3g
27 NG	
28 NG	
29 phi	L 5- 8
" phi	W 9- 6
30 phi	L 3- 5

END OF 1934

RUNS:	842
OPP RUNS:	669

CLUB VS. CLUB AND MONTHLY RECORDS OF THE
NEW YORK YANKEES' 1934 SEASON FOR HOME AND AWAY GAMES

CLUB:		APR	MAY	JUN	JUL	AUG	SEP	OCT	HOME	AWAY	TOTAL
BOST	H	1-1	xxx	xxx	3-1	1-1	2-1	xxx	7- 4	xxx	12-10
	A	1-1	xxx	1-2	1-1	2-2	xxx	xxx	xxx	5- 6	
CHIC	H	xxx	3-0	4-0	xxx	3-1	xxx	xxx	10- 1	xxx	17- 5
	A	xxx	1-2	xxx	4-1	xxx	2-1	xxx	xxx	7- 4	
CLEV	H	xxx	1-0	3-2	xxx	3-2	xxx	xxx	7- 4	xxx	11- 11
	A	xxx	0-3	xxx	2-2	xxx	2-2	xxx	xxx	4- 7	
DET	H	xxx	2-0	2-2	xxx	2-3	xxx	xxx	6- 5	xxx	10- 12
	A	xxx	1-2	xxx	1-3	xxx	2-2	xxx	xxx	4- 7	
PHIL	H	2-1	xxx	2-1	xxx	3-0	1-1	xxx	8- 3	xxx	15- 7
	A	2-1	xxx	2-1	1-2	xxx	2-0	xxx	xxx	7- 4	
STL	H	xxx	3-1	3-0	xxx	3-1	xxx	xxx	9- 2	xxx	17- 5
	A	xxx	2-1	xxx	3-1	xxx	3-1	xxx	xxx	8- 3	
WAS	H	xxx	1-2	xxx	3-1	2-0	0-2	xxx	6- 5	xxx	12-10
	A	1-0	1-1	1-0	1-0	1-2	1-2	xxx	xxx	6- 5	
TOTAL:	H	3-2	10- 3	14- 5	6- 2	17- 8	3- 4	xxx	53- 24	xxx	
	A	4-2	5- 9	4- 3	13-10	3- 4	12- 8	xxx	xxx	41-36	
GRAND TOT:		7-4	15-12	18- 8	19-12	20-12	15-12	xxx	xxx	xxx	
CUMUL TOT:		7-4	22-16	40-24	59-36	79-48	94-60	xxx	xxx	xxx	

TIE GAMES: NONE

1935

A FOURTH TEAM CAPTAIN

For the fifth time in seven seasons, the Yankees can do no better than second place. Being a runner-up again to Mickey Cochrane's Detroit club for the 2nd straight year, the Yanks won a fairly respectable total of 93 games, losing 58 (.616).

Lou Gehrig, who now must carry the burden of the team's offensive power practically on his own, assumed the role of the fourth team captain. He continued in this capacity until his eventual death in 1941. With Babe Ruth gone, the years of the Ruth-Gehrig power tandem were history. Gehrig led the league in runs scored with 125 and walks with 132, his personal best during his 17-year career.

For the first time in several years, the Yanks as a team did not finish first in any offensive statistical category. No pitchers topped A.L. lists, but the staff as a whole did lead the league in strikeouts (594) for the fifth straight season, extending their own club record of the previous year. The team also managed a first-ranked ERA of 3.60.

In 1935 the pitching staff was a bright spot, as was the consistency of Gehrig's play. However, Yankee Stadium attendance was at an all-time low attracting 657,508, which was to be the lowest total at Yankee Stadium until 1943. Next season would see an increase in team power and overall play.

The 1935 DAY BY DAY scores follow:

DAY BY DAY, 1935 NEW YORK YANKEES

April, 1935

16	BOS	L	0- 1
17	BOS	L	3- 4f
18	BOS	W	4- 0
19	PHI	L	5- 6
20	PHI	W	3- 1
21	PHI	W	4- 3
22	NG		
23	bos	L	4- 7
24	bos		*
25	bos	W	12- 4
26	phi	W	11- 2
27	phi	W	9- 8
28	phi	W	7- 5
29	WAS	W	2- 0
30	WAS	W	9- 8

May, 1935

1	WAS	L	6- 7
2	NG		
3	stl		*
4	stl		*
5	stl		*
6	chi		*
7	chi	L	3- 4
8	chi	L	4- 7
9	cle	L	0- 5a
10	cle	W	6- 3
11	cle	W	10- 4
12	det		*
13	det	L	0- 3
14	det	L	4-10
15	det	W	4- 0
16	CLE	W	10- 0
17	CLE	W	4- 2
18	CLE	W	3- 0
19	CLE	L	0- 1g
20	CHI	W	7- 2
21	CHI	L	2- 3
22	CHI	W	13- 5
23	STL		*
24	STL	L	3- 6
25	STL	W	3- 1
"	STL	W	8- 7
26	DET	W	2- 0
27	DET	W	3- 1
28	DET	L	3- 8
29	was	W	7- 4c
30	was	W	4- 0
"	was	W	9- 3
31	BOS		*

June, 1935

1	BOS	L	0- 6
"	BOS	W	4- 2
2	BOS	W	7- 2
3	PHI	W	7- 4
4	PHI		*
5	PHI	L	7- 9
6	PHI		*
7	bos	L	1- 2
8	bos	W	12- 6
"	bos	L	2- 4
9	bos		*
10	NG		
11	stl	W	7- 4
"	stl	W	9- 3
12	stl	W	11- 4
"	stl	L	6- 7
13	stl	W	8- 3
14	stl	W	4- 3i
15	chi	W	5- 3
16	chi		*
17	chi		*
18	chi		*
19	det	W	13- 3
"	det	W	7- 6h
20	det	W	5- 2
21	det	L	0- 7
22	cle	L	6-12
23	cle	L	5- 6
24	cle	W	4- 1
25	cle	L	4- 5
26	NG		
27	WAS	W	15- 5
28	NG		
29	WAS	W	6- 3
30	WAS	L	7- 8h

July, 1935

1	NG		
2	phi	W	8-5
3	phi	W	2-0
4	BOS	L	3-4
"	BOS	W	7- 1
5	was		*
6	was	L	3- 8
"	was	W	10-7g
7	was	W	11-1
8	ALL-STAR BREAK		
9	WON-45,LOST-26		
10	CLE		*
11	CLE	W	8-1
12	CLE	W	5-2
13	CHI	L	7-8
14	CHI	L	0- 3
"	CHI	W	5- 4
15	NG		
16	CHI	W	2-0
17	NG		
18	STL	L	1-4g
19	STL	L	6-7
20	STL		*
21	STL	W	2-0
"	STL	L	1- 2f
22	DET		*
23	DET	W	7- 5
"	DET	L	1-3
24	DET	L	0- 4
25	DET		*
26	WAS	L	3- 9
27	WAS	L	7-8
28	WAS	W	7-6
"	WAS	L	1-7
29	NG		
30	phi	L	5-6
31	phi		*

August, 1935

1	NG		
2	was	W	9-4
3	was	W	13- 2
4	was		L10-11
5	bos	W	10- 2a
6	bos		*
7	bos	L	5- 6
"	bos	W	6- 4
8	PHI	L	6- 9
9	PHI	W	3- 2
10	PHI	W	18- 7
"	PHI	W	7- 2
11	PHI	L	4- 8
"	PHI	L	4- 5
12	NG		
13	cle	W	8- 2
14	cle	L	6- 7
15	cle	W	3- 1
16	cle	L	5- 8
17	det	L	2- 3f
18	det	L	0- 6
19	det	W	7- 5
20	det	W	6- 5
21	stl	W	14- 2
"	stl	L	3-14
22	stl		9- 12
23	stl	W	6- 3i
24	stl	L	6- 7
25	chi	L	3- 6
"	chi	W	6- 1
26	chi	L	8- 9k
"	chi	W	7- 5c
27	chi	W	13-10
"	chi	L	3- 4
28	chi	W	9- 1
"	chi	W	5- 2
29	NG		
30	NG		
31	phi	W	6- 2
"	phi	W	3- 1

September, 1935

1	phi	W	5- 3
2	phi		*
3	phi		*
4	CHI		*
5	CHI		*
6	CHI		*
7	CHI	L	2- 3
"	CHI	W	5- 2
8	CLE	W	3- 2f
"	CLE	W	5- 4
9	CLE	W	5- 3
10	CLE	W	4- 1
11	CLE	L	4- 5
12	DET	L	5- 8
13	DET	L	5-13
14	DET	W	2- 1
"	DET	L	1- 5
15	DET	W	8- 7
16	STL	L	2- 5
17	STL	W	4- 3
18	STL	L	4- 7
"	STL	W	6- 3
19	NG		
20	NG		
21	bos	W	5- 2
22	bos	W	6- 4
"	bos	W	9- 0d
23	was	W	5- 1
24	was	W	14- 6
25	NG		
26	WAS	W	4- 2
27	BOS		*
28	BOS		*
29	BOS	L	3- 4
"	BOS	W	4- 0a

END OF 1935

RUNS: 818
OPP RUNS: 632

130 THE ULTIMATE NEW YORK YANKEES RECORD BOOK

CLUB VS. CLUB AND MONTHLY RECORDS OF THE NEW YORK YANKEES' 1935 SEASON FOR HOME AND AWAY GAMES

CLUB:		APR	MAY	JUN	JUL	AUG	SEP	OCT	HOME	AWAY	TOTAL
BOST	H	1-2	xxx	2-1	1-1	xxx	1-1	xxx	5-5	xxx	12-9
	A	1-1	xxx	1-2	xxx	2-1	3-0	xxx	xxx	7-4	
CHIC	H	xxx	2-1	xxx	2-2	xxx	1-1	xxx	5-4	xxx	11-9
	A	xxx	0-2	1-0	xxx	5-3	xxx	xxx	xxx	6-5	
CLEV	H	xxx	3-1	xxx	2-0	xxx	4-1	xxx	9-2	xxx	14-8
	A	xxx	2-1	1-3	xxx	2-2	xxx	xxx	xxx	5-6	
DET	H	xxx	2-1	xxx	1-2	xxx	2-3	xxx	5-6	xxx	11-11
	A	xxx	1-2	3-1	xxx	2-2	xxx	xxx	xxx	6-5	
PHIL	H	2-1	xxx	1-1	xxx	3-3	xxx	xxx	6-5	xxx	14-6
	A	3-0	xxx	xxx	2-1	2-0	1-0	xxx	xxx	8-1	
STL	H	xxx	2-1	xxx	1-3	xxx	2-2	xxx	5-6	xxx	12-10
	A	xxx	xxx	5-1	xxx	2-3	xxx	xxx	xxx	7-4	
WAS	H	2-0	0-1	2-1	1-3	xxx	1-0	xxx	6-5	xxx	15-7
	A	xxx	3-0	xxx	2-1	2-1	2-0	xxx	xxx	9-2	
TOTAL:	H	5-3	9-5	5-3	8-11	3-3	11-8	xxx	41-33	xxx	89-60
	A	4-1	6-5	11-7	4-2	17-12	6-0	xxx	xxx	48-27	
GRAND TOT:		9-4	15-10	16-10	12-13	20-15	17-8	xxx	xxx	xxx	TIE GAMES: NONE
CUMUL TOT:		9-4	24-14	40-24	52-37	72-52	89-60	xxx	xxx	xxx	

1936

RETURN TO POWER AND THE ARRIVAL OF JOE D.

The 1936 season was marked by the resurgence of power baseball as is characteristic of many great Yankee teams. The Yankees went on to win their 5th World Series in eight attempts, meeting and beating the New York Giants in the Fall Classic for the first time since 1923. Running roughshod over A.L. opponents throughout most of the season, New York finished 19½ games ahead of second place Detroit, to set a club and league record for games ahead of the runner-up team. The previous record was 19 games ahead by the '27 Yankees. Winning 102 and losing 51 (.667), the McCarthymen initiated a dynasty of sorts, clinching their first of 7 A.L. pennants in the next eight seasons.

A twenty-one-year-old rookie, Joe DiMaggio, fit perfectly in the Yankee scheme of things, bolstering the club's performance in many areas. Lou Gehrig won his first and only A.L. Most Valuable Player Award. Larrupin' Lou again led the A.L. in runs scored with 167, home runs with 49, and a .636 slugging mark. In addition to Gehrig's heroics, DiMaggio and Rolfe shared the A.L. lead with 15 triples apiece (Earl Averill of Cleveland had 15 3-baggers also). "Joltin' Joe" DiMaggio set an A.L. record by scoring 132 runs in his rookie season. His total (15) of three base hits tied an A.L. rookie record set previously in 1929 by Detroit's Dale Alexander.

Offensively, as a team, the Yankees set several club and Major League records, many of which were set by previous great Yankee teams. For example, five different players have 100 or more RBI, an A.L. and M.L. record. Among them, five players, Gehrig (152 RBI), Rolfe (116), Lazzeri (109), Dickey (107) and Selkirk (107), accounted for 591 of New York's 995 runs batted in, another M.L. record. Thus, five players were responsible for

59.4% of the Yanks' record RBI total. New York scored the most runs ever in A.L. history for a pennant winner (they scored 2 more runs in 1931 but finished in second place) by tallying 1,065. In one game against Philadelphia on May 24, the Yanks scored their most runs in history by drubbing the Athletics 25–2. The Bronx Bombers pounded out a Major League record 2,703 total bases on 1,096 singles, 630 on doubles, 249 bases on triples and 728 on homers. They set yet another Major League standard by getting 580 long hits (that is, doubles, triples, and homers) with 315 doubles, a club record, 83 triples and a league-leading 182 home runs. Their home run total surpassed their previous club high of 160 roundtrippers in 1930. Their 182 homer season broke the then Major League record 173, set by Philadelphia in 1932. Eventually, New York will break their record of 182 by hitting 190 in 1956. This was the last Yankee team to bat .300 as a club through the 1983 season. Their .483 team-slugging mark and 700 walks by Yankee batters were both A.L. highs for 1936.

On the mound, the New York pitching staff, for the sixth season in a row, a club record, led the American League with 624 strikeouts. Compositely, New York's ERA of 4.17 was the A.L. best. Individually, Monte Pearson's 19–7 record gave him the winning percentage lead with .731.

This was truly one of the greatest of all teams of baseball history, blending enormous power with consistent pitching and a steady defensive performance. Joe DiMaggio had much to do with the team's continued improvement, though not necessarily statistically, over the next few seasons.

The 1936 DAY BY DAY scores follow:

DAY BY DAY, 1936 NEW YORK YANKEES

April, 1936	May, 1936	July, 1936	August, 1936	September, 1936
14 was L 0- 1	24 phi W 25- 2	1 BOS W 5- 0	6 bos *	9 cle W 11- 3
15 was L 5- 6	25 phi L 7-10	2 BOS W 8- 7	7 NG	" cle W 12- 9
16 was W 6- 5	26 bos L 4- 5	3 BOS *	8 PHI W 4- 0	10 cle L 4- 5
17 BOS L 0- 8	27 bos W 9- 8g	4 was W 4- 3	9 PHI W 7- 6f	11 det W 14- 4
18 BOS W 3- 2	28 bos W 10- 6	" was W 5- 0	" PHI W 3- 0	12 det L 1-10
19 WAS W 9- 1	29 NG	5 was L 3- 9	10 WAS L 4-13	13 stl W 10- 7
20 phi L11-12	30 WAS W 7- 1	6 ALL-STAR BREAK	11 WAS L 3- 7	" stl W 13- 1
21 phi W 7- 6	" WAS W 6- 1	7 WON -51	12 WAS W 11- 7	14 NG
22 phi *	31 BOS W 5- 4h	8 LOST -23	13 NG	15 chi W 7- 1
" phi *	**June, 1936**	9 CLE L4- 11	14 phi L 5-10	16 chi *
23 WAS W 10- 6	1 NG	10 CLE W 18- 0	15 phi W 16- 2	17 NG
24 WAS W 10- 2	2 CHI L 9-11	11 CLE L2- 10	16 phi W 10- 2	18 NG
25 bos L 2- 7	3 CHI W 11- 1	12 CHI L 0- 5	" phi L 1- 2	19 WAS W 6- 5
26 bos W 12- 9	4 CHI L 3-16	" CHI W 5- 4	17 was L 5- 7	20 WAS L 1- 6
27 NG	5 CLE W 4- 3	13 CHI L 3- 6	18 was L 2- 9	" WAS W 3- 2
28 CLE W 2- 0	6 CLE L 2- 4	14 NG	19 was W 7- 4	21 NG
29 CLE W 6- 1	7 CLE W 5- 4L	15 DET L 1- 5	20 NG	22 PHI W 10- 3
30 CLE W 8- 1	8 STL W 12- 3	" DET W 7- 4	21 BOS W 4- 1	23 PHI W 12- 5
May, 1936	9 STL L 3- 5	16 DET W 5- 2	22 BOS W 3- 2i	24 PHI L 3- 4
1 CHI W 3- 2	10 STL *	17 DET W 9- 4	23 BOS W 5- 3	25 phi W 6- 5f
2 CHI L 4- 6	11 DET W 10- 9f	18 STL L 2- 7	" BOS L 3- 6	26 was W 3- 1
3 STL W 14- 5	12 DET W 9- 6	" STL W 15- 4	24 NG	27 was L 5-10
4 STL *	13 DET *	19 STL W 10- 3	25 STL W 13- 1	
5 STL W 8- 2	14 DET *	" STL L 4- 5	26 STL L 2- 5	END OF 1936
6 DET W 14- 3	15 NG	20 NG	27 STL W 7- 1	RUNS: 1065
7 DET W 6- 5	16 cle L 4- 8	21 stl L 4- 5	28 DET W 14- 5	OPP RUNS: 73l
8 PHI L 2- 3	17 cle W 15- 4	22 stl L 5- 6	" DET W 19- 4c	
9 PHI W 5- 2	" cle W 12- 2	23 stl W 15- 3	29 DET W 6- 4	
10 PHI W 7- 2	18 cle W 6- 5	24 NG	30 CHI W 8- 1	
11 NG	19 det W 5- 2	25 chi W 5- 3	" CHI W 4- 1	
12 stl L 0- 7	20 det L 0- 5	26 chi W 12- 3	31 CHI W 5- 1	
13 stl W 4- 1	21 det L 7- 8	" chi W 11- 8	**September, 1936**	
14 stl W 6- 1	22 chi W 9- 6	27 det L 1- 9	1 NG	
15 chi L7 - 9	23 chi L 4-13	28 det W 16- 6	2 CLE L 3- 4f	
16 chi W 8- 2	24 chi W 18-11	29 det W 13- 3	3 CLE W 6- 4	
17 cle W 8- 4	25 chi W 7- 6	30 det L 4- 5f	4 bos W 9- 6	
18 cle *	26 NG	31 cle W 11- 7	5 bos L 2- 3	
19 cle W 10- 4	27 stl W 10- 6	**August, 1936**	" bos TG 7- 7h	
20 det L 3- 4f	28 stl L 3- 6	1 cle W 5- 4	6 bos L5- 14	
21 det L 9-10	" stl W 7- 4	2 cle TG 4- 4L	" bos L 2- 4	
22 NG	29 NG	3 NG	7 PHI W 4- 3	
23 phi W 12- 6	30 BOS W 10- 5	4 bos W 4- 2	" PHI W 8- 3	
" phi W 15- 1	" BOS W 6- 3	5 bos W 7- 2	8 NG	

CLUB VS. CLUB AND MONTHLY RECORDS OF THE NEW YORK YANKEES' 1936 SEASON FOR HOME AND AWAY GAMES

CLUB:		APR	MAY	JUN	JUL	AUG	SEP	OCT	HOME	AWAY	TOTAL
BOST	H	1- 1	1- 0	2- 0	2- 0	3- 1	xxx	xxx	9- 2	xxx	
	A	1- 1	2- 1	xxx	xxx	2- 0	1- 3	xxx	xxx	6- 5	15- 7
CHIC	H	xxx	1- 1	1- 2	1- 2	3- 0	xxx	xxx	6- 5	xxx	
	A	xxx	1- 1	3- 1	3- 0	xxx	1- 0	xxx	xxx	8- 2	14- 7
CLEV	H	3- 0	xxx	2- 1	1- 2	xxx	1- 1	xxx	7- 4	xxx	
	A	xxx	2- 0	3- 1	1- 0	1- 0	2- 1	xxx	xxx	9- 2	16- 6
DET	H	xxx	2- 0	2- 0	3- 1	3- 0	xxx	xxx	10- 1	xxx	
	A	xxx	0- 2	1- 2	2- 2	xxx	1- 1	xxx	xxx	4- 7	14- 8
PHIL	H	xxx	2- 1	xxx	xxx	3- 0	4- 1	xxx	9- 2	xxx	
	A	1- 1	3- 1	xxx	xxx	2- 2	1- 0	xxx	xxx	7- 4	16- 6
STL	H	xxx	2- 0	1- 1	2- 2	2- 1	xxx	xxx	7- 4	xxx	
	A	xxx	2- 1	2- 1	1- 2	xxx	2- 0	xxx	xxx	7- 4	14- 8
WAS	H	3- 0	2- 0	xxx	xxx	1- 2	2- 1	xxx	8- 3	xxx	
	A	1- 2	xxx	xxx	2- 1	1- 2	1- 1	xxx	xxx	5- 6	13- 9
TOTAL:	H	10- 5	10- 2	8- 4	9- 7	15- 4	7- 3	xxx	56-21	xxx	
	A	10- 5	10- 6	9- 5	9- 5	6- 4	9- 6	xxx	xxx	46-30	102-51
GRAND TOT:		10- 5	20- 8	17- 9	18-12	21- 8	16- 9	xxx	xxx	xxx	
CUMUL TOT:		10- 5	30-13	47-22	65-34	86-42	102-51	xxx	xx x	xxx	

TIE GAMES: 2
cle-Aug; bos-Sep

1937

ONE MORE TIME

For the second straight year, the Bombers won their ninth A.L. pennant and again defeated the Giants in the World Series, the Yankees capturing their sixth World Championship. In 1937, New York won 100+ games (102) for the fifth time since 1927 and headed the A.L. by 13 games, Detroit coming in a distant second.

This 1937 New York club scored the most runs (979), hit the most homers (174), drove in the most runs (922), out-slugged their opponents (.456) and walked more often (709), all top marks for 1937. Individually, second year star, Joe DiMaggio, shined in leading four important A.L. categories: homers (46), runs scored (151), total bases (418) and slugging average (.673). Lou Gehrig became the only Yankee other than Ruth to lead the league in bases on balls three or more seasons. This was the third and final season that Gehrig led in total walks.

The mound staff continued to fare well, leading the Junior Circuit for the fourth straight year in team ERA, this year combining for a 3.65 mark. Yankee hurlers also paced the A.L. with 15 shutouts and 82 complete games. Lefty Gomez had another great year on the hill, topping all other A.L. pitchers with a 2.33 ERA, his second such title. Lefty also whitewashed his opponents 6 times, his second league-leading shutout mark, and became the *only* Yankee pitcher in history to win the strikeout crown three times, fanning 194 batters. Of the two 20-game winners in the A.L., both were Yanks (Gomez, 21 wins and Ruffing, 20 victories). This was the first time in A.L. history that the only 20-game winners were from the same team (the Chicago Cubs of the National League did it first in 1918).

The Yankees' continued success was facilitated by fine pitching and batting as well as with defensive adroitness. The Yankee Pennant Express will continue to roll as evidenced by their enduring excellence over the next two seasons.

The 1937 DAY BY DAY scores follow:

DAY BY DAY, 1937 NEW YORK YANKEES

April, 1937
20 WAS L 2- 3
21 WAS *
22 WAS *
23 bos *
24 bos W 6- 5f
25 bos W 9- 3
26 PHI W 7- 1
27 PHI *
28 was W 6- 1
29 was W 4- 2
30 was L 1- 4

May, 1937
1 BOS W 3- 2
2 BOS L 4- 5
3 NG
4 DET W 10- 1
5 DET W 7- 3
6 DET L6- 12
7 cle L 6- 7
8 cle L 0- 4
9 chi L 1- 2
10 chi W 7- 0
11 chi L 2- 7
12 stl *
13 stl W 4- 2
14 NG
15 phi W 6- 5
16 phi W 8- 4
17 phi L 2- 3
18 CHI W 4- 0
19 CHI *
20 CHI L 1- 3
21 STL W 4- 3g
22 STL W 14- 2
23 CLE W 7- 3
24 CLE W 14- 0
25 DET W 4- 3
26 DET W 7- 0
27 DET L 4- 5i
28 PHI *
29 PHI W 9- 4
" PHI W 10- 3

May, 1937
30 PHI W 13–1
31 bos W 4–3
" bos L 2- 8

June, 1937
1 NG
2 cle W 8- 4
3 cle L 2- 6
4 cle L 3- 5
5 det W 6- 5
6 det L 4- 5
7 det L 3- 4
8 chi L 4- 5
9 chi *
10 chi W 10-3
11 stl W 10-0
12 stl L 6- 7
13 stl W 16-9
" stl TG 8-8g
14 NG
15 CLE W 3-0
16 CLE W 4-1
17 CLE W 9-7
18 CHI *
19 CHI L 2- 5
20 CHI W 8-4
" CHI W 7-4
21 NG
22 STL W 8-5
23 STL L 3- 6
24 STL W 9-6
25 DET W 8-1
26 DET L 3-5
27 DET W 9-5
28 NG
29 phi W 3-2
30 phi W 5-1

July, 1937
1 phi W 12- 7
2 was L 3- 8
3 was W 5-4
4 was W 7-0

July, 1937
5 BOS W 15- 0
" BOS W 8- 4
6 ALL-STAR BREAK
7 WON -44
8 LOST -22
9 WAS W 16- 2
10 WAS W 12- 2
11 WAS W 4- 3
" WAS TG 5- 5e
12 PHI *
13 NG
14 det W 10- 2
15 det W 13- 6
16 det L 7-14
17 cle W 9- 6
18 cle W 5- 1
19 cle W 8- 5
20 stl W 5- 4f
" stl W 9- 6
21 stl W 6- 3
22 stl L 4-13
23 chi L 6- 9
24 chi L 5- 6f
25 chi W 12-11
" chi L 6- 7
26 NG
27 DET W 6- 5g
28 DET L 1- 8
29 DET W 7- 6
30 STL W 8- 2
31 STL L 6- 9f

August, 1937
1 STL W 14- 5
2 NG
3 CHI W 7- 2
" CHI W 5- 3
4 CHI W 10- 9
5 CHI W 13- 8
6 CLE-
VOID 7- 6f##
7 CLE W 6- 3
8 CLE W 6- 5
##GAME VOIDED
BUT SCORE COUNTS

August, 1937
9 NG
10 bos *
11 bos W 8- 5j
" bos W 10- 4c
12 bos L10-16
" bos W 5- 3
13 phi L 3- 4
14 phi L 6-12
15 phi L 4- 5
16 NG
17 WAS W 8- 0
" WAS W 6- 4
18 WAS W 7- 6
19 WAS W 4- 3h
20 PHI W 8- 7f
21 PHI L 2- 5
22 PHI W 4- 1b
" PHI *
23 NG
24 chi L 8- 9
25 chi W 10- 5
26 stl W 5- 1
27 stl W 4- 3
28 stl L 5- 9
29 det W 7- 4
30 det L 4- 5
31 cle W 7- 3

September, 1937
1 cle L 2- 4
2 cle L 2- 4
3 was L 2- 4
4 was W 6- 0
5 was W 10- 5
6 phi W 6- 3
" phi W 2- 1
7 NG
8 BOS W 3- 2
" BOS W 9- 6
9 BOS L7- 13
10 BOS L 3- 4
11 WAS W 6- 4

September, 1937
12 WAS L 1–2
" WAS W 2–1
13 NG
14 CLE W 17-5
15 CLE L 4- 5f
" CLE W 3-1
16 CLE W 8-0
17 CHI *
18 CHI W 12-8
" CHI W 4-0
19 DET L 1-8
20 DET W 5-0
21 STL *
22 STL W 4-1
" STL W 11-0
23 STL L 5-9
24 bos W 5-1
25 bos W 5- 2
26 bos L 2- 7
27 WAS *
28 WAS W 9-0
" WAS L 1-2
29 PHI W 15-4
" PHI L 0-3c
30 PHI L 3- 8
" PHI L 3- 6c

October, 1937
1 BOS L 2-4c
2 BOS W 11-3
3 BOS W 6- 1

END OF 1937
RUNS: 979
OPP RUNS: 671

CLUB VS. CLUB AND MONTHLY RECORDS OF THE NEW YORK YANKEES' 1937 SEASON FOR HOME AND AWAY GAMES

CLUB:		APR	MAY	JUN	JUL	AUG	SEP	OCT	HOME	AWAY	TOTAL
BOST	H	xxx	1–1	xxx	2–0	xxx	2–2	2–1	7–4	xxx	
	A	2–0	1–1	xxx	xxx	3–1	2–1	xxx	xxx	8–3	15–7
CHIC	H	xxx	1–1	2–1	xxx	4–0	2–0	xxx	9–2	xxx	
	A	xxx	1–2	1–1	1–3	1–1	xxx	xxx	xxx	4–7	13–9
CLEV	H	xxx	2–0	3–0	xxx	2–0	3–1	xxx	10–1	xxx	
	A	xxx	0–2	1–2	3–0	1–0	0–2	xxx	xxx	5–6	15–7
DET	H	xxx	2–1	2–1	2–1	xxx	1–1	xxx	7–4	xxx	
	A	xxx	2–1	1–2	2–1	1–1	xxx	xxx	xxx	6–5	13–9
PHIL	H	1–0	3–0	xxx	xxx	2–1	1–3	xxx	7–4	xxx	
	A	xxx	2–1	2–0	1–0	0–3	2–0	xxx	xxx	7–4	14–8
STL	H	xxx	2–0	2–1	1–1	1–0	2–1	xxx	8–3	xxx	
	A	xxx	1–0	2–1	3–1	2–1	xxx	xxx	xxx	8–3	16–6
WAS	H	0–1	xxx	xxx	3–0	4–0	2–1	xxx	9–2	xxx	
	A	2–1	xxx	xxx	2–1	xxx	3–2	xxx	xxx	7–4	16–6
TOTAL:	H	1–1	11–3	9–3	8–2	13–1	13–9	2–1	57–20	xxx	
	A	4–1	7–7	7–6	12–6	8–7	7–5	xxx	xxx	45–32	102–52
GRAND TOT:		5–2	18–10	16–9	20–8	21–8	20–14	2–1	57–20	45–32	102–52
CUMUL TOT:		5–2	23–12	39–21	59–29	80–37	100–51	102–52	xxx	xxx	

TIE GAMES: NONE

1938

THREE WORLD SERIES IN A ROW

Finishing 9½ games ahead of second place Boston, New York won its 3rd consecutive pennant and concluded the season with a 99–53 record. More importantly, the Yankees won their 7th World Series in ten visits, defeating the Chicago Cubs 4 games to none, thus becoming the first club in Major League history to win three successive world titles.

As has been the case for the past 15 years or so, the Yankees again dominated the A.L. club statistics in batting as well as pitching. Offensively, the New Yorkers led the American League in runs (966), homers (174), RBI (917), walks (749), slugging percentage (.446) and stolen bases (91). Individually, Frank Crosetti was the third Yank to lead the Junior Circuit in steals with 27.

The pitching staff again excelled, taking A.L. club ERA honors again (3.91) for the 5th straight season. New York hurlers spun 10 shutouts and combined for 91 complete games, both being tops in the league for 1938. Regarding winning percentage, Red Ruffing finished with a 21–7 ledger, a .750 winning clip, best in the A.L. Lefty Gomez won his third A.L. shutout title, blanking the opposition four times; thusly, Gomez is the only pitcher in Yankee history to lead the A.L. 3 times in shutouts pitched. On August 27, Monte Pearson hurled the fourth Yankee no-hitter, the first since Sam Jones' gem in 1923, the Bombers blasting Cleveland 13–0.

Three other records of note were set this season by the Yanks. New York set two American League records in the month of August: they won the most games in a month with 28 (they lost but 8) in 36 games. In August, the Yanks won 16 of 22 at home and 12 of 14 on the road and New York won 8 and lost but one against both Cleveland and Philadelphia. In addition, they scored 275 runs in 36 contests for an average of 7.6 tallies per game. The 275 runs scored in a month is also a Major League mark.

On May 30, 1938, 81,841 people were officially counted at Yankee Stadium, the largest crowd ever in that famous edifice. The Yanks beat the Red Sox both games of a twin-bill to celebrate the occasion.

Yankee domination of the American League continued with this season. They were World Champions for the seventh time and were preparing to add another such title the following year. 1939 was to have a tragic note as well with Lou Gehrig being stricken down in his prime with a fatal disease that will end his career and eventually his life.

The 1938 DAY BY DAY scores follow:

Frankie Crosetti—"The Crow" held down the shortstop position much of his 17 seasons with the Bombers. As player and coach, he was in pinstripes for 37 years, longer than any other Yankee in history.

DAY BY DAY, 1938 NEW YORK YANKEES

April, 1938			May, 1938			June, 1938			August, 1938			September, 1938		
18 bos	L	4- 8	28 phi	L	4-10	" PHI	W	13- 1	1 NG			1 DET	L	3- 6
19 bos	W	5- 3	29 phi	L	9-11	30 PHI	W	7- 1	2 det	L	3- 4	2 BOS	W	6- 4
" bos	L	0- 6	30 BOS	W	10- 0	**July, 1938**			3 det	W	10- 7g	3 BOS	L	3- 9
20 NG			" BOS	W	5- 4	1 WAS	W	8- 0	4 det	W	8- 4	4 WAS	W	7- 4
21 bos	L	2- 3	31 BOS	W	12- 5	2 WAS	W	12- 2	5 cle	W	6- 1	5 PHI	W	5- 2
22 WAS	W	7- 0	**June, 1938**			3 BOS	W	9- 3	6 cle	W	7- 3	" PHI	W	6- 3
23 WAS	L	4- 7	1 DET	L	4- 8	4 was	W	10- 5	7 cle	W	7- 0	6 NG		
24 WAS	W	4- 3	2 DET	W	5- 4	" was	TG	4- 4i	8 NG			7 bos	L	4-11b
25 phi	L	1- 6	" DET	W	5- 2	5 ALL-STAR BREAK			9 WAS	L	2- 4	8 bos	W	4- 0
26 phi	W	5- 3	3 DET	W	5- 1	6 WON - 41			10 WAS	W	12-11f	9 was	W	2- 0
27 phi	W	9- 2	4 STL		*	7 LOST - 25			11 WAS	W	9- 6	10 was	W	6- 5
28 BOS	L	1- 6	5 STL	L	5- 6	8 bos	L	8- 9	12 PHI	L	4- 5	11 was	L	3- 6
29 BOS	W	6- 4	" STL		*	9 bos	W	11- 6	" PHI	W	16- 3	12 NG		
30 was	W	8- 4	6 STL	W	6- 5	10 bos	L	4- 6	13 PHI	W	11- 4	13 cle	W	7- 1
May, 1938			7 CHI	L	5- 8	11 NG			14 PHI	W	4- 3	14 cle		*
1 was	L	3- 4	8 CHI		L10-11i	12 STL	W	7- 3	" PHI	W	9- 2	15 det	L	4- 6
2 was	W	3- 2	" CHI		L6- 10	" STL	W	10- 5	15 NG			16 det	W	6- 4
3 STL	W	5- 1	9 CHI	W	5- 3	13 STL	W	15-12f	16 was	W	16- 1	17 det	L	3- 7
4 STL	W	3- 2	10 CLE	W	8- 2	14 STL	W	5- 4c	" was	W	6- 2	18 stl	L	3- 4
5 STL	W	12-10	11 CLE		*	15 DET	W	3- 0b	17 was		*	" stl	L	7- 8
6 DET		*	12 CLE	W	7- 6	16 DET	W	7- 5	18 was	W	6- 5g	19 stl	L	1-13
7 DET	W	12- 8	13 NG			17 DET	W	16- 3	" was	L	3- 6	20 chi	L	4- 5
8 CHI	W	7- 3	14 chi	W	7- 4	18 NG			19 phi	W	5- 2	21 chi	L	2- 5
9 CHI		*	15 chi	W	6- 4	19 CLE	L	3- 5	20 phi	W	11- 3	22 chi	W	7- 4
10 CHI		*	16 chi	W	5- 1	20 CLE		*	21 phi	W	8- 4	23 NG		
11 CLE	W	4- 1	17 stl		*	21 CLE		*	" phi	W	8- 1	24 BOS	L	6- 7
12 CLE	L	2- 3	18 stl	L	0- 1	22 CHI		*	22 NG			25 BOS	L	3- 5f
13 PHI	L	6- 8	" stl		*	23 CHI		*	23 CHI	L	3-11	" BOS	TG	2- 2b
14 PHI	TG	1- 1a	19 stl	L	9-10	" CHI		*	" CHI	W	3- 1	26 BOS	W	4- 3
15 PHI		*	" stl	TG	7- 7d	24 CHI	W	2- 0	24 CHI	L	5- 8	27 WAS	W	5- 2
16 NG			20 stl	W	8- 4	" CHI	L	3- 8	" CHI	W	11- 1	28 WAS	L	1- 4
17 stl		*	21 cle		L5- 10	25 NG			25 CLE	W	5- 2	29 phi	W	7- 4
18 stl	W	11- 7	22 cle	L	1- 3	26 stl	W	10- 5	" CLE	W	15- 3	" phi	TG	1- 1a
19 stl		*	" cle	L	1- 7	" stl	W	12- 5d	26 CLE	W	15- 9	30 PHI	NG	
20 chi		*	23 cle	W	8- 6	27 stl	W	7- 5	" CLE	L	5- 8	**October, 1938**		
21 chi	W	1- 0	24 det		L8- 12	" stl		*	27 CLE	W	8- 7	1 bos	L	2- 9
22 cle	L	3- 8	25 det	W	9- 3	28 stl	L	3- 4	" CLE	W	13- 0	2 bos	W	6- 1
23 cle		*	26 det	W	10- 3	29 chi	W	4- 3	28 STL	W	4- 2	END OF 1938		
24 cle	L	5- 9	27 NG			30 chi	W	9- 6	29 STL	W	8- 4	RUNS:		966
25 det	L	3- 7	28 PHI		*	31 chi	W	5- 1	30 DET	W	3- 1	OPP RUNS		710
26 det	W	5- 1	" PHI		*	" chi	W	7- 3k	31 DET		L6- 12			
27 NG			29 PHI	W	10- 0									

CLUB VS. CLUB AND MONTHLY RECORDS OF THE
NEW YORK YANKEES' 1938 SEASON FOR HOME AND AWAY GAMES

CLUB:		APR	MAY	JUN	JUL	AUG	SEP	OCT	HOME	AWAY	TOTAL
BOST	H	1-1	3- 0	xxx	1- 0	xxx	2- 3	xxx	7- 4	xxx	11-11
	A	1-3	xxx	xxx	1- 2	xxx	1- 1	1- 1	xxx	4- 7	
CHIC	H	xxx	1- 0	1- 3	1- 1	2- 2	xxx	xxx	5- 6	xxx	14- 8
	A	xxx	1- 0	3- 0	4- 0	xxx	1- 2	xxx	xxx	9- 2	
CLEV	H	c	1- 1	2- 0	0- 1	5- 1	xxx	xxx	8- 3	xxx	13- 8
	A	xxx	0- 2	1- 3	xxx	3- 0	1- 0	xxx	xxx	5- 5	
DET	H	xxx	1- 0	3- 1	3- 0	1- 1	0- 1	xxx	8- 3	xxx	14- 8
	A	xxx	1- 1	2- 1	xxx	2- 1	1- 2	xxx	xxx	6- 5	
PHIL	H	xxx	0- 1	3- 0	xxx	4- 1	2- 0	xxx	9- 2	xxx	16- 5
	A	2-1	0- 2	xxx	xxx	4- 0	1- 0	xxx	xxx	7- 3	
STL	H	xxx	3- 0	1- 1	4- 0	2- 0	xxx	xxx	10- 1	xxx	15- 7
	A	xxx	1- 0	1- 2	3- 1	xxx	0- 3	xxx	xxx	5- 6	
WAS	H	2-1	xxx	xxx	2- 0	2- 1	2- 1	xxx	8- 3	xxx	16- 6
	A	1-0	1- 1	xxx	1- 0	3- 1	2- 1	xxx	xxx	8- 3	
TOTAL:	H	3-2	9- 2	10- 5	11- 2	16- 6	6- 5	xxx	55-22	xxx	99-53
	A	4-4	4- 6	7- 6	9- 3	12- 2	7- 9	1- 1	xxx	44-31	
GRAND TOT:		7-6	13- 8	17-11	20- 5	28- 8	13-14	1- 1	xxx	xxx	
CUMUL TOT:		7-6	20-14	37-25	57-30	85- 38	98-52	99-53	xxx		

TIE GAMES: 5
BOS-SEP;PHI-May;
phi-SEP;stl-June;
was-July

1939

FOURTH WORLD SERIES IN A ROW!

In 1939, the Yankees won an unprecedented fourth World Series consecutively, beating Cincinnati in the Fall Classic. They became the second New York team to win pennants in their respective leagues 4 years straight, the Giants accomplishing this previously in the N.L. from 1921 through 1924. The Yankees won 106 games, claiming the A.L. flag 17 games ahead of the Boston Red Sox. Of the 106 games won, 54 victories were away from home. They lost but twenty on enemy soil.

The success of this season was marred by two tragic events. The first involved the death of Colonel Ruppert, Yankee owner since 1915. Ed Barrow replaced Ruppert as club president, where he will serve until 1945. The heirs of the Ruppert estate will constitute the Yankee ownership up to that time. The second unfortunate event involved Lou Gehrig's illness which ended his incredible consecutive game streak on May 2. In one of the most memorable occasions in Yankee Stadium history, "Lou Gehrig Appreciation Day" was proclaimed on July 4, drawing some 61,808 in attendance. During the ceremony, Gehrig's uniform (#4) was the first to be retired in Yankee history. Lou's speech, in which he described himself as the "luckiest man on the face of the earth" in spite of his fatal illness, touched the hearts and soul of a nation. This much beloved ballplayer and human being so richly deserved the accolades bestowed upon him that day.

Even without Gehrig's potent bat in the lineup, the Yankees had a field day with opponent pitching. Pacing the A.L. with a fine .381 batting average was American League MVP Joe DiMaggio. Red Rolfe, Yankee third baseman, led the A.L. with 46 doubles. No Yankee player has led the A.L. in two-baggers since then, through the 1983 season. In addition, he was only one of two Yankees to lead the league in doubles, the other being Lou Gehrig who led twice (1928 and 1929), the latter year being tied with Manush of St. Louis. Rolfe also topped the A.L. with 213 hits and 139 runs scored.

As a team, the Bombers led the league in practically every major category, the team batting title escaping them. They notched the slugging crown (.451), club ERA 3.31 and fielded the best defensive team (.978), making the fewest errors with 126. Their league-leading club ERA was the last of 6 straight pitching titles, a club record. Offensively, the Yanks scored the most runs (967), hit the most homers (166), walked the most often (701) and had the most RBI (903). Attesting to their explosive power, New York scored 20 or more runs in a game, setting a then A.L. record, on 3 occasions, winning by such scores as 22–2, 23–2 and 21–0!

In the first game of a doubleheader at Philadelphia on June 28, the Bronx Bombers blasted eight home runs to become the first Major League club to accomplish this feat (other teams equalled this mark subsequently, but the Yanks were first). On July 26, the Yankees scored in all 8 innings (not batting in the bottom of the ninth) for the only time in their history in a 14–1 pasting of the St. Louis Brownies.

The pitching staff dominated the A.L. batters, shutting them down on twelve occasions, a league high. New York pitchers hurled 87 complete games, also tops in the A.L. Red Ruffing, Yankee portsider, led the circuit with five shutouts while teammate Johnny "Fireman" Murphy saved 19 games, first in the American League. Murphy, in total, led all his peers in the A.L. with saves on 4 different occasions, including this season's work.

The tragic losses of Colonel Jacob Ruppert and Lou Gehrig discolored a most eventful season for the Yankees. Gehrig's illness and his eventual death in June, 1941 demonstrated the human condition and mortal nature of us all.

The 1939 DAY BY DAY scores follow:

DAY BY DAY, 1939 NEW YORK YANKEES

April, 1939
17 was		*	
18 BOS		*	
19 BOS;		*	
20 BOS	W		2–0
21 was	W		6–3
22 was	L		1–3
23 was	W		7–4
24 PHI	W		2–1
25 PHI	W		8–4
26 PHI		*	
27 bos		*	
28 bos		*	
29 WAS	L		1–3
30 WAS	L		2–3

May, 1939
1 NG			
2 det	W		22–2
3 det	W		10–6
4 cle	W		10–6f
5 cle	L		1– 2g
6 cle	W		5–1
7 chi	W		15– 4
8 chi	L		3– 5
9 chi	W		8–6
10 stl	W		7–1
11 stl	W		10–8
12 NG			
13 phi		*	
14 phi	W		10–0
15 phi	W		3–0
16 STL	W		7–5
17 STL	W		4–3
18 STL	W		8–1
19 CHI	W		4–2
20 CHI	W		5–2
21 CLE	W		12–6
22 CLE		*	
23 CLE	W		7–3
24 DET	L		1–6
25 DET	W		5–2
26 PHI	W		1–0
27 PHI	W		8–2

May, 1939 (cont.)
" PHI	W		11–9
28 PHI	W		9–5
29 bos	W		6–1
30 bos	L		4– 8
" bos	W		17–9
31 NG			

June, 1939
1 cle	W		8–3
2 cle	W		17–5
3 cle	W		3–2
4 det	W		8–4
5 det	L		0–3
6 det	L		2–6
7 chi	W		5–2
8 chi	W		7–2
9 chi		*	
10 stl		*	
11 stl	W		8–5
" stl	W		5–1
12 NG			
13 NG			
14 CLE	L		2–4
15 CLE	W		1–0
16 CLE	W		4–3
17 DET	W		1–0
18 DET	L		5–8
19 DET	W		8–5
20 CHI	W		13–3
21 CHI	W		9–8
22 CHI	W		6–1
23 STL		*	
24 STL	W		2–1
25 STL	L		3–7
" STL	W		11–2
26 phi	L		2– 3
27 NG			
28 phi	W		23–2
" phi	W		10–0
29 was	L		1–2h
" was	W		7–0b
30 was	W		10–2

July, 1939
1 bos	L	3–	5
2 bos	L	3–	7
" bos	W	9–	3
3 NG			
4 WAS	L	2–	3
" WAS	W	11–	1
5 WAS	W	6–	4
6 NG			
7 BOS	L	3–	4
8 BOS	L	1–	3
" BOS	L	2–	3
9 BOS	L	3–	4
" BOS	L	3–	5
10 ALL-STAR BREAK			
11 WON	-	53	
12 LOST	-	22	
13 det	L	6–	10
14 det	W	6–	3
15 det	W	I0–	7
16 cle	W	5–	2
" cle	W	8–	3
17 cle	W	3–	0
18 stl	W	9–	0
" stl	W	4–	3
19 stl		*	
20 stl	W	2–	1
21 chi	L	1–	4
22 NG			
23 chi	L	5–	8
" chi	W	5–	4
24 NG			
25 STL	W	5–	1
26 STL	W	14–	1
27 STL		*	
28 CHI	W	2–	1
29 CHI		*	
30 CHI	W	4–	3
" CHI	L	1–	5
31 NG			

August, 1939
1 DET	L	2–	5
2 DET	L	2–	7
3 DET	W	12–	3
4 CLE	W	5–	4
5 CLE	W	6–	1
6 CLE	L	4–	5
" CLE	L	1–	7
7 NG			
8 was	L	4–	7
9 was	W	13–	8
10 was	L	5–	7
11 phi	W	9–	5
12 phi	W	18–	4
13 phi		L9–	12
" phi	W	21–	0d
14 NG			
15 WAS	W	3–	2f
16 WAS	W	4–	0
17 WAS	W	9–	8f
18 PHI	W	5–	0
19 PHI		*	
20 PHI	L	4–	5
" PHI	W	5–	1
21 NG			
22 chi	W	14–	5
23 chi	W	7–	2
" chi	W	16–	4
24 stl	W	11–	5
25 stl	W	11–	0
" stl	W	8–	2
26 stl	W	6–	1
27 det	W	13–	3
28 det	W	18–	2
29 det	L	6–	7
30 cle	L	3–	4f
31 NG			

September, 1939
1 cle	W	11–	8
2 bos	L	7–	12
3 bos		L11–	12
" bos	TG	5–	5c
4 phi	W	7–	6
" phi	W	2–	0
5 NG			

September, 1939 (cont.)
6 BOS	W		2–1
7 BOS	W		5–2
8 BOS	W		4–1c
9 WAS	W		5–2
10 WAS	W		4–3
" WAS	W		6–2
11 NG			
12 CLE	L		3–4f
13 CLE	L		4–9
14 DET	L		1–6
15 DET	W		10–3
16 DET	W		8–5
17 STL	L		4–8
" STL	L		1–3
18 STL	W		6–2
19 CHI	W		6–2
20 CHI	W		8–4
21 CHI	W		5–2
22 NG			
23 was	W		7–1
24 was	W		3–2
25 NG			
26 bos		*	
" bos		*	
27 bos		*	
" bos		*	
28 PHI	W		8–4
" PHI	L		4–5
29 NG			
30 BOS	W		5–4
" BOS	L		2–4c

October, 1939
1 NG	
END OF 1939	
RUNS:	967
OPP RUNS:	556

CLUB VS. CLUB AND MONTHLY RECORDS OF THE NEW YORK YANKEES' 1939 SEASON FOR HOME AND AWAY GAMES

CLUB:		APR	MAY	JUN	JUL	AUG	SEP	OCT	HOME	AWAY	TOTAL
BOST	H	1- 0	xxx	xxx	0- 5	xxx	4- 1	xxx	5- 6	xxx	
	A	xxx	2- 1	xxx	1- 2	xxx	0- 2	xxx	xxx	3- 5	8-11
CHIC	H	xxx	2- 0	3- 0	2- 1	xxx	3- 0	xxx	10- 1	xxx	
	A	xxx	2- 1	2- 0	1- 2	3- 0	xxx	xxx	xxx	8- 3	18- 4
CLEV	H	xxx	2- 0	2- 1	xxx	2- 2	0- 2	xxx	6- 5	xxx	
	A	xxx	2- 1	3- 0	3- 0	0- 1	1- 0	xxx	xxx	9- 2	15- 7
DET	H	xxx	1- 1	2- 1	xxx	1- 2	2- 1	xxx	6- 5	xxx	
	A	xxx	2- 0	1- 2	2- 1	2- 1	xxx	xxx	xxx	7- 4	13- 9
PHIL	H	2-0	4- 0	xxx	xxx	2- 1	1- 1	xxx	9- 2	xxx	
	A	xxx	2- 0	2- 1	xxx	3- 1	2- 0	xxx	xxx	9- 2	18- 4
STL	H	xxx	3- 0	2- 1	2- 0	xxx	1- 2	xxx	8- 3	xxx	
	A	xxx	2- 0	2- 0	3- 0	4- 0	xxx	xxx	xxx	11- 0	19- 3
WAS	H	0- 2	xxx	xxx	2- 1	3- 0	3- 0	xxx	8- 3	xxx	
	A	2-1	xxx	2- 1	xxx	1- 2	2- 0	xxx	xxx	7- 4	15- 7
TOTAL:	H	3-2	12- 1	9- 3	6- 7	8- 5	14- 7	xxx	52-25	xxx	
	A	2-1	12- 3	12- 4	10- 5	13- 5	5- 2	xxx	xxx	54- 20	106-45
GRAND TOT:		5-3	24- 4	21- 7	16-12	21-10	19- 9	xxx	xxx	xxx	
CUMUL TOT:		5-3	29- 7	50-14	66-26	87-36	106-45	xxx	xxx	xxx	

TIE GAMES: 1
bos-Sep.

1940

JOLTIN' JOE'S SECOND BATTING TITLE

The year 1940 spelled the end of four consecutive A.L. pennants for the Yanks. Finishing in third place but two games behind frontrunning Detroit, New York concluded its 38th season at 88–66, a .571 winning clip.

Joltin' Joe became the only Yankee in history to win consecutive batting titles, having won the previous season with a .381 mark. In 1940, his average dropped to .352. Charles "King Kong" Keller topped A.L. players with 106 bases on balls.

In comparison to previous seasons, New York's offensive statistics in 1940 were not up to their usual standards. However, the Bombers led in A.L. homers, with 155, for the 21st time since 1915. Although their pitching and fielding were very respectable, no Yankee players ranked first in the A.L. except Ernest "Tiny" Bonham who led league pitchers in ERA with 1.90, although pitching but 99 innings. (Note: Some baseball sources cite Bob Feller of Cleveland as the winner of the ERA Title because of Bonham's low innings pitched total.)

Losing by only two games to Detroit in 1940 was very disappointing. However, next season will again have the Yanks on top in their accustomed position.

The 1940 DAY BY DAY scores follow:

DAY BY DAY, 1940 NEW YORK YANKEES

April, 1940
```
16 phi    L  1- 2f
17 phi  W  4- 1
18 phi         *
19 WAS  W  5- 3
20 WAS         *
21 WAS         *
22 PHI         *
23 PHI     L  0- 3
24 PHI  W  9- 4
25 bos         *
26 bos     L  1- 8
27 was     L  2- 3
28 was     L  2- 3f
29 was  W  5- 4
30 STL     L  1- 2
```

May, 1940
```
 1 STL  W  5- 3
 2 STL         *
 3 CHI  W  8- 4
 4 CHI     L 3- 10
 5 DET     L  4- 6
 6 DET     L  4- 6
 7 DET     L  2- 4
 8 CLE     L  4-10
 9 CLE     L  0- 4
10 BOS     L  2- 3f
11 BOS     L  8- 9g
12 BOS  W  4- 0
13 NG
14 stl         *
15 stl         *
16 chi         *
17 chi  W  6- 1
18 chi  W  3- 0
19 cle     L  1- 5
20 cle     L  2-10
21 cle  W 10- 2
22 det  W  8- 2
23 det     L  2- 3
24 NG
25 bos         *
 " bos         *
26 bos  W  7- 2
27 WAS  W  5- 0
28 WAS  W 12- 4
 " WAS  W  3- 1
29 WAS  W  2- 1
30 BOS  W  4- 0
 " BOS     L  4-11
31 BOS         *
```

June, 1940
```
 1 STL  W  8- 5
 2 STL  W 13- 4
 " STL  W 11- 1
 3 STL  W  7- 1
 4 CHI     L  3- 7
 5 CHI  W  7- 5
 6 CHI     L  3- 4
 7 CLE  W  5- 4
 8 CLE     L  0- 3
 9 CLE  W  4- 3
10 DET         *
11 DET     L  1- 6
12 DET  W  7- 5
13 NG
14 stl   W 12- 3
15 stl   W  7- 6
16 stl      L 6- 12
 " stl       L  5- 6
17 NG
18 chi     L  3- 5
19 chi     L  0- 1
20 chi     L  0- 1g#
21 det  W 12- 7
22 det     L  2- 3
23 det     L  2- 9
24 cle     L  1- 7
25 cle     L  3- 5a
26 cle  W  3- 1
27 NG
28 PHI  W  4- 1
29 PHI  W 12- 9
30 PHI  W  4- 3
 " PHI      L  2- 3f
```

July, 1940
```
 1 was  W  8- 4
 2 was  W  6- 2
 3 was         *
 4 bos  W 12- 4
 " bos  W  7- 3
 5 phi     L  3- 6
 6 phi     L  7- 8f
 7 phi  W  6- 3
 " phi      L5- 10
 8 ALL-STAR BREAK
 9 WON  -  37
10 LOST  -  34
11 STL  W  6- 4
12 STL         *
13 STL  W 10- 4
 " STL  W 12- 6
14 CHI  W  4- 0
15 CHI     L  2- 3
16 CHI     L  1- 5
17 CLE  W  4- 3i
18 CLE  W  9- 6
19 CLE  W 15- 6
20 DET     L  1- 3
21 DET     L  3- 4
 " DET     L  2- 3
22 NG
23 stl     L  5- 9
24 stl     L 12-14
25 stl  W 13- 8
26 chi  W 10- 2
27 chi     L  5- 6h
28 chi  W 10- 9
 " chi      L  4- 8
29 NG
30 det  W  8- 6
31 det     L  6- 7g
```

August, 1940
```
 1 det     L  2-11
 2 cle  W 10- 2
 3 cle     L  1- 5
 4 cle     L  1- 3
 5 bos     L  1- 4
 6 bos     L  3- 8
 7 bos     L  7-10
 " bos  W  6- 3
 8 bos     L  5- 6
 9 PHI  W  2- 0
10 PHI  W 13- 0
11 PHI  W  7- 6g
12 NG
13 BOS  W  9- 1
 " BOS  W 19- 8b
14 BOS  W  8- 3
15 BOS     L  1-11
16 NG
17 phi         *
18 phi  W  9- 1
 " phi      L  3- 7
19 DET         *
20 DET  W  4- 3
 " DET  W  4- 2
21 DET  W  6- 5
22 CLE  W 15- 2
23 CLE  W  5- 3
24 CLE  W  3- 2
25 CHI     L  0- 1
 " CHI  W  3- 1
26 NG
27 CHI  W  5- 4f
28 STL         *
29 STL  W 10- 3
 " STL  W  6- 5i
30 WAS         *
31 WAS  W  7- 1
```

September, 1940
```
 1 WAS  W  3- 2
 " WAS  W  3- 0
 2 PHI  W  6- 3
 " PHI      L  0- 3
 3 NG
 4 was     L  5- 6
 5 was  W  2- 1
 " was  W  8- 1
 6 was     L  1- 3
 7 bos  W  4- 3
 8 bos  W  9- 4
 9 NG
10 CLE         *
11 cle  W  3- 1
 " cle      L  3- 5b
12 det     L  3- 6
13 det     L  0- 8
14 det  W 16- 7
15 stl     L  5-10
 " stl      L  1- 2
16 stl     L  4-16
17 stl  W  9- 0
18 chi     L  3- 6
 " chi  W  9- 8d
19 chi  W 10- 1
20 NG
21 BOS  W  5- 4
22 BOS  W  6- 3
23 NG
24 WAS  W  6- 5g
 " WAS  W  9- 4c
25 WAS         *
26 phi  W  5- 4
 " phi  W  2- 0
27 phi     L  2- 6
28 was     L  3- 4
 " was  W  7- 1d
29 was  W  4- 3g
END OF 1940
RUNS:           817
OPP RUNS:       671
```

#VOIDED AND REPLAYED

CLUB VS. CLUB AND MONTHLY RECORDS OF THE NEW YORK YANKEES' 1940 SEASON FOR HOME AND AWAY GAMES

CLUB:		APR	MAY	JUN	JUL	AUG	SEP	OCT	HOME	AWAY	TOTAL
BOST	H	xxx	2- 3	xxx	xxx	3- 1	2- 0	xxx	7- 4	xxx	xxx
	A	0-1	1- 0	xxx	2- 0	1- 4	2- 0	xxx	xxx	6- 5	13- 9
CHIC	H	xxx	1- 1	1- 2	1- 2	2- 1	xxx	xxx	5- 6	xxx	xxx
	A	xxx	2- 0	0- 2	2- 2	xxx	2- 1	xxx	xxx	6- 5	11- 11
CLEV	H	xxx	0- 2	2- 1	3- 0	3- 0	xxx	xxx	8- 3	xxx	xxx
	A	xxx	1- 2	1- 2	xxx	1- 2	1- 1	xxx	xxx	4- 7	12- 10
DET	H	xxx	0- 3	1- 1	0- 3	3- 0	xxx	xxx	4- 7	xxx	xxx
	A	xxx	1- 1	1- 2	1- 1	0- 1	1- 2	xxx	xxx	4- 7	8- 14
PHIL	H	1-1	xxx	3- 1	xxx	3- 0	1- 1	xxx	8- 3	xxx	xxx
	A	1-1	xxx	xxx	1- 3	1- 1	2- 1	xxx	xxx	5- 6	13- 9
STL	H	0-1	1- 0	4- 0	3- 0	2- 0	xxx	xxx	10- 1	xxx	xxx
	A	xxx	xxx	2- 2	1- 2	xxx	1- 3	xxx	xxx	4- 7	14- 8
WAS	H	1-0	4- 0	xxx	xxx	1- 0	4- 0	xxx	10- 0	xxx	xxx
	A	1-2	xxx	xxx	2- 0	xxx	4- 3	xxx	xxx	7- 5	17- 5
TOTAL:	H	2-2	8- 9	11- 5	7- 5	17- 2	7- 1	xxx	52-24	xxx	xxx
	A	2-4	5- 3	4- 8	9- 8	3- 8	13-11	xxx	xxx	36-42	88-66
GRAND TOT:		4-6	13-12	15-13	16- 13	20-10	20-12	xxx	xxx	xxx	**TIE GAMES:** NONE
CUMUL TOT:		4-6	17-18	32-31	48- 44	68-54	88-66	xxx	xxx	xxx	

1941

THE YEAR OF DIMAGGIO'S GREAT STREAK

After an off year (by Yankee standards, anyway), the McCarthymen began another streak of A.L. pennants. Making a shambles of the A.L. flag chase, the Yanks (101–53, .656) routed second place Boston by seventeen games. Winning their twelfth A.L. pennant, the Yanks vanquished the Brooklyn Dodgers in the World Series, claiming their ninth world title. The great DiMaggio became the first Yankee to win two Most Valuable Player Awards. He won also in 1939.

However, with all of this year's heroics, none could top the hitting streak of Joe DiMaggio. From May 15 to July 17, "The Yankee Clipper" hit safely in 56 consecutive games, an all-time Major League mark. During his famous streak, Joe D. got 91 hits in 223 at bats for a .408 average. Joe tallied 56 runs, 16 doubles, four triples, 15 homers and 55 RBI. In the course of the streak, the Yanks won 14 straight games, the last eleven coming at the start of July, and posted a 41–13 (.759) mark (with two ties included) during that time. DiMaggio also found the time to pace the league in total bases (348) and runs batted in (125) for the 1941 season.

In other statistical areas, the Yanks won their annual A.L. homer title, this time with 151 four-baggers. The pitching staff allowed the fewest opponents' runs (631) and finished .001 points behind first place Chicago in team ERA. During the 1941 season, the Bombers hit homers in 25 consecutive games, a Major League record. They hit 40 homers during those 25 games. Defensively, the Yanks turned the most double plays with 196. On the mound, Murphy topped the A.L. with 15 saves while Gomez topped in winning percentage (.750) with a 15–5 record. Throughout Yankee history only two New York pitchers had led the A.L. in winning percentage twice.

Gomez did it this season and 1934; Whitey Ford will do it three times (1956, 1961 and 1963), the only New York pitcher to do so.

A ninth World Championship culminated this fine New York season. In the midst of DiMaggio's great streak, a nation mourned the passing of Lou Gehrig on June 2. Lou's courage during his illness was indeed a testimonial to his character. With his passing, the enormity of his baseball legacy is magnified with each passing year.

The 1941 DAY BY DAY scores follow:

Joe DiMaggio—"The Yankee Clipper" rounds third base in the midst of his incredible 56-game consecutive hitting streak of 1941. With his classic swing, Joe D. plays his entire 13 seasons in pinstripes. This complete ballplayer was elected to the Hall of Fame in 1955.

DAY BY DAY, 1941 NEW YORK YANKEES

April, 1941

14 was	W	3– 0
15 PHI	L	1– 3
16 PHI	L	7–10
17 PHI	W	9– 4
18 was	L	4– 7
19 was	W	5– 2f
20 phi	W	19– 5
21 phi	W	14– 4
22 phi	L	5– 6
23 BOS	W	4– 2g
24 BOS	W	6– 3
25 WAS	W	6– 0
26 WAS	W	8– 3
27 WAS	L	3– 6
28 NG		
29 stl	L	2– 3
30 stl	W	7– 1

May, 1941

1 stl	W	14– 5
2 chi	L	1– 8
3 chi	W	6– 5i
4 det	L	1–10
5 det	L	3– 7
6 det	L	4– 7
7 cle	W	7– 5
8 cle	W	5– 4
9 NG		
10 bos		*
11 bos	L	5–13
12 bos	L	4– 8
13 CLE	L	1– 2f
14 CLE	L	1– 4
15 CHI	L	1–13
16 CHI	W	6– 5
17 CHI	L	2– 3
18 STL	W	12– 2
19 STL	L	1– 5
20 STL	W	10– 9
21 DET	W	5– 4f
22 DET	W	6– 5
23 BOS	TG	9– 9e

May, 1941

24 BOS	W	7– 6
25 BOS	L	3– 10
26 NG		
27 was	W	10– 8
28 was	W	6– 5
29 was	TG	2– 2a
30 bos	W	4– 3
31 cle		*

June, 1941

1 bos	W	2– 0
" bos	W	5– 3
2 bos	L	5– 7
3 det	L	2– 4
4 det		*
5 det	L	4– 5f
6 NG		
7 stl	W	11– 7
8 stl	W	9– 3
" stl	W	8– 3c
9 NG		
10 chi	W	8– 3
11 chi		*
12 chi	W	3– 2f
13 NG		
14 CLE	W	4– 1
15 CLE	W	3– 2
16 CLE	W	6– 4
17 CHI	L	7– 8
18 CHI	L	2– 3
19 CHI	W	7– 2
20 DET	W	14– 4
21 DET	L	2– 7
22 DET	W	5– 4
23 NG		
24 STL	W	9– 1
25 STL	W	7– 5
26 STL	W	4– 1
27 phi	L	6– 7
28 phi	W	7– 4
29 was	W	9– 4

June, 1941

" was	W	7–5
30 NG		

July, 1941

1 BOS	W	7–2
" BOS	W	9–2a
2 BOS	W	8–4
3 NG		
4 WAS		*
" WAS		*
5 PHI	W	10– 5
6 PHI	W	8– 4
" PHI	W	3–1
7 ALL-STAR BREAK		
8 WON - 48		
9 LOST - 26		
10 stl	W	1–0a
11 stl	W	6–2
12 stl	W	7–5
13 chi	W	8–1
" chi	W	1–0g
14 chi	L	1–7
15 chi	W	5–4
16 cle	W	10–3
17 cle	W	4–3
18 cle	L	1–2d
19 det	W	9–3
" det	W	6–2
20 det	W	12–6m
21 NG		
22 CLE	W	4–3
23 CLE	W	3–2
24 CLE	W	4–1
25 CHI	W	8–0
26 CHI	W	11–3
27 CHI	W	9–5
" CHI	L	3–7
28 NG		
29 DET	L	3–6
30 DET		*
31 DET	W	6–3i
" DET	W	5–0d

August, 1941

1 STL	W	9– 0
2 STL	W	2– 0
3 STL	L	2– 6
" STL	L	0– 5
4 was	W	7– 5
5 was	L	3– 4
6 bos	L	3– 6
" bos	W	3– 1
7 bos	L	5– 9
8 phi	L	3– 5
9 phi	W	8– 3
10 phi	W	11– 2
" phi	W	4– 1
11 BOS	L	0– 8
12 BOS	W	4– 0
13 WAS	L	3– 5g
" WAS	W	5– 1
14 WAS	W	7– 0
" WAS	W	10– 3
15 PHI		*
16 PHI	L	4– 6
17 PHI	W	2– 1
" PHI	W	4– 3
18 det		*
19 det	L	3–12
" det	W	8– 3
20 det	L	0– 1f
21 cle	L	0– 2
22 cle	L	4– 5
23 cle	W	7– 2
13 chi	W	5– 1
" chi	W	8– 5
25 chi	L	1– 9
26 NG		
27 stl	W	11– 1
28 stl	W	8– 5f
29 NG		
30 was	W	8– 1
31 was	W	5– 2

September, 1941

1 phi	W	13–11
" phi	L	1–5
2 NG		
3 bos	W	2–1g
4 bos	W	6–3
5 NG		
6 BOS	L	1–8
7 BOS	W	8–5
8 NG		
9 STL	W	1–0
10 NG		
11 DET	L	4–5h
12 DET	W	8–2
13 DET	L	3–5
14 CLE	W	6–3
" CLE	L	2–5d
15 CLE	W	4–2
16 NG		
17 CHI	W	5–3
18 NG		
19 NG		
20 bos	W	8–1
21 bos	L	1–4
22 NG		
23 PHI	L	8–9
24 PHI	W	7–2
25 NG		
26 WAS	W	4– 1
" WAS	W	1–0
27 WAS	L	3–4
28 WAS	L	0–5
END OF 1941		
RUNS:		830
OPP RUNS:		631

CLUB VS. CLUB AND MONTHLY RECORDS OF THE NEW YORK YANKEES' 1941 SEASON FOR HOME AND AWAY GAMES

CLUB:		APR	MAY	JUN	JUL	AUG	SEP	OCT	HOME	AWAY	TOTAL
BOST	H	2- 0	1- 1	xxx	3- 0	1- 1	1- 1	xxx	8- 3	xxx	13- 9
	A	xxx	1- 3	xxx	xxx	1- 2	3- 1	xxx	xxx	5- 6	
CHIC	H	xxx	1- 2	1- 2	3- 1	xxx	1- 0	xxx	6- 5	xxx	14- 8
	A	xxx	1- 1	2- 0	3- 1	2- 1	xxx	xxx	xxx	8- 3	
CLEV	H	xxx	0- 2	3- 0	3- 0	xxx	2- 1	xxx	8- 3	xxx	15- 7
	A	xxx	2- 0	2- 1	2- 1	1- 2	xxx	xxx	xxx	7- 4	
DET	H	xxx	2- 0	2- 1	2- 1	xxx	1- 2	xxx	7- 4	xxx	11-11
	A	xxx	0- 3	0- 2	3- 0	1- 2	xxx	xxx	xxx	4- 7	
PHIL	H	1- 2	xxx	xxx	3- 0	2- 1	1- 1	xxx	7- 4	xxx	14- 8
	A	2- 1	xxx	1- 1	xxx	3- 1	1- 1	xxx	xxx	7- 4	
STL	H	xxx	2- 1	3- 0	xxx	2- 2	1- 0	xxx	8- 3	xxx	18- 4
	A	1- 1	1- 0	3- 0	3- 0	2- 0	xxx	xxx	xxx	10- 1	
WAS	H	2- 1	xxx	xxx	xxx	3- 1	2- 2	xxx	7- 4	xxx	16- 6
	A	2- 1	2- 0	2- 0	xxx	3- 1	xxx	xxx	xxx	9- 2	
TOTAL:	H	5- 3	6- 6	9- 3	14- 2	8- 5	9- 7	xxx	51-26	xxx	101-53
	A	5- 3	7- 7	10- 4	11- 2	13- 9	4- 2	xxx	xxx	50-27	
GRAND TOT:		10- 6	13-13	19- 7	25- 4	21-14	13- 9	xxx	xxx	xxx	
CUMUL. TOT:		10- 6	23-19	42-26	67-30	88-44	101- 53	xxx	xxx	xxx	

TIE GAMES: 2
BOS-May; was-May

1942

LUCKY NUMBER THIRTEEN

New York won their thirteenth A.L. flag, heading second place Boston by nine full games. They won 103 games, while losing 51 for a .669 winning mark. Joe "Flash" Gordon, Yankee second baseman, was voted the American League's Most Valuable Player. His steady offensive play throughout the season earned him this award.

Offensively, their home run (and league-leading) total fell to 108, some 43 fewer than 1941. They led the way in runs scored (801) and RBI (744). New York hurlers pitched a league high 18 shutouts, the most by a Yankee staff since 1906. They also allowed but 507 opponent runs, an A.L. low for 1942. The staff totaled the greatest number of complete games (88) and led in club ERA for the 13th time since 1919. "Tiny" Bonham paved the A.L. way with a winning percentage of .808 (a 21–5 record), complete games (22) and six shutouts.

Defensively, New York finished first in the A.L., fielding at a .976 clip, making the fewest errors (142) and turning the most double plays (190). Their defensive skills were evident on August 14 versus Philadelphia when the New Yorkers turned 7 twin killings, an American League record. This record has not been equalled in the American League and required 27 more seasons (1969) for Houston to turn the trick against San Francisco. Atlanta had seven DPs also in 1982.

Although they lost to the St. Louis Cardinals in the World Series, the 1942 season, in which they won their thirteenth pennant, was a productive one for the men in pinstripes.

The 1942 DAY BY DAY scores follow:

DAY BY DAY, 1942 NEW YORK YANKEES

April, 1942

14	was	W	7- 0
15	was	W	9- 3
16	was	W	8- 5
17	BOS	W	1- 0
18	BOS	L	1- 5
19	BOS	L	2- 5
20	phi	*	
21	phi	W	10- 4
22	PHI	W	11- 5
23	PHI	W	6- 4
24	bos	W	8- 5
25	bos	L	2- 4
26	bos	W	7- 2
27	NG		
28	STL	L	1- 3
29	STL	L	6- 11
30	STL	W	3- 0

May, 1942

1	DET	L	2- 7
2	DET	L	1- 3
3	CHI	W	6- 4
"	CHI	W	3- 1
4	CHI	W	6- 1
5	CHI	W	5- 4f
6	CLE	W	3- 0
7	CLE	*	
8	NG		
9	WAS	*	
10	WAS	W	4- 3
"	WAS	W	3- 2f
11	NG		
12	cle	*	
13	cle	L	2- 7
14	det	*	
15	det	*	
16	det	W	6- 1
"	det	W	2- 1
17	stl	L	2- 4
"	stl	W	3- 2
18	stl	*	
19	NG		
20	chi	W	4- 1
21	chi	W	1- 0
22	NG		
23	was	W	8- 4
24	was	L	8- 9
25	BOS	W	3- 1
26	BOS	W	9- 2
27	PHI	W	8- 3
28	PHI	W	3- 2
29	WAS	W	16- 1
30	WAS	W	5- 1
"	WAS	W	6- 4
31	phi	W	11- 7
"	phi	L	2- 4

June, 1942

1	NG		
2	CHI	*	
3	CHI	W	4- 1
4	CHI	W	8- 2
5	CLE	W	6- 3
6	CLE	W	3- 0
7	CLE	L	4- 5
"	CLE	W	13- 1
8	CLE	W	11- 10g
9	DET	W	4- 1
10	DET	L	1- 4g
11	DET	*	
12	STL	*	
13	STL	W	4- 3f
14	STL	W	6- 1
"	STL	W	5- 4
15	NG		
16	det	L	6- 7
"	det	W	5- 3
17	det	L	0- 1
18	det	L	1- 3
19	cle	L	4- 5
20	cle	L	0- 1
21	cle	L	2- 3
"	cle	W	4- 0
22	NG		
23	stl	W	6- 5
24	stl	W	6- 4
25	stl	*	
26	chi	L	2- 4
27	chi	W	7- 3
28	chi	L	2- 6
"	chi	L	1- 13
29	NG		
30	phi	L	5- 8
"	phi	W	4- 3

July, 1942

1	phi	L	4- 5
2	phi	*	
3	bos	W	5- 3
4	bos	W	6- 3
"	bos	L	4- 6
5	PHI	L	4- 5
"	PHI	W	4- 2
6	ALL-STAR BREAK		
7	WON - 50		
8	LOST - 26		
9	STL	W	5- 2
10	STL	W	5- 2
11	STL	L	2- 5
12	DET	L	4- 6
"	DET	W	3- 1i
13	DET	W	4- 3
14	DET	W	3- 0
15	CLE	W	4- 0
16	CLE	W	8- 5
17	CLE	W	8- 1
18	CHI	W	7- 6f
19	CHI	W	9- 2
"	CHI	W	12- 0
20	NG		
21	cle	W	8- 3
22	cle	W	5- 1f
23	cle	L	2- 3g
24	det	W	3- 0
25	det	W	7- 2
26	det	W	5- 2
27	chi	*	
28	ci	W	8-3
29	chi	L	5- 6g
"	chi	L	5- 7
30	NG		
31	stl	L	8- 9
"	stl	W	8- 0

August, 1942

1	stl	L	3- 7
2	stl	W	4- 2
"	stl	W	10- 0
3	NG		
4	was	L	3- 4
5	was	*	
6	was	L	3- 6
7	NG		
8	PHI	W	8- 4
9	PHI	*	
10	PHI	L	1- 4
"	PHI	W	3- 2
11	BOS	L	2- 3g
12	BOS	W	8-4
13	NG		
14	phi	W	11- 2
15	phi	L	1- 3
"	phi	W	5- 3
16	phi	W	11- 2b
"	phi	*	
17	phi	W	15- 0
18	bos	L	7- 8f
19	bos	L	4- 6
"	bos	W	2- 1
20	bos	L	4-6
21	WAS	W	17- 7
22	WAS	W	1- 0
23	WAS	L	6- 7
"	WAS	W	3- 0
24	NG		
25	CHI	W	5- 3
26	CHI	L	3- 5
27	NG		
28	CLE	W	3-0
29	CLE	L	5-6
30	DET	W	7- 1
"	DET	W	4- 3f
31	DET	W	8- 3

September, 1942

1	NG		
2	STL	W	3- 2f
"	STL	W	6- 0
3	NG		
4	was	*	
5	was	W	6- 2
"	was	L	0- 1
6	was	W	11- 9
"	was	W	15- 2
7	PHI	W	6- 5
"	PHI	W	11- 2
8	NG		
9	stl	W	8- 3
10	stl	L	0- 9
11	chi	L	0- 1
12	chi	W	7-1
13	cle	W	9- 1
"	cle	W	4- 1
14	cle	W	8- 3
15	NG		
16	det	W	5- 1
17	det	W	7- 4
18	NG		
19	BOS	L	6- 9f
20	BOS	W	2- 1
"	BOS	L	2- 3d
21	BOS	L	2-3g
22	WAS	W	3- 1
23	WAS	W	4- 1
24	NG		
25	NG		
26	NG		
27	bos	L	6- 7

END of 1942

RUNS: 801
OPP RUNS: 507

CLUB VS. CLUB AND MONTHLY RECORDS OF THE NEW YORK YANKEES' 1942 SEASON FOR HOME AND AWAY GAMES

CLUB:		APR	MAY	JUN	JUL	AUG	SEP	OCT	HOME	AWAY	TOTAL
BOST	H	1- 2	2- 0	xxx	xxx	1- 1	1- 3	xxx	5- 6	xxx	10- 12
	A	2- 1	xxx	xxx	2- 1	1- 3	0- 1	xxx	xxx	5- 6	
CHIC	H	xxx	4- 0	2- 0	3- 0	1- 1	xxx	xxx	10- 1	xxx	15- 7
	A	xxx	2- 0	1- 3	1- 2	xxx	1- 1	xxx	xxx	5- 6	
CLEV	H	xxx	1- 0	4- 1	3- 0	1- 1	xxx	xxx	9- 2	xxx	15- 7
	A	xxx	0- 1	1- 3	2- 1	xxx	3- 0	xxx	xxx	6- 5	
DET	H	xxx	0- 2	1- 1	3- 1	3- 0	xxx	xxx	7- 4	xxx	15- 7
	A	xxx	2- 0	1- 3	3- 0	xxx	2- 0	xxx	xxx	8- 3	
PHIL	H	2- 0	2- 0	xxx	1- 1	2- 1	2- 0	xxx	9- 2	xxx	16- 6
	A	1- 0	1- 1	1- 1	0- 1	4- 1	xxx	xxx	xxx	7- 4	
STL	H	1- 2	xxx	3- 0	2- 1	xxx	2- 0	xxx	8- 3	xxx	15- 7
	A	xxx	1- 1	2- 0	1- 1	2- 1	1- 1	xxx	xxx	7- 4	
WAS	H	xxx	5- 0	xxx	xxx	3- 1	2- 0	xxx	10- 1	xxx	17- 5
	A	3- 0	1- 1	xxx	xxx	0- 2	3- 1	xxx	xxx	7- 4	
TOTAL:	H	4- 4	14- 2	10- 2	12- 3	11- 5	7- 3	xxx	58-19	xxx	103- 51
	A	6- 1	7- 4	6-10	9- 6	7- 7	10- 4	xxx	xxx	45-32	
GRAND TOT:		10- 5	21- 6	16-12	21- 9	18-12	17- 7	xxx	xxx	xxx	
CUMUL TOT:		10- 5	31-11	47-23	68-32	86-44	103-51	xxx	xxx	xxx	

TIE GAMES: NONE

1943

SEVENTH PENNANT IN EIGHT YEARS

The Yankees continued their unbelievable domination of the American League, winning yet another pennant, their fourteenth and seventh in the past 8 seasons. Their record of 98–56 (.636) put them ahead of 2nd place Washington by 13½ games. After losing to St. Louis in the World Series the preceding year, New York was not to be denied this year. After this season, the ledger showed 14 trips to the World Series for the Yanks with 10 victories.

This season, a pitcher dominated the season for the Yanks and as a result won the league's prestigious MVP Award, the only New York pitcher in history to receive such honor. His name was Spud Chandler. He anchored the sound New York pitching staff and won several A.L. statistical categories: percentage of games won(.833, 20–4), ERA (a fine 1.64) and wins and shutouts, 20 and 5, respectively, both tied with Detroit's Trout. As a whole, the Yankee pitching crew fared well with a league-leading 2.93 ERA, 83 complete games and 542 runs allowed, the latter being the fewest in the A.L.

From a batting standpoint, New York continued to flex its muscles, pacing the A.L. for the 8th straight year with 100 homers. The McCarthy-led team also scored the most runs (669), drove across the most runs (635) and received the most bases on balls (624). Their .376 slugging percentage was also tops in the league as was their 59 triples. Keller led the league in walks (102) and Johnny Lindell hit the most triples (12), being tied with Moses of Chicago for top honors.

This season was especially pleasing particularly if your name happened to be Spud Chandler. He won the Yanks their tenth World Series by blanking the Cardinals 2–0 in the fifth and final game of the 1943 Fall Classic. New York's domination of the American League was substantiated by the fact that three different Yankee players (DiMaggio, Gordon, and Chandler) won the MVP Award for the past three consecutive seasons. Starting in 1944, the Bombers would have to wait some three seasons to grab their 15th pennant.

The 1943 DAY BY DAY scores follow:

DAY BY DAY, 1943 NEW YORK YANKEES

April, 1943
21 WAS   *
22 WAS W 5- 4
23 NG
24 WAS W 1- 0
25 BOS W 7- 1
26 NG
27 bos L 1- 5
28 bos W 5- 0
29 bos W 7- 3h
30 was L 1- 2f

May, 1943
1 was W 9- 7g
2 was W 11- 3
" was L 1- 4
3 BOS *
4 BOS W 4- 3
5 BOS W 4- 3
6 BOS W 2- 1
" BOS W 5- 4
7 PHI W 6- 2
8 PHI L 4- 9
9 PHI W 13- 1
" PHI L 3- 4
10 NG
11 NG
12 chi L 1- 2f
13 chi *
14 chi L 0- 3
15 stl *
16 stl W 7- 3
" stl L 3- 4f
17 det *
18 det *
19 det *
20 det *
21 cle *
22 cle L 2- 9
23 cle L 1- 3
" cle L 2- 5
24 NG
25 NG
26 DET *

May, 1943
27 DET L 2- 3
28 DET W 2- 1
29 CLE W 9- 5
30 CLE W 4- 3
" CLE W 3- 2
31 CHI L5- 10f
" CHI W 10- 4

June, 1943
1 CHI *
2 CHI L 1- 2
3 STL W 2- 1
4 STL W 6- 4f
5 STL L 2- 3f
6 STL W 2- 1g
" STL W 10- 6
7 NG
8 NG
9 NG
10 phi W 8- 2
11 phi W 2- 1
12 phi W 14- 5
13 phi L 3- 5
" phi L 2- 3
14 was W 4- 1
15 was W 9- 5
16 was L 3- 8
17 was W 9- 8
18 BOS L 1- 3
19 BOS W 2- 1h
20 WAS L 3- 5
" WAS W 7- 6
21 NG
22 WAS L 2- 3
23 WAS L 0- 8
" WAS W 4- 0
24 NG
25 bos TG 2- 2g
26 bos L 1- 4
27 bos W 3- 2
" bos L 3- 4h
28 NG
29 NG

June, 1943
30 cle W 3- 0g

July, 1943
1 cle L 2- 3
2 cle L0- 12
3 det L 5- 6g
" det L 9- 10
4 det W 1- 0
" det L 0- 6
5 stl W 3- 2g
" stl W 8- 5
6 stl W 5- 4
7 stl W 2- 0
8 CHI L 0- 1
9 NG
10 chi W 9- 2
" chi W 8- 3
11 chi W 9- 0
" chi W 8- 6
12 ALL-STAR BREAK
13 WON - 43
14 LOST - 30
15 NG
16 PHI W 6- 5
17 PHI W 5- 4
18 PHI W 7- 2
" PHI W 4- 3f
19 NG
20 NG
21 STL L 0- 1
22 STL W 9- 5
23 STL W 1- 0
24 CHI W 5- 1
" CHI L 3- 5
25 CHI L 1- 2
" CHI W 6- 3
26 CHI W 5- 2
27 CLE W 4- 3i
28 CLE L 2- 6
29 CLE W 11- 1
30 CLE W 5- 4
31 DET L 6- 7

August, 1943
1 DET W 5- 4
" DET W 2- 1
2 NG
3 DET L 0- 4
" DET W 12- 4
4 NG
5 NG
6 phi L 0- 4
7 phi W 3- 1
8 phi W 7- 1
" phi W 8- 4f
9 NG
10 stl L 2- 10
11 stl L 1- 9
12 stl W 6- 2
13 stl W 4- 0
14 stl W 2- 1
15 chi W 7- 2
" chi L 3- 4d
16 chi W 7- 0
17 chi W 4- 2
18 cle L 8- 9
" cle L 5- 7j
19 cle W 2- 1i
20 cle W 10- 5
21 cle W 8- 3
22 det L 0-12
" det L 3- 8
23 det W 4- 1
" det *
24 det W 2- 1
" det L 1- 3
25 det W 7- 5
" det W 5- 1
26 NG
27 NG
28 BOS L 1- 2f
29 BOS W 6- 4f
" BOS W 5- 1
30 BOS W 3- 1
31 NG

September, 1943
1 NG
2 NG
3 WAS W 4- 0
4 WAS W 2- 1
5 WAS L 2- 3
" WAS L 1- 5
6 phi L 2-11
" phi W 11- 4
7 NG
8 NG
9 bos W 11- 3
10 bos W 9- 3
11 bos W 4- 0
12 bos W 1- 0
" bos W 9- 6
13 NG
14 PHI W 6- 5
15 PHI W 7- 3
16 PHI W 5- 1
17 was L 3- 6
18 NG
19 was L 2- 3f
" was L 1- 5
20 NG
21 NG
22 DET W 4- 2
23 DET W 1- 0
24 DET L 1- 2
25 DET W 2- 1j
26 CLE W 3- 2
" CLE W 6- 5f
27 CLE W 5- 2
28 CLE L 3- 11
29 CHI L 0- 3
" CHI W 4- 0
30 CHI L 3- 8

October, 1943
1 STL *
2 STL W 5- 1
" STL W 7- 6
3 STL W 5- 2

END OF 1943
RUNS: 669
OPP RUNS: 542

CLUB VS. CLUB AND MONTHLY RECORDS OF THE NEW YORK YANKEES' 1943 SEASON FOR HOME AND AWAY GAMES

CLUB:		APR	MAY	JUN	JUL	AUG	SEP	OCT	HOME	AWAY	TOTAL
BOST	H	1-0	4-0	1-1	xxx	3-1	xxx	xxx	9-2	xxx	17-5
	A	2-1	xxx	1-2	xxx	xxx	5-0	xxx	xxx	8-3	
CHIC	H	xxx	1-1	0-1	3-2	xxx	1-2	xxx	5-6	xxx	12-10
	A	xxx	0-2	xxx	4-1	3-1	xxx	xxx	xxx	7-4	
CLEV	H	xxx	3-0	xxx	3-1	xxx	3-1	xxx	9-2	xxx	13-9
	A	xxx	0-3	1-0	0-2	3-2	xxx	xxx	xxx	4-7	
DET	H	xxx	1-1	xxx	0-1	3-1	3-1	xxx	7-4	xxx	12-10
	A	xxx	xxx	xxx	1-3	4-3	xxx	xxx	xxx	5-6	
PHIL	H	xxx	2-2	xxx	4-0	xxx	3-0	xxx	9-2	xxx	16-6
	A	xxx	xxx	3-2	xxx	3-1	1-1	xxx	xxx	7-4	
STL	H	xxx	xxx	4-1	2-1	xxx	xxx	3-0	9-2	xxx	17-5
	A	xxx	1-1	xxx	4-0	3-2	xxx	xxx	xxx	8-3	
WAS	H	2-0	xxx	2-3	xxx	xxx	2-2	xxx	6-5	xxx	11-11
	A	0-1	2-1	3-1	xxx	xxx	0-3	xxx	xxx	5-6	
TOTAL:	H	3-0	11-4	7-6	12-5	6-2	12-6	3-0	54-23	xxx	98-56
	A	2-2	3-7	8-5	9-6	16-9	6-4	xxx	xxx	44-33	
GRAND TOT:		5-2	14-11	15-11	21-11	22-11	18-10	3-0	xxx	xxx	
CUMUL TOT:		5-2	19-13	34-24	55-35	77-46	95-56	98-56	xxx	xxx	

TIE GAMES: 1
bos-June

1944

MANHANDLED BY THE BROWNIES

After three consecutive A.L. pennants, New York fell to third place, six games behind the St. Louis Browns. St. Louis claimed their *only* pennant in history (they would later transfer to Baltimore in 1954 and go on to win A.L. flags as the Orioles).

A Yankee streak of sorts came to a halt this season. Since 1925, every New York team hit at least 100 homers. This year, the Bombers only got 96 roundtrippers, but still led the league. The Yankees also led the league in team slugging (.387). Stirnweiss won A.L. honors with 125 runs, 205 hits, 146 singles, and 55 stolen bases. Lindell paced the league with 297 total bases, one more than teammate Stirnweiss, and tied for the three-bagger lead (16) with Stirnweiss also. The 74 New York triples were a league high. Etten, Yank first baseman, powered the most homers with 22, which was the lowest total to lead the A.L. since Ruth's (Boston) and Walker's (Philadelphia) eleven in 1918. Nick Etten also walked the most frequently (97) in the Junior Circuit.

The pitching was not as dominant as in the previous seasons but their fielding netted them the league's fewest errors (156) and best average (.974). In 1944, the Yanks were beset by player losses due to the Second World War, as were other major league clubs. This was the year for St. Louis Brown fans to cherish forever.

The 1944 DAY BY DAY scores follow:

DAY BY DAY, 1944 NEW YORK YANKEES

April, 1944
18 bos W 3- 0
19 bos L 1- 6
" bos L 2- 5
20 NG
21 WAS *
22 WAS W 6- 3
23 WAS *
24 NG
25 PHI L 4- 8
26 PHI W 6- 2
27 PHI *
28 NG
29 was L 3- 9
30 w as W 2- 1
" was W 3- 2

May, 1944
1 NG
2 phi W 4- 1
3 phi W 3- 1
4 NG
5 BOS W 11- 7
6 BOS W 4- 3
7 BOS *
8 NG
9 NG
10 DET L 2- 4
11 DET W 5- 2
12 DET L 4-10
13 CLE W 5- 1
14 CLE W 4- 3
" CLE W 8- 4
15 CHI W 10- 2
16 CHI L4- 10
17 CHI L 0- 4
18 CHI L 4- 8f
19 STL L 5- 6
20 STL W 3- 2
21 STL W 4- 3
" STL W 8- 1h
22 NG
23 NG
24 chi *
25 chi *
26 chi W 4- 0
27 chi L 3- 4
28 stl W 6- 3g
" stl W 6- 2
29 stl L 3-11
30 det L 1- 2
" det L 1- 4
31 det L 2- 6

June, 1944
1 det L 3- 4
2 cle W 5- 1
3 cle L 4- 5
4 cle W 6- 4g
" cle L 3- 4
5 NG
6 NG
7 bos L 1- 8
8 bos L 7- 8
9 NG
10 bos *
11 bos L 1- 2
" bos L 1- 4
12 was L 3- 4g
13 was L 0- 3
14 was W 6- 2
15 wa s L 2- 3
16 PHI W 6- 1
17 PHI W 2- 1
" PHI L 3- 5
18 PHI L 0- 4
" PHI . L 6- 8
19 WAS *
20 WAS W 3- 1
21 WAS W 4- 3
" WAS L 4- 6
22 WAS W 4- 0
23 phi W 5- 1
24 phi *
25 phi W 4- 3
" phi W 5- 2
26 NG
27 NG
28 STL W 7- 2
29 STL W 1- 0
30 STL L 0- 3

July, 1944
1 CHI L 2- 3
2 CHI L 3- 7f
" CHI W 7- 6
3 NG
4 CLE L 1- 3
" CLE L 2- 7
5 CLE W 6- 2
6 CLE W 4- 0
7 DET W 3- 1
8 DET L 2- 6
9 DET W 4- 3
" DET W 8- 2
10 ALL-STAR BREAK
11 WON   39
12 LOST - 35
13 BOS W 4- 2
" BOS L 4- 8
14 BOS W 4- 3
15 BOS W 9- 7
16 BOS W 7- 1
" BOS *
17 NG
18 stl L 0- 8
19 stl W 6- 5
20 stl L 3- 7
21 stl W 8- 2
22 chi L 3- 9
" chi L 1- 4
23 chi W 7- 6
" chi L 6-10
24 chi W 11- 5
25 cle L 0-10
26 cle W 6- 3
27 cle L 1- 8
28 cle W 13- 7
29 det L 2- 3f
30 det W 10- 2
" det   L7- 13
31 NG

August, 1944
1 det   L 4- 8
2 NG
3 NG
4 phi   W 1- 0
5 phi   L 1- 2
" phi   L 0- 2
6 phi   W 6- 1
" phi   W 1- 0
7 NG
8 NG
9 STL   L 2- 3
10 STL   L 0- 3
11 STL W 6- 1
12 STL   L 3- 8
13 CHI W 10- 1
" CHI   L 3-11
14 CHI W 2- 1i
15 CHI W 3- 1
16 CLE W 11- 8
17 CLE W 10- 3
18 CLE   L 0- 2
19 CLE W 9- 3
20 DET   L 3- 4
" DET   L 8- 9
21 DET W 5- 1
22 DET W 9- 7
23 NG
24 NG
25 was W 4- 2
26 was W 10- 3
27 was W 4- 2
" was   L 4- 5
28 BOS   L 4- 7
29 BOS   L1- 8
" BOS W 11- 2
30 BOS W 9- 7
31 WAS W 9- 4
" WAS W 4- 3

September, 1944
1 WAS   L 7-10
2 WAS W 3- 1
3 WAS W 6- 5
" WAS W 11- 3
4 PHI W 10- 0
" PHI W 14- 0
5 NG
6 NG
7 NG
8 bos W 7- 6h
9 bos   L 1- 7
10 bos   L 2- 3
" bos W 4- 3
11 NG
12 NG
13 phi   *
14 phi   *
15 NG
16 PHI   L 3- 6
17 PHI   L 4- 5
" PHI   L 1- 2
18 NG
19 det   L 1- 4
20 det   L 2- 8
21 det W 5- 4f
22 cle W 7- 3
23 cle W 7- 2
24 cle   L 1- 4
25 chi W 3- 1h
" chi W 5- 4
26 chi W 9- 5
27 chi W 7- 2
28 stl   *
29 stl   L 1- 4
" stl   L 0- 1
30 stl   L 0- 2

October, 1944
1 stl   L 2- 5
END OF 1944
RUNS: 674
OPP RUNS: 617

CLUB VS. CLUB AND MONTHLY RECORDS OF THE
NEW YORK YANKEES' 1944 SEASON FOR HOME AND AWAY GAMES

CLUB:		APR	MAY	JUN	JUL	AUG	SEP	OCT	HOME	AWAY	TOTAL
BOST	H	xxx	2- 0	xxx	4- 1	2- 2	xxx	xxx	8- 3	xxx	11- 11
	A	1-2	xxx	0- 4	xxx	xxx	2- 2	xxx	xxx	3- 8	
CHIC	H	xxx	1- 3	xxx	1- 2	3- 1	xxx	xxx	5- 6	xxx	12-10
	A	xxx	1- 1	xxx	2- 3	xxx	4- 0	xxx	xxx	7- 4	
CLEV	H	xxx	3- 0	xxx	2- 2	3- 1	xxx	xxx	8- 3	xxx	14- 8
	A	xxx	xxx	2- 2	2- 2	xxx	2- 1	xxx	xxx	6- 5	
DET	H	xxx	1- 2	xxx	3- 1	2- 2	xxx	xxx	6- 5	xxx	8-14
	A	xxx	0- 3	0- 1	1- 2	0- 1	1- 2	xxx	xxx	2- 9	
PHIL	H	1-1	xxx	2- 3	xxx	xxx	2- 3	xxx	5- 7	xxx	13- 9
	A	xxx	2- 0	3- 0	xxx	3- 2	xxx	xxx	xxx	8- 2	
STL	H	xxx	3- 1	2- 1	xxx	1- 3	xxx	xxx	6- 5	xxx	10-12
	A	xxx	2- 1	xxx	2- 2	xxx	0- 3	0- 1	xxx	4- 7	
WAS	H	1-0	xxx	3- 1	xxx	2- 0	3- 1	xxx	9- 2	xxx	15- 7
	A	2-1	xxx	1- 3	xxx	3- 1	xxx	xxx	xxx	6- 5	
TOTAL:	H	2-1	10- 6	7- 5	10- 6	13- 9	5- 4	xxx	47-31	xxx	83-71
	A	3-3	5- 5	6-10	7- 9	6- 4	9- 8	0- 1	xxx	36-40	
GRAND TOT:		5-4	15-11	13-15	17-15	19-13	14-12	0- 1	xxx	xxx	83-71
CUMUL TOT:		5-4	20-15	33-30	50-45	69-58	83-70	83-71	xxx	xxx	

TIE GAMES: NONE

1945

SNUFFY STIRNWEISS' YEAR

In January 1945, a trio of investors purchased the Yankee franchise from the heirs of the late Jacob Ruppert for the sum of $2.8 million. The new owners were Larry MacPhail, Dan Topping and Del Webb with the former assuming the triple role of club president, general manager and co-owner.

Under this new directorship, the Yankees finished no better than fourth place, 6½ games behind A.L. champion Detroit. Although finishing only ten games above .500 at 81–71 (.533), they led the league in runs scored (676), home runs (93) and slugging percentage (.373).

New York's season practically belonged to second baseman George "Snuffy" Stirnweiss, leading the league in several major statistical categories. While leading the league with hits, Stirnweiss became the only Yankee player to lead the league in base hits for two consecutive seasons. Snuffy led the Junior Circuit with a .309 batting average, the lowest league-leading figure since Elmer Flick's .306 with Cleveland in 1905. In addition, Stirnweiss paced the league with 195 hits, 107 runs scored, 301 total bases, 22 triples, 33 stolen bases, 632 at bats and a .476 slugging average. The latter slugging figure was the lowest to lead the league since Ty Cobb's .475 in 1908. While Stirnweiss was busy leading the American League in 8 statistical departments, Etten won the RBI crown with 111 ribbies.

It could be speculated that Stirnweiss may have been the league's most valuable player had the Yankees finished in their usual top slot. Their domination of the American League would begin anew, however, with the arrival of one Charles "Casey" Stengel on the pinstripe scene several years hence.

In April 1945, Albert Chandler replaced Landis as baseball's second commissioner. Chandler will retain this duty until his resignation in July 1951.

All in all, 1945 proved to be a relatively uneventful year for the Yankee franchise on the playing field.

The 1945 DAY BY DAY scores follow:

DAY BY DAY, 1945 NEW YORK YANKEES

April, 1945
```
16 was            *
17 BOS   W   8- 4
18 BOS   W   6- 2
19 BOS   W   4- 3
20 was   W   6- 3
21 was   L   1- 2
22 was   W   5- 2
23 NG
24 NG
25 phi            *
26 phi   L   5- 7
27 WAS   L   4- 6
28 WAS   W   2- 1i
29 WAS   W  13- 4
 " WAS   L   1- 2
30 NG
```

May, 1945
```
 1 PHI            *
 2 PHI   W   6- 4
 3 PHI            *
 4 bos            *
 5 bos   W   7- 3
 6 bos   L   0- 5
 " bos   W   2- 0
 7 NG
 8 NG
 9 det   L   1- 4
10 det            *
11 det   W   7- 3
12 cle   W   7- 3c
13 cle   W   1- 0f
 " cle   L   2- 4
14 chi            *
15 chi            *
16 chi            *
17 chi            *
18 stl   L   1- 4
19 stl   L   2- 4
20 stl   L   1-10
 " stl   L   2- 5
21 NG
22 PHI   W   3- 0
23 CHI   W   5- 3
24 CHI   W   6- 3
25 CHI   W   5- 4
26 CHI   W  13- 0
27 STL   W  10- 9j
 " STL   W   3- 1d
28 STL            *
29 STL   W  11- 0
30 DET   L   2- 3
 " DET   W   3- 2
31 DET   L   0- 2
```

June, 1945
```
 1 CLE   W   9- 2
 2 CLE   L   0- 4
 3 CLE   W   8- 2
 " CLE   L   1- 4
 4 NG
 5 was   W  12- 3
 " was   L   3- 7
 6 was   L   0- 4
 7 NG
 8 BOS   L   4- 6
 9 BOS   W  13- 7
10 BOS   W   3- 2
 " BOS            *
11 NG
12 WAS   L   3- 5
13 NG
14 NG
15 phi   L   3- 4
16 phi   L   3- 4f
17 phi   W   7- 1
 " phi   L   2- 4
18 NG
19 bos   L   0- 1
20 bos            *
 " bos            *
21 bos   W  14- 4
22 PHI   W   2- 0
23 PHI   W   7- 6
24 PHI   W  13- 5
 " PHI   W   6- 3
25 NG
26 stl   W   5- 4
27 stl   W   7- 2
28 stl   L   4- 9
29 NG
30 chi   L   1- 5
```

July, 1945
```
 1 chi       L4- 11
 " chi   L   5- 6
 2 chi   L   6-11
 " chi   W   6- 1
 3 cle   L   2- 5
 4 cle   L   2- 4
 " cle   W   3- 2
 5 cle   L   1- 2g
 6 det   W   5- 4
 7 det   L   2- 3f
 8 det   W   8- 6
 " det       L2- 3
 9 ALL-STAR BREAK
10 WON  - 39
11 LOST   33
12 CLE   L   4- 7
13 CLE   L   4-16
14 CLE   W   4- 2
15 DET   W   5- 4
 " DET            *
16 DET   L   4- 9
17 DET            *
18 STL            *
 " STL            *
19 STL            *
 " STL            *
20 STL   L   3- 4
 " STL   L   2- 3
21 CHI   W  12- 3
22 CHI   L   5- 6h
23 CHI   L   0- 1g
24 NG
25 NG
26 PHI   W  13- 4
27 PHI   W   2- 0
28 PHI            *
29 PHI   W   2- 1f
 " PHI   W  11- 3
30 NG
31 bos   W   4- 2f
```

August, 1945
```
 1 bos   L   5- 7
 2 bos   W   3- 1
 3 phi   W   4- 1
 4 phi   W   5- 1
 5 phi   L3- 6
 " phi   L   3- 4
 6 NG
 7 NG
 8 cle   L   0- 1
 9 cle   W   3- 2
10 cle   W  10- 4
11 cle   L   3- 5
12 det   L   6- 9g
 " det   L   2- 8
13 det       L4- 15
 " det       L9- 11
14 det            *
15 stl       L4- 10
16 stl   L   2- 7
17 stl   L   1- 4
18 stl   L   1- 3
19 chi   W   4- 2
 " chi   L   0- 2
20 chi   W   4- 1
21 chi   W   3- 0
 " chi   W   6- 2
22 chi   L   5- 6g
23 NG
24 WAS            *
25 WAS   W   4- 2
 " WAS   W   5- 4f
26 WAS   W   3- 2
 " WAS   W   7- 1
27 NG
28 BOS   W   8- 7
29 BOS   L   0- 1
30 BOS   W   7- 1
31 was   W   3- 2
 " was   W   3- 1
```

September, 1945
```
 1 was   L   0- 3
 2 was   W   4- 2
 " was   L   0- 3
 3 phi   W   4- 1
 " phi   W   7- 6g
 4 DET   L   0-10
 5 DET   L   7-10
 " DET   W   5- 1
 6 DET   W  14- 5
 " DET   L   2- 5
 7 DET   L   0- 5
 8 DET   L   4-11
 9 CLE   L   3-10
 " CLE   L   3- 4c
10 CLE   W   5- 1
11 CLE            *
12 CHI   W   3- 1
 " CHI   W   9- 8f
13 CHI   L   0- 7f
14 CHI            *
15 STL   W   7- 4
 " STL   L   3- 8
16 STL   L   2- 6
 " STL   W   5- 4
17 STL            *
18 STL            *
 " STL            *
19 STL   L   5- 6f
 " STL   L   3- 4f
20 WAS   W   6- 1
21 WAS   W   5- 3
22 bos   W   2- 1
23 bos   L   5- 6j
 " bos   W   2- 1a
24 NG
25 NG
26 NG
27 PHI   W   8- 1
28 NG
29 BOS   W   5- 0
30 NG
```

October, 1945
```
 1 BOS   W  12- 2
END OF 1945
RUNS:        676
OPP RUNS:    606
```

CLUB VS. CLUB AND MONTHLY RECORDS OF THE NEW YORK YANKEES' 1945 SEASON FOR HOME AND AWAY GAMES

CLUB:		APR	MAY	JUN	JUL	AUG	SEP	OCT	HOME	AWAY	TOTAL
BOST	H	3-0	xxx	2- 1	xxx	2- 1	1- 0	1- 0	9- 2	xxx	16- 6
	A	xxx	2- 1	1- 1	1- 0	1- 1	2- 1	xxx	xxx	7- 4	
CHIC	H	xxx	4- 0	xxx	1- 2	xxx	2- 1	xxx	7- 3	xxx	12- 9
	A	xxx	xxx	0- 1	1- 3	4- 2	xxx	xxx	xxx	5- 6	
CLEV	H	xxx	xxx	2- 2	1- 2	xxx	1- 2	xxx	4- 6	xxx	9-12
	A	xxx	2- 1	xxx	1- 3	2- 2	xxx	xxx	xxx	5- 6	
DET	H	xxx	1- 2	xxx	1- 1	xxx	2- 5	xxx	4- 8	xxx	7-15
	A	xxx	1- 1	xxx	2- 2	0- 4	xxx	xxx	xxx	3- 7	
PHIL	H	xxx	2- 0	4- 0	4- 0	xxx	1- 0	xxx	11- 0	xxx	16- 6
	A	0- 1	xxx	1- 3	xxx	2- 2	2- 0	xxx	xxx	5- 6	
STL	H	xxx	3- 0	xxx	0- 2	xxx	2- 4	xxx	5- 6	xxx	7-15
	A	xxx	0- 4	2- 1	xxx	0- 4	xxx	xxx	xxx	2- 9	
WAS	H	2-2	xxx	0- 1	xxx	4- 0	2- 0	xxx	8- 3	xxx	14- 8
	A	2-1	xxx	1- 2	xxx	2- 0	1- 2	xxx	xxx	6- 5	
TOTAL:	H	5-2	10- 2	8- 4	7- 7	6- 1	11-12	1- 0	48-28	xxx	81-71
	A	2-2	5- 7	5- 8	5- 8	11-15	5- 3	xxx	xxx	33-43	
GRAND TOT:		7-4	15- 9	13-12	12-15	17-16	16-15	1- 0	xxx	xxx	**TIE GAMES:** NONE
CUMUL TOT:		7-4	22-13	35-25	47-40	64-56	80-71	81-71	xxx	xxx	

1946

THE DEPARTURE OF JOE McCARTHY

After guiding New York to eight A.L. pennants in 15 complete seasons as manager, Joe McCarthy resigned in May, being replaced by Bill Dickey and later by Johnny Neun, who concluded the season at the Yankee helm. New York came in at third place (87–67, .565), seventeen games off Boston's 1st place pace. In addition to 8 pennants and seven World Series Championships, McCarthy-led teams finished no worse than fourth place on one occasion, third place twice and four runner-up positions.

With World War II concluded, many Yankee players returned to the club from military duty. Players such as Joe DiMaggio, Spud Chandler, Charlie Keller and Tommy Henrich were back again in the New York lineup. No Yankee batters placed first in any major statistical departments. As a team, New York dominated the A.L. with 136 home runs. The pitching staff permitted the fewest opponent runs with 547. The Yanks also turned the most double plays with 174.

On April 30, Bob Feller tossed a no-hitter against New York, Cleveland winning 1–0. This marked the first time the Yanks were held hitless since Caldwell's gem in September, 1919.

This year's Yankee club had an off year due in part to the regrouping of players returning from military service. In 1947, the Yanks will return to their top slot in the American League.

The 1946 DAY BY DAY scores follow:

DAY BY DAY, 1946 NEW YORK YANKEES

April, 1946	May, 1946	June, 1946	August, 1946	September, 1946
16 phi W 5- 0	26 bos L 0- 1	30 PHI L 3- 6	3 NG	5 phi W 6- 2
17 phi L 1- 7	" bos W 4- 1c	**July, 1946**	4 cle W 2- 0	6 phi L 3- 4
18 phi W 8- 1	27 WAS *	1 NG	" cle *	7 was W 7- 4
19 WAS W 7- 6	28 WAS L 1- 2	2 BOS W 2- 1	5 NG	8 was L 1- 2g
20 WAS L 3- 7	29 WAS W 4- 0	3 BOS W 3- 2	6 was *	" was L 8- 9d
21 WAS W 6- 1	30 PHI W 6- 1	4 was L 0- 2	7 was L 3- 4	9 NG
22 PHI W 2- 1	" PHI W 6- 3	" was W 5- 0	8 w as W 9- 3	10 cle L 2- 4
23 PHI W 3- 0	31 PHI W 8- 1	5 was L 1- 6	" was W 13- 1	11 cle L 2-11
24 bos W 12- 5	**June, 1946**	6 phi W 8- 5	9 BOS L 3- 4	12 de t L 4- 6
25 bos L5- 12	1 STL L 3- 4	7 phi W 7- 3	10 BOS W 7- 5h	13 det W 5- 4
26 was W 11- 7	2 STL *	" phi L 1-4	11 BOS L 5-7	14 det L 4-7
27 wa s W 9- 0	" STL *	8 ALL-STAR BREAK	" BOS W 9- 1c	15 stl L 0- 1
28 was L 1- 3	3 STL W 12- 2	9 WON - 47	12 NG	" stl L 1- 2
29 CLE *	4 CHI W 2- 1	10 LOST - 31	13 WAS *	16 stl W 7- 5
30 CLE L 0- 1	5 CHI W 9- 6	11 CLE W 9- 1	14 WAS W 4- 1	17 NG
May, 1946	6 CHI W 4- 0	12 NG	15 WAS W 6- 1	18 chi W 4- 0
1 CLE W 6- 3	7 CLE W 6- 5g	13 CLE L 2- 3	" WAS W 7- 2	" chi L 7- 9
2 CLE W 8- 2	8 CLE L 1- 2	14 D ET L 1- 5	16 bos L 1- 4	19 NG
3 DET W 2- 0	9 CLE L 5- 9	" DET L 3- 6	17 bos L 4- 7	20 NG
4 DET W 4- 3	" CLE W 7- 4	15 DET L 0- 2	18 bos W 5- 0	21 PHI *
5 CHI W 4- 2	10 DET L 3-11	16 NG	" bos L 3- 4	22 PHI W 4- 3
6 CHI L 1- 2	11 DET L 3- 8	17 STL W 3- 2	19 CHI *	" PHI W 7- 4b
7 CHI *	12 DET L 5- 6	" STL W 8- 4	20 CHI L 2- 9	23 PHI W 9- 6
8 STL W 5- 1	13 NG	18 STL W 3- 1	21 CHI W 10- 1	24 bos L 4- 5
9 ST L L 1- 6	14 stl W 6- 1	19 NG	" CHI W 5- 4h	25 bos L 2- 5
10 BOS L 4- 5	15 stl L 3- 6	20 CHI W 7- 0	22 STL W 4- 3	26 NG
11 BOS W 2- 0	16 stl W 9- 2	21 CHI W 3- 2	" STL W 8- 2	27 NG
12 BOS L 1- 3	" stl W 7- 5f	" CHI L 3- 9	23 STL W 4- 1	28 NG
13 NG	17 NG	22 NG	24 STL L 2- 9	29 phi W 6- 0
14 stl W 6- 2	18 chi *	23 stl L 2- 8	25 DET L 2- 7	" phi W 2- 1c
15 stl L 2- 8	19 chi *	24 stl W 5- 3	26 DET W 10- 6	**END OF 1946**
16 chi *	20 chi L 1- 3	25 NG	27 DET L 4- 7f	RUNS: 684
17 chi W 4- 2	" chi W 6- 1	26 chi W 6- 2	28 CLE W 4- 0	OPP RUNS: 547
18 chi L 1- 5	21 det L 2- 6	27 chi W 10- 4	29 CLE W 9- 1	
19 cle W 2- 0	22 det W 5- 3	28 chi L 0- 2	30 NG	
" cle W 7- 1	23 det W 10- 8g	" chi W 7- 1	31 was W 4- 0	
20 cle L 3- 4	24 cle W 1- 0	29 chi L 3- 4h	**September, 1946**	
21 cle L 2- 7	25 cle L 3- 8	30 det L 5- 6	1 was W 7- 2	
22 det W 5- 3	26 cle W 8- 4	31 det L 0- 6	2 bos L 2- 5	
23 det W 12- 6	27 NG	**August, 1946**	" bos L 1- 3	
24 NG	28 PHI W 4- 1	1 det W 4- 2	3 NG	
25 bos L 4- 7	29 PHI L 0- 2	2 cle L 0- 3	4 phi L 3- 4	

CLUB VS. CLUB AND MONTHLY RECORDS OF THE NEW YORK YANKEES' 1946 SEASON FOR HOME AND AWAY GAMES

CLUB:		APR	MAY	JUN	JUL	AUG	SEP	OCT	HOME	AWAY	TOTAL
BOST	H	xxx	1- 2	xxx	2- 0	2- 2	0- 2	xxx	5- 6	xxx	8-14
	A	1-1	1- 2	xxx	xxx	1- 3	0- 2	xxx	xxx	3- 8	
CHIC	H	xxx	1- 1	3- 0	2- 1	2- 1	xxx	xxx	8- 3	xxx	14- 8
	A	xxx	1- 1	1- 1	3- 2	xxx	1- 1	xxx	xxx	6- 5	
CLEV	H	0-1	2- 0	2- 2	1- 1	2- 0	xxx	xxx	7- 4	xxx	12-10
	A	xxx	2- 2	2- 1	xxx	1- 1	0- 2	xxx	xxx	5- 6	
DET	H	xxx	2- 0	0- 3	0- 3	1- 2	xxx	xxx	3- 8	xxx	9-13
	A	xxx	2- 0	2- 1	0- 2	1- 0	1- 2	xxx	xxx	6- 5	
PHIL	H	2-0	3- 0	1- 2	xxx	xxx	3- 0	xxx	9- 2	xxx	16- 6
	A	2-1	xxx	xxx	2- 1	xxx	3- 2	xxx	xxx	7- 4	
STL	H	xxx	1- 1	1- 1	3- 0	3- 1	xxx	xxx	8- 3	xxx	14- 8
	A	xxx	1- 1	3- 1	1- 1	xxx	1- 2	xxx	xxx	6- 5	
WAS	H	2-1	1- 1	xxx	xxx	3- 0	1- 2	xxx	7- 4	xxx	14- 8
	A	2-1	xxx	xxx	1- 2	3- 1	1- 0	xxx	xxx	7- 4	
TOTAL:	H	4-2	11- 5	7- 8	8- 5	13- 6	4- 4	xxx	47-30	xxx	87-67
	A	5-3	7- 6	8- 4	7- 8	6- 5	7-11	xxx	xxx	40-37	
GRAND TOT:		9-5	18-11	15-12	15-13	19-11	11-15	xxx	xxx	xxx	TIE GAMES: NONE
CUMUL TOT:		9-5	27-16	42-28	57-41	76-52	87-67	xxx	xxx	xxx	

1947

BACK ON TOP AGAIN

The Yankees won their 15th A.L. pennant (and eleventh World Series by defeating the Brooklyn Dodgers) after a three year drought. Since their first A.L. championship in 1921, New York never went longer than four years without a pennant, through 1947. Bucky Harris, New York's fifteenth manager, guided his players to a 97–57 (.630) season, ending the year twelve games ahead of runner-up Detroit. Joe DiMaggio won his third and final MVP Award. Although not leading any major statistical areas, "The Yankee Clipper" placed in the top 5 in several departments. Tommy Henrich hit the most triples in the A.L. with 13.

Collectively, the Yankees led in almost every major category. As a hitting unit, New York led the A.L. in homers for the twelfth successive season, a Major League record. Their streak was snapped next season, finishing second to Cleveland in total homers. Through 1947, the Yanks led the American League 28 times since 1915, not hitting the most homers in but 5 seasons (1918, 1922, 1932, 1934 and 1935) during that span. Twenty-eight homer titles in 33 years works out to a percentage of 84.8%, quite an impressive figure! The Yankees, who through 1983 have never led the A.L. in doubles, finished only four shy of Detroit's 234 two-bagger total. This was their closest "almost" two base hit crown in their history.

In addition, New York paced the A.L. with 794 runs scored, 72 triples, 1,439 hits, 746 RBI, .407 slugging average and a .271 team batting figure. They had not led the American League in batting since 1931, then with a .297 mark.

In pitching, New York fared well also, having an A.L. leading 3.39 team ERA. The mound staff was led by Spud Chandler and Allie Reynolds, who finished first in the league with a 2.46 ERA and .704 winning percentage (19 wins, 8 defeats), respectively. The staff also led with 691 strikeouts and permitted the fewest enemy batters from crossing the plate with a 568 figure. The only major area not dominated by New York was in fielding, placing second in the A.L. behind Cleveland. Their 109 errors were the fewest in Yankee history for an entire season (this mark was later duplicated by the 1964 Yankees).

This season saw the longest Yankee winning streak in their history, some 19 straight games. The Yankees did not lose a game from June 29 through July 17, the streak coming to a halt at Detroit on July 18, the Tigers winning 8-0. The Yanks' longest victory skein prior to this season was sixteen back in 1926.

On May 26, "Babe Ruth Day" was held at Yankee Stadium before a gathering of 74,747 approving fans. It also marked the inaugural Old Timers' Day game at the Stadium.

At the end of the 1947 season, Larry MacPhail sold his one-third of Yankee ownership for about $2 million to Topping and Webb, who now became co-owners of the Yankees. The Webb-Topping ownership will exist until the Yanks are sold to CBS (Columbia Broadcasting System) in 1964.

Yankee fans approved of their team's performance in 1947. New York would not repeat as a pennant winner in 1948.

The 1947 DAY BY DAY scores follow:

In 1947, Joltin' Joe DiMaggio won his third and final MVP Award.

DAY BY DAY, 1947 NEW YORK YANKEES

April, 1947

14	was		*
15	PHI	L	1- 6
16	PHI		*
17	PHI	W	2- 1
18	was	W	7- 0
19	was	L	2- 4
20	phi	W	6- 2
"	phi	W	3- 2f
21	NG		
22	BOS	W	5- 4
23	BOS	W	3- 0
24	BOS	L	0- 1
25	WAS		*
26	WAS	W	3- 1
27	WAS	L	0- 1
28	NG		
29	stl		*
30	stl	L	5-15

May, 1947

1	chi		*
2	chi	W	5- 2
3	chi	L	1- 2
"	chi	L	3-10
4	det	TG	2- 2b
5	det		*
6	det	L	2- 3
7	cle		*
8	cle		*
"	cle		*
9	NG		
10	bos	W	9- 6
11	bos	L	7- 8
12	bos	L	3- 4
13	STL	W	9- 1
14	STL		*
15	CHI	L	2- 8
16	NG		
17	CHI	W	4- 3
"	CHI	W	4- 3
18	CLE	L	3- 5
19	CLE	L	4- 5
20	CLE	L	2- 4

May, 1947

21	DET	W	5-0
22	DET		*
23	BOS	W	9-0
24	BOS	W	5-0
25	BOS	W	17-2
26	BOS	W	9-3
27	was	L	4-5
28	was	W	9- 5
29	was	W	5- 2
30	phi	L	0-1
"	phi	L	0-4
31	cle	W	8-4

June, 1947

1	cle	W	11-9
"	cle		*
2	cle		*
"	cle		*
3	det	W	3-0
4	det	L	2-6
"	det	W	17-8
5	det	W	7-0
6	stl	L	3-4
7	stl	W	3-1
8	stl	L	2-9
"	stl	W	5- 4
9	chi	L	8- 9f
10	chi	W	5- 3
11	chi	L	2- 3g
12	NG		
13	STL	L	3-4 f
14	STL	W	12-4
15	STL	W	10-4
"	STL	W	2-1
16	CHI	W	4-3
17	NG		
18	CHI		*
19	CHI	L	4- 6
20	DET	W	5- 3
21	DET	W	5-4
"	DET	W	7-4
22	DET	W	6-5
23	CLE	W	8-5

June, 1947

24	CLE		*
25	CLE	W	3- 0
26	phi	L	2- 4
27	phi	W	7- 1
28	phi	W	5- 2
29	was	L	1- 5
"	was	W	3- 1
30	bos	W	3- 1

July, 1947

1	NG		
2	WAS	W	8- 1
3	NG		
4	WAS	W	7- 3
"	WAS	W	4- 2
5	PHI	W	5- 1
6	PHI	W	8- 2
"	PHI	W	9 - 2
7	ALL-STAR BREAK		
8	WON		47
9	LOST -		26
10	stl	W	4- 3
11	stl	W	3- 1
12	stl	W	12- 2
"	stl	W	8- 5
13	chi	W	10- 3
"	chi	W	6- 4
14	chi		*
15	cle	W	9- 4
"	cle	W	2- 1
16	cle	W	8- 2
17	cle	W	3- 1
"	cle	W	7- 2
18	det	L	0- 8
19	det	W	2- 1
20	det	L	1- 4
"	det		L11-12g
21	NG		
22	STL	W	6- 0
23	STL	L	2- 8
24	STL	W	14- 5
25	CHI	W	12- 4
26	CHI	L	1- 2

July, 1947

27	CHI	W	7- 4
"	CHI	L	4- 5
28	DET	W	5- 1
29	NG		
30	DET	W	8- 5
31	DET		*

August, 1947

1	CLE	L	3- 4
2	CLE	W	3- 2j
"	CLE	W	3- 0
3	CLE	W	5- 4
4	PHI	L	5- 9
5	phi	W	8- 5
6	phi	L	3- 5
7	NG		
8	bos	L	6- 9
9	bos	L	4- 6
10	bos	W	2- 1
11	PHI	L	2- 3
12	NG		
13	PHI	W	8- 2
14	PHI	W	8- 5
15	BOS	W	10- 6
16	BOS	W	1- 0
17	BOS	L	0- 3g
18	NG		
19	det	L	1- 2
20	det	W	14-13g
21	cle	W	9- 3
22	cle	L	3- 4
"	cle	L	1- 6
23	cle	W	13- 6
24	chi	L	2- 3
"	chi	W	16- 6c
25	chi	L	3- 4
26	stl	L	3- 4
27	stl	W	7- 6f
28	NG		
29	WAS	W	4- 3f
30	WAS	W	6- 5
31	WAS	W	6- 5
"	WAS	W	5- 1

September, 1947

1	bos	L	3- 6
"	bos	L	1- 4
2	bos		*
3	bos	W	11-2
"	bos	W	9-6
4	was	L	2-3
5	was	L	4- 5
6	was	L	6-9
7	was	W	7-1
8	CLE	L	3-4
9	NG		
10	CLE	W	7- 4
11	DET	L	2- 7
"	DET	W	11- 5
12	DET	L	2- 7
13	DET	W	5- 2
14	STL	W	6- 4
15	STL		*
16	STL	W	8-3
"	STL	L	2-8
17	CHI	W	5-0
18	CHI	W	3-1
19	NG		
20	phi	L	2-3
21	phi	W	6-0
22	WAS		*
23	WAS	W	2-0
"	WAS	W	3- 1
24	NG		
25	BOS		*
26	BOS	L	2- 3
27	PHI	L	1-2f
28	PHI	W	5-3
END OF 1947			
RUNS;			794
OPP RUNS:			568

CLUB VS. CLUB AND MONTHLY RECORDS OF THE NEW YORK YANKEES' 1947 SEASON FOR HOME AND AWAY GAMES

CLUB:		APR	MAY	JUN	JUL	AUG	SEP	OCT	HOME	AWAY	TOTAL
BOST	H	2-1	4-0	xxx	xxx	2-1	0-1	xxx	8-3	xxx	13-9
	A	xxx	1-2	1-0	xxx	1-2	2-2	xxx	xxx	5-6	
CHIC	H	xxx	2-1	1-1	2-2	xxx	2-0	xxx	7-4	xxx	12-10
	A	xxx	1-2	1-2	2-0	1-2	xxx	xxx	xxx	5-6	
CLEV	H	xxx	0-3	2-0	xxx	3-1	1-1	xxx	6-5	xxx	15-7
	A	xxx	1-0	1-0	5-0	2-2	xxx	xxx	xxx	9-2	
DET	H	xxx	1-0	4-0	2-0	xxx	2-2	xxx	9-2	xxx	14-8
	A	xxx	0-1	3-1	1-3	1-1	xxx	xxx	xxx	5-6	
PHIL	H	1-1	xxx	xxx	3-0	2-2	1-1	xxx	7-4	xxx	13-9
	A	2-0	0-2	2-1	xxx	1-1	1-1	xxx	xxx	6-5	
STL	H	xxx	1-0	3-1	2-1	xxx	2-1	xxx	8-3	xxx	15-7
	A	0-1	xxx	2-2	4-0	1-1	xxx	xxx	xxx	7-4	
WAS	H	1-1	xxx	xxx	3-0	4-0	2-0	xxx	10-1	xxx	15-7
	A 1-1	2-1	1-1	xxx	xxx	1-3	xxx	xxx	5-6		
TOTAL:	H	4-3	8-4	10-2	12-3	11-4	10-6	xxx	55-22	xxx	97-57
	A	3-2	5-8	11-7	12-3	7-9	4-6	xxx	xxx	42-35	
GRAND TOT:	H	7-5	13-12	21-9	24-6	18-13	14-12	xxx	xxx	xxx	
CUMUL TOT:		7-5	20-17	41-26	65-32	83-45	97-57	xxx	xxx	xxx	

TIE GAMES: 1
det-May

1948

THIRD PLACE AGAIN

In his second and final year at the Yankee helm, Bucky Harris' Yankees ended the campaign in third place, 2½ games behind Cleveland, the A.L. winner. Cleveland had to defeat Boston in a one game playoff, a first in American League history. In fact, the Yanks were only eliminated from the A.L. pennant chase on the next to last day of the season, losing at Boston 5–1 on October 2.

Joe DiMaggio paced the A.L. with 39 homers, 155 RBI and 355 total bases. Tommy "Old Reliable" Henrich got the most A.L. triples (14) for the second straight year. The Yankee team pounded out a league high 75 triples and .432 slugging mark. The pitching and defensive play were not up to the caliber of most recent Yankee clubs.

Two club records were set this season. Their 24 stolen base total was the lowest in their history (high was 288 steals in 1910). Phil Rizzuto, "The Scooter," led the club with but six stolen sacks. On a more positive note, New York batters hammered out seven grand slam homers, another club record (until tied by the Yankee 1980 team).

On June 13, Babe Ruth's uniform became the second to be retired in ceremonies at Yankee Stadium. Number 3 was never to be worn again by Yankee ballplayers. Gehrig's uniform (No. 4) had been previously retired in 1939.

On August 16, Babe Ruth succumbed to throat cancer after a gallant fight. A wake was held in Yankee Stadium with tens of thousands of mourners paying their last respects to this beloved man. His loss was felt throughout the nation.

At the conclusion of this season no one could have dreamed what was in store for the Yankees in the next several years. The emergence of Casey Stengel as New York manager extraordinaire was soon to be realized by the entire baseball world.

The 1948 DAY BY DAY scores follow:

DAY BY DAY, 1948 NEW YORK YANKEES

April, 1948
19 was W 12-4
20 was L 1-9
21 was L 3-6
22 NG
23 BOS L 0- 4
24 BOS W 7-2
25 BOS W 5-4
26 NG
27 phi W 4-2
28 WAS *
29 WAS W 5-4f
30 bos W 6- 0

May, 1948
1 bos L 6-8
2 bos L 1-7
3 NG
4 STL W 6-1
5 STL *
6 STL W 6-5
7 DET *
8 DET L 2-3
" DET W 9-1
9 CHI W 8-0
10 CHI W 9- 3
11 CLE W 4- 1
12 CLE *
13 CLE *
14 PHI W 3-0
15 PHI L 1-3
" PHI L 6-8
16 PHI *
17 NG
18 stl L 5-6
19 stl W 8-4
20 chi W 13-2
21 chi L 0-3
22 chi W 10-2
23 cle W 6-5
" cle L 1-5
24 NG
25 det W 16- 5
26 det L 3- 7

MAy, 1948
27 NG
28 phi L 3- 6
29 phi L 5- 6
30 phi L 6- 7f
" phi W 2- 1a
31 WAS W 10- 0
" WAS W 5- 4

June, 1948
1 WAS L 1- 4
2 DET W 1- 0
3 DET L 2- 6g
4 DET W 7- 4
5 STL W 7- 1
6 STL W 4- 3
" STL W 3- 0
7 STL L 3- 5
8 CHI W 3- 2h
9 CHI *
10 CHI *
11 CLE L 8-10
12 CLE L 5- 7
" CLE L 4- 9
13 CLE W 5- 3
14 NG
15 chi L 8- 9g
16 chi W 3- 1
17 NG
18 stl L 1- 2
19 stl W 10- 5
20 stl W 4- 2
" stl W 6- 2
21 cle W 13- 2
22 cle L 2- 5
23 cle W 5- 1g
24 cle W 4- 0
25 det L 2- 4
26 det W 8- 5
27 det W 7- 0
28 NG
29 BOS W 7- 0
30 .BOS L 3- 7

July, 1948
1 BOS W 10- 7
2 WAS L 1- 2h
3 WAS W 5- 3
4 WAS W 6- 5
5 bos L 5- 6
" bos L 7- 8
6 bos L 1- 2
7 PHI L 3- 4
8 PHI W 6- 5
9 was W 9- 0
10 was W 5- 2f
11 was L 4- 9
12 ALL-STAR BREAK
13 WON – 44
14 LOST – 32
15 STL W 4- 2
16 STL L 4-10
17 STL W 4- 0
18 DET L 3- 5
" DET W 12- 4c
19 DET *
20 DET L 1- 2
21 CLE W 7- 3
" CLE L 8-12
22 CLE W 6- 5
23 CLE *
24 CHI W 6- 2
" CHI L 4- 8f
25 CHI W 5- 3
" CHI W 7- 3
26 NG
27 stl L 0- 4
28 stl W 4– 0
29 NG
30 chi L 7- 8
31 chi W 4- 2

August, 1948
1 chi W 8- 2
" chi W 7- 5
2 NG
3 det W 15- 3
4 det *

August, 1948
5 det W 2- 1
6 cle L 7- 9
7 cle W 5- 0
8 cle L 6- 8
" cle L 1- 2
9 NG
10 BOS L 6- 9
11 BOS L 2- 5
12 BOS *
13 PHI W 8- 5
14 PHI W 14- 3
15 PHI L 3- 5f
" PHI L 3- 5
16 NG
17 was W 8- 1
18 was W 4- 1a
19 was W 8- 1
20 phi W 6- 2
21 phi W 6- 0
22 phi W 10- 0
" phi *
23 CHI W 11- 1
24 CHI L 5- 6
25 CHI W 8- 2
26 CHI W 6- 2
27 CLE L 1- 8
" CLE W 7- 2
28 CLE W 3- 2
29 DET L 6- 9
" DET W 11-10
30 DET W 3- 0
31 STL W 10- 9

September, 1948
1 STL W 5- 4h
2 NG
3 WAS W 6- 2
" WAS W 5- 2
4 WAS W 9- 7
5 WAS W 5- 3
6 PHI W 6- 4
" PHI L 2- 6
7 NG

September, 1948
8 bos L 6-10
9 bos L 4- 9
10 bos W 11- 6f
11 was W 6- 3
12 was W 10- 5
13 NG
14 cle W 6- 5
15 NG
16 det L 1- 2
" det W 8- 4
17 det W 13- 5
18 det l3- 4
19 stl L 6- 8
" stl W 9- 6
20 stl W 8- 7
21 NG
22 chi W 7- 2
23 chi L 2- 4
24 BOS W 9- 6
25 BOS L 2- 7
26 BOS W 6- 2
27 NG
28 phi L 2- 5
29 phi W 4- 2
30 phi W 9- 7

October, 1948
1 NG
2 bos L 1- 5
3 bos L 5-10
END OF 1948
RUNS: 857
OPP RUNS: 633

CLUB VS. CLUB AND MONTHLY RECORDS OF THE NEW YORK YANKEES' 1948 SEASON FOR HOME AND AWAY GAMES

CLUB:	APR	MAY	JUN	JUL	AUG	SEP	OCT	HOME	AWAY	TOTAL:
BOST H	2-1	xxx	1-1	1-0	0-2	2-1	xxx	6-5	xxx	8-14
A	1-0	0-2	xxx	0-3	xxx	1-2	0-2	xxx	2-9	
CHIC H	xxx	2-0	1-0	3-1	3-1	xxx	xxx	9-2	xxx	16-6
A	xxx	2-1	1-1	1-1	2-0	1-1	xxx	xxx	7-4	
CLEV H	xxx	1-0	1-3	2-1	2-1	xxx	xxx	6-5	xxx	12-10
A	xxx	1-1	3-1	xxx	1-3	1-0	xxx	xxx	6-5	
DET H	xxx	1-1	2-1	1-2	2-1	xxx	xxx	6-5	xxx	13-9
A	xxx	1-1	2-1	xxx	2-0	2-2	xxx	xxx	7-4	
PHIL H	xxx	1-2	xxx	1-1	2-2	1-1	xxx	5-6	xxx	12-10
A	1-0	1-3	xxx	xxx	3-0	2-1	xxx	xxx	7-4	
STL H	xxx	2-0	3-1	2-1	1-0	1-0	xxx	9-2	xxx	16-6
A	xxx	1-1	3-1	1-1	xxx	2-1	xxx	xxx	7-4	
WAS H	1-0	2-0	0-1	2-1	xxx	4-0	xxx	9-2	xxx	17-5
A	1-2	xxx	xxx	2-1	3-0	2-0	xxx	xxx	8-3	
TOTAL: H	3-1	9-3	8-7	12-7	10-7	8-2	xxx	50-27	xxx	94-60
A	3-2	6-9	9-4	4-6	11-3	11-7	0-2	xxx	44-33	
GRAND TOT:	6-3	15-12	17-11	16-13	21-10	19-9	0-2			TIE GAMES: NONE
CUMUL TOT:	6-3	21-15	38-26	54-39	75-49	94-58	94-60			

1949

CASEY STENGEL COMES TO NEW YORK

Beginning their 47th season, Casey Stengel assumed the Yankee reins and thus began his twelve year tenure as New York manager. The Yankees eked past Boston by one full game to capture their sixteenth pennant and were victorious over Brooklyn, winning their twelfth World Championship. With Stengel at the helm, the Yankees will go on to win an incredible 10 pennants and 7 World Series in but a dozen seasons.

Joe Page, "The Fireman," bolstered the pitching staff, gaining 27 saves in 60 relief appearances, a then Yankee record. The Yankee mound staff totaled 36 saves and 671 strikeouts, both American League highs for 1949.

After playing 17 years in pinstripes, Frankie Crosetti, "The Crow," remained with New York as third base coach. His tenure as player and coach lasted from 1932 through 1968, some 37 seasons, longer than any Yankee mainstay in history.

No Yankee pitchers or batters led the league in any statistical category, a rarity when considering they won the World Series from Brooklyn. It probably did demonstrate balance on the club that would go on to record World Series victories in each of the next four seasons.

The 1949 DAY BY DAY scores follow:

DAY BY DAY, 1949 NEW YORK YANKEES

April, 1949
19 WAS W 3- 2
20 WAS W 3- 0
21 WAS W 2- 1
22 bos W 5- 3
23 bos L 8-11
24 bos W 9- 4
25 PHI W 3- 2
26 PHI W 5- 4
27 was L 3- 4f
28 was W 6- 2
29 BOS W 7- 1
30 BOS W 4- 3

May, 1949
1 BOS L2- 11d
2 NG
3 stl W 5- 3
4 stl W 10- 5
5 chi W 7- 5
6 chi L 2- 6
7 chi W 8- 1
8 det W 12- 0
9 det L 1- 4
10 det W 6- 1
11 cle L 2- 3
12 NG
13 NG
14 phi L 5- 8
15 phi L 7- 8g
" phi L 6- 7b
16 NG
17 CLE W 4- 3
18 CLE W 6- 0
19 CLE L 2- 3
20 CHI *
21 CHI W 4- 3
22 STL *
" STL *
23 STL W 10- 3
24 STL W 13- 3
25 DET W 6- 2
26 DET *
27 PHI W 3- 0

May, 1949
28 PHI W 2- 1j
29 PHI L 1- 3
30 was L 2- 6
" was W 13- 3

June, 1949
1 chi W 3- 0
2 chi W 12- 7
3 chi W 9- 7
4 stl W 11- 3
5 stl W 6- 4
" stl L 6- 7
6 NG
7 det L 2- 5
8 det L 2- 3f
9 det L 5- 9
10 cle W 3- 2
11 cle W 12- 7
12 cle L 0- 6
" cle L 1- 3d
13 NG
14 CHI W 15- 3
15 CHI W 9- 4
16 CHI L 6-10
" CHI W 5- 4
17 CLE L 4-10
18 CLE W 6- 3
19 CLE L 2- 4g
20 STL W 4- 1
21 NG
22 STL L 1- 5
" STL W 10- 8
23 DET W 12- 0
24 DET W 5- 4
25 DET L 3- 9
26 DET W 6- 2
" DET L4- 12
27 NG
28 bos W 5- 4
29 bos W 9- 7
30 bos W 6- 3

July, 1949
1 was W 5- 4
2 was W 10- 2
3 was L 1- 2g
4 BOS W 3- 2
" BOS W 6- 4d
5 BOS L 2- 4
6 phi *
7 phi W 6- 2
8 WAS W 4- 3h
9 WAS L 5- 7
10 WAS *
" WAS *
11 ALL-STAR BREAK
12 WON - 50
13 LOST - 27
14 stl W 5- 0
15 stl W 6- 0
16 stl L 2- 4b
17 chi W 2- 1
" chi L 3- 7
18 chi L 5- 6f
19 cle L 4- 5
20 cle W 7- 3
21 cle W 5- 3
22 det W 8- 2
23 det L 1- 2
24 det W 6- 3g
25 CLE L 2- 4
26 NG
27 CLE *
28 CLE W 3- 2
29 CHI W 3- 2
30 CHI L 2- 9
31 CHI W 3- 2
" CHI L 1- 2f

August, 1949
1 NG
2 DET 2-10
3 DET W 7- 5
4 DET L 2- 3g
5 STL W 10- 2
" STL W 10- 5
6 STL W 9- 8

August, 1949
7 STL W 20- 2
" STL TG 2- 2f
8 NG
9 bos L 3- 6
10 bos W 3- 2
11 bos L 6- 7
12 phi W 7- 3
13 phi W 9- 7
14 phi W 4- 2
" phi L 3- 4
15 phi L 5- 9
16 WAS *
17 WAS W 4- 3
18 WAS W 5- 4
19 PHI W 7- 4
20 PHI W 7- 3
21 PHI L 7- 8
22 NG
23 det L 4- 8
24 det L 2-13
25 cle W 6- 3
26 cle L 3- 5
27 cle W 4- 0
28 chi W 8- 7
" chi W 7- 5d
29 NG
30 stl L 2- 6
31 stl L 3-10

September, 1949
1 stl W 4- 3
2 NG
3 was W 6- 0
4 was L 2- 3
5 phi W 13- 4
" phi W 5- 2c
6 NG
7 BOS W 5- 2
8 BOS *
9 BOS L 1- 7
10 WAS L 3- 4
" WAS W 8- 1d
11 WAS W 20- 5

September, 1949
" WAS W 2- 1b
12 NG
13 STL *
14 STL W 2- 0
" STL W 13- 7
15 CLE L 6-10
16 DET W 4- 1
17 DET W 5- 4
18 CLE W 7- 3
19 CLE W 6- 0
20 CHI W 3- 1
21 CHI L 9-10
22 was *
23 was L 8- 9f
" was W 7- 1c
24 bos L 0- 3
25 bos L 1- 4
26 BOS L 6- 7
27 PHI W 3- 1
28 PHI W 7- 5
29 PHI *
30 PHI L 1- 4

October, 1949
1 BOS W 5- 4
2 BOS W 5- 3
3 NG
4 NG
END OF 1949
RUNS: 829
OPP RUNS: 637

CLUB VS. CLUB AND MONTHLY RECORDS OF THE
NEW YORK YANKEES' 1949 SEASON FOR HOME AND AWAY GAMES

CLUB:		APR	MAY	JUN	JUL	AUG	SEP	OCT	HOME	AWAY	TOTAL
BOST	H	2-0	0- 1	xxx	2- 1	xxx	1- 2	2- 0	7- 4	xxx	13- 9
	A	2-1	xxx	3- 0	xxx	1- 2	0- 2	xxx	xxx	6- 5	
CHIC	H	xxx	1- 0	3- 1	2- 2	xxx	1- 1	xxx	7- 4	xxx	15- 7
	A	xxx	2- 1	3- 0	1- 2	2- 0	xxx	xxx	xxx	8- 3	
CLEV	H	xxx	2- 1	1- 2	1- 1	xxx	2- 1	xxx	6- 5	xxx	12-10
	A	xxx	0- 1	2- 2	2- 1	2- 1	xxx	xxx	xxx	6- 5	
DET	H	xxx	1- 0	3- 2	xxx	1- 2	2- 0	xxx	7- 4	xxx	11-11
	A	xxx	2- 1	0- 3	2- 1	0- 2	xxx	xxx	xxx	4- 7	
PHIL	H	2-0	2- 1	xxx	xxx	2- 1	2- 1	xxx	8- 3	xxx	14- 8
	A	xxx	0- 3	xxx	1- 0	3- 2	2- 0	xxx	xxx	6- 5	
STL	H	xxx	2- 0	2- 1	xxx	4- 0	2- 0	xxx	10- 1	xxx	17- 5
	A	xxx	2- 0	2- 1	2- 1	0- 2	1- 0	xxx	xxx	7- 4	
WAS	H	3-0	xxx	xxx	1- 1	2- 0	3- 1	xxx	9- 2	xxx	15- 7
	A	1-1	1- 1	xxx	2- 1	xxx	2- 2	xxx	xxx	6- 5	
TOTAL:	H	7- 0	8- 3	9- 6	6- 5	9- 3	13- 6	2- 0	54-23	xxx	97-57
	A	3-2	7- 7	10- 6	10- 6	8- 9	5- 4	xxx	xxx	43-34	
GRAND TOT:		10-2	15-10	19-12	16-11	17-12	18-10	2- 0	xxx	xxx	97-57
CUMUL TOT:		10-2	25-12	44-24	60-35	77-47	95-57	97-57	xxx	xxx	

TIE GAMES: 1
STL-Aug.

Phil Rizzuto displays his classy fielding abilities to the photographers. "The Scooter" played his entire 13-year career with the Yankees. A fine shortstop and flashy bunter, Phil won the A.L. MVP Award in 1950.

1950

THE YANKS RIDE THEIR "SCOOTER" TO VICTORY

The Yankees won their 17th pennant overall and second consecutive with a 98–56 (.636) record. They finished atop the league, besting Detroit by three games. They went on to defeat Philadelphia's "Whiz Kids" in the World Series, clinching their 13th Fall Classic in seventeen visits.

Phil Rizzuto copped the American League's Most Valuable Player Award. His steady shortstop play and timely hitting and bunting was just what the New Yorkers needed this season. He led the league in singles with 150 (the fourth Yankee player to do so) and placed second overall in hits (200) and RBI (125) on but seven home runs, disproving the notion that only power hitters can be the most valuable players in their league. For 13 steady seasons, "The Scooter" was a spark that ignited the Yankees and richly deserves to be in the Baseball Hall of Fame, an award which has somehow eluded him. Joe DiMaggio slugged for the best A.L. mark (.585), edging out Walt Dropo of Boston by .002 points. This all-around consistent team led the A.L. in triples with 70, their only league-leading offensive category.

In terms of pitching, the club paced the Junior Circuit with twelve shutouts and 712 strikeouts. Individually, Raschi's 21–8 record led all A.L. moundsmen with a .724 winning percentage. In addition, Raschi, "The Springfield Rifle," balked four times in a game versus Chicago on May 3rd to establish an American League record. Raschi's four balks in this game were two fewer than his season total of six, which tied an A.L. mark set in 1915. The Yankees set an A.L. record with fourteen total balks (ironically this mark was surpassed by the 1982 Yankees' total of fifteen balks).

Rizzuto's consistent play throughout the year earmarked this pennant-winning season. The success of the New York team against other league opponents would be unprecedented in this decade.

The 1950 DAY BY DAY scores follow:

DAY BY DAY, 1950 NEW YORK YANKEES

April, 1950
18 bos W 15-10
19 bos L 3- 6
" bos W 16- 7d
20 bos *
21 WAS W 14- 7
22 WAS L 6- 7f
23 WAS *
24 phi *
25 phi W 6- 3
26 BOS W 10- 2
27 BOS L 2- 7
28 was L 4- 5
29 was W 6- 2
30 was *

May, 1950
1 NG
2 CHI *
3 CHI W 4- 3
4 CHI L 0-15
5 CLE *
6 CLE L 4- 5
" CLE W 7- 4
7 DET W 6- 3
8 DET L 1- 7
9 STL W 4- 2
10 STL *
11 STL W 5- 1
" STL W 6- 5
12 PHI W 3- 2
13 PHI W 9- 3
14 PHI L 8- 9
15 NG
16 stl W 11- 0
17 stl W 11- 9
18 NG
19 chi W 2- 0
20 chi W 3- 1
21 cle W 14- 5
" cle W 12- 4
22 cle W 7- 2
23 NG

May, 1950
24 det *
25 det W 6- 4
26 phi W 2- 0
27 phi L 1- 6
28 phi W 6- 3
" phi L 5- 6c
29 NG
30 BOS W 11- 7
" BOS W 5- 3
31 NG

June, 1950
1 CHI W 6- 5f
2 CHI L 5- 6h
3 CHI W 3- 1
" CHI W 6- 3
4 CLE W 7- 0
5 CLE L 2- 3
6 CLE L 2-16
7 DET W 5- 4
8 DET W 11- 4
9 DET L7- 13
10 STL L 2- 7
11 STL W 1- 0
" STL W 4- 2
12 NG
13 chi L 5- 6
14 chi L 2- 5
15 chi L 0- 5
16 stl W 7- 5
17 stl L 3- 7
18 stl W 15- 5
" stl W 9- 0
19 NG
20 cle W 8- 2
21 cle L 1- 5
22 cle L 2- 6
23 det L9- 10
24 det L 1- 4
25 det W 8- 2
" det L 3- 6
26 NG

June, 1950
27 WAS L 3- 4h
28 WAS W 5- 1
29 WAS L 7-12
30 bos W 9- 6
" bos L 2-10

July, 1950
1 bos L 4-13
2 bos W 15- 9
3 was L 2- 7
4 was W 16- 9
" was TG 3- 3e
5 PHI W 12- 8
6 PHI W 5- 4
7 BOS W 5- 2
8 BOS L 2- 4
9 BOS W 3- 1
10 ALL-STAR BREAK
11 WON - 47
12 LOST - 30
13 CLE *
14 CLE L 1- 5
15 CLE W 4- 3f
16 CHI W 2- 1
" CHI L 2- 5
17 CHI W 4- 3
18 STL W 12- 1
19 STL W 16- 1
" STL W 4- 3
20 NG
21 DET W 14- 5
22 DET W 10- 4
23 DET L 5- 6
24 NG
25 stl L 3- 4
26 stl W 6- 3
27 stl L 2- 3
28 chi W 4- 1
29 chi W 11- 4
30 chi W 15- 7
" chi W 4- 3d
31 NG

August, 1950
1 det L 3- 7
2 det L 0- 4
3 det L 2- 5
4 cle W 1- 0
5 cle L 2- 4
6 cle W 9- 0
7 NG
8 BOS L 4- 7
9 BOS W 2- 1
10 PHI L 3- 5
11 PHI W 7- 6
12 PHI W 7- 2
13 PHI L 2- 5
14 NG
15 was L5- 10
" was W 9- 0
16 was W 9- 4
17 was L 1- 2
18 phi W 3- 2
19 phi W 6- 2
20 phi W 6- 4
" phi W 5- 2
21 NG
22 DET W 13- 6
23 DET W 7- 5
24 DET L 3- 6
25 STL W 10- 0
26 STL W 3- 2
27 CHI W 2- 1f
28 CHI L 4- 6
29 CLE W 6- 5f
" CLE *
30 CLE W 4- 3
" CLE W 3- 0
31 CLE W 7- 5

September, 1950
1 WAS W 6- 2
2 WAS W 9- 2
3 WAS *
" WAS *
4 PHI W 2- 1

September, 1950
" PHI L 3- 4
5 NG
6 bos L 2-11
7 bos L 8-10
8 NG
9 was *
10 was W 8- 1
" was *
11 was W 5- 1
" was W 6- 2
12 cle L 7- 8
13 cle W 10- 3
14 det W 7- 5
15 det L 7- 9
16 det W 8- 1
17 stl L 5- 6
" stl W 6- 1
18 NG
19 chi L 3- 4
20 chi W 8- 1
21 NG
22 NG
23 BOS W 8- 0
24 BOS W 9- 5
25 WAS W 8- 3
" WAS W 7- 4
26 WAS L9- 11
" WAS W 10- 7
27 phi L 7- 8
28 phi W 8- 6f
29 NG
30 bos W 6- 5

October, 1950
1 bos L 3- 7

END OF 1950
RUNS: 914
OPP RUNS: 691

CLUB VS. CLUB AND MONTHLY RECORDS OF THE NEW YORK YANKEES' 1950 SEASON FOR HOME AND AWAY GAMES

CLUB:		APR	MAY	JUN	JUL	AUG	SEP	OCT	HOME	AWAY	TOTAL
BOST	H	1- 1	2- 0	xxx	2- 1	1- 1	2- 0	xxx	8- 3	xxx	13- 9
	A	2- 1	xxx	1- 1	1- 1	xxx	1- 2	0- 1	xxx	5- 6	
CHIC	H	xxx	1- 1	3- 1	2- 1	1- 1	xxx	xxx	7- 4	xxx	14- 8
	A	xxx	2- 0	0- 3	4- 0	xxx	1- 1	xxx	xxx	7- 4	
CLEV	H	xxx	1- 1	1- 2	1- 1	4- 0	xxx	xxx	7- 4	xxx	14- 8
	A	xxx	3- 0	1- 2	xxx	2- 1	1- 1	xxx	xxx	7- 4	
DET	H	xxx	1- 1	2- 1	2- 1	2- 1	xxx	xxx	7- 4	xxx	11-11
	A	xxx	1- 0	1- 3	xxx	0- 3	2- 1	xxx	xxx	4- 7	
PHIL	H	xxx	2- 1	xxx	2- 0	2- 2	1- 1	xxx	7- 4	xxx	15- 7
	A	1- 0	2- 2	xxx	xxx	4- 0	1- 1	xxx	xxx	8- 3	
STL	H	xxx	3- 0	2- 1	3- 0	2- 0	xxx	xxx	10- 1	xxx	17- 5
	A	xxx	2- 0	3- 1	1- 2	xxx	1- 1	xxx	xxx	7- 4	
WAS	H	1- 1	xxx	1- 2	xxx	xxx	5- 1	xxx	7- 4	xxx	14- 8
	A	1- 1	xxx	xxx	1- 1	2- 2	3- 0	xxx	xxx	7- 4	
TOTAL:	H	2-2	10- 4	9- 7	12- 4	12- 5	8- 2	xxx	53-24	xxx	98- 56
	A	4-2	10- 2	6-10	7- 4	8- 6	10- 7	0- 1	xxx	45-32	
GRAND TOT:		6-4	20- 6	15-17	19- 8	20-11	18- 9	0- 1	xxx	xxx	**TIE GAMES:** 1
CUMUL TOT:		6-4	26-10	41-27	60-35	80-46	98-55	98- 56	xxx	xxx	was-July

1951

ENTER MICKEY MANTLE

The result of the 1951 season was the same as the two previous years—
the Yankees were the World Champions for the fourteenth time. Winning
their 18th A.L. pennant, they defeated the New York Giants in the World
Series. The Yanks beat runner-up Cleveland by five games and posted a
98–56 (.636) record. Casey Stengel's magic was working.

Yogi Berra, the fine Yankee catcher in his sixth season, won the A.L.
Most Valuable Player Award. This was Yogi's first of three such awards in
the next 5 years. His steady play, offensively and especially defensively,
aided the Yankee pennant cause. He led all A.L. catchers with 25 double
plays. He eventually led A.L. catchers on 6 occasions with the most DP's,
an American League record. He connected for 27 roundtrippers, 88 RBI
and batted a steady .294.

Gil McDougald, used mainly as a utility infielder this season, became the
first Yankee to win Rookie of the Year honors in the American League since
the award's inception in 1949. Gil batted .306 with 14 homers and 63 RBI.

Individually, no Yankee hitters placed first in any major A.L. areas.
However, as a team New York again led (as usual so it seems) the American
League in homers with 140, and with a .408 slugging average. Allie
Reynolds, Yankee portsider, was the talk of baseball this season. He
became the only pitcher in Yankee history to toss two no-hitters in one
season. His first was thrown at Cleveland July 12, coming immediately
after the traditional All-Star break. The Yanks won 1–0. In the thick of the
pennant race, Reynolds hurled his second no-hitter at home versus Boston
in the first game of a doubleheader on September 28, the New Yorkers
pounded the Red Sox, 8–0. Winning the second game of the twinbill 11–3
under Raschi's guidance, earned New York their 18th pennant. Yankee
fans would need to wait until 1983 for a New York hurler to toss a regular
season no-hitter. Their next no-hitter, a perfect game by Don Larsen, would
come in the 1956 World Series versus Brooklyn.

On the hill, the Bronx Bombers set a club record, tossing 24 combined shutouts. They whitewashed every A.L. club at least once with Washington leading the way with 7, followed by Cleveland and Boston with four each. The pitching staff hurled six shutouts in September, a major factor in the pennant race, and blanked Boston in three of the final five games of the season. Reynolds paced the A.L. in shutouts with seven while Raschi led in strikeouts with 164, as did the entire staff with 664. The Yankees had only one more pitcher (Al Downing in 1964) lead the A.L. in strikeouts through 1983. In October, Ford Frick replaced Albert "Happy" Chandler as the new commissioner of baseball. Frick, baseball's third commissioner, will serve until December 1965.

The end of 1951 marked a change of the Yankee guards, so to speak. A youngster from Spavinaw, Oklahoma, Mickey Charles Mantle, inherited Joe DiMaggio's venerable centerfield spot. In December, "Joltin' Joe" DiMaggio announced his voluntary retirement from baseball, after contributing thirteen years of his life to the Yankees.

With the end of 1951, the Yanks were once again World Champions. The awesome hitting power of Mickey Mantle, who is known for many so-called "tape measure" homers, was unleashed upon the rest of the American League.

The 1951 DAY BY DAY scores follow:

Mickey Mantle played his entire 18-year career with the Yankees. He won the American League's Most Valuable Player Award 3 times and the Triple Crown in 1956 with 52 homers, 130 RBI and a .353 batting average. His "tape measure" home runs are legend. He was inducted into the Hall of Fame in 1974.

DAY BY DAY, 1951 NEW YORK YANKEES

April, 1951
16 was   *
17 BOS W 5– 0
18 BOS W 6– 1
19 BOS   *
20 was   L 3– 5
 " was   L 4– 8
21 was W 8– 7
22 was   *
23 PHI W 5– 4
24 PHI W 3– 0
25 PHI W 4– 0
26 bos   L 7–13
27 bos   L 3– 4
28 WAS W 6– 4
29 WAS W 4– 0
30 NG

May, 1951
1 chi W 8– 3
2 chi W 6– 4
3 stl W 17– 3
4 stl W 8– 1
5 stl W 17– 6
6 det W 11– 6
7 det   L 6–10
8 det   L 5– 6g
9 cle W 9– 2
10 cle   *
11 NG
12 phi W 8– 4
13 phi   L 4– 5
 " phi   L 6– 9
14 CLE W 11– 4
15 NG
16 CLE W 11– 3
17 CLE W 1– 0
18 CHI   L 4– 7
19 CHI   *
20 STL W 7– 3
 " STL   *
21 STL W 2– 0
22 STL W 6– 1

May, 1951
23 DET   *
24 DET W 11– 1
25 PHI W 7– 5
26 PHI W 8– 5
27 PHI W 9– 0
 " PHI   L 4– 7
28 bos   L 2– 3
29 NG
30 bos L10–11k
 " bos   L 4– 9
31 NG

June, 1951
1 DET   *
2 DET W 8– 7h
3 cle   L 3– 8
 " cle   L 1– 4
4 cle   L 2– 8
5 cle W 8– 2
6 stl   L 4– 5
7 stl W 7– 5
8 chi W 4– 2
9 chi W 10– 5
10 chi W 2– 1
 " chi   L 7–11
11 NG
12 STL   L 1– 5
13 STL   *
14 STL   *
15 DET W 2– 0
16 DET   L 0– 4
17 DET W 5– 0
18 NG
19 CHI W 11– 9
 " CHI   L 4– 5
20 CHI W 2– 1
21 CHI   L 2– 5
22 CLE W 6– 0
23 CLE W 7– 6
24 CLE W 5– 3
25 NG
26 was   L 3– 7

June, 1951
27 was W 2– 0
28 was W 3– 0
29 BOS   *
 " BOS W 2– 1
30 BOS   L 1– 3

July, 1951
1 BOS W 5– 2
2 phi W 14– 5
3 NG
4 WAS   L 6– 9
 " WAS   L 5– 6
5 WAS W 8– 2
6 bos   L 2– 6
7 bos   L 4–10
8 bos   L 3– 6
9 ALL-STAR BREAK
10 WON - 45
11 LOST - 29
12 cle W 1– 0
13 cle   L8– 11
14 cle   L 0– 8
15 det   L 3– 5
 " det W 8– 7
16 det W 8– 6
17 chi   L 3– 4f
18 chi W 5– 1
19 chi   L 1– 2
20 stl W 1– 0
21 stl W 5– 3
22 stl W 9– 0
 " stl W 7– 3
23 NG
24 CLE W 3– 2
25 CLE W 2– 1
26 CLE   L 4– 9
27 CHI W 3– 1
28 CHI   *
29 CHI W 8– 3
 " CHI W 2– 0
30 DET W 5– 4
31 NG

August, 1951
1 DET   L 8– 9
 " DET W 10– 6
2 DET   L 0– 6
3 STL W 8– 4
 " STL   L 2–10
4 STL W 11– 3
5 STL W 6– 2
 " STL W 4– 3
6 WAS W 4– 0
7 WAS   *
8 WAS   L 1– 4
9 WAS W 6– 4
10 phi W 3– 1
11 phi W 7– 4g
12 phi   L 5– 9
 " phi   L 4– 7c
13 phi   L 8–16
14 was W 6– 3
15 was W 8– 5
16 was W 5– 3
17 PHI W 3– 2
18 PHI W 5– 1
19 PHI   L 1–15
20 det   L 3– 6
 " det W 12– 5
21 det W 11– 4
22 det   L 6– 7h
23 cle   L 1– 2
24 cle W 2– 0
25 cle W 7– 3
26 chi   L 2– 3
 " chi W 8– 6
27 NG
28 stl W 7– 5f
29 stl W 15– 2
30 NG
31 NG

September, 1951
1 was W 4– 0
2 was   *
3 phi W 3– 1
 " phi   L 2– 3

September, 1951
4 NG
5 BOS   L 2– 4
6 BOS   *
7 WAS W   4–2
8 WAS W   4–0
9 WAS W   7–5
 " WAS W 2– 0b
10 NG
11 STL   L 3–4
 " STL   L 3–6
12 NG
13 DET   L 2–9
14 DET W 5– 2
15 DET   L 4–7
16 CLE W 5– 1
17 CLE W   2–1
18 CHI   L 1– 7
19 CHI W   5–3
20 CHI W   5–4
21 bos W   5–1
22 bos   L 0–5
23 bos W   6–1
24 NG
25 PHI   *
26 PHI   L 1–4
27 NG
28 BOS W   8–0
 " BOS W 11– 3
29 BOS W 4– 0
 " BOS W   3–1
30 BOS W   3–0
END OF 1951
RUNS: 798
OPP RUNS: 621

CLUB VS. CLUB AND MONTHLY RECORDS OF THE NEW YORK YANKEES' 1951 SEASON FOR HOME AND AWAY GAMES

CLUB:		APR	MAY	JUN	JUL	AUG	SEP	OCT	HOME	AWAY	TOTAL
BOST	H	2-0	xxx	1- 1	1- 0	xxx	5- 1	xxx	9- 2	xxx	11-11
	A	0-2	0- 3	xxx	0- 3	xxx	2- 1	xxx	xxx	2- 9	
CHIC	H	xxx	0- 1	2- 2	3- 0	xxx	2- 1	xxx	7- 4	xxx	14- 8
	A	xxx	2- 0	3- 1	1- 2	1- 1	xxx	xxx	xxx	7- 4	
CLEV	H	xxx	3- 0	3- 0	2- 1	xxx	2- 0	x xx	10- 1	xxx	15- 7
	A	xxx	1- 0	1- 3	1- 2	2- 1	xxx	xxx	xxx	5- 6	
DET	H	xxx	1- 0	2- 1	1- 0	1- 2	1- 2	xxx	6- 5	xxx	12-10
	A	xxx	1- 2	1- 0	2- 1	2- 2	xxx	xxx	xxx	6- 5	
PHIL	H	3-0	3- 1	xxx	xxx	2- 1	0- 1	xxx	8- 3	xxx	13- 9
	A	xxx	1- 2	xxx	1- 0	2- 3	1- 1	xxx	xxx	5- 6	
STL	H	xxx	3- 0	0- 1	xxx	4-1	0- 2	xxx	7- 4	xxx	17- 5
	A	xxx	3- 0	1- 1	4- 0	2- 0	xxx	xxx	xxx	10- 1	
WAS	H	2-0	xxx	xxx	1- 2	2- 1	4- 0	xxx	9- 3	xxx	16- 6
	A	1-2	xxx	2- 1	xxx	3- 0	1- 0	xxx	xxx	7- 3	
TOTAL:	H	7-0	10- 2	8- 5	8- 3	9- 5	14 - 7	xxx	56-22	xxx	98-56
	A	1-4	8- 7	8- 6	9- 8	12- 7	4- 2	xxx	xxx	42-34	
GRAND TOT:		8-4	18- 9	16-11	17- 11	21-12	18- 9	xxx	xxx	xxx	
CUMUL TOT:		8-4	26-13	42-24	59-35	80-47	98-56	xxx	xxx	xxx	

TIE GAMES: NONE

1952

FOUR STRAIGHT WORLD SERIES AND COUNTING

Commemorating their 50th year in New York, the Yankees won their nineteenth overall and fourth consecutive A.L. pennant. This was the second time they had won 4 straight flags, having accomplished this previously from 1936 through 1939. Winning 95 and losing 59 (.617), the Yanks finished two games in front of second-place Cleveland. In addition to winning the A.L. pennant, the Bombers went on to capture their fifteenth World Series, defeating Brooklyn.

Statistically, the club dominated various categories. For the first time since 1947 (with .271), they led the A.L. in team batting with a .267 mark. They also led in total hits (1,411) and triples with 56. The Yanks placed no individual batters at the top of the A.L.

On the other hand, the pitching staff, anchored by the steady Allie Reynolds, combined for 17 shutouts and a 3.14 team ERA, both tops in the American League. Reynolds paced the League in three important categories: strikeouts (160), shutouts (6, tied with Mike Garcia of Cleveland) and ERA (2.06). For the first time since 1946 (and fifth time overall), the Yanks were held hitless in a game. At Yankee Stadium on August 25, Virgil "Fire" Trucks of Detroit no-hitted the Bombers in a 1-0 Tiger victory.

Defensively, New York finished second in the A.L. in team fielding. Their defense, as usual, showed consistent hitting and pitching performances. As a team, the Yanks turned over 199 league-leading double plays to establish a new club record up to that time (they had 196 twin-killings in 1941).

In 1952, DiMaggio's uniform (#5) became the third to be permanently retired. Lou Gehrig's and Babe Ruth's were the first and second. "Joltin' Joe" sure was in good company as far as this honor goes!

The 1952 season concluded with the Yankees winning their 19th pennant and 15th World Series. In an exciting flag fight to the finish, the Yanks clinched the pennant on the third to last day of the season. Their performance next season would set a precedent in baseball history.

The 1952 DAY BY DAY scores follow:

DAY BY DAY, 1952 NEW YORK YANKEES

April, 1952

15 phi		*
16 phi	W	8- 1
17 phi	L	1- 3
18 WAS	L	1- 3
19 WAS	L	0- 2
20 PHI	W	9- 6
21 PHI	W	5- 1
22 PHI	W	3- 1
23 bos	L	1- 3
24 bos	L	2- 3g
25 was		*
26 was		*
27 was		*
28 was		*
29 STL		*
30 STL	L	4- 9
" STL	W	4- 1

May, 1952

1 DET	L	4- 5
2 DET	W	4- 1
3 DET	L	3- 6
4 CHI	W	8- 0
" CHI	W	3- 1
5 NG		
6 CLE	L	0- 1
7 CLE	L	2- 7
8 CLE	L	5-12
9 BOS	W	7- 4
10 BOS	W	18- 3
11 BOS	W	1- 0
12 NG		
13 cle	L	6-10
14 cle	W	5- 3
15 cle		*
16 det	W	3- 2
17 det		*
18 stl	L	3- 4
" stl	W	8- 1
19 NG		
20 chi	W	4- 3
21 chi	W	5- 1
22 chi		*

May, 1952

23 NG		
24 bos	L	2- 5
25 bos		*
26 bos	L	3- 6
27 WAS	W	7- 2
28 NG		
29 PHI	W	3- 2
30 PHI	L	1- 2j
" PHI	L	2- 4
31 CLE		*

June, 1952

1 CLE		*
2 CLE	W	2- 0
3 CHI	W	4- 3i
4 CHI	W	6- 3
5 CHI	W	6- 4
6 STL	L	3- 9
7 STL	W	2- 1
8 STL	W	5- 2
" STL	W	3- 0
9 NG		
10 DET	W	4- 0
11 DET	W	7- 2
12 DET	W	3- 0
13 cle	L	1- 7
14 cle	W	11- 0
15 cle	W	8- 2
" cle	W	4- 3
16 NG		
17 det	L	6- 7g
18 det	W	10- 6
19 det	W	8- 0
20 chi	L	5- 8g
21 chi	L	1- 5
22 chi	W	3- 0
" chi	L	1- 2
23 stl	W	14-10
24 stl	W	8- 3
25 stl	L	9-10
26 NG		
27 PHI	W	10- 0
28 PHI	L	0-12

June, 1952

29 WAS	W	5- 0
" WAS	W	3- 1
30 BOS	L	3- 4

July, 1952

1 BOS	W	3- 2
2 BOS	L	4- 5
3 was	W	9- 6
" was	L	4- 6
4 was	W	9- 4
" was	W	4- 3
5 phi	W	3- 1
6 phi	W	5- 2
" phi	L	6- 7
7 ALL-STAR BREAK		
8 WON - 45		
9 LOST - 29		
10 STL	W	10- 2
11 STL	L	3- 6
12 STL	W	5- 4g
13 DET	W	11- 1
" DET	W	12- 2
14 DET	L	2- 8
15 CLE	L	3- 7
16 CLE	W	8- 7f
" CLE	W	7- 4
17 CLE	L	6-11
" CLE	W	5- 4
18 CHI	W	6- 3
19 CHI	W	4- 2
20 CHI	L	4- 5
21 NG		
22 cle	W	7- 3
" cle	W	8- 1
23 cle	L	3- 7
24 cle	L	2- 4
25 det	L	1- 2
26 det	L6-	10g
27 det	L	3- 8
" det	W	6- 0
28 det	L	2-12
29 chi	W	10- 7
30 chi	L	0- 7

July, 1952

31 chi	W	6- 2

August, 1952

1 stl	L	1- 2
2 stl	L	6-11
3 stl	W	6- 1
" stl	W	6- 4
4 was	W	1- 0
5 was	W	3- 2c
6 was	L	4- 6
7 was	L	2- 4
" was	W	7- 1
8 BOS		*
9 BOS	L	1- 3f
10 BOS		*
11 BOS	W	7- 0
12 WAS		*
13 WAS	L	4-12
" WAS	W	10- 9i
14 WAS	W	7- 2
15 bos	L	2- 3
16 bos	W	5- 4b
17 bos	W	3- 2
18 bos	W	4- 2
19 CHI	L	1- 3
20 CHI	L	3-12
21 CHI	L	1- 6
22 CLE	L	4- 6
23 CLE	W	1- 0
24 DET	W	4- 2
25 DET	L	0- 1
26 STL	W	6- 3
27 STL	W	12- 7
28 NG		
29 WAS	L	2- 3
30 WAS	W	6- 4
31 WAS	W	6- 1

September, 1952

1 BOS	W	5- 1
" BOS		*
2 BOS	W	5- 0
" BOS	W	4- 0
3 phi	L	0- 3

September, 1952

4 phi	W	12- 2
5 phi	L	2- 3
6 was	W	5- 2
7 was	W	5- 1
8 NG		
9 stl	L	4- 5
10 stl	W	6- 1
11 NG		
12 chi	W	6- 4
13 chi	W	6- 5
14 cle	W	7- 1
15 NG		
16 det	W	7- 0
17 det	W	12- 3
18 NG		
19 PHI	L	0- 2
20 PHI	W	2- 0
21 PHI	W	1- 0
22 NG		
23 bos		*
24 bos	W	3- 2f
" bos	W	8- 6
25 bos	W	3- 2
26 phi	W	5- 2g
27 phi	W	3- 0
28 phi	L	4- 9
END OF 1952		
RUNS:		727
OPP RUNS:		557

CLUB VS. CLUB AND MONTHLY RECORDS OF THE NEW YORK YANKEES' 1952 SEASON FOR HOME AND AWAY GAMES

CLUB:		APR	MAY	JUN	JUL	AUG	SEP	OCT	HOME	AWAY	TOTAL
BOST	H	xxx	3-0	0-1	1-1	1-1	3-0	xxx	8-3	xxx	
	A	0-2	0-2	xxx	xxx	3-1	3-0	xxx	xxx	6-5	14-8
CHIC	H	xxx	2-0	3-0	2-1	0-3	xxx	xxx	7-4	xxx	
	A	xxx	2-0	1-3	2-1	xxx	2-0	xxx	xxx	7-4	14-8
CLEV	H	xxx	0-3	1-0	3-2	1-1	xxx	xxx	5-6	xxx	
	A	xxx	1-1	3-1	2-2	xxx	1-0	xxx	xxx	7-4	12-10
DET	H	xxx	1-2	3-0	2-1	1-1	xxx	xxx	7-4	xxx	
	A	xxx	1-0	2-1	1-4	xxx	2-0	xxx	xxx	6-5	13-9
PHIL	H	3-0	1-2	1-1	xxx	xxx	2-1	xxx	7-4	xxx	
	A	1-1	xxx	xxx	2-1	xxx	3-3	xxx	xxx	6-5	13-9
STL	H	1-1	xxx	3-1	2-1	2-0	xxx	xxx	8-3	xxx	
	A	xxx	1-1	2-1	xxx	2-2	1-1	xxx	xxx	6-5	14-8
WAS	H	0-2	1-0	2-0	xxx	4-2	xxx	xxx	7-4	xxx	
	A	xxx	xxx	xxx	3-1	3-2	2-0	xxx	xxx	8-3	15-7
TOTAL:	H	4-3	8-7	13-3	10-6	9-8	5-1	xxx	49-28	xxx	
	A	1-3	5-4	8-6	10-9	8-5	14-4	xxx	xxx	46-31	95-59
GRAND TOT:		5-6	13-11	21-9	20-15	17-13	19-5	xxx	xxx	xxx	
CUMUL TOT:		5-6	18-17	39-26	59-41	76-54	95-59	xxx	xxx	xxx	

TIE GAMES: NONE

1953

WINNING PENNANT NO. 20

Casey Stengel's group won an unprecedented fifth World Series in a row defeating Brooklyn for the second straight year in the Fall Classic. Up to this point in their history, the Yanks had won 16 of twenty World Series in which they had appeared. Incredible! Thus, the Bronx Bombers broke their own previous record (established from 1936 through 1939) of four straight World Series titles. Stengel, "The Old Perfesser" (sic), proud of his team's accomplishment in 1953 would say in his own inimitable way, "you could look it up." The Yanks finished 8½ games ahead of runner-up Cleveland.

The Yanks, who finished with a 99–52 (.656) worksheet, again dominated league team statistics. As a unit, the club led the A.L. in the following departments: runs (801), RBI (762), walks (656), and batting and slugging averages, .273 and .417 respectively. Again as with last season, no individual Yankee hitters finished first in league statistics.

The pitching staff repeated as the A.L. ERA leader with a 3.20 mark. New York hurlers shut out their opponents a league high 16 times. "Steady Eddie" Lopat, Yankee southpaw, posted the best A.L. ERA with 2.42 as well as winning percentage (.800) with a 16–4 ledger. Whitey Ford finished second in the latter category with a .750 percentage, winning 18 and losing but six.

During the course of the 1953 season, the Yanks won 18 straight games, their second longest winning string in their history (19 is the longest, accomplished in 1947). The streak, begun at home versus Washington, May 27, was finally snapped June 16 with the lowly St. Louis Browns besting New York 3–1. Fifteen of the 18 straight victories came on enemy turf.

The death of Ed Barrow in December 1953 was a tragic date in New York Yankee history. The man who had built the first Yankee dynasty in the 1920's was now gone. A previous manager of the Boston Red Sox from 1918 through 1920, Barrow served as both Yankee general manager (1920–1945) and club president (1939–1945).

For the most part, 1953 was a season of superlatives for the Yankee franchise. NEVER again would a major league baseball club win five consecutive World Series titles (including the 1983 season).

The 1953 DAY BY DAY scores follow:

DAY BY DAY, 1953 NEW YORK YANKEES

April, 1953

13 was   *
14 PHI   L 0- 5
15 PHI   W 4- 1
16 was   W 6- 3
" was   *
17 was   W 7- 3
18 phi   *
19 phi   W 5- 2
" phi   L 0- 3
20 NG
21 BOS   W 1- 0
22 BOS   W 6- 2
23 BOS   W 6- 3
24 WAS   W 4- 1
25 WAS   W 4- 2
26 WAS   L 4- 5
27 NG
28 stl   W 7- 6f
29 stl   *
30 chi   W 6- 1

May, 1953

1 chi   L 5- 6
2 chi   L 7- 8
3 det   W 6- 5
4 det   L 8- 10
5 cle   W 11- 1
6 NG
7 NG
8 bos   L 1- 2g
9 bos   W 6- 4
10 bos   W 7- 4
11 NG
12 CLE   W 7- 0
13 CLE   W 9- 4
14 CHI   L 5- 7
15 CHI   *
16 CHI   L 3- 5
17 STL   W 6- 5f
" STL   *
18 NG
19 DET   W 4- 2g
20 DET   W 9- 8
21 was   W 6- 5
22 was   L 4- 12
23 BOS   W 3- 2
24 BOS   W 8- 4
25 BOS   L 10- 14
26 NG
27 WAS   W 3- 1
28 WAS   W 7- 2
29 phi   W 12- 7
30 phi   *
" phi   *
31 PHI   W 7- 1

June, 1953

1 NG
2 chi   W 4- 3
3 chi   W 18- 2
4 chi   W 9- 5f
5 stl   W 5- 0
6 stl   W 6- 2
7 stl   W 9- 2
" stl   W 7- 2
8 NG
9 det   W 3- 2
10 det   W 11- 4
11 det   W 6- 3
12 cle   W 4- 2
13 cle   W 9- 4
14 cle   W 6- 2
" cle   W 3- 0
15 NG
16 STL   L 1- 3
17 STL   W 5- 3
18 STL   W 5- 0
" STL   W 3- 0
19 DET   L 2- 3
20 DET   W 6- 2
21 DET   W 6- 3
" DET   L 3- 10
22 NG
23 CHI   L 3- 11
24 CHI   L 4- 8
25 CHI   L 2- 4
26 CLE   L 2- 7
27 CLE   L 0- 5
28 CLE   L 1- 4
29 NG
30 bos   L 4- 5

July, 1953

1 bos   L 0- 4
2 bos   W 5- 3f
3 PHI   W 4- 0
4 PHI   W 6- 3
" PHI   W 4- 0
5 was   L 0- 4
" was   L 4- 5
6 phi   W 10- 5
" phi   W 5- 3
7 phi   L 4- 5
8 BOS   W 4- 2
9 BOS   L 0- 4
10 WAS   W 6- 1
11 WAS   W 3- 2f
12 WAS   W 6- 5
13 ALL-STAR BREAK
14 WON - 56
15 LOST - 26
16 stl   L 6- 8
" stl   W 7- 3
17 stl   W 6- 4
18 stl   W 13- 2
19 chi   W 6- 2
" chi   W 3- 0
20 NG
21 cle   L 3- 8
22 cle   L 4- 6
23 cle   L 2- 10
24 det   L 1- 5
25 det   W 15- 11h
26 det   L 3- 5
" det   W 14- 4
27 NG
28 CLE   W 4- 2
29 CLE   W 7- 3
30 CLE   L 3- 4
31 STL   W 11- 5

August, 1953

1 STL   L 2- 3
2 STL   *
" STL   *
3 STL   W 11- 3
4 DET   W 15- 0
5 DET   W 5- 4
6 DET   W 5- 2
7 CHI   W 6- 1
8 CHI   W 1- 0
" CHI   W 3- 0
9 CHI   L 0- 5
10 NG
11 was   L 1- 2
12 was   W 22- 1
13 was   W 6- 1
14 phi   *
15 phi   L 8- 9
16 phi   W 8- 0
" phi   W 7- 3
17 phi   W 10- 3
" phi   W 9- 0
18 WAS   L 8- 10
19 WAS   W 2- 0
20 WAS   W 7- 0
21 PHI   W 5- 4g
22 PHI   L 4- 10
23 PHI   W 4- 0
24 NG
25 det   W 6- 3g
26 det   W 5- 4
27 cle   L 2- 4g
28 cle   L 2- 3
29 cle   L 0- 6
30 chi   W 10- 6
" chi   L 0- 1
31 NG

September, 1953

1 chi   W 3- 2
2 stl   W 9- 1
3 stl   W 8- 5
4 NG
5 was   *
6 was   *
" was   *
7 bos   L 4- 7
" bos   W 5- 3
8 NG
9 CHI   W 9- 3
10 CHI   W 1- 0
11 DET   L 2- 3f
12 DET   W 13- 4
13 CLE   W 6- 3
14 CLE   W 8- 5
15 CLE   L 0- 1
16 STL   L 3- 5
" STL   W 3- 2
17 STL   L 1- 7
18 NG
19 bos   L 0- 3
20 bos   W 10- 8
21 bos   *
22 PHI   W 7- 2
23 PHI   W 3- 1
24 NG
25 BOS   L 0- 5
26 BOS   L 1- 2g
27 BOS   L 1- 2
" BOS   *
END OF 1953
RUNS: 801
OPP RUNS: 547

CLUB VS. CLUB AND MONTHLY RECORDS OF THE
NEW YORK YANKEES' 1953 SEASON FOR HOME AND AWAY GAMES

CLUB:		APR	MAY	JUN	JUL	AUG	SEP	OCT	HOME	AWAY	TOTAL
BOST	H	3-0	2-1	xxx	1-1	xxx	0-3	xxx	6-5	xxx	
	A	xxx	2-1	0-1	1-1	xxx	2-2	xxx	xxx	5-5	11-10
CHIC	H	xxx	0-2	0-3	xxx	3-1	2-0	xxx	5-6	xxx	
	A	1-0	0-2	3-0	2-0	1-1	1-0	xxx	xxx	8-3	13-9
CLEV	H	xxx	2-0	0-3	2-1	xxx	2-1	xxx	6-5	xxx	
	A	xxx	1-0	4-0	0-3	0-3	xxx	xxx	xxx	5-6	11-11
DET	H	xxx	2-0	2-2	xxx	3-0	1-1	xxx	8-3	xxx	
	A	xxx	1-1	3-0	2-2	2-0	xxx	xxx	xxx	8-3	16-6
PHIL	H	1-1	1-0	xxx	3-0	2-1	2-0	xxx	9-2	xxx	
	A	1-1	1-0	xxx	2-1	4-1	xxx	xxx	xxx	8-3	17-5
STL	H	xxx	1-0	3-1	1-0	1-1	1-2	xxx	7-4	xxx	
	A	1-0	xxx	4-0	3-1	xxx	2-0	xxx	xxx	10-1	17-5
WAS	H	2-1	2-0	xxx	3-0	2-1	xxx	xxx	9-2	xxx	
	A	2-0	1-1	xxx	0-2	2-1	xxx	xxx	xxx	5-4	14-6
TOTAL:	H	6-2	10-3	5-9	10-2	11-4	8-7	xxx	50-27	xxx	
	A	5-1	6-5	14-1	10-10	9-6	5-2	xxx	xxx	49-25	99-52
GRAND TOT:		11-3	16-8	19-10	20-12	20-10	13-9	xxx	xxx	xxx	
CUMUL TOT:		11-3	27-11	46-21	66-33	86-43	99-52	xxx	xxx	xxx	

TIE GAMES: NONE

1954

WINNING 103 GAMES AND FINISHING SECOND!

It doesn't seem possible for any baseball team to win 103 games without clinching a pennant. Well, the Yankees did just that in 1954, finishing in the runner-up slot to Cleveland, some eight games behind the surprising Indians. The Yank's percentage of .669 (103–51) set an American League mark for a second-place club.

In spite of Cleveland's A.L. domination that season, Yogi Berra, Yankee catcher, won his second MVP Award (his first was in 1951). Yogi batted .307 and finished one RBI behind Larry Doby's league-leading total of 126. The emergence of Yankee righthander Bob Grim bolstered the pitching staff. Grim won 20 games in 26 decisions to become the first Yankee pitcher to win the coveted Rookie of the Year Award.

The New Yorkers scored 805 total runs with Mantle leading the way with 129 tallies, both A.L. highs in 1954. For the third straight year, a team record, the Yanks paced the Junior Circuit with a .268 club batting average. They also led in RBI (747) and slugging percentage (.408).

New York pitching and defense proved to be consistent overall. However, their pitching proved no match for Cleveland, who cinched the lowest club ERA standard (2.78) in 1954.

On September 12 at Cleveland's Municipal Stadium, a Major League *regular* season attendance mark was established. Some 86,563 spectators (of which 84,587 were paid admissions) witnessed a doubleheader between Cleveland and the Yankees. The Indians captured both games 4–1 and 3–2 to put a lock on their third and last A.L. pennant through the 1983 season. On the opposite side of the attendance spectrum, the Yanks drew but 1,912 on September 21 in a game versus Washington at Yankee Stadium.

During June, July and August, New York won 20 games in each month for the third time in a season in their history. They had accomplished this twice previously in 1932 (June, July and August) and 1937 (July, August and September). Such a feat demonstrated excellent consistency in overall play, as is the Yankee tradition.

The 1954 season proved quite frustrating for the men in pinstripes. Never would a Stengel-led club win more games than with this season. Despite winning 103 games, New York's effort fell short of Cleveland's masterful pitching.

The 1954 DAY BY DAY scores follow:

In spite of Cleveland's A.L. domination in 1954, Yogi Berra won his second MVP Award that season.

DAY BY DAY, 1954 NEW YORK YANKEES

April, 1954
13 was   L 3- 5f
14 was   W 2- 1
15 PHI   W 3- 0
16 NG
17 WAS   *
18 WAS   L 3- 9
19 bos   L 1- 2
" bos   W 5- 0
20 NG
21 BOS   W 5- 1
22 NG
23 phi   *
24 phi   L 0- 1
25 phi   W 6- 1
" phi   L 2- 4d
26 NG
27 CHI   L 3- 4
28 CHI   *
29 CHI   W 5- 4
30 CLE   L 4- 9f

May, 1954
1 CLE   L 2-10
2 DET   W 12- 4
" DET   L 0- 4a
3 NG
4 BAL   *
5 BAL   W 4- 2
6 BAL   W 9- 0
7 PHI   W 2- 0
8 PHI   *
9 PHI   W 7- 4
" PHI   TG 1- 1e
10 cle   L 7- 8
11 cle   W 5- 3
12 cle   W 5- 4
13 det   W 5- 3f
14 det   W 6- 4
15 det   W 7- 5
16 bal   W 2- 0
" bal   L 2- 6
17 NG

May, 1954
18 chi   W 4- 3
19 chi   W 3- 2
20 NG
21 BOS   L 3- 6
22 BOS   W 7- 0
23 BOS   L9- 10
24 PHI   W 7- 3
25 was   W 9- 3
26 was   L 1- 2
27 was   L 3- 7
28 bos   W 10- 9
29 bos   W 10- 2
30 bos   L 1- 3
31 WAS   L 0- 1
" WAS   W 7- 6f

June, 1954
1 WAS   W 9- 3
2 CLE   L 7- 8f
3 CLE   W 2- 1
4 CLE   W 8- 3
5 BAL   L 1- 2
" BAL   W 3- 1
6 BAL   L 5- 7
" BAL   W 5- 2
7 NG
8 DET   L 0- 8
9 DET   W 5- 1
10 DET   W 9- 5
11 CHI   W 3- 2
12 CHI   W 2- 0
13 CHI   W 4- 2
" CHI   L 0- 8
14 NG
15 bal   W 6- 4
16 bal   W 2- 0
17 bal   W 9- 2
18 chi   W 7- 6
19 chi   L 0- 3
20 chi   W 16- 6
" chi   L 3- 7d
21 NG

June, 1954
22 det   L 1- 4
23 det   W 9- 4
24 det   W 11- 2
25 cle   W 11- 0
26 cle   W 11- 9
27 cle   L 3- 4
28 NG
29 bos   W 14- 5
30 bos   L 1- 6

July, 1954
1 bos   W 8- 7
2 WAS   W 6- 5g
" WAS   L 4- 7
3 WAS   W 3- 2
4 WAS   W 3- 0
5 phi   W 7- 4
" phi   W 11- 2
6 BOS   W 4- 1
7 BOS   W 17- 9d
8 NG
9 was   W 6- 5
10 was   W 9- 1
11 was   W 7- 3
12 ALL-STAR BREAK
13 WON - 56
14 LOST 28
15 BAL   W 3- 1
16 BAL   W 3- 2
17 BAL   W 9- 3
18 DET   W 6- 0
" DET   L 6- 8
19 DET   W 8- 0
20 CHI   W 4- 1
21 CHI   L 3-15
22 CHI   W 4- 3f
" CHI   W 11- 1
23 CLE   L 2- 8
24 CLE   L 4- 5f
25 CLE   W 4- 3g
26 NG
27 chi   L 0- 4

July, 1954
28 chi   W 7- 5
29 chi   W 10- 0
30 bal   L 0-10
31 bal   W 6- 5

August, 1954
1 bal   W 8- 6
" bal   W 2- 1
2 NG
3 cle   W 2- 1
4 cle   L 2- 5
5 cle   W 5- 2
6 det   W 4- 3
7 det   L 1- 3
8 det   L 8-10f
9 NG
10 PHI   W 5- 2
11 PHI   W 3- 1
12 PHI   W 5- 4
" PHI   W 7- 1
13 BOS   W 8- 2
14 BOS   W 3- 1
15 BOS   W 14- 9
16 NG
17 phi   W 11- 1
18 phi   W 6- 1
19 phi   W 8- 5
20 bos   L 3- 4
21 bos   L9- 10h
22 bos   L 2- 8
23 NG
24 BAL   W 9- 2
25 BAL   W 5- 1
26 DET   W 11- 2
27 DET   W 4- 0
28 DET   W 4- 2
29 CHI   W 4- 1
30 NG
31 CLE   L 1- 6

September, 1954
1 CLE   W 4- 1
2 CLE   W 3- 2

September, 1954
3 was   W 9- 2
4 was   L 2- 5
5 was   L 4- 5
6 BOS   W 6- 5
" BOS   L 7- 8
7 NG
8 bal   W 8- 2
9 bal   L 0- 1
10 chi   W 6- 3
11 chi   L 5- 6f
12 cle   L 1- 4
" cle   L 2- 3
13 NG
14 det   W 11- 0
15 det   *
16 det   W 4- 2
17 phi   W 10- 3
18 phi   W 6- 3
19 phi   W 4- 2
20 WAS   L 2- 3
21 WAS   W 3- 1
22 WAS   W 3- 0
23 NG
24 PHI   L 1- 5
25 PHI   W 10- 2
26 PHI   L 6- 8
END OF 1954
RUNS: 805
OPP RUNS: 563

CLUB VS. CLUB AND MONTHLY RECORDS OF THE NEW YORK YANKEES' 1954 SEASON FOR HOME AND AWAY GAMES

CLUB:		APR	MAY	JUN	JUL	AUG	SEP	OCT	HOME	AWAY	TOTAL
BALT	H	xxx	2- 0	2- 2	3- 0	2- 0	xxx	xxx	9- 2	xxx	17- 5
	A	xxx	1- 1	3- 0	1- 1	2- 0	1- 1	xxx	xxx	8- 3	
BOST	H	1-0	1- 2	xxx	2- 0	3- 0	1- 1	xxx	8- 3	xxx	13- 9
	A	1-1	2- 1	1- 1	1- 0	0- 3	xxx	xxx	xxx	5- 6	
CHIC	H	1-1	xxx	3- 1	3- 1	1- 0	xxx	xxx	8- 3	xxx	15- 7
	A	xxx	2- 0	2- 2	2- 1	xxx	1- 1	xxx	xxx	7- 4	
CLEV	H	0-1	0- 1	2- 1	1- 2	0- 1	2- 0	xxx	5- 6	xxx	11-11
	A	xxx	2- 1	2- 1	xxx	2- 1	0- 2	xxx	xxx	6- 5	
DET	H	xxx	1- 1	2- 1	2- 1	3- 0	xxx	xxx	8- 3	xxx	16- 6
	A	xxx	3- 0	2- 1	xxx	1- 2	2- 0	xxx	xxx	8- 3	
PHIL	H	1- 0	3- 0	xxx	xxx	4- 0	1- 2	xxx	9- 2	xxx	18- 4
	A	1-2	xxx	xxx	2- 0	3- 0	3- 0	xxx	xxx	9- 2	
WAS	H	0-1	1- 1	1- 0	3- 1	xxx	2- 1	xxx	7- 4	xxx	13- 9
	A	1-1	1- 2	xxx	3- 0	xxx	1- 2	xxx	xxx	6- 5	
TOTAL:	H	3-3	8- 5	10- 5	14- 5	13- 1	6- 4	xxx	54- 23	xxx	103-51
	A	3-4	11- 5	10- 5	9- 2	8- 6	8- 6	xxx	xxx	49-28	
GRAND TOT:		6-7	19-10	20-10	23- 7	21- 7	14-10	xxx	xxx	xxx	
CUMUL TOT:		6-7	25-17	45-27	68-34	89-41	103-51	xxx	xxx	xxx	

TIE GAMES: 1

PHI-May

1955

YOGI'S THIRD MVP AWARD

The Yankees captured their 21st pennant in what turned out to be a real battle for the American League flag. Cleveland and Chicago, finishing behind New York 3 and 5 games, respectively, could not overcome the Yank's pennant express. New York ended the season with a respectable 96–58 (.623) worksheet.

Pacing the Yanks to the pennant (they were defeated by the Dodgers of Brooklyn in the World Series) was Yogi Berra, New York catcher par excellence. Winning his third (and final) MVP Award in his last five seasons, Yogi became the second Yankee to win this coveted award thrice (Joe DiMaggio was the first) and was the first of 3 Yankees to win this award in consecutive years. Mantle (1956 and 1957) and Maris (1960 and 1961) were the other two.

Elston Howard broke the Yankee color barrier, becoming the first black New York Yankee. Playing in his first Major League season, Ellie batted a respectable .290 in 97 games. He went on to become a mainstay in pinstripes, playing 12 full seasons and part of another with the Yanks. Starting out as an outfielder, catching became his eventual forte. He was known for his defensive skills and clutch hitting and was later to be honored as American League MVP in 1963.

Offensively, this Yankee club was the A.L. leader in triples (55), home runs (175) and slugging percentage (.418). Mickey Mantle paced the American League in homers (37), bases on balls (113) and slugging average (.611). Mantle and teammate Andy Carey tied for the league high in triples with eleven apiece.

On the mound, the New York club again finished first in the A.L. with a 3.23 team ERA and 19 shutouts of their opponents. Individually, Tommy Byrne led the A.L. hurlers with a .762 (16 wins, 5 losses) winning percentage. Whitey Ford had the most complete games (18) and wins (18, tied with Lemon of Cleveland and Boston's Sullivan). For the eighteenth time since 1920, the Yankee pitching staff won A.L. honors with a 3.23 ERA. The nineteen shutouts by the New York moundsmen was also the league's best.

Although placing third defensively in the Junior Circuit in 1955, the Yanks committed the fewest errors afield with 180. The Yankees again demonstrated fine defensive play throughout the season. A new club record was set this season with 46 Yankee batters being hit by a pitched ball. Hank Bauer and Yogi Berra were hit 8 and 7 times, respectively.

The season opened on April 13 (the opening game scheduled the previous day was postponed) with the Senators of Washington invading Yankee Stadium. The crowd of 11,251 was the smallest to witness an opening game in Yankee Stadium history. By the way, the Bombers pounded the Nats mercilessly, 19–1.

This season proved no exception to the overall greatness of Stengel-led teams. Next year especially will be one to remember, particularly if your name is Mickey Charles Mantle.

The 1955 DAY BY DAY scores follow:

DAY BY DAY, 1955 NEW YORK YANKEES

April, 1955
```
12 WAS              *
13 WAS  W  19- 1
14 bos  L   4- 8
15 bos  W   6- 4
16 was  W   5- 2
17 was  L   3- 7
18 bal  W   6- 0
19 NG
20 BAL  L   3- 6
21 BAL  W  14- 2
22 BOS  W   3- 0
23 BOS  W   7- 2
24 BOS  L   0- 1
25 NG
26 chi  W   5- 0
27 chi  L4- 13
28 kc   W  11- 4
29 kc   L   0- 6
30 NG
```

May, 1955
```
 1 det  W   6- 1
 2 det  L   1- 7
 3 cle  L   4- 7
 4 cle  W  11- 5
 5 NG
 6 bos  W   6- 0
 7 bos  W   9- 6
 8 bos  W   5- 0
 9 NG
10 CLE  L   6- 9
11 CLE  L   3- 4
12 NG
13 DET  W   5- 2
14 DET  W   7- 6
15 KC   L   3- 4
 " KC   W   8- 4
16 NG
17 CHI  W   1- 0
18 CHI  W  11- 6
19 NG
20 BAL  W   7- 5
21 BAL  W   9- 4
22 BAL  W   5- 0
 " BAL  W   7- 5
23 NG
24 WAS  L   2- 3
25 WAS  W   6- 2
26 WAS  W   8- 4
 " WAS  W   7- 3
27 bal  W   6- 2
28 bal  W   3- 2
29 bal  W   1- 0
30 was  L   2- 3f
 " was  W   5- 3
31 NG
```

June, 1955
```
 1 kc   W   3- 1
 " kc   W   6- 1
 2 kc   W  12- 6
 3 chi  L   2- 3
 4 chi  W   4- 3
 5 chi  L   3- 5
 " chi  W   3- 2f
 6 det  W   7- 5
 7 det  L   3- 4h
 8 det  L   1- 3
 9 det  W   7- 3
10 cle  W   3- 2
11 cle  L   6- 7
12 cle  L   2-10
 " cle  L   3- 7
13 NG
14 DET  W   7- 6f
15 DET  L   6- 8
16 DET  W   3- 2
17 CHI  L   1- 2
18 CHI  L   3- 6
19 CHI  W   7- 1
 " CHI  W   5- 2
20 NG
21 KC   W   6- 2
22 KC   W   6- 1
23 KC   W   4- 0
24 CLE  W   2- 1f
25 CLE  W   3- 2
26 CLE  L   0- 5
 " CLE  W   2- 0
27 NG
28 NG
29 BAL  W   9- 2
 " BAL  W   7- 3
30 NG
```

July, 1955
```
 1 WAS  W   7- 2
 2 WAS  W  12- 0
 3 WAS  L   0- 5
 4 BOS  L   2- 4
 " BOS  L5- 10
 5 NG
 6 bal  L   0- 4
 7 NG
 8 was  W   3- 0b
 9 was  W   4- 0
10 was  L   4- 6
 " was  W   8- 3
11 ALL-STAR BREAK
12 WON  - 55
13 LOST - 29
14 cle  L   4- 5
15 cle  W   4- 3f
16 det  L   3- 6
 " det  L   1- 2
17 det  L   5- 6f
18 NG
19 chi  W   4- 3
20 chi  L   6- 8
21 chi  L   6- 9
22 kc   L   1- 3
23 kc   L   7- 8f
24 kc   W   7- 3
 " kc   W   2- 0
25 NG
26 CHI  W   1- 0
27 CHI  L   4- 7
28 CHI  L   2- 3
29 KC   W   3- 2
30 KC   L   2-12
31 KC   W   5- 2
 " KC   L   1- 7
```

August, 1955
```
 1 NG
 2 CLE  W   2- 1f
 3 CLE  L   1- 2
 4 CLE  L   3- 6
 5 DET  W   3- 0
 6 DET  L   5- 7
 7 DET  L   2- 4
 " DET  W   3- 2f
 8 NG
 9 BOS  L   1- 4
10 BOS  W   3- 2i
11 BOS  W   5- 3
12 bal           *
13 bal           *
 " bal           *
14 bal  W   7- 2
 " bal  W  20- 6
15 bal  W   5- 4
 " bal  W  12- 6
16 bos  W  13- 6
17 bos  L   1- 7
18 bos           *
19 BAL  W   8- 0
20 BAL  W   3- 2
21 BAL  W   6- 1
22 NG
23 det  L   2- 7
24 det  W   3- 2
25 cle  W   5- 2
26 cle  L   2- 5
27 cle  L   6- 7
28 chi  W   6- 1
 " chi  L   2- 3
29 NG
30 kc   L   3- 4
31 kc   W  11- 6
```

September, 1955
```
 1 NG
 2 WAS  W   4- 2
 3 WAS  L5- 10
 4 WAS  W   8- 3
 5 bal  L   5- 6g
 " bal  W   5- 3
 6 NG
 7 KC   W   2- 1
 8 KC   W  13- 0
 9 CHI  W   5- 4
10 CHI  L   8- 9f
11 CLE  W   6- 1
 " CLE  L   2- 3
12 NG
13 DET  W   6- 0
14 DET  W   6- 4
15 NG
16 BOS  W   5- 4
17 BOS  W   4- 1
18 BOS  W   3- 2
19 was           *
20 was  W   6- 3
 " was  W   9- 7
21 was  W   7- 3
22 NG
23 bos  L   4- 8
 " bos  W   3- 2
24 bos           *
25 bos  W   9- 2
 " bos  L   1- 8
END OF 1955
RUNS:       762
OPP RUNS:   569
```

CLUB VS. CLUB AND MONTHLY RECORDS OF THE NEW YORK YANKEES' 1955 SEASON FOR HOME AND AWAY GAMES

CLUB:		APR	MAY	JUN	JUL	AUG	SEP	OCT	HOME	AWAY	TOTAL
BALT	H	1– 1	4– 0	2– 0	xxx	3– 0	xxx	xxx	10– 1	xxx	19– 3
	A	1–0	3– 0	xxx	0– 1	4– 0	1– 1	xxx	xxx	9– 2	
BOST	H	2–1	xxx	xxx	0– 2	2– 1	3– 0	xxx	7– 4	xxx	14– 8
	A	1– 1	3– 0	xxx	xxx	1– 1	2– 2	xxx	xxx	7– 4	
CHIC	H	xxx	2– 0	2– 2	1– 2	xxx	1– 1	xxx	6– 5	xxx	11– 11
	A	1–1	xxx	2– 2	1– 2	1– 1	xxx	xxx	xxx	5– 6	
CLEV	H	xxx	0– 2	3– 1	xxx	1– 2	1– 1	xxx	5– 6	xxx	9–13
	A	xxx	1– 1	1– 3	1– 1	1– 2	xxx	xxx	xxx	4– 7	
DET	H	xxx	2– 0	2– 1	xxx	2– 2	2– 0	xxx	8– 3	xxx	12–10
	A	xxx	1– 1	2– 2	0– 3	1– 1	xxx	xxx	xxx	4– 7	
KC	H	xxx	1– 1	3– 0	2– 2	xxx	2– 0	xxx	8– 3	xxx	15– 7
	A	1– 1	xxx	3– 0	2– 2	1– 1	xxx	xxx	xxx	7– 4	
WAS	H	1–0	3– 1	xxx	2– 1	xxx	2– 1	xxx	8– 3	xxx	16– 6
	A	1–1	1– 1	xxx	3– 1	xxx	3– 0	xxx	xxx	8– 3	
TOTAL:	H	4–2	12– 4	12– 4	5– 7	8– 5	11– 3	xxx	52–25	xxx	96– 58
	A	5–4	9– 3	8– 7	7–10	9– 6	6– 3	xxx	xxx	44–33	
GRAND TOT:		9-6	21– 7	20–11	12–17	17–11	17– 6	xxx	xxx	xxx	
CUMUL TOT:		9-6	30–13	50– 24	62–41	79–52	96–58	xxx	xxx	xxx	

TIE GAMES: NONE

1956

THE MICK WINS THE TRIPLE CROWN

Pacing the Yankees to their 22nd pennant, Mickey Mantle became the second Yankee (Lou Gehrig was the first in 1934) to win the triple crown. The Mick batted .353 (no Yankee player has won a batting crown since that time through the 1983 season), with 52 home runs and 130 RBI. The Mick did everything this season but sell programs. His season's work earned him a well-deserved (and first of 3) MVP Award by a landslide over other A.L. competitors. Speaking of landslide victories, the Yankees (97–57, .630) headed second place Cleveland by nine full games.

In addition to leading the league in the previously cited departments, Mickey had the best slugging mark (.705), the highest in the A.L. since Ted Williams' .735 in 1941 with Boston. The Mick also led the Junior Circuit with 132 runs scored and 376 total bases.

As a club, the Yankees led in four areas offensively: runs (857), RBI (788), slugging percentage (.434) and homers (190). That home run total established an American League record for roundtrippers, the previous mark being 182 by, you guessed it, the Yankees, the 1936 edition.

The pitching of the Yankees was again excellent. Although not leading in any major statistical areas as a team, Whitey Ford continued to demonstrate his fine pitching abilitites that contributed so greatly to the Yank's cause in this decade, as well as the next. His winning percentage of .760 (19–6) and 2.47 ERA were the league's best in 1956. Ford's percentage of games won in his career, .690, (236 wins, 106 losses) is the best in Major League history with pitchers winning 200+ games.

Defensively, the Yanks finished third overall in the A.L. in fielding. However, for the third consecutive season, Yankee clubs led the A.L. in double plays, this time pulling off a still-standing club record 214 twin-killings.

The 1956 baseball season concluded with the Yanks beating Brooklyn in the World Series. This victory was the Yank's 17th in twenty-two Fall Classic visits. The Series was culminated by Don Larsen's perfect game in the fifth game, October 8. Requiring just 97 pitches, Larsen's "no wind-up" delivery baffled the Dodgers throughout the contest. Larsen's perfecto and Mantle's triple crown capped a fantastic Yankee year.

The 1956 DAY BY DAY scores follow:

Don Larsen is about to achieve baseball immortality by striking out pinch-hitter Dale Mitchell in the World Series of 1956. Don retired all 27 of the Dodgers that he faced on this October 8 afternoon. His 97-pitch perfect game is the only one in World Series history.

DAY BY DAY, 1956 NEW YORK YANKEES

April, 1956

17 was W 10- 4
18 was W 9- 5
19 was L 3- 7
20 BOS W 7- 1
21 BOS W 14-10
22 BOS W 13- 6
23 NG
24 was W 4- 1
25 bal W 4- 2
26 bal L 5- 7
27 bos W 5- 2
28 bos L 4- 6
29 bos *
30 NG

May, 1956

1 DET W 9- 2
2 DET L 1- 8
3 KC   L 7- 8
4 KC   W 10- 6
5 KC   W 5- 2
6 CHI W 4- 0
" CHI W 4- 0
7 NG
8 CLE W 4- 3
9 CLE L 5- 6
10 CLE L 2- 7
11 BAL W 3- 2
12 BAL L 0- 1
13 BAL W 11- 2
" BAL L 1- 5
14 cle L 2- 3
15 cle *
16 cle W 4- 1
17 chi W 10- 3
18 chi W 8- 7f
19 chi W 6- 4
20 kc W 4- 2
21 kc W 8- 5
22 det L 2- 3
23 det W 13- 5
24 det W 11- 4
25 bal W 10- 2

May, 1956

26 bal L 4- 9
27 bal *
28 BOS W 2- 0
29 BOS L 3- 7
30 WAS W 4- 3
" WAS   W 12- 5
31 WAS W 9- 6

June, 1956

1 DET L 3- 6
2 DET *
3 DET L 3- 6
" DET L 4- 7f
4 NG
5 KC   L 4- 7
6 KC   W 10- 5
7 KC   W 9- 1
8 CLE L 0- 9
9 CLE L 8-15
10 CLE W 6- 0
11 NG
12 CHI W 4- 2
13 CHI L 5- 7
14 CHI W 5- 1
15 cle W 6- 2
16 cle W 3- 1
17 cle W 9- 4
18 det W 7- 4
19 det W 5- 3
20 det W 4- 1
21 NG
22 chi L 4- 5h
23 chi L 0- 2
24 chi L 2-14
" chi L 3- 6
25 kc W 9- 3
26 kc W 8- 4
27 kc W 5- 2
28 NG
29 WAS W 3- 1
30 WAS L 1- 5

July, 1956

1 WAS W 3- 2
" WAS W 8- 6

July, 1956

2 NG
3 BAL W 4- 3h
4 bos L 6- 7g
" bos W 9- 4
5 bos W 6- 1
" bos *
6 was W 8- 4
7 was W 8- 3
8 was W 8- 2
9 ALL-STAR BREAK
10 WON - 52
11 LOST - 26
12 CLE W 9- 5
13 CLE W 10- 0
14 CLE W 5- 4f
15 CHI W 2- 1
" CHI W 6- 5f
16 CHI *
17 DET W 4- 0
18 DET L 4- 8
" DET L 3- 4
19 DET W 7- 3
20 KC W 6- 2
21 KC *
22 KC L 4- 7
" KC   W 13- 4
23 NG
24 chi L 5-11
25 chi W 10- 1
26 chi W 8- 5
27 kc W 10- 9j
28 kc W 14- 3
29 kc W 5- 3
30 cle W 13- 6
31 cle L 0- 5

August, 1956

1 cle L 1- 5
2 cle L 0- 4
3 det L 4-10
4 det L 4- 5
5 det L 5- 8
6 bos W 4- 3

August, 1956

7 bos L 0- 1g
8 was W 12- 2
9 was W 15- 7
10 BAL W 5- 4
11 BAL L5- 10
12 BAL W 6- 2
" BAL W 4- 2
13 NG
14 BOS W 12- 2
15 BOS W 6- 4
16 BOS L 1- 2
17 bal L 4- 6
18 bal W 4- 1
" bal W 6- 2
19 bal L 2- 3
20 NG
21 CLE L 0- 3
22 CLE W 3- 2
23 CHI L 3- 8
" CHI L 4- 6
24 CHI W 2- 0
25 CHI L 2- 4
26 DET W 7- 0
" DET L 4- 5
27 NG
28 KC W 4- 0b
29 KC W 7- 6
30 NG
31 was W 6- 4

September, 1956

1 was L 3- 4
2 was L 3- 4
3 BAL W 6- 1
" BAL W 5- 0
4 NG
5 bos W 5- 3
6 NG
7 WAS L 5- 6
8 WAS W 16- 2
9 WAS W 2- 1
10 NG
11 kc W 9- 5

September, 1956

12 kc L 4- 7
13 kc W 3- 2
14 det W 5- 1
15 det L 2- 6
16 cle W 10- 3
" cle L 3- 4
17 NG
18 chi W 3- 2g
19 NG
20 NG
21 bos L 7-13
22 bos W 2- 1
23 bos W 7- 4
24 bal L 4- 5
25 bal W 11- 6
26 bal L 0- 1
27 NG
28 BOS W 7- 2
29 BOS L 5- 7i
30 BOS L 4- 7f
END OF 1956
RUNS: 857
OPP RUNS: 631

CLUB VS. CLUB AND MONTHLY RECORDS OF THE NEW YORK YANKEES' 1956 SEASON FOR HOME AND AWAY GAMES

CLUB:		APR	MAY	JUN	JUL	AUG	SEP	OCT	HOME	AWAY	TOTAL
BALT	H	xxx	2– 2	xxx	1– 0	3– 1	2– 0	xxx	8– 3	xxx	13– 9
	A	1–1	1– 1	xxx	xxx	2– 2	1– 2	xxx	xxx	5– 6	
BOST	H	3–0	1– 1	xxx	xxx	2– 1	1– 2	xxx	7– 4	xxx	14– 8
	A	1–1	xxx	xxx	2– 1	1– 1	3– 1	xxx	xxx	7– 4	
CHIC	H	xxx	2– 0	2– 1	2– 0	1– 3	xxx	xxx	7– 4	xxx	13– 9
	A	xxx	3– 0	0– 4	2– 1	xxx	1– 0	xxx	xxx	6– 5	
CLEV	H	xxx	1– 2	1– 2	3– 0	1– 1	xxx	xxx	6– 5	xxx	12–10
	A	xxx	1– 1	3– 0	1– 1	0– 2	1– 1	xxx	xxx	6– 5	
DET	H	xxx	1– 1	0– 3	2– 2	1– 1	xxx	xxx	4– 7	xxx	10–12
	A	xxx	2– 1	3– 0	xxx	0– 3	1– 1	xxx	xxx	6– 5	
KC	H	xxx	2– 1	2– 1	2– 1	2– 0	xxx	xxx	8– 3	xxx	18– 4
	A	xxx	2– 0	3– 0	3– 0	xxx	2– 1	xxx	xxx	10– 1	
WAS	H	1–0	3– 0	1– 1	2– 0	xxx	2– 1	xxx	9– 2	xxx	17– 5
	A	2–1	xxx	xxx	3– 0	3– 0	0– 2	xxx	xxx	8– 3	
TOTAL:	H	4–0	12– 7	6– 8	12– 3	10– 7	5– 3	xxx	49–28	xxx	97–57
	A	4–3	9– 3	9– 4	11– 3	6– 8	9– 8	xxx	xxx	48–29	
GRAND TOT:		8–3	21–10	15–12	23– 6	16– 15	14–11	xxx	xxx	xxx	**TIE GAMES:** NONE
CUMUL TOT:		8–3	29– 13	44–25	67–31	83–46	97–57	xxx	xxx	xxx	

1957

THEIR 23RD PENNANT

In this, their 55th season, the Yankees captured their 23rd A.L. pennant, but were beaten in the World Series by the Milwaukee Braves. Finishing eight games ahead of runner-up Chicago, New York won 98 games while losing 56 for a .636 winning figure. For the fourth straight year, the league's MVP belonged to a Yankee. This season, Mickey Mantle won his second MVP Award after having won the previous year as well. This was the first time in Major League history that players from the same team won the MVP Award in four consecutive seasons. The Yanks matched this feat again 1960 through 1963.

Tony Kubek, Yankee shortstop, walked away with the Rookie of the Year Award, the third Yankee to be so honored (Gil McDougald in 1951 and Bob Grim in 1954 were the previous winners).

As far as offensive team stats, New York led the American League in runs (723), hits (1,412), triples (54), batting average (.268) and slugging percentage (.409).

Mantle led the league in runs scored as well as walks with 121 and 146 respectively. Yankee teammates Gil McDougald, Hank Bauer and Harry "Suitcase" Simpson tied for the A.L. honors with nine triples apiece. Simpson had started the season with the Kansas City Athletics.

As usual, the Yanks fared exceptionally in the pitching department. The Bombers paced the league with a 3.00 team ERA as well as in total strikeouts, 810. Two Yankees finished 1–2 in individual ERA, Bobby Shantz leading the A.L. with 2.45 and Tom Sturdivant following with a 2.54 ERA. Sturdivant also tied for the league lead in winning percentage (.727) with Chicago's Dick Donavan, both winning 16 and losing six games.

The defense continued to shine, leading the league in double plays (183) again for the fourth straight year. In 1957, the fine Yankee infield, as in the previous several seasons, aided the pennant cause with slick fielding and consistent play.

As in many previous seasons, 1957 proved very fruitful for the New York franchise. Although losing to Milwaukee in the World Series this season, the Yanks will get revenge besting the Braves in next season's Fall Classic.

The 1957 DAY BY DAY scores follow:

DAY BY DAY, 1957 NEW YORK YANKEES

April, 1957	May, 1957	July, 1957	August, 1957	September, 1957
16 WAS W 2- 1	26 WAS L 7- 9	1 bal W 3- 2f	5 CLE L 2-7	12 NG
17 NG	" WAS W 7- 6	2 bal W 6- 4g	6 WAS W 4-0	13 CHI W 7-1
18 bos W 3- 2	27 bos W 17- 8	3 BOS W 10-0	7 WAS L 2-3	14 CHI L 2-5
19 NG	28 bos W 8- 5f	4 BOS L 2-3	8 WAS L 1-6	15 KC W 5-3
20 bos W 10- 7h	29 was L 2- 6	" BOS W 4-1	9 bal L 3-4	" KC W 3-0
21 bos L 4- 5	30 was L 1- 5	5 was W 5-3f	10 bal W 6-3	16 NG
22 was W 15- 6	" was W 9- 0	6 was W 10-6	11 bal W 7-2	17 DET W 7-1
23 was L 1- 3	31 BAL L 1- 3	7 was W 7-5	12 NG	18 DET W 4-3
24 BAL W 3- 2	**June, 1957**	8 ALL-STAR BREAK	13 bos W 3- 2	19 NG
25 NG	1 BAL L 3- 4	9 WON - 51	14 bos L 4-6	20 BOS W 7- 4
26 BOS L 2- 6	2 BAL L 2- 3	10 LOST - 26	15 bos W 6-3	21 BOS L 3- 8
27 BOS L 1- 2	" BAL W 4- 0	11 kc W 3-2g	16 BAL L 3- 4g	22 BOS W 5-1
28 BOS W 3- 2f	3 NG	12 kc W 4-2	17 BAL W 6- 2	23 NG
29 NG	4 cle W 7- 4	13 kc L 4-6	18 BAL W 7- 0	24 NG
30 det L 1- 2f	5 cle W 13- 3	14 chi L 1-3	" BAL W 3- 2	25 BAL W 5-1
May, 1957	6 cle W 14- 5	" chi W 6- 4	19 NG	" BAL L 2-4
1 det W 7- 4	7 det L 3- 6	15 NG	20 kc L 0- 1	26 NG
2 kc W 3- 1	8 det L 4- 7	16 det W 10-4f	21 kc L 3- 6	27 bos W 10-2
3 kc W 8- 5	9 det W 5- 4	17 det W 5-1	22 kc W 11- 4	28 bos W 2-0
4 chi W 3- 2	10 det L 4- 9	18 det W 3-2	23 cle L 4- 5f	29 bos L 2-3
5 chi W 4- 2	11 chi W 3- 2	19 cle W 9- 1	24 cle W 10-4	END OF 1957
" chi W 3- 0	12 chi L 6- 7	20 cle L 2- 4	25 det L 2-7	RUNS: 723
6 NG	13 chi W 4- 3	21 cle W 4- 3	26 det L 2-5	OPP RUNS: 534
7 cle L 1- 2	14 kc W 10- 1	" cle L 4-7	27 chi W 12-6	
8 cle L 4-10	15 kc W 9- 2	22 NG	28 chi W 5-4	
9 NG	16 kc W 8- 6f	23 CHI W 10- 6	29 chi W 2-1g	
10 bal L 1- 4	17 NG	24 CHI L 2-7	30 WAS L 2- 4	
11 bal W 6- 4	18 DET W 2- 1	25 CHI L 2-6	31 WAS L 5- 6	
12 bal W 4- 3	19 DET W 10- 2	26 DET L 2-3	**September, 1957**	
13 NG	20 DET W 3- 1	27 DET W 4-3	1 WAS W 3- 2	
14 KC *	21 CHI W 4- 2	28 DET L 5-6	2 bal L 7- 8g	
15 KC W 3- 0	22 CHI W 6- 5i	" DET W 4- 3k	" bal L 1-6	
16 KC W 3- 0	23 CHI W 9- 2	29 NG	3 bal W 2- 0	
17 DET L 1- 4	" CHI L 3- 4	30 kc W 10-4	4 BOS L 5- 7g	
18 DET L 1- 2	24 NG	31 kc W 2-0	5 BOS W 5- 2	
19 CLE W 6- 3	25 CLE L 2-11	" kc W 5-4	6 was L 3- 4	
20 CLE *	26 CLE W 3- 1	**August, 1957**	7 was W 4- 1	
21 CHI L 1- 3	27 CLE L 0- 2	1 NG	8 was W 5- 2	
22 CHI L 4- 8	28 KC W 5- 4	2 CLE W 3- 2	9 NG	
23 NG	29 KC W 7- 6f	3 CLE W 5- 3	10 CLE *	
24 WAS W 8- 1	30 KC W 2- 1	4 CLE W 5-2	11 CLE W 5- 0	
25 WAS W 8- 1	" KC W 5- 1	" CLE W 6-5	" CLE L 1-4	

CLUB VS. CLUB AND MONTHLY RECORDS OF THE NEW YORK YANKEES' 1957 SEASON FOR HOME AND AWAY GAMES

CLUB:		APR	MAY	JUN	JUL	AUG	SEP	OCT	HOME	AWAY	TOTAL
BALT	H	1-0	0-1	1-2	xxx	3-1	1-1	xxx	6-5	xxx	13-9
	A	xxx	2-1	xxx	2-0	2-1	1-2	xxx	xxx	7-4	
BOST	H	1-2	xxx	xxx	2-1	xxx	3-2	xxx	6-5	xxx	14-8
	A	2-1	2-0	xxx	xxx	2-1	2-1	xxx	xxx	8-3	
CHIC	H	xxx	0-2	3-1	1-2	xxx	1-1	xxx	5-6	xxx	14-8
	A	xxx	3-0	2-1	1-1	3-0	xxx	xxx	xxx	9-2	
CLEV	H	xxx	1-0	1-2	xxx	4-1	1-1	xxx	7-4	xxx	13-9
	A	xxx	0-2	3-0	2-2	1-1	xxx	xxx	xxx	6-5	
DET	H	xxx	0-2	3-0	2-2	xxx	2-0	xxx	7-4	xxx	12-10
	A	0-1	1-0	1-3	3-0	0-2	xxx	xxx	xxx	5-6	
KC	H	xxx	2-0	4-0	3-0	xxx	2-0	xxx	11-0	xxx	19-3
	A	xxx	2-0	3-0	2-1	1-2	xxx	xxx	xxx	8-3	
WAS	H	1-0	3-1	xxx	xxx	1-4	1-0	xxx	6-5	xxx	13-9
	A	1-1	1-2	xxx	3-0	xxx	2-1	xxx	xxx	7-4	
TOTAL:	H	3-2	6-6	12-5	8-5	8-6	11-5	xxx	48-29	xxx	98-56
	A	3-3	11-5	9-4	13-4	9-7	5-4	xxx	xxx	50-27	
GRAND TOT:		6-5	17-11	21-9	21-9	17-13	16-9	xxx	xxx	xxx	
CUMUL TOT:		6-5	23-16	44-25	65-34	82-47	98-56	xxx	xxx	xxx	

TIE GAMES: NONE

1958

A GREAT GETAWAY

Clinching their unprecedented 24th pennant, the Yanks again pounded the opposition, this time winning comfortably by ten games over runner-up Chicago. The New Yorkers finished thirty games above .500 with a 92–62 (.597) mark. Getting off to one of their best starts in history, their record after 28 games was an incredible 23–5, a winning clip of .821! They won ten in a row in mid-May to contribute to this fast getaway. Making their twenty-fourth appearance in the World Series, the Yankees finally beat the Braves of Milwaukee for their eighteenth World Series title.

From a pitching standpoint, Bob Turley, Yankee righthander, became New York's first pitcher to claim the Cy Young Award for pitching excellence. "Bullet Bob" Turley led all A.L. hurlers in winning percentage (.750 with a 21–7 record), wins (21), and complete games (19, tied with Chicago's Billy Pierce and Frank "The Yankee Killer" Lary of Detroit). Ford (7, the A.L. high) and Turley (6) combined for thirteen of New York's league-leading 21 shutouts. Ryne Duren notched 20 of New York's 33 saves, both tops in the American League in '58.

For the sixth time since 1908, Hoyt Wilhelm fired a no-hitter at the Yanks on September 20. Playing at Baltimore, the Orioles won 1–0. Through the 1983 season, Wilhelm's ho-hitter marks the last time the Yanks were rendered hitless. For the record, no lefthander has ever tossed a no-hitter against the Yanks in their history.

Offensively, Mantle paced the league in homers (42), runs scored (127), bases on balls (129) and total bases (307). As a team, New York bested all opponents for the sixth straight season in slugging percentage (.416), a club record unmatched by previous great Yankee teams. The New Yorkers had led the A.L. in slugging since 1953. The Yankee club also led in runs (759), hits (1,418), homers (164), RBI (715) and team batting (.268).

Their field work continued to be exemplary. For the fifth straight year (a club record), the Yanks completed the most double plays in the league, this time making 182.

The Yanks were again the World Champions (this was getting to be a long-lasting habit and a pain to Yankee opponents). In 1959, the Yanks plummeted (for them, anyway) to third place.

The 1958 DAY BY DAY scores follow:

Whitey Ford pitched in more seasons (16) than any Yankee hurler in history. Whitey holds the most Yankee club pitching records and has won 236 games in his career. He won the American League's Cy Young Award for pitching excellence in 1961 and was inducted into the Hall of Fame in 1974.

DAY BY DAY, 1958 NEW YORK YANKEES

April, 1958

15 bos	W	3- 0
16 bos	L	1- 3
17 bos	W	3- 1
18 BAL	W	3- 1
19 BAL	W	4- 3
20 BAL	W	7- 0
21 BOS	W	4- 1
22 BOS	W	12- 7
23 was	L	4- 5f
24 was		*
25 bal	L	1- 2
26 bal	W	2- 0
27 bal		*
" bal		*
28 NG		
29 DET	W	5- 1
30 DET	L1-	10

May, 1958

1 NG		
2 KC	W	8- 1
3 KC		*
4 CHI		*
" CHI		*
5 NG		
6 CLE		*
7 CLE		*
8 CLE		*
9 WAS	W	9- 5
10 WAS	W	8- 0
11 WAS	W	4- 3
" WAS	L	0- 4
12 NG		
13 BAL	W	3- 0
14 BAL	W	1- 0
15 BAL		*
16 was	W	7- 2
17 was	W	6- 5
18 was	W	5- 2
" was	W	3- 0
19 NG		
20 chi	W	5- 1
21 chi	W	5- 2

May, 1958

22 det	W	5- 4
23 det	W	8- 1
24 det	L	2- 3
25 cle	W	6- 1
" cle	W	6- 3
26 NG		
27 kc	L	3- 7
28 kc	L	3- 4
29 NG		
30 WAS	L	8-13
" WAS	L	2- 7
31 bos	W	5- 4f

June, 1958

1 bos	W	10- 4
2 CHI	W	3- 0
3 CHI	W	13- 0
4 CHI	L	2- 7
5 CHI	W	12- 5
" CHI	L	2- 3
6 CLE	W	6- 5
7 CLE	W	6- 3
8 CLE	L	1-14
" CLE	L	4- 5
9 NG		
10 KC		*
11 KC	W	10- 2
" KC	W	2- 1
12 KC	L	1- 4
" KC	W	3- 2h
13 DET	L	2- 4
14 DET	L	4- 5
15 DET	L	0- 2
" DET	L	0- 3
16 NG		
17 cle	W	4- 0
18 cle	W	3- 2
19 cle	W	9- 3
20 det	L	1- 7
21 det	L	0- 1
22 det	W	15- 0
23 chi	L	0- 2
24 chi	W	6- 2

June, 1958

25 chi		*
26 chi	W	4- 3
27 kc	W	10- 3
28 kc	W	8- 0
29 kc	L	6-12
30 NG		

July, 1958

1 bal	L	5- 7
" bal	W	2- 1
2 bal	W	4- 1
3 was	W	11- 3
4 was	W	2- 1
" was	W	13- 2
5 BOS	TG	3- 3f
6 BOS	L	4-10
7 ALL-STAR BREAK		
8 WON-48;LOST-25		
9 CLE	L	2-12
10 CLE	W	7- 4
" CLE	W	4- 3
11 CLE	W	11- 3
12 CLE	W	10- 0
13 CHI	L	4- 7
" CHI	W	5- 4f
14 CHI	W	5- 0
15 DET	L5-	12
16 DET	W	3- 2
17 DET	W	4- 2
18 KC	L	1- 2
19 KC	L	4- 6h
20 KC	W	3- 1f
" KC	W	8- 0
21 NG		
22 det	W	13- 3
23 det	W	16- 4
24 det	W	10- 7
25 cle	W	6- 0
26 cle	W	8- 3
27 cle	L	2- 7
" cle	L	2- 7
28 kc	W	14- 7
29 kc	L	3- 7

July, 1958

30 kc	L	0- 2a
31 kc	W	8- 3

August, 1958

1 chi	W	7- 0
2 chi	W	6- 1
3 chi	L	1- 3
" chi	L	0- 4
4 bal	W	9- 4
5 bal	W	4- 1
6 bal	W	3- 1
7 NG		
8 BOS	W	2- 0
9 BOS	L	6- 9
10 BOS	W	7- 5
" BOS	L	3- 9
11 BAL	L	2- 3
" BAL	L	3- 9
12 BAL	W	7- 2
13 WAS	L	4- 9
14 bos	W	8- 2
15 bos	L	2- 6
16 bos	L	4- 7
17 bos	L	5- 6
18 NG		
19 CLE	L	6- 8
20 CLE	W	7- 1
21 CHI	W	6- 3
22 CHI	W	8- 5
23 CHI	L	1- 7
24 DET	L	3- 8
" DET	W	3- 2
25 NG		
26 KC	W	6- 2
27 KC	L	7-11
28 NG		
29 was	L	0- 3
30 was	L	1- 3
31 was	W	7- 6

September, 1958

1 BOS	L	2- 4
" BOS	W	4- 2
2 BOS	W	6- 1

September 1958

3 BOS	W	8-5
4 NG		
5 WAS	L	3-6
6 WAS	L	3-8
7 WAS	L	0-1
" WAS	W	7-0
8 NG		
9 cle	L	2-9a
10 cle	W	8- 3
11 NG		
12 chi	W	5-0
13 chi	W	5-4
14 kc	W	5-3
" kc	W	12-7
15 NG		
16 det	L	2-4
17 det	L	2- 5
18 NG		
19 bal	L	4-5
20 bal	L	0-1
21 bal	L	2-3
22 NG		
23 bos	L	8- 9
24 bos	W	7- 5
25 NG		
26 BAL	L	2-3h
27 BAL		*
28 BAL	W	7- 0
" BAL	W	6-3

END OF 1958

RUNS: 759

OPP RUNS: 577

		APR	MAY	JUN	JUL	AUG	SEP	OCT	HOME	AWAY	TOTAL
	H							xxx	3- 8	xxx	
	A			[illegible]	1- 2	2- 1	xxx	xxx	xxx	5- 6	8-14
KC	H	xxx	1- 1	2- 1	xxx	4- 0	2- 0	xxx	9- 2	xxx	
	A	xxx	2- 0	3- 1	1- 0	2- 2	xxx	xxx	xxx	8- 3	17- 5
WAS	H	xxx	2- 1	xxx	2- 2	0- 2	2- 0	xxx	6- 5	xxx	
	A	2-1	3- 0	xxx	xxx	2- 1	2- 0	xxx	xxx	9- 2	15- 7
TOTAL:	H	1- 3	5- 9	8- 6	8- 4	6- 7	12- 8	xxx	40-37	xxx	
	A	6-5	7- 6	10- 6	4-12	9- 8	3- 1	xxx	xxx	39-38	79-75
GRAND TOT:		7-8	12-15	18-12	12-16	15-15	15- 9	xxx	xxx	TIE GAMES:	1
CUMUL TOT:		7-8	19-23	37-35	49-51	64-66	79-75	xxx	xxx	chi-July	

CLUB VS. CLUB AND MONTHLY RECORDS OF THE NEW YORK YANKEES' 1958 SEASON FOR HOME AND AWAY GAMES

CLUB:		APR	MAY	JUN	JUL	AUG	SEP	OCT	HOME	AWAY	TOTAL
BALT	H	3-0	2- 0	xxx	xxx	1- 2	2- 1	xxx	8- 3	xxx	
	A	1-1	xxx	xxx	2- 1	3- 0	0- 3	xxx	xxx	6- 5	14- 8
BOST	H	2-0	xxx	xxx	0- 1	2- 2	3- 1	xxx	7- 4	xxx	
	A	2-1	1- 0	1- 0	xxx	1- 3	1- 1	xxx	xxxx6- 5	13- 9	
CHIC	H	xxx	xxx	3- 2	2- 1	2- 1	xxx	xxx	7- 4	xxx	
	A	xxx	2- 0	2- 1	xxx	2- 2	2- 0	xxx	xxx	8- 3	15- 7
CLEV	H	xxx	xxx	2- 2	4- 1	1- 1	xxx	xxx	7- 4	xxx	
	A	xxx	2- 0	3- 0	2- 2	xxx	1- 1	xxx	xxx	8- 3	15- 7
DET	H	1-1	xxx	0- 4	2- 1	1- 1	xxx	xxx	4- 7	xxx	
	A	xxx	2- 1	1- 2	3- 0	xxx	0- 2	xxx	xxx	6- 5	10-12
KC	H	xxx	1- 0	3- 1	2- 2	1- 1	xxx	xxx	7- 4	xxx	
	A	xxx	0- 2	2- 1	2- 2	xxx	2- 0	xxx	xxx	6- 5	13- 9
WAS	H	xxx	3- 3	xxx	xxx	0- 1	1- 3	xxx	4- 7	xxx	
	A	0-1	4- 0	xxx	3- 0	1- 2	xxx	xxx	xxx	8- 3	12-10
TOTAL:	H	6-1	6- 3	8- 9	10- 6	8- 9	6- 5	xxx	44- 33	xxx	
	A	3-3	11- 3	9- 4	12- 5	7- 7	6- 7	xxx	xxx	48-29	92-62
GRAND TOT:		9-4	17- 6	17-13	22-11	15-16	12-12	xxx	xxx	TIE GAMES:	1
CUMUL TOT:		9-4	26-10	43-23	65-34	80-50	92-62	xxx	xxx	BOS-July	

1959

WORST SEASON IN THIRTY-FOUR YEARS

Thank goodness for Al Lopez, the other American League
(except Casey Stengel) must have thought. In guiding the White S
first pennant since 1919, the year of the infamous Black Sox Sc
Lopez won his second pennant of the 1950's. He had led the
Indians to an American League flag back in 1954. Thus, one
Lopez, blocked the way of complete pennant domination by
Bombers in the 1950's.

The Yankees finished a disappointing third, some 15 games
White Sox. With their 79–75 won-lost ledger (.513), this marke
season since 1925 when they won 69 and lost 85 (.448).

The pitching staff led the league in strikeouts with 836 and ti
with a circuit-pacing 15 shutouts.

This season saw a new American League president, Jo
replacing William Harridge who had served in that capaci
1931. Cronin will remain as A.L. president for thirteen seaso

The 1959 season proved very disappointing to the Yan
ways. They will get back on track again next season.

The 1959 DAY BY DAY scores follow:

CLUB VS. CLUB AND MONTHLY RECORDS OF THE NEW YORK YANKEES' 1959 SEASON FOR HOME AND AWAY GAMES

CLUB:		APR	MAY	JUN	JUL	AUG	SEP	OCT	HOME	AWAY	TOTAL
BALT	H	0–3	1–1	xxx	xxx	xxx	2–4	xxx	3–8	xxx	10–12
	A	2–1	2–2	1–0	1–1	xxx	1–0	xxx	xxx	7–4	
BOST	H	1–0	1–1	xxx	1–0	1–3	2–1	xxx	6–5	xxx	9–13
	A	1–2	xxx	xxx	0–5	2–0	0–1	xxx	xxx	3–8	
CHIC	H	xxx	0–2	3–0	2–2	xxx	2–1	xxx	6–5	xxx	9–13
	A	1–1	xxx	1–3	0–2	1–2	0–1	xxx	xxx	3–8	
CLEV	H	xxx	0–1	2–2	3–0	xxx	1–1	xxx	7–4	xxx	11–11
	A	xxx	0–2	3–1	1–2	0–2	xxx	xxx	xxx	4–7	
DET	H	xxx	0–2	1–3	xxx	1–2	2–1	xxx			
	A	xxx	0–2		1–2						

1960

CASEY'S LAST SEASON

After winning eight of ten pennants in the 1950's, the new decade opened with the same result, an American League pennant for the Yanks, their 25th. As was the case in many previous seasons, the Yankees again ran away from the other A.L. clubs, winning by a very comfortable eight game margin over second-place Baltimore. New York won 97 while losing 57 for a .630 victory percentage. They eventually lost out to Pittsburgh in a most exciting and unusual World Series.

Roger Maris, in his first season with New York, won the American League's MVP Award. Leading the league with 112 runs batted in and slugging percentage, (.581), he finished second to Mantle in three categories (total bases, runs scored and home runs). Mickey headed all A.L. hitters with 40 homers, 294 total bases and 119 runs scored.

As a club, the Bronx Bombers swatted 193 homers, a new A.L. mark (the Yanks had previously set the old standard in 1956 with 190 roundtrippers). Little did anyone realize that New York would again break their league record next season with an incredible 240 home runs. In addition, the Yanks scored the most in the Junior Circuit (746 runs), knocked in the most runs (699) and slugged a league high .426.

In pitching, New York dominated the A.L. with a club ERA of 3.52 and 16 shutouts. Whitey Ford was tied for the league lead with Early Wynn of Chicago and Jim Perry of Cleveland in tossing 4 shutouts apiece.

The Yanks concluded the season winning their last 15 games in a row, which must be a Major League record. On September 16, the Yankees were but one game ahead in the pennant fight. That winning streak won them the flag as it enabled them to pull away from the rest of the American League clubs. Within ten days the New Yorkers were on top by some seven games.

Although outscoring the Pirates in the Series, 55 to 27, this was not enough to win in seven games as one Mr. Mazeroski brought the curtain down on the Yankee season with a dramatic 9th inning home run. The close of the season also ended Casey Stengel's incredible New York managerial reign, having won 10 pennants and 7 World Series in a dozen years at the Yankee helm. Later Casey, in 1962, will manage those amazin' Mets of New York.

The 1960 DAY BY DAY scores follow:

Casey Stengel—"The Old Professor," one of the greatest managers and strategists of all time, guided his Yanks to 10 A.L. pennants and 7 World Series Championships, 5 of them consecutive, in 12 years at the Yankee helm. He was elected into the Hall of Fame in 1966.

DAY BY DAY, 1960 NEW YORK YANKEES

April, 1960
19 bos	W	8-4
20 bos	L	1-7
21 bos	W	4-0
22 BAL	W	5-0
23 BAL	W	3-2
24 BAL	W	15-9
25 NG		
26 BOS	L	5-7
27 WAS	L	4-5
28 NG		
29 bal	L	1-2
30 bal	W	16-0

May, 1960
1 bal	L	5-9
2 NG		
3 DET	W	10-3
4 DET	W	4-2
5 NG		
6 KC	W	8-7
7 KC	W	4-1
8 CHI	L	3-8f
9 NG		
10 CLE	L	1-5f
11 CLE		*
12 CLE	L	2-3g
13 was	W	7-3
14 was	L	0-4
15 was	W	11-2
16 NG		
17 cle	L	6-7
18 cle	W	4-2
19 NG		
20 chi	L	3-5
21 chi	L	8-9
22 kc	W	9-7
23 kc	W	4-3
24 det	L	0-4
25 det	L	3-9
26 BAL	W	2-0
27 BAL	L	2-3
28 WAS	W	5-1
29 WAS	W	6-4g

May, 1960
30 WAS	L	1-2
" WAS	W	3-2
31 bal	L	2-3

June, 1960
1 bal	L	1-4
2 bal	L	5-6
3 BOS	W	4-3
4 BOS	L	2-8
5 BOS	W	5-4
" BOS	W	8-3
6 CHI	L	2-3
7 CHI	W	5-2
8 CHI	W	6-0
9 CHI	W	5-2
10 CLE	W	4-3
11 CLE	W	6-4
12 CLE		*
" CLE		*
13 kc	W	8-4
14 kc	W	6-2
15 kc	TG	7-7h
16 kc	L	1-9
17 chi	W	4-2
18 chi	W	12-5
19 chi	W	7-5
" chi	W	5-3
20 NG		
21 det	W	6-0
22 det	W	7-3
23 det	L	1-2
24 cle	W	10-6
25 cle	L	1-4
26 cle	W	6-2
" cle	L	6-7g
27 NG		
28 KC	W	5-2
29 KC	W	10-0
30 KC	W	10-3

July, 1960
1 DET		*
2 DET	W	7-6
3 DET	W	7-6

July, 1960
" DET	W	6-2
4 was	L	8-9
5 was	L	3-5f
6 bal	W	5-2
7 bal	W	6-3
8 bos	L	0-8
9 bos	L	5-6
10 bos	L	5-9
11 ALL-STAR		
12 BREAK		
13 WON - 45		
14 LOST - 30		
15 det	L	4-8
16 det	W	11-2
17 det	L	2-12
" det	L	2-3
18 cle	W	9-2
19 cle	W	13-11
20 cle	L	6-8
21 NG		
22 CHI	L	5-11
23 CHI	L	3-5
24 CHI	L	3-6
" CHI	W	8-2
25 NG		
26 CLE	W	6-1
27 CLE		*
" CLE		*
28 CLE	W	4-0
" CLE	W	9-2
29 KC	L	2-5
30 KC		*
31 KC	L	2-5g
" KC	W	6-0

August, 1960
1 DET	W	3-2
2 DET	W	3-2j
" DET	W	3-2f
3 DET	L	2-12
4 NG		
5 kc	W	4-3
6 kc	W	16-4

August, 1960
7 kc	W	3-2
" kc	L	3-13
8 chi	L	1-9
9 chi	W	7-4d
10 chi	W	6-0
11 NG		
12 WAS	L	7-12
13 WAS	W	1-0
14 WAS	L	4-5
" WAS	L	3-6k
15 BAL	W	4-3
16 BAL	W	1-0
17 bos	W	3-2f
18 bos	W	11-7
19 was	L	2-4
20 was	W	9-5g
21 was	L	4-7
22 NG		
23 CHI	L	1-5
24 CHI	W	3-2
25 NG		
26 CLE	W	7-6g
" CLE	W	7-5
27 CLE	W	7-4
" CLE	W	3-0
28 DET	L	2-6
" DET	W	8-5
29 NG		
30 KC	W	3-2
31 KC	W	1-0
" KC	L	0-6

September, 1960
1 NG		
2 bal	L	0-5
3 bal	L	0-2
4 bal	L	2-6
5 BOS	W	3-2
" BOS	W	3-2
6 BOS	L	1-7
7 chi	W	6-4
8 chi	L	4-5
9 det	W	4-1

September, 1960
10 det	W	5-1
11 cle	W	5-0
" cle	W	3-2g
12 NG		
13 kc	L	3-12
14 kc	L	1-2
15 NG		
16 BAL	W	4-2
17 BAL	W	5-3
18 BAL	W	7-3
" BAL	W	2-0
19 NG		
20 WAS	W	2-1g
21 WAS	W	10-3
22 NG		
23 bos	W	5-1
24 bos	W	6-5f
25 bos	W	4-3
26 was	W	4-2f
27 was	W	5-1
28 was	W	6-3
29 NG		
30 BOS	W	6-5

October, 1960
1 BOS	W	3-1
2 BOS	W	8-7

END OF 1960

RUNS:	746
OPP RUNS:	627

CLUB VS. CLUB AND MONTHLY RECORDS OF THE NEW YORK YANKEES' 1960 SEASON FOR HOME AND AWAY GAMES

CLUB:		APR	MAY	JUN	JUL	AUG	SEP	OCT	HOME	AWAY	TOTAL
BALT	H	3-0	1-1	xxx	xxx	2-0	4-0	xxx	10-1	xxx	13- 9
	A	1-1	0-2	0-2	2-0	xxx	0-3	xxx	xxx	3- 8	
BOST	H	0-1	xxx	3-1	xxx	2-0	3-1	2-0	8-3	xxx	15- 7
	A	2-1	xxx	xxx	0-3		3-0	xxx	xxx	7- 4	
CHIC	H	xxx	0-1	3-1	1-3	1-1	xxx	xxx	5-6	xxx	12-10
	A	xxx	0-2	4-0	xxx	2-1	1-1	xxx	xxx	7- 4	
CLEV	H	xxx	0-2	2-0	3-0	4-0	xxx	xxx	9-2	xxx	16- 6
	A	xxx	1-1	2-2	2-1	xxx	2-0	xxx	xxx	7- 4	
DET	H	xxx	2-0	xxx	3-0	4-2	xxx	xxx	9-2	xxx	14- 8
	A	xxx	0-2	2-1	1-3	xxx	2-0	xxx	xxx	5- 6	
KC	H	xxx	2-0	3-0	1-2	2-1	xxx	xxx	8-3	xxx	15- 7
	A	xxx	2-0	2-1	xxx	3-1	0-2	xxx	xxx	7- 4	
WAS	H	0-1	3-1	xxx	xxx	1-3	2-0	xxx	6-5	xxx	12-10
	A	xxx	2-1	xxx	0-2	1-2	3-0	xxx	xxx	6- 5	
TOTAL:	H	3-2	8-5	11- 2	8- 5	14- 7	9- 1	2- 0	55-22	xxx	97- 57
	A	3-2	5-8	10- 6	5- 9	8- 4	11- 6	xxx	xxx	42-35	
GRAND TOT:		6-4	13-13	21- 8	13-14	22-11	20- 7	2- 0	xxx	xxx	
CUMUL TOT:		6-4	19-17	40-25	53-39	75-50	95-57	97-57	xxx	xxx	

TIE GAMES: 1
kc-June

1961

GIVE THAT MAN A STAR AND THE ARRIVAL OF THE MAJOR

This season went down as one of the most remarkable in Yankee (and baseball) history. The Bombers captured A.L. pennant No. 26 (and 19th World Series in defeating Cincinnati) under the guidance of their seventeenth manager, Ralph Houk, "The Major." The New Yorkers won 109 games (one short of their club record set in 1927) and went down to defeat 53 times for a fantastic .673 winning mark. Even second place Detroit, with 101 victories, finished some eight full games behind the Yanks.

Roger Maris eclipsed baseball's most cherished record, hitting out 61 homers and thus beating the Babe's venerable mark by one. Baseball Commissioner Ford Frick decided it was best to "minimize" this feat by requiring an asterisk (*) to indicate that Maris' record was accomplished in a 162 game season, as opposed to one of 154 as was the case in 1927, the year of Ruth's 60 homers. To proselytize for a moment, it seemed absurd that such a decision transpired at all since one could rule *every* record-breaking performance on this same basis. Imagine how absolutely absurd this could become. Roger Maris hit more homers in a season (albeit in a longer one) than did Babe Ruth. Period. As Casey Stengel would say, "You could look it up." Enough said.

In winning his second consecutive MVP Award, Maris led all A.L. hitters with 366 total bases and 142 RBI. Thus, Maris became the last Yankee to lead the A.L. in RBI through the 1983 season. Mantle won the slugging crown with a .687 mark as well as scoring the most A.L. runs (132) and accepting the most walks (126). The 115 combined homers of Maris (61) and Mantle (54) is the all-time Major League mark for two teammates in the same season.

Roger Maris—At Yankee Stadium on October 1, 1961, Maris connects for his record-breaking 61st home run off Boston's Tracy Stallard in the 4th inning. In 1961, Roger won his 2nd consecutive MVP Award with 142 RBI and 132 runs scored, both A.L. highs in '61.

As a hitting unit, the Yankee power was awesome to put it mildly. Their 240 homers set a Major League record which remains unsurpassed through 1983. Of those 240 homers, 128 (53%) were hit on the road in 82 games, another all-time mark. Six Yankees hit twenty or more homers, Maris leading the way with 61. The Yanks led the league with a .441 slugging mark and 782 RBI. New York also established a then A.L. record with 10 pinch-hit homers (Baltimore broke this record with eleven in 1982).

This year the Yankees set an unusual club record for consistency. For four consecutive months, the Yanks won twenty or more games, beginning in June. The record of those four fantastic months follows: after going 14–12 in May, they are 22–10 in June, 20–9 in July, 22–9 in August, and 21–8 in September. In 89 total games during that span, the Yanks won 63 and lost but 26 for a .708 winning clip.

Anchoring the fine pitching staff, Whitey Ford won the Cy Young Award becoming the second New York hurler to do so (Bob Turley was the first in 1958). Three Yankees topped American League pitchers with the highest winning percentage with Ford leading the way with an .862 mark. Ford won a remarkable league-leading 25 games, losing but four. The Yanks combined for an A.L. high 39 saves, Luis Arroyo having 29 to lead all A.L. pitchers.

Defensively, the Yanks ranked first overall in the A.L. with a .980 fielding mark. They also committed the league's fewest errors (124) and turned over the most double plays with 180.

This season was highlighted by the home run race between Maris and Mantle, the M & M boys. In 1961, Ralph Houk emerged as a first-rate manager, leading New York to pennants the next two seasons.

The 1961 DAY BY DAY scores follow:

DAY BY DAY, 1961 NEW YORK YANKEES

April, 1961
11 MIN L 0- 6
12 NG
13 MIN *
14 NG
15 KC W 5- 3
16 KC *
17 KC W 3- 0
18 LA *
19 LA *
20 LA W 7- 5
" LA W 4- 2
21 bal W 4- 2
22 bal L 3- 5
" bal TG 5- 5c
23 bal L 1- 4
24 det L 3- 4
25 det *
26 det W 13-11f
27 CLE W 4- 3
28 CLE *
29 CLE W 4- 2
30 was W 4- 3
" was L 1- 2

May, 1961
1 was *
2 min W 6- 4f
3 min W 7- 3
4 min W 5- 2
5 la W 5- 4
6 la L 3- 5
7 la L 3- 5
8 NG
9 kc L 4- 5
10 kc W 9- 4
11 NG
12 DET L 3- 4
13 DET L 3- 8
14 DET W 5- 4g
" DET W 8- 6
15 NG
16 WAS L 2- 3
17 WAS L 7- 8
18 NG
19 cle L 7- 9
20 cle L 3- 4
21 BAL W 4- 2
" BAL L 2- 3
22 BAL W 8- 2
23 NG
24 BOS W 3- 2
25 BOS W 6- 4
26 CHI *
27 CHI *
28 CHI L 9-14
" CHI W 5- 3
29 bos L 1- 2
30 bos W 12- 3
31 bos W 7- 6

June, 1961
1 bos L 5- 7
2 chi W 6- 2
3 chi L 5- 6i
4 chi W 10- 1
5 MIN W 6- 2
" MIN W 6- 1
6 MIN W 7- 2
7 MIN W 5- 1
8 KC W 6- 1
" KC L 6- 9
9 KC W 8- 6
10 KC W 5- 3
11 LA W 2- 1
" LA W 5- 1
12 LA W 3- 1
13 cle L 2- 7
14 cle W 11- 5
15 cle W 3- 2g
16 det L 2- 4
17 det L10-12
18 det W 9- 0
19 kc L 3- 4
20 kc W 6- 2
21 kc W 5- 3
22 kc W 8- 3
23 min L 0- 4
24 min W 10- 7
25 min W 8- 4
26 la W 8- 6
27 la L 6- 7
28 la L 3- 5
29 NG
30 WAS W 5- 1

July, 1961
1 WAS W 7- 6
2 WAS W 13- 4
3 NG
4 DET W 6- 2
" DET L 3- 4f
5 CLE W 6- 0
6 CLE W 4- 0
7 BOS W 14- 3
8 BOS W 8- 5
9 BOS W 3- 0
" BOS L 6- 9
10 ALL-STAR BREAK
11 WON - 53
12 LOST - 29
13 chi W 6- 2
14 chi L 1- 6
15 chi W 9- 8f
16 bal W 2- 1
17 bal W 5- 0
" bal *
18 was W 5- 3
19 was L 4- 8
" was L2- 12
20 NG
21 bos W 11- 8
22 bos W 11- 9
23 bos L 4- 5
24 NG
25 CHI W 5- 1
" CHI W 12- 0
26 CHI W 5- 2
27 CHI W 4- 3
28 BAL L 0- 4
29 BAL W 5- 4
30 BAL L 0- 4
" BAL L 1- 2
31 ALL-STAR BREAK
WON-65,LOST36

August, 1961
1 ALL-STAR BREAK
2 KC W 6- 5
" KC W 12- 5
3 KC L 1- 6
4 MIN W 8- 5f
5 MIN W 2- 1
6 MIN W 7- 6k
" MIN W 3- 2
7 LA W 4- 1
8 LA W 5- 4f
9 LA W 2- 0
10 LA W 3- 1
11 was W 12- 5
12 was L 1- 5
13 was L 2-12
" was W 9- 4
14 NG
15 CHI L 1- 2
16 CHI W 5- 4
17 CHI W 5- 3
18 cle L 1- 5
19 cle W 3- 2f
20 cle W 6- 0
" cle W 5- 2
21 NG
22 LA L 3- 4
23 LA W 8- 6f
24 LA L 4- 6
25 kc W 3- 0
26 kc W 5- 1
27 kc W 8- 7
28 NG
29 min L 0- 3
30 min W 4- 0
31 min L 4- 5

September, 1961
1 DET W 1- 0
2 DET W 7- 2
3 DET W 8- 5
4 WAS W 5- 3
" WAS W 3- 2
5 WAS W 6- 1
6 WAS W 8- 0
7 CLE W 7- 3
8 CLE W 9- 1
9 CLE W 8- 7
10 CLE W 7- 6
" CLE W 9- 3
11 NG
12 chi W 4- 3b
13 chi *
14 chi L 3- 8
" chi L 3- 4
15 det W 11- 1
" det L 2- 4
16 det L 4-10
17 det W 6- 4h
18 NG
19 bal L 0- 1
" bal W 3- 1
20 bal W 4- 2
21 bal L 3- 5
22 NG
23 bos W 8- 3
24 bos L 1- 3
25 NG
26 BAL W 3- 2
27 BAL L 2- 3
28 NG
29 BOS W 2- 1
30 BOS W 3- 1

October, 1961
1 BOS W 1- 0

END OF 1961
RUNS: 827
OPP RUNS: 612

CLUB VS. CLUB AND MONTHLY RECORDS OF THE NEW YORK YANKEES' 1961 SEASON FOR HOME AND AWAY GAMES

CLUB:		APR	MAY	JUN	JUL	AUG	SEP	OCT	HOME	AWAY	TOTAL
BALT	H	xxx	2-1	xxx	1-3	xxx	1-1	xxx	4-5	xxx	9-9
	A	1-2	xxx	xxx	2-0	xxx	2-2	xxx	xxx	5-4	
BOST	H	xxx	2-0	xxx	3-1	xxx	2-0	1-0	8-1	xxx	13-5
	A	xxx	2-1	0-1	2-1	xxx	1-1	xxx	xxx	5-4	
CHIC	H	xxx	1-1	xxx	4-0	2-1	xxx	xxx	7-2	xxx	12-6
	A	xxx	xxx	2-1	2-1	xxx	1-2	xxx	xxx	5-4	
CLEV	H	2-0	xxx	xxx	2-0	xxx	5-0	xxx	9-0	xxx	14-4
	A	xxx	0-2	2-1	xxx	3-1	xxx	xxx	xxx	5-4	
DET	H	xxx	2-2	xxx	1-1	xxx	3-0	xxx	6-3	xxx	10-8
	A	1-1	xxx	1-2	xxx	xxx	2-2	xxx	xxx	4-5	
KC	H	2-0	xxx	3-1	xxx	2-1	xxx	xxx	7-2	xxx	14-4
	A	xxx	1-1	3-1	xxx	3-0	xxx	xxx	xxx	7-2	
LA	H	2-0	xxx	3-0	xxx	4-0	xxx	xxx	9-0	xxx	12-6
	A	xxx	1-2	1-2	xxx	1-2	xxx	xxx	xxx	3-6	
MINN	H	0-1	xxx	4-0	xxx	4-0	xxx	xxx	8-1	xxx	14-4
	A	xxx	3-0	2-1	xxx	1-2	xxx	xxx	xxx	6-3	
WAS	H	xxx	0-2	1-0	2-0	xxx	4-0	xxx	7-2	xxx	11-7
	A	1-1	xxx	xxx	1-2	2-2	xxx	xxx	xxx	4-5	
TOTAL:	H	6-1	7-6	11-1	13-5	12-2	15-1	1-0	65-16	xxx	109-53
	A	3-4	7-6	11-9	7-4	10-7	6-7	xxx	xxx	44-37	
GRAND TOT:		9-5	14-12	22-10	20-9	22-9	21-8	1-0	xxx	xxx	
CUMUL TOT:		9-5	23-17	45-27	65-36	87-45	108-53	109-53	xxx	xxx	

TIE GAMES: 1
balt-Apr.

1962

MVP #3 FOR MICKEY

Beginning their 60th season in New York, the Yanks won pennant No. 27 and went on to whip the San Francisco Giants for their 20th World Series title. The Yanks finished 30 games over .500 with a 96–66 (.593) mark, five games ahead of runner-up Minnesota.

Mantle won his third Most Valuable Player Award (the third Yank to do so) and outfielder Tom Tresh became the fourth Yankee player to take Rookie of the Year honors. The club demonstrated power, hitting 199 homers, second to Detroit's 209. Eight Yanks had 10 or more homers, led by Maris with 33. The Yanks paced the A.L. in runs scored (817), hits (1,509), team batting (.267) and team slugging (.426). In the latter two categories, the Yanks have not again led the A.L. through the 1983 season. Individually, Mantle led in walks (122) and second baseman Bobby Richardson got the most base hits with 209 and placed fourth in doubles with 38. Through 1983, no Yankee led the league again in total hits or slugging percentage, as did Richardson and Mantle, respectively, this season.

On the hill, Whitey Ford and Ralph Terry anchored the pitching staff. Ford came in second in winning percentage with .680 (17–8) and Terry finished 5th with a .657 (23–12) mark. Terry posted the most A.L. innings pitched with 298⅔ as well as victories with 23. Ford was the third best in ERA (2.90) and Terry was third in strikeouts with 176. Terry was probably the best pitcher in the A.L. this season. The club finished second overall in ERA with a 3.70, being tied with the Los Angeles Angels.

On June 24 at Detroit, the Yanks and Tigers played the longest game *by time* in American League history, consuming 7 hours flat and some 22 innings. This is the longest game by time as well as by innings in Yankee history. Detroit had played a 24 inning game in 1945 at Philadelphia. In this game, outfielder Jack Reed hit his only Major League homer in the top of the 22nd inning with the score knotted at 7-all. Reed played in 222 games in his 3-year career, all with the Yankees. Bobby Richardson had 11 at bats (3 hits) and the team totaled 85 with 20 hits. In this unusual game, the Yanks scored 6 runs in the top of the first inning with Detroit countering with 3 in their home half of the initial frame. Bouton won the game pitching seven full innings of scoreless ball while Phil "The Vulture" Regan lost the marathon affair. Some 35,638 were there to witness this historic game, although probably not many had the stamina to await its completion.

This season marked the last World Series title for New York until 1977. They will, however, appear in three more Fall Classics prior to that time.

The 1962 DAY BY DAY scores follow:

DAY BY DAY, 1962 NEW YORK YANKEES

April, 1962			
10 BAL	W	7- 6	
11 NG			
12 NG			
13 det	L	3- 5	
14 det	W	11- 5	
15 det		*	
16 NG			
17 bal	W	8- 3	
18 bal	L	0- 1	
19 bal	W	3- 1	
20 NG			
20 NG			
21 CLE	W	3- 1	
22 CLE	L	5- 7	
" CLE	L	3- 9	
23 NG			
24 CHI	L	1- 3	
25 CHI	W	7- 6	
26 NG			
27 was	W	10- 8	
28 was	W	10- 3	
29 was	W	3- 2	
" was	W	11- 6	
30 NG			

May, 1962			
1 chi	W	6- 1	
2 chi	W	4- 3	
3 chi	L	0- 1	
4 NG			
5 WAS	W	7- 6	
6 WAS	L	2- 4	
" WAS	W	8- 0	
7 NG			
8 BOS		*	
9 BOS	W	4- 1	
10 NG			
11 cle	L	1- 7	
12 cle	W	9- 6	
13 cle	L	4- 6	
" cle	L	5- 8	
14 NG			
15 bos	L	4-14	
16 bos	W	9- 8	
17 bos	W	2- 1	

May, 1962			
18 MIN	L	3- 4	
19 MIN	W	2- 1	
20 MIN	W	4- 3	
" MIN	L	2- 4i	
21 NG			
22 LA	W	2- 1h	
23 KC	W	13- 7	
24 KC	W	9- 4	
25 DET	L	4- 5	
26 DET	L	1- 2	
27 DET	W	4- 1	
" DET	L	1- 5	
28 kc		*	
28 kc		*	
29 kc	L	1- 2	
30 min	W	10- 1	
" min	L	4- 5g	
31 NG			

June, 1962			
1 LA	W	6- 2	
2 LA	L	1- 6	
3 LA	W	6- 3	
4 NG			
5 CLE		*	
6 CLE	W	5- 0	
7 CLE	W	4- 0	
8 BAL	W	1- 0	
9 BAL	W	7- 3	
10 BAL	L	1- 5	
" BAL	L	2- 7	
11 BAL	L	3- 5	
12 DET	W	2- 1	
13 DET		*	
14 NG			
15 cle	L	0- 3	
16 cle	L	9-10	
17 cle	L	1- 6	
" cle	L	3- 6	
18 NG			
19 bal	L	1- 3	
20 bal		*	
21 bal	W	3- 0	
22 det	L	5- 7	
23 det	W	8- 4	

June, 1962			
" det	L	4- 5	
24 det	W	9- 7q	
25 det	W	2- 0	
26 MIN	L	0- 5	
27 MIN	W	7- 3	
28 MIN	W	4- 2	
29 LA	W	6- 3	
30 LA	L	3- 5	

July, 1962			
1 LA	W	6- 3	
" LA	L	5-12	
2 KC	W	8- 4	
3 KC	W	8- 7	
4 KC	L	1-11	
" KC	W	7- 3	
" KC	W	7- 3	
5 NG		✓	
6 min	W	7- 5	
7 min	W	6- 3	
8 min	W	9- 8	
9 ALL-STAR BREAK			
10 WON - 46			
11 LOST - 33			
12 la	L	4- 5	
13 la	L	2- 5	
14 la	W	9- 8f	
15 kc	W	8- 6f	
" kc	W	11- 3	
16 kc	W	3- 1	
17 bos	W	1- 0	
18 bos	W	12- 4	
19 bos	W	10- 6	
20 WAS	W	3- 2	
21 WAS	W	4- 3	
22 WAs	L	2- 3	
" WAS	L	3- 8	
23 NG			
24 BOS	W	5- 3	
25 BOS	L	2- 4	
" BOS	W	6- 4	
26 BOS	W	13- 3	
27 CHI	W	4- 3h	
28 CHI	W	4- 3	
29 CHI	W	7- 4	

July, 1962			
" CHI	L	2- 6	
30 ALL-STAR BREAK			
	WON-61,LOST-39		
31 was	W	9- 5	

August, 1962			
1 was	W	6- 4	
" was	W	5- 2g	
2 NG			
3 chi	W	10- 2	
4 chi	L	1- 2	
5 chi	L	2- 3i	
6 MIN	L	4- 5	
7 MIN	W	14- 1	
8 BAL	W	3- 2	
" BAL	L	3- 4	
9 BAL		*	
10 DET	W	8- 0	
11 DET	L	2- 7	
11 DET	L	2- 7	
" DET	W	3- 2f	
12 DET	W	2- 0	
13 min	L	4- 6	
14 min	W	5- 2	
15 min	W	9- 3	
16 min	L	8- 9f	
17 kc	L	2- 7	
18 kc	L	4- 5	
" kc	W	11- 7	
19 kc	W	21- 7	
20 kc	L	3- 7	
21 la	W	4- 3	
22 la	W	11- 4f	
23 la	L	4- 5i	
24 bal	L	2- 6	
" bal	L	2-14	
25 bal	L	6- 8	
" bal	L	3- 4	
26 bal	L	1- 2	
27 CLE	W	5- 0	
28 CLE	W	2- 1	
" CLE		*	
29 CLE	L	2- 3	
" CLE	L	5- 9	
30 NG			
31 KC	W	5- 1	

September, 1962			
1 KC	W	3- 1	
2 KC	W	2- 1	
3 LA	W	8- 2	
" LA	L	5- 6	
4 LA	L	6- 7	
5 LA		*	
6 LA	W	6- 5	
7 BOS	W	5-4	
8 BOS	W	6-1	
9 BOS	L	3- 9	
" BOS	L	4- 5L	
10 det	W	3-1	
11 det	W	8-7f	
12 cle	W	5-2	
13 NG			
14 bos	L	1-4	
15 bos	W	9-6	
16 bos	L	3-4	
16 bos	L	3-4	
17 NG			
18 was	W	7-1	
19 was	W	8- 5	
20 NG			
21 chi	L	6- 7	
22 chi	L	2-6	
23 chi	W	5-1f	
24 NG			
25 WAS	W	8-3	
26 WAS	W	9-5	
27 NG			
28 CHI	W	7-3	
29 CHI	W	8-6	
30 CHI	L	4-8	

END OF 1962

RUNS: 817

OPP RUNS: 680

CLUB VS. CLUB AND MONTHLY RECORDS OF THE
NEW YORK YANKEES' 1962 SEASON FOR HOME AND AWAY GAMES

CLUB:		APR	MAY	JUN	JUL	AUG	SEP	OCT	HOME	AWAY	TOTAL
BALT	H	1-0	xxx	2- 3	xxx	1- 1	xxx	xxx	4- 4	xxx	
	A	2-1	xxx	1- 1	xxx	0- 5	xxx	xxx	xxx	3- 7	7-11
BOST	H	xxx	1- 0	xxx	3- 1	xxx	2- 2	xxx	6- 3	xxx	
	A	xxx	2- 1	xxx	3- 0	xxx	1- 2	xxx	xxx	6- 3	12- 6
CHIC	H	1- 1	xxx	xxx	3- 1	xxx	2- 1	xxx	6- 3	xxx	
	A	xxx	2- 1	xxx	xxx	1- 2	1- 2	xxx	xxx	4- 5	10- 8
CLEV	H	1- 2	xxx	2- 0	xxx	2- 2	xxx	xxx	5- 4	xxx	
	A	xxx	1- 3	0- 4	xxx	xxx	1- 0	xxx	xxx	2- 7	7-11
DET	H	xxx	1- 3	1- 0	xxx	3- 1	xxx	xxx	5- 4	xxx	
	A	1-1	xxx	3- 2	xxx	xxx	2- 0	xxx	xxx	6- 3	11- 7
KC	H	xxx	2- 0	xxx	3- 1	1- 0	2- 0	xxx	8- 1	xxx	
	A	xxx	0- 1	xxx	3- 0	2- 3	xxx	xxx	xxx	5- 4	13- 5
LA	H	xxx	1- 0	1- 1	1- 1	xxx	2- 2	xxx	5- 4	xxx	
	A	xxx	xxx	2- 1	1- 2	2- 1	xxx	xxx	xxx	5- 4	10- 8
MINN	H	xxx	2- 2	2- 1	xxx	1- 1	xxx	xxx	5- 4	xxx	
	A	xxx	1- 1	xxx	3- 0	1- 2	xxx	xxx	xxx	6- 3	11- 7
WAS	H	xxx	2- 1	xxx	2- 2	xxx	2- 0	xxx	6- 3	xxx	
	A	4-0	xxx	xxx	1- 0	2- 0	2- 0	xxx	xxx	9- 0	15- 3
TOTAL:	H	3-3	9- 6	8- 5	12- 6	8- 5	10- 5	xxx	50- 30	xxx	
	A	7-2	6- 7	6- 8	11- 2	9-13	7- 4	xxx	xxx	46-36	96-66
GRAND TOT:		10-5	15-13	14-13	23- 8	17-18	17- 9	xxx	x x x	xxx	96-66
CUMUL TOT:		10-5	25-18	39-31	62-39	79-57	96-66	xxx	xxx	xxx	**TIE GAMES:** NONE

1963

THE MAJOR WINS HIS THIRD PENNANT

Under the guidance of Ralph Houk, the Major, in his third year as New York manager, the Yanks blasted the opposition, finishing 10½ games ahead of runner-up Chicago. Winning 104 games while losing 57 (for a .646 winning mark), the Yankees were beaten by the Dodgers in four straight games in their 28th World Series appearance. This had not happened since the Giants turned the trick in the 1922 Fall Classic (there was one tie also). Through 1963, on the other hand, New York had beaten National league opponents four games to none six times (1927, 1928, 1932, 1938, 1939 and 1950) previously.

Stat-wise, the club led the A.L. in no offensive categories. In pitching, they had the most complete games (59) and were tied for second in fielding percentage. This was an extremely adept defensive club, especially the infield.

Ellie Howard, fine Yankee catcher, won the MVP Award. Howard hit 28 homers, 5th in the A.L., had a .528 slugging mark, 3rd league-wise, and had 85 RBI. His catching expertise bolstered an already solid fielding team. For the second time in Major League history (1954 through 1957 was the first), the MVP went to a player of the same club in four consecutive seasons. Berra won the MVP in 1954 and 1955, while Mantle copped the award in 1956 and 1957. Then in 1960 and 1961, Maris won the MVP followed by Mantle and now Howard.

Individually, Whitey Ford became the only Yankee in history to lead the A.L. 3 times in winning percentage. Having led previously in 1956 (.760) and 1961 (.862, his best mark ever), Ford had a winning mark of .774, having won a league high 24 games, while losing 7. Finishing second to Whitey Ford's league high 269⅓ innings pitched, Ralph Terry had 268 and tied Pascual of Minnesota with the league lead in complete games (18). Jim Bouton came in second to Ford's winning percentage with a .750 mark (21–7). He finished second (tied with Pascual) with 21 wins and had 6 shutouts, second in A.L. His ERA of 2.53 was the league's fourth best. Al Downing had a good season also with a 2.56 ERA, fifth overall in the Junior Circuit. The Yankee southpaw had a high strikeout ratio per 9 innings throughout his career, averaging 6½ whiffs per game over his 17 year career.

The Major, Ralph Houk, stepped down as Yankee manager at the end of this season. He returned again as New York skipper in May 1966. Yogi Berra assumed the managerial duties the next season.

The 1963 DAY BY DAY scores follow:

Elston Howard was the winner of the MVP award in the American League in 1963. As a fine fielding catcher, Elston made but 2 errors in 146 games in 1964. He played in 13 Yankee campaigns and was the first black to appear in pinstripes, in 1955.

DAY BY DAY, 1963 NEW YORK YANKEES

April, 1963			May, 1963			June, 1963			August, 1963			September, 1963		
9 kc	W	8-2	21 KC	W	7-4	28 BOS	L	3-4	3 BAL	W	3-2	7 DET	W	11-6
10 kc	W	5-3	22 KC	W	8-7g	29 BOS	W	2-0	4 BAL	L	2-7	8 DET	W	5-3
11 BAL	L	1-4	23 NG			30 BOS	W	4-2	" BAL	W	11-10f	9 kc	L	6-7
12 NG			24 WAS	W	5-3	" BOS	W	11-4	5 NG			10 kc	L	0-2
13 BAL	W	6-1	25 WAS	W	5-1	**July, 1963**			6 was	L	5-8	11 kc	W	8-2
14 BAL	W	5-1	26 WAS	W	7-1	1 BOS	W	7-5	" was	W	1-0	12 kc	W	5-2
15 NG			" WAS	L	6-7	2 CHI	W	3-0	7 was	W	9-1	13 min	W	2-0
16 DET	L	2-7	27 NG			3 CHI	W	5-4	8 was	W	3-1	14 min	L	2-6
17 DET	L	2-4	28 bos	L	6-11	4 CHI	W	9-1	9 la	W	1-0	" min	W	3-1
18 NG			29 bos	W	6-5f	" CHI	L	2-4	10 la	W	2-1	15 min	W	2-1
19 was	W	8-4	30 bos		*	5 cle	L	1-4	11 la	W	6-4f	16 NG		
20 was	L	1-7	31 cle	W	4-0	6 cle	W	11-6	12 NG			17 cle	L	2-3f
21 was	W	7-6	**June, 1963**			7 cle		L3-11	13 bos		*	18 NG		
22 NG			1 cle	W	5-2	" cle	W	7-4f	14 bos	L	7-14	19 NG		
23 BOS		*	2 cle	L	0-5	8 ALL-STAR BREAK			" bos	L	4-5	20 KC	W	5-4i
24 CHI	L	4-6h	" cle	L	2-7	9 WON - 50			15 bos	W	10-2	" KC	L	3-4
25 NG			3 NG			10 LOST - 31			16 chi	W	4-2	21 KC	L	3-5
26 NG			4 bal	L	1-3	11 la	W	3-2f	17 chi	L	0-2	22 KC	W	4-3
27 CLE	W	8-1	5 bal	W	4-3	12 la	W	4-3	18 chi	W	8-2	23 NG		
28 CLE	W	5-0	6 bal	L	2-4	13 la	L	1-3	" chi	W	8-4	24 LA	W	8-1
29 chi		*	7 det	L	4-8	14 kc	W	11-6	19 NG			25 LA	W	3-1
30 la	L	3-6	8 det	L	4-8	" kc	W	5-0	20 CLE	L	1-2	26 NG		
May, 1963			9 det	W	6-2	15 kc		L10-11h	21 CLE	W	3-1	27 MIN	L	3-4
1 la	L	3-5	10 was	W	7-0	16 min		*	" CLE	W	3-1	28 MIN	L	3-6
2 la	W	7-0	" was	L	0-1	17 min	W	4-0	22 CLE	L	4-7	29 MIN		*
3 min	W	4-3f	11 NG			18 min	L	3-9	23 CHI	W	7-2			
4 min	W	3-2	12 BAL	W	3-2f	19 CLE		*	24 CHI	W	3-0	END OF 1963		
5 min	L	1-4	13 BAL	L	4-5	20 CLE	W	5-4	25 CHI	W	4-0	RUNS:		714
6 det	W	10-3	14 DET	W	4-2	21 CLE	W	5-2	" CHI	L	1-2h	OPP RUNS:		547
7 det	L	2-6	15 DET	W	9-2	" CLE	W	5-4g	26 NG					
8 det	L	6-7	16 DET	W	4-0	22 LA	W	8-4	27 BOS	W	5-0			
9 chi	L	0-2	" DET	W	6-3	23 LA	W	7-0	" BOS	W	3-0			
10 bal	L	3-6	17 NG			24 LA	W	8-4	28 BOS	W	4-1			
11 bal	W	13-1	18 WAS	W	10-5	25 LA	L	0-5	29 BOS	L	3-4			
12 bal	W	2-0	19 WAS	W	3-2	26 MIN	W	6-5	30 bal	W	4-1			
13 NG			20 WAS	W	5-4	27 MIN	W	5-1	31 bal	W	5-3			
14 MIN	W	2-1	21 bos	L	4-7	28 MIN	L	1-5	**September, 1963**					
15 MIN	W	4-3	22 bos	W	6-5	" MIN	W	3-2	1 bal	W	5-4			
16 NG			" bos	W	3-2	29 KC	L	0-5	2 det	W	5-4			
17 LA	W	4-3	23 bos	W	8-0	30 KC	W	6-2	" det	L	1-2			
18 LA		*	24 chi	L	2-5	31 KC	W	3-2	3 det	L	2-3k			
19 LA	L	2-6	25 chi	L	1-2	**August, 1963**			4 WAS	W	5-4			
" LA	W	10-4	26 chi	W	3-2	1 NG			5 WAS	W	3-2h			
20 NG			27 chi	L	0-6	2 BAL	L	3-5	6 DET	W	2-1			

CLUB VS. CLUB AND MONTLY RECORDS OF THE NEW YORK YANKEES' 1963 SEASON FOR HOME AND AWAY GAMES

CLUB		APR	MAY	JUN	JUL	AUG	SEP	OCT	HOME	AWAY	TOTAL
BALT	H	2-1	xxx	1- 1	xxx	2- 2	xxx	xxx	5- 4	xxx	11- 7
	A	xxx	2- 1	1- 2	xxx	2- 0	1- 0	xxx	xxx	6- 3	
BOST	H	xxx	xxx	3- 1	1- 0	3- 1	xxx	xxx	7- 2	xxx	12- 6
	A	xxx	1- 1	3- 1	xxx	1- 2	xxx	xxx	xxx	5- 4	
CHIC	H	0-1	xxx	xxx	3- 1	3- 1	xxx	xxx	6- 3	xxx	10- 8
	A	xxx	0- 1	1- 3	xxx	3- 1	xxx	xxx	xxx	4- 5	
CLEV	H	2-0	xxx	xxx	3- 0	2- 2	xxx	xxx	7- 2	xxx	11- 7
	A	xxx	1- 0	1- 2	2- 2	xxx	0- 1	xxx	xxx	4- 5	
DET	H	0-2	xxx	4- 0	xxx	xxx	3- 0	xxx	7- 2	xxx	10- 8
	A	xxx	1- 2	1- 2	xxx	xxx	1- 2	xxx	xxx	3- 6	
KC	H	xxx	2- 0	xxx	2- 1	xxx	2- 2	xxx	6- 3	xxx	12- 6
	A	2-0	xxx	xxx	2- 1	xxx	2- 2	xxx	xxx	6- 3	
LA	H	xxx	2- 1	xxx	3- 1	xxx	2- 0	xxx	7- 2	xxx	13- 5
	A	0-1	1- 1	xxx	2- 1	3- 0	xxx	xxx	xxx	6- 3	
MINN	H	xxx	2- 0	xxx	3- 1	xxx	0- 2	xxx	5- 3	xxx	11- 6
	A	xxx	2- 1	xxx	1- 1	xxx	3- 1	xxx	xxx	6- 3	
WAS	H	xxx	3- 1	3- 0	xxx	xxx	2- 0	xxx	8- 1	xxx	14- 4
	A	2-1	xxx	1- 1	xxx	3- 1	xxx	xxx	xxx	6- 3	
TOTAL:	H	4-4	9- 2	11- 2	15- 4	10- 6	9- 4	xxx	58-22	xxx	104-57
	A	4-2	8- 7	8- 11	7- 5	12- 4	7- 6	xxx	xxx	46-35	
GRAND TOT:	H	8-6	17- 9	19-13	22- 9	22-10	16-10	xxx	xxx	xxx	
CUMUL TOT:	A	8-6	25-15	44-28	66-37	88-47	104-57	xxx	xxx	xxx	

TIE GAMES: NONE

1964

ENTER YOGI BERRA: MANAGER

In Yogi Berra's only season as Yankee manager, New York had to scratch and claw to win their 29th pennant. The Yanks eventually fell to the St. Louis Cardinals in the World Series. The Cardinals had not made an appearance in the Fall Classic since 1946. Finishing at 99–63 (.611), the Yanks beat the Chicago White Sox by only one full game and the Baltimore Orioles, in third place by 2 games. The pennant was clinched for New York on the second-to-last day of the season (October 3) in defeating Cleveland at Yankee Stadium, 8–3, with the Yanks tallying five runs in the bottom of the 8th inning. An eleven game winning streak starting from September 16 through September 26 definitely aided the Yankee pennant cause. From August 29 through the end of the season (October 4), the Yanks won 27 of their final 36 games, a .750 winning clip, including a 22–6 mark in the month of September.

The Yanks paced the American League with 1,442 hits. Their team batting mark of .253 tied for second in the league with Detroit. They led in no other major statistical category in batting, pitching or fielding.

However, they set a few club marks this season: most errorless games–91, fewest errors–107 (tying the 1947 mark), most at bats (5,705) and highest fielding mark in their history–.983.

Individually, the Yanks placed two batters in the top 4 in the A.L., with Elston Howard's .313 mark (3rd) and Mantle's .303, the fourth best in the A.L. The Mick also finished second in league slugging (.591) and walks (99), and third in both homers (35) and RBI (111).

On the mound, Jim "Bulldog" Bouton paced the staff with an 18–13 mark. Whitey Ford finished second overall in the league in winning percentage–

.739 (17–6), shutouts (8), and third in ERA, with a fine 2.13 mark. Becoming only the fifth Yankee pitcher to lead the Junior Circuit in strikeouts (and the first since Reynolds led in 1952 with 160 whiffs), Al Downing fanned 217 enemy batters. A very bright move this season by Yankee management was that Mel Stottlemyre, Yankee sinker ball pitcher, was brought up from Richmond of the minor leagues on August 11. Mel's consistency (won 9 and lost 3) during the remainder of the season bolstered the Yankee staff. Stot would go on to pitch another 10 seasons as a Yankee, winning 164 (and losing 139) games. At the conclusion of his career after the 1974 season, Mel's name ranked in the top 10 of many Yankee all-time pitching categories, including 40 shutouts, second only to Whitey Ford's 45 whitewashes.

On August 14, the Columbia Broadcasting System purchased 80% of the Yankee franchise from Dan Topping and Del Webb. In 1965, CBS purchased the remaining 20% of Yankee stock to become sole owners.

Although successful pennant-wise, Yogi's only year at the Yankee helm was apparently not successful enough with Berra being released as New York manager October 16, the day after the final World Series game. Johnny Keane, pilot of the World Champion St. Louis Cardinals, became the 19th Yankee manager.

At the conclusion of the 1964 season, the Yanks had won 29 pennants in forty-four American League seasons, or 66% of the A.L. flags since 1921. During that same time-frame, the Bombers won 20 of 44 World Series (45.5%) as American League representative in the Fall Classic.

Who could have realized that 1964 would mark the end of the Yanks' incredible sports dynasty? It will take a dozen long seasons for the Bombers to achieve their long-awaited 30th American League pennant.

The 1964 DAY BY DAY scores follow:

DAY BY DAY, 1964 NEW YORK YANKEES

April, 1964			
14 BOS	*		
15 NG			
16 BOS	L	3-	4g
17 bal	L	3-	4g
18 bal	L	1-	2h
19 bal	W	5-	3
20 bos	L	0-	4
" bos	*		
21 NG			
22 chi	W	3-	0
23 NG			
24 NG			
25 BAL	W	4-	1
26 BAL	W	5-	4
27 NG			
28 CHI	*		
29 CHI	*		
30 NG			

May, 1964			
1 WAS	W	1-	0
2 WAS	L	4-	5f
3 WAS	W	4-	0
" WAS	L	5-	6
4 NG			
5 DET	W	4-	3f
6 was	W	9-	2
" was	L	4-	5
7 was	W	9-	6
8 cle	W	10-	3
9 cle	W	6-	2
10 cle	W	12-	2
" cle	W	3-	2f
11 NG			
12 det	L	2-	7
13 det	TG	1-	1b
14 det	L	3-	7
15 KC	L	0-	11
16 KC	W	10-	6
17 KC	W	11-	9
" KC	W	8-	0
18 NG			
19 MIN	L	2-	7i
20 MIN	L	4-	7
21 NG			

May, 1964			
22 LA	W		4-3
23 LA	L		5-9
24 LA	L		0-3
" LA	W		8-5
25 NG			
26 CLE	W		3-2
27 CLE	W		7-2
28 NG			
29 kc	L		1-4
30 kc	W		9-1
31 kc	L		2-4

June, 1964			
1 min	L		1-2
2 min	L	2-	6
3 min	W	3-	0
4 min	W		9-7
5 la	L		2-3
6 la	W		2-0k
7 la	W		9-3
8 NG			
9 bos	L		2-5
10 bos	L		6-7f
" bos	W		10-6
11 bos	W		8-4
12 CHI	W		6-1
" CHI	W		3-0
13 CHI	W	6-	3
14 CHI	W	8-	3
" CHI	W	4-	3f
15 NG			
16 BOS	L		5-6
" BOS	W		7-5
17 BOS	L	3-	4h
18 BOS	W		6-3
19 chi	*		
20 chi	W	1-	0g
21 chi	W	2-	0
" chi	W	2-	1m
22 chi	W	6-	5
23 bal	L		8-9
24 bal	L		4-7
25 bal	L		1-3
26 DET	L		0-1g
27 DET	W		5-4

June, 1964			
28 DET	W	8-	6
" DET	L	5-	6
29 NG			
30 LA	W	4-	0
" LA	W	3-	2

July, 1964			
1 KC	L	4-	5g
2 KC	W	4-	3k
3 MIN	L	0-	1f
4 MIN	W	7-	5
" MIN	W	2-	1
5 MIN	L	2-	9
6 ALL-STAR BREAK			
7 WON - 45			
8 LOST - 31			
9 was	W	6-	5
10 was	W	4-	1
11 was	W	3-	2
12 cle	TG	2-	2c
" cle	*		
13 cle	W	10-	4
14 BAL	W	4-	3
15 BAL	W	2-	0
16 BAL	L	1-	6
17 CLE	W	8-	4
18 CLE	L	4-	6k
19 CLE	W	6-	2
" CLE	L	0-	3
20 NG			
21 WAS	W	7-	1
22 WAS	W	6-	3
23 WAS	L	1-	2
24 det	L	5-	10
" det	W	6-	3
25 det	W	14-	2
26 det	W	11-	6
" det	W	5-	4
27 la	W	3-	0
28 la	L	1-	3
29 la	W	5-	0
30 NG			
31 min	L	3-	4

August, 1964			
1 min	W	6-	4
2 min	W	2-	0

August, 1964			
3 NG			
4 kc	L	1-	5
5 kc		L1-	10
6 kc	W	5-	3
7 BAL	L	0-	2
8 BAL	L	5-	6f
9 BAL	W	2-	1
" BAL	L	2-	4
10 NG			
11 CHI	L	4-	6
" CHI	L	2-	8
12 CHI	W	7-	3
13 CHI	W	5-	2
14 bal	L	4-	5
15 bal	W	8-	1
16 bal	W	3-	1
17 chi	L	1-	2
18 chi	L	3-	4f
19 chi	L	2-	4
20 chi	L	0-	5
21 bos	L	0-	7
22 bos	L	3-	5
" bos	W	8-	0
23 bos	W	4-	3
24 NG			
25 WAS	W	4-	1
26 WAS	L	0-	2
27 NG			
28 BOS	L	3-	5
29 BOS	W	10-	2
" BOS	W	6-	1
30 BOS	W	9-	3
31 NG			

September, 1964			
1 la	W	4-	1
2 la	L	0-	4
3 la	L	2-	4
4 kc	W	9-	7f
5 kc	W	9-	7
6 kc	W	3-	2
7 min	W	5-	4g
" min	*		
8 min	W	2-	1
9 det	L	0-	4

September, 1964			
10 det	W		5-2
11 MIN	L		3-5
12 MIN	W		4-3
13 MIN	W		5-2
14 NG			
15 LA	L		0-7
16 LA	W		9-4
17 LA	W		6-2
18 KC	W		6-0
19 KC	W		8-3
20 KC	W		4-0
21 NG			
22 cle	W		5-3
" cle	W		8-1
23 cle	W	4-	3g
" cle	W	6-	4
24 NG			
25 was	W		6-5
26 was	W		7-0
27 was	L		2-3g
28 NG			
29 DET	*		
" DET	*		
30 DET	W		7-6
" DET	W		11-8

October, 1964			
1 DET	L		2-4
" DET	L		2-5
2 CLE	W		5-2
3 CLE	W		8-3
4 CLE	L	1-	2i

END OF 1964

RUNS:	730
OPP RUNS:	577

CLUB VS. CLUB AND MONTHLY RECORDS OF THE NEW YORK YANKEES' 1964 SEASON FOR HOME AND AWAY GAMES

CLUB:		APR	MAY	JUN	JUL	AUG	SEP	OCT	HOME	AWAY	TOTAL
BALT	H	2-0	xxx	xxx	2-1	1-3	xxx	xxx	5-4	xxx	8-10
	A	1-2	xxx	0-3	xxx	2-1	xxx	xxx	xxx	3-6	
BOST	H	0-1	xxx	2-2	xxx	3-1	xxx	xxx	5-4	xxx	9-9
	A	0-1	xxx	2-2	xxx	2-2	xxx	xxx	xxx	4-5	
CHIC	H	xxx	xxx	5-0	xxx	2-2	xxx	xxx	7-2	xxx	12-6
	A	1-0	xxx	4-0	xxx	0-4	xxx	xxx	xxx	5-4	
CLEV	H	xxx	2-0	xxx	2-2	xxx	xxx	2-1	6-3	xxx	15-3
	A	xxx	4-0	xxx	1-0	xxx	4-0	xxx	xxx	9-0	
DET	H	xxx	1-0	2-2	xxx	xxx	2-0	0-2	5-4	xxx	10-8
	A	xxx	0-2	xxx	4-1	xxx	1-1	xxx	xxx	5-4	
KC	H	xxx	3-1	xxx	1-1	xxx	3-0	xxx	7-2	xxx	12-6
	A	xxx	1-2	xxx	xxx	1-2	3-0	xxx	xxx	5-4	
LA	H	xxx	2-2	2-0	xxx	xxx	2-1	xxx	6-3	xxx	11-7
	A	xxx	xxx	2-1	2-1	xxx	1-2	xxx	xxx	5-4	
MINN	H	xxx	0-2	xxx	2-2	xxx	2-1	xxx	4-5	xxx	10-8
	A	xxx	xxx	2-2	0-1	2-0	2-0	xxx	xxx	6-3	
WAS	H	xxx	2-2	xxx	2-1	1-1	xxx	xxx	5-4	xxx	12-6
	A	xxx	2-1	xxx	3-0	xxx	2-1	xxx	xxx	7-2	
TOTAL:	H	2-1	10-7	11-4	9-7	7-7	9-2	2-3	50-31	xxx	99-63
	A	2-3	7-5	10-8	10-3	7-9	13-4	xxx	xxx	49-32	
GRAND TOT:		4-4	17-12	21-12	19-10	14-16	22-6	2-3	xxx	xxx	
CUMUL TOT:		4-4	21-16	42-28	61-38	75-54	97-60	99-63	xxx	x xx	

TIE GAMES: 2
det-May; cle-Jul.

1965

THE FALL OF THE YANKEE EMPIRE

After winning 29 pennants since 1921, the New Yorkers found themselves in sixth place, 25 games off Minnesota's pennant-clinching pace. The Yankees faltered to their worst record since 1925 when they finished at 69–85 (.448). In 1965, the Yanks won but 77 games, losing 85 for a .475 winning percentage. Under New York's nineteenth manager, Johnny Keane, the beginning of the end of the Yankee dynasty was very evident in the team's everyday play. Keane managed for this full season plus a part of 1966, until replaced by Ralph Houk.

The club batted a lowly .235, the worst since 1915 (.233), to finish ninth out of ten A.L. teams. Their run total of 611 was their lowest since scoring 582 in 1919, as was their slugging mark of .364 and RBI total (576). However, they did continue to show some muscle, knocking out 149 homers. Tom Tresh was the main offensive power this year, ending second in A.L. total bases (287), third in runs scored (94) and led the club with 28 homers and 74 RBI.

Yankee righthander Mel Stottlemyre was the brightest spot on the pitching staff. Mel gained 20 victories (second in the league) and finished first in A.L. complete games (18) and innings pitched (291). Stot's winning mark of .690 (20–9) was 3rd in the A.L. A club record was set by the pitching staff striking out 1,001 batters. Downing led the way with 179.

Defensively, the Yankees turned the most A.L. double plays with 166.

The attendance at Yankee Stadium dwindled to some 1.2 million, the lowest total in some twenty years.

The new baseball commissioner, William Eckert, replaced Ford Frick as the fourth czar of the national pastime. Eckert will serve in that capacity until Bowie Kuhn assumes that duty in February, 1969.

With 1965, the Yankee empire was beginning to crumble. Next year, the Yanks finished in last place for the first time since 1912.

The 1965 DAY BY DAY scores follow:

DAY BY DAY, 1965 NEW YORK YANKEES

April, 1965
12 min L 4- 5f
13 min *
14 cal L 3- 4
15 cal W 4- 0
16 NG
17 kc W 5- 2
18 kc W 10- 4
19 kc L 2- 8
20 NG
21 MIN L 2- 7
22 MIN L 2- 8
23 CAL *
24 CAL L 3- 6
25 CAL W 3- 2
" CAL W 1- 0
26 NG
27 KC *
28 KC W 5- 1
29 NG
30 BAL L 4-10

May, 1965
1 BAL W 9- 4
2 BAL L 2- 4f
" BAL L 0- 5
3 NG
4 cle W 5- 3
5 cle L 0- 4
6 cle *
7 was L 3- 4
" was L 3- 7
8 was W 7- 3
9 was L 4- 5
10 bos L 2- 3
11 bos W 5- 3
12 bos L 0- 2
13 bos L 1- 4
14 bal W 9- 3
15 bal W 3- 2
16 bal L 5- 7
17 bal L 2- 9
18 BOS W 4- 3h
19 BOS L 0- 3
20 BOS W 6- 3
21 WAS L 4- 5

May, 1965
22 WAS W 6- 0
23 WAS L 3- 7
" WAS W 3- 2
24 CLE W 15- 5
25 CLE L 1- 5
26 det *
27 det L 1- 4
28 chi L 0- 2
29 chi L 3- 6
30 chi W 3- 2h
31 DET W 3- 1
" DET L 1- 5

June, 1965
1 NG
2 DET
3 NG
4 CHI L 0- 2k
5 CHI W 4- 3f
6 CHI W 6- 1
" CHI W 12- 0
7 kc W 4- 2
8 kc L 2- 3
9 kc W 5- 1
10 NG
11 cal W 6- 4
12 cal L3- 13
13 cal W 3- 0
14 cle L 4- 5
15 BAL L 1- 2f
16 BAL L 1- 5
17 BAL L 1- 2L
18 MIN W 10- 2
19 MIN W 5- 3
20 MIN L 4- 6
" MIN L 4- 7
21 NG
22 KC L 2- 6
" KC W 4- 2
23 KC W 8- 3
24 KC L 2- 6
25 CAL W 5- 1
26 CAL W 10- 3
27 CAL W 7- 2
28 was W 3- 0
" was W 4- 3

June, 1965
29 was L 1- 2
30 bal W 5- 4

July, 1965
1 bal L 3-4
2 BOS W 16-2
3 BOS W 6-2
4 BOS L 3-5
5 det W 7-2
" det L 4-5
6 det L 0-8
7 det W 4-3
8 det L 1- 6
9 min L 3- 8
10 min L 1- 4
" min W 8-6
11 min L 5-6
12 ALL-STAR BREAK
13 WON: - 41
14 LOST: - 46
15 WAS W 2- 1h
16 WAS W 9-5
17 WAS W 5-4
18 WAS L 0-3
19 BOS L 1-3
20 BOS W 6-3
21 CHI W 7-6f
22 CHI W 3-1
23 cle L 2- 5
24 cle L 0-3
25 cle W 3-0
" cle L 4-7
26 NG
27 DET W 4- 3
" DET L 0-3
28 DET L 3-4
29 DET W 7-3
30 CLE L 0-5
31 CLE W 7-6

August, 1965
1 CLE W 10-6
" CLE L 1-4
2 NG
3 chi L 2- 3
4 chi W 4- 3i
5 chi W 3-0

August, 1965
6 det L 4-5
7 det W 6-5
8 det W 6-5
9 NG
10 MIN L 3-7
11 MIN W 5-4
12 MIN L 2-8
13 KC W 3-1
14 KC W 3-2
15 KC L 1- 4
" KC W 7- 3
16 NG
17 CAL W 6-1
18 CAL L 3-7
19 CAL W 3- 1
20 bal W 1-0
21 bal *
22 bal *
23 min L 3- 4f
24 min W 2-1
25 min L 4-5
26 min L 2-9
27 kc L 0-1
28 kc L 0-4
29 kc W 4-3
30 cal W 4-2
31 cal L 0-1

September, 1965
1 cal L 6-7h
2 cal W 8-1
3 BOS W 9-0
4 BOS L 0-1
" BOS L 2-7
5 BOS L 3- 4h
6 BAL L 1- 2
" BAL L 2-6
7 BAL L 2-4
" BAL L 5-9
8 WAS W 6-5
9 NG
10 chi W 3-1
11 chi W 3-1
12 chi L 1-4
13 NG
14 was W 3- 1

September, 1965
15 was W 5-3
16 NG
17 DET L 3-4f
18 DET L 3- 4f
19 DET W 3-0
20 NG
21 CLE W 9-4
22 CLE L 3- 4
23 CLE L 1- 2
24 CHI *
25 CHI L 1-3
" CHI L 0-2
26 CHI L 3-5
27 NG
28 cle L 3-6
29 cle L 3- 5
30 NG

October, 1965
1 NG
2 bos W 6-4
3 bos W 11-5

END OF 1965
RUNS: 611
OPP RUNS: 604

CLUB VS. CLUB AND MONTHLY RECORDS OF THE NEW YORK YANKEES' 1965 SEASON FOR HOME AND AWAY GAMES

CLUB:		APR	MAY	JUN	JUL	AUG	SEP	OCT	HOME	AWAY	TOTAL
BALT	H	0-1	1- 2	0- 3	xxx	xxx	0- 4	xxx	1-10	xxx	5-13
	A	xxx	2- 2	1- 0	0-1	1- 0	xxx	xxx	xxx	4- 3	
BOST	H	xxx	2- 1	xxx	1- 1	xxx	1- 3	xxx	4- 5	xxx	9- 9
	A	xxx	1- 3	xxx	2- 1	xxx	xxx	2- 0	xxx	5- 4	
CAL	H	2- 1	xxx	3- 0	xxx	2- 1	xxx	xxx	7- 2	xxx	12- 6
	A	1-1	xxx	2-1	xxx	1- 1	1- 1	xxx	xxx	5- 4	
CHIC	H	xxx	xxx	3- 1	2- 0	xxx	0- 3	xxx	5- 4	xxx	10- 8
	A	xxx	1- 2	xxx	xxx	2- 1	2-1	xxx	xxx	5- 4	
CLEV	H	xxx	1- 1	xxx	1- 1	1- 1	1- 2	xxx	4- 5	xxx	6-12
	A	xxx	1- 1	0- 1	1- 3	xxx	0- 2	xxx	xxx	2- 7	
DET	H	xxx	1- 1	xxx	2- 2	xxx	1- 2	xxx	4- 5	xxx	8-10
	A	xxx	0- 1	xxx	2- 3	2- 1	xxx	xxx	xxx	4- 5	
KC	H	1- 0	xxx	2- 2	xxx	3- 1	xxx	xxx	6- 3	xxx	11- 7
	A	2-1	xxx	2- 1	xxx	1- 2	xxx	xxx	xxx	5- 4	
MINN	H	0- 2	xxx	2- 2	xxx	1- 2	xxx	xxx	3- 6	xxx	5-13
	A	0-1	xxx	xxx	1- 3	1- 3	xxx	xxx	xxx	2- 7	
WAS	H	xxx	2- 2	xxx	3- 1	xxx	1- 0	xxx	6- 3	xxx	11- 7
	A	xxx	1- 3	2- 1	xxx	xxx	2- 0	xxx	xxx	5- 4	
TOTAL:	H	3-4	7- 7	10- 8	9- 5	7- 5	4-14	xxx	40- 43	xxx	77-85
	A	3-3	6-12	7- 4	6-11	8- 8	5- 4	2- 0	xxx	37-42	
GRAND TOT:		6-7	13-19	17-12	15-16	15-13	9-18	2- 0	xxx	xxx	
CUMUL TOT:		6-7	19-26	36-38	51-54	66-67	75-85	77-85	xxx	xxx	

TIE GAMES: NONE

1966

FIRST LAST-PLACE FINISH IN FIFTY-FOUR YEARS

In 1966, the once proud Yanks concluded the season in tenth and last place. It had not been since 1912 that the team finished at the bottom of the American League. Managerial duties were divided between Johnny Keane and Ralph Houk, the latter beginning his second tenure as New York field manager. Finishing at 70–89 (.440), the Yanks ended 1966 but ½ game behind the 9th place Boston Red Sox. The New Yorkers had not played all 162 games, the Bostons did. This "cellar team" was probably one of the best last place teams in baseball history, if one could make such a statement. As a matter of fact, (you could look it up) their winning percentage of .440 represents the best mark for a cellar-dweller in A.L. history (excluding divisional play begun in 1969).

No individual Yankee players came close to leading the league in any statistical areas, nor did the club as a team. Well, to find a bright spot, Joe Pepitone did hit 31 homers, fifth in the league.

On the negative side statistically, the Yanks lost the most often in the league with 89 setbacks. Mel Stottlemyre became the first Yankee pitcher to lead the A.L. in losses (20) since "Sad Sam" Jones lost 21 in 1925.

Ending the season on a sour note, only 413 people witnessed a game at Yankee Stadium on September 22, the smallest crowd in the stadium's history. The White Sox beat the Yanks 4 to 1. With the loss at Baltimore, 3–2, on September 7, the Yanks fell into last place in the month of September. This had not occurred since 1913.

Ralph Houk would be with the Yanks as manager during one of the most dismal periods of this incredible baseball franchise. They would fare but a bit better in 1967.

The 1966 DAY BY DAY scores follow:

DAY BY DAY, 1966 NEW YORK YANKEES

April, 1966

12	DET	L	1–2
13	DET		*
14	DET	L	2–3
"	DET	L	2–5
15	bal	W	3–2
16	bal	L	2–7
17	bal	L	4–5
18	NG		
19	cle	L	1–3
20	cle	L	2–4
21	NG		
22	NG		
23	BAL	L	3–4
24	BAL	L	1–2
25	BOS	L	5–8
26	BOS	W	7–6
27	WAS	L	0–2
28	WAS		*
29	NG		
30	KC	W	6–0

May, 1966

1	KC	L	0–1
"	KC	W	10–4
2	NG		
3	CLE	L	0–1
4	CLE	L	1–2
5	CLE	L	0–4
6	cal	L	4–7
7	cal	W	3–1
8	cal	W	5–2
9	min	W	3–2
10	min		*
11	min		*
12	kc	L	3–4
13	kc	W	4–2
14	kc	L	2–4
15	kc	W	5–2
"	kc	W	3–1
16	NG		
17	det	L	2–7
18	det	W	7–2
19	NG		
20	MIN	W	2–1
21	MIN	W	4–2

May, 1966

22	MIN	W	5–3
"	MIN	W	2–1
23	NG		
24	CAL	L	2–4
25	CAL	W	11–6
26	NG		
27	CHI	W	4–1
28	CHI	TG	2–2a
29	CHI	L	0–2
30	was	W	4–2
"	was	L	1–2
31	was	L	1–5

June, 1966

1	chi	L	2–6
2	chi	W	5–3
3	bos	W	15–5
4	bos	L	3–6L
5	bos	W	5–3
6	NG		
7	cle	W	7–2
8	cle	L	1–2
9	cle		*
10	det	L	2–6
11	det	W	6–3
12	det	L	5–7
"	det	W	12–10
13	bal	L	0–8
14	bal	L	1–2
15	CLE	L	5–8
16	CLE	W	7–6
17	DET	W	5–2
18	DET	L	3–4
19	DET	L	1–2
20	NG		
21	BAL	L	5–7
"	BAL	W	8–3
22	BAL	L	0–3
23	BAL	L	2–5
24	CHI	W	5–2
25	CHI	L	1–2
26	CHI	W	7–2
"	CHI	W	2–0
27	NG		
28	bos	L	3–5

June, 1966

29	bos	W	6–5
30	bos	L	2–3

July, 1966

1	was	W	8–6
2	was	L	4–10
3	was	W	6–5g
4	CHI	L	0–5
"	CHI	W	5–2
5	BOS	L	1–7
6	BOS	L	3–5
"	BOS	L	4–5
7	BOS	W	5–2
8	WAS	L	6–7
"	WAS	W	7–5
9	WAS	L	0–3
10	WAS	L	2–3
"	WAS	L	2–9
11	ALL-STAR BREAK		
12	WON:	36	
13	LOST:	- 48	
14	kc	W	5–4
15	kc	L	4–5
16	kc	W	9–5f
17	min	W	4–2
"	min	W	9–6
18	min	W	6–4
19	KC		*
20	KC	W	4–0
21	KC	W	4–3g
22	CAL	L	4–6
23	CAL	L	6–7
24	CAL	W	9–1
"	CAL	W	4–1
25	NG		
26	MIN	L	3–6
27	MIN	W	6–3
28	NG		
29	chi	W	2–1
30	chi	L	0–6
31	chi	L	1–4
"	chi	L	0–5

August, 1966

1	cal	L	3–4
2	cal	L	5–6g

August, 1966

3	cal	W	9–0
4	cal	L	7–11
5	cle	L	4–5
"	cle	W	3–0
6	cle	W	5–4
7	cle	L	4–6
"	cle	L	3–5
8	NG		
9	BAL	W	4–1
10	BAL	L	4–9
11	BAL	L	5–6g
12	CLE	L	2–3
13	CLE	L	1–2
14	CLE	W	7–3
"	CLE	W	6–4
15	det	L	5–6
16	det	L	3–6
17	det	L	2–4
18	NG		
19	KC	W	7–5
"	KC	L	0–1
20	KC	W	8–5
21	KC	W	7–3
22	NG		
23	CAL	L	0–1
24	CAL	L	1–2
25	CAL	L	1–5
26	DET	W	6–5
27	DET	W	11–1
28	DET	W	8–1
29	kc	W	7–2
30	kc	L	1–4
31	cal	L	2–5

September, 1966

1	cal	W	5–2
2	min	L	5–8
3	min	L	1–6
"	min	W	7–4
4	min	L	2–9
5	bal	L	4–5
"	bal	L	4–7
6	bal	L	1–4
7	bal	L	2–3
8	NG		

September, 1966

9	bos	W	2–1
10	bos	W	5–1
11	bos	W	4–2f
12	NG		
13	WAS	L	2–3
14	WAS		*
15	WAS	L	4–5
"	WAS	W	10–5
16	MIN	L	1–2
17	MIN	L	2–4
18	MIN	L	3–5f
19	NG		
20	CHI		*
21	CHI		*
22	CHI	L	1–4
23	BOS	L	1–2
24	BOS	W	1–0
25	BOS	W	3–1
26	NG		
27	was		*
28	was		*
"	was		*
29	was		*
"	was		*
30	chi	L	5–6g

October, 1966

1	chi	W	5–3
2	chi	W	2–0

END OF 1966

RUNS: 611

OPP RUNS: 612

CLUB VS. CLUB AND MONTHLY RECORDS OF THE NEW YORK YANKEES' 1966 SEASON FOR HOME AND AWAY GAMES

CLUB:		APR	MAY	JUN	JUL	AUG	SEP	OCT	HOME	AWAY	TOTAL
BAL	H	0- 2	xxx	1- 3	xxx	1- 2	xxx	xxx	2- 7	xxx	
	A	1- 2	xxx	0- 2	xxx	xxx	0- 4	xxx	xxx	1- 8	3-15
BOS	H	1- 1	xxx	xxx	1- 3	xxx	2- 1	xxx	4- 5	xxx	
	A	xxx	xxx	3- 3	xxx	xxx	3- 0	xxx	xxx	6- 3	10- 8
CAL	H	xxx	1- 1	xxx	2- 2	0- 3	xxx	xxx	3- 6	xxx	
	A	xxx	2- 1	xxx	xxx	1- 4	1- 0	xxx	xxx	4- 5	7-11
CHI	H	xxx	1- 1	3- 1	1- 1	xxx	0- 1	xxx	5- 4	xxx	
	A	xxx	xxx	1- 1	1- 3	xxx	0- 1	2- 0	xxx	4- 5	9- 9
CLE	H	xxx	0- 3	1- 1	xxx	2- 2	xxx	xxx	3- 6	xxx	
	A	0- 2	xxx	1- 1	xxx	2- 3	xxx	xxx	xxx	3- 6	6-12
DET	H	0- 3	1- 1	1- 2	xxx	3- 0	xxx	xxx	4- 5	xxx	
	A	xxx	1- 1	2- 2	xxx	0- 3	xxx	xxx	xxx	3- 6	7- 11
KC	H	1- 0	1- 1	xxx	2- 0	3- 1	xxx	xxx	7- 2	xxx	
	A	xxx	3- 1	xxx	2- 1	1- 1	xxx	xxx	xxx	6- 3	13- 5
MIN	H	xxx	4- 0	xxx	1- 1	xxx	0- 3	xxx	5- 4	xxx	
	A	xxx	1- 1	xxx	3- 0	xxx	1- 3	xxx	xxx	5- 4	10- 8
WAS	H	0- 1	xxx	xxx	1- 4	xxx	1- 2	xxx	2- 7	xxx	
	A	xxx	1- 2	xxx	2- 1	xxx	xxx	xxx	xxx	3- 3	5-10
TOTAL:	H	2- 7	7- 6	6- 7	8-11	9- 8	3- 7	xxx	35-46	xxx	
	A	1- 4	8- 6	7- 9	8- 5	4-11	5- 8	2- 0	xxx	35-43	70-89
GRAND TOT:		3-11	15-12	13-16	16- 16	13-19	8-15	2- 0	70-89	xxx	
CUMUL TOT:		3-11	18- 23	31-39	47-55	60-74	68-89	70-89	xxx	70-89	

TIE GAMES: 1
CHI-May

1967

UP FROM THE CELLAR

The Yanks moved up a notch to ninth place (!) with a 72–90 (.444) ledger, twenty games behind pennant-winning Boston. This season was noted as the year Mantle was switched from his usual outfield position to first base. The Mick did not fare poorly, making eight errors in 131 games at the initial sack. His .993 (with 1,188 total chances at first base) fielding average ranked third overall in the American League in 1967 with players in more than one hundred games at that position. Only Norm Cash (.995) of Detroit and Don Mincher of California (.994) were ahead of Mantle.

As with last season, no Yankee players won any major statistical crown. Horace Clarke, Yankee second baseman, did get the most singles in the A.L. with 140. New York batters struck out a club record 1,043 times. In addition, the club managed but 17 triples, a club record for futility (they would later match this total in 1973). For the first time since 1912, New York finished dead last (tenth) in American League fielding percentage with a .976 mark. The team's lowly .225 club batting average set a club record in this department. They needed only to wait but one season to break this unspectacular batting mark.

Although playing a little better this season, the effort was nowhere near the usual Yankee standard of the past several decades. The 1968 edition would finish a much improved fifth place.

The 1967 DAY BY DAY scores follow:

DAY BY DAY, 1967 NEW YORK YANKEES

April, 1967

10 was	W	8-	0
11 NG			
12 was	L	4-10	
13 NG			
14 BOS	L	0-	3
15 BOS	W	1-	0
16 BOS	W	7-	6n
17 WAS	*		
18 NG			
19 chi	W	3-	0
20 NG			
21 bos	L	1-	6
22 bos	L	4-	5
23 bos	W	7-	5
24 NG			
25 CHI	W	11-	2
26 CHI	L	1-	5
27 NG			
28 CAL	W	5-	4
29 CAL	W	5-	2
30 CAL	W	4-	1f
" CAL	L	2-	4

May, 1967

1 min	*		
2 min	L	4-13	
3 min	L	3-	4
4 NG			
5 kc	*		
6 kc	*		
7 kc	L	1-	4
" kc	W	8-	3
8 cal	L	2-	3
9 cal	W	2-	1
10 cal	L	2-	3
11 NG			
12 BAL	L	0-14	
13 BAL	L	3-	5
14 BAL	W	6-	5
15 NG			
16 CLE	W	4-	3g
17 CLE	L	7-	8
18 NG			
19 det	L	2-	4
20 det	L	1-	3
21 det	L	4-	9
" det	W	6-	5

May, 1967

22 bal	L	0-	7
23 bal	L	0-	1
24 bal	W	2-	0
25 NG			
26 cle	L	3-	4
27 cle	L	3-	5
28 cle	W	5-	0
29 NG			
30 MIN	W	4-	3
" MIN	L	0-	3
31 KC	W	3-	0

June, 1967

1 NG			
2 DET	L	5-	9
3 DET	W	3-	1
4 DET	W	5-	0
" DET	L7-	11i	
5 WAS	W	4-	2
6 WAS	W	7-	1
7 WAS	W	7-	1
" WAS	L	1-	2
8 WAS	W	6-	0
9 CHI	W	2-	1f
10 CHI	L	0-	9
11 CHI	L	1-	2
" CHI	L	2-	3
12 bos	L	1-	3
13 bos	W	5-	3
14 was	W	7-	1
" was	L	2-	3
15 was	W	2-	0
16 chi	*		
17 chi	L	0-	1
18 chi	L	3-	7
" chi	L	0-	4
19 BOS	*		
20 BOS	L	1-	7
21 BOS	L	1-	8
22 NG			
23 DET	W	3-	1
24 DET	W	4-	3
25 DET	W	3-	2
26 kc	W	5-	2
27 kc	L	2-10	
" kc	W	2-	1

June, 1967

28 kc	L	0-	2
29 NG			
30 cal	L	2-	6

July, 1967

1 cal	W	6-	3
2 cal	L	4-	6
3 min	L	0-	3
4 min	L	3-	8
" min	L	6-	7
5 min	L	4-10	
6 NG			
7 bal	W	3-	0
8 bal	L	5-12	
" bal	W	3-	1
9 bal	L	1-	2
1 0 ALL-STAR BREAK			
11 WON: · 36			
12 LOST: · 45			
13 CLE	L	3-	4k
14 CLE	W	2-	1
" CLE	W	2-	0
15 CLE	W	4-	1
16 BAL	L	1-	2j
17 BAL	L	1-	6
18 cle	*		
19 cle	L	2-	5
20 cle	L	0-	4
21 det	L	2-	4
22 det	L4-	11	
23 det	W	4-	2
" det	L	3-	7
24 NG			
25 MIN	TG	1-	1e
26 MIN	W	6-	1
" MIN	L	2-	3n
27 MIN	W	6-	2
28 KC	*		
29 KC	L	2-	6
30 KC	W	7-	2
" KC	W	5-	2
31 KC	L	6-	8

August, 1967

1 CAL	W	6-	1
2 CAL	L	4-	5
3 CAL	*		

August, 1967

4 kc	L	1-	2
5 kc	L	2-	3h
6 kc	W	9-	6
7 cal	L	4-	8
8 cal	W	1-	0
9 cal	L	0-	7
10 NG			
11 cle	W	5-	3
" cle	W	4-	1
12 cle	L	2-	6
13 cle	W	15-11	
14 BAL	W	5-	4
15 BAL	L10-11i		
16 BAL	L	4-	5
17 BAL	L	1-	4
18 MIN	W	1-	0
" MIN	L	3-	4
19 MIN	L	0-	1
20 MIN	W	7-	3
21 chi	L	3-	4
22 chi	L	2-	3
" chi	W	2-	1
23 chi	L	2-	5
24 chi	W	5-	0
25 was	W	7-	5
" was	W	2-	1
26 was	L	3-	4
27 was	W	8-	2
28 BOS	L	0-	3
29 BOS	L	1-	2
" BOS	W	4-	3p
30 BOS	L	1-	2g
31 WAS	L	0-	6h

September, 1967

1 WAS	W	2-	1
2 WAS	W	2-	1
3 WAS	L	3-	6
4 CHI	W	3-	2
" CHI	L	2-	3f
5 CHI	L	3-	5
6 NG			
7 bos	L	1-	3
8 bos	W	5-	2
9 bos	L	1-	7
10 bos	L	1-	9

September, 1967

11 NG			
12 CAL	L	1-	2h
" CAL	W	2-	1
13 CAL	W	6-	4
14 NG			
15 CLE	W	5-	1
16 CLE	L	1-	6
17 CLE	L	2-	4
18 bal	L	0-	2
19 bal	L	0-	3
20 det	L1-	10	
21 NG			
22 min	L	2-	8
23 min	W	6-	2
24 min	L	4-	9
25 DET	W	2-	0
26 DET	L	0-	1
27 NG			
28 NG			
29 KC	W	4-	3
" KC	W	1-	0
30 KC	W	5-	4

October, 1967

1 KC	W	4-	3

END OF 1967

RUNS:	522
OPP RUNS:	621

CLUB VS. CLUB AND MONTHLY RECORDS OF THE NEW YORK YANKEES' 1967 SEASON FOR HOME AND AWAY GAMES

CLUB:		APR	MAY	JUN	JUL	AUG	SEP	OCT	HOME	AWAY	TOTAL
BAL	H	xxx	1- 2	xxx	0- 2	1- 3	xxx	xxx	2- 7	xxx	
	A	xxx	1- 2	xxx	2- 2	xxx	0- 2	xxx	xxx	3- 6	5-13
BOS	H	2-1	xxx	0- 2	xxx	1- 3	xxx	xxx	3- 6	xxx	
	A	1-2	xxx	1- 1	xxx	xxx	1- 3	xxx	xxx	3- 6	6-12
CAL	H	3- 1	xxx	xxx	xxx	1- 1	2- 1	xxx	6- 3	xxx	
	A	xxx	1- 2	0- 1	1- 1	1- 2	xxx	xxx	xxx	3- 6	9- 9
CHI	H	1-1	xxx	1- 3	xxx	xxx	1- 2	xxx	3- 6	xxx	
	A	1-0	xxx	0- 3	xxx	2- 3	xxx	xxx	xxx	3- 6	6- 12
CLE	H	xxx	1- 1	xxx	3- 1	xxx	1- 2	xxx	5- 4	xxx	
	A	xxx	1- 2	xxx	0- 2	3- 1	xxx	xxx	xxx	4- 5	9- 9
DET	H	xxx	xxx	5- 2	xxx	xxx	1- 1	xxx	6- 3	xxx	
	A	xxx	1- 3	xxx	1- 3	xxx	0- 1	xxx	xxx	2- 7	8-10
KC	H	xxx	1- 0	xxx	2- 2	xxx	3- 0	1- 0	7- 2	xxx	
	A	xxx	1- 1	2- 2	xxx	1- 2	xxx	xxx	xxx	4- 5	11- 7
MIN	H	xxx	1- 1	xxx	2- 1	2- 2	xxx	xxx	5- 4	xxx	
	A	xxx	0- 2	xxx	0- 4	xxx	1- 2	xxx	xxx	1- 8	6-12
WAS	H	xxx	xxx	4- 1	xxx	0- 1	2- 1	xxx	6- 3	xxx	
	A	1-1	xxx	2- 1	xxx	3- 1	xxx	xxx	xxx	6- 3	12- 6
TOTAL:	H	6-3	4- 4	10- 8	7- 6	5-10	10- 7	1- 0	43-38	xxx	
	A	3-3	5-12	5- 8	4-12	10- 9	2- 8	xxx	xxx	29-52	72-90
GRAND TOT:		9-6	9-16	15-16	11-18	15-19	12-15	1- 0	72-90	xxx	
CUMUL TOT:		9-6	18- 22	33-38	44-56	59-75	71-90	72-90	xxx	29-52	72-90

TIE GAMES: 1
min-July

1968

MANTLE'S LAST SEASON

Continuing to improve in the standings gradually, the Yanks moved up to fifth place at 83–79 (.512) some 20 games behind front-running Detroit. Last season, the New Yorkers finished the same number of games behind the first place team but could do no better than ninth place.

Mickey Mantle, concluding his fantastic Yankee career, continued to do a creditable job at first base. Statistically, the best any Yankee could do was finish third in runs scored (Roy White, 89) and second in bases on balls (Mantle, 106). The club batting average of a paltry .214 with but 1,137 hits were all-time lows for the Yankee team. Catcher Jake Gibbs led all club regulars with but a .267 average. Joe Pepitone was next at .245. The team's fielding and pitching improved by leaps and bounds but their hitting was anemic.

Stan Bahnsen, a bright spot on the Yankee pitching staff, won as A.L. Rookie of the Year, the fifth Yankee to win this award, and first since Tom Tresh in 1962. Finishing with a 17–12 mark, Stan placed 6th in A.L. ERA with a fine 2.05, one of the best in Yankee history. One must remember that pitching really dominated each league unbelievably with Tiant of Cleveland posting a 1.60 ERA and Bob Gibson an incredible 1.12 ERA with St. Louis in the National League. In addition, Denny McLain of Detroit became the first pitcher since Dizzy Dean of the National League St. Louis entry to win 30 games in a season. In the American League, Lefty Grove of Philadelphia won 31 in 1931, the last A.L. pitcher to do so prior to McLain's fine effort of this season.

The conclusion of 1968 marked the end of the line for one of the most legendary players that ever graced a baseball diamond, Mickey Mantle. Finishing his 18th and final season, Mantle will have played in 2,401 games with some 102 at bats, both all-time Yankee records, a truly remarkable feat when realizing the enormous numbers of injuries that plagued him throughout most of his career. Only Yogi Berra's 18 seasons with New York compared with the Mick's longevity in the famous pinstripes.

The 1968 DAY BY DAY scores follow:

DAY BY DAY, 1968 NEW YORK YANKEES

April, 1968			May, 1968			June, 1968			August, 1968			September, 1968		
9 CAL		*	19 bos	W	11- 3	26 DET		*	1 bos	W	1- 0	7 WAS	W	16- 2
10 CAL	W	1- 0	20 was	W	6- 1	27 NG			2 BAL	L	1- 4	" WAS	W	10- 0
11 NG			21 was	W	2-1	28 OAK	L	2- 3	3 BAL	W	3- 1	8 WAS	W	7- 2
12 NG			22 BAL	L	3-4	29 OAK	L	2- 5	4 BAL	L	3- 5	9 NG		
13 MIN	L	0- 6	23 NG			" OAK	W	5-4	5 BAL	L	3- 5f	10 CHI	W	2- 1
14 MIN	L	3- 4	24 CHI	W	1-0i	30 OAK	W	4- 2	6 NG			" CHI	W	5-0
15 OAK	L	3- 6	25 CHI	W	1-0f	**July, 1968**			7 OAK	W	3- 0	11 CHI	W	7- 2
16 OAK	L	3- 4	26 CHI	W	5- 1	1 was	L	1-3	" OAK	L	3- 4f	12 NG		
17 cal	W	3- 2	" CHI	W	7- 6	2 was		*	8 OAK	L	4- 6	13 was	W	4- 2
18 cal	W	6- 1	27 NG			3 was	W	4-1	9 MIN	L	3- 4g	" was	W	2- 1
19 NG			28 WAS		*	4 was	L	2-4	10 MIN	L	2- 3	14 was	W	4- 1
20 min	W	4- 2	29 NG			5 BAL	W	2-1	11 MIN	L	2-11	15 was	W	3- 2
21 min	L	2- 5	30 WAS	W	13-4	6 BAL	L	1-5	12 cal	W	5- 2	16 det	L	1- 9
22 oak	W	2- 1	" WAS	L	2-6	7 BAL	W	3-1	13 cal	W	3- 2	17 det	L	1- 2
23 oak	W	6- 3	31 det	L	0-1	" BAL	L	2-3	14 cal	W	5- 2	18 det		*
24 oak	L	3- 4	**June, 1968**			8 ALL-STAR BREAK			15 oak	L	3- 4	19 det	L	2- 6
25 NG			1 det	L	4- 5	9 WON: - 36			16 oak	W	2- 1	20 BOS	L	3- 4
26 DET	W	5- 0	2 det	W	4- 3	10 LOST: - 43			17 oak	W	3- 1	21 BOS	L	0- 2
27 DET	L	0- 7	" det	L	1- 8	11 chi	W	5-4#	18 oak	W	7- 5f	22 BOS	L	1- 5
28 DET	W	2- 1	3 MIN	L	3- 4	#Milwaukee, Wisc			19 min	L	0- 1	23 NG		
" DET	L	2- 3	4 MIN	L	0- 3	12 chi	W	2-1	20 min	W	5- 0	24 CLE	W	5- 1
29 NG			5 MIN	W	7-2	13 chi	W	4-2	21 min	W	2- 1	" CLE	L	2- 5
30 bal	L	5- 6	6 MIN	L	0-2	14 bal	L	4-6	22 min	L	1- 3	25 CLE	L	0- 3
May, 1968			7 CAL	W	4-1	15 bal	L	2-8	23 DET	W	2- 1	26 NG		
1 bal	L	1- 6	" CAL	L	4-8	16 WAS	W	4-0	" DET	TG	3- 3o	27 bos	L	2-12
2 bal	L	3- 7	8 CAL		*	" WAS	W	4-3	24 DET	W	2- 1	28 bos	W	4- 3
3 chi	W	3- 2	9 CAL	W	8-1	17 WAS	L	1-2	25 DET	W	6- 5	29 bos	W	4- 3
4 chi	L	1- 4	" CAL	W	3-2	18 WAS	W	4-1	" DET	W	5- 4			
5 chi	L	1- 5	10 CHI	L	2-5	19 CLE		*	26 CAL	W	6- 1	**END OF 1968**		
" chi	W	4- 1	11 CHI	L	5-9	20 CLE	L	0-3	" CAL		L2- 10	RUNS:		536
6 CLE	L	2- 3	12 CHI		*	21 CLE	L	1-4	27 CAL	W	2- 0	OPP RUNS:		531
7 CLE	L	0- 8	13 NG			" CLE	W	8-4	" CAL	L	0- 2			
8 CLE	W	2- 1	14 oak	W	5-4f	22 BOS	L	6-7	28 chi	L	0- 3			
9 NG			15 oak	W	3-2	23 BOS	W	4-1	29 chi	L	0- 1			
10 BOS	W	2- 1	16 cal	W	4-3	24 BOS		*	30 cle	W	1- 0			
11 BOS	W	1- 0	17 cal	L	1-2h	25 NG			" cle	L	2- 3f			
12 BOS	L	1- 8	18 cal	L	1-3	26 cle	W	5-0	31 cle	W	3- 1			
" BOS	L	2- 4	19 cal	L	2-3	27 cle	W	6-3	**September, 1968**					
13 NG			20 NG			28 cle	L	2-3	1 cle	W	5- 1			
14 cle	L	2- 4	21 min	W	11-6	" cle	L	1-4	2 bal	W	4- 2			
15 cle	TG	2- 2d	22 min	W	5-2	29 det	W	7-2	" bal	L	3- 4f			
16 bos		L10-11	23 min	L	3-6	30 det	L	0-5	3 bal	W	6- 1			
17 bos	L	4- 6	24 NG			31 bos	W	7-3	4 bal	L	3- 6			
18 bos	L	0- 4	25 DET	L	5- 8				5 NG					
									6 WAS		*			

CLUB VS. CLUB AND MONTHLY RECORDS OF THE
NEW YORK YANKEES' 1968 SEASON FOR HOME AND AWAY GAMES

CLUB:		APR	MAY	JUN	JUL	AUG	SEP	OCT	HOME	AWAY	TOTAL
BAL	H	xxx	0– 1	xxx	2– 2	1– 3	xxx	xxx	3– 6	xxx	5–13
	A	0–1	0– 2	xxx	0– 2	xxx	2– 2	xxx	xxx	2– 7	
BOS	H	xxx	2– 2	xxx	1– 1	xxx	0– 3	xxx	3– 6	xxx	8–10
	A	xxx	1– 3	xxx	1– 0	1– 0	2– 1	xxx	xxx	5– 4	
CAL	H	1– 0	xxx	3– 1	xxx	2– 2	xxx	xxx	6– 3	xxx	12– 6
	A	2–0	xxx	1– 3	xxx	3– 0	xxx	xxx	xxx	6– 3	
CHI	H	xxx	4– 0	0– 2	xxx	xxx	3– 0	xxx	7– 2	xxx	12– 6#
	A	xxx	2– 2	xxx	3– 0#	0– 2	xxx	xxx	xxx	5– 4#	
CLE	H	xxx	1– 2	xxx	1– 2	xxx	1– 2	xxx	3– 6	xxx	8–10
	A	xxx	0– 1	xxx	2– 2	2– 1	1– 0	xxx	xxx	5– 4	
DET	H	2–2	xxx	0– 1	xxx	4– 0	xxx	xxx	6– 3	xxx	8–10
	A	xxx	0– 1	1– 2	1– 1	xxx	0– 3	xxx	xxx	2– 7	
MIN	H	0–2	xxx	1– 3	xxx	0– 3	xxx	xxx	1– 8	xxx	6–12
	A	1–1	xxx	2– 1	xxx	2– 2	xxx	xxx	xxx	5– 4	
OAK	H	0–2	xxx	2– 2	xxx	1– 2	xxx	xxx	3– 6	xxx	10– 8
	A	2–1	xxx	2– 0	xxx	3– 1	xxx	xxx	xxx	7– 2	
WAS	H	xxx	1– 1	xxx	3– 1	xxx	3– 0	xxx	7– 2	xxx	14– 4
	A	xxx	2– 0	xxx	1– 2	xxx	4– 0	xxx	xxx	7– 2	
TOTAL:	H	3–6	8– 6	6– 9	7– 6	8–10	7– 5	xxx	39– 42	xxx	83–79
	A	5–3	5– 9	6– 6	8– 7	11– 6	9– 6	xxx	xxx	44–37	
GRAND TOT:		8– 9	13–15	12–15	15–13	19–16	16–11	xxx	83– 79	xxx	
CUMUL TOT:		8– 9	21–24	33–39	48–52	67–68	83–79	xxx	xxx	44–37	

TIE GAMES: 2
DET-Aug; cle-May

#INCLUDES ONE WIN AT MILWAUKEE, WISCONSIN, JULY 11

Bobby Murcer was a favorite with Yankee fans for many seasons. He had many great years when the Yanks were losing regularly. Bobby played 13 seasons with New York and retired in 1983.

1969

MANTLE'S RETIREMENT

Beginning divisional play for the first time in American League history, the Yankees finished in 5th place in the East with an 80–81(.497) mark. They concluded the season some 28½ games behind front-running Baltimore.

Prior to the start of the 1969 season, Mickey Mantle ended his Yankee years, announcing his retirement from baseball. On June 8 at Yankee Stadium before 60,096 fans, Mick's uniform (#7) was retired, the fourth Yankee to be so honored.

Statistically, the Yanks hit less than 100 homers for the first time since 1945 when they hit 93 four-baggers. Beginning in 1920, the Yanks had hit the century mark in homers 58 times (or 58 of 64 seasons) through 1983. For the first time since 1957, the New Yorkers led the A.L. in triples with 44. Only Horace Clarke's 146 one-base hits led the A.L. in any batting category. The club did set a team record with only 14 Yanks being hit by a pitched ball.

The pitching was fairly sound,showing periodic consistency but was not sufficient to clinch a pennant. The same held true for the defensive area. Mel Stottlemyre, Yankee pitcher, had the most complete games in the league, totaling 24 rout jobs.

This season brought with it a new Commissioner, Bowie Kuhn, who is expected to be replaced as of this writing. Kuhn, baseball's fourth commissioner, replaced William Eckert.

The Yankees officially bade farewell to Mickey Mantle during the course of the season. His departure left a void the Yanks could never seem to fill. Next season, the Yanks will have a fairly creditable season.

The 1969 DAY BY DAY scores follow:

DAY BY DAY, 1969 NEW YORK YANKEES

April, 1969			May, 1969			June, 1969			August, 1969			September, 1969		
7 was	W	8– 4	17 CAL	W	6–0	24 det	L	1– 2	1 sea	W	4–2	11 was	L	3–7
8 NG			18 CAL	W	3–1	25 det	L	1– 6	2 sea	W	5– 4	12 BOS	W	5–3
9 was	L	4– 6	" CAL	W	1–0	26 det	W	6– 0	3 sea	W	5– 3	" BOS	L	3–4
10 was	L	6– 9	19 NG			27 cle	L	1– 5	4 NG			13 BOS	L	2– 5
11 det	W	9– 4	20 OAK	W	2–1	28 cle	L	3– 7	5 CAL	W	3–2	14 BOS	W	3– 2
12 det	W	4– 0	21 OAK	W	6–5g	29 cle	L	1– 5	6 CAL	W	3– 1	15 DET	L	0–2
13 det	L	2– 6	22 NG			" cle	W	6– 3	7 NG			16 DET	W	7– 6i
14 NG			23 MIN	W	3–1	30 NG			8 OAK	L	3–5f	17 WAS	W	2– 1a
15 WAS	W	8– 2	24 MIN	L	1–2	**July, 1969**			" OAK	W	5– 0	18 WAS	W	4–3
16 WAS		*	25 MIN	L	1–2	1 BAL	W	10– 9	9 OAK	W	2– 1	19 bal	L	2–4
17 WAS	W	7– 3f	" MIN	L	2–3	2 BAL	W	3– 2	10 OAK	W	5–1	20 bal	L	7–8
" WAS	L	2– 5	26 NG			3 NG			11 NG			21 NG		
18 NG			27 chi	W	5–3	4 CLE	W	5– 4	12 MIN	W	10–3	22 bos	L	3–4
19 DET		*	28 chi	L	6–7#	" CLE	L	1– 4	13 MIN	L	2–5	23 bos	L	3–8
20 DET	L	2– 5	#Milwaukee, Wisc			5 CLE	L	2– 4	14 chi	W	3–2	24 bos	L	0–1j
" DET	W	2– 0	29 NG			6 CLE	W	4– 2	15 chi	W	2–1	25 bos	L	3–4
21 bos	W	6– 4	30 kc	W	6–2	7 NG			16 chi	L	4–5	26 BAL	W	4–2
22 bos	L	3– 8	" kc	W	5–4k	8 bal	L	3–10	17 chi	W	5–2	27 BAL	W	1– 0
23 cle		*	31 kc	TG	2–2c	" bal	L	1– 4	18 kc	L	1–6	28 BAL	W	3– 2
24 cle	W	11– 3	**June, 1969**			9 bal	L	5– 6	19 kc	W	5– 1	29 NG		
25 bal	W	7– 2	1 kc	W	8–5	10 NG			20 kc	L	0–5	30 CLE	W	8– 2
26 bal	W	6– 5f	2 min	L	2–3	11 was	W	4– 3	21 NG			**October, 1969**		
27 bal	L	0– 6	3 min	L	0–4	12 was	W	3– 1	22 min	L	0–6	1 CLE	W	4– 3
" bal	L	5–10	4 min	L	2–4	13 was	L	4– 5	23 min	L	3– 8	2 CLE		*
28 BOS	W	1– 0	5 NG			" was	L	1–10	24 min	L	0– 1			
29 BOS	L	1– 2	6 CHI	W	3–2	14 NG			25 NG			END OF 1969		
30 CLE	L	0– 3	7 CHI	W	6–2	15 BOS	L	6– 7	26 CHI	L	2– 3f	RUNS:		562
May, 1969			8 CHI	W	3–1	" BOS	W	4– 1	27 CHI	W	6–3	OPP RUNS:		587
1 CLE	L	2– 6	" CHI	W	11– 2	16 BOS	L	2– 6	28 NG					
2 BAL	L	1– 5	9 KC	L	1– 7	17 BOS		*	29 KC	W	6– 1			
3 BAL	L	4– 5	10 KC	L	6–7	18 WAS	W	5– 0	30 KC	L	0–2			
4 BAL	L	3– 5	11 KC	W	5–4g	19 WAS	W	9– 0	31 KC	W	5–3			
" BAL	L	2–14	12 NG			" WAS	L	0– 4	**September, 1969**					
5 NG			13 SEA	L	1–2	20 WAS	W	3– 2g	1 SEA	W	6– 1			
6 cal	W	2– 1	14 SEA	L	4–5	21 ALL-STAR BREAK			" SEA	L	1– 5i			
7 cal	L	2– 4	15 S EA	W	4–0a	22 WON: - 46			2 SEA	W	5– 4k			
8 NG			16 DET	L	2– 3	23 LOST: - 52			3 NG					
9 oak	L	2– 3	17 DET	L	0–8	24 cal	W	3– 1	4 NG					
10 oak	L	3– 4	" DET	L	3–6	25 cal	L	0– 6	5 cle	L	1–2			
11 oak	L	0– 2	18 DET	W	4–2	26 cal	W	3– 1	" cle	W	2– 0			
12 sea	L	4– 8	19 DET	W	5–3	27 cal	L	4– 5	6 cle	W	1– 0			
13 sea	L	3– 5	20 bos		*	28 NG			7 cle	L	3–7			
14 sea	W	5– 4	21 bos	L	5–6g	29 oak	L	5– 6	8 det	W	3– 2			
15 NG			" bos	W	6–3	30 oak	W	3– 2	9 det	L	0–2			
16 CAL	W	2– 1	22 bos	W	5–3f	31 oak	L	2– 3	10 was	L	1–6			
			23 det	L	5– 6									

CLUB VS. CLUB AND MONTHLY RECORDS OF THE NEW YORK YANKEES' 1969 SEASON FOR HOME AND AWAY GAMES

CLUB:		APR	MAY	JUN	JUL	AUG	SEP	OCT	HOME	AWAY	TOTAL
BAL	H	xxx	0- 4	xxx	2- 0	xxx	3- 0	xxx	5- 4	xxx	7-11
	A	2- 2	xxx	xxx	0- 3	xxx	0- 2	xxx	xxx	2- 7	
BOS	H	1- 1	xxx	xxx	1- 2	xxx	2- 2	xxx	4- 5	xxx	7-11
	A	1- 1	xxx	2- 1	xxx	xxx	0- 4	xxx	xxx	3- 6	
CAL	H	xxx	4- 0	xxx	xxx	2- 0	xxx	xxx	6- 0	xxx	9- 3
	A	xxx	1- 1	xxx	2- 2	xxx	xxx	xxx	xxx	3- 3	
CHI	H	xxx	xxx	4- 0	xxx	1- 1	xxx	xxx	5- 1	xxx	9- 3#
	A	xxx	1- 1#	xxx	xxx	3- 1	xxx	xxx	xxx	4- 2#	
CLE	H	0- 1	0- 1	xxx	2- 2	xxx	1- 0	1- 0	4- 4	xxx	8- 9
	A	1- 0	xxx	1- 3	xxx	xxx	2- 2	xxx	xxx	4- 5	
DET	H	1- 1	xxx	2- 3	xxx	xxx	1- 1	xxx	4- 5	xxx	8-10
	A	2- 1	xxx	1- 3	xxx	xxx	1- 1	xxx	xxx	4- 5	
KC	H	xxx	xxx	1- 2	xxx	2- 1	xxx	xxx	3- 3	xxx	7- 5
	A	xxx	2- 0	1- 0	xxx	1- 2	xxx	xxx	xxx	4- 2	
MIN	H	xxx	1- 3	xxx	xxx	1- 1	xxx	xxx	2- 4	xxx	2-10
	A	xxx	xxx	0- 3	xxx	0- 3	xxx	xxx	xxx	0- 6	
OAK	H	xxx	2- 0	xxx	xxx	3- 1	xxx	xxx	5- 1	xxx	6- 6
	A	xxx	0- 3	xxx	1- 2	xxx	xxx	xxx	xxx	1- 5	
SEAT	H	xxx	xxx	1- 2	xxx	xxx	2- 1	xxx	3- 3	xxx	7- 5
	A	xxx	1- 2	xxx	xxx	3- 0	xxx	xxx	xxx	4- 2	
WAS	H	2- 1	xxx	xxx	3- 1	xxx	2- 0	xxx	7- 2	xxx	10- 8
	A	1- 2	xxx	xxx	2- 2	xxx	0- 2	xxx	xxx	3- 6	
TOTAL:	H	4- 4	7- 8	8- 7	8- 5	9- 4	11- 4	1- 0	48-32	xxx	80-81
	A	7- 6	5- 7	5-10	5- 9	7- 6	3-11	xxx	xxx	32-49	
GRAND TOT:		11-10	12-15	13-17	13-14	16-10	14-15	1- 0	80-81		**TIE GAMES:** 1
CUMUL TOT:		11-10	23-25	36-42	49-56	65-66	79-81	80-81		32-49	kc-May

#INCLUDES ONE LOSS AT MILWAUKEE, WISCONSIN, MAY 28

1970

A CREDITABLE SEASON

After several years of mediocre play, the 1970 Yanks finished with a very respectable 93–69 (.574) winning mark. Unfortunately, the Baltimore Orioles won 15 more games than did the Yanks. Baltimore concluded the season having won two-thirds of their games.

No individual Yank pitchers or batters finished first in the league. However, the team did manage to pace the A.L. in triples (41) for the second consecutive year. The pitching staff also gave the opposition the fewest bases on balls in the league with 451. Between them, Bahnsen, Stottlemyre and Peterson won 49 of the Yanks' 93 wins, or 52.7%

The sixth Yankee to win the Rookie of the Year Award, Thurman Munson, brought a ray of hope to the Yanks' chances of remaining a contender over the next several campaigns. Thurman led the league with 60 assists as a catcher, batting .302 with 6 homers and 53 RBI.

In 1970, Casey Stengel's uniform was retired at Old-Timers' Day ceremonies, August 8. Never again would No. 37 grace a Yankee uniform. Casey thus became the fifth Yank to have his number retired.

This season had been the most productive for the Yanks in some time. However, the New Yorkers would not win 90 or more games again 'til their return to glory some six years hence.

The 1970 DAY BY DAY scores follow:

DAY BY DAY, 1970 NEW YORK YANKEES

April, 1970
7	BOS	L	3– 4
8	NG		
9	BOS	W	4– 3
10	NG		
11	CLE	L	0– 3
12	CLE	L	1– 2
"	CLE	W	5– 4
13	NG		
14	bos	L	3– 8
15	bos	L	2– 6
16	bos	L	5– 8
17	bal	W	4– 1g
18	bal	L	4– 5
19	bal	L	3– 4
"	bal	W	8– 5
20	was	W	11– 2
21	was	L	5– 7
22	was	L	1– 2n
23	was	W	11– 6
24	OAK	*	
25	OAK	L	0– 3
26	OAK	W	8– 3
27	NG		
28	CAL	W	7– 5
29	CAL	L	2– 3
30	CAL	W	1– 0

May, 1970
1	MIL	W	6– 3
2	MIL	W	7– 6
3	MIL	W	8– 7
"	MIL	W	4– 2
4	NG		
5	oak	L	3–11
6	oak	W	7– 6
7	oak	W	7– 3
8	cal	L	3– 4
9	cal	L	3– 11
10	cal	W	4– 3
11	mil	TG	5– 5e
12	mil	W	9– 5g
13	mil	L	1– 3
14	NG		
15	DET	W	4– 1
16	DET	W	7– 4
17	DET		*–
"	DET		*
18	BAL	W	10– 4
19	BAL	L	1– 5
20	WAS	L	0– 2
21	WAS	W	2– 0
22	CLE	W	7– 4
23	cle	L	3– 4i
24	cle	W	6– 5
"	cle	W	8– 7g
25	det	L	3– 4
26	det	L	0– 3
27	det	W	4– 2
28	NG		
29	min	W	4– 2
30	min	L	6– 10
31	min	L	6– 7f

June, 1970
1	NG		
2	KC	W	3– 2
3	KC	W	5– 3
4	KC	W	2– 1h
5	CHI	W	10– 1
6	CHI	W	3– 1
7	CHI	L	3– 4h
8	NG		
9	MIN	W	5– 2
10	MIN	W	2– 1
11	NG		
12	kc	W	5– 0
13	kc	W	9– 4h
14	kc	W	3– 2
15	NG		
16	chi	W	6– 2
17	chi	L	3– 6
18	bos	W	3– 2
19	bos	L	4– 7
20	bos	W	8– 3
21	bos	W	14–10g
22	NG		
23	NG		
24	CLE	L	2– 7
"	CLE	W	5– 4
25	CLE	W	3– 1
26	BOS	*	
27	BOS	L	0– 4
28	BOS	L	3– 5
"	BOS	W	8– 2
29	NG		
30	det	L	3– 5

July, 1970
1	det	L	5– 6g
2	det	L	0– 5
3	WAS	L	3– 4
4	WAS	W	4– 2
5	WAS	L	3– 7
"	WAS	L	3– 7
6	NG		
7	bal	L	2– 6f
8	bal	L	8– 9
9	bal	W	7– 5
10	was	L	1– 2
11	was	W	3– 1
12	was	L	3– 7
13	ALL-STAR BREAK		
14	WON: - 46		
15	LOST: - 39		
16	OAK	L	2– 8
"	OAK	W	4– 1
17	OAK	W	7– 1
18	OAK	W	7– 2
19	CAL	L	2– 5
"	CAL	L	1– 3
20	CAL	W	6– 1
21	MIL	W	4– 2
22	MIL	L	1– 4
23	NG		
24	oak	L	0–11
25	oak	L	0– 1
26	oak	L	3– 4
27	cal	W	5– 2f
28	cal	W	6– 5
29	cal	W	8– 3
30	NG		
31	mil	W	7– 3
"	mil	W	5– 3

August, 1970
1	mil	W	4– 1h
2	mil	L	5– 9
3	NG		
4	cle	L	1– 6
5	cle	W	7– 3
6	DET	L	1– 2
"	DET	W	7– 5
7	DET	W	5– 1
8	BAL	L	2– 4
9	BAL	W	6– 4g
"	BAL	L	9– 12g
10	NG		
11	CHI	L	7– 1
12	CHI	L	1– 5
13	CHI	W	4– 3
14	KC	W	3– 2f
15	KC	W	5– 4
16	KC	W	5– 1
17	NG		
18	min	L	7– 8
19	min	L	0– 3
20	min	W	4– 3
21	chi	W	4– 2
22	chi	L	2– 3
23	chi	L	0– 2
"	chi	W	7– 5
24	kc	L	7– 8
25	kc	W	2– 1
26	kc	W	3– 0
27	NG		
28	MIN	W	6– 0
"	MIN	W	2– 1
29	MIN	L	1– 3
30	MIN	W	5– 2
31	BAL	L	2–10

September, 1970
1	BAL	W	4– 2
2	BAL	W	3– 2
3	BAL	L	4– 8
4	CLE	W	3– 2
5	CLE	W	3– 1
6	CLE	W	4– 1
7	was	W	4– 3
8	was	W	7– 3
9	bal	L	0– 1
10	bal	L	1–2
11	cle	L	2– 3
12	cle	L	3– 4g
13	cle	L	1– 3
14	NG		
15	BOS	W	8–6
"	BOS	W	3–2
16	BOS	L	1–3
17	BOS	L	4– 5f
18	det	W	5– 0
19	det	W	7–6
20	det	W	5–1
21	WAS	W	5–2
22	WAS	W	2–1
23	WAS	W	6–4
24	NG		
25	DET	L	1–3
"	DET	W	8– 3
26	DET	W	2– 1
27	DET	W	4– 2
28	NG		
29	bos	L	4–5
30	bos	W	4–3

END OF 1970
RUNS: 680
OPP RUNS: 612

CLUB VS. CLUB AND MONTHLY RECORDS OF THE NEW YORK YANKEES' 1970 SEASON FOR HOME AND AWAY GAMES

CLUB:		APR	MAY	JUN	JUL	AUG	SEP	OCT	HOME	AWAY	TOTAL
BAL	H	xxx	1– 1	xxx	xxx	1– 3	2– 1	xxx	4– 5	xxx	7–11
	A	2– 2	xxx	xxx	1– 2	xxx	0– 2	xxx	xxx	3– 6	
BOS	H	1– 1	xxx	1– 2	xxx	xxx	2– 2	xxx	4– 5	xxx	8–10
	A	0– 3	xxx	3– 1	xxx	xxx	1– 1	xxx	xxx	4– 5	
CAL	H	2– 1	xxx	xxx	1– 2	xxx	xxx	xxx	3– 3	xxx	7– 5
	A	xxx	1– 2	xxx	3– 0	xxx	xxx	xxx	xxx	4– 2	
CHI	H	xxx	xxx	2– 1	xxx	2– 1	xxx	xxx	4– 2	xxx	7– 5
	A	xxx	xxx	1– 1	xxx	2– 2	xxx	xxx	xxx	3– 3	
CLE	H	1– 2	xxx	2– 1	xxx	xxx	3– 0	xxx	6– 3	xxx	10– 8
	A	xxx	3– 1	xxx	xxx	1– 1	0– 3	xxx	xxx	4– 5	
DET	H	xxx	2– 0	xxx	xxx	2– 1	3– 1	xxx	7– 2	xxx	11– 7
	A	xxx	1– 2	0– 1	0– 2	xxx	3– 0	xxx	xxx	4– 5	
KC	H	xxx	xxx	3– 0	xxx	3– 0	xxx	xxx	6– 0	xxx	11– 1
	A	xxx	xxx	3– 0	xxx	2– 1	xxx	xxx	xxx	5– 1	
MIL	H	xxx	4– 0	xxx	1– 1	xxx	xxx	xxx	5– 1	xxx	9– 3
	A	xxx	1– 1	xxx	2– 0	1– 1	xxx	xxx	xxx	4– 2	
MIN	H	xxx	xxx	2– 0	xxx	3– 1	xxx	xxx	5– 1	xxx	7– 5
	A	xxx	1– 2	xxx	xxx	1– 2	xxx	xxx	xxx	2– 4	
OAK	H	1– 1	xxx	xxx	3– 1	xxx	xxx	xxx	4– 2	xxx	6– 6
	A	xxx	2– 1	xxx	0– 3	xxx	xxx	xxx	xxx	2– 4	
WAS	H	xxx	1– 1	xxx	1– 3	xxx	3– 0	xxx	5– 4	xxx	10– 8
	A	2– 2	xxx	xxx	1– 2	xxx	2– 0	xxx	xxx	5– 4	
TOTAL:	H	5– 5	8– 2	10– 4	6– 7	11– 6	13– 4	xxx	53–28	xxx	93–69
	A	4– 7	9– 9	7– 3	7– 9	7– 7	6– 6	xxx	xxx	40–41	
GRAND TOT: H		9– 12	17–11	17– 7	13–16	18–13	19–10	xxx	93–69	xxx	
CUMUL TOT: A		9– 12	26–23	43–30	56–46	74–59	93– 69	xxx	xxx	40–41	

TIE GAMES: 1
MIL-May

1971

SLIPPING BACK DOWN AGAIN

After a respectable year previously, the Yanks finished disappointingly in fourth place, again behind the dynasty-minded Baltimore club. With an 82–80 (.506) worksheet, the Yanks fell 21 games behind the O's.

The offense was less productive than 1970 but Bobby Murcer had a very Yankee-like season. He finished second in league batting (.331), slugging (.543) and runs scored (94, tied with Tovar of Minnesota). Bobby was also third in total bases (287) and fourth in RBI with 94, being tied with Oakland's Sal Bando in the latter category. For the third consecutive season, the Yanks led the league in triples with 43 three-baggers. This marked the only time in Yankee history that they led the A.L. in triples three years running.

No Yankee pitcher won more than 16 games (Stottlemyre) and the defense placed in a second-place tie for fielding average.

On September 30, Washington bid adieu to the American League, forfeiting a game to New York. Playing their last game ever, the Senators, before a home crowd of 14,460, could not complete the game due to disenchanted fans swarming on the field. The Washington club, led by Manager Ted Williams, was leading with two out in the top of the ninth when the fans went crazy. Next season, the franchise was switched to Arlington, Texas, becoming the Texas Rangers. Thus, for the first time in A.L. history, beginning in 1901, the nation's capitol was not represented with an A.L. franchise.

Bobby Murcer, the expected successor to Mickey Mantle's previous fame, emerged as a favorite with Yankee fans. However, in spite of Murcer's fabulous season, the club continued to wallow in mediocrity. The next four seasons saw no drastic improvements in style of play.

The 1971 DAY BY DAY scores follow:

DAY BY DAY, 1971 NEW YORK YANKEES

April, 1971

6	bos	L 1- 3
7	NG	
8	NG	
9	was	L 4- 5f
10	was	W 6- 0
11	was	W 1- 0
"	was	L 3- 4
12	NG	
13	DET	W 5- 2
14	DET	W 8- 4
15	DET	L 2- 3
16	bal	L 1- 6
17	bal	W 5- 3f
18	bal	L 6-11
19	NG	
20	WAS	L 2- 7
21	WAS	L 6- 9
22	NG	
23	MIN	W 7- 3
24	MIN	L8- 11g
25	MIN	L 0- 8
26	NG	
27	CHI	W 6- 5h
28	CHI	*
29	NG	
30	MIL	W 5- 1

May, 1971

1	MIL	L 0- 1
2	MIL	W 2- 1
"	MIL	W 5- 4
3	NG	
4	min	L 5- 6f
5	min	L 3- 5
6	min	L 3- 5
7	chi	W 4- 3
8	chi	W 2- 1g
9	chi	W 6- 1
10	NG	
11	mil	*
12	mil	W 3- 0
13	mil	W 4- 3f
14	CLE	L 1- 2
15	CLE	L 2- 4
16	CLE	*
"	CLE	*

May, 1971

17	BAL	W 6- 3
18	BAL	L 2- 6
19	bos	L 2- 7
20	bos	L 2- 5
21	cle	L 7- 8
22	cle	L 1- 2
23	cle	W 6- 3
"	cle	L 1- 2
24	NG	
25	det	L 4- 7
26	det	W 2- 1
27	det	L 3- 4
28	CAL	L 6- 9
29	CAL	W 6- 1
30	CAL	W 7- 4
31	OAK	W 5- 3
"	OAK	L 3- 6

June, 1971

1	OAK	L 2- 5
2	BOS	W 6- 1
3	BOS	L 2- 3
4	KC	L 2- 6
5	KC	L 7-11
6	KC	W 5- 2
7	NG	
8	cal	W 3- 0
9	cal	L 3- 4
10	cal	W 3- 2
11	oak	W 6- 4
12	oak	L 3-13
13	oak	W 5- 1
14	kc	L 1- 4
15	kc	W 2- 1
16	kc	W 3- 2
17	bal	L 1- 3
18	bal	L 4- 6
19	bal	W 6- 4f
20	bal	L 4-10
21	NG	
22	DET	L 4- 7
"	DET	W 2- 1
23	DET	W 6- 5i
24	NG	
25	WAS	W 12- 2
26	WAS	W 4- 0

June, 1971

27	WAS	L 1- 2
"	WAS	L 0- 8
28	CLE	L 0- 3
"	CLE	L 2- 5
29	CLE	W 9- 2
30	was	L 1- 2

July, 1971

1	was	L 1- 3
2	bos	W 6- 0
3	bos	W 2- 1
4	bos	L 4- 7
5	bos	L 7-12
6	det	L7- 12
7	det	W 5- 3g
8	det	L 1- 3
9	BOS	W 5- 2
10	BOS	W 5- 3
11	BOS	W 3- 2
12	ALL-STAR BREAK	
13	WON - 41	
14	LOST - 47	
15	MIL	L 0- 1
16	MIL	W 7- 4
17	CHI	W 4- 2
18	CHI	W 3- 2
"	CHI	W 6- 1
19	CHI	L 3- 8f
"	CHI	L 1- 3
20	MIN	W 6- 5
21	MIN	L 1- 2
22	MIN	W 13- 4
23	mil	W 6- 2
24	mil	W 4- 3
25	mil	W 6- 2g
"	mil	W 11- 9
26	NG	
27	chi	L 6- 9h
28	chi	L 4- 5
29	chi	L 0- 4
30	min	W 11- 9
31	min	L 4- 5

August, 1971

1	min	L 7-10
2	cle	W 7- 0
3	cle	W 8- 1

August, 1971

4	cle	W 7- 3
5	BAL	W 5- 0
6	BAL	W 12- 3
7	BAL	L 1- 3
8	BAL	W 2- 1
9	NG	
10	CAL	L 6- 7
11	CAL	*
12	CAL	W 3- 0
"	CAL	W 2- 1g
13	OAK	L 2- 5
14	OAK	L 0- 1
15	OAK	L 4- 6
16	NG	
17	KC	W 2- 0
"	KC	W 8- 5
18	KC	W 3- 1
19	NG	
20	cal	L 0- 6
21	cal	L 1- 2i
22	cal	L 0-3
23	oak	L 2- 8
24	oak	W 1- 0
25	oak	W 4- 2
26	NG	
27	KC	L 0- 4
28	kc	L 3- 4
29	kc	W 10- 3
30	NG	
31	WAS	L 5- 6

September, 1971

1	WAS	L 0- 2
2	WAS	W 11- 1
3	DET	L 1- 3
4	DET	L 1- 9
5	DET	W 6- 5
6	BOS	W 5- 3
"	BOS	W 3- 0
7	BOS	L 3- 9
8	BOS	W 2- 1g
9	NG	
10	NG	
11	cle	W 10- 8
12	cle	L 2- 5
13	bos	W 4- 0

September, 1971

14	bos	W 6- 3
15	bal	W 4- 2
16	bal	L 2- 6
17	CLE	W 1- 0
"	CLE	W 7- 1
18	CLE	W 9- 0
19	CLE	W 3- 2
20	BAL	L 4- 8
21	BAL	L 0- 5
22	BAL	L1- 10
23	NG	
24	det	L 5- 8
25	det	L 7-10
26	det	W 3- 2
27	NG	
28	was	L 2- 4
29	was	W 6- 3
30	was	W 9- 0F

F = FORFEIT TO
NEW YORK WITH
OUT TOP OF
NINTH, YANKS
LOSING 5-7.

END OF 1971
RUNS: 648
OPP RUNS: 641

CLUB VS. CLUB AND MONTHLY RECORDS OF THE
NEW YORK YANKEES' 1971 SEASON FOR HOME AND AWAY GAMES

CLUB:		APR	MAY	JUN	JUL	AUG	SEP	OCT	HOME	AWAY	TOTAL
BALT	H	xxx	1- 1	xxx	xxx	3- 1	0- 3	xxx	4- 5	xxx	7- 11
	A	1- 2	xxx	1- 3	xxx	xxx	1- 1	xxx	xxx	3- 6	
BOST	H	xxx	xxx	1- 1	3- 0	xxx	3- 1	xxx	7- 2	xxx	11- 7
	A	0- 1	0- 2	xxx	2- 2	xxx	2- 0	xxx	xxx	4- 5	
CAL	H	xxx	2- 1	xxx	xxx	2- 1	xxx	xxx	4- 2	xxx	6- 6
	A	xxx	xxx	2- 1	xxx	0- 3	xxx	xxx	xxx	2- 4	
CHIC	H	1- 0	xxx	xxx	3- 2	xxx	xxx	xxx	4- 2	xxx	7- 5
	A	xxx	3- 0	xxx	0- 3	xxx	xxx	xxx	xxx	3- 3	
CLEV	H	xxx	0- 2	1- 2	xxx	xxx	4- 0	xxx	5- 4	xxx	10- 8
	A	xxx	1- 3	xxx	xxx	3- 0	1- 1	xxx	xxx	5- 4	
DET	H	2- 1	xxx	2- 1	xxx	xxx	1- 2	xxx	5- 4	xxx	8- 10
	A	xxx	1- 2	xxx	1- 2	xxx	1- 2	xxx	xxx	3- 6	
KC	H	xxx	xxx	1- 2	xxx	3- 0	xxx	xxx	4- 2	xxx	7- 5
	A	xxx	xxx	2- 1	xxx	1- 2	xxx	xxx	xxx	3- 3	
MIL	H	1- 0	2- 1	xxx	1- 1	xxx	xxx	xxx	4- 2	xxx	10- 2
	A	xxx	2- 0	xxx	4- 0	xxx	xxx	xxx	xxx	6- 0	
MIN	H	1- 2	xxx	xxx	2- 1	xxx	xxx	xxx	3- 3	xxx	4- 8
	A	xxx	0- 3	xxx	1- 1	0- 1	xxx	xxx	xxx	1- 5	
OAK	H	xxx	1- 1	0- 1	xxx	0- 3	xxx	xxx	1- 5	xxx	5- 7
	A	xxx	xxx	2- 1	xxx	2- 1	xxx	xxx	xxx	4- 2	
WAS	H	0- 2	xxx	2- 2	xxx	0- 1	1- 1	xxx	3- 6	xxx	7- 11
	A	2- 2	xxx	0- 1	0- 1	xxx	2- 1	xxx	xxx	4- 5	
TOTAL:	H	5- 5	6- 6	7- 9	9- 4	8- 6	9- 7	xxx	44-37	xxx	82-80
	A	3- 5	7-10	7- 7	8- 9	6- 7	7- 5	xxx	xxx	38-43	
GRAND TOT:		8-10	13-16	14-16	17-13	14-13	16- 12	xxx	xxx	xxx	
CUMUL TOT:		8-10	21-26	35-42	52-55	66- 68	82-80	xxx	xxx	xxx	

TIE GAMES: NONE

1972

ANOTHER SOLID PERFORMANCE BY MURCER

Continuing to play only average baseball, the Yanks mustered but a record of 79–76 (.510). However, they finished but 6½ games behind the surprising Detroit Tigers of Billy Martin, future manager of New York, again, again and again. This season was marred by the first players' strike in Major League history. Seven Yankee games at the start of the campaign were cancelled, five against Baltimore, of which 4 were at New York.

In spite of Murcer's decline in batting average, from .331 in 1971 to .292 this season, he put together another fine season. This time around, he led the league in total bases (314) and runs scored (102); placed second in homers (33); and third in RBI (96), hits (171), doubles (30) and slugging percentage (.537). Roy White, an all-time favorite with this writer, tied Richie Allen of Chicago with 99 bases on balls.

The pitching staff and defensive play faltered in 1972. However, the Yankee infield combination made a league high 179 double plays. Sparky Lyle, obtained from the Boston Red Sox, paced the A.L. in saves with 35. Mel Stottlemyre's performance etched his name in the Yankee record book. With 18 losses (tied with Pat Dobson of Baltimore), Stot became the only Yank hurler in history to lead A.L. in losses for *two* seasons. Only Orth (1907), Lake (1908), Russell Ford (1912) and Jones (1925) had been the league's losingest pitchers previously.

Yogi Berra and Bill Dickey, both excellent Yankee catchers in their glory years, had their uniforms permanently retired. Both wearing #8 in their playing days, Missouri's Yogi and Louisiana's Dickey were richly deserving of this honor.

In 1972, Murcer proved again to be the Yank's most consistent player. Next season, Mr. Steinbrenner purchased the Yankees from CBS.

The 1972 DAY BY DAY scores follow:

DAY BY DAY, 1972 NEW YORK YANKEES

April, 1972	May, 1972	June, 1972	July, 1972	September, 1972
6 BAL *	14 cal L 2- 6	23 cle W 4- 1	31 bal W 5- 2	4 bal L 3- 4
7 BAL *	15 NG	24 cle *	" bal W 2- 1	" bal W 5- 2
8 BAL *	16 cle W 3- 1	25 cle L 3- 4	**August, 1972**	5 bal W 7- 6
9 BAL *	17 cle L 1- 2	" cle L 1- 5	1 bos W 10- 4	6 bos L 0- 2
10 NG	18 NG	26 det L 3- 4	2 bos W 5- 1	7 bos L 4-10
11 det *	19 BOS W 6- 0	27 det L 2- 5	" bos L 4- 7	8 bos L 2- 4
12 NG	20 BOS *	28 BAL L 0- 4	3 bos L 2- 7	9 det W 3- 1
13 det *	21 BOS W 6- 3	29 BAL W 4- 3	4 mil W 9- 4	10 det W 5- 0
14 bal *	" BOS W 3- 2	30 CLE W 1- 0	5 mil L 0- 4	11 det W 4- 2b
FIRST SEVEN	22 NG	**July, 1972**	6 mil W 3- 0	12 BOS W 3- 2
GAMES CAN-	23 CLE L 0- 3	1 CLE W 5- 1	" mil W 6- 4f	13 BOS L 2- 7
CELLED,	24 CLE W 4- 2	2 CLE W 6- 1	7 NG	14 NG
PLAYER'S STRIKE	25 CLE W 2- 0	" CLE W 5- 2	8 DET W 4- 2	15 BAL L 1- 3
15 bal *	26 DET L 2- 8	3 NG	9 DET L 0- 6	16 BAL L 3- 7
16 bal L 1- 3c	27 DET L 1- 2	4 oak L 2- 4	" DET W 2- 1	17 BAL W 2- 1
" bal *	28 DET L 4- 5	5 oak W 4- 1	10 DET W 1- 0	18 NG
17 bal L 0- 4	29 DET W 5- 1	6 oak W 6- 2	11 MIL L 2- 4	19 mil L 2- 7
18 MIL W 2- 0	" DET W 4- 2	7 min L 2- 5	12 MIL W 10- 6	20 mil *
19 MIL W 3- 2	30 mil L 1- 3	8 min W 1- 0g	13 MIL W 5- 3	21 mil L 4- 6
20 mil *	31 mil W 5- 4	9 min W 9- 6	" MIL W 5- 4	22 cle L 1- 4
21 bos L 4- 5	**June, 1972**	10 cal L 3- 4	14 kc L 0- 3	23 cle W 5- 2c
22 bos L 7-11	1 mil L 8- 9h	11 cal W 7- 3	15 kc L 6- 7	24 cle W 5- 4g
23 bos *	2 chi L 1- 6	12 cal W 5- 0	16 kc L 2- 3	" cle W 8- 3
24 NG	3 chi W 18-10i	13 NG	17 NG	25 NG
25 OAK L 3- 4h	4 chi L 1- 6	14 OAK L 3- 9	18 TEX L 2-11	26 NG
26 OAK W 4- 2	" chi L 4- 5	" OAK L 0- 1	19 TEX W 6- 2	27 det L 5- 6
27 NG	5 NG	15 OAK L 2- 6	20 TEX 2- 0f	28 det W 3- 2h
28 MIN L 1- 4	6 TEX L 3- 6	16 OAK L 2- 5	21 NG	29 NG
29 MIN L 0- 2	7 TEX W 7- 5	17 NG	22 chi L 4- 5	30 CLE *
30 MIN W 5- 4	8 TEX L 2- 6	18 MIN W 6- 0	23 chi L 2- 5	**October, 1972**
" MIN L 4- 5	9 kc L 0- 1	19 MIN W 13- 3	24 NG	1 CLE L 1- 2g
May, 1972	10 kc W 8- 4	20 CAL *	25 KC W 4- 1	" CLE L 3- 4
1 NG	11 kc L 0- 1	21 CAL W 6- 0	" KC L 1- 5	2 MIL L 1- 6
2 CAL W 5- 0	12 NG	" CAL W 3- 0	26 KC L 3- 6	3 MIL L 2- 3
3 CAL *	13 CHI L 0- 2	22 CAL L 0- 1	27 KC W 7- 6	4 MIL L 0- 1
4 CAL *	14 CHI W 3- 0	" CAL W 7- 1	" KC W 9- 8L	
5 oak L 1- 3	15 CHI W 8- 1	23 CAL L 3- 6	28 NG	END OF 1972
6 oak L 1- 4	16 TEX *	24 ALL-STAR BREAK	29 TEX W 7- 6g	RUNS: 557
7 oak L 5- 7	17 TEX W 2- 0	25 WON - 42	" TEX L 4- 7	OPP RUNS: 527
8 min W 5- 3	" TEX W 3- 2	26 LOST - 43	30 TEX W 3- 1	
9 min L 2- 4	18 TEX *	27 BOS W 6- 2	31 TEX W 7- 0	
10 min L 0- 2	19 NG	28 BOS L 5- 6	**September, 1972**	
11 NG	20 KC W 4- 2	" BOS W 3- 1	1 CHI W 4- 0	
12 cal W 6- 3	21 KC *	29 BOS W 8- 1	2 CHI W 2- 1	
13 cal W 3- 0	22 cle *	30 bal L 0- 5	3 CHI L 0- 5	

CLUB VS. CLUB AND MONTHLY RECORDS OF THE NEW YORK YANKEES' 1972 SEASON FOR HOME AND AWAY GAMES

CLUB:		APR	MAY	JUN	JUL	AUG	SEP	OCT	HOME	AWAY	TOTAL
BALT	H	xxx	xxx	1-1	xxx	xxx	1-2	xxx	2-3	xxx	6-7
	A	0-2	xxx	xxx	2-1	xxx	2-1	xxx	xxx	4-4	
BOST	H	xxx	3-0	xxx	3-1	xxx	1-1	xxx	7-2	xxx	9-9
	A	0-2	xxx	xxx	xxx	2-2	0-3	xxx	xxx	2-7	
CAL	H	xxx	1-0	xxx	3-2	xxx	xxx	xxx	4-2	xxx	8-4
	A	xxx	2-1	xxx	2-1	xxx	xxx	xxx	xxx	4-2	
CHIC	H	xxx	xxx	2-1	xxx	xxx	2-1	xxx	4-2	xxx	5-7
	A	xxx	xxx	1-3	xxx	0-2	xxx	xxx	xxx	1-5	
CLEV	H	xxx	2-1	1-0	3-0	xxx	xxx	0-2	6-3	xxx	11-7
	A	xxx	1-1	1-2	xxx	xxx	3-1	xxx	xxx	5-4	
DET	H	xxx	2-3	xxx	xxx	3-1	xxx	xxx	5-4	xxx	9-7
	A	xxx	xxx	0-2	xxx	-xxx	4-1	xxx	xxx	4-3	
KC	H	xxx	xxx	1-0	xxx	3-2	xxx	xxx	4-2	xxx	5-7
	A	xxx	xxx	1-2	xxx	0-3	xxx	xxx	xxx	1-5	
MIL	H	2-0	xxx	xxx	xxx	3-1	xxx	0-3	5-4	xxx	9-9
	A	xxx	1-1	0-1	xxx	3-1	0-2	xxx	xxx	4-5	
MIN	H	1-3	xxx	xxx	2-0	xxx	xxx	xxx	3-3	xxx	6-6
	A	xxx	1-2	xxx	2-1	xxx	xxx	xxx	xxx	3-3	
OAK	H	1-1	xxx	xxx	0-4	xxx	xxx	xxx	1-5	xxx	3-9
	A	xxx	0-3	xxx	2-1	xxx	xxx	xxx	xxx	2-4	
TEX	H	xxx	xxx	2-0	xxx	3-1	xxx	xxx	5-1	xxx	8-4
	A	xxx	xxx	1-2	xxx	2-1	xxx	xxx	xxx	3-3	
TOTAL:	H	4-4	8-4	7-2	11-7	12-5	4-4	0-5	46-31	xxx	79-76
	A	0-4	5-8	4-12	8-4	7-9	9-8	xxx	xxx	33-45	
GRAND TOT:		4-8	13-12	11-14	19-11	19-14	13-12	0-5	xxx	79-76	
CUMUL TOT:		4-8	17-20	28-34	47-45	66-59	79-71	79-76	xxx		

TIE GAMES: NONE

1973

ENTER GEORGE STEINBRENNER

In January 1973, George Steinbrenner purchased the Yankee franchise from CBS, reportedly paying a sum of around $12 million. (By comparison, the club sold for around $18,000 in January, 1903, when transferred from Baltimore.) Mr. Steinbrenner's open pocketbook later leads New York back on top of the baseball world.

However, the Yanks again finished another average year, losing more than 50% of their games played at 80–82 (.494). Baltimore again dominated the A.L. East, the Yanks ending in fourth place, 17 games behind the Birds.

In the most significant rule change in the modern era of baseball, the American League adopted the "designated hitter" rule. Yankee Ron Blomberg became the first DH in the A.L. when he came to the plate versus Luis Tiant at Boston on April 6. The BoSox pounded New York pitching, winning handily, 15–5. In 55 games as DH in 1973, Blomberg batted .269 (45 for 167) with 7 homers and 27 RBI. As a club, New York had a composite "DH" average of .249 (149 for 599) with 20 roundtrippers and 89 runs batted in.

No Yankee players demonstrated any statistical clout by leading the American League. Hitting but 17 triples as a club, the Yanks tied a mark previously set in 1967. Defensively, the Yanks finished ninth overall in A.L. fielding (.976), their second worst showing (they were 10th of the ten clubs in 1967) in the field in their history.

The conclusion of 1973 marked two historic occasions in Yankee history. First of all, Ralph Houk stepped down as New York's field "Major" general after eleven consecutive seasons at the Yankee helm. Secondly, the last game of 1973 at Yankee Stadium, September 30 versus Detroit, was the final contest in the "Old" Stadium. The Tigers beat the Yanks in that last game at the Stadium, 8–5. Plans were drawn to completely refurbish "The House That Ruth Built." Thank God, this magnificent edifice was not demolished to make way for a parking lot or condominiums. With much foresight, caring and planning, this stadium was saved for the enjoyment of future generations.

This season commemorated the 50th anniversary of the opening of Yankee Stadium, April 18, 1923. Too bad the New Yorkers couldn't celebrate the occasion with another pennant. Fans had to wait 'til next year and the next, and then success again, finally.

The 1973 DAY BY DAY scores follow:

George Steinbrenner has been the owner of the Yankees since January 1973. He brought respectability back to the Yankee franchise in the fine Yankee tradition.

DAY BY DAY, 1973 NEW YORK YANKEES

April, 1973		May, 1973		June, 1973		August, 1973		September, 1973	
6 bos	L 5–15	17 MIL W 4– 2g		26 cle W 10– 2		1 bos L 2– 3		12 BOS L 1– 7	
7 bos	L5– 10	18 MIL L 5– 6		27 bal L 0– 4		2 bos L 0–10		13 BOS W 2– 1h	
8 bos	L 3– 4	19 cle L 4– 6		28 bal L 3– 6		3 det L 2– 7		14 bal *	
9 CLE	L 1– 3	20 cle W 4– 2		29 CLE W 7– 2		4 det W 3– 2j		15 bal W 3– 0	
10 NG		" cle W 7– 3		30 CLE W 7– 3		5 det L 6– 8		16 bal L 0– 3	
11 CLE W 4– 0		21 cle L 5–10		**July, 1973**		6 det L 4– 5f		" bal W 7– 5	
12 CLE W 5– 0		22 det W 7– 2		1 CLE W 5– 2		7 TEX L 1– 2		17 bal L 4– 5f	
13 NG		23 det W 6– 5		" CLE W 11– 3		" TEX W 3– 1		18 bos L 2– 4	
14 BOS L 1– 3		24 det L 0– 4		2 BOS L 0– 1		8 TEX W 3– 2		19 bos L 1– 3	
15 BOS W 6– 2		25 TEX W 9– 7		3 BOS W 3– 1		9 NG		20 NG	
16 NG		26 TEX W 10– 5		4 BOS L 1– 2		10 OAK W 10– 9		21 NG	
17 bal L 2– 4		27 TEX L 2– 5		" BOS L 0– 1		11 OAK L 3– 7		22 cle L 1– 5	
18 bal W 7– 4		28 TEX *		5 BOS L 4– 9		12 OAK L12–13		23 cle W 9– 1	
19 bal W 6– 1		29 OAK W 7– 1		6 min W 5– 2		13 CAL W 6– 0		" cle W 2– 1	
20 mil L 0– 2		30 OAK W 4– 3		7 min L 1– 9		14 CAL W 7– 2		24 NG	
21 mil *		31 OAK L 0– 6		" min L 2– 6		15 CAL L 1– 3		25 mil L 2–3i	
22 mil L 3– 4		**June, 1973**		8 min W 7– 0		16 NG		26 mil L 2– 5	
23 mil W 5– 2		1 CAL L 2– 5		9 chi L 3– 4		17 tex L 1– 8		27 mil W 2– 0	
24 CHI L 4– 8		2 CAL W 2– 0		10 chi L 1– 2		18 tex W 5– 3		28 DET W 4– 1	
25 CHI L 0– 3		3 CAL W 3– 2		11 chi W 2– 1		19 tex W 6– 2		29 DET W 3– 0	
26 NG		4 NG		12 KC W 10– 3		20 kc L 2– 6		30 DET L 5– 8	
27 MIN *		5 tex W 8– 6		13 KC w 5– 0		21 kc L 4– 5		END OF 1973	
28 MIN W 11– 3		6 tex W 5– 2		14 KC L 2– 4		22 kc L 7– 8f		RUNS: 641	
29 MIN W 6– 3		7 tex L 5– 7		15 KC W 2– 0		23 NG		OPP RUNS: 610	
" MIN W 11– 1		8 kc W 8– 1		16 NG		24 oak L 1– 5			
30 NG		9 kc W 6– 4		17 MIN W 4– 3h		25 oak L 0– 2			
May, 1973		10 kc L 4– 7		" MIN W 4– 1		26 oak L 0– 1			
1 KC W 6– 1		11 NG		18 MIN L 0– 3		27 NG			
2 KC L 3– 4		12 oak L 2– 4		19 NG		28 cal L 2– 5			
3 NG		13 oak W 8– 3		20 CHI W 12– 2		29 cal L 0– 5			
4 chi L 0– 5		14 oak L 0– 3		" CHI W 7– 0b		30 NG			
5 chi L 0– 4		15 cal W 4– 3f		21 CHI *		31 BAL W 5– 2			
6 chi L2– 11		16 cal L 2– 5		22 CHI L 2– 4		**September, 1973**			
7 min *		17 cal L 0– 8		" CHI W 2– 0		1 BAL L 6–10			
8 min W 14– 4		" cal W 5– 1		23 ALL-STAR BREAK		2 BAl L 0– 1			
9 min W 2– 0		18 NG		24 WON - 57		3 det W 4– 3			
10 NG		19 BAL W 5– 4		25 LOST - 44		4 det L 1– 2			
11 BAL L 0– 3		20 BAL W 2– 1		26 MIL W 1– 0h		5 NG			
12 BAL W 8– 0		21 DET W 5– 1b		27 MIL W 7– 6		6 MIL W 8– 6			
13 BAL W 4– 0		22 DET W 5– 4		28 mil L 4– 5		7 MIL L 0– 5			
" BAL L 6– 9		23 DET W 3– 2		29 mil L 2– 7		8 MIL W 15– 1			
14 DET L 0– 8		24 DET W 3– 2		" mil L 3– 6		9 MIL L 3–10			
15 DET *		" DET W 2– 1		30 bos L 3– 4		10 CLE L 2– 3			
16 MIL W 11– 4		25 cle L 2– 4		31 bos W 5– 4		11 CLE L 3– 7			

CLUB VS. CLUB AND MONTHLY RECORDS OF THE NEW YORK YANKEES' 1973 SEASON FOR HOME AND AWAY GAMES

CLUB:		APR	MAY	JUN	JUL	AUG	SEP	OCT	HOME	AWAY	TOTAL
BAL	H	xxx	2-2	2-0	xxx	1-0	0-2	xxx	5-4	xxx	9-9
	A	2-1	xxx	0-2	xxx	xxx	2-2	xxx	xxx	4-5	
BOST	H	1-1	xxx	xxx	1-4	xxx	1-1	xxx	3-6	xxx	4-14
	A	0-3	xxx	xxx	1-1	0-2	0-2	xxx	xxx	1-8	
CAL	H	xxx	xxx	2-1	xxx	2-1	xxx	xxx	4-2	xxx	6-6
	A	xxx	xxx	2-2	xxx	0-2	xxx	xxx	xxx	2-4	
CHIC	H	0-2	xxx	xxx	3-1	xxx	xxx	xxx	3-3	xxx	4-8
	A	xxx	0-3	xxx	1-2	xxx	xxx	xxx	xxx	1-5	
CLEV	H	2-1	xxx	2-0	2-0	xxx	0-2	xxx	6-3	xxx	11-7
	A	xxx	2-2	1-1	xxx	xxx	2-1	xxx	xxx	5-4	
DET	H	xxx	0-1	5-0	xxx	xxx	2-1	xxx	7-2	xxx	11-7
	A	xxx	2-1	xxx	xxx	1-3	1-1	xxx	xxx	4-5	
KC	H	xxx	1-1	xxx	3-1	xxx	xxx	xxx	4-2	xxx	6-6
	A	xxx	xxx	2-1	xxx	0-3	xxx	xxx	xxx	2-4	
MIL	H	xxx	2-1	xxx	2-0	xxx	2-2	xxx	6-3	xxx	8-10
	A	1-2	xxx	xxx	0-3	xxx	1-2	xxx	xxx	2-7	
MIN	H	3-0	xxx	xxx	2-1	xxx	xxx	xxx	5-1	xxx	9-3
	A	xxx	2-0	xxx	2-2	xxx	xxx	xxx	xxx	4-2	
OAK	H	xxx	2-1	xxx	xxx	1-2	xxx	xxx	3-3	xxx	4-8
	A	xxx	xxx	1-2	xxx	0-3	xxx	xxx	xxx	1-5	
TEX	H	xxx	2-1	xxx	xxx	2-1	xxx	xxx	4-2	xxx	8-4
	A	xxx	xxx	2-1	xxx	2-1	xxx	xxx	xxx	4-2	
TOTAL:	H	6-4	9-7	11-1	13-7	6-4	5-8	xxx	50-31	xxx	80-82
	A	3-6	6-6	8-9	4-8	3-14	6-8	xxx	xxx	30-51	80-82
GRAND TOT:		9-10	15-13	19-10	17-15	9-18	11-16	xxx	xxx	xxx	
CUMUL. TOT:		9-10	24-23	43-33	60-48	69-66	80-82	xxx	xxx	xxx	

TIE GAMES: NONE

1974

MANAGER NUMBER TWENTY

Playing at Shea Stadium this season (and next), the Yanks had one of their best finishes in many a season. Bill Virdon, the twentieth Yankee field manager, guided New York to a surprising second place showing. The Yanks wound up but two games behind pennant-winning Baltimore. The Yanks concluded the season at 89–73, a .549 winning mark.

This season marked Bobby Murcer's last with New York until his reunion with the Yanks again in 1979.

Statistically, no New Yorker led the A.L. in any batting or pitching category. Neither did the club as a whole.

Whitey Ford became the eighth Yankee player to have his uniform permanently retired. As one of the best southpaws in Yankee (and baseball) history, number 16 was honored in the same company as the likes of Ruth, Gehrig, DiMaggio, etc. Quite an honor for "The Chairman of the Board," Edward Charles "Whitey" Ford.

Leland MacPhail, in January 1974, assumed the role of fifth American League president. MacPhail, the Yanks' general manager from 1966 through 1973, remained an A.L. president until replaced by former Yankee, Doctor Bobby Brown in 1983. Lee's father, Larry MacPhail, had served concurrently as Yankee club president as well as general manager in 1945, 1946 and 1947.

Playing on "foreign soil," Shea Stadium, this season and next, the Yanks continued to improve in their overall play, heading for respectability again in 1976.

The 1974 DAY BY DAY scores follow:

DAY BY DAY, 1974 NEW YORK YANKEES

April, 1974	May, 1974	June, 1974	August, 1974	September, 1974
6 CLE W 6- 1	15 DET L 5- 6	24 CLE L3- 10	3 BOS W 6- 2	11 bal L 2- 3m
7 CLE W 7- 1	16 NG	25 CLE *	4 BOS L 3- 7	" bal W 5- 1
8 CLE W 5- 3	17 mil W 3- 2	26 CLE L 2- 3	" BOS *	12 bal W 3- 0
9 det W 3- 0	18 mil L 2- 5	27 NG	5 BOS W 8- 0	13 det L 3- 6
10 NG	19 mil W 6- 2	28 bal *	6 BAL L 1- 4	14 det W 10- 7
11 det L 1- 4	" mil L 1- 3	29 bal L 0- 2	7 BAL W 4- 3	15 det W 10- 2
12 cle L 1- 9	20 NG	30 bal L 0- 3	8 NG	16 NG
13 cle L 5- 8	21 bos L 6-14	**July, 1974**	9 cal L 1- 7	17 BAL L 0- 4
14 cle W 9- 5	22 bos L 3- 6	1 det L 3- 4	10 cal W 2- 1	18 BAL L 4-10
" cle L 6- 9	23 NG	2 det L 2- 4	11 cal W 5- 4	19 BAL L 0- 7
15 NG	24 BAL L 3- 6	3 det L 6- 8	12 oak L 2- 3	20 CLE W 5- 4
16 BOS W 2- 1	25 BAL L 1- 5	4 det W 6- 4	13 oak L 1- 6	" CLE W 3- 0
17 BOS L 3- 4	26 BAL W 6- 5	5 tex W 14- 2	14 oak W 4- 1	21 CLE W 14- 7
18 BOS W 6- 1	" BAL W 7- 5	6 tex W 9- 3	15 NG	22 CLE W 2- 1
19 bal L 3- 5	27 CHI L 3- 5	7 tex L 2- 3	16 CHI W 9- 8i	23 NG
20 bal W 4- 3	28 CHI W 3- 2f	8 tex W 12- 5	" CHI L 2- 4	24 BOS L 0- 4
21 bal L 5- 6i	29 CHI *	9 kc W 8- 2	17 CHI W 2- 1c	" BOS L 2- 4
" bal W 3- 0	30 NG	10 kc W 9- 4	18 CHI W 9- 4	25 BOS W 1- 0f
22 NG	31 min L 2- 5	11 kc W 2- 1	19 MIN L 2- 6	26 NG
23 NG	**June, 1974**	12 OAK W 3- 0	20 MIN W 2- 1	27 cle *
24 KC W 4- 3	1 min W 6- 5i	13 OAK W 12- 6	21 MIN W 4- 1	28 cle W 9- 3
25 KC L 1- 6	2 min W 11- 1	14 OAK L 3- 7	22 NG	" cle W 9- 7
26 TEX W 4- 3	3 NG	" OAK L 1- 6	23 CAL W 10- 4	29 cle W 10- 0
27 TEX L 1- 6	4 chi L 2- 9	15 NG	24 CAL W 3- 1	30 NG
28 TEX W 11- 2	5 chi L 6- 7k	16 TEX W 2- 0	25 CAL W 2- 1	**October, 1974**
" TEX L 5- 8	6 chi W 5- 1	17 TEX L 0- 2	26 min L 6- 7	1 mil L 2- 3f
29 NG	7 MIN L 2- 3	18 KC W 10- 6	27 min W 4- 2	2 mil W 2- 1
30 OAK W 4- 3	8 MIN W 3- 1	19 KC L 4- 5	28 min W 5- 0	END OF 1974
May, 1974	9 MIN W 4- 3	20 KC W 6- 2	29 NG	RUNS: 671
1 OAK W 4- 3	10 CAL W 7- 5	21 KC W 5- 4	30 chi W 8- 5	OPP RUNS: 623
2 NG	11 CAL L 4- 5	22 ALL-STAR BREAK	31 chi W 18- 6	
3 kc W 5- 4	12 CAL W 6- 4	23 WON 48	**September, 1974**	
4 kc L 1- 5	13 NG	24 LOST - 47	1 chi W 7- 5	
5 kc L 2- 8	14 oak W 5- 1	25 MIL W 1- 0	2 MIL W 3- 1	
6 tex W 6- 4	15 oak L 1- 9	26 MIL W 5- 1	" MIL L 2- 3	
7 tex W 4- 3h	16 oak W 5- 3	27 bos L 4- 5	3 NG	
8 bos L 0- 4	17 cal W 5- 1	28 bos L 3- 8	4 MIL W 3- 0	
9 bos L 0- 2	18 cal L 0- 3	29 bos L 1- 2g	5 NG	
10 MIL W 7- 2	19 cal W 2- 1	30 mil L 2- 3f	6 DET W 6- 2c	
11 MIL L 2- 3	20 NG	" mil L 0- 4	7 DET L 3- 8	
12 MIL L 3- 7	21 DET L 2- 3	31 mil W 4- 3	" DET W 1- 0	
" MIL L 1- 5d	22 DET L 1- 4	**August, 1974**	8 DET L 3-11	
13 NG	23 DET W 4- 1	1 cle L 2- 9	9 bos W 6- 3	
14 DET L 2- 5	" DET *	2 cle L 2- 8	10 bos W 2- 1h	

CLUB VS. CLUB AND MONTHLY RECORDS OF THE NEW YORK YANKEES' 1974 SEASON FOR HOME AND AWAY GAMES

CLUB:		APR	MAY	JUN	JUL	AUG	SEP	OCT	HOME	AWAY	TOTAL
BAL	H	xxx	2-2	xxx	xxx	1-1	0-3	xxx	3-6	xxx	7-11
	A	2-2	xxx	0-2	xxx	xxx	2-1	xxx	xxx	4-5	
BOS	H	2-1	xxx	xxx	xxx	2-1	1-2	xxx	5-4	xxx	7-11
	A	xxx	0-4	xxx	0-3	xxx	2-0	xxx	xxx	2-7	
CAL	H	xxx	xxx	2-1	xxx	3-0	xxx	xxx	5-1	xxx	9-3
	A	xxx	xxx	2-1	xxx	2-1	xxx	xxx	xxx	4-2	
CHI	H	xxx	1-1	xxx	xxx	3-1	xxx	xxx	4-2	xxx	8-4
	A	xxx	xxx	1-2	xxx	2-0	1-0	xxx	xxx	4-2	
CLE	H	3-0	xxx	0-2	xxx	xxx	4-0	xxx	7-2	xxx	11-7
	A	1-3	xxx	xxx	xxx	0-2	3-0	xxx	xxx	4-5	
DET	H	xxx	0-2	1-2	xxx	xxx	2-2	xxx	3-6	xxx	7-11
	A	1-1	xxx	xxx	1-3	xxx	2-1	xxx	xxx	4-5	
KC	H	1-1	xxx	xxx	3-1	xxx	xxx	xxx	4-2	xxx	8-4
	A	xxx	1-2	xxx	3-0	xxx	xxx	xxx	xxx	4-2	
MIL	H	xxx	1-3	xxx	2-0	xxx	2-1	xxx	5-4	xxx	9-9
	A	xxx	2-2	xxx	1-2	xxx	xxx	1-1	xxx	4-5	
MIN	H	xxx	xxx	2-1	xxx	2-1	xxx	xxx	4-2	xxx	8-4
	A	xxx	0-1	2-0	xxx	2-1	xxx	xxx	xxx	4-2	
OAK	H	1-0	1-0	xxx	2-2	xxx	xxx	xxx	4-2	xxx	7-5
	A	xxx	xxx	2-1	xxx	1-2	xxx	xxx	xxx	3-3	
TEX	H	2-2	xxx	xxx	1-1	xxx	xxx	xxx	3-3	xxx	8-4
	A	xxx	2-0	xxx	3-1	xxx	xxx	xxx	xxx	5-1	
TOTAL:	9-4 H	5-8	5-6	8-4	11-4	9-8	xxx	47-34	xxx		89-73
	A	4-6	5-9	7-6	8-9	7-6	10-2	1-1	xxx	42-39	
GRAND TOT:		13-10	10-17	12-12	16-13	18-10	19-10	1-1	xxx	xxx	**TIE GAMES: NONE**
CUMUL TOT:		13-10	23-27	35-39	51-52	69-62	88-72	89-73	xxx	xxx	

1975

THE ARRIVAL OF BILLY MARTIN AND THE LANDING OF A CATFISH

The Yankees concluded the 1975 season in third place in the A.L. with an 83-77 (.519) mark, twelve games behind the pennant-clinching BoSox. The season's managerial reins were divided between Billy Virdon (53–51, .510) and one Alfred Manuel Pesano, more commonly known as Billy Martin. Billy guided the New Yorkers to a 30–26 (.536) ledger to conclude the year. Martin remained for three seasons until replaced by Bob Lemon in July 1978.

Bobby Bonds, playing his only season in Yankee pinstripes, was obtained from the San Francisco Giants of the National League in a straight swap for the Yanks' Bobby Murcer prior to the 1975 season. Bonds finished third in A.L. runs scored (93) and fourth in both slugging percentage (.512) and home runs (32). Munson, the steady Yankee catcher, was third in A.L. hits (190) and batting average (.318). Thurman led in most singles with 151. Compositely, the team won no A.L. statistical crowns except complete games (70), being tied with Baltimore for A.L. honors.

Jim "Catfish" Hunter, acquired through free agency prior to 1975, dominated the Yanks' mound staff, which finished second in team ERA (3.29). Hunter tied Baltimore's Jim Palmer for the A.L. high in wins with 23, led the A.L. in complete games (30) and innings pitched (328). In addition, his 2.58 ERA and 7 shutouts were second best in the A.L., behind Jim Palmer.

During the latter part of this season, Billy Martin set the wheels in motion to an A.L. championship next year.

The 1975 DAY BY DAY scores follow:

DAY BY DAY, 1975 NEW YORK YANKEES

April, 1975	May, 1975	June, 1975	August, 1975	September, 1975
8 cle L 3- 5	19 KC W 5- 1	30 mil L 4- 5	4 mil W 2- 1	" CLE W 4- 3
9 NG	20 KC W 6- 0	**July, 1975**	5 mil W 4- 3	14 CLE W 6- 2
10 NG	21 KC L 1- 4f	1 mil L 3- 6	6 cle L 3- 5	15 NG
11 DET L 3- 5	22 NG	2 cle L 2- 3	7 cle W 6- 3	16 mil L 2- 5
12 DET L 2- 7	23 TEX W 11- 7	3 cle L 2- 3	8 cal W 4- 3	17 mil W 6- 5g
13 DET W 6- 0	24 TEX W 9- 5	4 BAL L 4- 5	9 cal L 1- 8	18 NG
" DET L 2- 5	25 TEX W 5- 4	5 BAL L 2- 5	10 cal L 0- 1	19 cle L 2- 3
14 NG	26 kc L 5- 6g	6 BAL W 6- 1	11 cal L 1- 8	20 cle W 4- 1
15 BOS L 3- 5	27 kc L 0- 3	" BAL *	12 oak W 7- 2	21 cle L 2- 3
16 BOS L 2- 4	28 kc W 6- 2	7 TEX W 5- 2	13 oak W 3- 1	" cle W 11- 5
17 NG	29 tex W 7- 5	8 TEX W 4- 0	14 oak L 1- 5	22 BOS L 4- 6
18 det W 11- 3	30 tex L 5- 6	9 TEX L 0- 4	15 kc W 5- 4	23 BOS *
19 det L 3- 8	31 tex W 6- 0	10 MIN L 3- 6	16 kc L 3- 4	24 BOS *
20 det W 7- 1	**June, 1975**	11 MIN L 1-11	17 kc L 3- 5	" BOS *
21 bos W 12- 1	1 tex W 8- 4	" MIN W 4- 3	18 NG	25 NG
22 bos W 5- 0	2 NG	12 NG	19 CHI L 6- 7g	26 BAL *
23 bos L 7-11	3 min W 5- 4	13 NG	20 CHI L 3- 5	" BAL *
24 NG	4 min W 6- 3	14 ALL-STAR BREAK	21 CHI L 1- 2	27 BAL W 3- 2f
25 MIL *	5 min W 7- 4	15 WON · 45	22 CAL W 5- 2	" BAL W 7- 3
26 MIL W 10- 1	6 chi W 5- 1	16 LOST · 41	23 CAL W 12- 4	28 BAL L 0- 3
27 MIL L 0- 7	7 chi W 6- 3	17 tex L 2- 7	24 CAL L 0- 9	" BAL W 3- 2
" MIL W 10- 1	8 chi W 4- 1	18 tex L 0- 1	" CAL L 3- 4	END OF 1975
28 CLE W 6- 1	9 CAL L 3- 5	19 min W 8- 7L	25 NG	RUNS: 681
29 CLE L 1- 3	10 CAL W 6- 4	" min L 1- 2	26 OAK W 7- 1	OPP RUNS: 588
30 BAL W 6- 4	11 MIN W 5- 1	20 min W 14- 2	27 OAK L 2- 3	
May, 1975	12 MIN *	" min W 5- 4	28 OAK W 3- 2	
1 BAL W 5- 0	13 CHI W 2- 1	21 min L 0- 3	29 KC W 6- 5f	
2 mil L 2- 4	14 CHI L 2- 7	22 chi W 11- 6	30 KC L 2- 5	
3 mil L 3- 4	15 CHI W 3- 0	23 chi *	31 KC L 0- 7	
4 mil L 4-11	16 MIL W 10- 7	24 chi L 3- 4g	**September, 1975**	
5 bal *	17 MIL L 3- 4	" chi L 0- 1	1 bos W 4- 2	
6 bal L 1- 3	" MIL W 4- 2	25 BOS W 8- 6	2 bos L 4- 7	
7 bal L 3- 4	18 MIL L 3- 5	26 BOS L 2- 4	3 det W 8- 0	
8 NG	19 det W 9- 2	27 BOS L 0- 1	4 det W 8- 1	
9 oak L 3- 4	20 det L 9-10	" BOS L 0- 6	5 bal L 4- 5	
10 oak W 3- 0	21 det W 4- 1	28 DET L 0- 3	" bal L 1- 2	
11 oak L 5- 7	22 det W 5- 3	29 DET W 4- 2	6 bal L 6- 7i	
12 NG	23 bal W 6- 1	30 DET W 2- 1	7 bal W 2- 0	
13 cal L 0- 5	24 bal W 3- 1	31 NG	8 DET W 3- 0	
14 cal W 4- 3f	25 bal W 2- 1	**August, 1975**	9 DET W 9- 6	
15 NG	26 bos L 1- 6	1 CLE W 5- 4	10 MIL W 8- 2	
16 OAK L 2- 4	27 bos L 1- 9	2 CLE W 5- 3	11 MIL W 10- 2	
17 OAK L 1- 6	28 bos W 8- 6	3 CLE W 12- 1	12 CLE *	
18 OAK W 9- 1	29 bos L 2- 3	" CLE L 2- 3	13 CLE L 1- 7	

CLUB VS. CLUB AND MONTHLY RECORDS OF THE NEW YORK YANKEES' 1975 SEASON FOR HOME AND AWAY GAMES

CLUB:		APR	MAY	JUN	JUL	AUG	SEP	OCT	HOME	AWAY	TOTAL
BAL	H	1- 0	1- 0	xxx	1- 2	xxx	3- 1	xxx	6- 3	xxx	
	A	xxx	0- 2	3- 0	xxx	xxx	1- 3	xxx	xxx	4- 5	10- 8
BOS	H	0- 2	xxx	xxx	1- 3	xxx	0- 1	xxx	1- 6	xxx	
	A	2- 1	xxx	1- 3	xxx	xxx	1- 1	xxx	xxx	4- 5	5-11
CAL	H	xxx	xxx	1- 1	xxx	2- 2	xxx	xxx	3- 3	xxx	
	W	xxx	1- 1	xxx	xxx	1- 3	xxx	xxx	xxx	2- 4	5- 7
CHI	H	xxx	xxx	2- 1	xxx	0- 3	xxx	xxx	2- 4	xxx	
	A	xxx	xxx	3- 0	1- 2	xxx	xxx	xxx	xxx	4- 2	6- 6
CLE	H	1- 1	xxx	xxx	xxx	3- 1	2- 1	xxx	6- 3	xxx	
	A	0- 1	xxx	xxx	0- 2	1- 1	2- 2	xxx	xxx	3- 6	9- 9
DET	H	1- 3	xxx	xxx	2- 1	xxx	2- 0	xxx	5- 4	xxx	
	A	2- 1	xxx	3- 1	xxx	xxx	2- 0	xxx	xxx	7- 2	12- 6
KC	H	xxx	2- 1	xxx	xxx	1- 2	xxx	xxx	3- 3	xxx	
	A	xxx	1- 2	xxx	xxx	1- 2	xxx	xxx	xxx	2- 4	5- 7
MIL	H	2- 1	xxx	2- 2	xxx	xxx	2- 0	xxx	6- 3	xxx	
	A	xxx	0- 3	0- 1	0- 1	2- 0	1- 1	xxx	xxx	3- 6	9- 9
MIN	H	xxx	xxx	1- 0	2- 2	xxx	xxx	xxx	3- 2	xxx	
	A	xxx	xxx	3- 0	2- 2	xxx	xxx	xxx	xxx	5- 2	8- 4
OAK	H	xxx	1- 2	xxx	xxx	2- 1	xxx	xxx	3- 3	xxx	
	A	xxx	1- 2	xxx	xxx	2- 1	xxx	xxx	xxx	3- 3	6- 6
TEX	H	xxx	3- 0	xxx	2- 1	xxx	xxx	xxx	5- 1	xxx	
	A	xxx	2- 1	1- 0	0- 2	xxx	xxx	xxx	xxx	3- 3	8- 4
TOTAL:	H	5- 7	7- 3	6- 4	8- 9	8- 9	9- 3	xxx	43-35	xxx	83-77
	A	4- 3	5-11	14- 5	3- 9	7- 7	7- 7	xxx	xxx	40- 42	
GRAND TOT:		9-10	12-14	20- 9	11-18	15-16	16-10	xxx	xxx	xxx	
CUMUL TOT:		9-10	21-24	41-33	52-51	67-67	83-77	xxx	xxx	xxx	

TIE GAMES: NONE

1976

AT LONG LAST, PENNANT NO. 30

After a pennant drought of eleven seasons, the American League crown was again worn by the Yankee franchise. This was their 30th American League pennant. The Yanks, despite losing to Cincinnati in the World Series, had an extremely fruitful year. In their first full season under Billy Martin, New York clinched the A.L. East with a 97–62 (.610) record, 10½ games ahead of long-time nemesis, Baltimore. At the start of the season, the club returned to the friendly confines of renovated Yankee Stadium after playing the two previous seasons at Shea Stadium. Attendance at the stadium passed two million (2,012,434) for the first time since 1950.

Catcher Thurman Munson, who became the first Yankee since 1963 (Elston Howard) to win the Most Valuable Player Award in the American League, was also privileged to serve as the fifth official team captain. Thurm secured that honorary position until his tragic death in August, 1979. Up to this season, the Yanks had no team captain since June 1941 when Lou Gehrig served in that privileged capacity. Munson's all-around consistent play (17 homers and 105 RBI, the latter second in the A.L.) earned him a well-deserved MVP Award.

Graig Nettles led the A.L. in homers (32) and was the first Yankee to do so since Maris hit 61 roundtrippers in 1961. Nettles was also third in slugging with a percentage of .475. Steady Roy White, Chris Chambliss and Mickey Rivers all significantly aided the pennant cause. White scored the most Junior Circuit runs (104) with Rivers coming in third overall with 95 tallies. First sacker Chris Chambliss was tied for third in the A.L. with 96 ribbies and was second in total bases (283) behind Kansas City's George Brett. Chris was also third in total hits with 188. The club as a whole won no A.L. offensive stat honors.

The pitching staff allowed the fewest opponents' runs in the league with 575. The team also had the lowest A.L. team ERA with a fine 3.19 mark. This was their 22nd league ERA title and their first since 1960. Although without a 20-game winner on the mound, Hunter, Figueroa, Doc Ellis and Sparky Lyle proved a formidable pitching quartet. Lyle led the A.L. in saves with 23.

Defensively, the Yanks finished second overall in the A.L. (tied with Boston) for the 2nd straight season. The infield was solid throughout the season with Chambliss at first, Randolph at second, Fred Stanley at short and consistent Graig Nettles at third.

To cap this fantastic season, Chambliss clinched the pennant for New York by sending a Mark Littell pitch over the right field fence at Yankee Stadium. This all happened on October 14 versus Kansas City in the fifth and final game of the A.L. Championship Series. There were none out in the bottom of the ninth inning. After Chris hit the ball, he stood up on his toes to watch its pennant-clinching flight. Immediately after, pandemonium was witnessed in Yankee Stadium with fans inundating the infield to celebrate the momentous occasion. This homer was without a doubt one of the most significant in all Yankee history.

The wait for this pennant was very frustrating and represented the longest gap between *repeat* pennants in Yankee history. Yankee fans hope the wait will never be that long again! Next season, the Yanks will be world champions once more.

The 1976 DAY BY DAY scores follow:

DAY BY DAY, 1976 NEW YORK YANKEES

April, 1976	May, 1976	July, 1976	August, 1976	September, 1976
8 mil L 0- 5	21 BOS W 6- 5h	1 cle L 2- 3	9 kc L 2- 8	19 mil W 2- 1
9 NG	22 BOS w 1- 0g	2 cle W 7- 1	10 kc W 2- 1g	20 mil L 2- 4
10 mil W 9- 7	23 BOS L 6- 7	3 cle W 7- 3	11 kc W 5- 3	21 BAL L8- 11f
11 mil *	24 MIL W 5- 2	4 cle W 4- 3	12 min W 12- 5	22 BAL L 0- 2
12 bal W 3- 0	25 MIL L 0- 1	5 KC L 1- 2	13 min W 9- 3	" BAL L 2- 5
13 bal W 7- 1	26 CLE W 4- 3	6 KC L 1- 3	14 min W 5- 4	23 BAL L 1- 2
14 NG	27 CLE L 3- 5	" KC W 7- 4	15 min L 8- 9	24 det L 0- 3
15 MIN W 11- 4	28 det W 9- 5	7 KC L 1- 2	16 TEX W 5- 1	" det W 8- 0
16 NG	29 det L 1- 4	8 CHI W 6- 0	17 TEX W 2- 1	25 det W 10- 6
17 MIN W 10- 0	30 det W 4- 0	9 CHI W 2- 1	18 TEX W 8- 6	26 det *
18 MIN L 4- 5	31 bos W 8- 3	10 CHI L 1- 4	19 NG	27 NG
19 NG	**June, 1976**	11 CHI W 5- 0	20 CAL L 3- 5	28 bos L 5- 7
20 CHI W 5- 4	1 bos *	12 ALL-STAR BREAK	21 CAL L 3- 4	29 bos W 9- 6
21 CHI W 10- 7	2 bos W 7- 2	13 WON 50	22 CAL L 8-11	30 NG
22 NG	3 bos L 2- 8	14 LOST - 31	23 MIN W 9- 4	**October, 1976**
23 KC L 2- 3	4 OAK L 4- 6g	15 tex W 7- 6	24 MIN W 5- 4	1 CLE *
24 KC W 9- 8g	5 OAK L 6- 7	" tex W 6- 4f	25 MIN W 5- 4o	" CLE *
25 KC *	6 OAK L 2- 3	16 tex W 3- 0	26 NG	2 CLE W 6- 5
26 NG	" OAK W 5- 2	17 tex W 7- 5	27 cal W 5- 0k	" CLE W 4- 3
27 tex W 1- 0	7 NG	18 tex L 2- 3h	28 cal W 8- 1	3 CLE *
28 tex *	8 CAL W 4- 2	19 chi W 3- 2	29 cal L 4- 5g	" CLE *
29 NG	9 CAL W 4- 3	20 chi W 14- 9g	30 oak W 5- 2	END OF 1976
30 kc W 5- 3	10 CAL L 0- 2	21 OAK W 10- 1	31 oak W 2- 1	RUNS: 730
May, 1976	11 TEX W 7- 5	22 OAK L 5- 6	**September, 1976**	OPP RUNS: 575
1 kc L 1- 4	12 TEX L 1- 2	23 BOS W 9- 1	1 oak L 0- 5	
2 kc L 1- 2g	13 TEX L 1- 7	24 BOS W 4- 1	2 NG	
3 NG	14 NG	25 BOS W 6- 5	3 bal W 3- 1	
4 cal W 2- 1	15 min W 4- 2	26 bal L 1- 3	4 bal W 4- 2	
5 cal W 10- 4	16 min W 9- 4	27 bal L 1- 4	" bal L 2- 6	
6 cal W 4- 2	17 chi W 5- 4	28 bal L 3- 4	5 bal L 3- 5	
7 oak W 14- 4	18 chi W 3- 2j	29 NG	6 BOS W 6- 5	
8 oak W 8- 4	19 chi W 4- 3	30 bos W 6- 4	7 BOS W 4- 2	
9 oak L 3- 4h	20 chi W 6- 3	31 bos L 2- 4	8 MIL W 8- 0	
10 NG	21 CLE W 6- 0	" bos L 4- 6	9 MIL W 4- 2	
11 DET L 3- 4	22 CLE L 2- 3	**August, 1976**	10 MIL W 6- 4	
12 DET W 7- 6	23 CLE L 1- 4	1 bos L 4- 5	11 DET L 5- 6	
13 DET L 2- 3	24 CLE W 6- 5	2 DET W 1- 0	12 DET 0- 6	
14 BAL L 2- 6	25 MIL W 1- 0	3 DET W 4- 3	" DET W 3- 1	
15 BAL W 7- 3	26 MIL W 6- 3	4 mil L 3- 4	13 DET L 1- 3	
16 BAL L 0- 7	27 MIL W 6- 2	" mil W 7- 2	14 cle W 8- 2	
17 cle *	" MIL W 10- 2	5 mil L 3- 9b	15 cle W 2- 0	
18 cle W 11- 6L	28 det L 1- 5	6 BAL *	16 cle *	
19 cle W 3- 2	29 det L 5- 7	7 BAL L 4- 7	17 mil W 5- 3g	
20 BOS L 2- 8	30 det *	8 BAL L 5- 8	18 mil W 5- 3	

CLUB VS. CLUB AND MONTHLY RECORDS OF THE NEW YORK YANKEES' 1976 SEASON FOR HOME AND AWAY GAMES

CLUB:		APR	MAY	JUN	JUL	AUG	SEP	OCT	HOME	AWAY	TOTAL
BAL	H	xxx	1- 2	xxx	xxx	0- 2	0- 4	xxx	1- 8	xxx	5- 13
	A	2- 0	xxx	xxx	0- 3	xxx	2- 2	xxx	xxx	4- 5	
BOS	H	xxx	2- 2	xxx	3- 0	xxx	2- 0	xxx	7- 2	xxx	11- 7
	A	xxx	1- 0	1- 1	1- 2	0- 1	1- 1	xxx	xxx	4- 5	
CAL	H	xxx	xxx	2- 1	xxx	0- 3	xxx	xxx	2- 4	xxx	7- 5
	A	xxx	3- 0	xxx	xxx	2- 1	xxx	xxx	xxx	5- 1	
CHI	H	2- 0	xxx	xxx	3- 1	xxx	xxx	xxx	5- 1	xxx	11- 1
	A	xxx	xxx	4- 0	2- 0	xxx	xxx	xxx	xxx	6- 0	
CLE	H	xxx	1- 1	2- 2	xxx	xxx	xxx	2- 0	5- 3	xxx	12- 4
	A	xxx	2- 0	xxx	3- 1	xxx	2- 0	xxx	xxx	7- 1	
DET	H	xxx	1- 2	xxx	xxx	2- 0	1- 3	xxx	4- 5	xxx	8- 9
	A	xxx	2- 1	0- 2	xxx	xxx	2- 1	xxx	xxx	4- 4	
KC	H	1- 1	xxx	xxx	1- 3	xxx	xxx	xxx	2- 4	xxx	5- 7
	A	1- 0	0- 2	xxx	xxx	2- 1	xxx	xxx	xxx	3- 3	
MIL	H	xxx	1- 1	4- 0	xxx	xxx	3- 0	xxx	8- 1	xxx	13- 5
	A	1- 1	xxx	xxx	xxx	1- 2	3- 1	xxx	xxx	5- 4	
MIN	H	2- 1	xxx	xxx	xxx	3- 0	xxx	xxx	5- 1	xxx	10- 2
	A	xxx	xxx	2- 0	xxx	3- 1	xxx	xxx	xxx	5- 1	
OAK	H	xxx	xxx	1- 3	1- 1	xxx	xxx	xxx	2- 4	xxx	6- 6
	A	xxx	2- 1	xxx	xxx	2- 0	0- 1	xxx	xxx	4- 2	
TEX	H	xxx	xxx	1- 2	xxx	3- 0	xxx	xxx	4- 2	xxx	9- 3
	A	1- 0	xxx	xxx	4- 1	xxx	xxx	xxx	xxx	5- 1	
TOTAL:	H	5- 2	6- 8	10- 8	8- 5	8- 5	6- 7	2- 0	45-35	xxx	97-62
	A	5- 1	10- 4	7- 3	10- 7	10- 6	10- 6	xxx	xxx	52-27	
GRAND TOT:		10- 3	16-12	17-11	18-12	18-11	16- 13	2- 0	45-35	52-27	
CUMUL TOT:		10- 3	26-15	43-26	61- 38	79-49	95-62	97-62	xxx	xxx	

TIE GAMES: NONE

1977

REGGIE COMES TO THE BIG APPLE

Celebrating their 75th anniversary in the American League, the Yankees again reigned as World Series champs for the 21st time in thirty-one appearances. This time around they defeated the Dodgers of Los Angeles in six games. For the twelfth time since 1927, the Yankees won 100+ games, this season getting one hundred victories even. They lost 62 for a winning mark of .617 and finished 2½ games ahead of both Baltimore and Boston, who tied for second place in the A.L. East. The Yanks, for the second straight year, emerged victorious over the Kansas City Royals, champions of the A.L. West in the 1977 A.L. Championship Series.

Acquiring Reggie Jackson prior to the start of 1977 proved most beneficial for the Yankees. Reggie's awesome display of power in the World Series, especially demonstrated in the sixth and final game at New York, October 18, was one of the most stirring moments in the history of sports in America. The great Reggie hit 3 homers on three first pitch swings, a Reggian, not Ruthian, feat. In total, Jax had hit four home runs in four successive official times at bat! He had homered in his last at bat in the 5th game and walked his first time up in the sixth game. Only the Babe had three homers in a World Series game prior to Jackson's feat. The Babe did it twice, once in 1926 (game 4) and then again in 1928 (game 4). Reggie, in this World Series, had set records for most home runs (5), most runs (10), most total bases (25). His slugging percentage in the Series was 1.250 (25 total bases in but 20 official at bats) which was a record for a 6-game Series.

During the regular season, Reggie was second in the A.L. with 39 doubles, third in slugging percentage (.550) and fifth in homers with 32.

Mickey Rivers placed fourth in A.L. batting (.326) and Nettles was second to Boston's Jim Rice in home runs with 37. The club did not finish first in any offensive category.

Pitching was a definite strength this season, especially their relief corps led by Sparky Lyle. Of their 34 total saves, Lyle's 26 was 2nd best in the A.L. Lyle, with a fine 2.17 ERA, pitched in 72 games (high in the A.L.) and set a club record for appearances by a pitcher and won the Cy Young Award (the third for a Yankee pitcher). Whitey Ford had been the last Yank to be so honored in 1961. Ron Guidry in his first full season as a Yankee finished fourth in A.L. ERA with 2.82, second in winning percentage (.696, 16–7), and tied for second in shutouts (5) with Blyleven of Texas and Leonard of Kansas City. The club overall allowed the fewest opposition runs (651) for the second consecutive year.

This season proved even more remarkable than the last. Could any season be more exciting for Yankee fans? Well, just wait 'til next year!

The 1977 DAY BY DAY scores follow:

Reggie Jackson strikes his feared batting stance during batting practice. In his 5 seasons as a Yankee, Reg hit 144 homers and clubbed a record-tying 3 round trippers in the 6th game of the 1977 World Series against the Los Angeles Dodgers.

DAY BY DAY, 1977 NEW YORK YANKEES

April, 1977
7 MIL W 3-0
8 NG
9 MIL L 2-3
10 MIL L 1-2
11 kc L 4-5i
12 NG
13 kc W 5-3
14 NG
15 mil L 4-7
16 mil L 3-4
17 mil L 0-2
18 TOR L 1-5
19 TOR L 3-8
20 TOR W 7-5
21 TOR W 8-6
22 cle *
23 cle W 9-3
" cle *
24 cle W 10-1
" cle W 7-1
25 bal W 9-6
26 bal L 2-6
27 bal W 4-3
28 NG
29 SEA W 3-0
30 SEA W 7-2

May, 1977
1 SEA W 5-2
2 NG
3 CAL W 8-1
4 CAL *
5 OAK L 2-5
6 OAK W 4-1
7 OAK W 11-2
8 OAK W 10-5
9 NG
10 NG
11 SEA L 2-5
12 SEA L 6-8
13 cal W 3-0
14 cal W 4-1
15 cal L 2-8
16 oak L 4-8
17 oak W 5-2k

May, 1977
18 NG
19 BAL W 9-1
20 BAL L 5-6
21 BAL L 3-4h
22 BAL L 1-5
" BAL W 8-2
23 BOS L 3-4
24 BOS W 6-5
25 TEX W 3-2
" TEX L 0-1
26 NG
27 CHI W 8-6
28 CHI L 4-9
29 CHI W 5-2
30 bos W 5-4
31 bos L 1-5

June, 1977
1 min L 3-4
2 min W 10-3
3 chi L 5-9
4 chi W 8-6
5 chi W 8-6
6 tex W 9-2
7 tex L 3-7
8 mil W 9-2
9 mil W 10-1
10 MIN W 4-1
11 MIN W 6-5
12 MIN L 1-6
13 KC L 3-8
14 KC W 4-2
15 NG
16 KC W 7-0
17 bos L 4-9
18 bos L 4-10
19 bos L1-11
20 det L 1-2
21 det L 2-5
22 det W12-11

June, 1977
28 tor L 5-8
" tor W 5-1g
29 NG
30 tor W 11-5

July, 1977
1 DET L 1-5
2 DET W 6-4
3 DET W 2-0
" DET L 6-10
4 CLE W 7-5
5 CLE W 5-4
6 CLE *
7 CLE W 8-2
8 bal W 7-5
9 bal L 5-6
10 bal L 0-6
11 bal L 3-4
12 mil W 5-2
13 mil L 8-9
14 mil W 6-3
15 kc L 4-7
16 kc L 1-5
17 kc L 4-8
18 ALL-STAR BREAK
19 WON - 50
20 LOST - 42
21 MIL W 7-0
" MIL L 4-5f
22 MIL L 3-6
23 MIL W 3-1
24 KC W 3-1
25 KC *
26 BAL W 5-4f
27 BAL L 4-6
28 BAL W 14-2
29 oak W 4-0
30 oak W 9-3
31 oak W 9-2

August, 1977
1 cal L 1-4
2 cal W 9-3
3 cal L 3-5
4 NG
5 sea L 3-5

August, 1977
6 sea L 2-9
7 sea W 7-1
8 NG
9 NG
10 OAK W 6-3
11 OAK W 3-0
12 CAL W 10-1
" CAL W 9-3
13 CAL L 5-6
14 CAL W 15-3
15 CHI W 6-2
16 CHI W 11-10
17 det W 7-5
18 det W 5-4
19 tex W 8-1
20 tex W 6-2
21 tex W 2-1
22 chi L 3-5
23 chi W 8-3
24 MIN W 11-1
25 MIN W 6-4
26 TEX W 6-5
27 TEX L 2-8
28 TEX W 1-0
29 KC W 5-3
30 SEA W 6-5g
31 SEA W 5-4

September, 1977
1 NG
2 min W 4-0
3 min W 7-4
4 min W 4-0
5 cle L 3-4
" cle L 4-5
6 cle W 8-3
7 cle W 4-3f
8 cle W 4-3
9 TOR W 2-0
10 TOR L 3-19
11 TOR W 4-3
" TOR L 4-6
12 NG
13 BOS W 4-2
14 BOS W 2-0

September, 1977
15 BOS L 3-7
16 det W 5-4
17 det W 9-4
18 det W 6-5
19 bos L 3-6
20 bos *
21 bos L 2-3
22 NG
23 tor W 5-3
24 tor *
25 tor W 15-0
" tor W 2-0
26 CLE W 4-2
27 CLE W 2-1
28 CLE W 10-0
29 CLE L 1-4
30 DET L 2-5

October, 1977
1 DET L 7-10
2 DET W 8-7
END OF 1977
RUNS: 831
OPP RUNS: 651

CLUB VS. CLUB AND MONTHLY RECORDS OF THE NEW YORK YANKEES' 1977 SEASON FOR HOME AND AWAY GAMES

CLUB:		APR	MAY	JUN	JUL	AUG	SEP	OCT	HOME	AWAY	TOTAL
BAL	H	xxx	2– 3	xxx	2– 1	xxx	xxx	xxx	4– 4	xxx	7– 8
	A	2–1	xxx	xxx	1– 3	xxx	xxx	xxx	xxx	3– 4	
BOS	H	xxx	1– 1	3– 0	xxx	xxx	2– 1	xxx	6– 2	xxx	7– 8
	A	xxx	1– 1	0– 3	xxx	xxx	0– 2	xxx	xxx	1– 6	
CAL	H	xxx	1– 0	xxx	xxx	3– 1	xxx	xxx	4– 1	xxx	7– 4
	A	xxx	2– 1	xxx	xxx	1– 2	xxx	xxx	xxx	3– 3	
CHI	H	xxx	2– 1	xxx	xxx	2– 0	xxx	xxx	4– 1	xxx	7– 3
	A	xxx	xxx	2– 1	xxx	1– 1	xxx	xxx	xxx	3– 2	
CLE	H	xxx	xxx	xxx	3– 0	xxx	3– 1	xxx	6– 1	xxx	12– 3
	A	3–0	xxx	xxx	xxx	xxx	3– 2	xxx	xxx	6– 2	
DET	H	xxx	xxx	xxx	2– 2	xxx	0– 1	1– 1	3– 4	xxx	9– 6
	A	xxx	xxx	1– 2	xxx	2– 0	3– 0	xxx	xxx	6– 2	
KC	H	xxx	xxx	2– 1	1– 0	1– 0	xxx	xxx	4– 1	xxx	5– 5
	A	1–1	xxx	xxx	0– 3	xxx	xxx	xxx	xxx	1– 4	
MIL	H	1–2	xxx	xxx	2– 2	xxx	xxx	xxx	3– 4	xxx	7– 8
	A	0–3	xxx	2– 0	2– 1	xxx	xxx	xxx	xxx	4– 4	
MIN	H	xxx	xxx	2– 1	xxx	2– 0	xxx	xxx	4– 1	xxx	8– 2
	A	xxx	xxx	1– 1	xxx	xxx	3– 0	xxx	xxx	4– 1	
OAK	H	xxx	3– 1	xxx	xxx	2– 0	xxx	xxx	5– 1	xxx	9– 2
	A	xxx	1– 1	xxx	3– 0	xxx	xxx	xxx	xxx	4– 1	
SEA	H	2–0	1– 0	xxx	xxx	2– 0	xxx	xxx	5– 0	xxx	6– 4
	A	xxx	0– 2	xxx	xxx	1– 2	xxx	xxx	xxx	1– 4	
TEX	H	xxx	1– 1	xxx	xxx	2– 1	xxx	xxx	3– 2	xxx	7– 3
	A	xxx	xxx	1– 1	xxx	3– 0	xxx	xxx	xxx	4– 1	
TOR	H	2–2	xxx	xxx	xxx	xxx	2– 2	xxx	4– 4	xxx	9– 6
	A	xxx	xxx	2– 2	xxx	xxx	3– 0	xxx	xxx	5– 2	
TOTAL:	H	5–4	11– 7	7– 2	10– 5	14– 2	7– 5	1– 1	55–26	xxx	100–62
	A	6–5	4– 5	9–10	6– 7	8– 5	12– 4	xxx	xxx	45–36	
GRAND TOT:		11–9	15–12	16–12	16–12	22– 7	19– 9	1– 1	xxx	xxx	
CUMUL TOT:		11– 9	26–21	42–33	58–45	80–52	99–61	100–62	xxx	xxx	

TIE GAMES: NONE

1978

THE GREATEST COMEBACK
OF ALL AND DOING IT THE
CAJUN WAY

If the two previous seasons were exciting, then attempts to label 1978 would summon such adjectives as phenomenal, incredible, unbelievable as apropos descriptions. The Yankees' pennant-clinching (their 32nd A.L. flag) highlighted this season. A one-game playoff victory at Boston's Fenway Park on October 2 was sweet indeed for the Yanks and just as disheartening for the Red Sox and their loyal Fenway fans. Such a one-game playoff happened only once prior in A.L. history in 1948. Ironically, it was Boston (at Fenway park) that came up without a pennant, losing to Lou Boudreau's Cleveland Indians.

With New York's one game playoff victory, 5–4 over the BoSox, the Yanks were again at the century mark in victories for the thirteenth time since "Murderer's Row" back in 1927. Billy Martin's bunch went on to vanquish the Royals of Kansas City for the third straight year to earn their 32nd World Series berth. As fate would have it, the Bombers won their 22nd Fall Classic against their previous cross-town rivals, the Dodgers. After losing the first two games to LA, the Yanks stormed back (in much the same manner as their great comebacks throughout the season) to win the next four games, clinching the Series in six games.

Now some words about baseball's greatest comeback in history. Led by Ron Guidry's incomparable pitching performance all season long, the Bombers were 14 games behind Boston on July 18 when New York was 47–42 (.528) and the Red Sox 61–28 (.685), both having played the same number of games (89) up to that point in the campaign. Excluding the one-game playoff versus Boston, New York won 52 of their remaining 73 games, a .712 winning clip. Manager Billy Martin, under much pressure to produce a winner, resigned on July 24 with a 52–42 (.553) won-lost ledger. Dick Howser managed but one game, losing at Kansas City that same evening. Bob Lemon, the Yanks' 22nd manager, began his tenure July 25 amid much controversy and led his club to a 48–20 (.706) record. Lemon, a thirteen season pitcher with the Cleveland Indians as his only club, later was replaced in an unexpected move by Billy Martin in June of next year. To complicate matters further, Lemon also eventually replaced another New York manager, Gene Michael, in September 1981.

By guiding the Yankees to an A.L. pennant, Bob Lemon was the only manager in Junior Circuit history to win a flag after managing a different club earlier in the same season (he went 34–40 [.459] with the Chicago White Sox until June 30). A large factor in the pennant race was the so-called "Boston Massacre" at Fenway Park from September 7 through 10. In four games, the Yanks pounded Boston pitchers for 42 runs and 67 basehits. The Red Sox managed but 9 runs and 21 hits during that four game series. The Bombers won by scores of 15–3, 13–2, 7–0, and 7–4. As a result of the sweep, the Yanks and Boston were deadlocked with identical 86–56 (.606) records with twenty games left on the regular season schedule. To digress for a moment, much has been said about the 1914 comeback of the "Miracle Braves." Although they came back to overcome the Giants after being in last place, the Braves of 1914 were not 14 games behind the leader as were the Yanks of 1978. There is a definite difference between making up games behind and improving one's position when one club is above another.

While New York was generally given most of the glory and press ink this season, the Red Sox should be commended since they made a comeback themselves, later in the season. The BoSox overcame a 3½ game deficit held by New York on September 16 by winning 12 of their final fourteen regular season games to tie the Yanks on October 1. On that final day of the regular season, both clubs shared identical 99–63 (.611) marks. The season Jim Rice of Boston had was fantastic and earned him the A.L. MVP Award, winning over Ron Guidry 352 votes to 291.

All Yankee individual performances in 1978 were greatly overshadowed by Louisiana's Ronald Ames Guidry. Of French and Cajun descent (as is the author), Louisiana Lightnin' posted an incredible 25–3 mark and 1.74 ERA, both best in the A.L. His ERA was the third best in Yankee history for a season, trailing Chandler (1.64) in 1943 and Russell Ford's 1.65 in 1910. It was, however, the best ERA by a lefty in Yankee history. In only his second full season as a Yankee, Guidry's .893 winning percentage was the highest in Major League history for pitchers winning more than twenty games.

Ron's nine shutouts, the most in the Majors this season, tied Babe Ruth's 1916 A.L. record with Boston as the most whitewashes by a lefthanded hurler in the American League. Finishing second in total strikeouts in the league with 248 (a new club record eclipsing Jack Chesbro's long-standing 1904 mark of 239) to Nolan Ryan (260) of California, Guidry established an American League record for a southpaw by fanning 18 Angels in a June 17 game at the "Big A" at Anaheim, California. He pitched a 4–0 shutout as well in that game. Overall, Guidry became the first Yankee to lead the A.L. in winning percentage since 1963 (Ford); the first to lead in ERA since 1958 (Ford); and the first to lead in shutouts since 1960 (Ford again).

The pitching staff had the best A.L. ERA (3.18), allowing the fewest runs (582) the third straight season, and had the most total saves (36), led by Goose Gossage with 27, another A.L. high in 63 relief stints. For the only time in their history so far, Yankees won the coveted Cy Young Award two straight years. Ron Guidry took the award this year while Sparky Lyle won the previous season.

No individual Yankee hitters placed first in any offensive department, but were consistent enough to do the main job—win. However, the club as a whole was much, much sounder afield and on the mound than at the plate.

In summation, this season was truly incredible. From Billy Martin's resignation in July to Bob Lemon's leadership the remainder of the campaign; from Guidry's incomparable season to the "Boston Massacre" in September; from the Yank's one-game playoff victory over Boston to the third straight defeat of the Kansas City Royals in the American League Championship Series. All of this finally culminated with yet another comeback, this time in the World Series. What a season it was! As us Cajuns would say, "poo yiee!" (or holy cow).

The 1978 DAY BY DAY scores follow:

DAY BY DAY, 1978 NEW YORK YANKEES

April, 1978	May, 1978	June, 1978	August, 1978	September, 1978
8 tex L 1– 2	21 tor W 2– 1	30 DET W 10– 2	7 NG	18 MIL W 4– 3
9 tex W 7– 1	" tor W 9– 1	**July, 1978**	8 MIL W 3–0	19 MIL L 0– 2
10 tex L 2– 5	22 NG	1 DET L 4– 8	9 MIL W 8– 7	20 tor L 1– 8
11 mil L 6– 9	23 CLE W 10– 1	2 DET W 3– 2	10 MIL W 9– 0	" tor W 3– 2
12 mil L 3– 5	24 CLE *	" DET W 5– 3	11 BAL W 2–1b	21 tor W 7– 1
13 CHI W 4– 2	25 CLE W 9– 3	3 bos L 5– 9	12 BAL L 4–6	22 cle L 7– 8f
14 NG	26 TOR W 4– 3	4 bos *	13 BAL L 0– 3b	23 cle L 1–10
15 CHI W 3– 2	27 TOR L 1– 4	5 tex L 2– 3	14 BAL W 4–1	24 cle W 4– 0
16 CHI W 3– 0	28 TOR W 5– 3	6 tex W 7– 2	15 oak W 6–0	25 NG
17 BAL L 1– 6	" TOR W 6– 5i	7 mil L 0– 6	16 oak W 5–3	26 TOR W 4– 1
18 BAL W 4– 3	29 cle W 2– 0	8 mil L 5– 6	17 NG	27 TOR W 5– 1
19 tor L 3– 4	30 cle L 1– 5	9 mil L 4– 8	18 sea W 6–1	28 TOR W 3– 1
20 tor *	31 BAL L 2– 3	10 ALL-STAR BREAK	19 sea L 1– 4	29 CLE W 3– 1
21 MIL L 2– 9	**June, 1978**	11 WON - 46	20 sea L 4– 5	30 CLE W 7– 0
22 MIL W 4– 3h	1 BAL L 0– 1	12 LOST - 38	21 NG	**October, 1978**
23 MIL L 2– 3	2 oak W 3– 1	13 CHI L 1– 6	22 cal W 6–2	1 CLE L 2– 9
24 bal W 8– 2	3 oak L 1– 5	14 CHI W 7– 6g	23 cal L 3–6	2 bos W 5– 4
25 bal W 4– 3	4 oak L 4– 6	15 KC L 2– 8	24 NG	END OF 1978
26 NG	5 sea L 3– 7	16 KC L 1– 3	25 OAK W 7– 1	RUNS: 735
27 NG	6 sea L 3– 4	17 KC L 7– 9g	26 OAK W 5– 4	OPP RUNS: 582
28 min W 3– 1	7 sea W 9– 1	18 NG	27 OAK W 6– 2	
29 min L 1– 3	8 NG	19 min W 2– 0	28 CAL W 4– 1	
30 min W 3– 2	9 cal W 3– 1	20 min W 4– 0	29 CAL W 4– 3g	
May, 1978	10 cal L 3– 4h	21 chi W 7– 4	30 bal W 5–4	
1 KC W 8– 4	11 cal L 6– 9	22 chi W 7– 2	31 bal W 6–2	
2 KC W 4– 2	12 OAK W 2– 0	23 chi W 3– 1	**September, 1978**	
3 KC W 6– 5	13 OAK W 5– 3	24 kc L 2– 5	1 SEA L 0–3	
4 NG	14 SEA W 11– 9f	25 kc W 4– 0	2 SEA W 6–2	
5 TEX W 5– 2	15 SEA W 5– 2	26 CLE W 3– 1	3 SEA W 4–3	
6 TEX L 5– 9	16 CAL L 7–10	27 CLE W 11– 0	4 DET W 9–1	
7 TEX W 3– 2h	17 CAL W 4– 0	" CLE L5– 17	" DET L 4–5	
8 MIN *	18 CAL L 2– 3	28 MIN L 5– 7f	5 DET W 4–2	
9 MIN W 3– 1	19 bos L 4–10	29 MIN W 7– 3	6 DET W 8–2	
10 NG	20 bos W 10– 4	30 MIN W 4– 3	7 bos W 15– 3	
11 NG	21 bos L 2– 9	" MIN L 0– 2	8 bos W 13– 2	
12 kc L 3– 4	22 det W 4– 2	31 TEX W 6– 1	9 bos W 7– 0	
13 kc W 5– 2	23 det W 12– 3	**August, 1978**	10 bos W 7– 4	
14 kc L 9–10	24 det L 3– 4	1 TEX W 8– 1	11 NG	
15 chi W 4– 1	25 det W 4– 2	2 NG	12 det L 4– 7	
16 chi W 8– 3	26 BOS L 1– 4	3 BOS L 5– 7m	13 det W 7– 3	
17 cle L 4– 5f	27 BOS W 6– 4j	" BOS L 1– 8c	14 det W 4–2	
18 cle W 5– 3	28 mil L 0– 5	4 BAL L 1– 2	15 BOS W 4–0	
19 tor W 11– 3	" mil L 2– 7	5 BAL W 3– 2	16 BOS W 3–2	
20 tor L 8–10	29 NG	6 BAL W 3– 0	17 BOS L 3– 7	

NEW YORK YANKEES' 1978 SEASON FOR HOME AND AWAY GAMES

CLUB:		APR	MAY	JUN	JUL	AUG	SEP	OCT	HOME	AWAY	TOTAL
BAL	H	1-1	0-1	0-1	xxx	2-1	xxx	xxx	3-4	xxx	9-6
	A	2-0	xxx	xxx	xxx	4-2	xxx	xxx	xxx	6-2	
BOS	H	xxx	xxx	1-1	xxx	0-2	2-1	xxx	3-4	xxx	9-7
	A	xxx	xxx	1-2	0-1	xxx	4-0	1-0	xxx	6-3	
CAL	H	xxx	xxx	1-2	xxx	2-0	xxx	xxx	3-2	xxx	5-5
	A	xxx	xxx	1-2	xxx	1-1	xxx	xxx	xxx	2-3	
CHI	H	3-0	xxx	xxx	1-1	xxx	xxx	xxx	4-1	xxx	9-1
	A	xxx	2-0	xxx	3-0	xxx	xxx	xxx	xxx	5-0	
CLE	H	xxx	2-0	xxx	2-1	xxx	2-0	0-1	6-2	xxx	9-6
	A	xxx	2-2	xxx	xxx	xxx	1-2	xxx	xxx	3-4	
DET	H	xxx	xxx	1-0	2-1	xxx	3-1	xxx	6-2	xxx	11-4
	A	xxx	xxx	3-1	xxx	xxx	2-1	xxx	xxx	5-2	
KC	H	xxx	3-0	xxx	0-3	xxx	xxx	xxx	3-3	xxx	5-6
	A	xxx	1-2	xxx	1-1	xxx	xxx	xxx	xxx	2-3	
MIL	H	1-2	xxx	xxx	xxx	3-0	1-1	xxx	5-3	xxx	5-10
	A	0-2	xxx	0-2	0-3	xxx	xxx	xxx	xxx	0-7	
MIN	H	xxx	1-0	xxx	2-2	xxx	xxx	xxx	3-2	xxx	7-3
	A	2-1	xxx	xxx	2-0	xxx	xxx	xxx	xxx	4-1	
OAK	H	xxx	xxx	2-0	xxx	3-0	xxx	xxx	5-0	xxx	8-2
	A	xxx	xxx	1-2	xxx	2-0	xxx	xxx	xxx	3-2	
SEA	H	xxx	xxx	2-0	xxx	xxx	2-1	xxx	4-1	xxx	6-5
	A	xxx	xxx	1-2	xxx	1-2	xxx	xxx	xxx	2-4	
TEX	H	xxx	2-1	xxx	1-0	1-0	xxx	xxx	4-1	xxx	6-4
	A	1-2	xxx	xxx	1-1	xxx	xxx	xxx	xxx	2-3	
TOR	H	xxx	3-1	xxx	xxx	xxx	3-0	xxx	6-1	xxx	11-4
	A	0-1	3-1	xxx	xxx	xxx	2-1	xxx	xxx	5-3	
TOTAL:	H	5-3	11-3	7-4	8-8	11-3	13-4	0-1	55-26	xxx	100-63
	A	5-6	8-5	7-11	7-6	8-5	9-4	1-0	xxx	45-37	**TIE GAMES:** NONE
GRAND TOT:		10-9	19-8	14-15	15-14	19-8	22-8	1-1			
CUMUL TOT:		10-9	29-17	43-32	58-46	77-54	99-62	100-63			

1979

THE LOSS OF A CAPTAIN

In a Yankee version of musical chairs, Billy Martin unexpectedly replaced Bob Lemon as New York manager on June 19. Lemon, who had taken over for Martin the previous season, led New York to a 34–30 (.531) mark prior to being replaced. Martin finished the year as Yankee field mentor, winning 55 and losing 41 for a .573 worksheet. The Yanks finished fourth in the A.L. East race, falling 13½ games behind pennant-winning Baltimore.

Thurman Munson, the Yankees' 5th team captain appointed at the beginning of the 1976 season, lost his life tragically in an airplane crash, August 2. All of the Yankee players attended Thurman's funeral on August 6, with many openly expressing their grief and great sense of loss. Later that evening a game was played versus Baltimore at Yankee Stadium. Bobby Murcer, who had eulogized Thurman earlier in the day and with hardly any sleep, knocked in all of New York's 5 runs to beat the Birds 5–4. The Yanks had been losing 4–0 'til the seventh inning. I guess one could say that Bobby Murcer played his heart out for his beloved companion who was now gone. Thurman, who was just barely into his thirty-second year of life, is sadly missed by all baseball fans who appreciated this fine man's courage, desire, and raw natural abilities.

In 1979, the Yankees fielded the most players (47) in their history. Of those total number of players, 19 were pitchers. At the gate, New York broke a club attendance mark, drawing 2,537,765 to Yankee Stadium, breaking the old mark of 2,373,901 set at the "old" Yankee Stadium in 1948. Next year will be even better. This year's attendance was, up to that point, the second highest in A.L. history. Cleveland's 2,620,627 in 1948 was the highest. This year, the Yanks play before 4,762,147 for both home and away games, an incredible total, illustrating the enormous drawing power this incomparable sports franchise has.

For the first time since 1961, the Yanks finished with the best fielding mark (.981) in the league. The defense was for the most part very sound. The club's ERA of 3.83 was second to Baltimore's 3.26 mark. As a unit, the Yanks were 10th in batting average of fourteen clubs.

Ron Guidry, "The Ragin' Cajun," (the nickname of his Alma Mater, the University of Southwestern Louisiana in Lafayette) had another fine year leading the A.L. again in ERA with a 2.78 mark. Ron became the only Yankee hurler in history to win consecutive ERA titles! Guidry finished second in strikeouts (201) again to Nolan Ryan's 223 with the Angels. Tommy John, acquired during the off season from the Dodgers, had a fine year also. He and Guidry combined for 39 victories with John winning 21 to rank second overall behind Flanagan's 23 with Baltimore. In addition, John (2.97) was only headed by teammate Ron Guidry's ERA as the league's best.

All in all, this year was one of the most tragic in Yankee history. Munson's uniform (no. 15) was the 9th to be retired in Yankee history. How fitting it was that this great player was remembered in this manner. How he had given of himself to his team and his family will never be forgotten.

The 1979 DAY BY DAY scores follow:

In 1979, Ron Guidry had another fine year, leading the A.L. again in ERA with a 2.78 mark. Ron became the only Yankee in history to win consecutive ERA titles.

DAY BY DAY, 1979 NEW YORK YANKEES

April, 1979	May, 1979	June, 1979	August, 1979	September, 1979
5 MIL L 1– 5	19 bos L 3– 4	30 BOS L 2– 3	11 bal *	21 tor L 2–3
6 NG	20 bos W 2– 0	**July, 1979**	12 bal *	22 tor W 7–4
7 MIL L 3– 4	21 det L 1– 3	1 BOS W 6– 5	" bal *	23 tor W 7–5
8 MIL W 2– 1	22 det W 12– 8	2 BOS W 7– 2	13 TEX W 3– 2	24 NG
9 NG	23 det L 3– 4	3 MIL L 2– 7	14 TEX W 6– 5	25 CLE W 7–5
10 bal W 7– 6	24 NG	4 MIL W 4– 3	15 TEX W 4– 3	26 CLE W 6–3
11 bal L 5– 6f	25 cle *	5 MIL L 0– 3	16 MIN L 1– 5	27 CLE W 5–2
12 bal W 5– 0	26 cle L 4– 8	6 oak W 4– 3	17 MIN L 2– 5	28 TOR W 7–3
13 chi L 2–12	27 cle L 0– 5	" oak W 3– 0	18 MIN W 5– 3	29 TOR W 9–4
14 chi W 8– 5	" cle W 5– 4	7 oak W 8– 3	19 MIN W 4– 3	30 TOR W 9–2
15 chi W 6– 5	28 mil W 2– 1	8 oak W 2– 0	20 kc W 17– 4	
16 NG	29 mil L 3– 7	9 NG	21 kc W 6– 2	END OF 1979
17 BAL W 5– 1	30 mil W 5– 2g	10 sea L 1– 5	22 kc L 1– 3	RUNS: 734
18 BAL W 3– 1	31 mil L 4– 5	11 sea L1– 16	23 NG	OPP RUNS: 672
19 BAL L 3– 6	**June, 1979**	12 sea W 14– 2	24 min W 7– 5	
20 TEX W 5– 3	1 CHI W 4– 0	13 cal L 1– 6	25 min L 1– 4	
21 TEX L 0– 5	2 CHI L 0– 7	14 cal L 7– 8h	26 min *	
22 TEX W 5– 1	3 CHI W 3– 2g	15 cal L 4– 5	27 tex W 7– 4	
23 NG	4 KC W 8– 3	16 ALL-STAR BREAK	28 tex L 2–10	
24 oak W 3– 1	5 KC L 1– 3	17 WON - 49	29 tex W 7– 5	
25 oak L 0– 1	6 MIN W 3– 2	18 LOST - 43	30 KC L 3– 8	
26 oak *	7 MIN L 1– 4	19 OAK W 10– 2	31 KC W 7– 3	
27 sea L 5– 6	8 kc W 11–10g	20 OAK L 1– 5	**September, 1979**	
28 sea L 2– 3	9 kc L 8– 9i	21 OAK W 12– 4	1 KC L 8– 9	
29 sea L 5– 6	10 kc W 10– 4	22 SEA W 4– 0	2 KC W 6– 5f	
30 cal L 1– 2	11 NG	23 SEA W 6– 2	3 BOS W 10– 6	
May, 1979	12 min W 4– 1	24 CAL W 6– 5	4 BOS W 3– 2	
1 cal W 12– 8g	13 min L 7– 8	25 CAL L 5– 9	5 BOS L 0– 5	
2 cal L 0– 1	14 min L 2– 4	26 CAL W 2– 0	6 det W 3– 1f	
3 NG	15 tex L 5– 9	27 mil L 5– 6	7 det L 0– 6	
4 OAK L 5–11	16 tex W 3– 2f	28 mil L 2– 9	8 det W 5– 4	
5 OAK W 5– 4	17 tex L 3– 6	29 mil L 3– 5	9 det L 1– 3	
6 OAK W 6– 5f	18 NG	30 chi W 7– 2	10 NG	
7 SEA L 4–12	19 TOR L 4– 5	31 chi W 7– 3	11 bos W 8– 3	
8 SEA W 5– 3	20 TOR W 2– 1	**August, 1979**	12 bos L 2– 9	
9 SEA W 5– 0	" TOR L 2– 3	1 chi W 9– 1	13 bos W 10– 3	
10 SEA W 8– 1	21 TOR W 3– 1	2 NG	14 DET *	
11 CAL L 1– 4	22 CLE W 3– 2	3 BAL L 0– 1	15 DET L 3– 4	
12 CAL W 6– 5	23 CLE W 6– 5f	4 BAL L 4– 5	" DET W 7– 1	
13 CAL W12– 10	24 CLE W 8– 2	5 BAL W 3– 2	16 DET L 4– 8h	
14 DET L 1– 3	25 tor L 1– 3	6 BAL W 5– 4	17 cle L 1– 5	
15 DET W 11– 3	26 tor W 11– 2	7 CHI L 5– 9	" cle L 5– 6	
16 DET W 6– 2	27 NG	8 CHI W 4– 3	18 cle L 3–16	
17 NG	28 tor W 5– 3f	9 CHI L 1– 5	19 cle W 2– 0	
18 bos W 10– 0	29 BOS L 2– 3i	10 bal L 6– 8	20 min L 1– 3	

NEW YORK YANKEES' 1979 SEASON FOR HOME AND AWAY GAMES

CLUB		APR	MAY	JUN	JUL	AUG	SEP	OCT	HOME	AWAY	TOTAL
BAL	H	2-1	xxx	xxx	xxx	2-2	xxx	xxx	4-3	xxx	6-5
	A	2-1	xxx	xxx	xxx	0-1	xxx	xxx	xxx	2-2	
BOS	H	xxx	xxx	0-2	2-0	xxx	2-1	xxx	4-3	xxx	8-5
	A	xxx	2-1	xxx	xxx	xxx	2-1	xxx	xxx	4-2	
CAL	H	xxx	2-1	xxx	2-1	xxx	xxx	xxx	4-2	xxx	5-7
	A	0-1	1-1	xxx	0-3	xxx	xxx	xxx	xxx	1-5	
CHI	H	xxx	xxx	2-1	xxx	1-2	xxx	xxx	3-3	xxx	8-4
	A	2-1	xxx	xxx	2-0	1-0	xxx	xxx	xxx	5-1	
CLE	H	xxx	xxx	3-0	xxx	xxx	3-0	xxx	6-0	xxx	8-5
	A	xxx	1-2	xxx	xxx	xxx	1-3	xxx	xxx	2-5	
DET	H	xxx	2-1	xxx	xxx	xxx	1-2	xxx	3-3	xxx	6-7
	A	xxx	1-2	xxx	xxx	xxx	2-2	xxx	xxx	3-4	
KC	H	xxx	xxx	1-1	xxx	1-1	1-1	xxx	3-3	xxx	7-5
	A	xxx	xxx	2-1	xxx	2-1	xxx	xxx	xxx	4-2	
MIL	H	1-2	xxx	xxx	1-2	xxx	xxx	xxx	2-4	xxx	4-9
	A	xxx	2-2	xxx	0-3	xxx	xxx	xxx	xxx	2-5	
MIN	H	xxx	xxx	1-1	xxx	2-2	xxx	xxx	3-3	xxx	5-7
	A	xxx	xxx	1-2	xxx	1-1	0-1	xxx	xxx	2-4	
OAK	H	xxx	2-1	xxx	2-1	xxx	xxx	xxx	4-2	xxx	9-3
	A	1-1	xxx	xxx	4-0	xxx	xxx	xxx	xxx	5-1	
SEA	H	xxx	3-1	xxx	2-0	xxx	xxx	xxx	5-1	xxx	6-6
	A	0-3	xxx	xxx	1-2	xxx	xxx	xxx	xxx	1-5	
TEX	H	2-1	xxx	xxx	xxx	3-0	xxx	xxx	5-1	xxx	8-4
	A	xxx	xxx	1-2	xxx	2-1	xxx	xxx	xxx	3-3	
TOR	H	xxx	xxx	2-2	xxx	xxx	3-0	xxx	5-2	xxx	9-4
	A	xxx	xxx	2-1	xxx	xxx	2-1	xxx	xxx	4-2	
TOTAL:	H	5-4	9-4	9-7	9-4	9-7	10-4	xxx	51-30	xxx	89-71
	A	5-7	7-8	6-6	7-8	6-4	7-8	xxx	xxx	38-41	
GRAND TOT:		10-11	16-12	15-13	16-12	15-11	17-12	xxx	xxx	xxx	89-71
CUMUL TOT:		10-11	26-23	41-36	57-48	72-59	89-71	xxx	xxx	xxx	

TIE GAMES: NONE

1980

MOST WINS SINCE 1963

Under the guidance of New York's 23rd manager, Dick Howser, the Yankees won 103 games while losing 59 (.636) for the best record in both leagues. Baltimore's second best record in baseball with 100 wins even fell three full games short of catching the Yanks. This was New York's fourteenth season with one hundred or more wins. After besting Kansas City in the American League Championship Series in 1976, 1977 and 1978, the Royals turned the tables on the Yanks, beating New York in three straight games.

Reggie Jackson tied for the league lead in homers (41) with Milwaukee's Ben Oglivie. Jax also finished second in slugging average (with a .597 mark) to George Brett of Kansas City. Second baseman Willie Randolph had the most bases on balls in the league with 119. The offensive unit was anchored by a solid veteran bench as well as by consistent play of its regulars. The club did not finish on top of the league in any significant hitting department. The team hit 7 grand slams to tie a previous club record set in 1948.

On the mound, Tommy John, Ron Guidry, Rudy May, and "Goose" Gossage were league standouts. Thirteen-year veteran and former Yankee Rudy May led in A.L. ERA with a 2.47 mark. This marked the third consecutive season that a Yankee had won this title (Guidry won the previous two). May's (15–5) .750 winning percentage was second in the A.L.; Tommy John (.710) was fourth overall with a 22–9 mark, his victory total second only to Baltimore's Steve Stone (25). Mike Norris of Oakland also had 22 wins to tie John for A.L. second best. Tommy tossed the most league shutouts (6) as did the club as a whole with 15. Guidry came in at third place with 166 strikeouts. "The Goose," Gossage tied Dan Quisenberry of Kansas City with 33 saves. This season the Yanks posted a club (and league) high 50 saves, being led by Gossage.

The Bombers set all kinds of attendance marks this season. They set a club (and league) record by drawing 2,627,417 to Yankee Stadium. Only the previous season had they set a new club season attendance figure. The total crowd at the Stadium set an A.L. mark (which was broken by California in 1982). In addition, the Yanks played before the greatest number of people on the road in Major League history, drawing some 2,451,240 in 79 away dates, an average of some 31,155 per opening. The Yanks' total attendance for both home and away games passed the 5 million mark for the first time in A.L. history. In a total of 158 playing dates (there were 4 total doubleheaders, 2 each at home and away), they attracted 5,078,657, an average of 32,143!

In December, tragedy again struck, with former Yankee A.L. MVP and catcher par excellence Elston Howard succumbing to a heart attack. Ellie, New York's first black player in 1955, was but 51 years of age.

Although winning the A.L. Eastern Division, the Yanks could not win another pennant. Next year, a players' strike creates a "split season" for the first time in American League history, dating back to 1901.

The 1980 DAY BY DAY scores follow:

DAY BY DAY, 1980 NEW YORK YANKEES

April, 1980			May, 1980			July, 1980			August, 1980			September, 1980		
10 tex	L	0- 1h	22 tor	W	5- 1	3 cle	L	0- 7	15 bal	W	4-3	28 det	L	5- 6f
11 tex	L	7-11	23 tor	W	7- 3	4 cle	W	11- 5	16 bal	W	4-1	29 NG		
12 tex		*	24 tor	W	6- 2	5 cle	W	3- 2	17 bal	L	0-1	30 cle	L	9-12
13 tex	W	9- 4	25 tor	L	6- 9	6 cle	L	3- 5	18 bal	L	5-6g	**October, 1980**		
" tex	W	8- 2	26 DET	W	13- 5	7 ALL-STAR BREAK			19 sea	W	3-1	1 cle	W	18- 7
14 chi		*	27 DET	W	9- 6	8 WON - 51			20 sea	W	6-4	2 DET	W	3- 2
15 chi	L	3- 4j	28 DET	L	3- 6	9 LOST - 27			21 sea	L	4- 6	3 DET		*
16 chi	W	6- 0	29 NG			10 tex	W	13- 5	22 cal	L	4- 8	4 DET	W	5- 2
17 chi	L	6- 8	30 TOR	W	6- 0	11 tex	L	8-10	23 cal	W	5- 2	" DET	L	6- 7
18 MIL	L	2- 3	31 TOR	W	8- 6g	12 chi	W	8- 0	24 cal	W	4-2	5 DET	W	2- 1
19 MIL	L	1- 5	**June, 1980**			13 chi	W	3- 1	25 oak	L	1-9			
20 MIL	W	9- 5	1 TOR	W	11- 7	14 chi	W	7- 6	26 oak	L	1-3			
21 BAL	W	3- 2	2 kc	W	5- 3	15 MIN	L	4- 5	27 NG			**END OF 1980**		
22 BAL	W	5- 4	3 kc	L	5- 6f	16 MIN	W	11- 1	28 SEA	W	6-5	RUNS:		820
23 BAL	W	6- 5	4 kc	L	3- 9	17 MIN	W	10- 3	29 SEA	W	5-1	OPP RUNS:		662
24 NG			5 NG			18 KC	L	1-13	30 SEA	W	9- 3			
25 CHI	L	0- 6	6 sea	W	3- 0	19 KC	W	13- 7	31 SEA	L	0-1			
26 CHI	L	7- 8h	7 sea	W	1- 0	20 KC	L	3-14	**September, 1980**					
27 CHI	W	1- 0	8 sea	L	0- 5	21 MIL	L	4- 7	1 OAK	W	5- 0			
28 bal		*	9 cal	W	8- 7f	22 MIL	W	3- 0	2 OAK	W	6- 1			
29 bal	W	4- 3	10 cal	L	4- 5	" MIL	L	1- 4	3 OAK	W	8- 3			
30 bal	L	4- 7	11 cal	W	9- 7g	23 MIL	W	4- 0	4 CAL	W	5- 3			
May, 1980			12 NG			24 NG			5 CAL	W	6- 5f			
1 NG			13 oak	L	3- 4	25 kc	L	1- 6	6 CAL	W	7- 4			
2 min	W	9- 6	" oak	W	6- 4	26 kc	W	5- 4	7 CAL	W	4- 1			
3 min	W	7- 3	14 oak	W	2- 1	27 kc	L	0- 8	8 tor	W	7- 4			
4 min	W	10- 1	15 oak	W	8- 2	28 min	W	7- 6f	9 tor	L	4- 6			
5 NG			16 sea	W	6- 3	29 min	L	2- 3	10 tor	W	7- 6			
6 mil	W	6- 5	17 sea	W	8- 2	30 min	L	1- 2f	11 bos	W	8- 5f			
7 mil	W	4- 1	18 CAL	W	5- 0	31 mil	W	7- 6g	12 bos	W	4- 2			
8 NG			19 CAL	W	7- 5	**August, 1980**			13 bos	W	4- 3			
9 MIN	W	5- 2	20 OAK	W	15- 7	1 mil	W	9- 4	14 bos	W	5- 3			
10 MIN	L	0- 1g	21 OAK	W	5- 3	2 mil	W	5- 3	15 NG					
11 MIN	W	5- 0	22 OAK	L	2- 5	3 mil	L	0- 2	16 TOR	W	5- 4			
12 KC	L	3-12	23 BOS	L	2- 7	4 TEX	W	10- 4	17 TOR	W	8- 7i			
13 KC	L	1- 4	24 BOS	W	10- 5	5 TEX	L	1- 8	18 TOR	L	1- 2			
14 KC	W	16- 3	25 BOS	L	3- 4f	6 TEX	W	2- 1	19 BOS	W	2- 1			
15 NG			26 NG			7 NG			20 BOS	L	1-4			
16 TEX	W	6- 2	27 CLE	L	0- 2	8 BAL	L	2- 5	21 BOS	W	3-0			
17 TEX	W	3- 0	28 CLE	W	11-10	9 BAL	L	2- 4	22 CLE	W	4-3			
18 TEX	L	4- 5f	29 CLE	W	7- 2	10 BAL	L	5- 6	23 CLE	W	5-4			
19 det	W	1- 0	30 bos	W	6- 3	11 CHI	W	3- 1	24 CLE	W	7-3			
20 det		L8- 12	**July, 1980**			12 CHI	W	8- 4f	25 CLE	L	0-5			
21 det	W	9- 5g	1 bos	W	3- 2	13 CHI	L	1- 4	26 det	W	7-5			
			2 bos	W	6- 0	14 bal	L	1- 6	27 det	L	1-5			

NEW YORK YANKEES' 1980 SEASON FOR HOME AND AWAY GAMES

CLUB:		APR	MAY	JUN	JUL	AUG	SEP	OCT	HOME	AWAY	TOTAL
BALT	H	3-0	xxx	xxx	xxx	0-3	xxx	xxx	3-3	xxx	6-7
	A	1-1	xxx	xxx	xxx	2-3	xxx	xxx	xxx	3-4	
BOST	H	xxx	xxx	1-2	xxx	xxx	2-1	xxx	3-3	xxx	10-3
	A	xxx	xxx	1-0	2-0	xxx	4-0	xxx	xxx	7-0	
CAL	H	xxx	xxx	2-0	xxx	xxx	4-0	xxx	6-0	xxx	10-2
	A	xxx	xxx	2-1	xxx	2-1	xxx	xxx	xxx	4-2	
CHIC	H	1-2	xxx	xxx	xxx	2-1	xxx	xxx	3-3	xxx	7-5
	A	1-2	xxx	xxx	3-0	xxx	xxx.	xxx	xxx	4-2	
CLEV	H	xxx	xxx	2-1	xxx	xxx	3-1xxx	5-2	xxx	3-3	8-5
	A	xxx	xxx	xxx	xxx	xxx	0-1	1-0	xxx	3-3	
DET	H	xxx	2-1	xxx	xxx	xxx	xxx	3-1	5-2	xxx	8-5
	A	xxx	2-1	xxx	xxx	xxx	1-2	xxx	xxx	3-3	
KC	H	xxx	1-2	xxx	1-2	xxx	xxx	xxx	2-4	xxx	4-8
	A	xxx	xxx	1-2	1-2	xxx	xxx	xxx	xxx	2-4	
MILW	H	1-2	2-0	xxx	2-2	xxx	xxx	xxx	3-4	xxx	8-5
	A	xxx	xxx	xxx	1-0	2-1	xxx	xxx	xxx	5-1	
MINN	H	xxx	2-1	xxx	2-1	xxx	xxx	xxx	4-2	xxx	8-4
	A	xxx	3-0	xxx	1-2	xxx	xxx	xxx	xxx	4-2	
OAK	H	xxx	xxx	2-1	xxx	xxx	3-0	xxx	5-1	xxx	8-4
	A	xxx	xxx	3-1	xxx	0-2	xxx	xxx	xxx	3-3	
SEA	H	xxx	xxx	2-0	xxx	3-1	xxx	xxx	5-1	xxx	9-3
	A	xxx	xxx	2-1	xxx	2-1	xxx	xxx	xxx	4-2	
TEX	H	xxx	2-1	xxx	xxx	2-1	xxx	xxx	4-2	xxx	7-5
	A	2-2	xxx	xxx	1-1	xxx	xxx	xxx	xxx	3-3	
TOR	H	xxx	2-0	1-0	xxx	xxx	2-1	xxx	5-1	xxx	10-3
	A	xxx	3-1	xxx	xxx	xxx	2-1	xxx	xxx	5-2	
TOTAL:	H	5-4	9-5	10-4	5-5	7-6	14-3	3-1	53-28	xxx	103-59
	A	4-5	10-2	9-5	11-7	8-8	7-4	1-0	xxx	50-31	
GRAND TOT:		9-9	19-7	19-9	16-12	15-14	21-7	4-1	xxx	xxx	
CUMUL TOT:		9-9	28-16	47-25	63-37	78-51	99-58	103-59	xxx	xxx	

TIE GAMES: NONE

1981

THE SPLIT SEASON

The 1981 season will be remembered as the year of the "split season" due to the players' strike in mid-season during which some 55 Yankee games were cancelled and never played. The strike began on June 12 and lasted through August 8. The 50-day strike wiped out 712 Major League games and cost the players around $28 million in individual salary losses. In addition, the 712 cancelled games cost the 26 Major League Clubs some $116 million in lost ticket sales and concessions.

The Yanks, thanks to a 9-game winning skein just before the strike was called, won the "first half" of the season with a 34–22 (.607) mark, two games ahead of Baltimore. The Yanks fared poorly in the so-called "second half" with a 25–26 (.490) ledger, 5 games off Milwaukee's pace. The Yanks concluded the "second half" in 5th place, 2½ games ahead of Toronto in the A.L. East cellar. The "split season" seemed an impropriety to some clubs, especially to the Cincinnati Reds in the National League. The Reds finished with the best combined (1st half and 2nd half) record in both leagues yet did not figure in any championship games at all! The Reds concluded each "half season" in second place in the N.L. Western Division. Cincinnati fans will forever remember this season as one of disappointment.

The Yanks' pitching corps shored the club throughout the season, led by Gossage (20 saves, 2nd in the A.L.) and Guidry's club-high 11 victories, the Yanks finished with the best A.L. Club ERA mark with 2.90. In addition, the New York mound staff allowed the fewest A.L. runs (343), struck out the most A.L. batters (606) and hurled 13 shutouts to tie both Detroit and Texas for the A.L. lead. Tommy John's 2.64 ERA was the American League's fourth best. Louisiana Lightnin', Ron Guidry, placed fifth in the A.L. in winning percentage with a .688 (11–5) mark and in strikeouts with 104.

Dave Righetti earned the American League Rookie of the Year Award becoming the seventh Yank to cop this honor and the first since Thurman Munson in 1970. Righetti posted an 8–4 record with a 2.06 ERA.

Offensively, the Yanks tied for second in club slugging percentage (.391) and managed exactly 100 homers, thus reaching the century plateau for the 56th time in 62 seasons since the Babe arrived on the Yankee scene in 1920. Dave Winfield, making his debut as a Yankee and as a millionaire many times over, finished fifth in the A.L. with 68 RBI.

The Yanks entered their 33rd World Series after defeating the Milwaukee Brewers, the "second half" winners, in 5 games and by downing the A.L. West winner, Oakland, three games to none in the American League Championship Series. The Yanks were beaten by the Los Angeles Dodgers in the World Series four games to two. After their 33rd World Series appearance, the Yanks had won 22 Fall Classics, a .667 winning mark in an incredible 187 World Series games. This represents about 40% of all American League World Series contests. Second in the A.L. to the Yanks' staggering total of 187 Fall Classic games, are the Boston Red Sox with 53 games. The Giants of San Francisco and New York are second overall in World Series games with 89, still some 98 contests fewer than the Yanks!

This was one of the strangest seasons in baseball history, especially with regard to the players' strike that forced a "split season." The Yanks will falter next season, not even winning half of their games.

The 1981 DAY BY DAY scores follow:

Graig Nettles, all-star third baseman and 6th official team captain, holds the American League homer record for third sackers with over 300 round trippers.

DAY BY DAY, 1981 NEW YORK YANKEES

April, 1981

```
 9 TEX  W  10-3
10 NG
11 TEX  W   5- 1
12 TEX  L   4-6
13 tor  L   1-5
14 tor      *-
15 tor  W   6-3
16 NG
17 tex  W   2-1
18 tex  L   4-6
19 tex  L   0-4
20 DET  W   6-2
21 DET  W   2- 0
22 DET  W   7-2
23 TOR      *
24 TOR  W   4-2
25 TOR  L   2-7
26 TOR  L   1-2
27 DET  W   3-1
28 DET  W   4-1
29 DET  W   3-2
30 NG
```

May, 1981

```
 1 oak  L   6- 8
 2 oak  L   3-6
 3 oak  W   3-2f
 " oak  W   2-0
 4 cal  W   4-2
 5 cal  L   2-6
 6 cal  W   5- 2
 7 cal  L   1-2
 8 sea  L   2-3
-9 sea  L   5- 6
10 sea  W   5-2
11 NG
12 OAK  W   4-1
13 OAK  L   4- 5
14 OAK  W   9-5
15 SEA      *
16 SEA  W   7-5
17 SEA  L   0-1
18 KC   W   2-1
19 KC   W   6-5
20 KC   W   5- 4g
17 NG
```

May, 1981

```
21 NG
22 CLE  L   3- 7
23 CLE  W   3- 2
24 CLE  L5- 12
25 bal  L   1-10
26 bal  L   4- 6
27 bal  L   5- 6
28 NG
29 cle  W   5- 2
30 cle  W   1- 0
31 cle  L   2- 7
```

June, 1981

```
 1 cle  W   5- 3
 2 BAL  W   5- 3g
 3 BAL  W   2- 0g
 4 BAL  W  12- 3
 5 CHI  W   6- 5h
 6 CHI  W   2- 0
 7 CHI  W   3- 1
 8 kc   W   8- 3
-9 kc   W   8- 5
10 chi  L   5- 6
11 chi  L   2- 3
1st HALF: W-34,L-22
PLAYERS STRIKE
CAUSED 52 GAMES
TO BE CANCELLED,
STRIKE LASTED
FROM JUNE 12
THROUGH AUGUST 8

SEASON RESUMED
WITH THE ALL-STAR
GAME AT CHICAGO
AUGUST 9.
```

August, 1981

```
 9 ALL-STAR
   BREAK
10 TEX  W   2-0
11 TEX  L   0-1
12 TEX  W   5- 4
13 det  W   3-0
14 det  L   0-1
15 det  L   5-8
16 det  L   4-5
17 CHI  L   1- 4
18 CHI  W   4-0
19 CHI  L   5-6
20 NG
21 KC   L   0-4
22 KC   W   5-0
23 KC   W   8- 0
24 MIN  L   2- 3h
25 MIN  L   0-3
26 MIN  W   3-2
27 chi  L   1-3d
28 chi  W   6- 1
29 chi  W  12-2
30 chi  W   5-1
31 min  W   7-0
```

September, 1981

```
 1 min  W  11-6
 2 min  L   3- 4
 3 kc   L   2-3
 4 kc   W   4-0
 5 kc   W   2- 1
 6 kc   W   6-1
 7 MIL  W   4-2
 8 MIL      *
 9 MIL  W   5- 2
 " MIL  L   3-5
10 NG
11 BOS  W   4- 1
12 BOS  L   1-2
13 BOS  W  10- 6
14 mil  W  10-2
15 mil  L   1- 2
16 mil  L   2-3
```

September, 1981

```
18 bos  W   6- 4
19 bos  L   5-8
20 bos  L   1-4
21 CLE  L   0-5
22 CLE  L   4-6
23 CLE  W   6- 1
24 BAL  L   1- 5
25 BAL  L   0-1
26 BAL  W   6-4
27 BAL  W   5-2
28 cle  L   2- 6
29 cle  L   2-3
30 cle      *
```

October, 1981

```
 1 NG
 2 bal  W   9-0
 3 bal  L   0-3
 4 bal  L   2- 5
2nd HALF: W-25,L-26
END OF 1981
RUNS:        421
OPP RUNS:    343
```

NEW YORK YANKEES' 1981 SEASON FOR HOME AND AWAY GAMES

CLUB:		APR	MAY	JUN	JUL	AUG	SEP	OCT	HOME	AWAY	TOTAL
BALT	H	xxx	xxx	3-0	xxx	xxx	2-2	xxx	5-2	xxx	6-7
	A	xxx	0-3	xxx	xxx	xxx	xxx	1-2	xxx	1-5	
BOST	H	xxx	xxx	xxx	xxx	xxx	2-1	xxx	2-1	xxx	3-3
	A	xxx	xxx	xxx	xxx	xxx	1-2	xxx	xxx	1-2	
CAL	H	xxx	xxx	xxx	xxx	xxx	xxx	xxx	xxx	xxx	2-2
	A	xxx	2-2	xxx	xxx	xxx	xxx	xxx	xxx	2-2	
CHIC	H	xxx	xxx	3-0	xxx	1-2	xxx	xxx	4-2	xxx	7-5
	A	xxx	xxx	0-2	xxx	3-1	xxx	xxx	xxx	3-3	
CLEV	H	xxx	1-2	xxx	xxx	xxx	1-2	xxx	2-4	xxx	5-7
	A	xxx	2-1	1-0	xxx	xxx	0-2	xxx	xxx	3-3	
DET	H	3-0	xxx	xxx	xxx	xxx	xxx	xxx	3-0	xxx	7-3
	A	3-0	xxx	xxx	xxx	1-3	xxx	xxx	xxx	4-3	
KC	H	xxx	3-0	xxx	xxx	2-1	xxx	xxx	5-1	xxx	10-2
	A	xxx	xxx	2-0	xxx	xxx	3-1	xxx	xxx	5-1	
MILW	H	xxx	xxx	xxx	xxx	xxx	2-1	xxx	2-1	xxx	3-3
	A	xxx	xxx	xxx	xxx	xxx	1-2	xxx	xxx	1-2	
MINN	H	xxx	xxx	xxx	xxx	1-2	xxx	xxx	1-2	xxx	3-3
	A	xxx	xxx	xxx	xxx	1-0	1-1	xxx	xxx	2-1	
OAK	H	xxx	2-1	xxx	xxx	xxx	xxx	xxx	2-1	xxx	4-3
	A	xxx	2-2	xxx	xxx	xxx	xxx	xxx	xxx	2-2	
SEA	H	xxx	1-1	xxx	xxx	xxx	xxx	xxx	1-1	xxx	2-3
	A	xxx	1-2	xxx	xxx	xxx	xxx	xxx	xxx	1-2	
TEX	H	2-1	xxx	xxx	xxx	2-1	xxx	xxx	4-2	xxx	5-4
	A	1-2	xxx	xxx	xxx	xxx	xxx	xxx	xxx	1-2	
TOR	H	1-2	xxx	xxx	xxx	xxx	xxx	xxx	1-2	xxx	2-3
	A	1-1	xxx	xxx	xxx	xxx	xxx	xxx	xxx	1-1	
TOTAL:	H	6-3	7-4	6-0	STRIKE	6-6	7-6	xxx	32-19	xxx	59-48
	A	5-3	7-10	3-2	STRIKE	5-4	6-8	1-2	xxx	27-29	
GRAND TOT:		11-6	14-14	9-2	xxx	11-10	13-14	1-2			
CUMUL TOT:		11-6	25-20	34-22	34-22	45-32	58-46	59-48			

TIE GAMES: NONE

1982

THREE YANKEE MANAGERS

For the first time since 1946 (and the second time in their history), managerial duties were shared between three men: Bob Lemon, Gene Michael, and Clyde King, the latter being at the helm at the finish of the 1982 season. Beginning their 80th year in the American League, the Yankees finished fourth place in the A.L. East, sixteen games behind Milwaukee, with a 79–83 (.488) worksheet. In addition, they finished but one full game ahead of Cleveland and Toronto, who shared the A.L. East cellar with identical 78–64 marks.

Graig Nettles was appointed as the sixth official Yankee captain prior to the start of the '82 campaign. Steady Nettles hit 18 homers and had 55 RBI. The homer total extended his American League mark for third basemen to 300 roundtrippers.

Offensively, the club faltered with a .256 batting mark, 11th in the league. They did display power, a long time Yankee trademark, by hitting 161 homers, being led by Winfield's 37, whose total was third in the league behind Gorman Thomas of Milwaukee and Reggie Jackson of California who were tied for the lead with 39 four-baggers. Winfield was runner-up with a .560 mark to Robin Yount's (Milwaukee) .578 slugging mark. Winfield also had 105 RBI and 15 game winning RBI to lead the club in those departments. In September, the Yanks suffered through 9 consecutive losses, the most by New York since 1953 when the Bombers dropped nine straight in June.

As a whole, the pitching was unsteady, finishing eighth overall in team ERA (3.99). Goose Gossage's 29 saves, second in the A.L., was a bright spot on the otherwise inconsistent mound staff. The Yanks managed to strike out 939 batters, second in the league, being led by Righetti's 163 and Guidry's 162, who finished third and fourth in the A.L., respectively. The

Yanks managed to set an A.L. record with 15 balks, adding one to their previous Junior Circuit standard set in 1950.

Defensively, the team finished no better than 10th place in the A.L. with a .979 mark. The Yanks established a Major League mark by having a game winning RBI in every one of the 162 games played.

To begin the season, the Yanks' first four games were postponed, all due to snow. This was the first time in Yankee history that the season opener was delayed for so long. In addition, the Yanks opened the campaign with a doubleheader for the first time in their history, losing both games to the Chicago White Sox at Yankee Stadium.

This season proved to be fairly uneventful, with three different managers and generally inconsistent overall play.

The 1982 DAY BY DAY scores follow:

Rich Gossage—"The Goose" is one of the best relief pitchers in all of baseball. His 90+ per hour fastball is not a welcome sight to opposing batters. In 1983, Gossage filed for free agency after 6 seasons in pinstripes.

DAY BY DAY, 1982 NEW YORK YANKEES

April, 1982

6 TEX		*
7 NG		
8 TEX		*
9 CHI		*
10 CHI		*
11 CHI	L	6- 7h
" CHI	L	0- 2
12 tex	W	10- 7
13 tex	W	6- 3
14 tex	L	1- 4
15 NG		
16 det	W	10-2
17 det	L	3-5
18 det	L	2-5
19 NG		
20 chi	W	11-2
21 chi	W	1-0
22 DET	L	1-3
23 DET	L	1-9
24 DET	L	2-7
25 DET	W	3-1
26 NG		
27 CAL	L	1-3c
28 CAL	W	6-0
29 CAL	L	0-2
30 SEA	L	3-6

May, 1982

1 SEA	W	5-1
2 SEA	W	4-2
3 OAK	L	2-5
4 OAK	L	7-9i
5 NG		
6 sea	L	3-7
7 sea	L	2-5
8 sea	W	9-4
9 sea	W	3-0
10 cal	L	1-2
11 cal	W	3-2
12 cal	W	6-5
13 oak	W	6-4
14 oak	W	7-4
15 oak	L	3-7
16 oak	L	6-7
17 kc	L	0-7
18 kc	W	6- 2

May, 1982

19 kc	W	3- 2
20 NG		
21 MIN	W	12- 1
22 MIN	W	1- 0
23 MIN	W	4- 2
24 NG		
25 TOR	W	8- 0
26 TOR	L	0- 7
27 NG		
28 min	W	10- 5
29 min	W	6- 4
30 min	W	8- 6f
31 tor	L	4- 5

June, 1982

1 tor	L	2- 5
2 tor	W	12- 6i
3 tor	L	1- 3
4 KC	L	3- 4
5 KC		*
6 KC	L	1-14
7 NG		
8 bos	L	3- 4f
9 bos	L	2- 3
10 bos	W	5- 3
11 bal	L	4- 9
12 bal	L	3- 5
13 bal		*
14 BOS	W	5- 1
15 BOS	W	5- 4
16 BOS	W	4- 1b
17 NG		
18 BAL	L	1- 4
19 BAL	W	4- 3L
20 BAL	L	3- 5f
21 mil	L	2- 6
22 mil	L	2- 3
23 mil	W	3- 2
24 CLE	L	2- 5
25 CLE	W	11- 3
26 CLE	W	4- 3m
27 CLE	L	3- 4
28 NG		
29 MIL	L	4-11
30 MIL	L	7- 9h

July, 1982

1 MIL	W	5- 3
2 cle	W	3- 1
3 cle	W	10- 6
4 cle	W	3- 2
5 sea	L	4- 5
6 sea	W	8- 7h
7 oak	W	5- 3
8 oak		3- 6
9 cal	L	1- 4
10 cal	L	6-12
11 cal	L	1- 2
12 ALL-STAR BREAK		
13 WON		39
14 LOST -		42
15 OAK	W	2- 1
16 OAK	W	6- 2
17 OAK	W	4- 1
18 OAK	W	7- 3
19 SEA	W	5- 3
20 SEA	L	5- 6
21 SEA	L	5- 6h
22 TEX	W	4- 3
23 CAL	W	6- 3
24 CAL	W	6- 5
25 CAL	L	4- 6
26 DET	L	3- 5
27 DET	W	6- 5
28 DET	W	8- 7
29 NG		
30 tex	W	4- 0
31 tex	L	2- 3

August, 1982

1 tex	L	2- 4
2 NG		
3 CHI	L	0- 1
" CHI	L	2-14
4 CHI	W	6- 2
" CHI	L	0- 7
5 TEX	L	2- 7
6 TEX	W	6- 0
7 TEX	W	9- 1
8 TEX	L	4- 6
" TEX	W	8- 5

August, 1982

9 det	W	9- 7
10 det	L	1-10
11 det	L	2- 3
12 chi	L	1- 2
13 chi	W	4- 3
14 chi	L	0- 6
15 chi	L	4- 6
16 KC	W	2- 0
" KC	W	4- 3
17 KC	L	4- 8
18 KC	W	9- 2
19 NG		
20 TOR	W	4- 2
21 TOR	L	1- 3
22 TOR	W	3- 1
23 TOR	W	4- 3
24 MIN	L	0- 5
25 MIN	W	8- 1
26 MIN	W	7- 2
27 tor	L3-	10
28 tor	L	2- 3g
29 tor	W	8- 2
30 min	W	8- 2
31 min	W	3- 1

September, 1982

1 min	L	2- 7
2 NG		
3 kc	L	3- 5
4 kc	W	3- 2
5 kc	W	18- 7
6 BAL	L	2- 8
7 BAL	L	2- 7
8 BAL	W	10- 5
9 MIL	W	5- 4f
10 MIL	L	3- 5
11 MIL	W	14- 2
12 MIL	W	9- 8
13 bal	L	7- 8
14 bal	L	4- 5
" bal	L	3- 5
15 bal	L	5- 8
16 bal	L	1- 3
17 mil	L0-	14
18 mil	L	4- 6

September, 1982

19 mil	L	1-14
20 CLE		*
21 CLE	L	8- 9
" CLE	W	6- 2
22 CLE	L	0- 5c
23 NG		
24 bos	L	2- 4
25 bos	W	6- 2
26 bos	L	2- 5
27 bos	W	10- 3
28 cle	W	6- 4
29 cle	W	13- 6
30 cle	W	7- 5

October, 1982

1 BOS	L	2- 3h
2 BOS	L	0- 5
3 BOs	L	3- 5g

END OF 1982

RUNS: 709

OPP RUNS: 716

CLUB vs. CLUB AND MONTHLY RECORDS OF THE
NEW YORK YANKEES' 1982 SEASON FOR HOME AND AWAY GAMES

CLUB:		APR	MAY	JUN	JUL	AUG	SEP	OCT	HOME	AWAY	TOTAL
BALT	H	xxx	xxx	1-2	xxx	xxx	1-2	xxx	2-4	xxx	2-11
	A	xxx	xxx	0-2	xxx	xxx	0-5	xxx	xxx	0-7	
BOST	H	xxx	xxx	3-0	xxx	xxx	xxx	0-3	3-3	xxx	6-7
	A	xxx	xxx	1-2	xxx	xxx	2-2	xxx	xxx	3-4	
CAL	H	1-2	xxx	xxx	2-1	xxx	xxx	xxx	3-3	xxx	5-7
	A	xxx	2-1	xxx	0-3	xxx	xxx	xxx	xxx	2-4	
CHIC	H	0-2	xxx	xxx	xxx	1-3	xxx	xxx	1-5	xxx	4-8
	A	2-0	xxx	xxx	xxx	1-3	xxx	xxx	xxx	3-3	
CLEV	H	xxx	xxx	2-2	xxx	xxx	1-2	xxx	3-4	xxx	9-4
	A	xxx	xxx	xxx	3-0	xxx	3-0	xxx	xxx	6-0	
DET	H	1-3	xxx	xxx	2-1	xxx	xxx	xxx	3-4	xxx	5-8
	A	1-2	xxx	xxx	xxx	1-2	xxx	xxx	xxx	2-4	
KC	H	xxx	xxx	0-2	xxx	3-1	xxx	xxx	3-3	xxx	7-5
	A	xxx	2-1	xxx	xxx	xxx	2-1	xxx	xxx	4-2	
MILW	H	xxx	xxx	0-2	1-0	xxx	3-1	xxx	4-3	xxx	5-8
	A	xxx	xxx	1-2	xxx	xxx	0-3	xxx	xxx	1-5	
MINN	H	xxx	3-0	xxx	xxx	2-1	xxx	xxx	5-1	xxx	10-2
	A	xxx	3-0	xxx	xxx	2-0	0-1	xxx	xxx	5-1	
OAK	H	xxx	0-2	xxx	4-0	xxx	xxx	xxx	4-2	xxx	7-5
	A	xxx	2-2	xxx	1-1	xxx	xxx	xxx	xxx	3-3	
SEA	H	0-1	2-0	xxx	1-2	xxx	xxx	xxx	3-3	xxx	6-6
	A	xxx	2-2	xxx	1-1	xxx	xxx	xxx	xxx	3-3	
TEX	H	xxx	xxx	xxx	1-0	3-2	xxx	xxx	4-2	xxx	7-5
	A	2-1	xxx	xxx	1-1	0-1	xxx	xxx	xxx	3-3	
TOR	H	xxx	1-1	xxx	xxx	3-1	xxx	xxx	4-2	xxx	6-7
	A	xxx	0-1	1-2	xxx	1-2	xxx	xxx	xxx	2-5	
TOTAL:	H	2-8	6-3	6-8	11-4	12-8	5-5	0-3	42-39	xxx	79-83
	A	5-3	11-7	3-8	6-6	5-8	7-12	xxx	xxx	37-44	
GRAND TOT:		7-11	17-10	9-16	17-10	17-16	12-17	0-3	xxx	xxx	
CUMUL TOT:		7-11	24-21	33-37	50-47	67-63	79-80	79-83	xxx	xxx	79-83

TIE GAMES: NONE

1983

BILLY'S BACK

In 1983, Billy Martin returned to manage the Yanks for the third time since 1975. The Bombers concluded the campaign in third place with a 91–71 record, a .562 winning mark, some 7 games behind Baltimore, the A.L. East winner.

The highlight of this season was southpaw Dave Righetti's no-hitter versus Boston at Yankee Stadium on July 4th. The Yanks, behind Righetti's gem, beat the BoSox 4–0 before a crowd of 41,077. This was the first regular season no-hitter by a Yankee hurler since Allie Reynolds turned the trick on September 28, 1951 (Don Larsen's perfect game in the 1956 World Series was the last no-hitter overall). In addition, Righetti became the first Yankee lefthander to hold the opposition hitless since George Mogridge no-hit Boston at Fenway Park way back in April 24, 1917!

Two controversies emerged in 1983. First there was Dave Winfield accidentally killing a seagull with a thrown ball from the outfield in a game at Toronto on August 4. Although charged with cruelty to animals by the local police, the charges were dropped the following day.

The other incident of note was the infamous (if you are a Yankee fan) "pine tar" game of August 24 versus Kansas City at Yankee Stadium. Kansas City's George Brett had hit an apparent game-leading home run in the top of the ninth to put the Royals ahead 5–4. Brett's bat was then immediately examined by the home plate umpire and the home run was disallowed because of the pine tar extending over the legal limit on Brett's bat, the Yanks being declared as 4–3 winners. Brett protested vehemently to the umpire's decision and the Royals filed a dispute of the outcome to A.L. President Larry MacPhail, Jr. On 7-28-83, MacPhail overruled the umpire and the game became a suspended contest to be completed on August 18, prior to the regularly scheduled game. The Yanks had to wait almost a month amid enormous national media coverage to play the final 3 outs in their home-half of the 9th inning. Instead of winning 4–3, the Yanks lost this contest officially 5–4. The "tar war's" saga had ended. "May the bat be with you."

Statistically, the Yanks finished fourth overall in club batting with .273,

3rd in total hits, 1,535, and blasted the century mark in homers (153) for the 58th time since 1920. Dave Winfield had another fine year: he was third in A.L. RBI (116) and triples (8), second in game winning RBI (21), fifth with 307 total bases, tied for fifth in homers (32) and placed seventh in A.L. slugging percentage with a .513 mark. He led the club in most statistical categories. Ken Griffey and Don Baylor placed 1–2 in club batting with .306 and .303, respectively. Baylor led the club with 17 stolen bases and 33 doubles.

In pitching, the Yanks were fifth in club ERA (3.86), first in A.L. complete games (47), tied for third with 12 shutouts and finished second overall in total strikeouts with 892. Individually, Ron Guidry led the league with 21 complete games, was third with 21 victories, fifth in winning percentage (.700) with a 21–9 ledger, and placed sixth with 156 strikeouts. Reliable Goose Gossage, who has filed for free agency as of this writing, was 6th in saves (22), and second in winning percentage (.722), winning 13 and losing 5, all in relief. "Rags" Righetti came in fourth in A.L. strikeouts with 169 whiffs.

Rookie lefthander Ray Fontenot (pronounced Fon-tin-know) of Lake Charles, Louisiana, posted an 8–2 worksheet in but 15 games since being recalled from the Minor Leagues on June 20. He pitched his first Major League shutout, with a 5–0,6-hitter at Texas on July 26. For the first time in their history, the Yankees have 2 Cajuns on the same club, both starting pitchers and both southpaws. I guess that means that more crawfish, bouding and gumbo will be eaten by the Yankees because of Guidry and Fontenot! Pooo Yieee!

Another rookie player who showed a lot of promise this season was Don Mattingly. He hit a steady .283 in 91 games with four homers and 32 RBI and demonstrated good all-around play. Fontenot and Mattingly are indeed two sound prospects for the Yankee future.

This season was quite frustrating in its outcome with the seagull incident, the "pine tar" game and numerous key injuries including shortstop Andre Robertson's serious neck injury sustained in an auto accident on August 18. Hopefully, this fine athlete can overcome his disability and again contribute to the Yankee cause in the very near future.

The season was ended on a sour note when 3 Oriole pitchers held New York to but one hit (a single by Griffey) at Baltimore on October 2. The Yanks prevented a no-hitter from being tossed against them for the first time since Hoyt Wilhelm held New York hitless (again at Baltimore) September 20, 1958, in defeating the Yankees,1–0.

Hopefully, 1984 shall be more productive than this season. I guess all us Yankee fans can do is wait 'til next year and hope that Yogi Berra, the new Yankee skipper, can lead the Bombers to yet another World Series.

The 1983 DAY BY DAY scores follow:

DAY BY DAY, 1983 NEW YORK YANKEES

April, 1983			May, 1983			July, 1983			August, 1983			September, 1983		
5 sea	L	4- 5	19 NG			1 BOS	W	12- 8	11 det	W	6- 5f	22 NG		
6 sea	L	2- 6	20 oak	L	4- 8	2 BOS	L4-	10	12 det	L	6- 7f	23 CLE	W	7-4
7 sea	W	8- 1	21 oak	W	1- 0	3 BOS	L	3- 7	13 det	L	3- 6	24 CLE	W	9-1
8 NG			22 oak	W	4- 2	4 BOS	W	4- 0	14 det	W	4- 1	25 CLE	W	6-4
9 tor	L	4- 7	23 cal	L	0- 3	5 ALL-STAR BREAK			15 CHI	L	0- 1	26 CLE	L	0-7
10 tor	W	3- 0	24 cal	L	6- 7f	6 WON - 41			16 CHI	L	3- 5	27 BOS	W	7- 2
11 NG			25 cal	L	1- 7	7 LOST - 35			17 CHI	L	5- 7i	28 BOS	L	2- 3
12 DET	L	2-13	26 NG			8 kc	W	9- 2	18 KC	L	4- 5	29 BOS	W	4- 3
13 DET	L	5- 7	27 OAK	W	4- 2	9 kc	L	2- 3h	19 CAL	W	11- 6	30 bal	W	6-4
14 DET	W	6- 3	28 OAK	W	5- 2	10 kc	W	6- 4	20 CAL	W	6- 2	" bal	L	2-3
15 TOR	L	5- 6	29 OAK	W	5- 0	11 min	L	2- 4	21 CAL	W	2- 1	**October, 1983**		
16 TOR	*		30 OAK	W	10- 5	12 min	W	4- 3	22 OAK	L	2- 3j	1 bal	W	5-4
17 TOR	W	7- 5	31 CAL	W	5- 3	13 min	L	1- 6	23 OAK	L	3- 9	2 bal	L	0-2
18 TOR	W	3- 0	**June, 1983**			14 TEX	L	2-11	24 SEA	W	6- 3			
19 chi	L	3-13	1 CAL	W	3- 0	15 TEX	W	7- 5	25 SEA	W	7- 4	END OF 1983		
20 chi	W	6- 4	2 CAL	L	8- 9	16 TEX	W	3- 1	26 cal	W	3- 2	RUNS:		770
21 NG			3 SEA	L	0- 5	17 TEX	W	8- 6	27 cal	L	6- 7	OPP RUNS:		703
22 MIN	L	3- 5	4 SEA	L	4- 5	18 MIN	W	4- 2	28 cal	W	7- 3			
23 MIN	W	7- 4	5 SEA	L	7- 8	19 MIN	W	4- 0	29 NG					
24 MIN	*		6 SEA	W	6- 2	20 MIN	W	6- 4f	30 oak	W	8- 5			
25 MIN	W	2- 1	7 CLE	L	1- 2f	21 KC	*		31 oak	W	6- 4			
26 KC	L	4-10	8 CLE	W	6- 5	22 KC	W	7- 6	**September, 1983**					
27 KC	W	6- 0	9 NG			" KC	L	2- 3	1 oak	L	0- 2			
28 NG			10 mil	W	7- 1	23 KC	W	5- 1	2 sea	W	5- 4			
29 tex	L	3- 8	11 mil	L	2- 6	24 NG			3 sea	W	5- 3			
30 tex	L	3- 6	12 mil	L	5- 6h	25 tex	W	6- 5	4 sea	W	4- 3			
May, 1983			13 cle	L	0- 9	26 tex	W	5- 0	5 mil	L	1- 3			
1 tex	W	8- 4	14 cle	L	6- 9	27 tex	W	4- 3	6 mil	L	3- 6			
2 kc	L	1- 4	15 cle	W	8- 5	28 NG			7 mil	W	11- 5			
3 kc	L	2- 5	16 cle	W	8- 1	29 chi	L	2- 7	8 mil	W	6- 5			
4 kc	W	8- 1	17 MIL	W	7- 2	30 chi	L	1- 5	9 BAL	W	5- 3			
5 NG			18 MIL	W	5- 4	31 chi	W	12- 6g	10 BAL	L	4- 8			
6 min	W	8- 4	19 MIL	W	8- 3	**August, 1983**			" BAL	L	1- 3			
7 min	W	8- 7	20 bal	*		1 chi	L	1- 4	11 BAL	L	3- 5			
8 min	L	5- 6	21 bal	L	2- 5	2 tor	L9-	10g	12 MIL	W	1- 0			
9 NG			22 bal	W	5- 2	" tor	L6-	13	13 MIL	W	2- 1			
10 TEX	L	2- 4	23 NG			3 tor	L	2- 6	14 MIL	W	4- 1			
11 TEX	L	1- 3	24 bos	L	4- 5	4 tor	W	3- 1	15 NG					
12 NG			25 bos	W	4- 1	5 DET	W	12- 3	16 cle	*				
13 CHI	W	3- 1	26 bos	L	5-12	6 DET	W	13- 3	17 cle	L	6- 7			
14 CHI	W	8- 5	27 BAL	W	4- 3g	7 DET	L	5- 8	18 cle	L	6-10			
15 CHI	L	3- 7	28 BAL	*		8 TOR	W	8- 3	" cle	W	13- 8			
16 det	W	7- 0	29 BAL	W	7- 0	" TOR	W	11- 3	19 bos	L	3- 5			
17 det	W	7- 5g	30 BAL	W	4- 3h	9 TOR	L	0- 8	20 bos	W	3- 2			
18 det	W	6- 4				10 TOR	W	8- 3	21 bos	L	1- 3			

CLUB VS. CLUB AND MONTHLY RECORDS OF THE
NEW YORK YANKEES' 1983 SEASON FOR HOME AND AWAY GAMES

CLUB:		APR	MAY	JUN	JUL	AUG	SEP	OCT	HOME	AWAY	TOTAL
BAL	H	xxx	xxx	3-0	xxx	xxx	1-3	xxx	4-3	xxx	7-6
	A	xxx	xxx	1-1	xxx	xxx	1-1	1-1	xxx	3-3	
BOS	H	xxx	xxx	xxx	2-2	xxx	2-1	xxx	4-3	xxx	6-7
	A	xxx	xxx	1-2	xxx	xxx	1-2	xxx	xxx	2-4	
CAL	H	xxx	1-0	1-1	xxx	3-0	xxx	xxx	5-1	xxx	7-5
	A	xxx	0-3	xxx	xxx	2-1	xxx	xxx	xxx	2-4	
CHI	H	xxx	2-1	xxx	xxx	0-3	xxx	xxx	2-4	xxx	4-8
	A	1-1	xxx	xxx	1-2	0-1	xxx	xxx	xxx	2-4	
CLE	H	xxx	xxx	1-1	xxx	xxx	3-1	xxx	4-2	xxx	7-6
	A	xxx	xxx	2-2	xxx	xxx	1-2	xxx	xxx	3-4	
DET	H	1-2	xxx	xxx	xxx	2-1	xxx	xxx	3-3	xxx	8-5
	A	xxx	3-0	xxx	xxx	2-2	xxx	xxx	xxx	5-2	
KC	H	1-1	xxx	xxx	2-1	0-1	xxx	xxx	3-3	xxx	6-6
	A	xxx	1-2	xxx	2-1	xxx	xxx	xxx	xxx	3-3	
MIL	H	xxx	xxx	3-0	xxx	xxx	3-0	xxx	6-0	xxx	9-4
	A	xxx	xxx	1-2	xxx	xxx	2-2	xxx	xxx	3-4	
MIN	H	2-1	xxx	xxx	3-0	xxx	xxx	xxx	5-1	xxx	8-4
	A	xxx	2-1	xxx	1-2	xxx	xxx	xxx	xxx	3-3	
OAK	H	xxx	4-0	xxx	xxx	0-2	xxx	xxx	4-2	xxx	8-4
	A	xxx	2-1	xxx	xxx	2-0	0-1	xxx	xxx	4-2	
SEA	H	xxx	xxx	1-3	xxx	2-0	xxx	xxx	3-3	xxx	7-5
	A	1-2	xxx	xxx	xxx	xxx	3-0	xxx	xxx	4-2	
TEX	H	xxx	0-2	xxx	3-1	xxx	xxx	xxx	3-3	xxx	7-5
	A	0-2	1-0	xxx	3-0	xxx	xxx	xxx	xxx	4-2	
TOR	H	2-1	xxx	xxx	xxx	3-1	xxx	xxx	5-2	xxx	7-6
	A	1-1	xxx	xxx	xxx	1-3	xxx	xxx	xxx	2-4	
TOTAL:	H	6-5	7-3	9-5	10-4	10-8	9-5	xxx	51-30	xxx	91-71
	A	3-6	9-7	5-7	7-5	7-7	8-8	1-1	xxx	40-41	
GRAND TOT:		9-11	16-10	14-12	17-9	17-15	17-13	1-1	xxx	xxx	
CUMUL TOT:		9-11	25-21	39-33	56-42	73-57	90-70	91-71	xxx	xxx	

TIE GAMES: NONE

Three-time American League MVP Award Winner (1951, 1954, and 1955) Yogi Berra reassumed the Yankees' managerial reins to begin the 1984 season. In his only previous season as Yankee manager, Berra piloted the Yankees to an American League pennant.

1984

Yogi Returns to the Yankee Helm

After having piloted the Yankees to an American League pennant previously in 1964 (his only season as Yank manager), Yogi Berra again assumes the managerial reins of the Bronx Bombers to begin the 1984 season. Yogi has accepted the terms of a two-year contract. Hopefully, this three-time American League Most Valuable Player (1951, 1954 and 1955) can work his magic on his pinstriped crew and attain the achievement which has eluded him as manager—a World Series Championship.

SUMMARY

With the conclusion of the Yankees' 81st season in the American League, they had won 7,119 games for an average of about 88 victories per season. On the other side of the ledger, the Bombers lost 5,341 contests for an 81 year mean of 66 defeats per season. Their combined 7,119 wins and 5,341 losses (totalling 12,460 games) figures out to an all-time winning percentage of .5713. Their phenomenal record reveals (you could look it up) that they are 1,778 games above the .500 mark; this translates into almost eleven 162-games seasons in which the Yanks could lose every game and still finish with close to a .500 winning percentage! Amazing! If such would happen, hypothetically, that is, their record at the end of that 11th season would be 7,119 wins and 7,123 losses, only 5 games below the .500 mark, even after losing 1,778 consecutive hypothetical games!

In their 81 seasons, the Yankees have compiled a record for 3,841 wins and 2,393 losses at home for a .6161 winning mark; away from home, the Bombers have been victorious in 3,278 and went down to 2,948 defeats for a .5265 road-winning percentage.

Following is an all-time list of wins, losses and ties against all 20 American League opponents playing against the Yankees from 1903 through 1983. Immediately following that list is the all-time records against those twenty American League Yankee opponents both at home as well as on the road. These all-time home and away lists exclude tie games.

ALL-TIME WON-LOST-TIE RECORDS OF ALL YANKEE GAMES VERSUS EVERY AMERICAN LEAGUE OPPONENT
(1903 THROUGH 1983)

CLUB:	DATES:	TOTAL YEARS:	TOTAL WON:	TOTAL LOST:	GRAND TOTAL:	% WON:	TIE GAMES:	GRAND TOTAL-GAMES:
BALTIMORE ORIOLES	1954–NOW	30	253	277	530	.4774	1	531
BOSTON RED SOX	1903– NOW	81	905	725	1630	.5552	13	1643
CALIFORNIA ANGELS	1965– NOW	19	138	103	241	.5726	0	241
CHICAGO WHITE SOX	1903– NOW	81	899	680	1579	.5693	12	1592##
CLEVELAND INDIANS	1903– NOW	81	902	736	1638	.5507	12	1651%%
DETROIT TIGERS	1903– NOW	81	862	781	1643	.5247	9	1653&&
KANSAS CITY ATHLETICS	1955– 1967	13	183	75	258	.7093	1	259
KANSAS CITY ROYALS	1969– NOW	15	98	79	177	.5537	1	178
LOS ANGELES ANGELS	1961– 1964	4	46	26	72	.6389	0	72
MILWAUKEE BREWERS	1970– NOW	14	108	94	202	.5347	1	203
MINNESOTA TWINS	1961– NOW	23	176	137	313	.5623	1	314
OAKLAND ATHLETICS	1968– NOW	16	106	84	190	.5579	0	190
PHILADELPHIA ATHLETICS	1903– 1954	52	665	445	1110	.5991	8	1118
SAINT LOUIS BROWNS	1903– 1953	51	711	399	1110	.6405	11	1121
SEATTLE MARINERS	1977– NOW	7	42	32	74	.5676	0	74
SEATTLE PILOTS	1969 ONLY	1	7	5	12	.5833	0	12
TEXAS RANGERS	1972– NOW	12	88	49	137	.6423	0	137
TORONTO BLUE JAYS	1977– NOW	7	54	33	87	.6207	0	87
WASHINGTON SENATORS	1903– 1960	58	755	507	1262	.5983	12	1274
WASHINGTON SEANTORS	1961– 1971	11	121	74	195	.6205	0	195
GRAND TOTAL, 20 CLUBS:	81 YEARS	81	7119	5341	12460	.5713	82	12545

INCLUDES ONE VOIDED AND REPLAYED GAME AT CHICAGO, JUNE 20, 1940 (YANKS LOSE 0–1 IN 11 INN)

%% INCLUDES ONE VOIDED AND REPLAYED GAME CLEVELAND AT NY, AUGUST 6, 1937 (NY WINS 7–6 IN 10 INN)

&& INCLUDES ONE VOIDED AND REPLAYED GAME AT DETROIT, AUGUST 1, 1932 (NEW YORK WINS 6–3)

ALL-TIME WON-LOST RECORDS OF YANKEE HOME GAMES VERSUS EVERY AMERICAN LEAGUE OPPONENT
1903 THROUGH 19830

CLUB:	DATES:	TOTAL YEARS	HOME WON	HOME LOST	HOME TOTAL	HOME % WON
BALTIMORE ORIOLES	1954–NOW	30	135	131	266	.5075
BOSTON RED SOX	1903–NOW	81	489	322	811	.6030
CALIFORNIA ANGELS	1965–NOW	19	78	40	118	.6610
CHICAGO WHITE SOX	1903–NOW	81	481	308	789	.6096
CLEVELAND INDIANS	1903–NOW	81	492	327	819	.6007
DETROIT TIGERS	1903–NOW	81	465	358	823	.5650
KANSAS CITY ATHLETICS	1955–1967	13	99	30	129	.7674
KANSAS CITY ROYALS	1969–NOW	15	53	36	89	.5955
LOS ANGELES ANGELS	1961–1964	4	27	9	36	.7500
MILWAUKEE BREWERS	1970–NOW	14	64	37	101	.6336
MINNESOTA TWINS	1961–NOW	23	91	64	155	.5871
OAKLAND ATHLETICS	1968–NOW	16	55	40	95	.5789
PHILADELPHIA ATHLETICS	1903–1953	51	384	172	556	.6906
SEATTLE MARINERS	1977–NOW	7	26	10	36	.7222
SEATTLE PILOTS	1969 ONLY	1	3	3	6	.5000
TEXAS RANGERS	1972–NOW	12	48	22	70	.6857
TORONTO BLUE JAYS	1977–NOW	7	30	14	44	.6818
WASHINGTON SENATORS	1903–1960	58	403	227	630	.6397
WASHINGTON SENATORS	1961–1971	11	62	37	99	.6263
GRAND TOTALS–HOME GAMES:		81	3841	2393	6234	.6161

ALL-TIME WON-LOST RECORDS OF YANKEE AWAY GAMES VERSUS EVERY AMERICAN LEAGUE OPPONENT
(1903 THROUGH 1983)

CLUB:	DATES:	TOTAL YEARS	AWAY WON	AWAY LOST	AWAY TOTAL	AWAY % WON
BALTIMORE ORIOLES	1954–NOW	30	118	146	264	.4470
BOSTON RED SOX	1903–NOW	81	416	403	819	.5079
CALIFORNIA ANGELS	1965–NOW	19	60	63	123	.4878
CHICAGO WHITE SOX	1903–NOW	81	418	372	790	.5291
CLEVELAND INDIANS	1903–NOW	81	410	409	819	.5006
DETROIT TIGERS	1903–NOW	81	397	423	820	.4841
KANSAS CITY ATHLETICS	1955–1967	13	84	45	129	.6512
KANSAS CITY ROYALS	1969–NOW	15	45	43	88	.5114
LOS ANGELES	1961–1964	4	19	17	36	.5278
MILWAUKEE BREWERS	1970–NOW	14	44	57	101	.4356
MINNESOTA TWINS	1961–NOW	23	85	73	158	.5380
OAKLAND ATHLETICS	1968–NOW	16	51	44	95	.5368
PHILADELPHIA ATHLETICS	1903–1954	52	309	239	548	.5639
SAINT LOUIS BROWNS	1903–1953	51	327	227	554	.5903
SEATTLE MARINERS	1977–NOW	7	16	22	38	.4211
SEATTLE PILOTS	1969 ONLY	1	4	2	6	.6667
TEXAS RANGERS	1972–NOW	12	49	27	67	.5970
TORONTO BLUE JAYS	1977–NOW	7	24	19	43	.5581
WASHINGTON SENATORS	1903–1960	58	352	280	632	.5570
WASHINGTON SENATORS	1961–1971	11	59	37	96	.6146
GRAND TOTALS–AWAY GAMES:		81	3278	2948	6226	.5265

Babe Ruth embraces Lou Gehrig in a memorable scene in 1939. The occasion was Lou Gehrig Appreciation Day at Yankee Stadium on July 4, 1939. The great Gehrig will be stricken down in his prime of life by a fatal muscular disease.

SPECIAL RECORDS SECTION

HISTORIC FIRST GAMES AND OPENING-DAY SCORES

THE YANKEES' FIRST GAME EVER (1903 EXHIBITION SEASON)

The Yankees (nee the Highlanders) played the first game in their history in Atlanta, Georgia, March 26, 1903, playing an exhibition game against the Atlanta Crackers of the Southern Association. Abner Powell's Atlanta club was no match in this contest, the Yankees shutting out the Crackers, 9-0. This was the first game of a five game series between these two teams. All of the games were played at Piedmont Park. New York won the second game, March 28, 6-0; New York won the third contest, March 30, 9-0; the Yanks won the fourth game, April 1, 12-4, Atlanta scoring its first run in the 6th inning; and the fifth and final game also went to the New Yorkers (April 4), 9-3. This made the series a sweep. As was customary in the early days, the Yankees batted last in spite of being the visiting club.

THE FIRST GAME BOX SCORE:

ATLANTA (SOUTHERN ASSOCIATION)	POS	AB	R	H	PO	A	E	NEW YORK (AMERICAN LEAGUE)	POS	AB	R	H	PO	A	E
Winters	rf	1	0	0	0	0	0	Courtney	cf	5	0	0	1	0	0
Petit	lf	1	0	0	0	0	0	Keeler	rf	5	2	2	3	0	0
Gruebner	ss	4	0	0	2	6	2	McFarland	lf	4	2	1	1	0	0
Taylor	3b	4	0	1	1	3	0	Williams	2b	5	1	2	3	4	0
Lauzon	1b	4	0	3	13	0	1	Ganzel	1b	4	0	2	10	0	0
Baird	2b	4	0	1	2	2	1	Conroy	3b	3	2	0	2	0	0
Koehler	cf	4	0	0	0	0	1	Long	ss	4	1	1	1	4	1
Voght	lf	3	0	1	2	1	0	Beville	c	3	0	2	6	0	0
Kennedy	c	3	0	0	4	4	0	Powell	p	3	0	0	0	2	0
Vittur	p	2	0	0	0	1	0	Wiltse	p	2	1	1	0	1	0
Russell	p	1	0	0	0	1	0								
Totals:		31	0	6	24	18	5	Totals:		38	9	11	27	11	1

Score by Innings:

```
Atlanta.....................................0 0 0   0 0 0   0 0 0—0
New York....................................2 0 1   1 1 0   0 4 x—9
```

Two base hits-Williams, Keeler, Lauzon. Stolen bases-Keeler, Ganzel, Conroy. Sacrifice hits-Long, Wiltse. Bases on balls-off Howell, 3; off Wiltse, 1; off Vittur, 4; off Russell, 0. Double plays-Long to Williams to Ganzel (2). Time of game-1:50. Umpire-Jack O'Connor. Attendance-2000.

At the conclusion of this five-game series, the Yanks moved on to play the New Orleans Pelicans prior to the start of the regular season.

THE FINAL EXHIBITION SERIES PRIOR TO THE REGULAR SEASON

After the Atlanta series, the Yanks played another five game set, this time pitted against New Orleans of the Southern Association. All five games were played at New Orleans' Athletic Park. The first game was played on April 8, 1903, with the Yanks coming out on top, 8–2. The scores of the next four games were as follows: 2nd-Yanks, 7–2 (April 11); 3rd-Pelicans, 5–4 (April 12); 4th-Yanks, 3–0 (April 15); and 5th game-Pelicans, 4–0 (April 16). The Yanks won the series from the New Orleans Pelicans, three games to two. After the final game, the Yanks headed to Washington D.C. where they open their inaugural season on April 22, 1903. The first game box score is dedicated to a friend, Arthur Schott, of New Orleans.

THE FIRST GAME BOX:

NEW ORLEANS (SOUTHERN ASSOCIATION)	POS	AB	R	H	PO	A	E		NEW YORK (AMERICAN LEAGUE)	POS	AB	R	H	PO	A	E
Montgomery	lf	4	0	1	4	0	0		Davis	lf	4	1	1	3	0	0
Atz	2b	3	0	0	1	4	1		Keeler	rf	5	2	2	0	0	0
J. Smith	ss	4	1	1	1	2	1		Fultz	cf	4	1	1	1	0	0
Law	1b	2	0	0	12	0	1		Williams	2b	5	1	1	4	2	0
Sheehan	3b	4	0	1	0	1	1		Ganzel	1b	3	0	0	8	1	0
Miller	rf	3	0	0	0	0	0		Conroy	3b	3	1	0	1	3	0
Hutchcroft	cf	4	1	2	2	0	0		Long	ss	4	1	1	3	1	1
Hurley	c	4	0	0	3	1	1		Beville	c	4	1	2	7	0	0
C. Smith	p	2	0	1	0	2	0		Chesbro	p	1	0	1	0	0	0
Adams	p	1	0	0	1	2	0		Griffith	p	2	0	0	0	3	0
Haslem	p	1	0	0	0	1	1									
									Totals:		35	8	9	27	10	1
Totals:		32	2	6	24	13	6									

Score by Innings:

New Orleans . . . . .0 1 1   0 0 0   0 0 0—2
New York . . . . .0 0 0   0 2 0   0 6 x—8

Sacrifice hits-Atz, Law, Davis, Chesbro, Ganzel. Stolen bases-Davis, Keeler, Conroy, Miller. Struck out-By Chesbro, 4; Griffith, 1; C. Smith, 1; Adams, 1. Bases on balls-Off Chesbro, 3; Griffith, 1; Adams, 1; Haslem, 1. Hit by pitched ball-By Chesbro (Miller). Double plays-Atz to Law. Umpire-Phelan. Time of game-1:45. Attendance-1200.

After the series in New Orleans, the Yanks began their preparation for the opening game at Washington April 22. In that first regular season game at the Washington park, the home-standing Senators beat New York, 3–1, before 11,950 people. Willie Keeler scored the first Yankee run in history in the first inning, coming home on a fielder's choice.

THE YANKEES' FIRST REGULAR SEASON BOX SCORE
(AT WASHINGTON: APRIL 22, 1903)

NEW YORK	POS	AB	R	H	PO	A
Davis	lf	4	0	0	2	0
Keeler	rf	3	1	0	0	0
Fultz	cf	4	0	2	0	0
Williams	2b	3	0	0	0	3
Ganzel	1b	4	0	1	11	1
Conroy	3b	4	0	1	4	3
Long	ss	4	0	1	1	4
O'Connor	c	4	0	1	5	2
Chesbro	p	3	0	0	1	5
aCourtney	ph	1	0	0	0	0
Totals:		34	1	6	24	18

WASHINGTON	POS	AB	R	H	PO	A
Robinson	ss	3	1	1	3	7
Selbach	rf	3	1	1	0	0
Delahanty	lf	3	0	1	1	0
Ryan	cf	2	0	0	2	0
Carey	1b	4	1	1	7	0
Coughlin	3b	4	0	1	3	2
Demontreville	2b	3	0	1	6	2
Clark	c	4	0	0	3	2
Orth	p	4	0	0	2	2
Totals:		30	3	6	27	15

a-Batted for Chesbro in ninth.

Score by Innings:

New York . . . . .1 0 0   0 0 0   0 0 0—1
Washington . . . . .0 0 0   1 2 0   0 0 x—3

E-Williams, Long. Robinson 2, Orth. ER-Washington 2.2B-Demontreville, Fultz, Coughlin. S-Ryan, Demontreville. SB-Delahanty. LOB-New York 8, Washington 6. DP-Chesbro, O'Connor and Ganzel. BB-Chesbro 4, Orth 3. SO-Chesbro 3, Orth 2. WP-Chesbro 2, Orth 1. Umpire-Connolly. Time-1:45. Attendance-11,950.

The following day, again at Washington, the New Yorkers won their first regular season game in their history. The Yankees, behind the pitching of Harry Howell, defeated the Washington club, 7–2, for their first of 7119 victories through the 1983 season.

Following the presentation of that first game victory box score is a listing of all opening days scores in New York Yankee history.

THE BOX SCORE OF THE FIRST YANKEE REGULAR SEASON VICTORY
(AT WASHINGTON: APRIL 23, 1903)

WASHINGTON	POS	AB	R	H	PO	A	E	NEW YORK	POS	AB	R	H	PO	A	E
Robinson	ss	4	0	1	2	3	1	Davis	lf	5	1	1	1	0	0
Selbach	rf	4	1	2	4	1	0	Keeler	rf	5	1	1	3	0	0
Delehanty	lf	3	1	0	0	0	0	Fultz	cf	4	1	1	3	0	0
Ryan	cf	4	0	0	2	0	2	Williams	2b	5	1	1	4	6	0
Carey	1b	4	0	2	13	0	0	Ganzel	1b	3	1	2	12	0	0
Coughlin	3b	4	0	1	1	3	0	Conroy	3b	5	0	2	2	4	0
Demont	2b	4	0	0	1	2	1	Long	ss	3	1	1	0	2	3
Clarke	c	4	0	1	3	1	1	Courtney	ss	2	0	0	0	1	0
Lee	p	3	0	1	1	4	0	O'Connor	c	3	0	0	2	1	0
								Howell	p	4	1	2	0	1	0
Totals:		34	2	8	27	14	5			39	7	11	27	15	3

Score by Innings:

```
Washington . . . . . . . . . . . . . . . . . . . . . . . . . . . . . . . .0 0 0   0 0 2   0 0 0—2
New York . . . . . . . . . . . . . . . . . . . . . . . . . . . . . . . . .0 0 1   1 1 1   2 1 0—7
```

Earned runs-New York, 2. Two-base hits-Ganzel, Conroy. Three-base hits-Howell. Sacrifice hits-Ganzel, O'Connor. Double plays-Conroy to Williams, Courtney, Williams, Ganzel. First base on balls-off Lee, 2. Hit by pitched ball Delehanty. Struck out by Lee, 2; by Howell, 2. Left on bases-Washington, 4; New York, 9. Time of Game-1:50. Umpire-Connolly. Attendance-2,240.

NEW YORK YANKEE OPENING-DAY GAMES

From 1903 through 1983, the Yankees have played 81 opening-day games in as many seasons. Of those 81 openers, the Yankees have won 45, lost 35, with one game ending in a tie. Opening at home, New York has been victorious 24 of 39 times with one tie game. On the road, the Bombers record is even at 21–21. The earliest opening was on April 5 (1979 and 1983) and the latest opener was played on April 23, 1919. There have been 10 extra-inning opening day contests, the longest being the 4–4 tie versus Boston in 1910. Only one game was less than nine full innings, the 1972 seven-inning contest with Baltimore. Nineteen openers involved shutouts, the Yankees winning 11 while losing 8. In 1–0 games, the Yanks won two (1908 and 1968) and lost three (1935, 1936 and 1980). The most runs scored by New York was 19 in the 1955 opener versus Washington at Yankee Stadium. The final tally was a 19–1 Yankee rout of the Senators. The most runs scored by an opponent on the season's first day was the Red Sox' 15–5 pasting of the Yanks at Fenway Park on April 6, 1973. The most common Yankee opponent on opening day was the Boston Red Sox with 26 games, the New Yorkers winning 16, losing 9, with one game ending in a tie.

It is interesting to note that from 1903 through 1960, the only Yankee opponents in openers had been Boston, Philadelphia, and Washington. This string was broken when the Yanks played host to the then first-year Minnesota Twins in 1961, the first year of expansion in the American League. The Yanks have opened only once in their history with a double-header, this occurring in 1982, playing host to the Chicago White Sox in an opening game for the first time in the 80 year Yankee-White Sox rivalry. The most consecutive opening game victories was 7 straight from 1923 through 1929; the most consecutive losses on opening day was 5 from 1934 through 1938. In addition, the Yankees have won six straight openers on two different occasions.

The most successful Yankee pitcher on opening day has been Mel Stottlemyre with 4 wins (a club record) and 3 defeats in 7 opening day decisions, another club record. Chesbro and Stottlemyre are the only two Yankee hurlers to win three consecutive opening games, while Gomez is the only one to lose 3 straight. The next best records are: Chesbro (3–1), Ruffing (3–2), Ford and Gomez (2–3), and Caldwell (0–3) with pitchers having three or more opening game decisions. Walter Johnson has the best opponent record with a 3–1 mark. Grove has a 1–3 mark, Ehmke, 0–3. Babe Ruth (1–0) defeated the Yanks on opening day, April 11, 1917.

Jack Chesbro—"Happy Jack" won an American League record 41 games with New York in 1904. In 7 seasons with New York, he won 128 games. He was inducted into the Hall of Fame in 1946.

Bill Dickey played all 17 seasons with New York and has a lifetime batting average of .313. He became the Yanks'13th manager upon Joe McCarthy's resignation in 1946. The Louisiana native was a close personal friend to Lou Gehrig and was elected to the Hall of Fame in 1954.

ALL-TIME NEW YORK YANKEE
OPENING DAY SCORES:

DATE	OPP	SCORE	W	L	WINNING PITCHER	LOSING PITCHER
Apr 22, 1903	was	1– 3		L	Orth	*Chesbro*
Apr 14, 1904	BOS	8– 2	W		*Chesbro*	Doyle
Apr 14, 1905	was	4– 2	W		*Chesbro*	Patten
Apr 14, 1906	BOS	2– 1h	W		*Chesbro*	Young
Apr 11, 1907	was	3– 2	W		*Orth*	Hughes
Apr 14, 1908	PHI	1– 0h	W		*Doyle*	Carter
Apr 12, 1909	was	1– 4		L	Smith	*Newton*
Apr 14, 1910	BOS	4– 4j	TG		None	None
Apr 12, 1911	phi	2– 1	W		*Vaughn*	Bender
Apr 11, 1912	BOS	3– 5		L	Wood	*Caldwell*
Apr 12, 1916	WAS	2– 3g		L	Johnson	*Caldwell*
Apr 11, 1917	BOS	3–10		L	Johnson	*Caldwell*
Apr 14, 1914	PHI	8– 2	W		*McHale*	Bush
Apr 14, 1915	was	0– 7		L	Johnson	*Warhop*
Apr 12, 1916	WAS	2- 3g		L	Johnson	*Caldwell*
Apr 11, 1917	BOS	3-10		L	Ruth	*Caldwell*
Apr 15, 1918	was	6– 3	W		*Mogridge*	Johnson
Apr 23, 1919	BOS	0–10		L	Mays	*Mogridge*
Apr 14, 1920	phi	1– 3		L	Perry	*Shawkey*
Apr 13, 1921	PHI	11– 1	W		*Mays*	Perry
Apr 12, 1922	was	5– 6		L	Mogridge	*Jones*
Apr 18, 1923	BOS	4– 1	W		*Shawkey*	Ehmke
Apr 15, 1924	bosb	2– 1	W		*Hoyt*	Ehmke
Apr 14, 1925	WAS	5– 1	W		*Shocker*	Mogridge
Apr 13, 1926	bos	12–11	W		*Shawkey*	Ehmke
Apr 12, 1927	PHI	8– 3	W		*Hoyt*	Grove
Apr 11, 1928	phi	8– 3	W		*Pennock*	Grove
Apr 18, 1929	BOS	7– 3	W		*Pipgras*	Ruffing
Apr 15, 1930	phi	2– 6		L	Grove	*Pipgras*
Apr 14, 1931	BOS	6– 3	W		*Ruffing*	Moore
Apr 12, 1932	phi	12– 6	W		*Gomez*	Earnshaw
Apr 13, 1933	BOS	4– 3	W		*Gomez*	Andrews
Apr 17, 1934	phi	5– 6		L	Cascarella	*Smythe*
Apr 16, 1935	BOS	0– 1		L	Ferrell	*Gomez*
Apr 14, 1936	was	0– 1		L	Newsom	*Gomez*
Apr 20, 1937	WAS	2– 3		L	Weaver	*Gomez*
Apr 18, 1938	bos	4– 8		L	Bagby	*Ruffing*
Apr 20, 1939	BOS	2– 0	W		*Ruffing*	Grove
Apr 16, 1940	phi	1– 2f		L	Dean	*Ruffing*
Apr 14, 1941	was	3– 0	W		*Russo*	Leonard
Apr 14, 1942	was	7– 0	W		*Ruffing*	Hudson
Apr 22, 1943	WAS	5– 4	W		*Murphy*	Haeffner
Apr 18, 1944	bos	3– 0	W		*Borowy*	Terry
Apr 17, 1945	BOS	8– 4	W		*Donald*	Cecil

ALL-TIME NEW YORK YANKEE
OPENING DAY SCORES: (cont.)

DATE	OPP	SCORE	W	L	WINNING PITCHER	LOSING PITCHER
Apr 16, 1946	phi	5– 0	W		*Chandler*	Christopher
Apr 15, 1947	PHI	1– 6		L	Marchildon	*Chandler*
Apr 19, 1948	was	12– 4	W		*Reynolds*	Wynn
Apr 19, 1949	WAS	3– 2	W		*Lopat*	Hudson
Apr 18, 1950	bos	15–10	W		*Johnson*	Masterson
Apr 17, 1951	BOS	5– 0	W		*Raschi*	Wight
Apr 16, 1952	phi	8– 1	W		*Raschi*	Kellner
Apr 14, 1953	PHI	0– 5		L	Kellner	*Raschi*
Apr 13, 1954	was	3– 5f		L	Dixon	*Reynolds*
Apr 13, 1955	WAS	19– 1	W		*Ford*	McDermott
Apr 17, 1956	was	10– 4	W		*Larsen*	Pascua!
Apr 16, 1957	was	2– 1	W		*Fʻord*	Stobbs
Apr 15, 1958	bos	3– 0	W		*Larsen*	Nixon
Apr 12, 1959	BOS	3– 2	W		*Turley*	Brewer
Apr 19, 1960	bos	8– 4	W		*Coates*	Brewer
Apr 11, 1961	MIN	0– 6		L	Ramos	*Ford*
Apr 10, 1962	BAL	7– 6	W		*Terry*	Brown
Apr 9, 1963	kc	8– 2	W		*Terry*	Segui
Apr 16, 1964	BOS	3– 4g		L	Radatz	*Ford*
Apr 12, 1965	min	4– 5f		L	Fosnow	*Ramos*
Apr 12, 1966	DET	1– 2		L	Lolich	*Ford*
Apr 10, 1967	was	8– 0	W		*Stottlemyre*	Richert
Apr 10, 1968	CAL	1– 0	W		*Stottlemyre*	Brunet
Apr 7, 1969	was	8– 4	W		*Stottlemyre*	Pascual
Apr 7, 1970	BOS	3– 4		L	Peters	*Stottlemyre*
Apr 6, 1971	bos	1– 3		L	Culp	*Bahnsen*
Apr 16, 1972	bal	1– 3		L	Dobson	*Stottlemyre*
Apr 6, 1973	bos	5–15		L	Tiant	*Stottlemyre*
Apr 6, 1974	CLE	6– 1	W		*Stottlemyre*	Perry
Apr 8, 1975	cle	3– 5		L	Perry	*Medich*
Apr 8, 1976	mil	0– 5		L	Slaton	*Hunter*
Apr 7, 1977	MIL	3– 0	W		*Hunter*	Travers
Apr 8, 1978	tex	1– 2		L	Matlack	*Gossage*
Apr 5, 1979	MIL	1– 5		L	Caldwell	*Guidry*
Apr 10, 1980	tex	0– 1h		L	Lyle	*Underwood*
Apr 9, 1981	TEX	10– 3	W		*John*	Matlack
Apr 11, 1982	CHI	6– 7h		L	Hickey	*Gossage*
Apr 5, 1983	sea	4– 5		L	Clark	*Erickson*

SYMBOL LEGEND:
f = 10 inning game; g = 11 inning game; h = 12 inning game
j = 14 inning game; TG = Tie game (1910)
Pitcher = New York Yankee pitcher of record (won or lost)

THE ULTIMATE NEW YORK YANKEES RECORD BOOK

THE BOX SCORE OF THE YANKEES' FIRST HOME GAME IN HISTORY:
(AT NEW YORK: APRIL 30,1903)

NEW YORK	POS	AB	R	H	PO	A	E	WASHINGTON	POS	AB	R	H	PO	A	E
Davis	lf	4	1	1	0	0	2	Robinson	ss	4	0	2	2	2	0
Keeler	rf	2	3	2	1	0	0	Selbach	rf	5	1	0	0	0	0
McFarland	cf	3	1	0	0	0	0	Delahanty	lf	4	0	0	3	0	0
Williams	2b	4	0	2	2	3	0	Ryan	cf	4	0	2	3	1	0
Ganzel	1b	3	0	0	12	1	0	Carey	1b	4	0	0	8	0	0
Conroy	3b	4	1	2	5	1	0	Coughlin	3b	4	1	2	2	1	1
Courtney	ss	3	0	1	2	1	1	DeMontreville	2b	4	0	1	0	3	0
O'Conner	c	4	0	1	4	1	0	Drill	c	4	0	0	5	1	0
Chesbro	p	4	0	0	1	5	0	Townsend	p	3	0	0	1	2	0
								*Holmes		1	0	0	0	0	0
Totals:			31	6	9	27	12	3	Totals:		37	2	7	24	10	1

*Batted for Townsend in ninth inning.

Washington . . . . .0 0 0   0 0 0 1   1 0—2
New York . . . . .1 1 0   0 2 0   2 0 x—6

Earned runs-New York, 2. Two base hits-Keeler, 2; Williams, 2; Conroy, 2; Coughlin, Robinson. Sacrifice hits-McFarland, Courtney. Stolen baseO'Conner. Double play-Ryan and Drill. Left on bases-New York, 7; Washington, 9. First base on balls-off Chesbro, 1; off Townsend, 3. First base on errors-New York, 1; Washington, 3. Hit by pitched ball-by Townsend, 1. Struck out-by Chesbro, 1; by Townsend, 4. Time-1:30. Umpires-Connolly and Caruthers.

THE FIRST GAME EVER AT FENWAY PARK

Fenway Park was dedicated on April 20, 1912 before a crowd of some 27,000. How fitting it was that the Red Sox should play the Yankees in this inaugural game at Fenway. This park would see many an exciting game over the next several decades. The BoSox emerged as winners, defeating the Yanks in 11 innings, 7–6.

THE BOX SCORE:

	BOSTON								NEW YORK						
	POS	AB	R	H	PO	A	E		POS	AB	R	H	PO	A	E
Hooper	rf	5	0	0	4	0	0	Zinn	lf	5	1	0	3	0	0
Yerkes	2b	7	3	5	4	3	3	Wolter	rf	4	1	1	0	0	0
Speaker	cf	6	0	3	2	0	0	Kauff	cf	1	1	0	0	0	0
Stahl	1b	6	0	1	6	1	1	Chase	1b	4	0	2	13	0	0
Gardner	3b	6	1	2	1	1	0	Hartzell	ss	5	1	1	2	2	1
Lewis	1f	4	1	1	3	1	0	Daniels	cf,rf	5	1	0	4	0	0
Wagner	ss	5	1	1	5	3	1	Dolan	3b	4	1	1	0	0	2
Nunamaker	c	4	0	0	6	1	0	E. Gardner	2b	5	0	1	1	3	0
Carrigan	c	0	0	0	0	1	0	Street	c	5	0	1	9	3	0
O'Brien	p	1	0	0	0	1	1	Caldwell	p	2	0	1	0	1	0
Hall	p	3	1	1	2	2	1	Quinn	p	2	0	0	0	3	0
*Hendricksen	ph	0	0	0	0	0	0	Vaughn	p	1	0	0	0	0	0
#Engle	ph	1	0	0	0	0	0								
Total:		48	7	14	33	14	7	Total:		43	6	8	32a	12	3

*Batted for O'Brien in 4th inning
#Batted for Nunamaker in 10th inning
aTwo out when winning run was scored

```
Boston . . . . . . . . . . . . . . . . . . . . . . . . . . . . . .1 0 0   3 0 1   0 1 0   0 1—7
New York . . . . . . . . . . . . . . . . . . . . . . . . . .3 0 2   0 0 0   0 1 0   0 0—6
```

Two-base hits-Yerkes (2), Speaker, Stahl, Hall. Hits-Off O'Brien, 5 in 4 innings; off Hall, 3 in 7 innings; off Caldwell, 5 in 3 1/3 innings; off Quinn, 6 in 5 innings; off Vaughn, 3 in 2 1/3 innings. Sacrifice hits-Chase, Hooper. Stolen bases-Hartzell, Chase, Daniels (2), Lewis, Wolter, Wagner. Left on bases-Boston-18; New York-14. First base on balls-Off O'Brien, off Hall, 3; off Caldwell, 4; off Quinn, 4; off Vaughn, 1. First base on errors-Boston, 3; New York, 4. Hit by pitchers-Daniels, zChase (by O'Brien); Nunamaker (by Quinn). Struck out-By O'Brien, 4; by Hall, 2; by Caldwell, 2; by Quinn, 4; by Vaughn, 2. Passed ball-Street. Wild pitch-O'Brien. Time of game-3:10. Umpires-Messrs. Connolly and Hart. Attendance-27,000.

THE BOX SCORE OF THE FIRST GAME EVER BETWEEN THE YANKEES AND THE BOSTON RED SOX:
(AT BOSTON: MAY 7, 1903)

BOSTON	POS	AB	R	H	PO	A	E	NEW YORK	POS	AB	R	H	PO	A	E
Dougherty	lf	5	1	2	3	0	0	Davis	lf	3	1	0	1	0	0
Collins	3b	3	1	1	0	3	0	Keeler	rf	3	0	0	0	0	0
Stahl	cf	4	1	3	1	0	0	Fultz	cf	4	0	1	2	0	0
Freeman	rf	4	1	2	1	0	0	Williams	2b	4	0	1	2	7	0
Parent	ss	4	1	2	3	5	1	Ganzel	1b	4	0	0	11	2	0
Lachance	lb	3	0	1	11	1	0	Conroy	3b	4	1	1	2	1	0
Ferris	2b	4	1	1	3	0	0	Long	ss	3	0	0	2	5	2
Griger	c	4	0	1	5	1	0	Beville	c	3	0	1	3	2	0
Dineen	p	4	0	0	0	1	0	Wiltze	p	3	0	2	1	1	0
Totals:			35	6	13	27	11	1	Totals:			31	2	6	24	18	2

```
Boston...................................1 1 0   0 0 1   3 0 x—6
New York................................1 0 0   0 1 0   0 0 0—2
```

Earned runs-Boston, 5; New York, 1. Two-base hits-Parent, Wiltze. Three-base hits-Stahl, 2. Home run-Ferris. Stolen bases-Dougherty, Conroy. Double plays-Long, Williams and Ganzel. Bases on balls-off Dineen, 1; off Wiltze, 1. Struck out-by Dineen, 5, by Wiltze, 1. Time-1:33. Umpire-Caruthers. Attendance-5,402.

BABE RUTH'S FIRST GAME AS A YANKEE

Babe Ruth's first appearance in a Yankee regular season game was at Philadelphia on April 14, 1920. In the game, the Bambino went two for four, both hits being of the one base variety. Playing at Shibe Park on a very cold and windy day, some twelve thousand brave fans witnessed the Yankee debut of the man who probably put baseball back on its feet after the recent Black Sox fiasco in the 1919 World Series. Ruth, in his first of 2,084 Yankee games, made a costly error from his centerfield position that did not help the Yankee cause. Dugan hit a fly ball to center which Ruth judged nicely but dropped the ball as it struck his glove. Making this error in the eighth inning of a 1–1 game, two runners scored on Babe's bobble, putting the Athletics ahead to stay, 3–1. If Ruth had caught the ball the inning would have been history as there were two outs when the muff was made. Bob Shawkey took the loss while Scott Perry picked up his first win of the season.

Ruth went on to terrorize American League pitchers that season, batting .376 and hitting a then unprecedented 54 homers. Ruth's slugging mark of .847 was the best in Major League history! Not bad for a Yankee first year player, huh?

THE BOX SCORE OF BABE RUTH'S FIRST GAME AS A YANKEE
(AT PHILADELPHIA: APRIL 14, 1920)

	NEW YORK POS	AB	R	H	PO	A	E		PHILADELPHIA POS	A	B	R	H	PO	A	E
Gleich	rf	4	0	0	2	0	0	Witt	cf	4	0	2	3	0	0	
Peckinpaugh	ss	4	0	0	1	1	0	Strunk	rf	2	0	0	2	0	0	
Pipp	1b	3	1	2	8	1	0	C. Walker	lf	4	1	3	2	0	0	
Ruth	cf	4	0	2	4	0	1	Griffin	1b	3	1	1	8	0	0	
Lewis	lf	4	0	1	1	0	0	Dugan	2b	4	0	0	2	3	0	
Meusel	3b	4	0	0	0	4	0	Galloway	ss	4	0	0	1	2	1	
Pratt	2b	4	0	2	0	1	0	Dykes	3b	3	0	0	3	2	0	
Ruel	c	3	0	0	7	0	0	Perkins	c	3	1	1	6	0	0	
Shawkey	p	2	0	0	1	3	0	Perry	p	3	0	0	0	1	0	
Totals:		32	1	7	24	10	1	Totals:		30	3	7	27	8	1	

```
New York . . . . . . . . . . . . . . . . . . . . . . . . . . . . . . . . .1 0 0   0 0 0   0 0 0—1
Philadelphia . . . . . . . . . . . . . . . . . . . . . . . . . . . . . . .0 0 0   0 1 0   0 2 x—3
```

Home runs-Pipp, Perkins. Sacrifices-Griffin, Strunk. Double plays-Dugan and Galloway; Dykes and Griffin. Left on bases-New York, 6; Philadelphia, 6. Bases on balls-off Shawkey, 1; off Perry, 1. Hit by pitcher-by Perry (Shawkey). Struck out-by Shawkey, 6; by Perry, 6. Umpires-Dinneen and Nallin. Time of game-1:30.

Babe Ruth smashes his then record-shattering 60th homer in 1927 off Washington's Tom Zachary at Yankee Stadium on September 30. The famous homer was hit with one runner on base and broke his previous record of 59 home runs hit in 1921.

Babe Ruth addresses the Yankee Stadium crowd of 60,000. It is April 27, 1947, and the mighty Babe is waging a heroic battle with cancer. "Babe Ruth Day" at Yankee Stadium was one of the most memorable moments in the annals of sports. Babe will lose his gallant fight for life on August 16, 1948.

THE BOX SCORE OF THE END OF LOU GEHRIG'S 2130 CONSECUTIVE GAME STREAK
(AT DETROIT: MAY 2, 1939)

NEW YORK	POS	AB	H	O	A		DETROIT	POS	AB	H	O	A
Crosetti	ss	5	2	5	1		McCosky	cf	5	0	3	0
Rolfe	3b	6	2	1	0		Walker	lf	3	0	1	0
Henrich	cf	4	1	1	0		Gehringer	2b	4	1	3	1
Dickey	c	5	2	4	0		Greenberg	1b	3	0	6	1
Keller	lf	5	2	3	0		Fox	rf	4	1	4	0
Selkirk	rf	3	2	3	0		Tebbett	c	4	1	4	0
Gordon	2b	4	2	3	4		Rogell	3b	3	2	2	4
Dahlgren	1b	5	2	7	0		Croucher	ss	3	2	3	3
Ruffins	p	6	2	0	0		Kennedy	p	0	0	0	1
							Eisenstat	p	0	0	1	0
Totals:		43	17	27	5		*Cullenbine		1	0	0	0
							Lynn	p	1	0	0	0
							Hutchinson	p	0	0	0	0
							Gill	p	1	0	0	0
							°Fleming		1	0	0	0
							Totals:		33	7	27	10

*Batted for Eisenstat in third inning.
°Batted for Gill in ninth inning.

```
New York .................................6 0 2  0 2 3  9 0 0—22
Detroit ..................................0 0 0  0 0 0  2 0 0— 2
```

Runs–Crosetti (3), Rolfe (2), Henrich (3), Dickey (2), Keller (4), Selkirk (2), Gordon (3), Dahlgren (2), Ruffing, Rogell, Greenberg. Error-Greenberg. Runs batted in-Keller (6), Gordon, Ruffing (3), Dahlgren (2), Selkirk (2), Henrich (3), Rolfe (3), Dickey, Croucher, Rogell. Two-base hits-Dahlgren, Tebbetts, Rolfe (2), Rogell, Croucher, Selkirk. Three-base hit-Keller. Home runs-Dahlgren, Selkirk, Henrich, Keller. Sacrifice-Henrich. Double play-Gordon to Crosetti to Dahlgren. Left on bases-New York, 7; Detroit, 8. First on base on balls- off Ruffing, 4; off Lynn, 3; off Kennedy, 2; off Eisenstat, 1; off Gill, 1; off Hutchinson, 5. Struck out-by Ruffing, 2; by Eisenstat, 1; by Lynn, 2. Hits-off Kennedy, 2 in 1 inning; off Eisenstat, 4 in 2⅔ innings; off Lynn, 3 in 2⅔ innings; off Hutchinson, 4 in ⅔ inning; off Gill, 2 in 2⅔ innings. Balk-Lynn. Passed ball-Tebbetts. Losing pitcher-Kennedy. Umpires-Basil, Ormsby and Summers. Time of game- two hours and 22 minutes. Attendance- 11, 379.

RUN-SCORING RECORDS

THE GREATEST NUMBER OF RUNS
SCORED BY THE YANKEES IN A GAME

On May 24, 1936, the Yankees scored a club record 25 runs at Philadelphia. The 25–2 pounding of the Athletics was also the greatest winning margin (23) in their history. Second baseman Tony Lazzeri became the first player in Major League history to hit two grand slams in the same game. All total, Lazzeri had an American League record 11 RBI in a single game. The previous day, Tony had 4 runs batted in. Thus, in two games Lazzeri had 15 RBI, a Major League record. Prior to "Poosh 'Em Up" Lazzeri's RBI performance in this game, Jimmy Foxx was the RBI leader in a game, knocking in nine runs August 14, 1933 with Philadelphia. The all-time RBI man in a single game is "Sunny Jim" Bottomly with twelve ribbies on September, 16, 1924. Bottomly played with the St. Louis Cardinals.

The box score of the 25–2 Philadelphia massacre to be presented next is followed with a listing of all nineteen 20-run games in Yankee history. After the twenty-run game listing is the greatest winning and losing margins in New York Yankee history.

THE BOX SCORE OF THE MOST RUNS SCORED BY THE YANKEES IN ONE GAME (AT PHILADELPHIA: MAY 24, 1936)

NEW YORK	POS	AB	R	H	RBI	PO	A	E	PHILADELPHIA	POS	AB	R	H	RBI	PO	A	E
Crosetti	ss	6	2	2	3	3	5	0	Finney	1b	3	1	2	0	5	0	0
Rolfe	3b	4	2	0	0	3	2	0	Dean	1b	1	0	1	0	0	0	0
DiMaggio	1f	7	2	3	3	2	0	0	Warstler	2b	2	1	1	0	3	3	0
Gehrig	1b	4	3	2	1	7	0	0	Peters	ss	1	0	0	0	1	0	0
Dickey	c	5	3	2	2	3	0	1	Moses	cf	4	0	0	0	4	0	0
Chapman	cf	2	4	2	2	2	0	0	Puccinelli	rf	3	0	1	0	1	0	0
Selkirk	rf	5	3	1	2	2	0	0	Higgins	3b	4	0	1	1	3	1	0
Lazzeri	2b	5	4	4	11	2	1	0	Johnson	lf	2	0	0	0	1	0	0
Pearson	p	5	2	3	2	0	1	0	Mailho	lf	2	0	0	0	2	0	0
Jorgens	c	1	0	0	0	0	0	1	Newsome	ss,2b	4	0	0	0	1	4	0
Saltzgaver	1b	1	0	0	0	3	0	0	Berry	c	4	0	0	0	6	0	0
									Turbeville	p	0	0	0	0	0	0	0
Total:		45	25	19	24	27	9	2	Dietrich	p	1	0	1	0	0	0	0
									aNiemiec	ph	0	0	0	0	0	0	0
									Bullock	p	0	0	0	0	0	0	0
									Fink	p	0	0	0	0	0	0	0
									Upchurch	p	1	0	0	0	0	0	0
									bHayes	ph	1	0	0	0	0	0	0
									Totals:		33	2	7	1	27	8	0

a Batted for Dietrich in fourth
b Batted for Upchurch in ninth

Score by Innings:

New York . . . . .0 5 0 5 6 1 2 6 0—25
Philadelphia . . . . .2 0 0 0 0 0 0 0 0— 2

Two base hits-DiMaggio, Chapman (2), Dean. Three base hits-Dickey (2), Lazzeri. Two runs-Lazzeri (3), DiMaggio, Crosetti (2). Double plays-Newsome to Warstler to Finney, Crosetti to Gehrig. Left on bases-New York, 9; Philadelphia, 7. First bases on balls-Off Turbeville, 5; off Pearson, 3; off Dietrich, 5; off Bullock, 4; off Upchurch, 2. Struck out-By Dietrich, 3; by Pearson, 3; by Upchurch, 2. Hits-Off Turbeville, 1 in 1⅓ innings; off Dietrich, 6 in 2⅔ innings; off Bullock, 1 in ⅓ innings; off Fink, 3 in ⅔ innings; Upchurch, 8 in 4 innings. Wild pitches-Pearson, Bullock (2). Losing pitcher-Turbeville. Umpires-Summers and Johnston, Time of game-2:34.

SCORING TWENTY (20) OR MORE RUNS IN A SINGLE GAME (19 TIMES)

DATE:	SCORE	OPP	1	2	3	4	5	6	7	8	9	Total	NOTES
Jul 14, 1904	21– 3	CLE	0	8	2	1	0	0	0	10	0	21	21 hits, 10 runs 8th inning
Aug 31, 1906	20– 5	WAS	5	5	5	1	0	4	–	–		20	6 inning game, 2nd game
July 17, 1920	20– 5	CHI	2	4	0	0	2	3	8	1	x	20	22 hits
Sep 25, 1921	21– 7	CLE	0	5	2	8	0	3	1	2	x	21	20 hits
Sep 28, 1923	24– 4	bos	4	0	1	0	1	11	2	3	2	24	30 hits, 11 runs 6th inning
Jul 4, 1927	21– 1	WAS	4	1	0	0	2	9	3	2	x	21	2nd game
May 22, 1930	20–13	phi	7	2	0	0	2	1	2	1	5	20	23 hits, 2nd game
May 18, 1931	20 8	det	1	0	5	1	0	0	0	8	5	20	Yanks were walked 16 times
Jul 26, 1931	22– 5	CHI	3	6	9	4	0	0	0	0	x	22	2nd game, all runs in 4 innings
Jun 3, 1932	20–13	phi	2	0	0	2	3	2	3	2	6	20	23 hits, Gehrig 4 home runs
May 24, 1936	25– 2	phi	0	5	0	5	6	1	2	6	0	25	Lazzeri 11 RIB's-A.L. record
May 2, 1939	22– 2	det	6	0	2	0	2	3	9	0	0	22	End of Gehrig's 2130 streak
Jun 28, 1939	23– 2	phi	0	1	5	9	0	4	4	0	0	23	NY: 8 homers, 27 hits, 2nd game
Aug 13, 1939	21– 0	phi	0	5	5	2	1	5	0	3	–	21	8 innings, 2nd game, 23 hits
Aug 7, 1949	20– 2	STL	3	0	9	0	0	3	0	5	x	20	22 hits, lst game
Sep 11, 1949	20– 5	WAS	0	0	12	0	2	0	5	1	x	20	12 runs 3rd inning, 1st game
Aug 12, 1953	22– 1	was	4	0	3	2	3	0	5	5	0	22	28 hits
Aug 14, 1955	20– 6	bal	1	4	0	4	0	0	0	5	6	20	20 hits, 2nd game
Aug 19, 1962	21– 7	kc	4	0	1	5	0	4	0	4	3	21	20 hits

20 RUNS BY THE YANKEES—19 TIMES
(ACCOMPLISHED 8 TIMES AT HOME, 11 TIMES ON THE ROAD)

GREATEST YANKEE WINNING AND LOSING MARGINS IN HISTORY:
(15 or more RUN minus OPP RUN difference was accomplished 44 times)

DATE	SCORE	DIFF.	OPPONENT	DATE	SCORE	DIFF.	OPPONENT
May 24, 1936	25–2	23	phi	Apr 30, 1960	16–0	16	bal
Jun 28, 1939	23–2	21	phi (1)	Aug 31, 1906	20–5	15	WAS (2) (6 Inn)
Aug 12, 1953	22–1	21	was	Jul 17, 1920	20–5	15	CHI
Aug 13, 1939	21–0	21	phi (2) (8 Inn)	Sep 11, 1949	20–5	15	WAS (1)
Sep 28, 1923	24–4	20	bos	Aug 28, 1936	19–4	15	DET (2) (7 Inn)
May 2, 1939	22–2	20	det	May 10, 1952	18–3	15	BOS
Jul 4, 1927	21–1	20	WAS (2)	Jun 9, 1929	17–2	15	STL
Jul 14, 1904	21–3	18	CLE	Jun 17, 1930	17–2	15	cle
Aug 7, 1949	20–2	18	STL (1)	May 25, 1947	17–2	15	BOS
Apr 13, 1955	19–1	18	WAS	Aug 11, 1903	16–1	15	WAS
Jul 10, 1936	18–0	18	CLE	Sep 13, 1924	16–1	15	chi
Jul 26, 1931	22–5	17	CHI (2)	Aug 16, 1938	16–1	15	was (1)
Jul 21, 1910	19–2	17	STL	May 29, 1942	16–1	15	WAS
Jul 14, 1931	19–2	17	CLE (1)	Jul 19, 1950	16–1	15	STL (1)
Aug 12, 1931	18–1	17	cle (1)	Jun 23, 1930	15–0	15	STL (1)
Apr 24, 1909	17–0	17	WAS	Jul 5, 1937	15–0	15	BOS (1)
Jul 6, 1920	17–0	17	was	Aug 17, 1942	15–0	15	phi
Sep 17, 1931	17–0	17	STL (1)	Aug 4, 1953	15–0	15	DET
Jun 18, 1916	19–3	16	cle	Jun 22, 1958	15–0	15	det
Jul 30, 1920	19–3	16	stl	Sep 25, 1977	15–0	15	tor (1)
Sep 10, 1921	19–3	16	phi				
Aug 28, 1939	18–2	16	det				
Jun 3, 1953	18–2	16	chi	(1) = 1st game of doubleheader			
Apr 25, 1933	16–0	16	was	(2) = 2nd game of doubleheader			

GREATEST YANKEE LOSING MARGINS IN HISTORY
(15 or more RUN minus OPP RUN difference was accomplished 7 times)

DATE	SCORE	DIFF.	OPPONENT
Jul 29, 1928	6–24	18	cle (1)
Jun 17, 1925	1–19	18	DET
Sep 10, 1977	3–19	16	TOR
Jul 15, 1908	1–16	15	CLE (1)
Jul 30, 1921	1–16	15	CLE
Jul 15, 1907	0–15	15	chi
May 4, 1950	0–15	15	CHI

(1) = 1st game of doubleheader

ALL-TIME YANKEE VICTORIES AND LOSSES, BOTH CLUBS SCORING 10 OR MORE RUNS IN A GAME:

ALL-TIME YANKEE VICTORIES (BOTH CLUBS):			TEN OR MORE RUNS ACCOMPLISHED 51 TIMES			
DATE	**SCORE**	**OPPONENT**	**DATE**	**SCORE**	**OPPONENT**	
May 22, 1930	20–13	phi (2)	Jul 19, 1960	13–11	cle	
Jun 3, 1932	20–13	phi	April 26, 1961	13–11	det	(10 Inn)
Sep 16, 1930	19–10	stl	Sep 25, 1905	13–10	STL	
Sep 28, 1911	18–12	STL	Jul 15, 1920	13–10	STL	(11 Inn)
Jun 24, 1936	18–11	chi	Jul 22, 1926	13–10	CHI	
Jun 3, 1933	17–11	PHI	Aug 27, 1935	13–10	chi (1)	
Jun 15, 1930	17–10	cle	April 13, 1926	12–11	bos	
Jul 1, 1907	16–15	WAS (1)	Jun 8, 1927	12–11	CHI	(11 Inn)
Apr 21, 1908	16–13	WAS	Jul 25, 1937	12–11	chi (1)	
Sep 23, 1933	16–12	bos	Aug 10, 1938	12–11	WAS	(10 Inn)
May 14, 1923	16–11	det (12 Inn)	Jun 22, 1977	12–11	det	
Jul 29, 1903	15–14	bos	Jul 28, 1924	12–10	chi (2)	
Jul 13, 1938	15–12	STL (10 Inn)	Sep 7, 1927	12–10	bos	
May 27, 1933	15–11	CHI	May 5, 1938	12–10	STL	
Jul 25, 1953	15–11	det (12 Inn)	Jun 12, 1966	12–10	det (2)	
Aug 13, 1967	15–11	cle	May 13,1979	12–10	CAL	
Apr 18, 1950	15–10	bos	May 12, 1921	11–10	det	
Jul 31, 1930	14–13	bos	Sep 25, 1929	11–10	bos	(11 Inn)
Aug 20, 1947	14–13	det (11 Inn)	Sep 10, 1932	11–10	det (1)	
Sep 18, 1928	14–11	stl	Jun 8, 1942	11–10	CLE	(11 Inn)
Aug 10, 1930	14–11	STL	Aug 29, 1948	11–10	DET (2)	
Jun 23, 1952	14–10	stl	Aug 4, 1963	11–10	BAL (2)	(10 Inn)
Apr 21, 1956	14–10	BOS	Aug 16, 1977	11–10	CHI	
Jun 21, 1970	14–10	bos (11 Inn)	Jun 8, 1979	11–10	kc	(11 Inn)
Jun 26, 1930	13–11	CLE	Jun 28, 1980	11–10	CLE	
Sep 1, 1941	13–11	phi (1)				

ALL-TIME YANKEE LOSSES (BOTH CLUBS):			TEN OR MORE RUNS ACCOMPLISHED 40 TIMES			
DATE	**SCORE**	**OPPONENT**	**DATE**	**SCORE**	**OPPONENT**	
May 11, 1925	10–19	stl	Aug 12, 1973	12–13	OAK	
Sep 29, 1928	10–19	det	Aug 7, 1923	10–12	STL	
Jul 19, 1925	12–18	det	Jul 27, 1932	10–12	cle (2)	
May 3, 1912	15–18	phi	Jun 17, 1961	10–12	det	
Jun 22, 1932	10–17	stl	Sep 5, 1927	11–12	bos (1)	(18 Inn)
Aug 14, 1929	13–17	det	Jul 14, 1934	11–12	det	
Aug 12, 1937	10–16	bos (1)	Apr 20, 1936	11–12	phi	
Sep 26, 1912	12–15	bos (8 Inn)	Sep 3, 1939	11–12	bos (1)	
Jul 18, 1934	14–15	cle	Jul 20, 1947	11–12	det (2)	(11 Inn)
May 9, 1926	10–14	DET	Jul 27, 1907	10–11	CLE	(11 Inn)
Jun 22, 1931	10–14	stl	Aug 3, 1911	10–11	CLE	
Jun 23, 1932	10–14	stl	Sep 30, 1912	10–11	phi	(11 Inn)
Jun 8, 1933	10–14	phi	Sep 13, 1930	10–11	det (1)	
May 25, 1953	10–14	BOS	Apr 24, 1933	10–11	was	
Jul 28, 1931	12–14	CHI	Aug 4, 1935	10–11	was	
Jul 24, 1940	12–14	stl	Jun 8, 1938	10–11	CHI (1)	(13 Inn)
Sep 9, 1932	13–14	det (1) (14 Inn)	May 30, 1951	10–11	bos (1)	(15 Inn)
Oct 3, 1913	10–13	PHI	Jul 15, 1963	10–11	kc	(12 Inn)
Jul 26, 1928	10–13	det (2)	Aug 15, 1967	10–11	BAL	(13 Inn)
Jun 30, 1933	12–13	cle	May 16, 1968	10–11	bos	

TIES: TEN OR MORE RUNS, BOTH CLUBS:
(Accomplished in only one game)

DATE	SCORE	OPPONENT	
Sep 12, 1931	13–13	CHI (2)	(10 Inn)

MOST YANKEE RUNS IN AN INNING

On July, 6, 1920, the Yankees scored a then American League record 14 runs in one inning. Playing at Washington, the Bombers pounded the Griffs (so called because of their ex-Yankee manager Clark Griffith) 17–0, scoring 14 times in the fifth frame. Carl Mays, Yankee righthander, tossed a three-hit complete game shutout at the Washington club.

The fourteen runs in the fifth resulted from five errors, three walks, seven hits, one hit batsman and a wild pitch thrown in (no pun intended) for good measure. Details of the big inning in which the Yanks batted around twice: Vick reached first safely on Ellerbee's error. Pipp doubled. Ruth was walked intentionally, the bases now loaded. *Vick* (players that score are italicized for clarity) scored on Meusel's fly to left, for the first out. Bodie singled to left, *Pipp* scoring. Milam, the leftfielder, made a poor throw home, *Ruth* scoring and Bodie went to third. *Bodie* scored when rightfielder Roth dropped a fly hit by Pratt. Ruel doubled and then pitcher Erickson was lifted, Snyder coming in to pitch. Pitcher Carl Mays singled, driving in *Pratt* and *Ruel*. Snyder hit Fewster with a pitch. Snyder uncorked a wild pitch. Snyder issued walks to both Vick and Pipp, *Mays* being forced home. *Fewster* and *Vick* crossed home on Ruth's single. *Pipp* scored on Meusel's single. *Ruth* scored as a result of Harris' (second base) error off the bat of Bodie. Pratt hit a three-run homer scoring *Meusel*, *Bodie*, and, of course, *Pratt*, who hit the homer. Ruel was retired by catcher Picinich. Rice, centerfielder, dropped Mays' fly for an error. Snyder struck out Fewster to finally end the fourteen run inning.

The fourteen run frame remained the A.L. record until tied by Boston in July, 1948 and was surpassed by the same Red Sox on June 18, 1953, when the BoSox tallied an incredible 17 runs against Detroit. The Major League mark of 18 runs in an inning appears safe for awhile, especially since it has been on the books since 1883. Chicago of the National League scored eighteen times against the Detroit club 100 years ago!

The box score of the July 6, 1920 Yankee game follows. Thereafter is a listing of the twenty innings in which the Yanks scored ten or more runs.

THE BOX SCORE

NEW YORK	POS	AB	R	H	PO	A	E
Fewster	ss	5	1	1	1	5	0
Vick	rf	4	3	1	4	0	0
Pipp	1b	4	2	1	11	1	0
Ruth	lf	5	2	2	2	0	0
Meusel	3b	5	2	3	0	0	1
Bodie	cf	4	3	2	1	0	0
Pratt	2b	4	2	2	1	4	0
Lucey	2b	1	0	0	0	1	0
Ruel	c	5	1	1	3	0	0
Hoffman	c	1	0	1	3	0	0
Mays	p	5	1	2	1	1	0
Totals:		43	17	16	27	12	1

WASHINGTON	POS	AB	R	H	PO	A	E
Judge	1b	4	0	0	13	0	0
Milan	lf	4	0	0	4	0	1
Rice	cf	3	0	1	0	0	0
Roth	rf	4	0	1	0	0	1
Harris	2b	4	0	0	4	3	2
Shanks	3b	2	0	1	1	1	0
Ellerbe	ss	3	0	0	1	4	1
Gharrity	c	1	0	0	2	1	0
Picinich	c	2	0	0	2	1	0
Erickson	p	1	0	0	0	1	0
Snyder	p	0	0	0	0	0	0
Courtney	p	2	0	0	0	1	0
Totals:		30	0	3	27	12	6

Score by Innings:

New York . . . . .0 1 1 0 14 0 1 0 0—17
Washington . . . . .0 0 0 0 0 0 0 0 0— 0

Two-base hits-Vick, Meusel, Pipp, Ruel. Home run-Pratt. Stolen base-Rice. Sacrifice hits-Bodie, Meusel, Mays. Double plays-Ellerbe to Harris to Judge; Fewster to Pratt to Pipp. Left on bases-New York, 11; Washington, 5. First base on balls-Off Erickson, 4; Snyder, 2; Courtney, 1; Mays, 1. Hits-Off Erickson, 8 in 4$\frac{1}{3}$ innings; off Snyder, 2 (none retired in fifth); off Courtney, 6 in 4$\frac{2}{3}$ innings. Hit with pitched ball-By Mays (Shanks); by Snyder (Fewster). Struck out-By Erickson, 1; Courtney, 1; Mays, 6. Wild pitch-Snyder. Passed ball-Picinich. Losing pitcher-Erickson.

TEN OR MORE RUNS IN AN INNING (20 TIMES)

DATE	OPP	SCORE	RUNS	INN	DATE	OPP	SCORE	RUNS	INN	
Jul 14, 1904	CLE	21– 3	10	8	Jun 24, 1936	chi	18–11	10	5	
May 3, 1912	cle	15–18	10	9	Aug 28, 1936*	DET	19– 4	11	2	(7 Inn)
May, 8, 1915	BOS	10– 3	10	4	Aug 27, 1939	det	13– 3	10	8	
Jul 6, 1920	was	17– 0	14	5	Aug 29, 1940#	STL	10– 3	10	5	
Sep 28, 1923	bos	24– 4	11	6	Jun 21, 1945	bos	14– 4	13	5	
Jul 28, 1924*	chi	12–10	10	1	May 24, 1949	STL	13– 3	10	5	
Jul 26, 1928#	det	12– 1	11	12	Sep 11, 1949	WAS	20– 5	12	3	
May 27, 1932	chi	12–10	12	8	May 3, 1951	stl	17– 3	11	9	
May 27, 1933	CHI	15–11	12	8	May 10, 1952	BOS	18– 3	11	7	
Jun 3, 1933	PHI	17–11	10	5	Jul 21, 1979	OAK	12– 4	10	5	

10 OR MORE RUNS: AT HOME–10 TIMES
                  AWAY   10 TIMES

*1st game of doubleheader
#2nd game of doubleheader

Following is the box score of the 11-run 12th inning (an American League Record then) by the Yanks at Detroit in 1928.

THE BOX SCORE OF THE 11-RUN 12TH INNING BY THE YANKEES (AN AMERICAN LEAGUE RECORD)
(AT DETROIT: JULY 26, 1928)

NEW YORK POS		AB	H	O	A		DETROIT POS		AB	H	O	A
Combs	cf	5	1	4	0		Warner	3b	3	1	0	2
Meusel	rf	6	4	0	0		Sweeney	1b	1	0	5	0
Ruth	lf	5	1	1	0		McManus	1b,3b	5	1	12	5
Gehrig	1b	4	1	16	0		Gehringer	2b	4	1	4	3
Lazzeri	2b	5	1	2	4		Rice	cf	5	0	3	0
Durocher	2b	0	0	1	0		W ingo	lf	4	2	4	0
Koenig	ss	6	2	3	3		Heilmann	rf	5	0	1	0
Robertson	3b	5	2	2	4		Tavener	ss	4	1	2	5
Bengough	c	3	0	5	0		Woodall	c	5	0	5	0
Grabowski	c	1	1	2	0		Sorrell	p	4	0	0	4
Hoyt	p	6	2	0	7		°Hargarve		1	1	0	0
*Durst		1	0	0	0							
Totals:		47	15	36	18		Totals:		41	7	36	19

*Batted for Bengough in tenth inning.
°Batted for Warner in ninth inning.

New York . . . . .0 0 0   0 0 1   0 0 0   0 0 11—12
Detroit . . . . .0 0 0   0 0 0   0 0 1   0 0 0— 1
Runs-Combs, Meusel (2), Ruth, Gehrig, Lazzeri, Durocher, Koenig, Robertson (2), Grabowski, Hoyt, Hargrove. Error-Tavener. Two-base hits-McManus, Meusel, Robertson, Grabowski, Ruth. Three-base hits-Gehringer, Tavener, Meusel, Lazzeri. Home runs-Meusel, Hargrave. Sacrifices-Ruth, Robertson, Tavener. Double plays-Tavener to Gehringer to McManus; McManus to Tavener to McManus; Sorrell to Tavener to Sweeney. Left on bases-Detroit, 7; New York, 6. First base on balls-off Sorrell, 5; off Hoyt, 2. Struck out-by Sorrell, 4; by Hoyt, 5. Umpires-Van Granflan, Connolly and Campbell.

MOST NEW YORK YANKEE HITS IN ONE GAME

On September 28, 1923, at Boston, the Yankees made their most hits in a game in their history. All total the Bombers made 30 safeties, with Ruth and Schang each getting 5 hits in six at bats. They managed 20 singles, 8 doubles and 2 home runs.

THE BOX SCORE

	NEW YORK POS	AB	R	H	PO	A	E		BOSTON POS	AB	R	H	PO	A	E
Witt	cf	4	3	2	1	0	0	Mitchell	ss	5	0	1	4	3	0
Haines	cf	2	1	0	2	0	0	Picinich	c	5	0	1	7	1	1
McNally	3b	1	1	1	0	0	0	Donahue	rf	4	1	0	1	1	0
Dugan	3b	5	2	3	2	0	0	Burns	1b	4	1	2	5	1	0
Ruth	lf	6	4	5	5	0	0	Reichle	1b	1	0	0	3	0	0
Gehrig	1b	7	3	4	5	1	2	Menosky	lf	4	1	1	2	0	0
Meusel	rf	2	0	0	0	0	0	Collins	cf	4	1	3	3	0	1
Smith	rf	4	2	3	0	0	0	Shanks	3b	4	0	1	1	2	0
Ward	2b	3	2	1	3	1	0	McMillan	2b	4	0	2	1	3	1
Gazella	2b	2	1	1	2	0	0	Ehmke	p	2	0	0	0	0	0
Schang	c	6	2	5	2	1	0	*Harris		1	0	0	0	0	0
Scott	ss	1	0	0	1	1	0	Blethen	p	1	0	0	0	0	0
Johnson	ss	6	2	2	4	1	0								
Jones	p	6	1	3	0	0	0	Totals:		39	4	11	27	11	3
Totals:		55	24	30	27	5	2								

*Batted for Ehmke in sixth inning.

New York . . . . .4 0 1   0 1 11   2 3 2—24
Boston . . . . .0 0 0   3 0 0   0 1 0— 4

Two-base hits-Gehrig(3), Ruth (2), Witt, Smith, Schang, Burns, Menosky, Shanks. Home runs-Ruth, Ward. Stolen bases-Haines, Smith. Sacrifice-Schang. Double play-Schang and Scott. Left on bases-New York, 11; Boston, 9. Bases on balls-off Jones, 1; off Ehmke, 4; off Blethen, 2. Struck out-by Jones, 1; by Ehmke, 6; by Blethen, 1. Hits-off Ehmke, *21 in 6 innings;* off Blethen, 9 in 3. Passed ball-Picinich. Losing pitcher-Ehmke. Umpires-Connolly, Dinneen and Rowland. Time-1:54.

Following is a box score and accompanying narrative of the Yankees' worst defeat in their history at the hands of the Cleveland Indians in 1928. But before that infamous game is presented, a word about the most hits in a game against the Yanks is in order. On September 29, 1928, the Yanks were mauled by the Detroit Tigers, at Detroit, 19–10. The Tigers pounded four Yankee hurlers for 28 hits, five by Charlie Gehringer and four each by McManus, Fothergill and Hargrave. All total, the Tigers made 21 one-base hits, three doubles and two triples and home runs. Detroit hurler Elam Vangilder pitched a complete game to pick up the win allowing 17 Yankee hits in the process. Tom Zachary was the starter and loser for the Yankees.

THE WORST DEFEAT IN YANKEE HISTORY

On July 29, 1928, at Cleveland, the Indians gave the Bombers their worst defeat in their illustrious history. The Tribe blasted the Yanks 24–6, pounding out 27 hits in the process. Former Yankee and then Cleveland manager Roger Peckinpaugh was delighted indeed at the final outcome. Lowly Cleveland finished in 7th place in 1928, thirty games under .500 with a 62–92 (.403) and some 39 games behind the eventual pennant-winning Yankees.

However, on this day, Cleveland played like real champions. Cleveland's third baseman Johnny Hodapp and Luke Sewell, the catcher, both made five hits, the latter going 5 for 6. Indian second baseman Carl Lind led the way with 5 RBI's in addition to making 4 hits in six at bats. Yankee starter George Pipgras could not get anyone out in the first inning and made way for four other Yankee hurlers who would not fare better than Pipgras did. An approximate crowd of 23,000 were on hand to witness the game (uh, that should be massacre) that took 2 hours and twenty-two minutes to complete.

THE BOX SCORE

NEW YORK	POS	AB	R	H	PO	A	E	RBI
Combs	cf	5	1	1	6	0	0	2
Meusel	lf	4	2	2	2	0	0	0
Ruth	rf	4	2	4	2	0	0	2
Gehrig	1b	5	0	0	2	0	0	0
Lazzeri	2b	1	0	1	0	2	2	1
Durocher	2b	3	0	2	1	0	0	1
Koenig	ss	5	0	2	2	1	1	0
Dugan	3b	4	0	1	2	0	0	0
Grabowski	c	4	1	1	7	0	0	0
Pipgras	p	0	0	0	0	0	0	0
Moore	p	1	0	0	0	1	0	0
Thomas	p	0	0	0	0	0	0	0
H. Johnson	p	2	0	0	0	1	0	0
Campbell	p	0	0	0	0	0	0	0
a Durst	ph	1	0	1	0	0	0	0
Total:		39	6	15	24	5	3	6

CLEVELAND	POS	AB	R	H	PO	A	E	RBI
Langford	lf	6	4	3	1	0	0	2
Lind	2b	6	3	4	4	5	0	5
J. Sewell	ss	7	2	3	1	5	0	3
Hodapp	3b	7	4	5	1	4	0	4
Morgan	1b	6	2	2	11	0	0	3
Summa	rf	5	1	2	1	0	1	1
Caldwell	rf	0	0	0	1	0	0	0
Gerken	cf	4	3	2	4	0	0	1
L. Sewell	c	6	3	5	3	0	0	3
Shaute	p	5	2	1	0	0	0	2
Total:		52	24	27	27	14	1	24

a Batted for Campbell in ninth.

```
NewYork . . . . . . . . . . . . . . . . . . . . . . . . . . . . . . 1 0 1   1 0 0   0 0 3— 6
Cleveland . . . . . . . . . . . . . . . . . . . . . . . . . . . . . 8 9 1   0 0 6   0 0 x—24
```

Two-base hits-Hodapp, Dugan, Ruth, Koenig, Combs, Summa, Meusel. Three-base hit-L. Sewell. Stolen bases-Langford, Hodapp. Sacrifices-Summa, Langford, Meusel. Double plays-Hodapp, Lind and Morgan; Hodapp and Morgan. Left on bases-New York: 9, Cleveland: 10. Bases on balls-Off Shaute 2, Pipgras 1, H. Johnson 3. Struck out-By Shaute 2, Moore 2, H. Johnson 2, Campbell 1. Hits-Off Pipgras 5 in no innings (none out in first), Moore 5 in 1 1/3, Thomas 3 in none, H. Johnson 10 in 4 1/3, Campbell 4 in 2 1/3. Losing pitcher— Pipgras. Umpires-Jennings, Nallin, McGowan. Time of game- two hours and twenty-two minutes.

THE WORST DEFEAT IN YANKEE STADIUM HISTORY THE MOST RUNS AGAINST THE YANKEES IN AN INNING AND GREATEST LOSING MARGIN

The above caption briefly summarizes the game played at Yankee Stadium on June 17, 1925, versus the Detroit Tigers. In this game, the Detroiters pounded the Yankees into submission, winning 19–1! Never had a Yankee opponent scored so many runs in "The House That Ruth Built." In 1977, the Blue Jays of Toronto will equal the Tigers' run total of 1925, but the Yankees managed to get three runs, as opposed to one in the 1925 massacre.

In addition to allowing the most runs in Yankee Stadium in its history, two additional club records were set in the Detroit fiasco. In the 6th inning, the Tigers mauled four Yankee hurlers for 13 runs, *eleven tallies crossed the dish plate before one batter could be retired*! The four New York pitchers issued seven walks in the inning, six hits, and Yankee fielders made two errors for good measure. The other club record established was the worst margin of defeat (later in 1928, the Yanks lost at Cleveland by a margin of 18 runs, or 24 [for Cleveland] minus 6 [for New York]), thus matching the 19–1 pounding by the Tigers. Prior to the Detroit game, the Yanks had never lost by more than 15 runs in any game since 1903! Hooks Dauss got the win while Shawkey suffered the humiliating loss.

THE BOX SCORE

DETROIT	POS	AB	R	H	PO	A	E		NEW YORK	POS	AB	R	H	PO	A	E
Haney	3b	4	2	2	0	1	0	Wanninger	ss	3	0	0	1	2	0
O'Rourke	2b	4	1	1	1	3	0	Shanks	3b	4	0	0	1	2	0
Burke	2b	1	1	1	2	0	0	Ruth	rf	4	0	0	6	0	0
Wingo	lf	5	3	3	3	0	0	Combs	cf	4	0	0	2	0	1
Cobb	cf	6	2	3	4	0	0	Meusel	lf	3	0	1	2	0	0
Fothergill	cf	0	0	0	0	0	0	Gehrig	1b	4	1	2	10	0	0
Heilmann	rf	4	1	2	3	0	0	Ward	2b	3	0	0	2	2	2
Manush	rf	2	1	1	2	0	0	Schang	c	3	0	1	3	1	0
Blue	1b	4	2	2	5	0	0	Shawkey	p	0	0	0	0	1	0
Neun	1b	1	0	0	2	0	0	#Witt		1	0	0	0	0	0
Tavener	ss	4	2	0	1	2	0	Ferguson	p	1	0	0	0	0	1
Bassler	c	4	3	1	3	0	0	Beall	p	0	0	0	0	0	0
Stanage	c	1	0	1	1	0	0	H. Johnson	p	0	0	0	0	0	0
Dauss	p	4	1	1	0	1	0	Jones	p	1	0	0	0	2	0
Totals:		44	19	18	27	7	0	Totals:		31	1	4	27	10	4

Batted for Shawkey in third inning

Score by Innings:

```
Detroit . . . . . . . . . . . . . . . . . . . . . . . . . . . . . . . . .0 0 4   0 0 13   0 0 2—19
New York . . . . . . . . . . . . . . . . . . . . . . . . . . . . . . . .0 0 0   0 0 0   1 0 0— 1
```

Two base hits-Wingo, Blue. Three base hits-Dauss, Heilmann, Gehrig. Home run-Cobb, Gehrig, Wingo. Sacrifice-Haney. Double play-Wanninger to Ward to Gehrig. Left on bases-New York, 6; Detroit, 6. Bases on balls-Off Dauss, 3; off Ferguson, 1; off Beall, 3; off H. Johnson, 3. Struck out-By Dauss, 4; by Shawkey, 2. Hits-Off Shawkey, 7 in 3 innings; off Ferguson, 3 in 2 (none out in 6th); off Beall, none (retired no batsmen); off Johnson, 2 (retired no batsmen); off Jones, 6 in 4 innings. Losing pitcher-Shawkey.

SHUTOUTS: VICTORIES AND LOSSES

MOST RUNS, SHUTOUT VICTORY

On August 13, 1939, the Yankees did not allow the home-standing Philadelphia Athletics to score any runs. Unfortunately for Philadelphia, the Bombers scored 21 times in the eight inning affair. The game was called after eight full innings because of Sunday curfew laws in the City of Brotherly Love. The Yanks pounded three Philly pitchers for 23 basehits, including four each by DiMaggio, Dickey and Ruffing, the winning pitcher. Dahlgren and DiMaggio had two homers each. This 21–0 debacle (sounds like an NFL score) set a club record for most runs in a shutout victory. The most runs scored by opponents in a Yankee shutout defeat is 15 on two occasions. On July 17, 1907, the White Sox pummeled the Yankees at Chicago winning 15–0. The Yanks managed 8 hits and the White Sox banged 16 safeties. The second 15–0 loss was duplicated again by the White Sox, this time beating the Bombers before their home crowd on May 4, 1950. This time, the ChiSox made 23 hits off 2 Yankee hurlers. Eddie Lopat picked up the loss while Chicago's Bob "Sugar" Cain tossed a five-hitter at New York.

The box score of the Yanks' 21–0 victory against the Athletics follows. Immediately afterwards, two shutout lists are presented. The first lists all Yankee shutout wins scoring 10 or more runs; the second details games in which Yankee opponents have scored ten or more runs against New York in a single game.

BOX SCORE OF MOST RUNS
IN A YANKEE SHUTOUT VICTORY
(August 13, 1939, at Philadelphia, 2nd game)

NEW YORK	POS	AB	R	H	RBI	PO	A	E	PHILADELPHIA	POS	AB	R	H	RBI	PO	A	E
Crosetti	ss	6	1	1	0	0	2	0	Moses	rf	1	0	1	0	1	0	1
Rolfe	3b	4	2	2	2	2	2	0	Miles	rf	2	0	0	0	2	0	0
Keller	rf	6	1	2	2	2	0	0	Newsome	ss	2	0	0	0	1	3	0
DiMaggio	cf	5	3	4	5	3	0	0	Johnson	lf	1	0	0	0	0	0	0
Dickey	c	6	3	4	0	5	0	0	Tipton	lf	2	0	0	0	1	0	0
Selkirk	lf	2	2	2	2	0	0	0	Brucker	c	3	0	1	0	2	0	0
Henrich	lf	3	2	1	1	4	0	0	Siebert	1b	2	0	1	0	8	0	0
Gordon	2b	5	2	1	2	4	0	0	Chapman	cf	3	0	0	0	3	1	0
Dahlgren	1b	4	4	2	4	4	1	0	Ambler	2b	2	0	0	0	4	1	0
Ruffing	p	6	1	4	3	0	1	0	Collins	2b	1	0	0	0	1	1	1
									Gantenbein	3b	3	0	0	0	1	3	1
Totals:		47	21	23	21	24	6	0	Pippen	p	1	0	0	0	0	0	0
									Potter	p	2	0	0	0	0	2	0
									Total:		25	0	3	0	24	11	3

Score by Innings:

New York . . . . .0 5 5 2 1 5 0 3—21
Philadelphia . . . . .0 0 0 0 0 0 0 0— 0

(Game called at the end of the eighth inning due to Sunday curfew laws)

Two base hits-Dickey, Siebert, Rolfe. Three base hits-Selkirk, Brucker. Home runs-Dahlgren(2), DiMaggio (2). Stolen base-Henrich. Sacrifice hit-DiMaggio. Left on bases-New York, 10; Philadelphia, 4. First base on balls-Off Ruffing, 3; off Pippen, 2; off Potter, 4. Struck out-By Pippen, 2; by Ruffing, 3. Hits-Opp Pippen, 6 in 2 innings; off Potter 17 in 6 innings. Hit by pitched ball-By Potter (Selkirk). Losing pitcher-Pippen. Umpires-Grieve, Quinn and McGowan. Time of game-2:05.

MOST RUNS, NEW YORK YANKEE SHUTOUT WIN
(10 RUNS OR MORE ACCOMPLISHED 73 TIMES)

DATE	SCORE	OPPONENT	DATE	SCORE	OPPONENT
Aug 13, 1939	21–0	phi (2) (8 inn)	Aug 25, 1939	11–0	stl (1)
Jul 10, 1936	18–0	CLE	May 26, 1945	11–0	STL
Apr 24, 1909	17–0	WAS	May 16, 1950	11–0	stl
Jul 6, 1920	17–0	was	Jun 14, 1952	11–0	cle
Sep 17, 1931	17–0	STL (1)	Jun 25, 1954	11–0	cle
Apr 25, 1933	16–0	was	Sep 14, 1954	11–0	det
Apr 30, 1960	16–0	bal	May 30, 1959	11–0	was (2)
Jun 23, 1930	15–0	STL (1)	Jul 27, 1978	11–0	CLE
Jul 5, 1937	15–0	BOS (1)	Sep 9, 1907	10–0	was (1)
Aug 17, 1942	15–0	phi	Sep 17, 1909	10–0	CLE
Aug 4, 1953	15–0	DET	Aug 23, 1920	10–0	DET
Jun 22, 1958	15–0	det	Jun 15, 1923	10–0	STL
Sep 25, 1977	15–0	tor (1)	Sep 9, 1926	10–0	BOS
May 14, 1910	14–0	STL	May 16, 1935	10–0	CLE
Jun 13, 1920	14–0	cle	Jun 11, 1937	10–0	stl
Jun 26, 1920	14–0	BOS	May 30, 1938	10–0	BOS (1)
Sep 21, 1926	14–0	chi	Jun 29, 1938	10–0	PHI
May 24, 1937	14–0	CLE (2)	May 14, 1939	10–0	phi
Sep 4, 1944	14–0	PHI (2)	Jun 28, 1939	10–0	phi (2)
Aug 27, 1938	13–0	CLE (2)	Aug 2, 1942	10–0	stl (2)
Aug 10, 1940	13–0	PHI	Sep 4, 1944	10–0	PHI (1)
May 26, 1945	13–0	CHI	May 31, 1948	10–0	WAS (1)
Sep 8, 1955	13–0	KC	Aug 22, 1948	10–0	phi
Jun 3, 1958	13–0	CHI	Aug 25, 1950	10–0	STL
May 8, 1925	12–0	stl	Jun 27, 1952	10–0	PHI
Aug 4, 1929	12–0	CLE (1)	Jul 29, 1954	10–0	chi
Jul 13, 1933	12–0	STL	Jul 13, 1956	10–0	CLE
Jul 19, 1942	12–0	CHI (2)	Jul 3, 1957	10–0	BOS
May 8, 1949	12–0	det	Jul 12, 1958	10–0	CLE
Jun 23, 1949	12–0	DET	Jun 29, 1960	10–0	KC
Jul 2, 1955	12–0	WAS	Sep 7, 1968	10–0	WAS (2)
Jul 25, 1961	12–0	CHI (2)	Sep 29, 1974	10–0	cle
Jun 6, 1965	12–0	CHI (2)	Apr 17, 1976	10–0	MIN
Sep 29, 1909	11–0	STL (2)	Sep 28, 1977	10–0	CLE
May 6, 1910	11–0	bos	May 18, 1979	10–0	bos
May 18, 1920	11–0	CLE			
May 18, 1930	11–0	bos			
Sep 22, 1937	11–0	STL (2)			

SUMMARY:
MOST RUNS, SHUTOUT WINS:
(Frequency with each club)

CLUB
Cleveland	15
St. Louis	14
Philadelphia	10
Boston	8
Chicago	7
Washington (Orig. Club)	7
Detroit	6
Kansas City Athletics	2
Baltimore	1
Minnesota	1
Toronto	1
Washington (Expansion)	1
TOTAL 10 + runs:	73

None: Kansas City Royals, Los Angeles and California Angels, Milwaukee, Oakland, Seattle Mariners, Seattle Pilots, and Texas

ALL CAPS—YANKEE HOME GAME
(1)—1st game of doubleheader
(2)—2nd game of doubleheader

MOST RUNS ALLOWED,
NEW YORK YANKEE SHUTOUT LOSS:
(ALLOWED 10 OR MORE 30 TIMES)

DATE	SCORE	OPPONENT
Aug 15, 1907	0–15	chi
May 4, 1950	0–15	CHI
May 12, 1967	0–14	BAL
Sep 17, 1982	0–14	mil
Jul 31, 1911	0–13	CHI
Jun 9, 1915	0–13	CHI
Jul 17, 1923	0–13	cle
May 30, 1941	0–13	bos (2)
Sep 26, 1908	0–12	chi
Jul 2, 1943	0–12	cle
Aug 22, 1943	0–12	det (2)
Jun 28, 1952	0–12	PHI
Sep 7, 1928	0–11	WAS (1)
May 15, 1964	0–11	KC
Jul 24, 1970	0–11	oak
Aug 18, 1906	0–10	CHI
May 9, 1910	0–10	bos
May 9, 1911	0–10	det
Oct 7, 1914	0–10	phi
Apr 23, 1919	0–10	BOS
Aug 21, 1921	0–10	stl (2)
Oct 2, 1925	0–10	phi
Apr 21, 1928	0–10	PHI
Aug 22, 1929	0–10	stl
Sep 15, 1929	0–10	CLE (2)
Jul 25, 1944	0–10	cle
Sep 4, 1945	0–10	DET
Jul 30, 1954	0–10	bal
May 17, 1959	0–10	KC (2)
Aug 2, 1973	0–10	bos

SUMMARY: MOST RUNS ALLOWED, SHUTOUT LOSS:

CLUB	
Chicago	6
Boston	4
Cleveland	4
Philadelphia	4
Detroit	3
Baltimore	2
Kansas City Athletics	2
St. Louis	2
Milwaukee	1
Oakland	1
Washington (Orig. Club)	1
TOTAL 10 + Runs:	30

None: Kansas City Royals, Los Angeles and California Angels, Minnesota, Seattle Mariners, Seattle Pilots, Texas, Toronto, and Washington (Expansion).

ALL CAPS—YANKEE HOME GAME
(1)—1st game of doubleheader
(2)—2nd game of doubleheader

1-0 GAMES

THE LONGEST 1–0 WIN
FOR THE YANKEES

On July 4, 1925, the Yankees won their longest 1–0 game in their history. In the first game of a doubleheader against Philadelphia at Yankee Stadium, the two teams battled for 15 long innings before the Yanks broke the scoring drought. With two out in the bottom of the 15th inning, outfielder Bobby Veach scored, giving the Yanks and Herb Pennock the victory. Pennock pitched the entire game for the Bombers.

The box score for this game is presented after this narration. Immediately following the longest 1–0 victory box score is a listing of every 1–0 win by the Yankees from 1903 through 1983. New York has won 158 1–0 contests over the years. The most 1–0 wins were in 1908 and 1968 with six. Twenty different Yankee seasons were played without a 1–0 victory.

THE BOX SCORE OF THE YANKEES' LONGEST 1-0 VICTORY
(AT NEW YORK: JUNE 24, 1925, 1ST GAME)

NEW YORK	POS	AB	R	H	PO	A	E		PHILADELPHIA	POS	AB	R	H	PO	A	E
Dugan	3b	7	0	1	1	5	0		Dykes	2b	6	0	2	7	4	0
Combs	cf	7	0	2	4	0	0		Hale	3b	5	0	0	0	5	0
Ruth	rf	5	0	2	6	0	0		Lamar	lf	5	0	0	0	0	0
***Witt		0	0	0	0	0	0		Simmons	cf	5	0	1	3	0	0
Veach	rf	1	1	1	0	1	0		Miller	rf	5	0	0	3	0	0
Meusel	lf	5	0	2	3	0	0		Perkins	c	5	0	0	12	1	0
Gehrig	1b	5	0	1	18	1	0		Poole	1b	5	0	1	16	1	0
Bengough	c	3	0	1	2	1	0		Galloway	ss	5	0	0	3	6	0
*Paschal		1	0	0	0	0	0		Grove	p	5	0	0	0	5	0
O'Neill	c	3	0	2	4	0	0									
Ward	2b	5	0	1	2	6	0		Total:		46	0	4 x44	22	0
Wanninger	ss	2	0	0	2	2	0									
**Shanks		1	0	0	0	0	0									
E. Johnson	ss	2	0	1	2	0	0									
Pennock	p	5	0	0	1	4	0									
Totals:		52	1	14	45	20	0									

*Batted for Bengough in ninth inning.
** Batted for Wanninger in ninth inning.
***Ran for Ruth in thirteenth inning.
xTwo out when winning run was scored.

```
Philadelphia . . . . . . . . . . . . . . . .0 0 0   0 0 0   0 0 0   0 0 0   0 0 0—0
New York . . . . . . . . . . . . . . . . . .0 0 0   0 0 0   0 0 0   0 0 0   0 0 1—1
```

Two-base hit-Meusel. Three-base hit-Dykes. Stolen base-Ward. Sacrifices- Hale, Gehrig, Pennock, Meusel. Double plays-Grove, Dykes and Poole; Dykes, Galloway and Poole. Left on bases-New York, 15; Philadelphia, 2. Bases on balls-off Grove, 5. Struck out-by Grove, 10; by Pennock, 5. Wild pitch-Grove. Umpires-Moriarity, Owens and McGowan. Time-2:5

ALL-TIME YANKEE 1-0 VICTORIES

DATE	OPPONENT		DATE	OPPONENT	
Jun 16, 1903	CHI		Jun 7, 1918	stl	
Jun 17, 1903	CHI		May 14, 1919	det	
Aug 18, 1903	det (1)		Jul 1, 1919	was	
Sep 8, 1903	BOS		Jul 10, 1919	cle (1)	
May 28, 1904	PHI		Apr 21, 1922	WAS	
Jul 25, 1904	CHI		Jul 7, 1922	CLE	
Aug 23, 1904	CHI		Aug 13, 1924	STL (1)	
Aug 30, 1904	CLE		Jul 3, 1925	PHI	
Oct 10, 1904	BOS (2)	(10 Inn)	Jul 4, 1925	PHI (1)	(15 Inn)
Apr 27, 1905	PHI		Sep 10, 1927	STL	
Aug 23, 1905	stl (2)	(12 Inn)	Jul 7, 1928	STL (2)	
Sep 2, 1905	BOS		Jun 3, 1929	CHI	
Sep 20, 1905	PHI		Sep 15, 1929	CLE (1)	
Jun 4, 1906	stl (7)		May 6, 1932	DET	
Jul 24, 1906	DET		Jun 19, 1932	chi	
Sep 4, 1906	bos (2)		Aug 13, 1932	was	
Sep 23, 1906	chi		May 24, 1934	PHI	
Aug 28, 1907	BOS (2)		Sep 23, 1934	BOS (1)	
Sep 10, 1907	was (1)		May 21, 1938	chi	
Apr 14, 1908	PHI	(12 Inn)	May 26, 1939	PHI	
Apr 27, 1908	BOS		Jun 15, 1939	CLE	
Aug 28, 1908	CHI		Jun 17, 1939	DET	
Sep 12, 1908	bos		Jul 10, 1941	stl	(5 Inn)
Sep 15, 1908	bos		Jul 13, 1941	chi (2)	(11 Inn)
Sep 24, 1908	chi		Sep 9, 1941	STL	
Apr 16, 1909	phi		Sep 26, 1941	was (2)	
Jul 22, 1909	cle		Apr 17, 1942	BOS	
Apr 21, 1910	phi		May 21, 1942	chi	
Aug 13, 1910	chi		Aug 22, 1942	WAS	
Aug 31, 1912	was		Apr 24, 1943	WAS	
Apr 29, 1914	BOS		Jul 4, 1943	det (1)	
Jul 10, 1914	CLE (2)	(6 Inn)	Jul 23, 1943	STL	
Jul 26, 1914	chi (1)		Sep 12, 1943	bos (1)	
Aug 13, 1914	bos		Sep 23, 1943	DET	
Jul 2, 1915	WAS		Jun 29, 1944	STL	
Aug 28, 1915	det (1)		Aug 4, 1944	phi	
Sep 2, 1915	was		Aug 6, 1944	phi (2)	
Jul 3, 1916	was		May 13, 1945	cle	(10 Inn)
Jul 4, 1916	was (1)		Jun 24, 1946	cle	
Jul 22, 1916	STL		Aug 16, 1947	BOS	
May 10, 1917	chi		Jun 2, 1948	DET	
Jun 25, 1917	PHI (1)		Jun 11, 1950	STL (1)	
Sep 3, 1917	bos (1)		Aug 4, 1950	cle	
Sep 11, 1917	phi (1)		May 17, 1951	CLE	
May 16, 1918	STL		Jul 12, 1951	cle	
May 22, 1918	CHI	(14 Inn)	Jul 20, 1951	stl	

111

ALL-TIME YANKEE 1-0 VICTORIES: Continued

DATE	OPPONENT		DATE	OPPONENT	
May 11, 1952	BOS		May 11, 1968	BOS	
Aug 4, 1952	was		May 24, 1968	CHI	(13 Inn)
Aug 23, 1952	CLE		May 25, 1968	CHI	(10 Inn)
Sep 21, 1952	PHI		Aug 1, 1968	bos	
Apr 21, 1953	BOS		Aug 30, 1968	cle (1)	
Aug 8, 1953	CHI (1)		Apr 28, 1969	BOS	
Sep 10, 1953	CHI		May 18, 1969	CAL (2)	
May 17, 1955	CHI		Sep 6, 1969	cle	
May 29, 1955	bal		Sep 27, 1969	BAL	
Jul 26, 1955	CHI		Apr 30, 1970	CAL	
May 14, 1958	BAL		Apr 11, 1971	was (1)	
Apr 22, 1959	was	(14 Inn)	Aug 24, 1971	oak	
Jul 14, 1959	CLE		Sep 17, 1971	CLE (1)	
Sep 13, 1959	CLE (2)		Jun 30, 1972	cle	
Aug 13, 1960	WAS		Jul 8, 1972	min	(11 Inn)
Aug 16, 1960	BAL		Aug 10, 1972	DET	
Aug 31, 1960	KC (1)		Jul 26, 1973	MIL	(12 Inn)
Sep 1, 1961	DET		Jul 25, 1974	MIL	
Oct 1, 1961	BOS		Sep 7, 1974	DET (2)	
Jun 8, 1962	BAL		Sep 25, 1974	BOS	(10 Inn)
Jul 17, 1962	bos		Apr 27, 1976	tex	
Aug 6, 1963	was (2)		May 22, 1976	BOS (11)	
Aug 9, 1963	LA		Jun 25, 1976	MIL	
May 1, 1964	WAS		Aug 2, 1976	DET	
Jun 20, 1964	chi	(11 Inn)	Aug 28, 1977	TEX	
Apr 25, 1965	CAL (2)		Apr 27, 1980	CHI	
Aug 20, 1965	bal		May 19, 1980	det	
Sep 24, 1966	BOS		Jun 7, 1980	sea	
Apr 15, 1967	BOS		May 30, 1981	cle	
Aug 8, 1967	cal		Apr 21, 1982	chi	
Aug 18, 1967	MIN (1)		May 22, 1982	MIN	
Sep 29, 1967	KC(2)		May 21, 1983	oak	
Apr 10, 1968	CAL		Sep 12, 1983	MIL	

THE FOLLOWING SEASONS HAD NO 1-0 VICTORIES:

1911	1931	1954
1913	1933	1956
1920	1935	1957
1921	1936	1975
1923	1937	1978
1926	1940	1979
1930	1949	

THE LONGEST 1–0 LOSS FOR THE YANKEES

On July 25, 1914, the Yankees suffered through their longest 1–0 defeat at the hands of the White Sox. Playing at Chicago, the Yanks went down to defeat in 13 innings. Outfielder Ray Demmitt scored the game's lone run in the bottom of the thirteenth frame with none out. Both pitchers for each club hurled complete games with Joe Benz picking up the White Sox win, and Jack Warhop suffering the disappointing defeat.

The box score for this game follows. Immediately thereafter, a list of every 1–0 Yankee loss is given. Over the years, the Yanks have been defeated 170 times in 1–0 games. The most 1–0 losses suffered in one season was nine (an American League record) in 1914 when the Yanks were shut out by opponents 27 times, a club record. There have been no 1-0 losses in 14 different seasons.

THE BOX SCORE:

	NEW YORK POS	AB	R	H	PO	A	E		CHICAGO POS	AB	R	H	PO	A	E
Boone	2b	4	0	2	3	5	0	Weaver	ss	5	0	0	3	2	1
Hartzell	lf	4	0	2	3	0	0	Blackburne	2b	5	0	0	2	4	0
Peckinpaugh	ss	4	0	0	4	6	0	Demmitt	lf	5	1	0	2	0	0
Cree	cf	5	0	1	1	0	0	Collins	rf	3	0	0	3	0	0
Mullen	1b	4	0	0	16	0	0	Fournier	1b	5	0	2	12	0	0
Cook	rf	5	0	0	1	0	0	Bodie	cf	4	0	0	2	1	1
Nunamaker	c	5	0	1	6	1	1	Schalk	c	4	0	2	13	5	0
Maisel	3b	5	0	1	2	1	0	Alcock	3b	3	0	0	2	2	0
Warhop	p	5	0	0	0	3	1	Benz	p	4	0	0	0	5	1
Totals:		41	0	7	36a	16	2	Total:		38	1	4	39	19	3

aNone out when winning run scored

Score by Innings:

New York . . . . .0 0 0   0 0 0   0 0 0   0 0 0   0 0 0—0
Chicago . . . . .0 0 0   0 0 0   0 0 0   0 0 0   0 0 1—1

Sacrifice hits-Mullen, Collins. Stolen bases-Alcock, Collins. Double plays- Benz to Schalk to Weaver; Boone to Peckinpaugh to Mullen (2); Schalk to Weaver. Left on bases-New York, 6; Chicago, 4. Bases on balls-Off Benz, 3; off Warhop, 1. Hit by pitcher-By Warhop (Collins). Struck out-By Benz, 9; by Warhop, 4. Time-2:17. Umpires-Hildebrand and Chill.

ALL-TIME YANKEE 1–0 LOSSES

DATE	OPPONENT		DATE	OPPONENT	
May 30, 1903	phi (1)	(10 Inn)	May 30, 1916	PHI	
May 30, 1904	PHI (2)		Jun 22, 1916	bos	
Jun 19, 1904	stl (2)		Jul 12, 1916	CLE (1)	
Aug 11, 1904	chi		Sep 30, 1916	bos	(10 Inn)
Oct 8, 1904	bos (2)	(7 Inn)	Apr 28, 1917	PHI	
May 26, 1905	cle	(10 Inn)	May 13, 1917	chi	
Jul 1, 1905	PHI (1)		May 20, 1917	det	
Aug 26, 1905	cle		Jun 18, 1917	STL	
Sep 29, 1905	CLE		Jul 7, 1917	stl	
Sep 30, 1905	CLE (2)	(5 Inn)	Aug 14, 1917	was (1)	
Jun 10, 1906	chi		Apr 23, 1918	bos	
May 16, 1907	det		Jul 11, 1918	CLE	
Jul 12, 1907	det (1)		May 22, 1919	chi	
Aug 19, 1907	stl		Jun 15, 1919	STL	
Sep 20, 1907	DET		Jul 3, 1919	was	
May 29, 1908	PHI (2)		Jul 28, 1920	stl	
Aug 29, 1908	CHI (1)		Aug 8, 1920	det	
Aug 31, 1908	PHI (1)		May 30, 1921	was (1)	
Oct 7, 1908	was (1)	(11 Inn)	Jun 28, 1922	was	
Apr 26, 1909	bos		Sep 29, 1922	bos	
Jun 11, 1909	CHI		May 24, 1923	phi	
Jul 11, 1909	stl (2)		Aug 27, 1924	cle (1)	
Aug 25, 1909	stl	(10 Inn)	May 3, 1925	PHI	
Jul 26, 1910	DET		May 14, 1925	chi	
Aug 9, 1910	stl (1)		Jun 25, 1925	was	
Sep 19, 1910	chi		Aug 26, 1925	chi	
Apr 21, 1911	WAS		Aug 28, 1925	stl	
Oct 5, 1911	phi		Sep 3, 1927	phi	
Apr 15, 1912	WAS		Aug 23, 1931	bos (1)	
Jun 8, 1912	cle		May 30, 1934	WAS (1)	
Sep 2, 1912	BOS (2)		Apr 16, 1935	BOS	
Jun 11, 1913	CHI		May 19, 1935	CLE	(11 Inn)
Sep 5, 1913	was (2)		Apr 14, 1936	was	
May 25, 1914	CHI		Jun 18, 1938	stl	
Jun 8, 1914	chi		Jun 19, 1940	chi	
Jun 29, 1914	was		Jun 20, 1940	chi	(11 Inn)*
Jul 3, 1914	phi (2)		Aug 25, 1940	CHI (1)	
Jul 25, 1914	chi	(13 Inn)	Aug 20, 1941	det	(10 Inn)
Aug 15, 1914	bos		Jun 17, 1942	det	
Aug 17, 1914	WAS (1)		Jun 20, 1942	cle	
Sep 4, 1914	WAS				
Sep 9, 1914	was		*GAME WAS VOIDED, BUT		
Aug 21, 1915	chi (1)	(11 Inn)	COUNTS AS A GAME PLAYED IN		
Sep 8, 1915	WAS		THE STATS		

ALL-TIME YANKEE 1-0 LOSSES: Continued

DATE	OPPONENT		DATE	OPPONENT	
Sep 5, 1942	was (2)		May 23, 1967	bal	
Sep 11, 1942	chi		Jun 17, 1967	chi	
Jul 8, 1943	chi		Aug 19, 1967	MIN	
Jul 21, 1943	STL		Sep 26, 1967	DET	
Sep 29, 1944	stl (2)		May 31, 1968	det	
Jun 19, 1945	bos		Aug 19, 1968	min	
Jul 23, 1945	CHI	(11 Inn)	Aug 29, 1968	chi	
Aug 8, 1945	cle		Aug 24, 1969	min	
Apr 30, 1946	CLE		Sep 24, 1969	bos	(14 Inn)
May 26, 1946	bos (1)		Jul 25, 1970	oak	
Sep 15, 1946	stl (1)		Sep 9, 1970	bal	
Apr 24, 1947	BOS		May 1, 1971	MIL	
Apr 27, 1947	WAS		Jul 15, 1971	MIL	
May 30, 1947	phi (1)		Aug 14, 1971	OAK	
May 6, 1952	CLE		Jun -9, 1972	kc	
Aug 25, 1952	DET		Jun 11, 1972	kc	
Aug 30, 1953	chi (2)		Jul 14, 1972	OAK (2)	
Sep 15, 1953	CLE		Jul 22, 1972	CAL (1)	
Apr 24, 1954	phi		Oct 4, 1972	MIL	
May 31, 1954	WAS (1)		Jul 2, 1973	BOS	
Sep 9, 1954	bal		Jul 4, 1973	BOS (2)	
Apr 24, 1955	BOS		Aug 26, 1973	oak	
May 12, 1956	BAL		Sep 2, 1973	BAL	
Aug 7, 1956	bos	(11 Inn)	Jul 18, 1975	tex	
Sep 26, 1956	bal		Jul 24, 1975	chi (2)	
Aug 20, 1957	kc		Jul 27, 1975	BOS (1)	
Jun 21, 1958	det		Aug 10, 1975	cal	
Sep 7, 1958	WAS (1)		May 25, 1976	MIL	
Sep 20, 1958	bal		May 25, 1977	TEX (2)	
Jul 26, 1959	det		Jun 1, 1978	BAL	
Sep 19, 1961	bal (1)		Apr 25, 1979	oak	
Apr 18, 1962	bal		May 2, 1979	cal	
May 3, 1962	chi		Aug 3, 1979	BAL	
Jun 10, 1963	was (2)		Apr 10, 1980	tex	(12 Inn)
Jun 26, 1964	DET	(11 Inn)	May 10, 1980	MIN	(11 Inn)
Jul 3, 1964	MIN	(10 Inn)	Aug 17, 1980	bal	
Aug 27, 1965	kc		Aug 31, 1980	SEA	
Aug 31, 1965	cal		May 17, 1981	SEA	
Sep 4, 1965	BOS (1)		Aug 11, 1981	TEX	
May 1, 1966	KC (1)		Aug 14, 1981	det	
May 3, 1966	CLE		Sep 25, 1981	BAL	
Aug 19, 1966	KC (2)		Aug 3, 1982	CHI (1)	
Aug 23, 1966	CAL		Aug 15, 1983	CHI	

THE FOLLOWING SEASONS HAD NO
1-0 LOSSES:

1926	1929	1932	1937	1948	1950	1960
1928	1930	1933	1939	1949	1951	1974

THE LONGEST GAMES IN NEW YORK YANKEES HISTORY
(by innings played)

From 1903 through 1983, the Yankees have participated in 32 games of sixteen innings or more. Of these thirty-two extra-inning contests, 15 have been played at New York and the remaining seventeen on the road. At home, the Yanks'record in these games is 8 wins, 5 losses and 2 ties; on the road, their mark is 6 victories, 8 defeats and 3 stalemates. The longest game by far in Yankee history is the 7-hour (an A.L. record) affair at Detroit on June 24,1962,when the Yanks emerged victorious 9–7 after playing 22 full innings. Jack Reed, Yankee rightfielder, clubbed his only Major League homer to win the game in the 22nd frame. Jim Bouton picked up the win for New York while Phil "The Vulture" Regan suffered the setback.

In the listing of these 16-plus inning games, the number of innings is cited first, followed immediately by the inning symbol used in the day by day score section earlier in this book. The date of the game is noted, as is the site of the game (ALL CAPITALS IS A YANKEE HOME GAME and vice versa), the decision (whether won, lost or tied), the final score and whether it was the first (1) or second (2) game of a doubleheader.

THE SCORES OF THE LONGEST GAMES
IN YANKEE HISTORY

INN	SYM	DATE	GAME SITE	DEC	SCORE
22	q	Jun 24, 1962	det	W	9– 7
20	p	Aug 29, 1967	BOS	W	4– 3(2)
19	o	May 24, 1918	CLE	L	2– 3
19	o	Aug 23, 1968	DET	TIE	3– 3(2)
19	o	Aug 25, 1976	MIN	W	5– 4
18	n	Jun 25, 1903	chi	TIE	6– 6
18	n	Sep 5, 1927	bos	L	11–12(1)
18	n	Aug 21, 1933	chi	TIE	3– 3
18	n	Apr 16, 1967	BOS	W	7– 6
18	n	Jul 26, 1967	MIN	L	2– 3(2)
18	n	Apr 22, 1970	was	L	1– 2
17	m	Jul 10, 1917	stl	W	7– 5
17	m	Jul 17, 1919	stl	L	6– 7
17	m	Jul 20, 1941	det	W	12– 6
17	m	Jun 21, 1964	chi	W	2– 1(2)
17	m	Aug 3, 1978	BOS	L	5– 7(1)
17	m	Jun 26, 1982	CLE	W	4– 3
16	L	Jul 5, 1912	was	L	5– 6
16	L	May 19, 1916	DET	TIE	2– 2
16	L	Jul 9, 1921	chi	L	9–10
16	L	Sep 29, 1923	bos	L	2– 3(2)
16	L	Aug 15, 1931	det	W	7– 5
16	L	Jun 1, 1932	phi	L	7– 8(1)
16	L	Jun 7, 1936	CLE	W	5– 4
16	L	Aug 2, 1936	cle	TIE	4– 4
16	L	Sep 9, 1962	BOS	L	4– 5(2)
16	L	Jun 17, 1965	BAL	L	1– 2
16	L	Jun 4, 1966	bos	L	3– 6
16	L	Aug 27, 1972	KC	W	9– 8(2)
16	L	Jul 12, 1975	MIN	W	8– 7####
16	L	May 18, 1976	cle	W	11– 6
16	L	Jun 19, 1982	BAL	W	4– 3

####Suspended at New York after 14 innings with score tied 6–6; game was concluded *Minnesota* prior to regularly scheduled game.

Following is the box score of the longest game in Yankee history, the 22 inning at Detroit in June, 1962.

BOX SCORE OF THE LONGEST GAME
IN YANKEE HISTORY
(AT DETROIT: JUNE 24, 1962)

NEW YORK	POS	AB	R	H	RBI	DETROIT	POS	AB	R	H	RBI
Tresh	ss	9	0	2	0	Boros	3b,2b	10	1	1	0
Richardson	2b	11	2	3	0	Bruton	cf	9	2	2	0
Maris	cf	9	2	2	2	Goldy	rf	10	1	1	3
Mantle	rf	3	1	1	0	Colavito	lf	10	1	7	1
Pepitone	rf	1	0	0	0	Cash	1b	8	1	2	0
*Linz		0	0	0	0	McAuliffe	2b	5	0	1	0
Reed	rf	4	1	1	2	aMorton		1	0	0	0
Blanchard	lf	10	1	1	0	Osborne	3b	1	0	0	0
Berra	c	10	0	3	1	Fernandez	ss	10	1	1	1
Skowron	1b	10	1	2	1	Roarke	c	5	0	2	2
Boyer	3b	9	1	3	3	bWood		0	0	0	0
Turley	p	1	0	0	0	Brown	c	4	0	1	0
Coates	p	0	0	0	0	Lary	p	0	0	0	0
cLopez		1	0	1	0	dMaxwell		1	0	1	0
Stafford	p	0	0	0	0	Casale	p	1	0	0	0
Bridges	p	0	0	0	0	eWertz		1	0	0	0
fHoward		1	0	0	0	Nischwitz	p	0	0	0	0
Clevenger	p	2	0	0	0	Kline	p	1	0	0	0
hCerv		1	0	0	0	Aguirre	p	2	0	0	0
Daley	p	1	0	0	0	Fox	p	2	0	0	0
Bouton	p	2	0	1	0	gMossi		1	0	0	0
						Regan	p	0	0	0	0
Totals:		85	9	20	9	Totals:		82	7	19	7

```
New York ..6 1 0  0 0 0  0 0 0  0 0 0  0 0 0  0 0 0  2—9
Detroit ....3 0 3  0 0 1  0 0 0  0 0 0  0 0 0  0 0 0  0—7
```

Pitcher	IP	H	R	ER	BB	SO
Turley	1/3	1	3	3	3	0
Coates	2²/3	4	3	3	1	6
Stafford	2²/3	4	1	1	1	3
Bridges	1/3	0	0	0	0	0
Clevenger	6¹/3	5	0	0	3	1
Daley	2²/3	2	0	0	0	2
Bouton (W. 2–1)	7	3	0	0	2	6
Lary	2	7	7	7	1	1
Casale	3	1	0	0	2	0
Nischwitz	1²/3	2	0	0	2	0
Kline	1	0	0	0	2	0
Aguirre	5¹/3⁺	2	0	0	1	8
Fox	8	7	0	0	0	1
Regan (L. 4–7)	1	1	2	2	1	2

⁺Pitched to one batter in fourteenth.
d Singled for Lary in second. c Singled for Coates in fourth. e Struck out for Casale in fifth. f Grounded out for Bridges in seventh. b Ran for Roarke in tenth. * Walked intentionally for Pepitone in thirteenth. a Flied out for McAuliffe in fifteenth. h Hit into force play for Daley in sixteenth. g Called out on strikes for Fox in twenty-first. 2B-Richardson, Roarke. 3B- Colavito. HR-Boyer, Reed, Goldy. SB-Tresh, Bruton. SH-Tresh, Fox, Brown. SF-Berra. E-Berra, Boyer, Daley, Tresh, Goldy, Fernandez, McAuliffe. PO-A- New York 66–20, Detroit 66–27. DP-Clevenger and Skowron; Berra and Boyer; Tresh, Richardson and Skowron; Boyer, Richardson and Skowron. LOB-New York 21, Detroit 22. HP-Daley (Goldy). WP-Kline, Fox. U-McKinley, Napp, Umont and Drummond. T-7:00. Attendance-35,638.

ALL-TIME STATISTICS

YANKEE SEASON VICTORIES

In their first 81 seasons in the American League (1903 through 1983), the Yanks had won more games (7,119) than any other A.L. club by far. This is well illustrated when considering that they had won 100+ games in 14 different seasons which is both the American League record as well as the standard for the entire Major Leagues. The Bombers have won 90 or more games in one season some 43 times or about 53% of the club's total eighty-one years since moving from Baltimore in 1903. The most victories were in 1927 (110) and the fewest wins occurred in 1912 when the Yanks won but 50 games. Through 1983, the Yanks have averaged 87.8 wins per season over 81 campaigns. The win mode (the most frequent) has been 98 victories in six different seasons of play.

ALL-TIME WIN LIST
(RANKED IN DESCENDING ORDER):

WINS	YEAR	WINS	YEAR	WINS	YEAR	WINS	YEAR
110	1927	99	1938	96	1962	89	1924
109	1961	99	1953	95	1920	89	1935
107	1932	99	1964	95	1952	89	1974
106	1939	98	1921	94	1922	89	1979
104	1963	98	1923	94	1931	88	1910
103	1942	98	1943	94	1934	88	1929
103	1954	98	1950	94	1948	88	1940
103	1980	98	1951	93	1970	87	1946
102	1936	98	1957	92	1904	86	1930
102	1937	97	1947	92	1958	83	1944
101	1928	97	1949	91	1926	83	1968
101	1941	97	1956	91	1933	83	1975
100	1977	97	1960	91	1983	82	1971
100	1978	97	1976	90	1906	81	1945
(100+ 14 YRS)		96	1955	(90+ 29 YRS)		80	1916

ALL-TIME WIN LIST: Continued

WINS	YEAR	WINS	YEAR	WINS	YEAR	WINS	YEAR
80	1919	77	1965	70	1907	60	1918
80	1969	76	1911	70	1914	(60 + 3 YRS)	
80	1973	74	1909	70	1966	59	1981
(80 + 18 YRS)		72	1903	(70 + 13 YRS)		51	1908
79	1959	72	1967	69	1915	50	1912
79	1972	71	1905	69	1925	(50 + 3 YRS)	
79	1982	71	1917				

VICTORY SUMMARY:

WINS	FREQ	TOT WINS	%
100 +	14	1451	20.38
90 +	29	2768	38.88
80 +	18	1525	21.42
70 +	13	960	13.49
60 +	3	198	2.78
50 +	4	217	3.05
–	81	7119	100.00

THERE HAVE BEEN 40 DIFFERENT WIN TOTALS

YANKEE SEASON LOSSES

From 1903 through 1983, the New York Yankees have lost 5,341 games or an average of 65.9 defeats per season. The most setbacks suffered in one year was 103 way back in 1908. The fewest losses in an entire season was 44 with the great '27 Yankees, "Murderer's Row." The most frequent loss total is 59 on seven separate occasions.

ALL-TIME LOSS LIST
(RANKED IN ASCENDING ORDER):

LOSSES	YEAR	LOSSES	YEAR	LOSSES	YEAR	LOSSES	YEAR
44	1927	57	1947	62	1958	74	1916
45	1939	57	1949	62	1976	75	1959
47	1932	57	1956	62	1977	76	1911
48	1981	57	1960	63	1910	76	1972
(40 + 4 YRS)		57	1963	63	1918	77	1909
		58	1955	63	1924	77	1975
51	1936	59	1904	63	1926	78	1905
51	1942	59	1919	63	1964	78	1907
51	1954	59	1920	63	1978	79	1968
52	1937	59	1931	66	1929	(70 + 14 YRS)	
52	1953	59	1933	66	1940		
53	1928	59	1952	66	1962	80	1971
53	1938	59	1980	67	1946	81	1969
53	1941	(50 + 28 YRS)		68	1930	82	1917
53	1961		69	1970		82	1973
54	1923			(60 + 21 YRS)		83	1915
55	1921	60	1922			83	1982
56	1943	60	1934	71	1944	84	1914
56	1950	60	1935	71	1945	85	1925
56	1951	60	1948	71	1979	85	1965
56	1957	61	1906	71	1983	89	1966
		62	1903			(80 + 10 YRS)	
						90	1967
						94	1913
						(90 + 2 YRS)	
						102	1912
						103	1908
						(100 + 2 YRS)	

LOSS SUMMARY

LOSSES	FREQ	TOTAL LOSSES	%
40 +	4	184	3.45
50 +	28	1558	29.17
60 +	21	1329	24.88
70 +	14	1047	19.60
80 +	10	834	15.61
90 +	2	184	3.45
100 +	2	205	3.84
–	81	5341	100.00

THERE HAVE BEEN 40 DIFFERENT LOSS TOTALS

THE NEW YORK YANKEES' BEST AND WORST SEASONS AT HOME

WINS				LOSSES			
MOST		FEWEST		MOST		FEWEST	
NO.	YEAR	NO.	YEAR	NO.	YEAR	NO.	YEAR
65	1961	27	1913	47	1908	15	1932
62	1932	30	1908	47	1913	16	1961
58	1942	31	1912	46	1966	19	1927
58	1963	32	1907	44	1912	19	1942
57	1927	32	1981B	43	1915	19	1981B
57	1937	35	1917	43	1943	20	1937
56	1936	35	1966	42	1968	21	1936
56	1951	36	1911	41	1907	22	1938
55	1938	36	1914	40	1911	22	1947
55	1947	37	1915	40	1914	22	1951
55	1960	37	1918A	40	1917	22	1960
55	1977	39	1968	39	1982	22	1963
55	1978	40	1905	38	1967	23	1906
54	1943	40	1959	37	1959	23	1933
54	1949	40	1965	37	1971	23	1943
54	1954	41	1903	36	1925	23	1949
53	1906	41	1909	35	1905	23	1954
53	1921	41	1935	35	1909	24	1934
53	1934	42	1925	35	1975	24	1940
53	1950	42	1982	35	1976	24	1950
53	1970						
53	1980						

A Shortened Season—World War I
B Shortened Season—Players' Strike

THE NEW YORK YANKEES' BEST AND WORST SEASONS ON THE ROAD

WINS				LOSSES			
MOST		FEWEST		MOST		FEWEST	
NO.	YEAR	NO.	YEAR	NO.	YEAR	NO.	YEAR
54	1939	19	1912	58	1912	20	1939
53	1927	21	1908	56	1908	24	1923
52	1923	23	1918A	52	1967	25	1927
52	1976	27	1925	51	1973	25	1953
50	1941	27	1981B	49	1925	27	1935
50	1957	29	1967	49	1969	27	1941
50	1980	30	1913	47	1913	27	1957
49	1928	30	1973	45	1972	27	1976
49	1953	31	1903	44	1914	28	1928
49	1954	31	1905	44	1982	28	1954
49	1964	32	1915	43	1905	29	1904
48	1935	32	1969	43	1916	29	1956
48	1956	33	1909	43	1945	29	1958
48	1958	33	1945	43	1966	29	1981B
47	1904	33	1972	43	1971	30	1921
46	1920	34	1914	42	1909	30	1936
46	1936	34	1916	42	1917	31	1920
46	1952	34	1919	42	1940	31	1924
46	1962	35	1966	42	1965	31	1938
46	1963	36	1917	42	1975	31	1952
		36	1940			31	1980
		36	1944				

A Shortened Season—World War I
B Shortened Season—Players' Strike

MOST RUNS SCORED BY AND AGAINST IN ONE MONTH

200 OR MORE RUNS SCORED IN A MONTH: (ACCOMPLISHED 21 TIMES)

DATE	RECORD*	RUNS	+	TOTAL GAMES	=	AVG/GAME
Aug 1938	28- 8-0	275#		36		7.6
Jun 1930	20- 8-0	261		28		9.3
Aug 1939	21-10-0	254		31		8.2
Jul 1931	22- 9-0	248		31		8.0
Jul 1930	17-18-0	241		35		6.9
Aug 1935	20-15-0	233		35		6.7
Jul 1927	24- 7-0	229		31		7.4
Jul 1920	20-14-0	223		34		6.6
Jul 1924	23-14-0	222		37		6.0
Jul 1937	20- 8-1	220		29		7.6
Jun 1933	18-13-0	219		31		7.1
May 1936	20- 8-0	218		28		7.8
Jul 1932	20-14-0	216		34		6.4
May 1939	24- 4-0	213		28		7.6
Jul 1936	18-12-0	207		30		6.9
Jun 1932	20- 8-0	206		28		7.4
Sep 1921	20- 9-0	203		29		7.0
Aug 1937	21- 8-0	203		29		7.0
May 1951	18- 9-0	202		27		7.5
Jul 1958	22-11-1	202		34		5.9
Aug 1948	21-10-0	200		31		6.5

*WON-LOST-TIE RECORD FOR THE MONTH
#AMERICAN LEAGUE RECORD FOR RUNS
IN A MONTH (MAJOR LEAGUE RECORD ALSO)

160 OR MORE RUNS SCORED AGAINST IN A MONTH: (ACCOMPLISHED 21 TIMES)

DATE	RECORD*	RUNS	+	TOTAL GAMES	=	AVG/GAME
Jul 1930	17-18- 0	225X		35		6.4
Jul 1928	20-15- 0	189		35		5.4
Jun 1933	18-13- 0	187		31		6.0
Jul 1925	12-17- 0	184		29		6.3
Jul 1932	20-14- 0	183		34		5.4
May 1941	13-13- 2	180		28		6.4
Aug 1935	20-15- 0	178		35		5.1
Jun 1912	6-21- 0	177		27		6.6
Jul 1908	6-24- 0XX	176		30		5.9
Sep 1930	13-13- 0	174		26		6.7
Aug 1933	13-15- 1	172		29		5.9
Jul 1924	23-14- 0	171		37		4.6
Jul 1911	13-18- 0	169		31		5.5
Sep 1982	12-17- 0	168		29		5.8
Jun 1950	15-17- 0	165		32		5.2
Jul 1952	20-15- 0	165		35		4.7
Jun 1931	13-14- 0	164		27		6.1
Jul 1944	17-15- 0	163		32		5.1
Aug 1931	16-14- 0	162		30		5.4
Jun 1930	20- 8- 0	160		28		5.7
Aug 1951	21-11- 0	160		33		4.8

*WON-LOST-TIE RECORD FOR THE MONTH
X IN ONLY THIS MONTH HAS YANKEE OPPOSITION
SCORED 200 OR MORE RUNS IN THEIR HISTORY
XX WORST MONTH IN YANKEE HISTORY, RECORD-WISE

MOST WINS AND LOSSES IN A MONTH

From 1903 through 1983, the Yankees have *won* 20 or more games in a month 78 times; they have *lost* 20 in a month but 7 times, the last time being in July 1919 when they lost 21 while winning 13!! The previously cited stat really attests to the enormous success of the Yankees over the decades. Only once have the Yankees in their history lost 20-plus games in consecutive months in the same season! This was accomplished in June and July of 1908, the two worst back-to-back months in Yankee history. Their combined record for those two months was a pitiful 12–43, a .218 winning percentage!

On a more positive note, the Yankees have won 20-plus games in three consecutive months on 4 different occasions. They won 20-plus in June, July and August 1932; July, August, and September 1937; June, July and August 1954; and June, July, August and September 1961, the latter accomplishment being a club record. The Maris-Mantle year of 1961 was the only season that the Bombers won 20-plus games in a month 4 times and they did it consecutively. Talk about a consistent performance!!

LOSING 20 OR MORE GAMES IN A MONTH
(ACCOMPLISHED 7 TIMES)

MONTH	RECORD	% WON
Jul 1908	6–24	.200
Sep 1912	4–21	.190
Jun 1912	6–21	.222
Jun 1908	7–21	.250
Jul 1919	13–21B	.382
Jun 1914	6–20T	.231
Aug 1917	7–20	.350

T = One tie this month
B = Last month to lose 20 or more games through 1983!!!!!!!!

WINNING 20 OR MORE GAMES IN A MONTH
(ACCOMPLISHED *78 TIMES* THROUGH '83)

MONTH	RECORD	% WON	MONTH	RECORD	% WON
Aug 1938	#28– 8	.777	Jun 1952	21– 9	.700
Jul 1941	X25– 4	.862	Jun 1957	21– 9	.700
May 1939	24– 4	.857	Jul 1957	21– 9	.700
May 1928	24– 5	.828	Aug 1939	21–10	.677
Jul 1947	24– 6	.800	Aug 1948	21–10	.677
Jul 1927	24– 7	.774	May 1956	21–10	.667
Aug 1932	23– 5	.821	Jul 1943	21–11	.656
Jul 1956	23– 6	.793	Aug 1951	21–12	.636
Jul 1954	23– 7	.767	Jun 1964	21–12	.636
Jul 1923	23– 8	.742	Aug 1941	21–14	.600
Jul 1962	23– 8	.742	Jul 1938	20– 5T	.800
Jul 1924	23–14	.622	Aug 1922	20– 6	.769
Sep 1964	22– 6	.786	May 1950	20– 6	.769
Jul 1929	22– 7	.759	Sep 1927	20– 7	.741
Aug 1977	22– 7	.759	Sep 1960	20– 7	.741
Sep 1978	22– 8	.733	Jun 1919	20– 8	.714
Jul 1931	22– 9	.710	Jun 1930	20– 8	.714
Aug 1961	22– 9	.710	Jun 1932	20– 8	.714
Jul 1963	22– 9	.710	May 1936	20– 8	.714
Jun 1961	22–10	.688	Jul 1937	20– 8T	.714
Aug 1963	22–10	.688	Sep 1921	20– 9	.690
Aug 1943	22–11	.667	Jul 1961	20– 9	.690
Jul 1958	22–11T	.667	Jun 1975	20– 9	.690
Aug 1960	22–11	.667	Aug 1940	20–10	.667
May 1923	21– 6	.777	Aug 1953	20–10	.667
Jun 1927	21– 6	.777	Jun 1954	20–10	.667
Sep 1931	21– 6T	.777	Sep 1906D	20–11	.645
May 1942	21– 6	.777	Aug 1950	20–11	.645
Jun 1939	21– 7	.750	Jun 1955	20–11	.645
Aug 1954	21– 7	.750	Aug 1934	20–12	.625
May 1955	21– 7	.750	Sep 1940	20–12	.625
Sep 1980	21– 7	.750	Jul 1953	20–12	.625
Jun 1920	21– 8	.724	Jul 1914	20–13TT	.606
Aug 1936	21– 8T	.724	Jul 1920	20–14	.588
Aug 1937	21– 8	.724	Jul 1932	20–14	.588
Jun 1960	21– 8T	.724	Sep 1937	20–14	.588
Sep 1961	21– 8	.724	Jul 1928	20–15	.571
Jul 1942	21– 9	.700	Aug 1935	20–15	.571
Jun 1947	21– 9	.700	Jul 1952	20–15	.571

T = One tie this month also
# = Major League record for most wins in a month
X = American League record for percentage of games won in a month

T = One tie this month
TT = two ties this month
D = First month in history to win 20–plus games

ALL-TIME SEASON SERIES BY CLUB AND DECADES
(1903 THROUGH 1983)

DECADE:	BALT	BOST	CAL	CHIC	CLEV	DET	KC A's	KC R's
	W L T	W L T	W L T	W L T	W L T	W L T	W L T	W L T
1903-09	xx	2- 5-0	x	1- 6-0	3- 4-0	1- 5-1	xx	xx
1910-19	xx	3- 5-2	x	2- 8-0	3- 7-0	2- 7- 1	xx	xx
1920-29	xx	9- 1-0	x	8- 2-0	7- 2-1	7- 2-1	xx	xx
1930-39	xx	8- 1-1	x	10- 0-0	8- 1-0	8- 1-1	xx	xx
1940-49	xx	6- 3-1	x	9- 0-1	9- 1-0	4- 4-2	xx	xx
1950-59	5- 1- 0	8- 1-1	x	8- 1-1	6- 1-3	6- 3-1	5- 0-0	xx
1960-69	2- 7-1	5- 3-2	3- 1-1	8- 1-1	4- 5-1	5- 5-0	8- 0-0	1- 0-0
1970-79	3- 6-1	4- 5-1	5- 2-3	7- 2-1	9- 0-1	6- 4-0	xx	4- 4-2
1980-83	1- 3-0	1- 2-1	2- 1-1	2- 2-0	3- 1-0	3- 1-0	xx	3- 1-1
GR. TOT:	11-17-2	46-26-9	10- 4-5	55-22-4	52-22-7	42-32-7	13- 0-0	8- 5- 3

DECADE:	LA	MILW	MINN	OAK	PHIL	STL	SEA M's	SEA P's
	W L T	W L T	W L T	W L T	W L T	W L T	W L T	W L T
1903-09	xx	xx	xx	x	4- 3-0	5- 2-0	xx	xx
1910-19	xx	xx	xx	x	5- 5-0	6- 3-1	xx	xx
1920-29	xx	xx	xx	x	7- 3-0	9- 0-1	xx	xx
1930-39	xx	xx	xx	x	8- 1-1	10- 0- 0	xx	xx
1940-49	xx	xx	xx	x	10- 0-0	8- 2-0	xx	xx
1950-59	xx	xx	xx	x	5- 0- 0	4- 0-0	xx	xx
1960-69	4- 0-0	xx	5- 4-0	1- 0-1	xx	xxx	xx	1- 0-0
1970-79	xx	3- 4-3	7- 2-1	4- 3-3	xx	xxx	2- 0-1	xx
1980-83	xx	2- 1-1	3- 0-1	4- 0- 0	xx	xxx	2- 1-1	xx
GR TOT:	4- 0-0	5- 5-4	15- 6-2	9- 3-4	39-12-1	42- 7-2	4- 1-2	1- 0-0

DECADE:	TEX	TOR	(OLD) WAS	(NEW) WAS	GRAND TOTAL ALL-TIME VS. 20 CLUBS: WON	LOST	TIED	TOTAL	TOTAL % WON
1903–1909	x	x	6– 1–0	x	22	26	1	49	.4583
1910–19	x	x	4– 6– 0	x	25	41	4	70	.3788
1920–29	x	x	7– 2–1	x	54	12	4	70	.8182
1930–39	x	x	7– 2–1	x	59	6	5	70	.9077
1940–49	x	x	9– 0– 1	x	55	10	5	70	.8462
1950–59	x	x	10– 0–0	x	57	7	6	70	.8906
1960–69	x	x	1– 0–0	8– 1– 0	56	27	7	90	.6747
1970–79	8– 0–0	3– 0–0	xxx	1– 1– 0	66	33	17	116	.6667
1980–83	4– 0–0	2– 2– 0	xxx	x	31	15	6	52	.6739
GR. TOT:	12– 0–0 W L T	5– 2–0 W L T	44–11–3 W L T	9– 2– 0 W L T	425	177 (602)	55	657	.7060

Roger Maris and Mickey Mantle pose for photographers in Florida during spring training. In 1961, the M & M boys combined for a Major League record 115 homers, Roger getting 61 and "The Mick" poling 54 4-baggers. The Bronx Bombers won 20-plus games in a month 4 times in 1961.

ALL-TIME YANKEE WON-LOST RECORDS BY MONTH FOR HOME AND AWAY GAMES

MONTH	HOME			AWAY					
	WON	LOST	%WON	WON	LOST	%WON	WON	LOST	%WON
April	327	214	.6044	273	260	.5122	600	474	.5587
May	662	376	.6378	567	506	.5284	1229	882	.5822
June	654	417	.6106	604	531	.5322	1258	948	.5703
July	742	466	.6142	622	549	.5312	1364	1015	.5734
August	727	449	.6182	602	595	.5029	1329	1044	.5601
September	673	439	.6052	584	473	.5525	1257	912	.5795
October	56	32	.6364	26	34	.4333	82	66	.5541
GR. TOT.	3841	2393	.6161	3278	2948	.5265	7119	5341	.5713

YANKEE RECORDS BY DECADES

DECADE	(W) WON	(L) LOST	(W+L) TOTAL	% WON	SCH TIES	UNPL GAMES*	% GAMES^bb	SCH^cc
03– 09	520	518	1038	.5010	20	1064	26	97.56
10– 19	701	780	1481	.4733	23	1526	45	97.05
20– 29	933	602	1535	.6078	5	1540	5	99.68
30– 39	970	554	1524	.6365	15	1540	16	98.96
40– 49	929	609	1538	.6040	5	1540	2	99.87
50– 59	955	582	1537	.6213	4	1540	3	99.80
60– 69	887	720	1607	.5520	9	1540	5	99.67
70– 79	892	715	1607	.5551	1	1612	14	99.14
80– 83	332	261	593	.5599	0	1621	55%%	91.51
81 YRS.	7119	5341	12460##	.5713	82	12631	171	98.65

##DOES NOT INCLUDE 3 GAMES PROTESTED AND REPLAYED
*TOTAL GAMES SCHEDULED DURING THIS PERIOD
AA-INCLUDES ONE PLAYOFF GAME AT BOSTON IN 1978
bb-TOTAL UNPLAYED GAMES DURING THIS PERIOD
cc-PERCENTAGE OF SCHEDULED GAMES THAT WERE PLAYED
%%-ALL 55 GAMES UNPLAYED WERE IN 1981 AS A RESULT OF PLAYERS' STRIKE

TOTAL SCHEDULED GAMES

GAMES		YRS		TOTAL
*140	@	2	=	280
154	@	56	=	8624
162	@	22	=	3564
**163	@	1	=	163
		81		12631

*140 (scheduled in 1903, 1919)
**163 (scheduled in 1978)

TIE GAMES

Through the years, the Yankees have played in 82 tie games. (They actually played one additional tie game in 1906 but it went into the record books as a forfeited 9-0 game instead of a 3-3 tie.) The most tie games played in one season were five each in 1910 and 1938. The Yankees and the Boston Red Sox rivalry, the greatest in sports, has yielded the most ties over the years with 13. The first official tie game for the Yanks *at home* did not come until 1907, the fourteen previous standoffs being all away from home.

Through 1983, the most recent Yankee tie was played on May 11, 1970, at Milwaukee, the score being knotted at 5-5 after nine innings. The highest total of runs in a New York game was a wild 13-13 affair September 12, 1931, versus Chicago at Yankee Stadium. This slugfest went ten innings before being called off. There was no other double-digit run total in a tie game in Yankee history. The longest contest ending in a deadlock occured on August 23, 1968 versus Detroit at Yankee Stadium. This game was halted after 19 innings had transpired with the score tied at 3-3. Of the 81 years of Yankee history beginning in 1903, 37 seasons had no tie games at all. These no-tie seasons are cited immediately after the all-time tie list. Of the 82 tie contests, 32 were played at New York while the remaining 50 were played in the opponent's ball-yard. The most common tie score was 2-2, happening 15 times, followed by 1-1, fourteen times. There have been only four scoreless (0-0) ties in New York Yankee history, the last being played in May 1919. Twenty-eight of the 82 ties occurred in the second game of a doubleheader. Since they played without lights in the A.L. prior to 1939, many games had to be called due to darkness. In addition, the most common mode of travel in the early years was by train, and so many contests were ended in a tie so one of the clubs could catch a train. There were no transcontinental flights back then and the furthest "west" the Yankees had to travel was St. Louis, Chicago and Detroit.

The all-time Yankee tie list that follows cites the date of the game, the site of the game (ALL CAPITALS IS A HOME GAME and vice versa), the score and the number of innings played, which is noted to the right of the score. As with the day by day scores presented earlier in this book, the Yankee score is always listed first. The standard club and month abbreviations are used and a (2) represents the tie was the second game of a doubleheader. This is found (if applicable) to the right of the innings column. Fractional innings are not noted and the list is in chronological order, beginning with 1903.

THE ALL-TIME YANKEE TIE LIST:

DATE	OPP	SCORE	INN	DATE	OPP	SCORE	INN
Jun 25, 1903	chi	6–6	18	May 11, 1919	WAS	0– 0	12
Sep 1, 1903	phi	1–1	9 (2)	May 12, 1919	WAS	4– 4	15
Aug 13, 1904	chi	3–3	5	Jun 21, 1924	cle	3– 3	5 (2)
Sep 14, 1904	bos	1–1	5 (2)	May 9, 1925	stl	1– 1	7
Sep 15, 1904	bos	1–1	9 (2)	Sep 27, 1925	DET	1– 1	5 (2)
Sep 23, 1904	cle	1–1	9	Jul 4, 1926	was	4– 4	6
May 13, 1905	chi	0–0	11	Apr 14, 1927	PHI	9– 9	10
Jul 8, 1905	was	5–5	14 (2)	Apr 28, 1931	was	7– 7	14
Sep 9, 1905	phi	7–7	9 (2)	Sep 12, 1931	CHI	13–13	10 (2)
Apr 18, 1906	bos	3–3	11	Sep 8, 1932	det	7– 7	7 (2)
Aug 13, 1906	chi	0–0	9	Aug 21, 1933	chi	3– 3	18
Sep 3, 1906	PHI	3–3	9 (2)#	Sep 9, 1933	STL	6– 6	9
#FORFEIT COUNTS AS A 9 to 0 WIN				Aug 2, 1936	cle	4– 4	16
Sep 20, 1906	stl	5–5	8	Sep 5, 1936	bos	7– 7	12 (2)
Sep 27, 1906	cle	2–2	6 (2)	June 13, 1937	stl	8– 8	11
Apr 13, 1907	was	4–4	10	Jul 11, 1937	WAS	5– 5	9
Aug 10, 1907	STL	6–6	9 (2)	May 14, 1938	PHI	1– 1	5
Sep 5, 1907	phi	2–2	9 (2)	Jun 19, 1938	stl	7– 7	8 (2)
Oct 5, 1907	BOS	3–3	10 (2)	Jul 4, 1938	was	4– 4	13 (2)
Jun 24, 1908	phi	6–6	9	Sep 25, 1938	BOS	2– 2	6 (2)
May 27, 1909	chi	2–2	10 (2)	Sep 29, 1938	phi	1– 1	5 (2)
Sep 30, 1909	STL	4–4	9	Sep 3, 1939	bos	5– 5	7 (2)
Apr 14, 1910	BOS	4–4	14	May 23, 1941	BOS	9– 9	9
Apr 23, 1910	was	0–0	6	May 29, 1941	was	2– 2	5
May 24, 1910	CHI	5–5	12	Jun 25, 1943	bos	2– 2	11
Jun 28, 1910	stl	4–4	7	May 4, 1947	det	2– 2	6
Aug 27, 1910	CHI	6–6	8 (2)	Aug 7, 1949	STL	2– 2	10 (2)
Sep 19, 1911	CLE	3–3	9	Jul 4, 1950	was	3– 3	9 (2)
Aug 26, 1912	CLE	8–8	9	May 9, 1954	PHI	1– 1	9 (2)
May 14, 1913	cle	2–2	15	Jul 5, 1958	BOS	3– 3	10
May 24, 1913	BOS	3–3	10	Jul 29, 1959	chi	4– 4	6
Jun 6, 1914	chi	1–1	8	Jun 15, 1960	kc	7– 7	12
Jul 9, 1914	CLE	3–3	10 (2)	Apr 22, 1961	bal	5– 5	7 (2)
Jul 23, 1914	DET	1–1	9	May 13, 1964	det	1– 1	6
Aug 7, 1915	STL	4–4	10	Jul 12, 1964	cle	2– 2	7
Aug 9, 1915	CLE	1–1	6	May 28, 1966	CHI	2– 2	5
May 19, 1916	DET	2–2	16	Jul 25, 1967	MIN	1– 1	9
Oct 3, 1916	WAS	9–9	11	May 15, 1968	cle	2– 2	8
May 19, 1917	det	9–9	11	Aug 23, 1968	DET	3– 3	19 (2)
Jul 2, 1917	bos	4–4	11	May 31, 1969	kc	2– 2	7
Jun 17, 1918	det	5–5	8	May 11, 1970	mil	5– 5	9
Jul 22, 1918	STL	4–4	15				
Jul 28, 1918	cle	2–2	10	TIES AT HOME:			32
				TIES ON ROAD:			50
				TOTAL TIES:			82

NO TIE GAMES WERE PLAYED IN THE FOLLOWING YEARS: (37 years)

1920	1929	1942	1951	1957	1972	1977	1982
1921	1930	1944	1952	1962	1973	1978	1983
1922	1934	1945	1953	1963	1974	1979	
1923	1935	1946	1955	1965	1975	1980	
1928	1940	1948	1956	1971	1976	1981	

NO-HITTERS BY AND AGAINST THE YANKEES

NO-HITTERS BY YANKEE PITCHERS

From 1903 through 1983, Yankee pitchers have tossed eight no-hitters against American League opposition. One pitcher, Tom Hughes, hurled hitless ball for 9$\frac{1}{3}$ innings, only to lose the game in the 11th inning. No other Yankee pitcher has gone more than nine full innings without yielding a hit. The Cleveland Indians and the Boston Red Sox were both involved in five New York no-hitters. Yankee moundsmen have no-hit Cleveland thrice while the Indians have tossed two hitless jobs at the New Yorkers. The Boston Red Sox figure prominently as well in Yankee no-hit history with Cy Young of Boston pitching the first hitless gem against the Yankees way back in 1908. The most recent no-hitter also involved the BoSox. On July 4, 1983, lefthander Dave Righetti held the Bostons hitless in the Yankee 4–0 victory. Righetti's performance was the first by a southpaw since George Mogridge (the only other Yankee lefty to hurl a no-hitter) held (you guessed it) the Red Sox in check with nary a hit.

Of course, the most famous no-hitter in New York Yankee history has to be Don Larsen's *perfect* World Series game in the 1956 Fall Classic. Larsen required 97 pitches to retire all 27 Brooklyn batters that he faced on that October afternoon before 64,519 Yankee Stadium rooters. Only in the first inning did Larsen go to a full count (three balls and two strikes) to any one batter, Pee Wee Reese.

The best season performance was turned in by Allie Reynolds. In 1951, he became the only Yankee hurler to fire two no-hitters in the same season. Allie's first was in a night game at Cleveland, July 12; his second helped the Yankee pennant cause, tossing the latter no-hitter on September 28 in the first game versus Boston. They won their 18th pennant by winning the nightcap as well.

THE BOX SCORES OF THE EIGHT YANKEE NO-HITTERS FOLLOW:

BOX SCORE OF TOM HUGHES' 9-INNING NO-HITTER
(AT NEW YORK; AUGUST 30, 1910—HUGHES LOST
THE GAME IN THE 11TH INNING, 0–5)

CLEVELAND	POS	AB	H	O	A	E		NEW YORK	POS	AB	H	O	A	E
Turner	3b	4	0	0	3	0		Daniels	lf	5	1	3	0	0
Thomason	rf	5	1	2	0	0		Wolter	rf	4	0	2	0	0
Niles	lf	5	2	2	0	0		Chase	1b	4	0	13	1	0
Lajoie	2b	5	2	3	2	0		Knight	ss	3	1	1	8	0
Stovall	1b	5	1	13	1	0		Laporte	2b	3	0	1	2	0
Birmingham	cf	4	0	4	0	0		Cree	cf	4	1	3	0	0
Ball	ss	4	0	2	0	0		Austin	3b	2	0	2	4	1
Land	c	4	0	6	2	0		Criger	c	4	0	8	0	0
Kaler	p	4	1	1	5	0		##Hughes	p	3	0	0	2	0
								*Roach	p	1	0	0	0	0
Totals:		40	7	33	13	0		Totals:		33	3	33	17	1

##Pitched 9⅓ innings no-hit ball

```
Cleveland..........................0 0 0   0 0 0   0 0 0   0 5 —5
New York...........................0 0 0   0 0 0   0 0 0   0 0 —0
```

Runs-Turner, Thomason, Niles, Lajoie, and Kaler. Sacrifice hits-Austin and Laporte. Stolen base-Lajoie. Left on bases-Cleveland, 3; New York, 4. First base on error-Cleveland, 1. Base on balls-off Kaler, 2; off Hughes, 1. Struck out-by Kaler, 6; by Hughes, 7. Umpires-Messrs. Egan and O'Laughlin. Time of game-1 hour and 58 mins.

THE BOX SCORE OF
GEORGE MOGRIDGE'S NO-HITTER
(AT BOSTON: APRIL 24, 1917)

NEW YORK	POS	AB	H	O	A	E		BOSTON	POS	AB	H	O	A	E
Gilhooley	rf	4	1	1	0	0		Hooper	rf	4	0	3	0	0
High	lf	3	0	2	0	0		Barry	2b	3	0	0	1	0
Miller	lf	1	0	0	0	0		Gainer	1b	4	0	10	0	0
Maisel	2b	3	1	5	7	1		Lewis	lf	3	0	1	0	1
Pipp	1b	2	0	12	2	0		Walker	cf	2	0	2	2	0
Aragon	3b	4	1	1	4	0		Gardner	3b	1	0	1	2	1
Magee	cf	4	2	1	0	0		McNally	3b	1	0	1	2	1
Peckinpaugh	ss	3	2	2	4	2		Scott	ss	3	0	0	0	0
Nunamaker	c	4	1	3	1	0		Cady	c	3	0	9	0	1
Mogridge	p	3	0	0	1	0		Leonard	p	3	0	0	3	0
*Bauman		1	0	0	0	0		°Walsh		0	0	0	0	0
Totals:		32	8	27	19	3		Totals:		27	0	27	10	4

*Batted for High in seventh inning.
°Batted for Gardner in seventh inning.

```
New York .............................0 0 0   0 0 1   0 0 1—2
Boston...............................0 0 0   0 0 0   1 0 0 —1
```

Runs-Aragon, Peckinpaugh and Barry. Errors-Maisel, Peckinpaugh (2), Lewis, Gardner, McNally and Cady. Two-base hit-Aragon. Stolen bases-Maisel and Peckinpaugh. Sacrifice hits-Peckinpaugh, Mogridge, Pipp, Walker and Lewis. Sacrifice fly-Walsh. Left on bases-New York, 9; Boston, 4. First base on errors-New York, 2; Boston, 2. First base on balls-off Mogridge, 3; off Leonard, 3. Struck out-by Mogridge, 3; by Leonard, 6. Umpires-Messrs. Connolly and McCormick. Time of game-2 hours and 1 minute.

THE BOX SCORE OF SAM JONES' NO-HITTER
(AT PHILADELPHIA: SEPTEMBER 4, 1923)

NEW YORK	POS	AB	H	O	A	E		PHILADELPHIA	POS	AB	H	O	A	E
Witt	cf	4	1	6	0	0		Matthews	cf	4	0	4	0	0
Dugan	3b	4	1	2	5	0		Galloway	ss	3	0	1	1	0
Ruth	lf	4	1	2	0	0		Hale	3b	3	0	0	4	0
Pipp	1b	4	0	13	0	0		Hauser	1b	3	0	10	0	0
Meusel	rf	4	2	1	0	0		Miller	lf	3	0	5	0	0
Ward	2b	4	0	1	0	0		Welch	rf	3	0	3	1	0
Hofmann	c	3	1	2	0	0		Dykes	2b	3	0	2	4	1
Scott	ss	4	1	0	8	1		Perkins	c	3	0	2	0	0
Jones	p	3	0	0	0	0		Hasty	p	2	0	0	1	0
								*McGowan		1	0	0	0	0
Totals:		34	7	27	13	1		Totals:		28	0	27	11	1

*Batted for Hasty in ninth.

New York . . . . .0 0 2 0 0 0 0 0 0—2
Philadelphia . . . . .0 0 0 0 0 0 0 0 0—0

Runs-Hofmann, Scott. Errors-Scott, Dykes. Two-base hit-Meusel. Double play-Welch to Perkins. Left on bases-Philadelphia, 2. Bases on balls-off Jones, 1; off Hasty, 1. Struck out-by Hasty, 1. Umpires-Dinneen, Ormsby, Moriarity.

BOX SCORE OF MONTE PEARSON'S NO-HITTER
(AT NEW YORK: AUGUST 27, 1938, 2ND GAME)

CLEVELAND	POS	AB	H	O	A		NEW YORK	POS	AB	H	O	A
Lary	ss	2	0	3	3		Crosetti	ss	4	0	1	2
*Pytlak		1	0	0	0		Rolfe	3b	5	2	2	0
Campbell	rf	3	0	2	0		Henrich	rf	5	3	1	0
Heath	lf	3	0	3	0		DiMaggio	cf	5	1	0	0
Averill	cf	2	0	1	0		Gehrig	1b	4	2	6	1
Weatherly	cf	1	0	0	0		Selkirk	lf	5	2	4	0
Trosky	1b	3	0	6	0		Gordon	2b	4	3	1	5
Hemsley	c	3	0	8	0		Glenn	c	4	0	9	0
Keltner	3b	3	0	0	3		Pearson	p	3	0	3	0
Hale	2b	3	0	1	0							
Humphries	p	1	0	0	0							
Galehouse	p	1	0	0	0		Totals:		39	13	27	8
°Solters		1	0	0	0							
Totals:		27	0	24	6							

*Batted for Galehouse in ninth.
°Batted for Lary in ninth.

Cleveland . . . . .0 0 0 0 0 0 0 0 0— 0
New York . . . . .5 0 2 3 0 2 1 0 x—13

Runs-Crosetti, Rolfe (2); Henrich (2); DiMaggio (2); Gehrig (3); Selkirk, Gordon (2). Errors-Lary (2). Runs batted in-Henrich (4), Gordon (6), Selkirk (2), Glenn. Three-base hit-Gordon. Home runs-Henrich (2), Gordon (2). Left on bases-New York, 6; Cleveland, 2. First base on balls-off Humphries, 3; off Pearson, 2; off Galehouse, 1. Struck out-by Humphries, 3; by Pearson, 7; by Galehouse, 5. Hits-off Humphries, 9 in 4 innings; off Galehouse, 4 in 4 innings. Losing pitcher-Humphries. Umpires-Kolls, Hubbard and Rue. Time of game-1 hour and 58 minutes.

THE BOX SCORE OF ALLIE REYNOLD'S
FIRST OF TWO 1951 NO-HITTERS
(AT CLEVELAND: JULY 12, 1951)

NEW YORK						CLEVELAND				
	POS	AB	H	O	A		POS	AB	H	O	A
Mantle	rf	3	1	0	0	Mitchell	lf	4	0	0	0
Rizzuto	ss	4	0	0	4	Avila	2b	4	0	3	4
Collins	1b	4	0	9	1	Doby	cf	1	0	0	0
Berra	c	4	1	4	1	Chapman	cf	1	0	1	0
Woodling	cf	4	1	2	0	Easter	1b	2	0	12	0
Bauer	lf	3	0	7	0	Rosen	3b	3	0	1	1
McDougald	3b	3	1	1	2	Simpson	rf	2	0	3	0
Coleman	2b	3	0	4	5	Boone	ss	3	0	1	1
Reynolds	p	2	0	0	0	Hegan	c	3	0	6	0
						Feller	p	2	0	0	1
Totals:		30	4	27	13	*Lemon		1	0	0	0
						Totals:		26	0	27	7

*Struck out for Feller in ninth.

New York . . . . .0 0 0   0 0 0   1 0 0—1
Cleveland . . . . .0 0 0   0 0 0   0 0 0—0

RunWoodling. Error-Rizzuto. Run batted in-Woodling. Two base hit-Mantle. Home run-Woodling. Double plays-Rizzuto to Coleman to Collins, Berra to Coleman to Collins, Boone to Avila to Easter. Left on bases-New York, 5; Cleveland, 2. Base on balls-Reynolds, 3; Feller, 3. Strikeouts-Reynolds, 4; Feller, 3. Winner-Reynolds (10–5). Loser-Feller (12–3). Umpires-McGowan, McKinley, Hurley, Honochick. Time-2:12. Attendance-39, 195.

THE BOX SCORE OF ALLIE REYNOLD'S
SECOND OF TWO 1951 NO-HITTERS
(AT NEW YORK: SEPTEMBER 28, 1951, 1ST GAME)

BOSTON								NEW YORK							
	POS	AB	R	H	RBI	O	A	E		POS	AB	R	H	RBI	O	A	E
DiMaggio	cf	2	0	0	0	2	0	1	Rizzuto	ss	5	1	1	0	1	2	0
Pesky	2b	4	0	0	0	1	2	0	Coleman	2b	3	2	1	1	2	3	0
Williams	lf	3	0	0	0	3	0	0	Bauer	rf	4	0	1	1	5	0	0
Vellmer	rf	2	0	0	0	0	0	1	DiMaggio	cf	4	0	1	0	0	0	0
Goodman	1b	3	0	0	0	12	0	0	McDougald	3b	3	1	1	1	0	1	0
Boudreau	ss	3	0	0	0	0	1	0	Berra	c	4	0	1	1	9	1	1
Hatfield	3b	3	0	0	0	3	2	1	Woodling	lf	4	2	2	1	2	0	0
Robinson	c	3	0	0	0	3	0	0	Collins	1b	4	2	2	2	8	0	0
Parnell	p	1	0	0	0	0	2	0	Reynolds	p	3	0	0	0	0	1	0
Scarborough	p	1	0	0	0	0	1	0									
Taylor	p	0	0	0	0	0	2	0	Totals:		34	8	10	7	27	8	1
*Maxwell		1	0	0	0	0	0	0									
Totals:		26	0	0	0	24	10	3									

*Grounded out for Taylor in ninth.

Boston . . . . .0 0 0   0 0 0   0 0 0—0
New York . . . . .2 0 2   1 0 2   0 1 x—8

Two-base Hit-Collins. Home Runs-Collins, Woodling. Stolen base-Coleman. Sacrifice-Reynolds. Double Plays-Hatfield to Goodman, Rizzuto to Collins. Left on bases-Boston, 3; New York, 5. Base on Balls-Parnell, 2; Reynolds, 4. Hits off-Parnell 5 in 3; Scarborough, 3 in 3; Taylor, 2 in 2. Winner-Reynolds (17– 8). Loser-Parnell (18–11). Strikeouts-Parnell, 2, Reynolds 9. UmpiresHubbard, McGowan, Berry, Hurley. Time-3:12.

Allie Reynolds—In 1951, Allie became the first American League pitcher to toss no-hitters in the same season. He had a won-lost record of 131-60 (.686) in 8 years as a Yankee.

DON LARSEN'S WORLD SERIES PERFECT GAME
(AT YANKEE STADIUM: OCTOBER 8, 1956—5TH GAME OF WORLD SERIES)

Yankee righthander Don Larsen pitched his way to immortality by facing 27 Brooklyn batters, retiring them all! Larsen required but 97 pitches to finish his masterpiece. He had a 3–2 count on only one batter, Pee Wee Reese in the first inning.

THE BOX SCORE:

BROOKLYN								NEW YORK							
	POS	AB	R	H	PO	A	E		POS	AB	R	H	PO	A	E
Gilliam	2b	3	0	0	2	0	0	Bauer	rf	4	0	1	4	0	0
Reese	ss	3	0	0	4	2	0	Collins	1b	4	0	1	7	0	0
Snider	cf	3	0	0	1	0	0	Mantle	cf	3	1	1	4	0	0
Robinson	3b	3	0	0	2	4	0	Berra	c	3	0	0	7	0	0
Hodges	1b	3	0	0	5	1	0	Slaughter	lf	2	0	0	1	0	0
Amoros	lf	3	0	0	3	0	0	Martin	2b	3	0	1	3	4	0
Furillo	rf	3	0	0	0	0	0	McDougald	ss	2	0	0	0	2	0
Campanella	c	3	0	0	7	2	0	Carey	3b	3	1	1	1	1	0
Maglie	p	2	0	0	0	1	0	Larsen	p	2	0	0	0	1	0
aMitchell	ph	1	0	0	0	0	0								
Totals:		27	0	0	24	10	0	Totals:		26	2	5	27	8	0

aCalled out on strikes for Maglie in ninth
 for 27th consecutive out and a perfect game for Larsen.

Score by Innings:

Brooklyn . . . . .0 0 0   0 0 0   0 0 0—0
New York . . . . .0 0 0   1 0 1   0 0 *—2

Runs batted in-Mantle, Bauer. Home run-Mantle. Sacrifice hit-Larsen. Double plays-Reese and Hodges; Hodges, Campanella, Robinson, Campanella and Robinson. Left on bases-Brooklyn 0, New York 3. Earned runs-New York 2, Brooklyn 0. Bases on balls-Off Maglie 2 (Slaughter, McDougald). Struck out-By Larsen 7 (Gilliam, Reese, Hodges, Campanella, Snider, Maglie, Mitchell); by Maglie 5 (Martin, Collins 2, Larsen, Bauer). Runs and earned runs-Off Larsen 0–0; off Maglie 2–2. Winning pitcher-Larsen; Losing pitcher-Maglie. Umpires-Pinelli (N.L.) at plate; Soar (A.L.) at first base; Boggess (N.L.) at second base; Napp (A.L.) at third base; Gorman (N.L.) in left field; Runge (A.L.) in right field. Time of game-2:06. Attendance-64,519.

BOX SCORE OF DAVE RIGHETTI'S NO-HITTER
(YANKEE STADIUM; JULY 4, 1983)

BOSTON	POS	AB	R	H	BI
Remy	2b	4	0	0	0
Boggs	3b	4	0	0	0
Rice	lf	1	0	0	0
Armas	cf	3	0	0	0
Evans	rf	3	0	0	0
Nichols	dh	2	0	0	0
Stapleton	1b	3	0	0	0
Newman	c	2	0	0	0
Hoffman	ss	3	0	0	0
Totals:		25	0	0	0

NEW YORK	POS	AB	R	H	BI
Campaneris	3b	3	0	2	0
Mattingly	1b	4	0	0	0
Winfield	cf	3	1	1	0
Piniella	lf	4	0	0	0
Baylor	dh	3	2	1	1
Wynegar	c	3	0	0	0
Kemp	rf	4	1	2	2
Smalley	ss	4	0	1	0
Robertson	2b	3	0	1	1
Totals:		31	4	8	4

Score by Innings:

Boston . . . . .0 0 0   0 0 0   0 0 0—0
New York . . . . .0 0 0   0 1 1   0 2 x—4

Game-winning RBI-Robertson (1). E-Boggs. DP-Boston 2, New York 1. LOB-Boston 2, New York 7. HR-Baylor (9). SB-Campaneris (3).

BOSTON

	IP	H	R	ER	BB	SO
Tudor (L 5– 5)	7²/₃	8	4	4	4	2
Stanley	¹/₃	0	0	0	0	0

NEW YORK

	IP	H	R	ER	BB	SO
Righetti (W 10–3)	9	0	0	0	4	9

Time-2:33. Attendance-41,077

NO-HITTERS AGAINST THE YANKEES

Opponent pitchers have no-hit the Yankees six times in their history. The great Cy Young tossed the first hitless game in 1908, the Red Sox winning 8–0. Each of the five subsequent authors of no-hit games against the Bombers were righthanded hurlers. Thus, no lefthander has ever turned the no-hit trick against New York.

The most recent no-hitter against the Yanks was thrown by Hoyt Wilhelm of Baltimore. At Baltimore's Memorial Stadium, Wilhelm fired his gem at New York on September 20, 1958. The Orioles won the game 1–0.

The 1983 season almost saw the Yanks being no-hit. On the final day of the regular season at Baltimore October 2, three Oriole pitchers combined for a one-hit 1–0 Baltimore win.

THE BOX SCORES OF THE SIX NO-HITTERS AGAINST THE YANKEES FOLLOW:

THE BOX SCORE OF CY YOUNG'S NO-HITTER
(AT NEW YORK: JUNE 30, 1908)

BOSTON	POS	AB	R	H	PO	A	E	NEW YORK	POS	AB	R	H	PO	A	E
Thoney	lf	0	0	0	0	0	0	Niles	2b	2	0	0	3	6	0
Cravath	lf	5	0	1	4	0	0	Keeler	rf	3	0	0	2	1	1
Sullivan	cf	5	1	1	1	0	0	Moriarity	1b	3	0	0	10	1	1
McConnell	2b	2	2	2	2	4	0	Hemphill	cf	3	0	0	0	0	0
Gessler	rf	3	0	1	2	0	0	Ball	ss	3	0	0	3	3	0
Laporte	3b	4	0	2	2	2	0	Stahl	lf	3	0	0	2	1	0
Unglaub	1b	4	2	2	13	0	0	Conroy	3b	3	0	0	0	1	0
Wagner	ss	4	2	1	0	3	0	Blair	c	3	0	0	7	2	0
Criger	c	3	0	0	3	2	0	Manning	p	0	0	0	0	2	0
Young	p	5	1	3	0	1	0	Newton	p	1	0	0	0	1	1
								Lake	p	2	0	0	0	0	0
Totals		35	8	13	27	12	0	Totals		26	0	0	27	18	3

```
Boston.....................................1 1 2   1 0 1   0 0 2—8
New York...................................0 0 0   0 0 0   0 0 0—0
```

Hits-off Manning, 3 in one and two-thirds innings; off Newton, 3 in two-thirds inning; off Lake, 7 in five and two-thirds innings. Sacrifice hits-McConnell, 2; Criger, 2. Stolen base-McConnell. Double play-Stahl and Blair. Left on bases-Boston, 11. First base on balls-off Manning, 3; off Newton, 1; off Lake, 1; off Young, 1. First base on errors-Boston, 2. Hit by pitcher-by Manning, 1; by Newton, 1. Struck out-by Manning, 1; by Newton, 1; by Lake, 4; by Young, 2. Time-2:00. Umpire-O'Laughlin.

THE BOX SCORE OF GEORGE FOSTER'S NO-HITTER
(AT BOSTON: JUNE 21, 1916)

BOSTON	POS	AB	H	O	A	E		NEW YORK	POS	AB	H	O	A	E
Hooper	rf	4	3	3	0	0		Gilhooley	rf	4	0	5	0	0
Janvrin	2b	3	2	1	1	0		High	lf	3	0	2	0	0
Lewis	lf	3	2	3	0	0		Peckinpaugh	ss	3	0	2	2	0
Hoblitzell	1b	3	0	6	1	0		Pipp	1b	3	0	6	0	0
Walker	cf	3	0	5	0	0		Baker	3b	3	0	0	1	0
Gardner	3b	3	0	3	0	0		Magee	cf	2	0	5	0	0
Scott	ss	3	1	1	0	0		Gedeon	2b	3	0	1	2	0
Carrigan	c	3	0	4	2	0		Nunamaker	c	2	0	3	2	0
Foster	p	3	0	1	3	0		Shawkey	p	1	0	0	1	0
								*Caldwell		1	0	0	0	0
Totals		28	8	27	7			Totals		25	0	24	8	

*Batted for Shawkey in ninth inning.

```
New York . . . . . . . . . . . . . . . . . . . . . . . . . . . . . . . . .0 0 0   0 0 0   0 0 0—0
Boston . . . . . . . . . . . . . . . . . . . . . . . . . . . . . . . . . . .1 0 0   0 0 1   0 0 x—2
```

Runs-Hooper, Janvrin. Two-base hit-Hooper. Three-base hit-Janvrin. Sacrifice hits-Janvrin, Shawkey. Sacrifice fly-Lewis. Left on bases-Boston, 4; New York, 2. First base on balls-Off Foster, 3. Struck out-by Foster, 3; by Shawkey, 2. Umpires-Messrs. Hildebrand and O'Longhlin. Time of game-1 hour and 31 minutes.

THE BOX SCORE OF RAY CALDWELL'S NO-HITTER
(AT NEW YORK: SEPTEMBER 10, 1919, 1ST GAME)

CLEVELAND	POS	AB	H	O	A	E		NEW YORK	POS	AB	H	O	A	E
Graney	lf	3	0	3	0	0		Fewster	rf	4	0	3	0	0
Chapman	ss	2	1	1	6	0		Peckinpaugh	ss	4	0	4	4	0
Speaker	cf	3	1	3	0	0		Baker	3b	3	0	0	2	0
Harris	1b	3	2	11	0	0		Pipp	1b	3	0	13	2	0
Gardner	3b	4	1	0	2	0		Pratt	2b	3	0	0	3	0
Wambsganss	2b	4	0	1	0	1		Lewis	lf	3	0	1	0	0
Smith	rf	4	0	2	0	0		Bodie	cf	3	0	2	0	0
O'Neill	c	3	0	6	1	0		Hannah	c	2	0	2	0	0
Caldwell	p	4	1	0	1	0		Mays	p	2	0	2	4	0
								*Vick		1	0	0	0	0
Totals		30	6	27	10	1		Totals		28	0	27	15	0

*Batted for Mays in ninth inning.

```
Cleveland . . . . . . . . . . . . . . . . . . . . . . . . . . . . . . . . .2 0 0   0 0 1   0 0 0—3
New York . . . . . . . . . . . . . . . . . . . . . . . . . . . . . . . . . .0 0 0   0 0 0   0 0 0—0
```

Runs-Graney, Chapman, Harris. Errors-Wambsganss. Two-base hits-Harris, Caldwell. Home run-Harris. Left on bases-New York, 2; Cleveland, 7. First base on balls-off Mays, 3; off Caldwell, 1. Hit by pitcher-by Mays (Graney). Struck out-by Mays, 2; by Caldwell, 5. Sacrifice hits-Speaker, Chapman, Harris.

THE BOX SCORE OF BOB FELLER'S NO-HITTER
(AT NEW YORK: APRIL 30, 1946)

CLEVELAND	POS	AB	H	O	A		NEW YORK	POS	AB	H	O	A
Case	lf	4	2	1	0		Rizzuto	ss	3	0	5	5
Lemon	cf	4	1	1	0		Stirnweiss	3b	3	0	1	2
Edwards	rf	2	0	0	0		Henrich	rf	1	0	0	0
Fleming	1b	3	1	9	0		DiMaggio	cf	4	0	1	0
Keltner	3b	1	0	0	3		Keller	lf	3	0	3	0
Boudreau	ss	3	0	0	4		Etten	1b	3	0	8	0
Hayes	c	4	2	12	1		Gordon	2b	3	0	3	3
Mack	2b	3	1	4	2		Dickey	c	2	0	6	3
Feller	p	4	0	0	1		Bevens	p	3	0	0	2
Totals		28	7	27	11		Totals		25	0	27	15

```
Cleveland.................................0 0 0  0 0 0  0 0 1—1
New York..................................0 0 0  0 0 0  0 0 0—0
```

Runs-Hayes. Errors-Rizzuto, Bevens, Keltner, Fleming. Runs batted in-Hayes. Home run-Hayes. Stolen bases-Case, Henrich. Sacrifices-Boudreau, Keltner, Stirnweiss, Edwards, Henrich. Double plays-Gordon to Rizzuto to Etten, Stirnweiss to Rizzuto to Etten, Dickey to Rizzuto. Left on bases-Cleveland, 8; New York, 5. Base on balls-Bevens, 5; Feller, 5. Strikeouts-Bevens, 5; Feller, 11. Umpires-Rommel, Boyer and Jones. Time-2:14. Attendance-37,144.

THE BOX SCORE OF VIRGIL TRUCK'S NO-HITTER
(AT NEW YORK: AUGUST 25, 1952)

DETROIT	POS	AB	R	H	RBI	O	A	E		NEW YORK	POS	AB	R	H	RBI	O	A	E
Groth	cf	4	0	0	0	2	0	0		Mantle	cf	3	0	0	0	3	0	0
Pesky	ss	4	0	0	0	3	2	1		Collins	1b	4	0	0	0	10	1	0
Hatfield	3b	3	0	1	0	2	0	0		Bauer	rf	4	0	0	0	1	0	0
Dropo	1b	4	1	2	0	5	3	0		Berra	c	3	0	0	0	7	0	0
Souchock	rf	4	0	1	1	3	0	0		Woodling	lf	3	0	0	0	3	0	0
Delsing	lf	4	0	0	0	2	1	0		Babe	3b	3	0	0	0	3	2	0
Batts	c	2	0	1	0	6	2	1		Martin	2b	3	0	0	0	1	4	0
Federoff	2b	3	0	0	0	0	1	0		Rizzuto	ss	2	0	0	0	0	5	0
Trucks	p	2	0	0	0	4	2	0		*Mize		1	0	0	0	0	0	0
										Brideweser	ss	0	0	0	0	0	0	0
Totals		30	1	5	1	27	11	2		Miller	p	1	0	0	0	0	1	0
										°Noren		1	0	0	0	0	0	0
										Scarborough	p	0	0	0	0	0	0	0
										Totals		28	0	0	0	27	14	0

*Fouled out for Rizzuto in 8th.
°Flied out for Miller in 8th.

```
Detroit...................................0 0 0  0 0 0  1 0 0—1
New York..................................0 0 0  0 0 0  0 0 0—0
```

2B-Dropo. S-Miller. DP-Babe, Martin and Collins. Left on bases-Detroit, 5; New York, 3. BB-Trucks, 1; Miller, 2. SO-Trucks, 8; Miller, 7. HO-Miller, 4 in 8 innings; Scarborough, 1 in 1. R and ER-Miller, 1-1; Scarborough, 0-0; Trucks, 0-0. HBP-Miller (Batts). Winner-Trucks (5-15). Loser-Miller (3-5). U-Robb, Grieve, Honochick and Paparella. Time-2:03. Attendance-13,442.

BOX SCORE OF HOYT WILHELM'S NO-HITTER
(AT BALTIMORE: SEPTEMBER 20, 1958)

NEW YORK	POS	AB	R	H
Bauer	rf	4	0	0
Lumpe	ss	2	0	0
Mantle	cf	3	0	0
Skowron	3b	3	0	0
Siebern	lf	3	0	0
Howard	c	3	0	0
Throneberry	1b	2	0	0
aBerra	1b	1	0	0
Richardson	2b	2	0	0
Larsen	p	2	0	0
Shantz	p	0	0	0
bSlaughter		1	0	0
Totals		26	0	0

BALTIMORE	POS	AB	R	H
Williams	3b1b	4	0	1
Boyd	1b	4	0	1
Woodling	rf	2	0	0
Busby	cf	1	0	1
Nieman	lf	3	0	0
Robinson	3b	1	0	0
Triandos	c	3	1	1
Tasby	cfrf	3	0	0
Gardner	2b	3	0	0
Castleman	ss	2	0	1
Miranda	ss	0	0	0
Wilhelm	p	3	0	0
Totals		29	1	5

a-Grounded out for Throneberry in eighth.
b-Flied out for Shantz in ninth.

Innings

New York . . . . .0 0 0   0 0 0   0 0 0—0
Baltimore . . . . .0 0 0   0 0 0   1 0 x—1

RBI-Triandos. E-Skowron 2. Left on bases-New York 1, Baltimore 6. 2B-Williams. HR-Triandos.

Baltimore	IP	H	R	ER	BB	SO
Wilhelm	9	0	0	0	2	8
(W, 3-10)						
New York						
Larsen	6	1	0	0	2	2
Shantz	2	4	1	1	0	2
(L, 7-6)						

PB-Triandos. U-Paparella, Chylak, Tobacchi and Stuart. Time of game-1:48. Attendance-10,941.

BIBLIOGRAPHY

The following newspapers (on microfilm) and reference works were used primarily in the compilation of my research. This listing is not intended to be all-inclusive since every source could not possibly be cited.

These newspapers greatly facilitated my research: the *New Orleans Times Picayune*, the *New York Times*, the *New York Herald Tribune*, the *St. Louis Post-Dispatch*, the *Washington Post*, the *Atlanta Constitution*, and the *Baton Rouge Morning Advocate*.

Research books found to be most helpful: *The Book of Baseball Records* by Seymour Siwoff, *The Baseball Encyclopedia* (MacMillan), *The Sports Encylopedia: Baseball* and finally two books by Mark Gallagher: *Day by Day in New York Yankees History* and *The Yankee Encyclopedia*. Also, the research material obtained from the Baseball Hall of Fame Library greatly facilitated my work specifically involving Yankee total runs versus those of their opponents.